The Expositor's Bible:
The Book of Isaiah Volumes I & II
By the Rev. George Adam Smith, M.A.
Edited by Anthony Uyl

Woodstock, Ontario, 2017

The Expositor's Bible: The Book of Isaiah Volumes I & II
By the Rev. George Adam Smith, M.A.
Edited by Anthony Uyl

Originally edited by the Rev. Sir W. Robertson Nicoli, M.A., LL.D.
Editor of "The Expositor," etc.

Hodder and Stoughton; London. MCMX
Printed by Hazell, Watson & Viney, Ltd., London and Aylesbury.

The text of The Expositor's Bible: The Book of Isaiah Volumes I & II is all in the Public Domain. This edition is published by Devoted Publishing a division of 2165467 Ontario Inc.

What kind of philosophies do you have?
Let us know!

Contact us at: devotedpub@hotmail.com
Visit us on Facebook: Devoted Publishing
Get more products via our website: www.devotedpublishing.com
Published in Woodstock, Ontario, Canada 2017.

For bulk educational rates, please contact us at the above email address.

ISBN: 978-1-988297-92-7

Rev. George Adam Smith, M.A.

Table of Contents

VOLUME I 6
INTRODUCTION 6
   TABLE OF DATES 8
BOOK I 9
   CHAPTER I 10
      Footnotes: 14
   CHAPTER II 15
   CHAPTER III 20
      Footnotes: 26
   CHAPTER IV 27
      Footnotes: 37
   CHAPTER V 38
      Footnotes: 41
   CHAPTER VI 42
      Footnotes: 50
   CHAPTER VII 51
      Footnotes: 55
BOOK II 56
      Footnotes: 57
   CHAPTER VIII 58
      Footnotes: 62
   CHAPTER IX 63
      Footnote: 66
   CHAPTER X 67
      Footnotes: 72
   CHAPTER XI 73
      Footnotes: 75
BOOK III 76
   CHAPTER XII 77
      Footnotes: 80
CHAPTER XIII 81
      Footnotes: 86
   CHAPTER XIV 87
   CHAPTER XV 91
      Footnotes: 95
   CHAPTER XVI 96
      Footnote: 98
   CHAPTER XVII 99
      Footnote: 104
   CHAPTER XVIII 105
BOOK IV 110
      Footnote: 110
   CHAPTER XIX 111

Footnotes:	115
CHAPTER XX	116
Footnotes:	119
CHAPTER XXI	120
Footnotes:	123
CHAPTER XXII	124
CHAPTER XXIII	127
Footnotes:	131
CHAPTER XXIV	132
CHAPTER XXV	135
Footnote:	139
CHAPTER XXVI	140
Footnotes:	142
BOOK V	143
CHAPTER XXVII	145
Footnotes:	149
CHAPTER XXVIII	150
Footnote:	153
CHAPTER XXIX	154
Footnotes:	158
CHAPTER XXX	159
Footnotes:	161
Volume II	162
INTRODUCTION	163
BOOK I	166
CHAPTER I	167
Footnotes:	173
CHAPTER II	174
Footnote:	176
CHAPTER III	177
Footnotes:	180
CHAPTER IV	181
Footnotes:	186
BOOK II	188
CHAPTER V	189
Footnotes:	194
CHAPTER VI	195
Footnotes:	200
CHAPTER VII	201
Footnotes:	208
CHAPTER VIII	210
Footnotes:	213
CHAPTER IX	214
Footnotes:	220

CHAPTER X	221
Footnotes:	225
CHAPTER XI	226
Footnotes:	229
CHAPTER XII	230
Footnotes:	235
CHAPTER XIII	236
Footnotes:	238
CHAPTER XIV	239
Footnotes:	243
BOOK III	245
CHAPTER XV	246
Footnotes:	250
CHAPTER XVI	251
Footnotes:	258
CHAPTER XVII	259
Footnotes:	262
CHAPTER XVIII	263
Footnotes:	269
CHAPTER XIX	270
Footnotes:	277
CHAPTER XX	278
Footnotes:	289
BOOK IV	292
CHAPTER XXI	294
Footnotes:	298
CHAPTER XXII	299
Footnotes:	302
CHAPTER XXIII	303
Footnotes:	308
CHAPTER XXIV	310
Footnotes:	314
CHAPTER XXV	316
Footnotes:	322

VOLUME I

INTRODUCTION

As the following Exposition of the Book of Isaiah does not observe the canonical arrangement of the chapters, a short introduction is necessary upon the plan which has been adopted.

The size and the many obscurities of the Book of Isaiah have limited the common use of it in the English tongue to single conspicuous passages, the very brilliance of which has cast their context and original circumstance into deeper shade. The intensity of the gratitude with which men have seized upon the more evangelical passages of Isaiah, as well as the attention which apologists for Christianity have too partially paid to his intimations of the Messiah, has confirmed the neglect of the rest of the Book. But we might as well expect to receive an adequate conception of a great statesman's policy from the epigrams and perorations of his speeches as to appreciate the message, which God has sent to the world through the Book of Isaiah, from a few lectures on isolated, and often dislocated, texts. No book of the Bible is less susceptible of treatment apart from the history out of which it sprang than the Book of Isaiah; and it may be added, that in the Old Testament at least there is none which, when set in its original circumstance and methodically considered as a whole, appeals with greater power to the modern conscience. Patiently to learn how these great prophecies were suggested by, and first met, the actual occasions of human life, is vividly to hear them speaking home to life still.

I have, therefore, designed an arrangement which embraces all the prophecies, but treats them in chronological order. I will endeavour to render their contents in terms which appeal to the modern conscience; but, in order to be successful, such an endeavour presupposes the exposition of them in relation to the history which gave them birth. In these volumes, therefore, narrative and historical exposition will take precedence of practical application.

Every one knows that the Book of Isaiah breaks into two parts between chaps. xxxix. and xl. Vol. I. of this Exposition covers chaps. i.-xxxix. Vol. II. will treat of chaps. xl.-lxvi. Again, within chaps. i.-xxxix. another division is apparent. The most of these chapters evidently bear upon events within Isaiah's own career, but some imply historical circumstances that did not arise till long after he had passed away. Of the five books into which I have divided Vol. I., the first four contain the prophecies relating to Isaiah's time (740-701 B.C.), and the fifth the prophecies which refer to later events (chaps. xiii.-xiv. 23; xxiv.-xxvii.; xxxiv.; xxxv.).

The prophecies, whose subjects fall within Isaiah's times, I have taken in chronological order, with one exception. This exception is chap. i., which, although it published near the end of the prophet's life, I treat of first, because, from its position as well as its character, it is evidently intended as a preface to the whole book. The difficulty of grouping the rest of Isaiah's oracles and orations is great. The plan I have adopted is not perfect, but convenient. Isaiah's prophesying was determined chiefly by four Assyrian invasions of Palestine: the first, in 734-732 B.C., by Tiglath-pileser II., while Ahaz was on the throne; the second by Salmanassar and Sargon in 725-720, during which Samaria fell in 721; the third by Sargon, 712-710; the fourth by Sennacherib in 701, which last three occurred while Hezekiah was king of Judah. But outside the Assyrian invasions there were three other cardinal dates in Isaiah's life: 740, his call to be a prophet; 727, the death of Ahaz, his enemy, and the accession of his pupil, Hezekiah; and 705, the death of Sargon, for Sargon's death led to the rebellion of the Syrian States, and it was this rebellion which brought on Sennacherib's invasion. Taking all these dates into consideration, I have placed in Book I. all the prophecies of Isaiah from his call in 740 to the death of Ahaz in 727; they lead up to and illustrate Tiglath-pileser's invasion; they cover what I have ventured to call the prophet's apprenticeship, during which the theatre of his vision was mainly the internal life of his people, but he gained also his first outlook upon the world beyond. Book II. deals with the prophecies from the accession of Hezekiah in 727 to the death of Sargon in 705--a long period, but few prophecies, covering both Salmanassar's and Sargon's campaigns. Book III. is filled with the prophecies from 705 to 702, a numerous group, called forth from Isaiah by the rebellion and political activity in Palestine consequent on Sargon's death and preliminary to Sennacherib's arrival. Book IV. contains the prophecies which refer to Sennacherib's actual invasion of Judah and siege of Jerusalem, in 701.

Of course, any chronological arrangement of Isaiah's prophecies must be largely provisional. Only some of the chapters are fixed to dates past possibility of doubt. The Assyriology which has helped us with these must yield further results before the controversies can be settled that exist with regard to the rest. I have explained in the course of the Exposition my reasons for the order which I have followed, and need only say here that I am still more uncertain about the generally received dates of chaps x. 5-xi., xvii. 12-14 and xxxii. The religious problems, however, were so much the same during the whole of Isaiah's career that uncertainties of date, if they are confined to the limits of that career, make little difference to the exposition of the book.

Isaiah's doctrines, being so closely connected with the life of his day, come up for statement at many points of the narrative, in which this Exposition chiefly consists. But here and there I have inserted chapters dealing summarily with more important topics, such as The World in Isaiah's Day; The Messiah; Isaiah's Power of Prediction, with its evidence on the character of Inspiration; and the question, Had Isaiah a Gospel for the Individual? A short index will guide the student to Isaiah's teaching on other important points of theology and life, such as holiness, forgiveness, monotheism, immortality, the Holy Spirit, etc.

Treating Isaiah's prophecies chronologically as I have done, I have followed a method which put me on the look-out for any traces of development that his doctrine might exhibit. I have recorded these as they occur, but it may be useful to collect them here. In chaps. ii.-iv. we have the struggle of the apprentice prophet's thoughts from the easy religious optimism of his generation, through unrelieved convictions of judgement for the whole people, to his final vision of the Divine salvation of a remnant. Again, chap. vii. following on chaps. ii.-vi. proves that Isaiah's belief in the Divine righteousness preceded, and was the parent of, his belief in the Divine sovereignty. Again, his successive pictures of the Messiah grow in contents, and become more spiritual. And again, he only gradually arrived at a clear view of the siege and deliverance of Jerusalem. One other fact of the same kind has impressed me since I wrote the exposition of chap. i. I have there stated that it is plain that Isaiah's conscience was perfect just because it consisted of two complementary parts: one of God the infinitely High, exalted in righteousness, far above the thoughts of His people, and the other of God the infinitely Near, concerned and jealous for all the practical details of their life. I ought to have added that Isaiah was more under the influence of the former in his earlier years, but that as he grew older and took a larger share in the politics of Judah it was the latter view of God, to which he most frequently gave expression. Signs of a development like these may be fairly used to correct or support the evidence which Assyriology affords for determining the chronological order of the chapters.

But these signs of development are more valuable for the proof they give that the Book of Isaiah contains the experience and testimony of a real life: a life that learned and suffered and grew, and at last triumphed. There is not a single word about the prophet's birth or childhood, or fortune, or personal appearance, or even of his death. But between silence on his origin and silence on his end—and perhaps all the more impressively because of these clouds by which it is bounded—there shines the record of Isaiah's spiritual life and of the unfaltering career which this sustained,—clear and whole, from his commission by God in the secret experience of his own heart to his vindication in God's supreme tribunal of history. It is not only one of the greatest, but one of the most finished and intelligible, lives in history. My main purpose in expounding the book is to enable English readers, not only to follow its course, but to feel, and to be elevated by, its Divine inspiration.

I may state that this Exposition is based upon a close study of the Hebrew text of Isaiah, and that the translations are throughout my own, except in one or two cases where I have quoted from the revised English version.

With regard to the Revised Version of Isaiah, which I have had opportunities of thoroughly testing, I would like to say that my sense of the immense service which it renders to English readers of the Bible is only exceeded by my wonder that the Revisers have not gone just a very little farther, and adopted one or two simple contrivances which are in the line of their own improvements and would have greatly increased our large debt to them. For instance, why did they not make plain by inverted commas such undoubted interruptions of the prophet's own speech as that of the drunkards in chap. xxviii. 9, 10? Not to know that these verses are spoken in mockery of Isaiah, a mockery to which he replies in vv. 10-13, is to miss the meaning of the whole passage. Again, when they printed Job and the Psalms in metrical form, as well as the Hymn of Hezekiah, why did they not do the same with other poetical passages of Isaiah, particularly the great Ode on the King of Babylon in chap. xiv.? This is utterly spoiled in the form in which the Revisers have printed it. What English reader would guess that it was as much a piece of metre as any of the Psalms? Again, why have they so consistently rendered by the misleading word "judgement" a Hebrew term that no doubt sometimes means an act of doom, but far oftener the abstract quality of justice? It is such defects, along with a frequent failure to mark the proper emphasis in a sentence, that have led me to substitute a more literal version of my own.

I have not thought it necessary to discuss the question of the chronology of the period. This has been done so often and so recently. See Robertson Smith's Prophets of Israel, pp. 145, 402, 413, Driver's Isaiah, p. 12, or any good commentary.

I append a chronological table, and an index to the canonical chapters will be found before the index of subjects. The publishers have added a map of Isaiah's world in illustration of chap. v.

TABLE OF DATES

B.C.
745. Tiglath-pileser II. ascends the Assyrian Throne.
740. Uzziah dies. Jotham becomes sole King of Judah. Isaiah's Inaugural Vision (Isa. vi.).
735. Jotham dies. Ahaz succeeds. League of Syria and Northern Israel against Judah.
734-732. Syrian Campaign of Tiglath-pileser II. Siege and Capture of Damascus. Invasion of Israel. Captivity of Zebulon, Naphtali and Galilee (Isa. ix. 1). Ahaz visits Damascus.
727. Salmanassar IV. succeeds Tiglath-pileser II. Hezekiah succeeds Ahaz (or in 725?).
725. Salmanassar marches on Syria.
722 or 721. Sargon succeeds Salmanassar. Capture of Samaria. Captivity of all Northern Israel.
720 or 719. Sargon defeats Egypt at Rafia.
711. Sargon invades Syria (Isa. xx.). Capture of Ashdod.
709. Sargon takes Babylon from Merodach-baladan.
705. Murder of Sargon. Sennacherib succeeds.
701. Sennacherib invades Syria. Capture of Coast Towns. Siege of Ekron and Battle of Eltekeh. Invasion of Judah. Submission of Hezekiah. Jerusalem spared. Return of Assyrians with the Rabshakeh to Jerusalem, while Sennacherib's Army marches on Egypt. Disaster to Sennacherib's Army near Pelusium. Disappearance of Assyrians from before Jerusalem--all happening in this order.
697 or 696. Death of Hezekiah. Manasseh succeeds.
681. Death of Sennacherib.
607. Fall of Nineveh and Assyria. Babylon supreme. Jeremiah.
599. First Deportation of Jews to Babylon by Nebuchadnezzar.
588. Jerusalem destroyed. Second Deportation of Jews.
538. Cyrus captures Babylon. First Return of Jewish Exiles, under Zerubbabel, happens soon after.
458. Second Return of Jewish Exiles, under Ezra.

Rev. George Adam Smith, M.A.

BOOK I

PREFACE AND PROPHECIES TO THE DEATH OF AHAZ, 727 B.C.

ISAIAH: i. The Preface. " ii.-iv. 740-735 B.C. " v., ix. 8-x. 4. 735 B.C. " vi. About 735 B.C. " vii.-ix. 7. 734-732 B.C.

CHAPTER I

THE ARGUMENT OF THE LORD AND ITS CONCLUSION.

Isaiah i.--His General Preface.

The first chapter of the Book of Isaiah owes its position not to its date, but to its character. It was published late in the prophet's life. The seventh verse describes the land as overrun by foreign soldiery, and such a calamity befell Judah only in the last two of the four reigns over which the first verse extends Isaiah's prophesying. In the reign of Ahaz, Judah was invaded by Syria and Northern Israel, and some have dated chapter i. from the year of that invasion, 734 B.C. In the reign again of Hezekiah some have imagined, in order to account for the chapter, a swarming of neighbouring tribes upon Judah; and Mr. Cheyne, to whom regarding the history of Isaiah's time we ought to listen with the greatest deference, has supposed an Assyrian invasion in 711, under Sargon. But hardly of this, and certainly not of that, have we adequate evidence, and the only other invasion of Judah in Isaiah's lifetime took place under Sennacherib, in 701. For many reasons this Assyrian invasion is to be preferred to that by Syria and Ephraim in 734 as the occasion of this prophecy. But there is really no need to be determined on the point. The prophecy has been lifted out of its original circumstance and placed in the front of the book, perhaps by Isaiah himself, as a general introduction to his collected pieces. It owes its position, as we have said, to its character. It is a clear, complete statement of the points which were at issue between the Lord and His own all the time Isaiah was the Lord's prophet. It is the most representative of Isaiah's prophecies, a summary, perhaps better than any other single chapter of the Old Testament, of the substance of prophetic doctrine, and a very vivid illustration of the prophetic spirit and method. We propose to treat it here as introductory to the main subjects and lines of Isaiah's teaching, leaving its historical references till we arrive in due course at the probable year of its origin, 701 B.C. [1]

Isaiah's preface is in the form of a Trial or Assize. Ewald calls it "The Great Arraignment." There are all the actors in a judicial process. It is a Crown case, and God is at once Plaintiff and Judge. He delivers both the Complaint in the beginning (vv. 2, 3) and the Sentence in the end. The Assessors are Heaven and Earth, whom the Lord's herald invokes to hear the Lord's plea (ver. 2). The people of Judah are the Defendants. The charge against them is one of brutish, ingrate stupidity, breaking out into rebellion. The Witness is the prophet himself, whose evidence on the guilt of his people consists in recounting the misery that has overtaken their land (vv. 4-9), along with their civic injustice and social cruelty--sins of the upper and ruling classes (vv. 10, 17, 21-23). The people's Plea-in-defence, laborious worship and multiplied sacrifice, is repelled and exposed (vv. 10-17). And the Trial is concluded--Come now, let us bring our reasoning to a close, saith the Lord--by God's offer of pardon to a people thoroughly convicted (ver. 18). On which follow the Conditions of the Future: happiness is sternly made dependent on repentance and righteousness (vv. 19, 20). And a supplementary oracle is given (vv. 24-31), announcing a time of affliction, through which the nation shall pass as through a furnace; rebels and sinners shall be consumed, but God will redeem Zion, and with her a remnant of the people.

That is the plan of the chapter--a Trial at Law. Though it disappears under the exceeding weight of thought the prophet builds upon it, do not let us pass hurriedly from it, as if it were only a scaffolding.

That God should argue at all is the magnificent truth on which our attention must fasten, before we inquire what the argument is about. God reasons with man--that is the first article of religion according to Isaiah. Revelation is not magical, but rational and moral. Religion is reasonable intercourse between one intelligent Being and another. God works upon man first through conscience.

Over against the prophetic view of religion sprawls and reeks in this same chapter the popular--religion as smoky sacrifice, assiduous worship, and ritual. The people to whom the chapter was addressed were not idolaters. [2] Hezekiah's reformation was over. Judah worshipped her own God, whom the prophet introduces not as for the first time, but by Judah's own familiar names for Him--Jehovah, Jehovah of Hosts, the Holy One of Israel, the Mighty One, or Hero, of Israel. In this hour of extreme danger the people are waiting on Jehovah with great pains and cost of sacrifice. They pray, they sacrifice, they solemnize to perfection. But they do not know, they do not consider; this is the burden of their offence. To use a better word, they do not think. They are God's grown-up children (ver. 2)--children, that is to say, like the son of the parable, with native instincts for their God, and grown up--that is to say, with reason and conscience developed. But they use neither, stupider than very beasts. Israel doth not know, my people doth not consider. In all their worship conscience is asleep, and they

Rev. George Adam Smith, M.A.

are drenched in wickedness. Isaiah puts their life in an epigram--wickedness and worship: I cannot away, saith the Lord, with wickedness and worship (ver. 13).

But the pressure and stimulus of the prophecy lie in this, that although the people have silenced conscience and are steeped in a stupidity worse than ox or ass, God will not leave them alone. He forces Himself upon them; He compels them to think. In the order and calmness of nature (ver. 2), apart from catastrophe nor seeking to influence by any miracle, God speaks to men by the reasonable words of His prophet. Before He will publish salvation or intimate disaster He must rouse and startle conscience. His controversy precedes alike His peace and His judgements. An awakened conscience is His prophet's first demand. Before religion can be prayer, or sacrifice, or any acceptable worship, it must be a reasoning together with God.

That is what mean the arrival of the Lord, and the opening of the assize, and the call to know and consider. It is the terrible necessity which comes back upon men, however engrossed or drugged they may be, to pass their lives in moral judgement before themselves; a debate to which there is never any closure, in which forgotten things will not be forgotten, but a man "is compelled to repeat to himself things he desires to be silent about, and to listen to what he does not wish to hear, ... yielding to that mysterious power which says to him, Think. One can no more prevent the mind from returning to an idea than the sea from returning to a shore. With the sailor this is called the tide; with the guilty it is called remorse. God upheaves the soul as well as the ocean."[3] Upon that ever-returning and resistless tide Hebrew prophecy, with its Divine freight of truth and comfort, rides into the lives of men. This first chapter of Isaiah is just the parable of the awful compulsion to think which men call conscience. The stupidest of generations, formal and fat-hearted, are forced to consider and to reason. The Lord's court and controversy are opened, and men are whipped into them from His Temple and His altar.

For even religion and religiousness, the common man's commonest refuge from conscience--not only in Isaiah's time--cannot exempt from this writ. Would we be judged by our moments of worship, by our temple-treading, which is Hebrew for church-going, by the wealth of our sacrifice, by our ecclesiastical position? This chapter drags us out before the austerity and incorruptibleness of Nature. The assessors of the Lord are not the Temple nor the Law, but Heaven and Earth--not ecclesiastical conventions, but the grand moral fundamentals of the universe, purity, order and obedience to God. Religiousness, however, is not the only refuge from which we shall find Isaiah startling men with the trumpet of the Lord's assize. He is equally intolerant of the indulgent silence and compromises of the world, that give men courage to say, We are no worse than others. Men's lives, it is a constant truth of his, have to be argued out not with the world, but with God. If a man will be silent upon shameful and uncomfortable things, he cannot. His thoughts are not his own; God will think them for him as God thinks them here for unthinking Israel. Nor are the practical and intellectual distractions of a busy life any refuge from conscience. When the politicians of Judah seek escape from judgement by plunging into deeper intrigue and a more bustling policy, Isaiah is fond of pointing out to them that they are only forcing judgement nearer. They do but sharpen on other objects the thoughts whose edge must some day turn upon themselves.

What is this questioning nothing holds away, nothing stills, and nothing wears out? It is the voice of God Himself, and its insistence is therefore as irresistible as its effect is universal. That is not mere rhetoric which opens the Lord's controversy: Hear, O heavens, and give ear, O earth, for the Lord hath spoken. All the world changes to the man in whom conscience lifts up her voice, and to the guilty Nature seems attentive and aware. Conscience compels heaven and earth to act as her assessors, because she is the voice, and they the creatures, of God. This leads us to emphasize another feature of the prophecy.

We have called this chapter a trial-at-law; but it is far more a personal than a legal controversy; of the formally forensic there is very little about it. Some theologies and many preachers have attempted the conviction of the human conscience by the technicalities of a system of law, or by appealing to this or that historical covenant, or by the obligations of an intricate and burdensome morality. This is not Isaiah's way. His generation is here judged by no system of law or ancient covenants, but by a living Person and by His treatment of them--a Person who is a Friend and a Father. It is not Judah and the law that are confronted; it is Judah and Jehovah. There is no contrast between the life of this generation and some glorious estate from which they or their forefathers have fallen; but they are made to hear the voice of a living and present God: I have nourished and brought up children, and they have rebelled against Me. Isaiah begins where Saul of Tarsus began, who, though he afterwards elaborated with wealth of detail the awful indictment of the abstract law against man, had never been able to do so but for that first confronting with the Personal Deity, Saul, Saul, why persecutest thou Me? Isaiah's ministry started from the vision of the Lord; and it was no covenant or theory, but the Lord Himself, who remained the prophet's conscience to the end.

But though the living God is Isaiah's one explanation of conscience, it is God in two aspects, the moral effects of which are opposite, yet complementary. In conscience men are defective by forgetting either the sublime or the practical, but Isaiah's strength is to do justice to both. With him God is first the infinitely High, and then equally the infinitely Near. The Lord is exalted in righteousness! yes, and sublimely above the people's vulgar identifications of His will with their own safety and success, but likewise concerned with every detail of their politics and social behaviour, not to be relegated to the Temple, where they were wont to confine Him, but by His prophet descending to their markets and councils, with His own opinion of their policies, interfering in their intrigues, meeting Ahaz at the conduit of the upper pool in the highway of the fuller's field, and fastening eyes of glory on every pin and point of the dress of the daughters of Zion. He is no merely transcendent God. Though He be the High and Holy One, He will discuss each habit of the people, and argue upon its merits every one of their policies. His constant cry to them is Come and let us reason together, and to hear it is to have a conscience. Indeed, Isaiah lays more stress on this intellectual side of the moral sense than on the other, and the frequency with which in this chapter he employs the expressions know, and consider, and reason, is characteristic of all his prophesying. Even the most superficial reader must notice how much this prophet's doctrine of conscience and repentance harmonizes with the metanoia of New Testament preaching.

This doctrine, that God has an interest in every detail of practical life and will argue it out with men, led Isaiah to a revelation of God quite peculiar to himself. For the Psalmist it is enough that his soul come to God, the living God. It is enough for other prophets to awe the hearts of their generations by revealing the Holy One; but Isaiah, with his intensely practical genius, and sorely tried by the stupid inconsistency of his people, bends himself to make them understand that God is at least a reasonable Being. Do not, his constant cry is, and he puts it sometimes in almost as many words--do not act as if there were a Fool on the throne of the universe, which you virtually do when you take these meaningless forms of worship as your only intercourse with Him, and beside them practise your rank iniquities, as if He did not see nor care. We need not here do more than mention the passages in which, sometimes by a word, Isaiah stings and startles self-conscious politicians and sinners beetle-blind in sin, with the sense that God Himself takes an interest in their deeds and has His own working-plans for their life. On the land question in Judah (v. 9): In mine ears, saith the Lord of hosts. When the people were paralyzed by calamity, as if it had no meaning or term (xxviii. 29): This also cometh forth from the Lord of hosts, which is wonderful in counsel and excellent in effectual working. Again, when they were panic-stricken, and madly sought by foolish ways their own salvation (xxx. 18): For the Lord is a God of judgement--i.e., of principle, method, law, with His own way and time for doing things--blessed are all they that wait for Him. And again, when politicians were carried away by the cleverness and success of their own schemes (xxxi. 2): Yet He also is wise, or clever. It was only a personal application of this Divine attribute when Isaiah heard the word of the Lord give him the minutest directions for his own practice--as, for instance, at what exact point he was to meet Ahaz (vii. 3); or that he was to take a board and write upon it in the vulgar character (viii. 1); or that he was to strip frock and sandals, and walk without them for three years (xx). Where common men feel conscience only as something vague and inarticulate, a flavour, a sting, a foreboding, the obligation of work, the constraint of affection, Isaiah heard the word of the Lord, clear and decisive on matters of policy, and definite even to the details of method and style.

Isaiah's conscience, then, was perfect, because it was two-fold: God is holy; God is practical. If there be the glory, the purity as of fire, of His Presence to overawe, there is His unceasing inspection of us, there is His interest in the smallest details of our life, there are His fixed laws, from regard for all of which no amount of religious sensibility may relieve us. Neither of these halves of conscience can endure by itself. If we forget the first we may be prudent and for a time clever, but will also grow self-righteous, and in time self-righteousness means stupidity too. If we forget the second we may be very devotional, but cannot escape becoming blindly and inconsistently immoral. Hypocrisy is the result either way, whether we forget how high God is or whether we forget how near.

To these two great articles of conscience, however--God is high and God is near--the Bible adds a greater third, God is Love. This is the uniqueness and glory of the Bible's interpretation of conscience. Other writings may equal it in enforcing the sovereignty and detailing the minutely practical bearings of conscience: the Bible alone tells man how much of conscience is nothing but God's love. It is a doctrine as plainly laid down as the doctrine about chastisement, though not half so much recognised--Whom the Lord loveth He chasteneth. What is true of the material pains and penalties of life is equally true of the inward convictions, frets, threats and fears, which will not leave stupid man alone. To men with their obscure sense of shame, and restlessness, and servitude to sin the Bible plainly says, "You are able to sin because you have turned your back to the love of God; you are unhappy because you do not take that love to your heart; the bitterness of your remorse is that it is love against which you are ungrateful." Conscience is not the Lord's persecution, but His jealous pleading, and not the fierceness of His anger, but the reproach of His love. This is the Bible's doctrine throughout, and it is not absent from the chapter we are considering. Love gets the first word even in the indictment of this austere assize: I have nourished and brought up children, and they have rebelled against Me. Conscience is already a Father's voice: the recollection, as it is in the parable of the prodigal, of a Father's mercy; the reproach, as it is with Christ's lamentation over Jerusalem, of outraged love. We shall find not a few passages in Isaiah, which prove that he was in harmony with all revelation upon this point, that conscience is the reproach of the love of God.

But when that understanding of conscience breaks out in a sinner's heart forgiveness cannot be far away. Certainly penitence is at hand. And therefore, because of all books the Bible is the only one which interprets conscience as the love of God, so is it the only one that can combine His pardon with His reproach, and as Isaiah now does in a single verse, proclaim His free forgiveness as the conclusion of His bitter quarrel. Come, let us bring our reasoning to a close, saith the Lord. Though your sins be as scarlet, they shall be white as snow; though they be red like crimson, they shall be as wool. Our version, Come, and let us reason together, gives no meaning here. So plain an offer of pardon is not reasoning together; it is bringing reasoning to an end; it is the settlement of a dispute that has been in progress. Therefore we translate, with Mr. Cheyne, Let us bring our reasoning to an end. And how pardon can be the end and logical conclusion of conscience is clear to us, who have seen how much of conscience is love, and that the Lord's controversy is the reproach of His Father's heart, and His jealousy to make His own consider all His way of mercy towards them.

But the prophet does not leave conscience alone with its personal and inward results. He rouses it to its social applications. The sins with which the Jews are charged in this charge of the Lord are public sins. The whole people is indicted, but it is the judges, princes and counsellors who are denounced. Judah's disasters, which she seeks to meet by worship, are due to civic faults, bribery, corruption of justice, indifference to the rights of the poor and the friendless. Conscience with Isaiah is not what it is with so much of the religion of to-day, a cul de sac, into which the Lord chases a man and shuts him up to Himself, but it is a thoroughfare by which the Lord drives the man out upon the world and its manifold need of him. There is little dissection and less study of individual character with Isaiah. He has no time for it. Life is too much about him, and his God too much interested in life. What may be called the more personal sins—drunkenness, vanity of dress, thoughtlessness, want of faith in God and patience to wait for Him—are to Isaiah more social than individual symptoms, and it is for their public and political effects that he mentions them. Forgiveness is no end in itself, but the opportunity of social service; not a sanctuary in which Isaiah leaves men to sing its praises or form doctrines of it, but a gateway through which he leads God's people upon the world with the cry that rises from him here: Seek justice, relieve the oppressed, judge the fatherless, plead for the widow.

Before we pass from this form in which Isaiah figures religion we must deal with a suggestion it raises. No modern mind can come into this ancient court of the Lord's controversy without taking advantage of its open forms to put a question regarding the rights of man there. That God should descend to argue with men, what licence does this give to men? If religion be reasonable controversy of this kind, what is the place of doubt in it? Is not doubt man's side of the argument? Has he not also questions to put—the Almighty from his side to arraign? For God has Himself here put man on a level with Him, saying, Come, and let us reason together.

A temper of this kind, though not strange to the Old Testament, lies beyond the horizon of Isaiah. The only challenge of the Almighty which in any of his prophecies he reports as rising from his own countrymen is the bravado of certain drunkards (chaps. v. and xxviii.). Here and elsewhere it is the very opposite temper from honest doubt which he indicts—the temper that does not know, that does not consider. Ritualism and sensualism are to Isaiah equally false, because equally unthinking. The formalist and the fleshly he classes together, because of their stupidity. What does it matter whether a man's conscience and intellect be stifled in his own fat or under the clothes with which he dresses himself? They are stifled, and that is the main thing. To the formalist Isaiah says, Israel doth not know, my people doth not consider; to the fleshly (chap. v.), My people are gone into captivity for want of knowledge. But knowing and considering are just that of which doubt, in its modern sense, is the abundance, and not the defect. The mobility of mind, the curiosity, the moral sensitiveness, the hunger that is not satisfied with the chaff of formal and unreal answers, the spirit to find out truth for one's self, wrestling with God—this is the very temper Isaiah would have welcomed in a people whose sluggishness of reason was as justly blamed by him as the grossness of their moral sense. And if revelation be of the form in which Isaiah so prominently sets it, and the whole Bible bears him out in this—if revelation be this argumentative and reasonable process, then human doubt has its part in revelation. It is, indeed, man's side of the argument, and as history shows, has often helped to the elucidation of the points at issue.

Merely intellectual scepticism, however, is not within Isaiah's horizon. He would never have employed (nor would any other prophet) our modern habits of doubt, except as he employs these intellectual terms, to know and to consider—viz., as instruments of moral search and conviction. Had he lived now he would have been found among those few great prophets who use the resources of the human intellect to expose the moral state of humanity; who, like Shakespeare and Hugo, turn man's detective and reflective processes upon his own conduct; who make himself stand at the bar of his conscience. And truly to have doubt of everything in heaven and earth, and never to doubt one's self, is to be guilty of as stiff and stupid a piece of self-righteousness as the religious formalists whom Isaiah exposes. But the moral of the chapter is plainly what we have shown it to be, that a man cannot stifle doubt and debate about his own heart or treatment of God; whatever else he thinks about and judges, he cannot help judging himself.

Note on the Place of Nature in the Argument of the Lord.--The office which the Bible assigns to Nature in the controversy of God with man is fourfold--Assessor, Witness, Man's Fellow-Convict, and Doomster or Executioner. Taking these backward:--1. Scripture frequently exhibits Nature as the doomster of the Lord. Nature has a terrible power of flashing back from her vaster surfaces the guilty impressions of man's heart; at the last day her thunders shall peal the doom of the wicked, and her fire devour them. In those prophecies of the book of Isaiah which relate to his own time this use is not made of Nature, unless it be in his very earliest prophecy in chap. ii., and in his references to the earthquake (v. 25). To Isaiah the sentences and scourges of God are political and historical, the threats and arms of Assyria. He employs the violences of Nature only as metaphors for Assyrian rage and force. But he often promises fertility as the effect of the Lord's pardon, and when the prophets are writing about Nature, it is difficult to say whether they are to be understood literally or poetically. But, at any rate, there is much larger use made of physical catastrophes and convulsions in those other prophecies which do not relate to Isaiah's own time, and are now generally thought not to be his. Compare chaps. xiii. and xiv. 2. The representation of the earth as the fellow-convict of guilty man, sharing his curse, is very vivid in Isaiah xxiv.-xxvii. In the prophecies relating to his own time Isaiah, of course, identifies the troubles that afflict the land with the sin of the people, of Judah. But these are due to political causes--viz., the Assyrian invasion. 3. In the Lord's court of judgement the prophets sometimes employ Nature as a witness against man, as, for instance, the prophet Micah (vi. 1, ff). Nature is full of associations; the enduring mountains have memories from old, they have been constant witnesses of the dealing of God with His people. 4. Or lastly, Nature may be used as the great assessor of the conscience, sitting to expound the principles on which God governs life. This is Isaiah's favourite use of Nature. He employs her to corroborate his statement of the Divine law and illustrate the ways of God to men, as in the end of chap. xxviii., and no doubt in the opening verse of this chapter.

Footnotes:

1. See p. 343.
2. At least those to whom the first twenty-three verses were addressed. There is distinct blame of worshipping in the groves of Asherah in the appended oracle (vv. 24-31), which is proof that this oracle was given at an earlier period than the rest of the chapter--a fair instance of the very great difficulty we have in determining the dates of the various prophecies of Isaiah.
3. Les Misérables: "a Tempest in a Brain."

Rev. George Adam Smith, M.A.

CHAPTER II

THE THREE JERUSALEMS.

Isaiah ii.-iv. (740-735 B.C.).

After the general introduction, in chap. i., to the prophecies of Isaiah, there comes another portion of the book, of greater length, but nearly as distinct as the first. It covers four chapters, the second to the sixth, all of them dating from the same earliest period of Isaiah's ministry, before 735 B.C. They deal with exactly the same subjects, but they differ greatly in form. One section (chaps. ii.-iv.) consists of a number of short utterances--evidently not all spoken at the same time, for they conflict with one another--a series of consecutive prophecies, that probably represent the stages of conviction through which Isaiah passed in his prophetic apprenticeship; a second section (chap. v.) is a careful and artistic restatement, in parable and oration, of the truths he has thus attained; while a third section (chap. vi.) is narrative, probably written subsequently to the first two, but describing an inspiration and official call, which must have preceded them both. The more one examines chaps. ii.-vi., and finds that they but express the same truths in different forms, the more one is confirmed in some such view of them as this, which, it is believed, the following exposition will justify. Chaps. v. and vi. are twin appendices to the long summary in ii.-iv.: chap. v. a public vindication and enforcement of the results of that summary, chap. vi. a private vindication to the prophet's heart of the very same truths, by a return to the secret moment of their original inspiration. We may assign 735 B.C., just before or just after the accession of Ahaz, as the date of the latest of these prophecies. The following is their historical setting.

For more than half a century the kingdom of Judah, under two powerful and righteous monarchs, had enjoyed the greatest prosperity. Uzziah strengthened the borders, extended the supremacy and vastly increased the resources of his little State, which, it is well to remember, was in its own size not larger than three average Scottish counties. He won back for Judah the port of Elath on the Red Sea, built a navy, and restored the commerce with the far East, which Solomon began. He overcame, in battle or by the mere terror of his name, the neighbouring nations--the Philistines that dwelt in cities, and the wandering tribes of desert Arabs. The Ammonites brought him gifts. With the wealth, which the East by tribute or by commerce poured into his little principality, Uzziah fortified his borders and his capital, undertook large works of husbandry and irrigation, organized a powerful standing army, and supplied it with a siege artillery capable of slinging arrows and stones. His name spread far abroad, for he was marvellously helped till he was strong. His son Jotham (740-735 B.C.) continued his father's policy with nearly all his father's success. He built cities and castles, quelled a rebellion among his tributaries, and caused their riches to flow faster still into Jerusalem. But while Jotham bequeathed to his country a sure defence and great wealth, and to his people a strong spirit and prestige among the nations, he left another bequest, which robbed these of their value--the son who succeeded him. In 735 Jotham died and Ahaz became king. He was very young, and stepped to the throne from the hareem. He brought to the direction of the government the petulant will of a spoiled child, the mind of an intriguing and superstitious woman. It was when the national policy felt the paralysis consequent on these that Isaiah published at least the later part of the prophecies now marked off as chaps. ii.-iv. of his book. My people, he cries--my people! children are their oppressors, and women rule over them. O my people, they which lead thee cause thee to err, and destroy the way of thy paths.

Isaiah had been born into the flourishing nation while Uzziah was king. The great events of that monarch's reign were his education, the still grander hopes they prompted the passion of his virgin fancy. He must have absorbed as the very temper of his youth this national consciousness which swelled so proudly in Judah under Uzziah. But the accession of such a king as Ahaz, while it was sure to let loose the passions and follies fostered by a period of rapid increase in luxury, could not fail to afford to Judah's enemies the long-deferred opportunity of attacking her. It was an hour both of the manifestation of sin and of the judgement of sin--an hour in which, while the majesty of Judah, sustained through two great reigns, was about to disappear in the follies of a third, the majesty of Judah's God should become more conspicuous than ever. Of this Isaiah had been privately conscious, as we shall see, for five years. In the year that king Uzziah died (740), the young Jew saw the Lord sitting upon a throne, high and lifted up. Startled into prophetic consciousness by the awful contrast between an earthly majesty that had so long fascinated men, but now sank into a leper's grave, and the heavenly, which rose sovereign and everlasting above it, Isaiah had gone on to receive conviction of his people's sin and certain punishment. With the accession of Ahaz, five years later, his own political experience was so far developed as to permit of his expressing in their exact historical effects the awful principles of which he had received foreboding when Uzziah died. What we find in chaps. ii.-iv. is a record of the struggle of his mind towards this expression; it is the summary, as we have already said, of Isaiah's apprenticeship.

The word that Isaiah, the son of Amoz, saw concerning Judah and Jerusalem. We do not know anything of Isaiah's family or of the details of his upbringing. He was a member of some family of Jerusalem, and in intimate relations with the Court. It has been believed that he was of royal blood, but it matters little whether this be true or not. A spirit so wise and masterful as his did not need social rank to fit it for that intimacy with princes which has doubtless suggested the legend of his royal descent. What does matter is Isaiah's citizenship in Jerusalem, for this colours all his prophecy. More than Athens to Demosthenes, Rome to Juvenal, Florence to Dante, is Jerusalem to Isaiah. She is his immediate and ultimate regard, the centre and return of all his thoughts, the hinge of the history of his time, the one thing worth preserving amidst its disasters, the summit of those brilliant hopes with which he fills the future. He has traced for us the main features of her position and some of the lines of her construction, many of the great figures of her streets, the fashions of her women, the arrival of embassies, the effect of rumours. He has painted her aspect in triumph, in siege, in famine and in earthquake; war filling her valleys with chariots, and again nature rolling tides of fruitfulness up to her gates; her moods of worship and panic and profligacy--till we see them all as clearly as the shadow following the sunshine and the breeze across the cornfields of our own summers.

If he takes wider observation of mankind, Jerusalem is his watch-tower. It is for her defence he battles through fifty years of statesmanship, and all his prophecy may be said to travail in anguish for her new birth. He was never away from her walls, but not even the psalms of the captives by the rivers of Babylon, with the desire of exile upon them, exhibit more beauty and pathos than the lamentations which Isaiah poured upon Jerusalem's sufferings or the visions in which he described her future solemnity and peace.

It is not with surprise, therefore, that we find the first prophecies of Isaiah directed upon his mother city: The word that Isaiah the son of Amoz saw concerning Judah and Jerusalem. There is little about Judah in these chapters: the country forms but a fringe to the capital.

Before we look into the subject of the prophecy, however, a short digression is necessary on the manner in which it is presented to us. It is not a reasoned composition or argument we have here; it is a vision, it is the word which Isaiah saw. The expression is vague, often abused and in need of defining. Vision is not employed here to express any magical display before the eyes of the prophet of the very words which he was to speak to the people, or any communication to his thoughts by dream or ecstasy. They are higher qualities of "vision" which these chapters unfold. There is, first of all, the power of forming an ideal, of seeing and describing a thing in the fulfilment of all the promise that is in it. But these prophecies are much more remarkable for two other powers of inward vision, to which we give the names of insight and intuition--insight into human character, intuition of Divine principles--clear knowledge of what man is and how God will act--a keen discrimination of the present state of affairs in Judah, and unreasoned conviction of moral truth and the Divine will. The original meaning of the Hebrew word saw, which is used in the title to this series, is to cleave, or split; then to see into, to see through, to get down beneath the surface of things and discover their real nature. And what characterizes the bulk of these visions is penetrativeness, the keenness of a man who will not be deceived by an outward show that he delights to hold up to our scorn, but who has a conscience for the inner worth of things and for their future consequences. To lay stress on the moral meaning of the prophet's vision is not to grudge, but to emphasize its inspiration by God. Of that inspiration Isaiah was himself assured. It was God's Spirit that enabled him to see thus keenly; for he saw things keenly, not only as men count moral keenness, but as God Himself sees them, in their value in His sight and in their attractiveness for His love and pity. In this prophecy there occurs a striking expression--the eyes of the glory of God. It was the vision of the Almighty Searcher and Judge, burning through man's pretence, with which the prophet felt himself endowed. This then was the second element in his vision--to penetrate men's hearts as God Himself penetrated them, and constantly, without squint or blur, to see right from wrong in their eternal difference. And the third element is the intuition of God's will, the perception of what line of action He will take. This last, of course, forms the distinct prerogative of Hebrew prophecy, that power of vision which is its climax; the moral situation being clear, to see then how God will act upon it.

Under these three powers of vision Jerusalem, the prophet's city, is presented to us--Jerusalem in three lights, really three Jerusalems. First, there is flashed out (chap. ii. 2-5) a vision of the ideal city, Jerusalem idealized and glorified. Then comes (ii. 6-iv. 1) a very realistic picture, a picture of the actual Jerusalem. And lastly at the close of the prophecy (iv. 2-6) we have a vision of Jerusalem as she shall be after God has taken her in hand--very different indeed from the ideal with which the prophet began. Here are three successive motives or phases of prophecy, which, as we have said, in all probability summarize the early ministry of Isaiah, and present him to us first as the idealist or visionary, second as

Rev. George Adam Smith, M.A.

the realist or critic, and third as the prophet proper or revealer of God's actual will.

I. The Idealist (ii. 1-5).

All men who have shown our race how great things are possible have had their inspiration in dreaming of the impossible. Reformers, who at death were content to have lived for the moving forward but one inch of some of their fellow-men, began by believing themselves able to lift the whole world at once. Isaiah was no exception to this human fashion. His first vision was that of a Utopia, and his first belief that his countrymen would immediately realize it. He lifts up to us a very grand picture of a vast commonwealth centred in Jerusalem. Some think he borrowed it from an older prophet; Micah has it also; it may have been the ideal of the age. But, at any rate, if we are not to take verse 5 in scorn, Isaiah accepted this as his own. And it shall come to pass in the last days, that the mountain of the Lord's house shall be established in the top of the mountains, and exalted above the hills, and all nations shall flow unto it. The prophet's own Jerusalem shall be the light of the world, the school and temple of the earth, the seat of the judgement of the Lord, when He shall reign over the nations, and all mankind shall dwell in peace beneath Him. It is a glorious destiny, and as its light shines from the far-off horizon, the latter days, in which the prophet sees it, what wonder that he is possessed and cries aloud, O house of Jacob, come ye, and let us walk in the light of the Lord! It seems to the young prophet's hopeful heart as if at once that ideal would be realized, as if by his own word he could lift his people to its fulfilment.

But that is impossible, and Isaiah perceives so as soon as he turns from the far-off horizon to the city at his feet, as soon as he leaves to-morrow alone and deals with to-day. The next verses of the chapter--from verse 6 onwards--stand in strong contrast to those which have described Israel's ideal. There Zion is full of the law and Jerusalem of the word of the Lord, the one religion flowing over from this centre upon the world. Here into the actual Jerusalem they have brought all sorts of foreign worship and heathen prophets; they are replenished from the East, and are soothsayers like the Philistines, and strike hands with the children of strangers. There all nations come to worship at Jerusalem; here her thought and faith are scattered over the idolatries of all nations. The ideal Jerusalem is full of spiritual blessings, the actual of the spoils of trade. There the swords are beat into ploughshares and the spears into pruning-hooks; here are vast and novel armaments, horses and chariots. There the Lord alone is worshipped; here the city is crowded with idols. The real Jerusalem could not possibly be more different from the ideal, nor its inhabitants as they are from what their prophet had confidently called on them to be.

II. The Realist (ii. 6-iv. 1).

Therefore Isaiah's attitude and tone suddenly change. The visionary becomes a realist, the enthusiast a cynic, the seer of the glorious city of God the prophet of God's judgement. The recoil is absolute in style, temper and thought, down to the very figures of speech which he uses. Before, Isaiah had seen, as it were, a lifting process at work, Jerusalem in the top of the mountains, and exalted above the hills. Now he beholds nothing but depression. For the day of the Lord of hosts shall be upon every one that is proud and haughty, upon all that is lifted up, and it shall be brought low, and the Lord alone shall be exalted in that day. Nothing in the great civilization, which he had formerly glorified, is worth preserving. The high towers, fenced walls, ships of Tarshish, treasures and armour must all perish, even the hills lifted by his imagination shall be bowed down, and the Lord alone be exalted in that day. This recoil reaches its extreme in the last verse of the chapter. The prophet, who had believed so much in man as to think possible an immediate commonwealth of nations, believes in man now so little that he does not hold him worth preserving: Cease ye from man, whose breath is in his nostrils; for wherein is he to be accounted of?

Attached to this general denunciation are some satiric descriptions, in the third chapter, of the anarchy, to which society in Jerusalem is fast being reduced under its childish and effeminate king. The scorn of these passages is scathing; the eyes of the glory of God burn through every rank, fashion and ornament in the town. King and court are not spared; the elders and princes are rigorously denounced. But by far the most striking effort of the prophet's boldness is his prediction of the overthrow of Jerusalem itself (ver. 8). What it cost Isaiah to utter and the people to hear we can only partly measure. To his own passionate patriotism it must have felt like treason, to the blind optimism of the popular religion it doubtless appeared the rankest heresy--to aver that the holy city, inviolate and almost unthreatened since the day David brought to her the ark of the Lord, and destined by the voice of her prophets, including Isaiah himself, to be established upon the tops of the mountains, was now to fall into ruin. But Isaiah's conscience overcomes his sense of consistency, and he who has just proclaimed the eternal glory of Jerusalem is provoked by his knowledge of her citizens' sins to recall his words and intimate her destruction. It may have been, that Isaiah was partly emboldened to so novel a threat, by his knowledge of the preparations which Syria and Israel were already making for the invasion of Judah. The prospect of Jerusalem, as the centre of a vast empire subject to Jehovah, however natural it was under a successful ruler like Uzziah, became, of course, unreal when every one of Uzziah's and Jotham's tributaries had risen in revolt against their successor, Ahaz. But of these outward movements Isaiah tells us nothing. He is wholly engrossed with Judah's sin. It is his growing acquaintance with the corruption of his fellow-countrymen that has turned his back on the ideal city of his opening ministry, and changed him into a prophet of Jerusalem's ruin. Their tongue and their doings are against the Lord, to provoke the eyes of His glory. Judge, prophet and elder, all the upper ranks and useful guides of the people, must perish. It is a sign of the degradation to which society shall be reduced, when Isaiah with keen sarcasm pictures the despairing people choosing a certain man to be their ruler because he alone has a coat to his back! (iii. 6).

With increased scorn Isaiah turns lastly upon the women of Jerusalem (iii. 16-iv. 2), and here perhaps the change which has passed over him since his opening prophecy is most striking. One likes to think of how the citizens of Jerusalem took this alteration in their prophet's temper. We know how popular so optimist a prophecy as that of the mountain of the Lord's house must have been, and can imagine how men and women loved the young face, bright with a far-off light, and the dream of an ideal that had no quarrel with the present. "But what a change is this that has come over him, who speaks not of to-morrow, but of to-day, who has brought his gaze from those distant horizons to our streets, who stares every man in the face (iii. 9), and makes the women feel that no pin and trimming, no ring and bracelet, escape his notice! Our loved prophet has become an impudent scorner!" Ah, men and women of Jerusalem, beware of those eyes! The glory of God is burning in them; they see you through and through, and they tell us that all your armour and the show of your countenance, and your foreign fashions are as nothing, for there are corrupt hearts below. This is your judgement, that instead of sweet spices there shall be rottenness, and instead of a girdle a rope, and instead of well-set hair baldness, and instead of a stomacher a girding of sackcloth, and branding instead of beauty. Thy men shall fall by the sword, and thy mighty in the war. And her gates shall lament and mourn, and she shall be desolate and sit upon the ground!

This was the climax of the prophet's judgement. If the salt have lost its savour, wherewith shall it be salted? It is thenceforth good for nothing but to be cast out and trodden under foot. If the women are corrupt the state is moribund.

III. The Prophet of the Lord (iv. 2-6).

Is there, then, no hope for Jerusalem? Yes, but not where the prophet sought it at first, in herself, and not in the way he offered it--by the mere presentation of an ideal. There is hope, there is more--there is certain salvation in the Lord, but it only comes after judgement. Contrast that opening picture of the new Jerusalem with this closing one, and we shall find their difference to lie in two things. There the city is more prominent than the Lord, here the Lord is more prominent than the city; there no word of judgement, here judgement sternly emphasized as the indispensable way towards the blessed future. A more vivid sense of the Person of Jehovah Himself, a deep conviction of the necessity of chastisement: these are what Isaiah has gained during his early ministry, without losing hope or heart for the future. The bliss shall come only when the Lord shall have washed away the filth of the daughters of Zion, and shall have purged the blood of Jerusalem from the midst thereof by the spirit of judgement and the spirit of burning. It is a corollary of all this that the participants of that future shall be many fewer than in the first vision of the prophet. The process of judgement must weed men out, and in place of all nations coming to Jerusalem, to share its peace and glory, the prophet can speak now only of Israel--and only of a remnant of Israel. The escaped of Israel, the left in Zion, and he that remaineth in Jerusalem. This is a great change in Isaiah's ideal, from the supremacy of Israel over all nations to the bare survival of a remnant of his people.

***

Is there not in this threefold vision a parallel and example for our own civilisation and our thoughts about it? All work and wisdom begin in dreams. We must see our Utopias before we start to build our stone and lime cities.

> "It takes a soul
> To move a body; it takes a high-souled man
> To move the masses even to a cleaner stye;
> It takes the ideal to blow an inch inside
> The dust of the actual."

But the light of our ideals dawns upon us only to show how poor by nature are the mortals who are called to accomplish them. The ideal rises still as to Isaiah only to exhibit the poverty of the real. When we lift our eyes from the hills of vision, and rest them on our fellow-men, hope and enthusiasm die out of us. Isaiah's disappointment is that of every one who brings down his gaze from the clouds to the streets. Be our ideal ever so desirable, be we ever so persuaded of its facility, the moment we attempt to apply it we shall be undeceived. Society cannot be regenerated all at once. There is an expression which

Rev. George Adam Smith, M.A.

Isaiah emphasizes in his motive of cynicism: The show of their countenance doth witness against them. It tells us that when he called his countrymen to turn to the light he lifted upon them he saw nothing but the exhibition of their sin made plain. When we bring light to a cavern whose inhabitants have lost their eyes by the darkness, the light does not make them see; we have to give them eyes again. Even so no vision or theory of a perfect state--the mistake which all young reformers make--can regenerate society. It will only reveal social corruption, and sicken the heart of the reformer himself. For the possession of a great ideal does not mean, as so many fondly imagine, work accomplished; it means work revealed--work revealed so vast, often so impossible, that faith and hope die down, and the enthusiast of yesterday becomes the cynic of to-morrow. Cease ye from man, whose breath is in his nostrils, for wherein is he to be accounted? In this despair, through which every worker for God and man must pass, many a warm heart has grown cold, many an intellect become paralyzed. There is but one way of escape, and that is Isaiah's. It is to believe in God Himself; it is to believe that He is at work, that His purposes to man are saving purposes, and that with Him there is an inexhaustible source of mercy and virtue. So from the blackest pessimism shall arise new hope and faith, as from beneath Isaiah's darkest verses that glorious passage suddenly bursts like uncontrollable spring from the very feet of winter. For that day shall the spring of the Lord be beautiful and glorious, and the fruit of the land shall be excellent and comely for them that are escaped of Israel. This is all it is possible to say. There must be a future for man, because God loves him, and God reigns. That future can be reached only through judgement, because God is righteous.

To put it another way: All of us who live to work for our fellow-men or who hope to lift them higher by our word begin with our own visions of a great future. These visions, though our youth lends to them an original generosity and enthusiasm, are, like Isaiah's, largely borrowed. The progressive instincts of the age into which we are born and the mellow skies of prosperity combine with our own ardour to make our ideal one of splendour. Persuaded of its facility, we turn to real life to apply it. A few years pass. We not only find mankind too stubborn to be forced into our moulds, but we gradually become aware of Another Moulder at work upon our subject, and we stand aside in awe to watch His operations. Human desires and national ideals are not always fulfilled; philosophic theories are discredited by the evolution of fact. Uzziah does not reign for ever; the sceptre falls to Ahaz: progress is checked, and the summer of prosperity draws to an end. Under duller skies ungilded judgement comes to view, cruel and inexorable, crushing even the peaks on which we built our future, yet purifying men and giving earnest of a better future, too. And so life, that mocked the control of our puny fingers, bends groaning to the weight of an Almighty Hand. God also, we perceive as we face facts honestly, has His ideal for men; and though He works so slowly towards His end that our restless eyes are too impatient to follow His order, He yet reveals all that shall be to the humbled heart and the soul emptied of its own visions. Awed and chastened, we look back from His Presence to our old ideals. We are still able to recognize their grandeur and generous hope for men. But we see now how utterly unconnected they are with the present--castles in the air, with no ladders to them from the earth. And even if they were accessible, still to our eyes, purged by gazing on God's own ways, they would no more appear desirable. Look back on Isaiah's early ideal from the light of his second vision of the future. For all its grandeur, that picture of Jerusalem is not wholly attractive. Is there not much national arrogance in it? Is it not just the imperfectly idealized reflection of an age of material prosperity such as that of Uzziah's was? Pride is in it, a false optimism, the highest good to be reached without moral conflict. But here is the language of pity, rescue with difficulty, rest only after sore struggle and stripping, salvation by the bare arm of God. So do our imaginations for our own future or for that of the race always contrast with what He Himself has in store for us, promised freely out of His great grace to our unworthy hearts, yet granted in the end only to those who pass towards it through discipline, tribulation and fire.

***

This, then, was Isaiah's apprenticeship, and its net result was to leave him with the remnant for his ideal: the remnant and Jerusalem secured as its rallying-point.

CHAPTER III

THE VINEYARD OF THE LORD, OR TRUE PATRIOTISM THE CONSCIENCE OF OUR COUNTRY'S SINS.

Isaiah v.; ix. 8-x. 4 (735 B.C.).

The prophecy contained in these chapters belongs, as we have seen, to the same early period of Isaiah's career as chapters ii.-iv., about the time when Ahaz ascended the throne after the long and successful reigns of his father and grandfather, when the kingdom of Judah seemed girt with strength and filled with wealth, but the men were corrupt and the women careless, and the earnest of approaching judgement was already given in the incapacity of the weak and woman-ridden king. Yet although this new prophecy issues from the same circumstances as its predecessors, it implies these circumstances a little more developed. The same social evils are treated, but by a hand with a firmer grasp of them. The same principles are emphasized--the righteousness of Jehovah and His activity in judgement--but the form of judgement of which Isaiah had spoken before in general terms looms nearer, and before the end of the prophecy we get a view at close quarters of the Assyrian ranks.

Besides, opposition has arisen to the prophet's teaching. We saw that the obscurities and inconsistencies of chapters ii.-iv. are due to the fact that that prophecy represents several stages of experience through which Isaiah passed before he gained his final convictions. But his countrymen, it appears, have now had time to turn on these convictions and call them in question: it is necessary for Isaiah to vindicate them. The difference, then, between these two sets of prophecies, dealing with the same things, is that in the former (chapters ii.-iv.), we have the obscure and tortuous path of a conviction struggling to light in the prophet's own experience; here, in chapter v., we have its careful array in the light and before the people.

The point of Isaiah's teaching against which opposition was directed was of course its main point, that God was about to abandon Judah. This must have appeared to the popular religion of the day as the rankest heresy. To the Jews the honour of Jehovah was bound up with the inviolability of Jerusalem and the prosperity of Judah. But Isaiah knew Jehovah to be infinitely more concerned for the purity of His people than for their prosperity. He had seen the Lord exalted in righteousness above those national and earthly interests, with which vulgar men exclusively identified His will. Did the people appeal to the long time Jehovah had graciously led them for proof that He would not abandon them now? To Isaiah that gracious leading was but for righteousness' sake, and that God might make His own a holy people. Their history, so full of the favours of the Almighty, did not teach Isaiah as it did the common prophets of his time, the lesson of Israel's political security, but the far different one of their religious responsibility. To him it only meant what Amos had already put in those startling words, You only have I known of all the families of the earth: therefore I will visit upon you all your iniquities. Now Isaiah delivered this doctrine at a time when it brought him the hostility of men's passions as well as of their opinions. Judah was arming for war. Syria and Ephraim were marching upon her. To threaten his country with ruin in such an hour was to run the risk of suffering from popular fury as a traitor as well as from priestly prejudice as a heretic. The strain of the moment is felt in the strenuousness of the prophecy. Chapter v., with its appendix, exhibits more grasp and method than its predecessors. Its literary form is finished, its feeling clear. There is a tenderness in the beginning of it, an inexorableness in the end and an eagerness all through, which stamp the chapter as Isaiah's final appeal to his countrymen at this period of his career.

The chapter is a noble piece of patriotism--one of the noblest of a race who, although for the greater part of their history without a fatherland, have contributed more brilliantly than perhaps any other to the literature of patriotism, and that simply because, as Isaiah here illustrates, patriotism was to their prophets identical with religious privilege and responsibility. Isaiah carries this to its bitter end. Other patriots have wept to sing their country's woes; Isaiah's burden is his people's guilt. To others an invasion of their fatherland by its enemies has been the motive to rouse by song or speech their countrymen to repel it. Isaiah also hears the tramp of the invader; but to him is permitted no ardour of defence, and his message to his countrymen is that they must succumb, for the invasion is irresistible and of the very judgement of God. How much it cost the prophet to deliver such a message we may see from those few verses of it in which his heart is not altogether silenced by his conscience. The sweet description of Judah as a vineyard, and the touching accents that break through the roll of denunciation with such phrases as My people are gone away into captivity unawares, tell us how the prophet's love of country is struggling with his duty to a righteous God. The course of feeling throughout the prophecy is very striking. The tenderness of the opening lyric seems ready to flow into gentle pleading with the whole people. But as the prophet turns to particular classes and their sins his mood changes to indignation, the voice settles down to judgement; till when it issues upon that clear statement of the coming of the Northern hosts every trace of emotion has left it, and the sentences ring out as unfaltering as the tramp of the armies they describe.

I. The Parable of the Vineyard (v. 1-7).

Isaiah adopts the resource of every misunderstood and unpopular teacher, and seeks to turn the flank of his people's prejudices by an attack in parable on their sympathies. Did they stubbornly believe it impossible for God to abandon a State He had so long and so carefully fostered? Let them judge from an analogous case in which they were all experts. In a picture of great beauty Isaiah describes a vineyard upon one of the sunny promontories visible from Jerusalem. Every care had been given it of which an experienced vine-dresser could think, but it brought forth only wild grapes. The vine-dresser himself is introduced, and appeals to the men of Judah and Jerusalem to judge between him and his vineyard. He gets their assent that all had been done which could be done, and fortified with that resolves to abandon the vineyard. I will lay it waste; it shall not be pruned nor digged, but there shall come up briers and thorns. Then the stratagem comes out, the speaker drops the tones of a human cultivator, and in the omnipotence of the Lord of heaven he is heard to say, I will also command the clouds that they rain no rain upon it. This diversion upon their sympathies having succeeded, the prophet scarcely needs to charge the people's prejudices in face. His point has been evidently carried. For the vineyard of Jehovah of hosts is the house of Israel, and the men of Judah his pleasant plant; and He looked for judgement, but behold oppression, for righteousness, but behold a cry.

The lesson enforced by Isaiah is just this, that in a people's civilization there lie the deepest responsibilities, for that is neither more nor less than their cultivation by God; and the question for a people is not how secure does this render them, nor what does it count for glory, but how far is it rising towards the intentions of its Author? Does it produce those fruits of righteousness for which alone God cares to set apart and cultivate the peoples? On this depends the question whether the civilization is secure, as well as the right of the people to enjoy and feel proud of it. There cannot be true patriotism without sensitiveness to this, for however rich be the elements that compose the patriot's temper, as piety towards the past, ardour of service for the present, love of liberty, delight in natural beauty and gratitude for Divine favour, so rich a temper will grow rancid without the salt of conscience; and the richer the temper is, the greater must be the proportion of that salt. All prophets and poets of patriotism have been moralists and satirists as well. From Demosthenes to Tourgenieff, from Dante to Mazzini, from Milton to Russell Lowell, from Burns to Heine, one cannot recall any great patriot who has not known how to use the scourge as well as the trumpet. Many opportunities will present themselves to us of illustrating Isaiah's orations by the letters and speeches of Cromwell, who of moderns most resembles the statesman-prophet of Judah; but nowhere does the resemblance become so close as when we lay a prophecy like this of Jehovah's vineyard by the side of the speeches in which the Lord Protector exhorted the Commons of England, although it was the hour of his and their triumph, to address themselves to their sins.

So, then, the patriotism of all great men has carried a conscience for their country's sins. But while this is always more or less a burden to the true patriot, there are certain periods in which his care for his country ought to be this predominantly, and need be little else. In a period like our own, for instance, of political security and fashionable religion, what need is there in patriotic displays of any other kind? but how much for patriotism of this kind--of men who will uncover the secret sins, however loathsome, and declare the hypocrisies, however powerful, of the social life of the people! These are the patriots we need in times of peace; and as it is more difficult to rouse a torpid people to their sins than to lead a roused one against their enemies, and harder to face a whole people with the support only of conscience than to defy many nations if you but have your own at your back, so these patriots of peace are more to be honoured than those of war. But there is one kind of patriotism more arduous and honourable still. It is that which Isaiah displays here, who cannot add to his conscience hope or even pity, who must hail his country's enemies for his country's good, and recite the long roll of God's favours to his nation only to emphasize the justice of His abandonment of them.

II. The Wild Grapes of Judah (v. 8-24).

The wild grapes which Isaiah saw in the vineyard of the Lord he catalogues in a series of Woes (vv. 8-24), fruits all of them of love of money and love of wine. They are abuse of the soil (8-10, 17[4]), a giddy luxury which has taken to drink (11-16), a moral blindness and headlong audacity of sin which habitual avarice and drunkenness soon develop (18-21), and, again, a greed of drink and money--men's perversion of their strength to wine, and of their opportunities of justice to the taking of bribes (22-24).

These are the features of corrupt civilization not only in Judah, and the voice that deplores them cannot speak without rousing others very clamant to the modern conscience. It is with remarkable persistence that in every civilization the two main passions of the human heart, love of wealth and love of pleasure, the instinct to gather and the instinct to squander, have sought precisely these two forms denounced by Isaiah in which to work their social havoc--appropriation of the soil and indulgence in strong drink. Every civilized community develops sooner or later its land-question and its liquor-question. "Questions" they are called by the superficial opinion that all difficulties may be overcome by the cleverness of men; yet problems through which there cries for remedy so vast a proportion of our poverty, crime and madness, are something worse than "questions." They are huge sins, and require not merely the statesman's wit, but all the penitence and zeal of which a nation's conscience is capable. It is in this that the force of Isaiah's treatment lies. We feel he is not facing questions of State, but sins of men. He has nothing to tell us of what he considers the best system of land tenure, but he enforces the principle that in the ease with which land may be absorbed by one person the natural covetousness of the human heart has a terrible opportunity for working ruin upon society. Woe unto them that join house to house, that lay field to field, till there be no room, and ye be made to dwell alone in the midst of the land. We know from Micah that the actual process which Isaiah condemns was carried out with the most cruel evictions and disinheritances. Isaiah does not touch on its methods, but exposes its effects on the country--depopulation and barrenness,--and emphasizes its religious significance. Of a truth many houses shall be desolate, even great and fair, without an inhabitant. For ten acres of vineyard shall yield one bath, and a homer of seed shall yield but an ephah.... Then shall lambs feed as in their pasture, and strangers shall devour the ruins of the fat ones--i.e., of the luxurious landowners (9, 10, 17. See note on previous page). And in one of those elliptic statements by which he often startles us with the sudden sense that God Himself is acquainted with all our affairs, and takes His own interest in them, Isaiah adds, "All this was whispered to me by Jehovah: In mine ears--the Lord of hosts" (ver. 9).

During recent agitations in our own country one has often seen the "land laws of the Bible" held forth by some thoughtless demagogue as models for land tenure among ourselves; as if a system which worked well with a small tribe in a land they had all entered on equal footing, and where there was no opportunity for the industry of the people except in pasture and tillage, could possibly be applicable to a vastly larger and more complex population, with different traditions and very different social circumstances. Isaiah says nothing about the peculiar land laws of his people. He lays down principles, and these are principles valid in every civilization. God has made the land, not to feed the pride of the few, but the natural hunger of the many, and it is His will that the most be got out of a country's soil for the people of the country. Whatever be the system of land-tenure--and while all are more or less liable to abuse, it is the duty of a people to agitate for that which will be least liable--if it is taken advantage of by individuals to satisfy their own cupidity, then God will take account of them. There is a responsibility which the State cannot enforce, and the neglect of which cannot be punished by any earthly law, but all the more will God see to it. A nation's treatment of their land is not always prominent as a question which demands the attention of public reformers; but it ceaselessly has interest for God, who ever holds individuals to answer for it. The land-question is ultimately a religious question. For the management of their land the whole nation is responsible to God, but especially those who own or manage estates. This is a sacred office. When one not only remembers the nature of land--how it is an element of life, so that if a man abuse the soil it is as if he poisoned the air or darkened the heavens--but appreciates also the multitude of personal relations which the landowner or factor holds in his hand--the peace of homes, the continuity of local traditions, the physical health, the social fearlessness and frankness, and the thousand delicate associations which their habitations entwine about the hearts of men--one feels that to all who possess or manage land is granted an opportunity of patriotism and piety open to few, a ministry less honourable and sacred than none other committed by God to man for his fellow-men.

After the land-sin Isaiah hurls his second Woe upon the drink-sin, and it is a heavier woe than the first. With fatal persistence the luxury of every civilization has taken to drink; and of all the indictments brought by moralists against nations, that which they reserve for drunkenness is, as here, the most heavily weighted. The crusade against drink is not the novel thing that many imagine who observe only its late revival among ourselves. In ancient times there was scarcely a State in which prohibitive legislation of the most stringent kind was not attempted, and generally carried out with a thoroughness more possible under despots than where, as with us, the slow consent of public opinion is necessary. A horror of strong drink has in every age possessed those who from their position as magistrates or prophets have been able to follow for any distance the drifts of social life. Isaiah exposes as powerfully as ever any of them did in what the peculiar fatality of drinking lies. Wine is a mocker by nothing more than by the moral incredulity which it produces, enabling men to hide from themselves the spiritual and material effects of over-indulgence in it. No one who has had to do with persons slowly falling from moderate to immoderate drinking can mistake Isaiah's meaning when he says, They regard not the work of the Lord; neither have they considered the operation of His hands. Nothing kills the conscience like steady drinking to a little excess; and religion, even while the conscience is alive, acts on it only as an opiate. It is not, however, with the symptoms of drink in individuals so much as with its aggregate effects on the nation that Isaiah is concerned. So prevalent is excessive drinking, so entwined with the social customs of the country and many powerful interests, that it is extremely difficult to rouse public opinion to its effects. And so they go into captivity for lack of knowledge. Temperance reformers are often blamed for the strength of their language, but they may shelter themselves behind Isaiah. As he pictures it, the national destruction caused by drink is complete. It is nothing less than the people's captivity, and we know what that meant to an Israelite. It affects all classes: Their honourable men are famished, and their multitude parched with thirst.... The mean man is bowed down, and the great man is humbled. But the want and ruin of this earth are not enough to describe it. The appetite of hell itself has to be enlarged to suffice for the consumption of the spoils of strong drink. Therefore hell hath enlarged her desire and opened her mouth without measure; and their glory, and their multitude, and their pomp, and he that rejoiceth among them, descend into it. The very appetite of hell has to be enlarged! Does it not truly seem as if the wild and wanton waste of drink were preventable, as if it were not, as many are ready to sneer, the inevitable evil of men's hearts choosing this form of issue, but a superfluous audacity of sin, which the devil himself did not desire or tempt men to? It is this feeling of the infernal gratuitousness of most of the drink-evil--the conviction that here hell would be quiet if only she were not stirred up by the extraordinarily wanton provocatives that society and the State offer to excessive drinking--which compels temperance reformers at the present day to isolate drunkenness and make it the object of a special crusade. Isaiah's strong figure has lost none of its strength to-day. When our judges tell us from the bench that nine-tenths of pauperism and crime are caused by drink, and our physicians that if only irregular tippling were abolished half the current sickness of the land would cease, and our statesmen that the ravages of strong drink are equal to those of the historical scourges of war, famine and pestilence combined, surely to swallow such a glut of spoil the appetite of hell must have been still more enlarged, and the mouth of hell made yet wider.

The next three Woes are upon different aggravations of that moral perversity which the prophet has already traced to strong drink. In the first of these it is better to read, draw punishment near with cords of vanity, than draw iniquity. Then we have a striking antithesis--the drunkards mocking Isaiah over their cups with the challenge, as if it would not be taken up, Let Jehovah make speed, and hasten His work of judgement, that we may see it, while all the time they themselves were dragging that judgement near, as with cart-ropes, by their persistent diligence in evil. This figure of sinners jeering at the approach of a calamity while they actually wear the harness of its carriage is very striking. But the Jews are not only unconscious of judgement, they are confused as to the very principles of morality: Who call evil good, and good evil; that put darkness for light, and light for darkness; that put bitter for sweet, and sweet for bitter!

In his fifth Woe the prophet attacks a disposition to which his scorn gives no peace throughout his ministry. If these sensualists had only confined themselves to their sensuality they might have been left alone; but with that intellectual bravado which is equally born with "Dutch courage" of drink, they interfered in the conduct of the State, and prepared arrogant policies of alliance and war that were the distress of the sober-minded prophet all his days. Woe unto them that are wise in their own eyes and prudent in their own sight.

In his last Woe Isaiah returns to the drinking habits of the upper classes, from which it would appear that among the judges even of Judah there were "six-bottle men." They sustained their extravagance by subsidies, which we trust were unknown to the mighty men of wine who once filled the seats of justice in our own country. They justify the wicked for a bribe, and take away the righteousness of the righteous from him. All these sinners, dead through their rejection of the law of Jehovah of hosts and the word of the Holy One of Israel, shall be like to the stubble, fit only for burning, and their blossom as the dust of the rotten tree.

III. The Anger of the Lord (v. 25; ix. 8-x. 4; v. 26-30).

This indictment of the various sins of the people occupies the whole of the second part of the oration. But a third part is now added, in which the prophet catalogues the judgements of the Lord upon them, each of these closing with the weird refrain, For all this His anger is not turned away, but His hand is stretched out still. The complete catalogue is usually obtained by inserting between the 25th and 26th verses of chapter v. the long passage from chapter ix., ver. 8, to chapter x., ver. 4. It is quite true that as far as chapter v. itself is concerned it does not need this insertion; but ix. 8-x. 4 is decidedly out of place where it now lies. Its paragraphs end with the same refrain as closes v. 25, which forms, besides, a natural introduction to them, while v. 26-30 form as natural a conclusion. The latter verses describe an Assyrian invasion, and it was always in an Assyrian invasion that Isaiah foresaw the final calamity of Judah. We may, then, subject to further light on the exceedingly obscure subject of the arrangement of Isaiah's prophecies, follow some of the leading critics, and place ix. 8-x. 4 between verses 25-26 of chapter v.; and the more we examine them the more we shall be satisfied with our arrangement, for strung together in this order they form one of the most impressive series of scenes which even an Isaiah has given us.

From these scenes Isaiah has spared nothing that is terrible in history or nature, and it is not one of the least of the arguments for putting them together that their intensity increases to a climax. Earthquakes, armed raids, a great battle and the slaughter of a people; prairie and forest fires, civil strife and the famine fever, that feeds upon itself; another battle-field, with its cringing groups of captives and heaps of slain; the resistless tide of a great invasion; and then, for final prospect, a desolate land by the sound of a hungry sea, and the light is darkened in the clouds thereof. The elements of nature and the elemental passions of man have been let loose together; and we follow the violent floods, remembering that it is sin which has burst the gates of the universe, and given the tides of hell full course through it. Over the storm and battle there comes booming like the storm-bell the awful refrain, For all this His anger is not turned away, but His hand is stretched out still. It is poetry of the highest order, but in him who reads it with a conscience mere literary sensations are sobered by the awe of some of the most profound moral phenomena of life. The persistence of Divine wrath, the long-lingering effects of sin in a nation's history, man's abuse of sorrow and his defiance of an angry Providence, are the elements of this great drama. Those who are familiar with King Lear, will recognize these elements, and observe how similarly the ways of Providence and the conduct of men are represented there and here.

What Isaiah unfolds, then, is a series of calamities that have overtaken the people of Israel. It is impossible for us to identify every one of them with a particular event in Israel's history otherwise known to us. Some it is not difficult to recognize; but the prophet passes in a perplexing way from Judah to Ephraim and Ephraim to Judah, and in one case, where he represents Samaria as attacked by Syria and the Philistines, he goes back to a period at some distance from his own. There are also passages, as for instance x. 1-4, in which we are unable to decide whether he describes a present punishment or threatens a future one. But his moral purpose, at least, is plain. He will show how often Jehovah has already spoken to His people by calamity, and because they have remained hardened under these warnings, how there now remains possible only the last, worst blow of an Assyrian invasion. Isaiah is justifying his threat of so unprecedented and extreme a punishment for God's people as overthrow by this Northern people, who had just appeared upon Judah's political horizon. God, he tells Israel, has tried everything short of this, and it has failed; now only this remains, and this shall not fail. The prophet's purpose, therefore, being not an accurate historical recital, but moral impressiveness, he gives us a more or less ideal description of former calamities, mentioning only so much as to allow us to recognize here and there that it is actual facts which he uses for his purpose of condemning Israel to captivity, and vindicating Israel's God in bringing that captivity near. The passage thus forms a parallel to that in Amos, with its similar refrain: Yet ye have not returned unto Me, saith the Lord (Amos iv. 6-12), and only goes farther than that earlier prophecy in indicating that the instruments of the Lord's final judgement are to be the Assyrians.

Five great calamities, says Isaiah, have fallen on Israel and left them hardened: 1st, earthquake (v. 25); 2nd, loss of territory (ix. 8-12); 3rd, war and a decisive defeat (ix. 13-17); 4th, internal anarchy (ix. 18-21); 5th, the near prospect of captivity (x. 1-4).

1. The Earthquake (v. 25).--Amos closes his series with an earthquake; Isaiah begins with one. It may be the same convulsion they describe, or may not. Although the skirts of Palestine both to the east and west frequently tremble to these disturbances, an earthquake in Palestine itself, up on the high central ridge of the land, is very rare. Isaiah vividly describes its awful simplicity and suddenness. The Lord stretched forth His hand and smote, and the hills shook, and their carcases were like offal in the midst of the streets. More words are not needed, because there was nothing more to describe. The Lord lifted His hand; the hills seemed for a moment to topple over, and when the living recovered from the shock there lay the dead, flung like refuse about the streets.

2. The Loss of Territory (ix. 8-21).--So awful a calamity, in which the dying did not die out of sight nor fall huddled together on some far off battle-field, but the whole land was strewn with her slain, ought to have left indelible impression on the people. But it did not. The Lord's own word had been in it for Jacob and Israel (ix. 8), that the people might know, even Ephraim and the inhabitants of Samaria. But unhumbled they turned in the stoutness of their hearts, saying, when the earthquake had passed: [5] The bricks are fallen, but we will build with hewn stones; [6] the sycamores are cut down, but we will change them into cedars. Calamity did not make this people thoughtful; they felt God only to endeavour to forget Him. Therefore He visited them the second time. They did not feel the Lord shaking their land, so He sent their enemies to steal it from them: the Syrians before and the Philistines behind; and they devour Israel with open mouth. What that had been for appalling suddenness this was for lingering and harassing--guerilla warfare, armed raids, the land eaten away bit by bit. Yet the people do not return unto Him that smote them, neither seek they the Lord of hosts.

3. War and Defeat (ix. 13-17).--The next consequent calamity passed from the land to the people themselves. A great battle is described, in which the nation is dismembered in one day. War and its horrors are told, and the apparent want of Divine pity and discrimination which they imply is explained.

Rev. George Adam Smith, M.A.

Israel has been led into these disasters by the folly of their leaders, whom Isaiah therefore singles out for blame. For they that lead these people cause them to err, and they that are led of them are destroyed. But the real horror of war is that it falls not upon its authors, that its victims are not statesmen, but the beauty of a country's youth, the helplessness of the widow and orphan. Some question seems to have been stirred by this in Isaiah's heart. He asks, Why does the Lord not rejoice in the young men of His people? Why has He no pity for widow and orphan, that He thus sacrifices them to the sin of the rulers? It is because the whole nation shares the ruler's guilt; every one is an hypocrite and an evil-doer, and every mouth speaketh folly. As ruler so people, is a truth Isaiah frequently asserts, but never with such grimness as here. War brings out, as nothing else does, the solidarity of a people in guilt.

4. Internal Anarchy (ix. 18-21).--Even yet the people did not repent; their calamities only drove them to further wickedness. The prophet's eyes are opened to the awful fact that God's wrath is but the blast that fans men's hot sins to flame. This is one of those two or three awful scenes in history, in the conflagration of which we cannot tell what is human sin and what Divine judgement. There is a panic wickedness, sin spreading like mania, as if men were possessed by supernatural powers. The physical metaphors of the prophet are evident: a forest or prairie fire, and the consequent famine, whose fevered victims feed upon themselves. And no less evident are the political facts which the prophet employs these metaphors to describe. It is the anarchy which has beset more than one corrupt and unfortunate people, when their misleaders have been overthrown: the anarchy in which each faction seeks to slaughter out the rest. Jealousy and distrust awake the lust for blood, rage seizes the people as fire the forest, and no man spareth his brother. We have had modern instances of all this; these scenes form a true description of some days of the French Revolution, and are even a truer description of the civil war that broke out in Paris after her late siege.

> *"If that the heavens do not their visible spirits*
> *Send quickly down to tame these vile offences,*
> *'T will come,*
> *Humanity must perforce prey on itself*
> *Like monsters of the deep."* [7]

5. The Threat of Captivity (x. 1-4).--Turning now from the past, and from the fate of Samaria, with which it would appear he has been more particularly engaged, the prophet addresses his own countrymen in Judah, and paints the future for them. It is not a future in which there is any hope. The day of their visitation also will surely come, and the prophet sees it close in the darkest night of which a Jewish heart could think--the night of captivity. Where, he asks his unjust countrymen--where will ye then flee for help? and where will you leave your glory? Cringing among the captives, lying dead beneath heaps of dead--that is to be your fate, who will have turned so often and then so finally from God. When exactly the prophet thus warned his countrymen of captivity we do not know, but the warning, though so real, produced neither penitence in men nor pity in God. For all this His anger is not turned away, but His hand is stretched out still.

6. The Assyrian Invasion (v. 26-30).--The prophet is, therefore, free to explain that cloud which has appeared far away on the northern horizon. God's hand of judgement is still uplifted over Judah, and it is that hand which summons the cloud. The Assyrians are coming in answer to God's signal, and they are coming as a flood, to leave nothing but ruin and distress behind them. No description by Isaiah is more majestic than this one, in which Jehovah, who has exhausted every nearer means of converting His people, lifts His undrooping arm with a flag to the nations that are far off, and hisses or whistles for them from the end of the earth. And, behold, they come with speed, swiftly: there is no weary one nor straggler among them; none slumbers nor sleeps; nor loosed is the girdle of his loins, nor broken the latchet of his shoes; whose arrows are sharpened, and all their bows bent; their horses' hoofs are like the flint, and their wheels like the whirlwind; a roar have they like the lion's, and they roar like young lions; yea, they growl and grasp the prey, and carry it off, and there is none to deliver. And they growl upon him that day like the growling of the sea; and if one looks to the land, behold, dark and distress, and the light is darkened in the cloudy heaven.

Thus Isaiah leaves Judah to await her doom. But the tones of his weird refrain awaken in our hearts some thoughts which will not let his message go from us just yet.

It will ever be a question, whether men abuse more their sorrows or their joys; but no earnest soul can doubt, which of these abuses is the more fatal. To sin in the one case is to yield to a temptation; to sin in the other is to resist a Divine grace. Sorrow is God's last message to man; it is God speaking in emphasis. He who abuses it shows that he can shut his ears when God speaks loudest. Therefore heartlessness or impenitence after sorrow is more dangerous than intemperance in joy; its results are always more tragic. Now Isaiah points out that men's abuse of sorrow is twofold. Men abuse sorrow by mistaking it, and they abuse sorrow by defying it.

Men abuse sorrow by mistaking it, when they see in it nothing but a penal or expiatory force. To many men sorrow is what his devotions were to Louis XI., which having religiously performed, he felt the more brave to sin. So with the Samaritans, who said in the stoutness of their hearts, The bricks are fallen down, but we will build with hewn stones; the sycomores are cut down, but we will change them into cedars. To speak in this way is happy, but heathenish. It is to call sorrow "bad luck;" it is to hear no voice of God in it, saying, "Be pure; be humble; lean upon Me." This disposition springs from a vulgar conception of God, as of a Being of no permanence in character, easily irritated but relieved by a burst of passion, smartly punishing His people and then leaving them to themselves. It is a temper which says, "God is angry, let us wait a little; God is appeased, let us go ahead again." Over against such vulgar views of a Deity with a temper Isaiah unveils the awful majesty of God in holy wrath: For all this His anger is not turned away, but His hand is stretched out still. How grim and savage does it appear to our eyes till we understand the thoughts of the sinners to whom it was revealed! God cannot dispel the cowardly thought, that He is anxious only to punish, except by letting His heavy hand abide till it purify also. The permanence of God's wrath is thus an ennobling, not a stupefying doctrine.

Men also abuse sorrow by defying it, but the end of this is madness. "It forms the greater part of the tragedy of King Lear, that the aged monarch, though he has given his throne away, retains his imperiousness of heart, and continues to exhibit a senseless, if sometimes picturesque, pride and selfishness in face of misfortune. Even when he is overthrown he must still command; he fights against the very elements; he is determined to be at least the master of his own sufferings and destiny. But for this the necessary powers fail him; his life thus disordered terminates in madness. It was only by such an affliction that a character like his could be brought to repentance, ... to humility, which is the parent of true love, and that love in him could be purified. Hence the melancholy close of that tragedy." [8] As Shakespeare has dealt with the king, so Isaiah with the people; he also shows us sorrow when it is defied bringing forth madness. On so impious a height man's brain grows dizzy, and he falls into that terrible abyss which is not, as some imagine, hell, but God's last purgatory. Shakespeare brings shattered Lear out of it, and Isaiah has a remnant of the people to save.

Footnotes:

4. Ewald happily suggests that verse 17 has dropped out of, and should be restored to, its proper position at the end of the first "woe," where it contributes to the development of the meaning far more than from where it stands in the text.

5. Read past tenses, as in the margin of Revised Version, for all the future tenses, or better, the historical present, down to the end of the chapter.

6. It is part of the argument for connecting ix. 8 with v. 25 that this phrase would be very natural after the earthquake described in v. 25.

7. King Lear, act iv., sc. 2.

8. Ulrici: Shakespeare's Dramatic Art.

Rev. George Adam Smith, M.A.

CHAPTER IV

ISAIAH'S CALL AND CONSECRATION.

Isaiah vi. (740 B.C.; WRITTEN 735? OR 725?).

It has been already remarked that in chapter vi. we should find no other truths than those which have been unfolded in chapters ii.-v.: the Lord exalted in righteousness, the coming of a terrible judgement from Him upon Judah, and the survival of a bare remnant of the people. But chapter vi. treats the same subjects with a difference. In chapters ii.-iv. they gradually appear and grow to clearness in connection with the circumstances of Judah's history; in chapter v. they are formally and rhetorically vindicated; in chapter vi. we are led back to the secret and solemn moments of their first inspiration in the prophet's own soul. It may be asked why chapter vi. comes last and not first in this series, and why in an exposition, attempting to deal, as far as possible, chronologically with Isaiah's prophecies, his call should not form the subject of the first chapter. The answer is simple, and throws a flood of light upon the chapter. In all probability chapter vi. was written after its predecessors, and what Isaiah has put into it is not only what happened in the earliest moments of his prophetic life, but that spelt out and emphasized by his experience since. The ideal character of the narrative, and its date some years after the events which it relates, are now generally admitted. Of course the narrative is all fact. No one will believe that he, whose glance penetrated with such keenness the character of men and movements, looked with dimmer eye into his own heart. It is the spiritual process which the prophet actually passed through before the opening of his ministry. But it is that, developed by subsequent experience, and presented to us in the language of outward vision. Isaiah had been some years a prophet, long enough to make clear that prophecy was not to be for him what it had been for his predecessors in Israel, a series of detached inspirations and occasional missions, with short responsibilities, but a work for life, a profession and a career, with all that this means of postponement, failure, and fluctuation of popular feeling. Success had not come so rapidly as the prophet in his original enthusiasm had looked for, and his preaching had effected little upon the people. Therefore he would go back to the beginning, remind himself of that to which God had really called him, and vindicate the results of his ministry, at which people scoffed and his own heart grew sometimes sick. In chapter vi. Isaiah acts as his own remembrancer. If we keep in mind, that this chapter, describing Isaiah's call and consecration to the prophetic office, was written by a man who felt that office to be the burden of a lifetime, and who had to explain its nature and vindicate its results to his own soul--grown somewhat uncertain, it may be, of her original inspiration--we shall find light upon features of the chapter that are otherwise most obscure.

1. The Vision (vv. 1-4).

Several years, then, Isaiah looks back and says, In the year King Uzziah died. There is more than a date given here; there is a great contrast suggested. Prophecy does not chronicle by time, but by experiences, and we have here, as it seems, the cardinal experience of a prophet's life.

All men knew of that glorious reign with the ghastly end--fifty years of royalty, and then a lazar-house. There had been no king like this one since Solomon; never, since the son of David brought the Queen of Sheba to his feet, had the national pride stood so high or the nation's dream of sovereignty touched such remote borders. The people's admiration invested Uzziah with all the graces of the ideal monarch. The chronicler of Judah tells us that God helped him and made him to prosper, and his name spread far abroad, and he was marvellously helped till he was strong; he with the double name--Azariah, Jehovah-his-Helper; Uzziah, Jehovah-his-Strength. How this glory fell upon the fancy of the future prophet, and dyed it deep, we may imagine from those marvellous colours, with which in later years he painted the king in his beauty. Think of the boy, the boy that was to be an Isaiah, the boy with the germs of this great prophecy in his heart--think of him and such a hero as this to shine upon him, and we may conceive how his whole nature opened out beneath that sun of royalty and absorbed its light.

Suddenly the glory was eclipsed, and Jerusalem learned that she had seen her king for the last time: The Lord smote the king so that he was a leper unto the day of his death, and dwelt in a several house, and he was cut off from the house of the Lord. Uzziah had gone into the temple, and attempted with his own hands to burn incense. Under a later dispensation of liberty he would have been applauded as a brave Protestant, vindicating the right of every worshipper of God to approach Him without the intervention of a special priesthood. Under the earlier dispensation of law his act could be regarded only as one of presumption, the expression of a worldly and irreverent temper, which ignored the infinite distance between God and man. It was followed, as sins of wilfulness in religion were always followed under the old covenant, by swift disaster. Uzziah suffered as Saul, Uzzah, Nadab and Abihu did. The wrath, with which he burst out on the opposing priests, brought on, or made evident as it is believed to have done in other cases, an attack of leprosy. The white spot stood out unmistakeably from the flushed forehead, and he was thrust from the temple--yea, himself also hasted to go out.

We can imagine how such a judgement, the moral of which must have been plain to all, affected the most sensitive heart in Jerusalem. Isaiah's imagination was darkened, but he tells us that the crisis was the enfranchisement of his faith. In the year King Uzziah died--it is as if a veil had dropped, and the prophet saw beyond what it had hidden, the Lord sitting on a throne high and lifted up. That it is no mere date Isaiah means, but a spiritual contrast which he is anxious to impress upon us, is made clear by his emphasis of the rank and not the name of God. It is the Lord sitting upon a throne--the Lord absolutely, set over against the human prince. The simple antithesis seems to speak of the passing away of the young man's hero-worship and the dawn of his faith; and so interpreted, this first verse of chapter vi. is only a concise summary of that development of religious experience which we have traced through chapters ii.-iv. Had Isaiah ever been subject to the religious temper of his time, the careless optimism of a prosperous and proud people, who entered upon their religious services without awe, trampling the courts of the Lord, and used them like Uzziah, for their own honour, who felt religion to be an easy thing, and dismissed from it all thoughts of judgement and feelings of penitence--if ever Isaiah had been subject to that temper, then once for all he was redeemed by this stroke upon Uzziah. And, as we have seen, there is every reason to believe that Isaiah did at first share the too easy public religion of his youth. That early vision of his (ii. 2-5), the establishment of Israel at the head of the nations, to be immediately attained at his own word (v. 5) and without preliminary purification, was it not simply a less gross form of the king's own religious presumption? Uzziah's fatal act was the expression of the besetting sin of his people, and in that sin Isaiah himself had been a partaker. I am a man of unclean lips, and I dwell in the midst of a people of unclean lips. In the person of their monarch the temper of the whole Jewish nation had come to judgement. Seeking the ends of religion by his own way, and ignoring the way God had appointed, Uzziah at the very moment of his insistence was hurled back and stamped unclean. The prophet's eyes were opened. The king sank into a leper's grave, but before Isaiah's vision the Divine majesty arose in all its loftiness. I saw the Lord high and lifted up. We already know what Isaiah means by these terms. He has used them of God's supremacy in righteousness above the low moral standards of men, of God's occupation of a far higher throne than that of the national deity of Judah, of God's infinite superiority to Israel's vulgar identification of His purposes with her material prosperity or His honour with the compromises of her politics, and especially of God's seat as their Judge over a people, who sought in their religion only satisfaction for their pride and love of ease.

From this contrast the whole vision expands as follows.

Under the mistaken idea that what Isaiah describes is the temple in Jerusalem, it has been remarked, that the place of his vision is wonderful in the case of one who set so little store by ceremonial worship. This, however, to which our prophet looks is no house built with hands, but Jehovah's own heavenly palace (ver. 1--not temple); only Isaiah describes it in terms of the Jerusalem temple which was its symbol. It was natural that the temple should furnish Isaiah not only with the framework of his vision, but also with the platform from which he saw it. For it was in the temple that Uzziah's sin was sinned and God's holiness vindicated upon him. It was in the temple that, when Isaiah beheld the scrupulous religiousness of the people, the contrast of that with their evil lives struck him, and he summed it up in the epigram wickedness and worship (i. 13). It was in the temple, in short, that the prophet's conscience had been most roused, and just where the conscience is most roused there is the vision of God to be expected. Very probably it was while brooding over Uzziah's judgement on the scene of its occurrence that Isaiah beheld his vision. Yet for all the vision contained the temple itself was too narrow. The truth which was to be revealed to Isaiah, the holiness of God, demanded a wider stage and the breaking down of those partitions, which, while they had been designed to impress God's presence on the worshipper, had only succeeded in veiling Him. So while the seer keeps his station on the threshold of the earthly building, soon to feel it rock beneath his feet, as heaven's praise bursts like thunder on the earth, and while his immediate neighbourhood remains the same familiar house, all beyond is glorified. The veil of the temple falls away, and everything behind it. No ark nor mercy-seat is visible, but a throne and a court--the palace of God in heaven, as we have it also pictured in the eleventh and twenty-ninth Psalms. The Royal Presence is everywhere. Isaiah describes no face, only a Presence and a Session: the Lord sitting on a throne, and His skirts filled the palace.

> "No face; only the sight
> Of a sweepy garment vast and white
> With a hem that I could recognize." [9]

Rev. George Adam Smith, M.A.

Around (not above, as in the English version) were ranged the hovering courtiers, of what shape and appearance we know not, except that they veiled their faces and their feet before the awful Holiness,--all wings and voice, perfect readinesses of praise and service. The prophet heard them chant in antiphon, like the temple choirs of priests. And the one choir cried out, Holy, holy, holy is Jehovah of hosts; and the other responded, The whole earth is full of His glory.

It is by the familiar name Jehovah of hosts--the proper name of Israel's national God--that the prophet hears the choirs of heaven address the Divine Presence. But what they ascribe to the Deity is exactly what Israel will not ascribe, and the revelation they make of His nature is the contradiction of Israel's thoughts concerning Him.

What, in the first place, is HOLINESS? We attach this term to a definite standard of morality or an unusually impressive fulness of character. To our minds it is associated with very positive forces, as of comfort and conviction--perhaps because we take our ideas of it from the active operations of the Holy Ghost. The original force of the term holiness, however, was not positive but negative, and throughout the Old Testament, whatever modifications its meaning undergoes, it retains a negative flavour. The Hebrew word for holiness springs from a root which means to set apart, make distinct, put at a distance from. When God is described as the Holy One in the Old Testament it is generally with the purpose of withdrawing Him from some presumption of men upon His majesty or of negativing their unworthy thoughts of Him. The Holy One is the Incomparable: To whom, then, will ye liken Me, that I should be equal to him? saith the Holy One (xl. 25). He is the Unapproachable: Who is able to stand before Jehovah, this holy God? (1 Sam. vi. 20). He is the Utter Contrast of man: I am God, and not man, the Holy One in the midst of thee (Hosea xi. 9). He is the Exalted and Sublime: Thus saith the high and lofty One that inhabiteth eternity, whose name is Holy: I dwell in the high and holy place (lvii. 15). Generally speaking, then, holiness is equivalent to separateness, sublimity--in fact, just to that loftiness or exaltation which Isaiah has already so often reiterated as the principal attribute of God. In their thrice-repeated Holy the seraphs are only telling more emphatically to the prophet's ears what his eyes have already seen, the Lord high and lifted up. Better expression could not be found for the full idea of Godhead. This little word Holy radiates heaven's own breadth of meaning. Within its fundamental idea-- distance or difference from man--what spaces are there not for every attribute of Godhead to flash? If the Holy One be originally He who is distinct from man and man's thoughts, and who impresses man from the beginning with the awful sublimity of the contrast in which He stands to him, how naturally may holiness come to cover not only that moral purity and intolerance of sin to which we now more strictly apply the term, but those metaphysical conceptions as well, which we gather up under the name "supernatural," and so finally, by lifting the Divine nature away from the change and vanity of this world, and emphasizing God's independence of all beside Himself, become the fittest expression we have for Him as the Infinite and Self-existent. Thus the word holy appeals in turn to each of the three great faculties of man's nature, by which he can be religiously exercised--his conscience, his affections, his reason; it covers the impressions which God makes on man as a sinner, on man as a worshipper, on man as a thinker. The Holy One is not only the Sinless and Sin-abhorring, but the Sublime and the Absolute too.

But while we recognize the exhaustiveness of the series of ideas about the Divine Nature, which develop from the root meaning of holiness, and to express which the word holy is variously used throughout the Scriptures, we must not, if we are to appreciate the use of the word on this occasion, miss the motive of recoil which starts them all. If we would hear what Isaiah heard in the seraphs' song, we must distinguish in the three-fold ascription of holiness the intensity of recoil from the confused religious views and low moral temper of the prophet's generation. It is no scholastic definition of Deity which the seraphim are giving. Not for a moment is it to be supposed that to that age, whose representative is listening to them, they are attempting to convey an idea of the Trinity. Their thrice-uttered Holy is not theological accuracy, but religious emphasis. This angelic revelation of the holiness of God was intended for a generation, some of whom were idol-worshippers, confounding the Godhead with the work of their own hands or with natural objects, and none of whom were free from a confusion in principle of the Divine with the human and worldly, for which now sheer mental slovenliness, now a dull moral sense, and now positive pride was to blame. To worshippers who trampled the courts of the Lord with the careless feet, and looked up the temple with the unabashed faces, of routine, the cry of the seraphs, as they veiled their faces and their feet, travailed to restore that shuddering sense of the sublimity of the Divine Presence, which in the impressible youth of the race first impelled man, bowing low beneath the awful heavens, to name God by the name of the Holy. To men, again, careful of the legal forms of worship, but lawless and careless in their lives, the song of the seraphs revealed not the hard truth, against which they had already rubbed conscience trite, that God's law was inexorable, but the fiery fact that His whole nature burned with wrath towards sin. To men, once more, proud of their prestige and material prosperity, and presuming in their pride to take their own way with God, and to employ like Uzziah the exercises of religion for their own honour, this vision presented the real sovereignty of God: the Lord Himself seated on a throne there--just where they felt only a theatre for the display of their pride, or machinery for the attainment of their private ends. Thus did the three-fold cry of the angels meet the three-fold sinfulness of that generation of men.

But the first line of the seraph's song serves more than a temporary end. The Trisagion rings, and has need to ring, for ever down the Church. Everywhere and at all times these are the three besetting sins of religious people--callousness in worship, carelessness in life, and the temper which employs the forms of religion simply for self-indulgence or self-aggrandisement. These sins are induced by the same habit of contentment with mere form; they can be corrected only by the vision of the Personal Presence who is behind all form. Our organization, ritual, law and sacrament--we must be able to see them fall away, as Isaiah saw the sanctuary itself disappear, before God Himself, if we are to remain heartily moral and fervently religious. The Church of God has to learn that no mere multiplication of forms, nor a more æsthetic arrangement of them, will redeem her worshippers from callousness. Callousness is but the shell which the feelings develop in self-defence when left by the sluggish and impenetrative soul to beat upon the hard outsides of form. And nothing will fuse this shell of callousness but that ardent flame, which is kindled at the touching of the Divine and human spirits, when forms have fallen away and the soul beholds with open face the Eternal Himself. As with worship, so with morality. Holiness is secured not by ceremonial, but by a reverence for a holy Being. We shall rub our consciences trite against moral maxims or religious rites. It is the effluence of a Presence, which alone can create in us, and keep in us, a clean heart. And if any object that we thus make light of ritual and religious law, of Church and sacrament, the reply is obvious. Ritual and sacrament are to the living God but as the wick of a candle to the light thereof. They are given to reveal Him, and the process is not perfect unless they themselves perish from the thoughts to which they convey Him. If God is not felt to be present, as Isaiah felt Him to be, to the exclusion of all forms, then these will be certain to be employed, as Uzziah employed them, for the sake of the only other spiritual being of whom the worshipper is conscious--himself. Unless we are able to forget our ritual in spiritual communion with the very God, and to become unconscious of our organization in devout consciousness of our personal relation to Him, then ritual will be only a means of sensuous indulgence, organization only a machinery for selfish or sectarian ends. The vision of God--this is the one thing needful for worship and for conduct.

But while the one verse of the antiphon reiterates what Jehovah of hosts is in Himself, the other describes what He is in revelation. The whole earth is full of His glory. Glory is the correlative of holiness. Glory is that in which holiness comes to expression. Glory is the expression of holiness, as beauty is the expression of health. If holiness be as deep as we have seen, so varied then will glory be. There is nothing in the earth but it is the glory of God. The fulness of the whole earth is His glory, is the proper grammatical rendering of the song. For Jehovah of hosts is not the God only of Israel, but the Maker of heaven and earth, and not the victory of Israel alone, but the wealth and the beauty of all the world is His glory. So universal an ascription of glory is the proper parallel to that of absolute Godhead, which is implied in holiness.

II. The Call (vv. 4-8).

Thus, then, Isaiah, standing on earth, on the place of a great sin, with the conscience of his people's evil in his heart, and himself not without the feeling of guilt, looked into heaven, and beholding the glory of God, heard also with what pure praise and readiness of service the heavenly hosts surround His throne. No wonder the prophet felt the polluted threshold rock beneath him, or that as where fire and water mingle there should be the rising of a great smoke. For the smoke described is not, as some have imagined, that of acceptable incense, thick billows swelling through the temple to express the completion and satisfaction of the seraphs' worship; but it is the mist which ever arises where holiness and sin touch each other. It has been described both as the obscurity that envelops a weak mind in presence of a truth too great for it, and the darkness that falls upon a diseased eye when exposed to the mid-day sun. These are only analogies, and may mislead us. What Isaiah actually felt was the dim-eyed shame, the distraction, the embarrassment, the blinding shock of a personal encounter with One whom he was utterly unfit to meet. For this was a personal encounter. We have spelt out the revelation sentence by sentence in gradual argument; but Isaiah did not reach it through argument or brooding. It was not to the prophet what it is to his expositors, a pregnant thought, that his intellect might gradually unfold, but a Personal Presence, which apprehended and overwhelmed him. God and he were there face to face. Then said I, Woe is me, for I am undone, because a man unclean of lips am I, and in the midst of a people unclean of lips do I dwell; for the King, Jehovah of hosts, mine eyes have beheld.

The form of the prophet's confession, uncleanness of lips, will not surprise us as far as he makes it for himself. As with the disease of the body, so with the sin of the soul; each often gathers to one point of pain. Every man, though wholly sinful by nature, has his own particular consciousness of guilt. Isaiah being a prophet felt his mortal weakness most upon his lips. The inclusion of the people, however, along with himself under this form of guilt, suggests a wider interpretation of it. The lips are, as it were, the blossom of a man. Grace is poured upon thy lips, therefore God hath blessed thee for ever. If any man offend not in word, the same is a perfect man, able to bridle the whole body also. It is in the blossom of a plant that the plant's defects become conspicuous; it is when all a man's faculties combine for the complex and delicate office of expression that any fault which is in him will come to the surface. Isaiah had been listening to the perfect praise of sinless beings, and it brought into startling relief the defects of his own people's worship. Unclean of lips these were indeed when brought against that heavenly choir. Their social and political sin--sin of heart and home and market--came to a head in their worship, and what should have been the blossom of their life fell to the ground like a rotten leaf beneath the stainless beauty of the seraphs' praise.

While the prophet thus passionately gathered his guilt upon his lips, a sacrament was preparing on which God concentrated His mercy to meet it. Sacrament and lips, applied mercy and presented sin, now come together. Then flew unto me one of the seraphim, and in his hand a glowing stone--with tongs had he taken it off the altar--and he touched my mouth and said, Lo, this hath touched thy lips, and so thy iniquity passeth away and thy sin is atoned for.

The idea of this function is very evident, and a scholar who has said that it "would perhaps be quite intelligible to the contemporaries of the prophet, but is undoubtedly obscure to us," appears to have said just the reverse of what is right; for so simple a process of atonement leaves out the most characteristic details of the Jewish ritual of sacrifice, while it anticipates in an unmistakeable manner the essence of the Christian sacrament. In a scene of expiation laid under the old covenant, we are struck by the absence of oblation or sacrificial act on the part of the sinner himself. There is here no victim slain, no blood sprinkled; an altar is only parenthetically suggested, and even then in its simplest form, of a hearth on which the Divine fire is continually burning. The glowing stone, not live coal as in the English version, was no part of the temple furniture, but the ordinary means of conveying heat or applying fire in the various purposes of household life. There was, it is true, a carrying of fire in some of the temple services, as, for example, on the great Day of Atonement, but then it was effected by a small grate filled with living embers. In the household, on the other hand, when cakes had to be baked, or milk boiled, or water warmed, or in fifty similar applications of fire, a glowing stone taken from off the hearth was the invariable instrument. It is this swift and simple domestic process which Isaiah now sees substituted for the slow and intricate ceremonial of the temple--a seraph with a glowing stone in his hand, with tongs had he taken it off the altar. And yet the prophet feels this only as a more direct expression of the very same idea, with which the elaborate ritual was inspired--for which the victim was slain, and the flesh consumed in fire, and the blood sprinkled. Isaiah desires nothing else, and receives no more, than the ceremonial law was intended to assure to the sinner--pardon of his sin and reconciliation to God. But our prophet will have conviction of these immediately, and with a force which the ordinary ritual is incapable of expressing. The feelings of this Jew are too intense and spiritual to be satisfied with the slow pageant of the earthly temple, whose performances to a man in his horror could only have appeared so indifferent and far away from himself as not to be really his own nor to effect what he passionately desired. Instead therefore of laying his guilt in the shape of some victim on the altar, Isaiah, with a keener sense of its inseparableness from himself, presents it to God upon his own lips. Instead of being satisfied with beholding the fire of God consume it on another body than his own, at a distance from himself, he feels that fire visit the very threshold of his nature, where he has gathered the guilt, and consume it there. The whole secret of this startling nonconformity to the law, on the very floor of the temple, is that for a man who has penetrated to the presence of God the legal forms are left far behind, and he stands face to face with the truth by which they are inspired. In that Divine Presence Isaiah is his own altar; he acts his guilt in his own person, and so he feels the expiatory fire come to his very self directly from the heavenly hearth. It is a replica of the fifty-first Psalm: For Thou delightest not in sacrifice, else would I give it; Thou hast no pleasure in burnt offering. The sacrifices of God are a broken spirit. This is my sacrifice, my sense of guilt gathered here upon my lips: my broken and contrite heart, who feel myself undone before Thee, Lord, Thou wilt not despise.

It has always been remarked as one of the most powerful proofs of the originality and Divine force of Christianity, that from man's worship of God, and especially from those parts in which the forgiveness of sin is sought and assured, it did away with the necessity of a physical rite of sacrifice; that it broke the universal and immemorial habit by which man presented to God a material offering for the guilt of his soul. By remembering this fact we may measure the religious significance of the scene we now contemplate. Nearly eight centuries before there was accomplished upon Calvary that Divine Sacrifice for sin, which abrogated a rite of expiation, hitherto universally adopted by the conscience of humanity, we find a Jew, in the dispensation where such a rite was most religiously enforced, trembling under the conviction of sin, and upon a floor crowded with suggestions of physical sacrifice; yet the only sacrifice he offers is the purely spiritual one of confession. It is most notable. Look at it from a human point of view, and we can estimate Isaiah's immense spiritual originality; look at it from a Divine, and we cannot help perceiving a distinct foreshadow of what was to take place by the blood of Jesus under the new covenant. To this man, as to some others of his dispensation, whose experience our Christian sympathy recognizes so readily in the Psalms, there was granted aforetime boldness to enter into the holiest. For this is the explanation of Isaiah's marvellous disregard of the temple ritual. It is all behind him. This man has passed within the veil. Forms are all behind him, and he is face to face with God. But between two beings in that position, intercourse by the far off and uncertain signals of sacrifice is inconceivable. It can only take place by the simple unfolding of the heart. It must be rational, intelligent and by speech. When man is at such close quarters with God what sacrifice is possible but the sacrifice of the lips? Form for the Divine reply there must be some, for even Christianity has its sacraments, but like them this sacrament is of the very simplest form, and like them it is accompanied by the explanatory word. As Christ under the new covenant took bread and wine, and made the homely action of feeding upon them the sign and seal to His disciples of the forgiveness of their sins, so His angel under the old and sterner covenant took the more severe, but as simple and domestic form of fire to express the same to His prophet. And we do well to emphasize that the experimental value of this sacrament of fire is bestowed by the word attached to it. It is not a dumb sacrament, with a magical efficacy. But the prophet's mind is persuaded and his conscience set at peace by the intelligible words of the minister of the sacrament.

Isaiah's sin being taken away, he is able to discern the voice of God Himself. It is in the most beautiful accordance with what has already happened that he hears this not as command, but request, and answers not of compulsion, but of freedom. And I heard the voice of the Lord saying, Whom shall I send? and who will go for us? And I said, Here am I; send me. What spiritual understanding alike of the will of God and the responsibility of man, what evangelic liberty and boldness, are here! Here we touch the spring of that high flight Isaiah takes both in prophecy and in active service for the State. Here we have the secret of the filial freedom, the life-long sense of responsibility, the regal power of initiative, the sustained and unfaltering career, which distinguish Isaiah among the ministers of the old covenant, and stamp him prophet by the heart and for the life, as many of them are only by the office and for the occasion. Other prophets are the servants of the God of heaven; Isaiah stands next the Son Himself. On others the hand of the Lord is laid in irresistible compulsion; the greatest of them are often ignorant, by turns headstrong and craven, deserving correction, and generally in need of supplementary calls and inspirations. But of such scourges and such doles Isaiah's royal career is absolutely without a trace. His course, begun in freedom, is pursued without hesitation or anxiety; begun in utter self-sacrifice, it knows henceforth no moment of grudging or disobedience. Esaias is very bold, because he is so free and so fully devoted. In the presence of mind with which he meets each sudden change of politics during that bewildering half-century of Judah's history, we seem to hear his calm voice repeating its first, Here am I. Presence of mind he always had. The kaleidoscope shifts: it is now Egyptian intrigue, now Assyrian force; now a false king requiring threat of displacement by God's own hero, now a true king, but helpless and in need of consolation; now a rebellious people to be condemned, and now an oppressed and penitent one to be encouraged:--different dangers, with different sorts of salvation possible, obliging the prophet to promise different futures, and to say things inconsistent with what he had already said. Yet Isaiah never hesitates; he can always say, Here am I. We hear that voice again in the spontaneousness and versatility of his style. Isaiah is one of the great kings of literature, with every variety of style under his sway, passing with perfect readiness, as subject or occasion calls, from one to another of the tones of a superbly endowed nature. Everywhere this man impresses us with his personality, with the wealth of his nature and the perfection of his control of it. But the personality is consecrated. The Here am I is followed by the send me. And its health, harmony and boldness, are derived, Isaiah being his own witness, from this early sense of pardon and purification at the Divine hands. Isaiah is indeed a king and a priest unto God--a king with all his powers at his own command, a priest with them all consecrated to the service of Heaven.

One cannot pass away from these verses without observing the plain answer which they give to the question, What is a call to the ministry of God? In these days of dust and distraction, full of party cries, with so many side issues of doctrine and duty presenting themselves, and the solid attractions of so many other services insensibly leading men to look for the same sort of attractiveness in the ministry, it may prove a relief to some to ponder the simple elements of Isaiah's call to be a professional and life-long prophet. Isaiah got no "call" in our conventional sense of the word, no compulsion that he must go, no articulate voice describing him as the sort of man needed for the work, nor any of those similar "calls" which sluggish and craven spirits so often desire to relieve them of the responsibility or the strenuous effort needed in deciding for a profession which their conscience will not permit them to refuse. Isaiah got no such call. After passing through the fundamental religious experiences of forgiveness and cleansing, which are in every case the indispensable premises of life with God, Isaiah was left to himself. No direct summons was addressed to him, no compulsion was laid on him; but he heard the voice of God asking generally for messengers, and he on his own responsibility answered it for himself in particular. He heard from the Divine lips of the Divine need for messengers, and he was immediately full of the mind that he was the man for the mission, and of the heart to give himself to it. So great an example cannot be too closely studied by candidates for the ministry in our own day. Sacrifice is not the half-sleepy, half-reluctant submission to the force of circumstance or opinion, in which shape it is so often travestied among us, but the resolute self-surrender and willing resignation of a free and reasonable soul. There are many in our day who look for an irresistible compulsion into the ministry of the Church; sensitive as they are to the material bias by which men roll off into other professions, they pray for something of a similar kind to prevail with them in this direction also. There are men who pass into the ministry by social pressure or the opinion of the circles they belong to, and there are men who adopt the profession simply because it is on the line of least resistance. From which false beginnings rise the spent force, the premature stoppages, the stagnancy, the aimlessness and heartlessness, which are the scandals of the professional ministry and the weakness of the Christian Church in our day. Men who drift into the ministry, as it is certain so many do, become mere ecclesiastical flotsam and jetsam, incapable of giving carriage to any soul across the waters of this life, uncertain of their own arrival anywhere, and of all the waste of their generation, the most patent and disgraceful. God will have no drift-wood for His sacrifices, no drift-men for His ministers. Self-consecration is the beginning of His service, and a sense of our own freedom and our own responsibility is an indispensable element in the act of self-consecration. We--not God--have to make the decision. We are not to be dead, but living, sacrifices, and everything which renders us less than fully alive both mars at the time the sincerity of our surrender and reacts for evil upon the whole of our subsequent ministry.

III. The Commission (vv. 9-13).

A heart so resolutely devoted as we have seen Isaiah's to be was surely prepared against any degree of discouragement, but probably never did man receive so awful a commission as he describes himself to have done. Not that we are to suppose that this fell upon Isaiah all at once, in the suddenness and distinctness with which he here records it. Our sense of its awfulness will only be increased when we realize that Isaiah became aware of it, not in the shock of a single discovery, sufficiently great to have carried its own anæsthetic along with it, but through a prolonged process of disillusion, and at the pain of those repeated disappointments, which are all the more painful that none singly is great enough to stupefy. It is just at this point of our chapter, that we feel most the need of supposing it to have been written some years after the consecration of Isaiah, when his experience had grown long enough to articulate the dim forebodings of that solemn moment. Go and say to this people, Hearing, hear ye, but understand not; seeing, see ye, but know not. Make fat the heart of this people, and its ears make heavy, and its eyes smear, lest it see with its eyes, and hear with its ears, and its heart understand, and it turn again and be healed. No prophet, we may be sure, would be asked by God to go and tell his audiences that in so many words, at the beginning of his career. It is only by experience that a man understands that kind of a commission, [10] and for the required experience Isaiah had not long to wait after entering on his ministry. Ahaz himself, in whose death-year it is supposed by many that Isaiah wrote this account of his consecration--the conduct of Ahaz himself was sufficient to have brought out the convictions of the prophet's heart in this startling form, in which he has stated his commission. By the word of the Lord and an offer of a sign from Him, Isaiah did make fat that monarch's heart and smear his eyes. And perverse as the rulers of Judah were in the examples and policies they set, the people were as blindly bent on following them to destruction. Every one, said Isaiah, when he must have been for some time a prophet--every one is a hypocrite and an evildoer, and every mouth speaketh folly.

But if that clear, bitter way of putting the matter can have come to Isaiah only with the experience of some years, why does he place it upon the lips of God, as they give him his commission? Because Isaiah is stating not merely his own singular experience, but a truth always true of the preaching of the word of God, and of which no prophet at the time of his consecration to that ministry can be without at least a foreboding. We have not exhausted the meaning of this awful commission when we say that it is only a forcible anticipation of the prophet's actual experience. There is more here than one man's experience. Over and over again are these words quoted in the New Testament, till we learn to find them true always and everywhere that the Word of God is preached to men,--the description of what would seem to be its necessary effect upon many souls. Both Jesus and Paul use Isaiah's commission of themselves. They do so like Isaiah at an advanced stage in their ministry, when the shock of misunderstanding and rejection has been repeatedly felt, but then not solely as an apt description of their own experience. They quote God's words to Isaiah as a prophecy fulfilled in their own case--that is to say, as the statement of a great principle or truth of which their own ministry is only another instance. Their own disappointments have roused them to the fact, that this is always an effect of the word of God upon numbers of men--to deaden their spiritual faculties. While Matthew and the book of Acts adopt the milder Greek version of Isaiah's commission, John gives a rendering that is even stronger than the original. He hath blinded, he says of God Himself, their eyes and hardened their hearts, lest they should see with their eyes and perceive with their hearts. In Mark's narrative Christ says that He speaks to them that are outside in parables, for the purpose that seeing they may see, and not perceive, and hearing they may hear, and not understand, lest haply they should turn again and it should be forgiven them. We may suspect, in an utterance so strange to the lips of the Lord of salvation, merely the irony of His baffled love. But it is rather the statement of what He believed to be the necessary effect of a ministry like His own. It marks the direction, not of His desire, but of natural sequence.

With these instances we can go back to Isaiah and understand why he should have described the bitter fruits of experience as an imperative laid upon him by God. Make fat the heart of this people, and its ears make heavy, and its eyes do thou smear. It is the fashion of the prophet's grammar, when it would state a principle or necessary effect, to put it in the form of a command. What God expresses to Isaiah so imperatively as almost to take our breath away; what Christ uttered with such abruptness that we ask, Does He speak in irony? what Paul laid down as the conviction of a long and patient ministry, is the great truth that the Word of God has not only a saving power, but that even in its gentlest pleadings and its purest Gospel, even by the mouth of Him who came, not to condemn, but to save the world, it has a power that is judicial and condemnatory.

It is frequently remarked by us as perhaps the most deplorable fact of our experience, that there exists in human nature an accursed facility for turning God's gifts to precisely the opposite ends from those for which He gave them. So common is man's misunderstanding of the plainest signs, and so frequent his abuse of the most evident favours of Heaven, that a spectator of the drama of human history might imagine its Author to have been a Cynic or Comedian, portraying for His own amusement the loss of the erring at the very moment of what might have been their recovery, the frustration of love at the point of its greatest warmth and expectancy. Let him look closer, however, and he will perceive, not a comedy, but a tragedy, for neither chance nor cruel sport is here at work, but free will and the laws of habit, with retribution and penalty. These actors are not puppets in the hand of a Power that moves them at will; each of them plays his own part, and the abuse and contradiction, of which he is guilty, are but the prerogative of his freedom. They are free beings who thus reject the gift of Divine assistance, and so piteously misunderstand Divine truth. Look closer still, and you will see that the way they talk, the impression they accept of God's goodness, the effect of His judgements upon them, is determined not at the moment of their choice, and not by a single act of their will, but by the whole tenor of their previous life. In the sudden flash of some gift or opportunity, men reveal the stuff of which they are made, the disposition they have bred in themselves. Opportunity in human life is as often judgement as it is salvation. When we perceive these things, we understand that life is not a comedy, where chance governs or incongruous situations are invented by an Almighty Satirist for his own sport, but a tragedy, with all tragedy's pathetic elements of royal wills contending in freedom with each other, of men's wills clashing with God's: men the makers of their own destinies, and Nemesis not directing, but following their actions. We go back to the very fundamentals of our nature on this dread question. To understand what has been called "a great law in human degeneracy," that "the evil heart can assimilate good to itself and convert it to its nature," we must understand what free will means, and take into account the terrible influence of habit.

Now there is no more conspicuous instance of this law, than that which is afforded by the preaching of the Gospel of God. God's Word, as Christ reminds us, does not fall on virgin soil; it falls on soil already holding other seed. When a preacher stands up with the Word of God in a great congregation, vast as Scripture warrants us for believing his power to be, his is not the only power that is operative. Each man present has a life behind that hour and place, lying away in the darkness, silent and dead as far as the congregation are concerned, but in his own heart as vivid and loud as the voice of the preacher, though he be preaching never so forcibly. The prophet is not the only power in the delivery of God's Word, nor is the Holy Spirit the only power. That would make all preaching of the Word a mere display. But the Bible represents it as a strife. And now it is said of men themselves that they harden their hearts against the Word, and now--because such hardening is the result of previous sinning, and has therefore a judicial character--that God hardens their hearts. Simon, Simon, said Christ to a face that spread out to His own all the ardour of worship, Satan is desiring to have you, but I have prayed that your faith fail not. God sends His Word into our hearts; the Mediator stands by, and prays that it make us His own. But there are other factors in the operation, and the result depends on our own will; it depends on our own will, and it is dreadfully determined by our habits.

Now this is one of the first facts to which a young reformer or prophet awakes. Such an awakening is a necessary element in his education and apprenticeship. He has seen the Lord high and lifted up. His lips have been touched by the coal from off the altar. His first feeling is that nothing can withstand that power, nothing gainsay this inspiration. Is he a Nehemiah, and the hand of the Lord has been mighty upon him? Then he feels that he has but to tell his fellows of it to make them as enthusiastic in the Lord's work as himself. Is he a Mazzini, aflame from his boyhood with aspirations for his country, consecrated from his birth to the cause of duty? Then he leaps with joy upon his mission; he has but to show himself, to speak, to lead the way, and his country is free. Is he--to descend to a lower degree of prophecy--a Fourier, sensitive more than most to how anarchic society is, and righteously eager to settle it upon stable foundations? Then he draws his plans for reconstruction, he projects his phalanges and phalansteres, and believes that he has solved the social problem. Is he--to come back to the heights--an Isaiah, with the Word of God in him like fire? Then he sees his vision of the perfect state; he thinks to lift his people to it by a word. O house of Jacob, he says, come ye, and let us walk in the light of the Lord!

Rev. George Adam Smith, M.A.

For all of whom the next necessary stage of experience is one of disappointment, with the hard commission, Make the heart of this people fat. They must learn that, if God has caught themselves young, and when it was possible to make them entirely His own, the human race to whom He sends them is old, too old for them to effect much upon the mass of it beyond the hardening and perpetuation of evil. Fourier finds that to produce his perfect State he would need to re-create mankind, to cut down the tree to the very roots, and begin again. After the first rush of patriotic fervour, which carried so many of his countrymen with him, Mazzini discovers himself in "a moral desert," confesses that the struggle to liberate his fatherland, which has only quickened him to further devotion in so great a cause, has been productive of scepticism in his followers, and has left them withered and hardened of heart, whom it had found so capable of heroic impulses. He tells us how they upbraided and scorned him, left him in exile, and returned to their homes, from which they had set out with vows to die for their country, doubting now whether there was anything at all worth living or dying for outside themselves. Mazzini's description of the first passage of his career is invaluable for the light which it throws upon this commission of Isaiah. History does not contain a more dramatic representation of the entirely opposite effects of the same Divine movement upon different natures. While the first efforts for the liberty of Italy materialized the greater number of his countrymen, whom Mazzini had persuaded to embark upon it, the failure and their consequent defection only served to strip this heroic soul of the last rags of selfishness, and consecrate it more utterly to the will of God and the duty that lay before it.

A few sentences from the confessions of the Italian patriot may be quoted, with benefit to our appreciation of what the Hebrew prophet must have passed through.

"It was the tempest of doubt, which I believe all who devote their lives to a great enterprise, yet have not dried and withered up their soul--like Robespierre--beneath some barren intellectual formula, but have retained a loving heart, are doomed, once at least, to battle through. My heart was overflowing with and greedy of affection, as fresh and eager to unfold to joy as in the days when sustained by my mother's smile, as full of fervid hope for others, at least, if not for myself. But during these fatal months there darkened round me such a hurricane of sorrow, disillusion and deception as to bring before my eyes, in all its ghastly nakedness, a foreshadowing of the old age of my soul, solitary in a desert world, wherein no comfort in the struggle was vouchsafed to me. It was not only the overthrow for an indefinite period of every Italian hope, ... it was the falling to pieces of that moral edifice of faith and love from which alone I had derived strength for the combat; the scepticism I saw arising round me on every side; the failure of faith in those who had solemnly bound themselves to pursue unshaken the path we had known at the outset to be choked with sorrows; the distrust I detected in those most dear to me, as to the motives and intentions which sustained and urged me onward in the evidently unequal struggle.... When I felt that I was indeed alone in the world, I drew back in terror at the void before me. There, in that moral desert, doubt came upon me. Perhaps I was wrong, and the world right? Perhaps my idea was indeed a dream?... One morning I awoke to find my mind tranquil and my spirit calmed, as one who has passed through a great danger. The first thought that passed across my spirit was, Your sufferings are the temptations of egotism, and arise from a misconception of life.... I perceived that although every instinct of my heart rebelled against that fatal and ignoble definition of life which makes it to be a search after happiness, yet I had not completely freed myself from the dominating influence exercised by it upon the age.... I had been unable to realize the true ideal of love--love without earthly hope.... Life is a mission, duty therefore its highest law. From the idea of God I descended to faith in a mission and its logical consequence--duty the supreme rule of life; and having reached that faith, I swore to myself that nothing in this world should again make me doubt or forsake it. It was, as Dante says, passing through martyrdom to peace--'a forced and desperate peace.' I do not deny, for I fraternized with sorrow, and wrapped myself in it as in a mantle; but yet it was peace, for I learned to suffer without rebellion, and to live calmly and in harmony with my own spirit. I reverently bless God the Father for what consolations of affection--I can conceive of no other--He has vouchsafed to me in my later years; and in them I gather strength to struggle with the occasional return of weariness of existence. But even were these consolations denied me, I believe I should still be what I am. Whether the sun shine with the serene splendour of an Italian noon, or the leaden, corpse-like hue of the northern mist be above us, I cannot see that it changes our duty. God dwells above the earthly heaven, and the holy stars of faith and the future still shine within our souls, even though their light consume itself unreflected as the sepulchral lamp."

Such sentences are the best commentary we can offer on our text. The cases of the Hebrew and Italian prophets are wonderfully alike. We who have read Isaiah's fifth chapter know how his heart also was "overflowing with and greedy of affection," and in the second and third chapters we have seen "the hurricane of sorrow, disillusion and deception darken round him." "The falling to pieces of the moral edifice of faith and love," "scepticism rising on every side," "failure of faith in those who had solemnly bound themselves," "distrust detected in those most dear to me"--and all felt by the prophet as the effect of the sacred movement God had inspired him to begin:--how exact a counterpart it is to the cumulative process of brutalizing which Isaiah heard God lay upon him, with the imperative Make the heart of this people fat! In such a morally blind, deaf and dead-hearted world Isaiah's faith was indeed "to consume itself unreflected like the sepulchral lamp." The glimpse into his heart given us by Mazzini enables us to realize with what terror Isaiah faced such a void. O Lord, how long? This, too, breathes the air of "a forced and desperate peace," the spirit of one who, having realized life as a mission, has made the much more rare recognition that the logical consequence is neither the promise of success nor the assurance of sympathy, but simply the acceptance of duty, with whatever results and under whatever skies it pleases God to bring over him.

> *Until cities fall into ruin without an inhabitant,*
> *And houses without a man,*
> *And the land be left desolately waste,*
> *And Jehovah have removed man far away,*
> *And great be the desert in the midst of the land;*
> *And still if there be a tenth in it,*
> *Even it shall be again for consuming.*
> *Like the terebinth, and like the oak,*
> *Whose stock when they are felled remaineth in them,*
> *The holy seed shall be its stock.*

The meaning of these words is too plain to require exposition, but we can hardly over-emphasize them. This is to be Isaiah's one text throughout his career. "Judgement shall pass through; a remnant shall remain." All the politics of his day, the movement of the world's forces, the devastation of the holy land, the first captivities of the holy people, the reiterated defeats and disappointments of the next fifty years--all shall be clear and tolerable to Isaiah as the fulfilling of the sentence to which he listened in such "forced and desperate peace" on the day of his consecration. He has had the worst branded into him; henceforth no man nor thing may trouble him. He has seen the worst, and knows there is a beginning beyond. So when the wickedness of Judah and the violence of Assyria alike seem most unrestrained--Assyria most bent on destroying Judah, and Judah least worthy to live--Isaiah will yet cling to this, that a remnant must remain. All his prophecies will be variations of this text; it is the key to his apparent paradoxes. He will proclaim the Assyrians to be God's instrument, yet devote them to destruction. He will hail their advance on Judah, and yet as exultingly mark its limit, because of the determination in which he asked the question, O Lord, how long? and the clearness with which he understood the until, that came in answer to it. Every prediction he makes, every turn he seeks to give to the practical politics of Judah, are simply due to his grasp of these two facts--a withering and repeated devastation, in the end a bare survival. He has, indeed, prophecies which travel farther; occasionally he is permitted to indulge in visions of a new dispensation. Like Moses, he climbs his Pisgah, but he is like Moses also in this, that his lifetime is exhausted with the attainment of the margin of a long period of judgement and struggle, and then he passes from our sight, and no man knoweth his sepulchre unto this day. As abruptly as this vision closes with the announcement of the remnant, so abruptly does Isaiah disappear on the fulfilment of the announcement--some forty years subsequent to this vision--in the sudden rescue of the holy seed from the grasp of Sennacherib.

***

We have now finished the first period of Isaiah's career. Let us catalogue what are his leading doctrines up to this point. High above a very sinful people, and beyond all their conceptions of Him, Jehovah, the national God, rises holy, exalted in righteousness. From such a God to such a people it can only be judgement and affliction that pass; and these shall not be averted by the fact that He is the national God, and they His worshippers. Of this affliction the Assyrians gathering far off upon the horizon are evidently to be the instruments. The affliction shall be very sweeping; again and again shall it come; but the Lord will finally save a remnant of His people. Three elements compose this preaching--a very keen and practical conscience of sin; an overpowering vision of God, in whose immediate intimacy the prophet believes himself to be; and a very sharp perception of the politics of the day.

One question rises. In this part of Isaiah's ministry there is no trace of that Figure whom we chiefly identify with his preaching, the Messiah. Let us have patience; it is not time for him; but the following is his connection with the prophet's present doctrines.

Isaiah's great result at present is the certainty of a remnant. That remnant will require two things--they will require a rallying-point, and they will require a leader. Henceforth Isaiah's prophesying will be bent to one or other of these. The two grand purposes of his word and work will be, for the sake of the remnant, the inviolateness of Zion, and the coming of the Messiah. The former he has, indeed, already intimated (chap. iv.); the latter is now to share with it his hope and eloquence.

Footnotes:

9. A Browning's "Christmas Eve."

10. Even Calvin, though in order to prove that Isaiah had been prophesying for some time before his inaugural vision, says that his commission implies some years' actual experience of the obstinacy of the people.

CHAPTER V

THE WORLD IN ISAIAH'S DAY AND ISRAEL'S GOD.

735-730 B.C.

Up to this point we have been acquainted with Isaiah as a prophet of general principles, preaching to his countrymen the elements of righteousness and judgement, and tracing the main lines of fate along which their evil conduct was rapidly forcing them. We are now to observe him applying these principles to the executive politics of the time, and following Judah's conduct to the issues he had predicted for it in the world outside herself. Hitherto he has been concerned with the inner morals of Jewish society; he is now to engage himself with the effect of these on the fortunes of the Jewish State. In his seventh chapter Isaiah begins that career of practical statesmanship, which not only made him "the greatest political power in Israel since David," but placed him, far above his importance to his own people, upon a position of influence over all ages. To this eminence Isaiah was raised, as we shall see, by two things. First, there was the occasion of his times, for he lived at a juncture at which the vision of the World, as distinguished from the Nation, opened to his people's eyes. Second, he had the faith which enabled him to realize the government of the World by the One God, whom he has already beheld exalted and sovereign within the Nation. In the Nation we have seen Isaiah led to emphasize very absolutely the righteousness of God; applying this to the whole World, he is now to speak as the prophet of what we call Providence. He has seen Jehovah ruling in righteousness in Judah; he is now to take possession of the nations of the World in Jehovah's name. But we mistake Isaiah if we think it is any abstract doctrine of providence which he is about to inculcate. For him God's providence has in the meantime but one end: the preservation of a remnant of the holy people. Afterwards we shall find him expecting besides, the conversion of the whole World to faith in Israel's God.

The World in Isaiah's day was practically Western Asia. History had not long dawned upon Europe; over Western Asia it was still noon. Draw a line from the Caspian to the mouth of the Persian Gulf; between that line and another crossing the Levant to the west of Cyprus, and continuing along the Libyan border of Egypt, lay the highest forms of religion and civilisation which our race had by that period achieved. This was the World on which Isaiah looked out from Jerusalem, the furthest borders of which he has described in his prophecies, and in the political history of which he illustrated his great principles. How was it composed?

There were, first of all, at either end of it, north-east and south-west, the two great empires of Assyria and Egypt, in many respects wonderful counterparts of each other. No one will understand the history of Palestine, who has not grasped its geographical position relative to these similar empires. Syria, shut up between the Mediterranean sea and the Arabian desert, has its outlets north and south into two great river-plains, each of them ending in a delta. Territories of that kind exert a double force on the world with which they are connected, now drawing across their boundaries the hungry races of neighbouring highlands and deserts, and again sending them forth, compact and resistless armies. This double action summarises the histories of both Egypt and Assyria from the earliest times to the period which we are now treating, and was the cause of the constant circulation, by which, as the Bible bears witness, the life of Syria was stirred from the Tower of Babel downwards. Mesopotamia and the Nile valley drew races as beggars to their rich pasture grounds, only to send them forth in subsequent centuries as conquerors. The century of Isaiah fell in a period of forward movement. Assyria and Egypt were afraid to leave each other in peace; and the wealth of Phoenicia, grown large enough to excite their cupidity, lay between them. In each of these empires, however, there was something to hamper this aggressive impulse. Neither Assyria nor Egypt was a homogeneous State. The valleys of the Euphrates and the Nile were, each of them the home of two nations. Beside Assyria lay Babylonia, once Assyria's mistress, and now of all the Assyrian provinces by far the hardest to hold in subjection, although it lay the nearest to home. In Isaiah's time, when an Assyrian monarch is unable to come into Palestine, Babylon is generally the reason; and it is by intriguing with Babylon that a king of Judah attempts to keep Assyria away from his own neighbourhood. But Babylon only delayed the Assyrian conquest. In Egypt, on the other hand, power was more equally balanced between the hardier people up the Nile and the wealthier people down the Nile--between the Ethiopians and the Egyptians proper. It was the repeated and undecisive contests between these two during the whole of Isaiah's day, which kept Egypt

Rev. George Adam Smith, M.A.

from being an effective force in the politics of Western Asia. In Isaiah's day no Egyptian army advanced more than a few leagues beyond its own frontier.

Next in this world of Western Asia come the Phoenicians. We may say that they connected Egypt and Assyria, for although Phoenicia proper meant only the hundred and fifty miles of coast between Carmel and the bay of Antioch, the Phoenicians had large colonies on the delta of the Nile and trading posts upon the Euphrates. They were gathered into independent but more or less confederate cities, the chief of them Tyre and Sidon; which, while they attempted the offensive only in trade, were by their wealth and maritime advantages capable of offering at once a stronger attraction and a more stubborn resistance to the Assyrian arms, than any other power of the time. Between Phoenicia proper and the mouths of the Nile, the coast was held by groups of Philistine cities, whose nearness to Egypt rather than their own strength was the source of a frequent audacity against Assyria, and the reason why they appear in the history of this period oftener than any other State as the object of Assyrian campaigns.

Behind Phoenicia and the Philistines lay a number of inland territories: the sister-States of Judah and Northern Israel, with their cousins Edom, Moab, and Aram or Syria. Of which Judah and Israel were together about the size of Wales; Edom a mountain range the size and shape of Cornwall; Moab, on its north, a broken tableland, about a Devonshire; and Aram, or Syria, a territory round Damascus, of uncertain size, but considerable enough to have resisted Assyria for a hundred and twenty years. Beyond Aram, again, to the north, lay the smaller State of Hamath, in the mouth of the pass between the Lebanons, with nothing from it to the Euphrates. And then, hovering upon the east of these settled States, were a variety of more or less Nomadic Tribes, whose refuges were the vast deserts of which so large a part of Western Asia consists.

Here was a world, with some of its constituents wedged pretty firmly by mutual pressure, but in the main broken and restless--a political surface that was always changing. The whole was subject to the movements of the two empires at its extremes. One of them could not move without sending a thrill through to the borders of the other. The approximate distances were these:--from Egypt's border to Jerusalem, about one hundred miles; from Jerusalem to Samaria, forty-five; from Samaria to Damascus, one hundred and fifteen; from Damascus to Hamath, one hundred and thirty; and from Hamath to the Euphrates, one hundred; in all from the border of Egypt to the border of Assyria four hundred and ninety English statute miles. The main line of war and traffic, coming up from Egypt, kept the coast to the plain of Esdraelon, which it crossed towards Damascus, travelling by the north of the sea of Galilee, the way of the sea. Northern Israel was bound to fall an early prey to armies, whose easiest path thus traversed her richest provinces. Judah, on the other hand, occupied a position so elevated and apart, that it was likely to be the last that either Assyria or Egypt would achieve in their subjugation of the States between them.

Thus, then, Western Asia spread itself out in Isaiah's day. Let us take one more rapid glance across it. Assyria to the north, powerful and on the offensive, but hampered by Babylon; Egypt on the south, weakened and in reserve; all the cities and States between turning their faces desperately northwards, but each with an ear bent back for the promises of the laggard southern power, and occasionally supported by its subsidies; Hamath, their advanced guard at the mouth of the pass between the Lebanons, looking out towards the Euphrates; Tyre and Sidon attractive to the Assyrian king, whose policy is ultimately commercial, by their wealth, both they and the Philistine cities obstructing his path by the coast to his great rival of Egypt; Israel bulwarked against Assyria by Hamath and Damascus, but in danger, as soon as they fall, of seeing her richest provinces overrun; Judah unlikely in the general restlessness to retain her hold upon Edom, but within her own borders tolerably secure, neither lying in the Assyrian's path to Egypt, nor wealthy enough to attract him out of it; safe, therefore, in the neutrality which Isaiah ceaselessly urges her to preserve, and in danger of suction into the whirlpool of the approach of the two empires only through the foolish desire of her rulers to secure an utterly unnecessary alliance with the one or the other of them.

For a hundred and twenty years before the advent of Isaiah, the annals of the Assyrian kings record periodical campaigns against the cities of "the land of the west," but these isolated incursions were followed by no permanent results. In 745, however, five years before King Uzziah died, a soldier ascended the throne of Assyria, under the title of Tiglath-pileser II.,[11] who was determined to achieve the conquest of the whole world and its organization as his empire. Where his armies came, it was not simply to chastise or demand tribute, but to annex countries, carry away their populations and exploit their resources. It was no longer kings who were threatened; peoples found themselves in danger of extinction. This terrible purpose of the Assyrian was pursued with vast means and the utmost ferocity. He has been called the Roman of the East, and up to a certain degree we may imagine his policy by remembering all that is familiar to us of its execution by Rome: its relentlessness, impetus and mysterious action from one centre; the discipline, the speed, the strange appearance, of his armies. But there was an Oriental savagery about Assyria, from which Rome was free. The Assyrian kings moved in the power of their brutish and stormy gods--gods that were in the shape of bulls and had the wings as of the tempest. The annals of these kings, in which they describe their campaigns, are full of talk about trampling down their enemies; about showering tempests of clubs upon them, and raining a deluge of arrows; about overwhelming them, and sweeping them off the face of the land, and strewing them like chaff on the sea; about chariots with scythes, and wheels clogged with blood; about great baskets stuffed with the salted heads of their foes. It is a mixture of the Roman and Red Indian.

Picture the effect of the onward movement of such a force upon the imaginations and policies of those little States that clustered round Judah and Israel. Settling their own immemorial feuds, they sought alliance with one another against this common foe. Tribes, that for centuries had stained their borders with one another's blood, came together in unions, the only reason for which was that their common fear had grown stronger than their mutual hate. Now and then a king would be found unwilling to enter such an alliance or eager to withdraw from it, in the hope of securing by his exceptional conduct the favour of the Assyrian, whom he sought further to ingratiate by voluntary tribute. The shifting attitudes of the petty kings towards Assyria bewilder the reader of the Assyrian annals. The foes of one year are the tributaries of the next; the State, that has called for help this campaign, appears as the rebel of that. In 742, Uzziah of Judah is cursed by Tiglath-pileser as an arch-enemy; Samaria and Damascus are recorded as faithful tributaries. Seven years later Ahaz of Judah offers tribute to the Assyrian king, and Damascus and Samaria are invaded by the Assyrian armies. What a world it was, and what politics! A world of petty clans, with no idea of a common humanity, and with no motive for union except fear; politics without a noble thought or long purpose in them, the politics of peoples at bay--the last flicker of dying nationalities,--stumps of smoking firebrands, as Isaiah described two of them.

When we turn to the little we know of the religions of these tribes, we find nothing to arrest their restlessness or broaden their thoughts. These nations had their religions, and called on their gods, but their gods were made in their own image, their religion was the reflex of their life. Each of them employed, rather than worshipped, its deity. No nation believed in its god except as one among many, with his sovereignty limited to its own territory, and his ability to help it conditioned by the power of the other gods, against whose peoples he was fighting. There was no belief in "Providence," no idea of unity or of progress in history, no place in these religions for the great world-force that was advancing upon their peoples.

From this condemnation we cannot except the people of Jehovah. It is undeniable that the mass of them occupied at this time pretty much the same low religious level as their neighbours. We have already seen (chap. i.) their mean estimate of what God required from themselves; with that corresponded their view of His position towards the world. To the majority of the Israelites their God was but one out of many, with His own battles to fight and have fought for Him, a Patron sometimes to be ashamed of, and by no means a Saviour in whom to place an absolute trust. When Ahaz is beaten by Syria, he says: Because the gods of the kings of Syria helped them, therefore will I sacrifice to them, that they may help me (2 Chron. xxviii. 23). Religion to Ahaz was only another kind of diplomacy. He was not a fanatic, but a diplomat, who made his son to pass through the fire to Moloch, and burnt incense in the high places and on the hills, and under every green tree. He was more a political than a religious eclectic, who brought back the pattern of the Damascus altar to Jerusalem. The Temple, in which Isaiah saw the Lord high and lifted up, became under Ahaz, and by the help of the priesthood, the shelter of various idols; in every corner of Jerusalem altars were erected to other gods. This religious hospitality was the outcome neither of imagination nor of liberal thought; it was prompted only by political fear. Ahaz has been mistaken in the same way as Charles I. was--for a bigot, and one who subjected the welfare of his kingdom to a superstitious regard for religion. But beneath the cloak of religious scrupulousness and false reverence, [12] there was in Ahaz the same selfish fear for the safety of his crown and his dynasty, as those who best knew the English monarch tell us, was the real cause of his ceaseless intrigue and stupid obstinacy.

Now that we have surveyed this world, its politics and its religion, we can estimate the strength and originality of the Hebrew prophets. Where others saw the conflicts of nations, aided by deities as doubtfully matched as themselves, they perceived all things working together by the will of one supreme God and serving His ends of righteousness. It would be wrong to say, that before the eighth century the Hebrew conception of God had been simply that of a national deity, for this would be to ignore the remarkable emphasis placed by the Hebrews from very early times upon Jehovah's righteousness. But till the eighth century the horizon of the Hebrew mind had been the border of their territory; the historical theatre on which it saw God working was the national life. Now, however, the Hebrews were drawn into the world; they felt movements of which their own history was but an eddy; they saw the advance of forces against which their own armies, though inspired by Jehovah, had no chance of material success. The perspective was entirely changed; their native land took to most of them the aspect of a petty and worthless province, their God the rank of a mere provincial deity; they refused the waters of Shiloah, that go softly, and rejoiced in the glory of the king of Assyria, the king of the great River and the hosts that moved with the strength of its floods. It was at this moment that the prophets of Israel performed their supreme religious service. While Ahaz and the mass of the people illustrated the impotence of the popular religion, by admitting to an equal place in the national temple the gods of their victorious foes, the prophets boldly took possession of the whole world in the name of Jehovah of hosts, and exalted Him to the throne of the supreme Providence. Now they could do this only by emphasizing and developing the element of righteousness in the old conception of Him. This attribute of Jehovah took absolute possession of the prophets; and in the strength of its inspiration they were enabled, at a time when it would have been the sheerest folly to promise Israel victory against a foe like Assyria, to asseverate that even that supreme world-power was in the hand of Jehovah, and that He must be trusted to lead up all the movements of which the Assyrians were the main force to the ends He had so plainly revealed to His chosen Israel. Even before Isaiah's time such principles had been proclaimed by Amos and Hosea, but it was Isaiah, who both gave to them their loftiest expression, and applied them with the utmost detail and persistence to the practical politics of Judah. We have seen him, in the preliminary stages of his ministry under Uzziah and Jotham, reaching most exalted convictions of the righteousness of Jehovah, as contrasted with the people's view of their God's "nationalism." But we are now to follow him boldly applying this faith--won within the life of Judah, won, as he tells us, by the personal inspiration of Judah's God--to the problems and movements of the whole world as they bear upon Israel's fate. The God, who is supreme in Judah through righteousness, cannot but be supreme everywhere else, for there is nothing in the world higher than righteousness. Isaiah's faith in a Divine Providence is a close corollary to his faith in Jehovah's righteousness; and of one part of that Providence he had already received conviction--A remnant shall remain. Ahaz may crowd Jerusalem with foreign altars and idols, so as to be able to say: "We have with us, on our side, Moloch and Chemosh and Rimmon and the gods of Damascus and Assyria." Isaiah, in the face of this folly, lifts up his simple gospel: "Immanu-El. We have with us, in our own Jehovah of hosts, El, the one supreme God, Ruler of heaven and earth."

Footnotes:

11. The Pul of 2 Kings xv. 19 and the Tiglath-pileser of 2 Kings xvi. are the same.
12. Isa. vii. 12.

CHAPTER VI

KING AND MESSIAH; PEOPLE AND CHURCH.

Isaiah vii., viii., ix. 1-8. 735-732 B.C.

This section of the book of Isaiah (vii.-ix. 7) consists of a number of separate prophecies uttered during a period of at least three years: 735-732 B.C. By 735 Ahaz had ascended the throne; Tiglath-pileser had been occupied in the far east for two years. Taking advantage of the weakness of the former and the distance of the latter, Rezin, king of Damascus, and Pekah, king of Samaria, planned an invasion of Judah. It was a venture they would not have dared had Uzziah been alive. While Rezin marched down the east of the Jordan and overturned the Jewish supremacy in Edom, Pekah threw himself into Judah, defeated the armies of Ahaz in one great battle, and besieged Jerusalem, with the object of deposing Ahaz and setting a Syrian, Ben-Tabeel, in his stead. Simultaneously the Philistines attacked Judah from the south-west. The motive of the confederates was in all probability anger with Ahaz for refusing to enter with them into a Pan-Syrian alliance against Assyria. In his distress Ahaz appealed to Tiglath-pileser, and the Assyrian swiftly responded. In 734--it must have been less than a year since Ahaz was attacked--the hosts of the north had overrun Samaria and swept as far south as the cities of the Philistines. Then, withdrawing his troops again, Tiglath-pileser left Hoshea as his vassal on Pekah's throne, and sending the population of Israel east of the Jordan into distant captivity, completed a two years' siege of Damascus (734-732) by its capture. At Damascus Ahaz met the conqueror, and having paid him tribute, took out a further policy of insurance in the altar-pattern, which he brought back with him to Jerusalem. Such were the three years, whose rapid changes unfolded themselves in parallel with these prophecies of Isaiah. The details are not given by the prophet, but we must keep in touch with them while we listen to him. Especially must we remember their central point, the decision of Ahaz to call in the help of Assyria, a decision which affected the whole course of politics for the next thirty years. Some of the oracles of this section were plainly delivered by Isaiah before that event, and simply seek to inspire Ahaz with a courage which should feel Assyrian help to be needless; others, again, imply that Ahaz has already called in the Assyrian: they taunt him with hankering after foreign strength, and depict the woes which the Assyrian will bring upon the land; while others (for example, the passage ix. 1-7) mean that the Assyrian has already come, and that the Galilean provinces of Israel have been depopulated, and promise a Deliverer. If we do not keep in mind the decision of Ahaz, we shall not understand these seemingly contradictory utterances, which it thoroughly explains. Let us now begin at the beginning of chapter vii. It opens with a bare statement, by way of title, of the invasion of Judah and the futile result; and then proceeds to tell us how Isaiah acted from the first rumour of the confederacy onward.

I. The King (chap. vii.).

And it came to pass in the days of Ahaz, the son of Jotham, the son of Uzziah, king of Judah, that Rezin, the king of Syria, and Pekah, the son of Remaliah, king of Israel, went up to Jerusalem to war against it, but could not prevail against it. This is a summary of the whole adventure and issue of the war, given by way of introduction. The narrative proper begins in verse 2, with the effect of the first news of the league upon Ahaz and his people. Their hearts were moved, like the trees of the forest before the wind. The league was aimed so evidently against the two things most essential to the national existence and the honour of Jehovah; the dynasty of David, namely, and the inviolability of Jerusalem. Judah had frequently before suffered the loss of her territory; never till now were the throne and city of David in actual peril. But that, which bent both king and people by its novel terror, was the test Isaiah expected for the prophecies he had already uttered. Taking with him, as a summary of them, his boy with the name Shear-Jashub--A-remnant-shall-return--Isaiah faced Ahaz and his court in the midst of their preparation for the siege. They were examining--but more in panic than in prudence--the water supply of the city, when Isaiah delivered to them a message from the Lord, which may be paraphrased as follows: Take heed and be quiet, keep your eyes open and your heart still; fear not, neither be faint-hearted, for the fierce anger of Rezin and Remaliah's son. They have no power to set you on fire. They are but stumps of expiring firebrands, almost burnt out. While you wisely look after your water supply, do so in hope. This purpose of deposing you is vain. Thus saith the Lord Jehovah: It shall not stand, neither shall it come to pass. Of whom are you afraid? Look those foes of yours in the face. The head of

Rev. George Adam Smith, M.A.

Syria is Damascus, and Damascus' head is Rezin: is he worth fearing? The head of Ephraim is Samaria, and Samaria's head is Remaliah's son: is he worth fearing? Within a few years they will certainly be destroyed. But whatever estimate you make of your foes, whatever their future may be, for yourself have faith in God; for you that is the essential thing. If ye will not believe, surely ye shall not be established. [13]

This paraphrase seeks to bring out the meaning of a passage confessedly obscure. It seems as if we had only bits of Isaiah's speech to Ahaz and must supply the gaps. No one need hesitate, however, to recognize the conspicuous personal qualities--the combination of political sagacity with religious fear, of common-sense and courage rooted in faith. In a word, this is what Isaiah will say to the king, clever in his alliances, religious and secular, and busy about his material defences: "Take unto you the shield of faith. You have lost your head among all these things. Hold it up like a man behind that shield; take a rational view of affairs. Rate your enemies at their proper value. But for this you must believe in God. Faith in Him is the essential condition of a calm mind and a rational appreciation of affairs."

It is, no doubt, difficult for us to realize that the truth which Isaiah thus enforced on King Ahaz-- the government of the world and human history by one supreme God--was ever a truth of which the race stood in ignorance. A generation like ours cannot be expected to put its mind in the attitude of those of Isaiah's contemporaries who believed in the real existence of many gods with limited sovereignties. To us, who are full of the instincts of Divine Providence and of the presence in history of law and progress, it is extremely hard even to admit the fact--far less fully to realize what it means--that our race had ever to receive these truths as fresh additions to their stock of intellectual ideas. Yet, without prejudice to the claims of earlier prophets, this may be confidently affirmed: that Isaiah where we now meet him stood on one side believing in one supreme God, Lord of heaven and earth, and his generation stood on the other side, believing that there were many gods. Isaiah, however, does not pose as the discoverer of the truth he preaches; he does not present it as a new revelation, nor put it in a formula. He takes it for granted, and proceeds to bring its moral influence to bear. He will infect men with his own utter conviction of it, in order that he may strengthen their character and guide them by paths of safety. His speech to Ahaz is an exhibition of the moral and rational effects of believing in Providence. Ahaz is a sample of the character polytheism produced; the state of mind and heart to which Isaiah exhorts him is that induced by belief in one righteous and almighty God. We can make the contrast clear to ourselves by a very definite figure.

The difference, which is made to the character and habits of men if the country they live in has a powerful government or not, is well known. If there be no such central authority, it is a case of every man's hand against his neighbour. Men walk armed to the teeth. A constant attitude of fear and suspicion warps the whole nature. The passions are excited and magnified; the intelligence and judgement are dwarfed. Just the same after its kind is life to the man or tribe, who believe, that the world in which they dwell and the life they share with others have no central authority. They walk armed with prejudices, superstitions and selfishnesses. They create, like Ahaz, their own providences, and still, like him, feel insecure. Everything is exaggerated by them; in each evil there lurks to their imagination unlimited hostility. They are without breadth of view or length of patience. But let men believe that life has a central authority, that God is supreme, and they will fling their prejudices and superstitions to the winds, now no more needed than the antiquated fortresses and weapons by which our forefathers, in days when the government was weak, were forced to defend their private interests. When we know that God reigns, how quiet and free it makes us! When things and men are part of His scheme and working out His ends, when we understand that they are not monsters but ministers, how reasonably we can look at them! Were we afraid of Syria and Ephraim? Why, the head of Syria is this fellow Rezin, the head of Ephraim this son of Remaliah! They cannot last long; God's engine stands behind to smite them. By the reasonable government of God, let us be reasonable! Let us take heed and be quiet. Have faith in God, and to faith will come her proper consequent of commonsense.

For the higher a man looks, the farther he sees: to us that is the practical lesson of these first nine verses of the seventh chapter. The very gesture of faith bestows upon the mind a breadth of view. The man, who lifts his face to God in heaven, is he whose eyes sweep simultaneously the farthest prospect of earth, and bring to him a sense of the proportion of things. Ahaz, facing his nearest enemies, does not see over their heads, and in his consternation at their appearance prepares to embark upon any policy that suggests itself, even though it be so rash as the summoning of the Assyrian. Isaiah, on the other hand, with his vision fixed on God as the Governor of the world, is enabled to overlook the dust that darkens Judah's frontier, to see behind it the inevitable advance of the Assyrians, and to be assured that, whether Ahaz calls them to his quarrel or no, they will very soon of their own motion overwhelm both of his enemies. From these two smoking firebrands there is then no real danger. But from the Assyrian, if once Judah entangle herself in his toils, there is the most extreme danger. Isaiah's advice is therefore not mere religious quietism; it is prudent policy. It is the best political advice that could have been offered at that crisis, as we have already been able to gather from a survey of the geographical and political dispositions of Western Asia, [14] apart altogether from religious considerations. But to Isaiah the calmness requisite for this sagacity sprang from his faith. Mr. Bagehot might have appealed to Isaiah's whole policy in illustration of what he has so well described as the military and political benefits of religion. Monotheism is of advantage to men not only by reason of "the high concentration of steady feeling" which it produces, but also for the mental calmness and sagacity, which surely spring from a pure and vivid conviction that the Lord reigneth. [15]

One other thing it is well we should emphasize, before we pass from Isaiah's speech to Ahaz. Nothing can be plainer than that Isaiah, though advocating so absolutely a quiescent belief in God, is no fatalist. Now other prophets there have been, insisting just as absolutely as Isaiah upon resignation to God the supreme, and the evident practical effect of their doctrine of the Divine sovereignty has been to make their followers, not shrewd political observers, but blind and apathetic fatalists. The difference between them and Isaiah has lain in the kind of character, which they and he have respectively attributed to the Deity, before exalting Him to the throne of absolute power and resigning themselves to His will. Isaiah, though as disciplined a believer in God's sovereignty and man's duty of obedience as any prophet that ever preached these doctrines, was preserved from the fatalism to which they so often lead by the conviction he had previously received of God's righteousness. Fatalism means resignation to fate, and fate means an omnipotence either without character, or (which is the same thing) of whose character we are ignorant. Fate is God minus character, and fatalism is the characterless condition to which belief in such a God reduces man. History presents it to our view amid the most diverse surroundings. The Greek mind, so free and sunny, was bewildered and benumbed by belief in an inscrutable Nemesis. In the East how frequently is a temper of apathy or despair bred in men, to whom God is nothing but a despot! Even within Christianity we have had fanatics, so inordinately possessed with belief in God's sovereignty of election, to the exclusion of all other Divine truths, as to profess themselves, with impious audacity, willing to be damned for His glory. Such instances are enough to prove to us the extreme danger of making the sovereignty of God the first article of our creed. It is not safe for men to exalt a deity to the throne of the supreme providence, till they are certified of his character. The vision of mere power intoxicates and brutalizes, no less when it is hallowed by the name of religion, than when, as in modern materialism, it is blindly interpreted as physical force. Only the people who have first learned to know their Deity intimately in the private matters of life, where heart touches heart, and the delicate arguments of conscience are not overborne by the presence of vast natural forces or the intricate movements of the world's history, can be trusted afterwards to enter these larger theatres of religion, without risk of losing their faith, their sensibility or their conscience.

The whole course of revelation has been bent upon this: to render men familiarly and experimentally acquainted with the character of God, before laying upon them the duty of homage to His creative power or submission to His will. In the Old Testament God is the Friend, the Guide, the Redeemer of men, or ever He is their Monarch and Lawgiver. The Divine name which the Hebrew sees excellent through all the earth is the name that he has learned to know at home as Jehovah, our Lord (Ps. viii.). Jehovah trains His people to trust His personal troth and lovingkindness within their own courts, before He tests their allegiance and discipline upon the high places of the world. And when, amid the strange terrors of these and the novel magnitudes with which Israel, facing the world, had to reckon, the people lost their presence of mind, His elegy over them was, My people are destroyed for lack of knowledge. Even when their temple is full and their sacrifices of homage to His power most frequent, it is still their want of moral acquaintance with Himself of which He complains: Israel doth not know; My people doth not consider. What else was the tragedy in which Jewish history closed, than just the failure to perceive this lesson: that to have and to communicate the knowledge of the Almighty's character is of infinitely more value than the attempt to vindicate in any outward fashion Jehovah's supremacy over the world? This latter, this forlorn, hope was what Israel exhausted the evening of their day in attempting. The former--to communicate to the lives and philosophies of mankind a knowledge of the Divine heart and will, gained throughout a history of unique grace and miracle--was the destiny which they resigned to the followers of the crucified Messiah.

For under the New Testament this also is the method of revelation. What our King desires before He ascends the throne of the world is that the world should know Him; and so He comes down among us, to be heard, and seen, and handled of us, that our hearts may learn His heart and know His love, unbewildered by His majesty. And for our part, when we ascribe to our King the glory and the dominion, it is as unto Him that loved us and washed us from our sins in His blood. For the chief thing for individuals, as for nations, is not to believe that God reigneth so much as to know what kind of God He is who reigneth.

***

Rev. George Adam Smith, M.A.

But Ahaz would not be persuaded. He had a policy of his own, and was determined to pursue it. He insisted on appealing to Assyria. Before he did so, Isaiah made one more attempt on his obduracy. With a vehemence, which reveals how critical he felt the king's decision to be, the prophet returned as if this time the very voice of Jehovah. And Jehovah spake to Ahaz, saying, Ask thee a sign of Jehovah thy God; ask it either in Sheol below or in the height above. But Ahaz said, I will not ask, neither will I tempt the Lord.

Isaiah's offer of a sign was one which the prophets of Israel used to make when some crisis demanded the immediate acceptance of their word by men, and men were more than usually hard to convince--a miracle such as the thunder that Samuel called out of a clear sky to impress Israel with God's opinion of their folly in asking for a king; [16] or as the rending of the altar which the man of God brought to pass to convict the sullen Jeroboam; [17] or as the regress of the shadow on the sun-dial, which Isaiah himself gave in assurance of recovery to the sick Hezekiah. [18] Such signs are offered only to weak or prejudiced persons. The most real faith, as Isaiah himself tells us, is unforced, the purest natures those which need no signs and wonders. But there are certain crises at which faith must be immediately forced, and Ahaz stood now at such a crisis; and there are certain characters who, unable to read a writ from the court of conscience and reason, must be served with one from a court--even though it be inferior--whose language they understand; and Ahaz was such a character. Isaiah knew his man, and prepared a pretty dilemma for him. By offering him whatever sign he chose to ask, Isaiah knew that the king would be committed before his own honour and the public conscience to refrain from calling in the Assyrians, and so Judah would be saved; or if the king refused the sign, the refusal would unmask him. Ahaz refused, and at once Isaiah denounced him and all his house. They were mere shufflers, playing fast and loose with God as well as men. Hear ye now, O house of David. Is it a small thing for you to weary men, that ye must weary my God also? You have evaded God; therefore God Himself will take you in hand: the Lord Himself shall give you a sign.

In order to follow intelligently the rest of Isaiah's address, we must clearly understand how the sign which he now promises differs in nature from the sign he had implored Ahaz to select, of whatever sort he may have expected that selection to be. The king's determination to call in Assyria has come between. Therefore, while the sign Isaiah first offered upon the spot was intended for an immediate pledge that God would establish Ahaz, if only he did not appeal to the foreigner, the sign Isaiah now offers shall come as a future proof of how criminal and disastrous the appeal to the foreigner has been. The first sign would have been an earnest of salvation; the second is to be an exposure of the fatal evil of Ahaz's choice. The first would have given some assurance of the swift overthrow of Ephraim and Syria; the second shall be some painful illustration of the fact that not only Syria and Ephraim, but Judah herself, shall be overwhelmed by the advance of the northern power. This second sign is one, therefore, which only time can bring round. Isaiah identifies it with a life not yet born.

A Child, he says, shall shortly be born to whom his mother shall give the name Immanu-El--God-with-us. By the time this Child comes to years of discretion, he shall eat butter and honey. Isaiah then explains the riddle. He does not, however, explain who the mother is, having described her vaguely as a or the young woman of marriageable age; for that is not necessary to the sign, which is to consist in the Child's own experience. To this latter he limits his explanation. Butter and honey are the food of privation, the food of a people, whose land, depopulated by the enemy, has been turned into pasture. Before this Child shall arrive at years of discretion not only shall Syria and Ephraim be laid waste, but the Lord Himself will have laid waste Judah. Jehovah shall bring upon thee, and upon thy people and upon thy father's house days, that have not come, from the day that Ephraim departed from Judah; even the king of Assyria. Nothing more is said of Immanuel, but the rest of the chapter is taken up with the details of Judah's devastation.

Now this sign and its explanation would have presented little difficulty but for the name of the Child--Immanuel. Erase that, and the passage reads forcibly enough. Before a certain Child, whose birth is vaguely but solemnly intimated in the near future, shall have come to years of discretion, the results of the choice of Ahaz shall be manifest. Judah shall be devastated, and her people have sunk to the most rudimentary means of living. All this is plain. It is a form which Isaiah used more than once to measure the near future. And in other literatures, too, we have felt the pathos of realizing the future results of crime and the length to which disaster lingers, by their effect upon the lives of another generation:--

> "The child that is unborn shall rue
> The hunting of that day!"

But why call the Child Immanuel? The name is evidently part of the sign, and has to be explained in connection with it. Why call a Child God-with-us who is not going to act greatly or to be highly honoured, who is only going to suffer, for whom to come to years of intelligence shall only be to come to a sense of his country's disaster and his people's poverty? This Child who is used so pathetically to measure the flow of time and the return of its revenges, about whom we are told neither how he shall behave himself in the period of privation, nor whether he shall survive it--why is he called Immanuel? or why, being called Immanuel, has he so sordid a fate to contrast with so splendid a name?

It seems to the present expositor quite impossible to dissociate so solemn an announcement by Jehovah to the house of David of the birth of a Child, so highly named, from that expectation of the coming of a glorious Prince which was current in this royal family since the days of its founder. Mysterious and abrupt as the intimation of Immanuel's birth may seem to us at this juncture, we cannot forget that it fell from Isaiah's lips on hearts which cherished as their dearest hope the appearance of a glorious descendant of David, and were just now the more sensitive to this hope that both David's city and David's dynasty were in peril. Could Ahaz possibly understand by Immanuel any other child than that Prince whose coming was the inalienable hope of his house? But if we are right in supposing that Ahaz made this identification, or had even the dimmest presage of it, then we understand the full force of the sign. Ahaz by his unbelief had not only disestablished himself (ver. 9): he had mortgaged the hope of Israel. In the flood of disaster, which his fatal resolution would bring upon the land, it mattered little what was to happen to himself. Isaiah does not trouble now to mention any penalty for Ahaz. But his resolve's exceeding pregnancy of peril is borne home to the king by the assurance that it will devastate all the golden future, and must disinherit the promised King. The Child, who is Israel's hope, is born; he receives the Divine name, and that is all of salvation or glory suggested. He grows up not to a throne or the majesty which the seventy-second Psalm pictures--the offerings of Sheba's and Seba's kings, the corn of his land shaking like the fruit of Lebanon, while they of the city flourish like the grass of the earth--but to the food of privation, to the sight of his country razed by his enemies into one vast common fit only for pasture, to loneliness and suffering. Amid the general desolation his figure vanishes from our sight, and only his name remains to haunt, with its infinite melancholy of what might have been, the thorn-choked vineyards and grass-grown courts of Judah.

But even if it were to prove too fine a point, to identify Immanuel with the promised Messiah of David's house, and we had to fall back on some vaguer theory of him, finding him to be a personification,--either a representative of the coming generation of God's people, or a type of the promised to-morrow,--the moral effect of the sign would remain the same; and it is with this alone that we have here to do. Be this an individual, or a generation, or an age,--by the Name bestowed upon it, it was to have been a glorious, God-inhabited age, generation, or individual, and Ahaz has prematurely spoiled everything about it but the Name. The future shall be like a boy cursed by his fathers, brought into the world with glorious rights that are stamped in his title, but only to find his kingdom and estates no longer in existence, and all the circumstances dissipated, in which he might have realized the glorious meaning of his name. Type of innocent suffering, he is born to an empty title, his name the vestige of a great opportunity, the ironical monument of an irreparable crime.

If Ahaz had any conscience left, we can imagine the effect of this upon him. To be punished for sin in one's own body and fortune, this is sore enough; but to see heaven itself blackened and all the gracious future frustrate, this is unspeakably terrible.

Ahaz is thus the Judas of the Old Testament, if that conception of Judas' character be the right one which makes his wilful desire to bring about the kingdom of God in his own violent fashion the motive of his betrayal of Jesus. Of his own obduracy Ahaz has betrayed the Messiah and Deliverer of his people. The assurance of this betrayal is the sign of his obduracy, a signal and terrible proof of his irretrievable sin in calling upon the Assyrians. The king has been found wanting.

II. The People (chap. viii.).

The king has been found wanting; but Isaiah will appeal to the people. Chap. viii. is a collection of addresses to them, as chap. vii. was an expostulation with their sovereign. The two chapters are contemporary. In chap. viii. ver. 1, the narrative goes back upon itself, and returns to the situation as it was before Ahaz made his final resolution of reliance on Assyria. Vv. 1-4 of chap. viii. imply that the Assyrian has not yet been summoned by Ahaz to his assistance, and therefore run parallel to chap. vii. vv. 3-9; but chap. viii. ver. 5 and following verses sketch the evils that are to come upon Judah and Israel, consequent upon the arrival of the Assyrians in Palestine, in answer to the appeal of Ahaz. These evils for land and nation are threatened as absolutely to the people, as they had been to the king. And then the people are thrown over (viii. 14), as the king had been; and Isaiah limits himself to his disciples (ver. 16)--the remnant that was foretold in chap. vi.

This appeal from monarch to people is one of the most characteristic features of Isaiah's ministry. Whatever be the matter committed to him, Isaiah is not allowed to rest till he has brought it home to the popular conscience; and however much he may be able to charge national disaster upon the folly of politicians or the obduracy of a king, it is the people whom he holds ultimately responsible. The statesman, according to Isaiah, cannot rise far above the level of his generation; the people set the fashion to their most autocratic rulers. This instinct for the popular conscience, this belief in the moral solidarity of a nation and their governors, was the motive of the most picturesque passages in Isaiah's career, and inspired some of the keenest epigrams in which he conveyed the Divine truth. We have here a case in illustration. Isaiah had met Ahaz and his court at the conduit of the upper pool, in the highway of the fuller's field, preparing for the expected siege of the city, and had delivered to them the Lord's message not to fear, for that Syria-Ephraim would certainly be destroyed. But that was not enough. It was now laid upon the prophet to make public and popular advertisement of the same truth.

Isaiah was told to take a large, smooth board, and write thereon in the character used by the common people--with the pen of a man--as if it were the title to a prophecy, the compound word "Maher-shalal-hash-baz." This was not only an intelligibly written, but a significantly sonorous, word--one of those popular cries in which the liveliest sensations are struck forth by the crowded, clashing letters, full to the dullest ears of rumours of war: speed-spoil-hurry-prey. The interpretation of it was postponed, the prophet meantime taking two faithful witnesses to its publication. In a little a son was born to Isaiah, and to this child he transferred the noisy name. Then its explanation was given. The double word was the alarm of a couple of invasions. Before the boy shall have knowledge to cry, My father, my mother, the riches of Damascus and the spoil of Samaria shall be carried away before the king of Assyria. So far nothing was told the people that had not been told their king; only the time of the overthrow of their two enemies was fixed with greater precision. At the most in a year, Damascus and Samaria would have fallen. The ground was already vibrating to the footfall of the northern hosts.

The rapid political changes, which ensued in Palestine, are reflected on the broken surface of this eighth chapter. We shall not understand these abrupt and dislocated oracles, uttered at short intervals during the two years of the Assyrian campaign, unless we realize that northern shadow passing and repassing over Judah and Israel, and the quick alternations of pride and penitence in the peoples beneath it. We need not try to thread the verses on any line of thought. Logical connection among them there is none. Let us at once get down into the currents of popular feeling, in which Isaiah, having left Ahaz, is now labouring, and casting forth these cries.

It is a period of powerful currents, a people wholly in drift, and the strongest man of them arrested only by a firm pressure of the Lord's hand. For Jehovah spake thus to me with a strong hand, and instructed me, that I should not walk in the way of this people. The character of the popular movement, the way of this people, which nearly lifted Isaiah off his feet, is evident. It is that into which every nation drifts, who have just been loosened from a primitive faith in God, and by fear or ambition have been brought under the fascination of the great world. On the one hand, such a generation is apt to seek the security of its outward life in things materially large and splendid, to despise as paltry its old religious forms, national aspirations and achievements, and be very desirous to follow foreign fashion and rival foreign wealth. On the other hand, the religious spirit of such an age, withdrawn from its legitimate objects, seeks satisfaction in petty and puerile practices, demeaning itself spiritually, in a way that absurdly contrasts with the grandeur of its material ambitions. Such a stage in the life of a people has its analogy in the growth of the individual, when the boy, new to the world, by affecting the grandest companions and models, assumes an ambitious manner, with contempt for his former circumstances, yet inwardly remains credulous, timid and liable to panic. Isaiah reveals that it was such a stage, which both the kingdoms of Israel had now reached. This people hath refused the waters of Shiloah, that go softly, and rejoice in Rezin and Remaliah's son.

It was natural, that when the people of Judah contrasted their own estate with that of Assyria, or even of Damascus, they should despise themselves. For what was Judah? A petty principality, no larger than three of our own counties. And what was Jerusalem? A mere mountain village, some sixty or seventy acres of barren rock, cut into tongues by three insignificant valleys, down which there sometimes struggled tiny threads of water, though the beds were oftener dry, giving the town a withered and squalid look--no great river to nourish, ennoble or protect. What were such a country and capital to compare with the empire of Assyria?--the empire of the two rivers, whose powerful streams washed the ramparts, wharves, and palace stairs of mighty cities! What was Jerusalem even to the capital of Rezin? Were not Abana and Pharpar, rivers of Damascus, better than all the waters of Israel, let alone these waterless wâdys, whose bleached beds made the Jewish capital so squalid? It was the Assyrian's vast water system--canals, embankments, sluices, and the wealth of water moving through them--that most impressed the poor Jew, whose streams failed him in summer, and who had to treasure up his scanty stores of rainwater in the cisterns, with which the rocky surface of his territory is still so thickly indented. There had, indeed, been at Jerusalem some attempt to conduct water. It was called The Shiloah--conduit or aqueduct, literally emissary in the old sense of the word--a rough, narrow tunnel of some thousand feet in length, hewn through the living rock from the only considerable spring on the east side of Jerusalem, to a reservoir within the walls. To this day The Shiloah presents itself as not by any means a first-class piece of engineering. Ahaz had either just made the tunnel or repaired it; but if the water went no faster than it travels now, the results were indeed ridiculous. Well might this people despise the waters of the Shiloah, that go trickling, when they thought upon the rivers of Damascus or the broad streams of Mesopotamia. Certainly it was enough to dry up the patriotism of the Judean, if he was capable of appreciating only material value, to look upon this bare, riverless capital, with its bungled aqueduct and trickling water supply. On merely material grounds, Judah was about the last country at that time, in which her inhabitants might be expected to show pride or confidence.

But woe to the people, whose attachment to their land is based upon its material advantages, who have lost their sense for those spiritual presences, from an appreciation of which springs all true love of country, with warrior's courage in her defence and statesman's faith in her destiny! The greatest calamity, which can befall any people, is to forfeit their enthusiasm for the soil, on which their history has been achieved and their hearths and altars lie, by suffering their faith in the presence of God, of which these are but the tokens, to pass away. With this loss Isaiah now reproaches Judah. The people are utterly materialized; their delights have been in gold and silver, chariots and horses, fenced cities and broad streams, and their faith has now followed their delights. But these things to which they flee will only prove their destruction. The great foreign river, whose waters they covet, will overflow them: even the king of Assyria and all his glory, and he shall come up over all his channels and go over all his banks; and he shall sweep onward into Judah; he shall overflow and pass through; he shall reach even to the neck; and the stretching out of his wings shall fill the breadth of thy land, O Immanuel, thou who art God-with-us. At the sound of the Name, which floats in upon the floods of invasion like the Ark on the waters of old, Isaiah pulls together his distraught faith in his country, and forgetting her faults, flings defiance at her foes. Associate yourselves, ye peoples, and ye shall be broken in pieces; and give ear, all ye of far-off countries, gird yourselves, and ye shall be broken in pieces. Take counsel together, and it shall be brought to nought; speak the word, and it shall not stand: for Immanu-El--"With us is God." The challenge was made good. The prophet's faith prevailed over the people's materialism, and Jerusalem remained inviolable till Isaiah's death.

Meantime the Assyrian came on. But the infatuated people of Judah continued to tremble rather before the doomed conspirators, Rezin and Pekah. It must have been a time of huge excitement. The prophet tells us how he was steadied by the pressure of the Lord's hand, and how, being steadied, the meaning of the word "Immanuel" was opened out to him. God-with-us is the one great fact of life. Amid all the possible alliances and all the possible fears of a complex political situation, He remains the one certain alliance, the one real fear. Say ye not, A conspiracy, concerning all whereof this people say, A conspiracy; neither fear ye their fear, nor be in dread thereof. Jehovah of hosts, Him shall ye sanctify; and let Him be your fear, and let Him be your dread. God is the one great fact of life, but what a double-edged fact--a sanctuary to all who put their trust in Him, but a rock of offence to both houses of Israel! The figure is very picturesque. An altar, a common stone on steps, one of those which covered the land in large numbers--it is easy to see what a double purpose that might serve. What a joy the sight would be to the weary wanderer or refugee who sought it, what a comfort as he leant his weariness upon it, and knew he was safe! But those who were flying over the land, not seeking Jehovah, not knowing indeed what they sought, blind and panic-stricken--for them what could that altar do but trip them up like any other common rock in their way? "In fact, Divine justice is something which is either observed, desired, or attained, and is then man's weal, or, on the other hand, is overlooked, rejected, or sought after in a wild, unintelligent spirit, and only in the hour of need, and is then their lasting ruin." [19]

The Assyrian came on, and the temper of the Jews grew worse. Samaria was indeed doomed from the first, but for some time Isaiah had been excepting Judah from a judgement for which the guilt of Northern Israel was certainly riper. He foresaw, of course, that the impetus of invasion might sweep the Assyrians into Judah, but he had triumphed in this: that Judah was Immanuel's land, and that all who arrayed themselves against her must certainly come to nought. But now his ideas have changed, as Judah has persisted in evil. He knows now that God is for a stumbling-block to both houses of Israel; nay, that upon Jerusalem herself He will fall as a gin and a snare. Only for a little group of individuals, separate from both States, and gathered round the prophet and the word of God given to him, is salvation certain. People, as well as king, have been found wanting. There remains only this remnant.

Isaiah then at last sees his remnant. But the point we have reached is significant for more than the fulfilment of his expectations. This is the first appearance in history of a religious community, apart from the forms of domestic or national life. "Till then no one had dreamed of a fellowship of faith dissociated from all national forms, bound together by faith in the Divine word alone. It was the birth of a new era in religion, for it was the birth of the conception of the Church, the first step in the emancipation of spiritual religion from the forms of political life." [20]

The plan of the seventh and eighth chapters is now fully disclosed. As the king for his unworthiness has to give place to the Messiah, so the nation for theirs have to give place to the Church. In the seventh chapter the king was found wanting, and the Messiah promised. In the eighth chapter the people are found wanting; and the prophet, turning from them, proceeds to form the Church among those who accept the Word, which king and people have refused. Bind thou up the testimony, and seal the teaching [21] among my disciples. And I will wait on Jehovah, who hideth His face from the house of Jacob, and I will look for Him. Behold, I and the children Jehovah hath given me are for signs and wonders in Israel from Jehovah of hosts, Him that dwelleth in Mount Zion.

This, then, is the situation: revelation concluded, the Church formed upon it, and the nation abandoned. But is that situation final? The words just quoted betray the prophet's hope that it is not. He says: I will wait. He says again: The Lord is only hiding His face from the house of Jacob. I will expect again the shining of His countenance. I will hope for Divine grace and the nation being once more conterminous. The rest of the section (to ix. 7) is the development of this hope, which stirs in the prophet's heart after he has closed the record of revelation.

The darkness deepened across Israel. The Assyrian had come. The northern floods kept surging among the little States of Palestine, and none knew what might be left standing. We can well understand Isaiah pausing, as he did, in face of such rapid and incontrollable movements. When Tiglath-pileser swept over the plain of Esdraelon, casting down the king of Samaria and the Philistine cities, and then swept back again, carrying off upon his ebb the populations east of the Jordan, it looked very like as if both the houses of Israel should fall. In their panic, the people betook themselves to morbid forms of religion; and at first Isaiah was obliged to quench the hope and pity he had betrayed for them in indignation at the utter contrariety of their religious practices to the word of God. There can be no Divine grace for the people as long as they seek unto them that have familiar spirits, and unto the wizards that chirp and that mutter. For such a disposition the prophet has nothing but scorn, Should not a people seek unto their God? On behalf of the living should they seek unto the dead? They must come back to the prophet's own word before hope may dawn. To the revelation and the testimony! If they speak not according to this word, surely there is no morning for them.

The night, however, grew too awful for scorn. There had been no part of the land so given to the idolatrous practices, which the prophet scathed, as the land of Zebulon and the land of Naphtali, by the sea beyond Jordan, Galilee of the Gentiles. But all the horrors of captivity had now fallen upon it, and it had received at the Lord's hand double for all its sins. The night had been torn enough by lightning; was there no dawn? The darkness of these provinces fills the prophet's silenced thoughts. He sees a people hardly bestead and hungry, fretting themselves, cursing their king, who had betrayed them, and their God, who had abandoned them, turning their faces upwards to heaven and downwards to the sacred soil from which they were being dragged, but, behold, distress and darkness, the gloom of anguish; and into thick darkness they are driven away. It is a murky picture, yet through the smoke of it we are able to discern a weird procession of Israelites departing into captivity. We date it, therefore, about 732 B.C., the night of Israel's first great captivity. The shock and the pity of this rouse the prophet's great heart. He cannot continue to say that there is no morning for those benighted provinces. He will venture a great hope for their people.

Over how many months the crowded verses, viii. 21-ix. 7, must be spread, it is useless now to inquire--whether the revulsion they mark arose all at once in the prophet's mind, or hope grew gradually brighter as the smoke of war died away on Israel's northern frontier during 731 B.C. It is enough that we can mark the change. The prophet's tones pass from sarcasm to pity (viii. 20, 21); from pity to hope (viii. 22-ix. 1); from hope to triumph in the vision of salvation actually achieved (ix. 2). The people that walked in darkness have seen a great light; they that dwelt in the land of the shadow of death, on them hath the light shined. For a mutilated, we see a multiplied, nation; for the fret of hunger and the curses of defeat, we hear the joy of harvest and of spoil after victory. For the yoke of his burden, and the staff of his shoulder, the rod of his oppressor, Thou hast broken as in the day of Midian. War has rolled away for ever over that northern horizon, and all the relics of war in the land are swept together into the fire. For all the armour of the armed man in the tumult, and the garments rolled in blood, shall even be for burning, and for fuel of fire. In the midday splendour of this peace, which, after the fashion of Hebrew prophecy, is described as already realized, Isaiah hails the Author of it all in that gracious and marvellous Child whose birth he had already intimated, Heir to the throne of David, but entitled by a fourfold name, too generous, perhaps, for a mere mortal, Wonderful-Counsellor, Hero-God, Father-Everlasting, Prince-of-peace, who shall redeem the realms of his great forerunner and maintain Israel with justice and righteousness from henceforth, even for ever.

When, finally, the prophet inquires what has led his thoughts through this rapid change from satisfaction (chap. viii. 16) with the salvation of a small remnant of believers in the word of God--a little kernel of patience in the midst of a godless and abandoned people--to the daring vision of a whole nation redeemed and established in peace under a Godlike King, he says: The zeal of the Lord of hosts hath performed this.

The zeal, translates our English version, but no one English word will give it. It is that mixture of hot honour and affection to which "jealousy" in its good sense comes near. It is that overflow of the love that cannot keep still, which, when men think God has surely done all He will or can do for an ungrateful race, visits them in their distress, and carries them forward into unconceived dispensations of grace and glory. It is the Spirit of God, which yearns after the lost, speaks to the self-despairing of hope, and surprises rebel and prophet alike with new revelations of love. We have our systems representing God's work up to the limits of our experience, and we settle upon them; but the Almighty is ever greater than His promise or than His revelation of Himself.

Footnotes:

13. There is a play upon words here, which may be reproduced in English by the help of a North-England term: If ye have not faith, ye cannot have staith.

14. Page 96.

15. Physics and Politics (International Scientific Series), pp. 75 ff. One of the finest modern illustrations of the connection between faith and common-sense is found in the Letters of General Gordon to His Sister. Gordon's coolness in face of the slave trade, the just survey he makes of it, and the sensible advice which he gives about meeting it stand well in contrast to the haste and rash proposals of philanthropists at home, and are evidently due to his conviction that the slave trade, like everything else in the world, is in the hands of God, and so may be calmly studied and wisely checkmated. Gordon's letters make very clear how much of his shrewdness in dealing with men was due to the same source. It is instructive to observe throughout, how his complete resignation to the will of God and his perfect obedience delivered him from prejudices and partialities, from distractions and desires, that make sober judgement impossible in other men.

16. 1 Sam. xii. 17.

17. 1 Kings xiii. 3.

18. Chap. xxxviii.

19. Ewald.

20. Robertson Smith, Prophets of Israel, p. 275.

21. English Version, "law," but not the law of Moses. Isaiah refers to the word that has come by himself.

Rev. George Adam Smith, M.A.

CHAPTER VII

THE MESSIAH.

We have now reached that point of Isaiah's prophesying at which the Messiah becomes the most conspicuous figure on his horizon. Let us take advantage of it, to gather into one statement all that the prophet told his generation concerning that exalted and mysterious Person. [22]

When Isaiah began to prophesy, there was current among the people of Judah the expectation of a glorious King. How far the expectation was defined it is impossible to ascertain; but this at least is historically certain. A promise had been made to David (2 Sam. vii. 4-17) by which the permanence of his dynasty was assured. His offspring, it was said, should succeed him, yet eternity was promised not to any individual descendant, but to the dynasty. Prophets earlier than Isaiah emphasized this establishment of the house of David, even in the days of Israel's greatest distress; but they said nothing of a single monarch with whom the fortunes of the house were to be identified. It is clear, however, even without the evidence of the Messianic Psalms, that the hope of such a hero was quick in Israel. Besides the documentary proof of David's own last words (2 Sam. xxiii.), there is the manifest impossibility of dreaming of an ideal kingdom apart from the ideal king. Orientals, and especially Orientals of that period, were incapable of realizing the triumph of an idea or an institution without connecting it with a personality. So that we may be perfectly sure, that when Isaiah began to prophesy the people not only counted upon the continuance of David's dynasty, as they counted upon the presence of Jehovah Himself, but were familiar with the ideal of a monarch, and lived in hope of its realization.

In the first stage of his prophecy, it is remarkable, Isaiah makes no use of this tradition, although he gives more than one representation of Israel's future in which it might naturally have appeared. No word is spoken of a Messiah even in the awful conversation, in which Isaiah received from the Eternal the fundamentals of his teaching. The only hope there permitted to him is the survival of a bare, leaderless few of the people, or, to use his own word, a stump, with no sign of a prominent sprout upon it. In connection, however, with the survival of a remnant, as we have said on chap. vi. (p. 89), it is plain that there were two indispensable conditions, which the prophet could not help having to state sooner or later. Indeed, one of them he had mentioned already. It was indispensable that the people should have a leader, and that they should have a rallying-point. They must have their King, and they must have their City. Every reader of Isaiah knows that it is on these two themes the prophet rises to the height of his eloquence--Jerusalem shall remain inviolable; a glorious King shall be given unto her. But it has not been so generally remarked, that Isaiah is far more concerned and consistent about the secure city than about the ideal monarch. From first to last the establishment and peace of Jerusalem are never out of his thoughts, but he speaks only now and then of the King to come. Through long periods of his ministry, though frequently describing the blessed future, he is silent about the Messiah, and even sometimes so groups the inhabitants of that future, as to leave no room for Him among them. Indeed, the silences of Isaiah upon this Person are as remarkable as the brilliant passages, in which he paints His endowments and His work.

If we consider the moment, chosen by Isaiah for announcing the Messiah and adding his seal to the national belief in the advent of a glorious Son of David, we find some significance in the fact that it was a moment, when the throne of David was unworthily filled and David's dynasty was for the first time seriously threatened. It is impossible to dissociate the birth of a boy called Immanuel, and afterwards so closely identified with the fortunes of the whole land (vii. 8), from the public expectation of a King of glory; and critics are almost unanimous in recognizing Immanuel again in the Prince-of-the-Four-Names in chap. ix. Immanuel, therefore, is the Messiah, the promised King of Israel. But Isaiah makes his own first intimation of Him, not when the throne was worthily filled by an Uzziah or a Jotham, but when a fool and traitor to God abused its power, and the foreign conspiracy to set up a Syrian prince in Jerusalem imperilled the whole dynasty. Perhaps we ought not to overlook the fact, that Isaiah does not here designate Immanuel as a descendant of David. The vagueness with which the mother is described has given rise to a vast amount of speculation as to what particular person the prophet meant by her. But may not Isaiah's vagueness be the only intention he had in mentioning a mother at all? The whole house of David shared at that moment the sin of the king (vii. 13); and it is not presuming too much upon the freedom of our prophet to suppose, that he shook himself loose from the tradition, which entailed the Messiah upon the royal family of Judah, and at least left it an open question, whether Immanuel might not, in consequence of their sin, spring from some other stock.

It is, however, far less with the origin, than with the experience, of Immanuel that Isaiah is concerned; and those who embark upon curious inquiries, as to who exactly the mother might be, are busying themselves with what the prophet had no interest in, while neglecting that in which really lay the significance of the sign that he offered.

Ahaz by his wilfulness has made a Substitute necessary. But Isaiah is far more taken up with this: that he has actually mortgaged the prospects of that Substitute. The Messiah comes, but the wilfulness of Ahaz has rendered His reign impossible. He, whose advent has hitherto not been foretold except as the beginning of an era of prosperity, and whose person has not been painted but with honour and power, is represented as a helpless and innocent Sufferer--His prospects dissipated by the sins of others, and Himself born only to share His people's indigence (p. 115). Such a representation of the Hero's fate is of the very highest interest. We are accustomed to associate the conception of a suffering Messiah only with a much later development of prophecy, when Israel went into exile; but the conception meets us already here. It is another proof that Esaias is very bold. He calls his Messiah Immanuel, and yet dares to present Him as nothing but a Sufferer--a Sufferer for the sins of others. Born only to suffer with His people, who should have inherited their throne--that is Isaiah's first doctrine of the Messiah.

Through the rest of the prophecies published during the Syro-Ephraitic troubles the Sufferer is slowly transformed into a Deliverer. The stages of this transformation are obscure. In chap. viii. Immanuel is no more defined than in chap. vii. He is still only a Name of hope upon an unbroken prospect of devastation. The stretching out of his wings--i.e., the floods of the Assyrian--shall fill the breadth of Thy land, O Immanuel. But this time that the prophet utters the Name, he feels inspired by new courage. He grasps at Immanuel as the pledge of ultimate salvation. Let the enemies of Judah work their worst; it shall be in vain, for Immanuel, God is with us. And then, to our astonishment, while Isaiah is telling us how he arrived at the convictions embodied in this Name, the personality of Immanuel fades away altogether, and Jehovah of hosts Himself is set forth as the sole sanctuary of those who fear Him. There is indeed a double displacement here. Immanuel dissolves in two directions. As a Refuge, He is displaced by Jehovah; as a Sufferer and a Symbol of the sufferings of the land, by a little community of disciples, the first embodiment of the Church, who now, with Isaiah, can do nothing except wait for the Lord (pp. 124-126).

Then, when the prophet's yearning thoughts, that will not rest upon so dark a closure, struggle once more, and struggling pass from despair to pity, and from pity to hope, and from hope to triumph in a salvation actually achieved, they hail all at once as the Hero of it the Son whose birth was promised. With an emphasis, which vividly reveals the sense of exhaustion in the living generation and the conviction that only something fresh, and sent straight from God Himself, can now avail Israel, the prophet cries: Unto us a Child is born; unto us a Son is given. The Messiah appears in a glory that floods His origin out of sight. We cannot see whether He springs from the house of David; but the government is to be upon His shoulder, and He shall reign on David's throne with righteousness for ever. His title shall be fourfold: Wonderful-Counsellor, God-Hero, Father-Everlasting, Prince-of-Peace.

These Four Names do certainly not invite us to grudge them meaning, and they have been claimed as incontrovertible proofs, that the prophet had an absolutely Divine Person in view. Some distinguished scholars insist that the promised Deliverer is nothing less than a God in the metaphysical sense of the word. [23] There are serious reasons, however, which make us doubt this conclusion, and, though we firmly hold that Jesus Christ was God, prevent us from recognizing these names as prophecies of His Divinity. Two of the names are capable of being used of an earthly monarch: Wonderful-Counsellor and Prince-of-Peace, which are, within the range of human virtue, in evident contrast to Ahaz, at once foolish in the conception of his policy and warlike in its results. It will be more difficult to get Western minds to see how Father-Everlasting may be applied to a mere man, but the ascription of eternity is not unusual in Oriental titles, and in the Old Testament is sometimes rendered to things that perish. When Hebrews speak of any one as everlasting, that does not necessarily imply Divinity. The second name, which we render God-Hero, is, it is true, used of Jehovah Himself in the very next chapter to this, but in the plural it is also used of men by Ezekiel (xxxii. 21). The part of it translated God is a frequent name of the Divine Being in the Old Testament, but literally means only mighty, and is by Ezekiel (xxxi. 11) applied to Nebuchadnezzar. We should hesitate, therefore, to understand by these names "a God in the metaphysical sense of the word."

We fall back with greater confidence on other arguments of a more general kind, which apply to all Isaiah's prophecies of the Messiah. If Isaiah had one revelation rather than another to make, it was the revelation of the unity of God. Against king and people, who crowded their temple with the shrines of many deities, Isaiah presented Jehovah as the one only God. It would simply have nullified the force of his message, and confused the generation to which he brought it, if either he or they had conceived of the Messiah, with the conceiving of Christian theology, as a separate Divine personality.

Again, as Mr. Robertson Smith has very clearly explained, [24] the functions assigned by Isaiah to the King of the future are simply the ordinary duties of the monarchy, for which He is equipped by the indwelling of that Spirit of God, that makes all wise men wise and valorous men valorous. "We believe in a Divine and eternal Saviour, because the work of salvation as we understand it in the light of the New Testament is essentially different from the work of the wisest and best earthly king." But such an earthly king's work is all Isaiah looks for. So that, so far from its being derogatory to Christ to grudge the sense of Divinity to these names, it is a fact that the more spiritual our notions are of the saving work of Jesus, the less inclined shall we be to claim the prophecies of Isaiah in proof of His Deity.

There is a third argument in the same direction, the force of which we appreciate only when we come to discover how very little from this point onwards Isaiah had to say about the promised king. In chaps. i.-xxxix. only three other passages are interpreted as describing the Messiah. The first of these, xi. 1-5, dating perhaps from about 720, when Hezekiah was king, tells us, for the first and only time by Isaiah's lips, that the Messiah is to be a scion of David's house, and confirms what we have said: that His duties, however perfectly they were to be discharged, were the usual duties of Judah's monarchy.[25] The second passage, xxxii. 1 ff., which dates probably from after 705, when Hezekiah was still king, is, if indeed it refers at all to the Messiah, a still fainter, though sweeter, echo of previous descriptions. While the third passage, xxxiii. 17: Thou shalt see thy king in his beauty, does not refer to the Messiah at all, but to Hezekiah, then prostrate and in sackcloth, with Assyria thundering at the gate of Jerusalem (701). The mass of Isaiah's predictions of the Messiah thus fall within the reign of Ahaz, and just at the point at which Ahaz proved an unworthy representative of Jehovah, and Judah and Israel were threatened with complete devastation. There is a repetition when Hezekiah has come to the throne. But in the remaining seventeen years, except perhaps for one allusion, Isaiah is silent on the ideal king, although he continued throughout that time to unfold pictures of the blessed future which contained every other Messianic feature, and the realization of which he placed where he had placed his Prince-of-the-Four-Names--in connection, that is, with the approaching defeat of the Assyrians. Ignoring the Messiah, during these years Isaiah lays all the stress of his prophecy on the inviolability of Jerusalem; and while he promises the recovery of the actually reigning monarch from the distress of the Assyrian invasion,--as if that were what the people chiefly desired to see, and not a brighter, stronger substitute,--he hails Jehovah Himself, in solitary and undeputed sovereignty, as Judge, Lawgiver, Monarch and Saviour (xxxiii. 22). Between Hezekiah, thus restored to his beauty, and Jehovah's own presence, there is surely no room left for another royal personage. But these very facts--that Isaiah felt most compelled to predict an ideal king when the actual king was unworthy, and that, on the contrary, when the reigning king proved worthy, approximating to the ideal, Isaiah felt no need for another, and indeed in his prophecies left no room for another--form surely a powerful proof that the king he expected was not a supernatural being, but a human personality, extraordinarily endowed by God, one of the descendants of David by ordinary succession, but fulfilling the ideal which his forerunners had missed. Even if we allow that the four names contain among them the predicate of Divinity, we must not overlook the fact that the Prince is only called by them. It is not that He is, but that He shall be called, Wonderful-Counsellor, God-Hero, Father-Everlasting, Prince-of-Peace. Nowhere is there a dogmatic statement that He is Divine. Besides, it is inconceivable that if Isaiah, the prophet of the unity of God, had at any time a second Divine Person in his hope, he should have afterwards remained so silent about Him. To interpret the ascription of the Four Names as a conscious definition of Divinity, at all like the Christian conception of Jesus Christ, is to render the silence of Isaiah's later life and the silence of subsequent prophets utterly inexplicable.

On these grounds, then, we decline to believe that Isaiah saw in the king of the future "a God in the metaphysical sense of the word." Just because we know the proofs of the Divinity of Jesus to be so spiritual, do we feel the uselessness of looking for them to prophecies, that manifestly describe purely earthly and civil functions.

But such a conclusion by no means shuts us out from tracing a relation between these prophecies and the appearance of Jesus. The fact, that Isaiah allowed them to go down to posterity, proves that he himself did not count them to have been exhausted in Hezekiah. And this fact of their preservation is ever so much the more significant, that their literal truth was discredited by events. Isaiah had evidently foretold the birth and bitter youth of Immanuel for the near future. Immanuel's childhood was to begin with the devastation of Ephraim and Syria, and to be passed in circumstances consequent on the devastation of Judah, which was to follow close upon that of her two enemies. But although Ephraim and Syria were immediately spoiled, as Isaiah foresaw, Judah lay in peace all the reign of Ahaz and many years after his death. So that had Immanuel been born in the next twenty-five years after the announcement of His birth, He would not have found in His own land the circumstances which Isaiah foretold as the discipline of His boyhood. Isaiah's forecast of Judah's fate was, therefore, falsified by events. That the prophet or his disciples should have allowed it to remain, is proof that they believed it to have contents, which the history they had lived through neither exhausted nor discredited. In the prophecies of the Messiah there was something ideal, which was as permanent and valid for the future as the prophecy of the Remnant or that of the visible majesty of Jehovah. If the attachment, at which the prophet aimed when he launched these prophecies on the stream of time, was denied them by their own age, that did not mean their submersion, but only their freedom to float further down the future and seek attachment there.

This boldness, to entrust to future ages a prophecy discredited by contemporary history, argues a profound belief in its moral meaning and eternal significance; and it is this boldness, in face of disappointment continued from generation to generation in Israel, that constitutes the uniqueness of the Messianic hope among that people. To sublimate this permanent meaning of the prophecies from the contemporary material, with which it is mixed, is not difficult. Isaiah foretells his Prince on the supposition that certain things are fulfilled. When the people are reduced to the last extreme, when there is no more a king to rally or to rule them, when the land is in captivity, when revelation is closed, when, in despair of the darkness of the Lord's face, men have taken to them that have familiar spirits and wizards that peep and mutter, then, in that last sinful, hopeless estate of man, a Deliverer shall appear. The zeal of the Lord of hosts will perform it. This is the first article of Isaiah's Messianic creed, and stands back behind the Messiah and all Messianic blessings, their exhaustless origin. Whatsoever man's sin and darkness be, the Almighty lives, and His zeal is infinite. Therefore it is a fact eternally true, that whatsoever Deliverer His people need and can receive shall be sent to them, and shall be styled by whatsoever names their hearts can best appreciate. Titles shall be given Him to attract their hope and their homage, and not a definition of His nature, of which their theological vocabulary would be incapable. This is the vital kernel of Messianic prophecy in Isaiah. The zeal of the Lord, kindling the dark thoughts of the prophet as he broods over his people's need of salvation, suddenly makes a Saviour visible--visible just as He is needed there and then. Isaiah hears Him hailed by titles that satisfy the particular wants of the age, and express men's thoughts as far up the idea of salvation and majesty as they of that age can rise. But the prophet has also perceived that sin and disaster will so accumulate before the Messiah comes, that, though innocent, He shall have to bear tribulation and pass to His prime through suffering. No one with open mind can deny, that in this moderate estimate of the prophet's meaning there is a very great deal of the essence of the Gospel as it has been fulfilled in the personal consciousness and saving work of Jesus Christ,--as much of that essence, indeed, as it was possible to communicate to so early a generation, and one whose religious needs were so largely what we call temporal. But if we grant this, and if at the same time we appreciate the uniqueness of such a hope as this of Israel, then surely it must be allowed to have the appearance of a special preparation for Christ's life and work; and so, to use very moderate words which have been applied to Messianic prophecy in general, it may be taken "as a proof of its true connection with the Gospel dispensation as part of one grand scheme in the counsels of Providence." [26]

***

Men do not ask when they drink of a streamlet high up on the hills, "Is this going to be a great river?" They are satisfied if it is water enough to quench their thirst. And so it was enough for Old Testament believers if they found in Isaiah's prophecy of a Deliverer--as they did find--what satisfied their own religious needs, without convincing them to what volumes it should swell. But this does not mean that in using these Old Testament prophecies we Christians should limit our enjoyment of them to the measure of the generation to whom they were addressed. To have known Christ must make the predictions of the Messiah different to a man. You cannot bring so infinite an ocean of blessing into historic connection with these generous, expansive intimations of the Old Testament without its passing into them. If we may use a rough figure, the Messianic prophecies of the Old Testament are tidal rivers. They not only run, as we have seen, to their sea, which is Christ; they feel His reflex influence. It is not enough for a Christian to have followed the historical direction of the prophecies, or to have proved their connection with the New Testament as parts of one Divine harmony. Forced back by the fulness of meaning to which he has found their courses open, he returns to find the savour of the New Testament upon them, and that where he descended shallow and tortuous channels, with all the difficulties of historical exploration, he is borne back on full tides of worship. To use the appropriate words of Isaiah, the Lord is with him there, a place of broad rivers and streams.

With all this, however, we must not forget that, beside these prophecies of a great earthly ruler, there runs another stream of desire and promise, in which we see a much stronger premonition of the fact that a Divine Being shall some day dwell among men. We mean the Scriptures in which it is foretold that Jehovah Himself shall visibly visit Jerusalem. This line of prophecy, taken along with the powerful anthropomorphic representations of God,--astonishing in a people like the Jews, who so abhorred the making of an image of the Deity upon the likeness of anything in heaven and earth,--we hold to be the proper Old Testament instinct that the Divine should take human form and tabernacle amongst men. But this side of our subject--the relation of the anthropomorphism of the Old Testament to the Incarnation--we postpone till we come to the second part of the book of Isaiah, in which the anthropomorphic figures are more frequent and daring than they are here.

Footnotes:

22. The Messiah, or Anointed, is used in the Old Testament of many agents of God: high-priest (Lev. iv. 3); ministers of the Word (Ps. cv. 15); Cyrus (Isa. xlv. 1); but mostly of God's king, actual (1 Sam. xxiv. 7), or expected (Dan. ix. 25). So it became in Jewish theology the technical term for the coming King and the Captain of salvation.

23. I regret very much that in previous editions I should have erroneously imputed this opinion to Dr. Hermann Schultz--through a mistranslation of his words on pp. 726, 727 of his A. T. Theologie.

24. Prophets of Israel, p. 306.

25. See further on this passage pp. 180-183. As is there pointed out, while these passages on the Messiah are indeed infrequent and unconnected, there is a very evident progress through them of Isaiah's conception of his Hero's character.

26. Stanton: The Jewish and Christian Messiah.

BOOK II

PROPHECIES FROM THE ACCESSION OF HEZEKIAH TO THE DEATH OF SARGON, 727-705 B.C.

Isaiah:-- xxviii. 725 B.C. x. 5-34. 721 B.C. xi., xii. About 720 B.C.? xx. 711 B.C. xxi. 1-10. 710 B.C. xxxviii., xxxix. Between 712 and 705 B.C.

The prophecies with which we have been engaged (chaps. ii.-x. 4) fall either before or during the great Assyrian invasion of Syria, undertaken in 734-732 by Tiglath-pileser II., at the invitation of King Ahaz. Nobody has any doubt about that. But when we ask what prophecies of Isaiah come next in chronological order, we raise a storm of answers. We are no longer on the sure ground we have been enjoying.

Under the canonical arrangement the next prophecy is "The Woe upon the Assyrian" (x. 5-34). In the course of this the Assyrian is made to boast of having overthrown Samaria (vv. 9-11): Is not Samaria as Damascus?... Shall I not, as I have done unto Samaria and her idols, so do to Jerusalem and her idols? If Samaria mean the capital city of Northern Israel--and the name is never used in these parts of Scripture for anything else--and if the prophet be quoting a boast which the Assyrian was actually in a position to make, and not merely imagining a boast, which he would be likely to make some years afterwards (an entirely improbable view, though held by one great scholar [27]), then an event is here described as past and over which did not happen during Tiglath-pileser's campaign, nor indeed till twelve years after it. Tiglath-pileser did not require to besiege Samaria in the campaign of 734-732. The king, Pekah, was slain by a conspiracy of his own subjects; and Hoshea, the ringleader, who succeeded, willingly purchased the stability of a usurped throne by homage and tribute to the king of kings. So Tiglath-pileser went home again, satisfied to have punished Israel by carrying away with him the population of Galilee. During his reign there was no further appearance of the Assyrians in Palestine, but at his death in 727 Hoshea, after the fashion of Assyrian vassals when the throne at Nineveh changed occupants, attempted to throw off the yoke of the new king, Salmanassar IV. Along with the Phoenician and Philistine cities, Hoshea negotiated an alliance with So, or Seve, the Ethiopian, a usurper who had just succeeded in establishing his supremacy over the land of the Pharaohs. In a year Salmanassar marched south upon the rebels. He took Hoshea prisoner on the borders of his territory (725), but, not content, as his predecessor had been, with the submission of the king, he came up throughout all the land, and went up to Samaria, and besieged it three years. [28] He did not live to see the end of the siege, and Samaria was taken in 722 by Sargon, his successor. Sargon overthrew the kingdom and uprooted the people. The northern tribes were carried away into a captivity, from which as tribes they never returned.

It was evidently this complete overthrow of Samaria by Sargon in 722-721, which Isaiah had behind him when he wrote x. 9-11. We must, therefore, date the prophecy after 721, when nothing was left as a bulwark between Judah and the Assyrian. We do so with reluctance. There is much in x. 5-34 which suits the circumstances of Tiglath-pileser's invasion. There are phrases and catch-words coinciding with those in vii.-ix. 7; and the whole oration is simply a more elaborate expression of that defiance of Assyria, which inspires such of the previous prophecies as viii. 9, 10. Besides, with the exception of Samaria, all the names in the Assyrian's boastful catalogue--Carchemish, Calno, Arpad, Hamath and Damascus--might as justly have been vaunted by the lips of Tiglath-pileser as by those of Sargon. But in spite of these things, which seem to vindicate the close relation of x. 5-34 to the prophecies which precede it in the canon, the mention of Samaria as being already destroyed justifies us in divorcing it from them. While they remain dated from before 732, we place it subsequent to 722.

Was Isaiah, then, silent these ten years? Is there no prophecy lying farther on in his book that treats of Samaria as still standing? Besides an address to the fallen Damascus in xvii. 1-11, which we shall take later with the rest of Isaiah's oracles on foreign states, there is one large prophecy, chap. xxviii., which opens with a description of the magnates of Samaria lolling in drunken security on their vine-crowned hill, but God's storms are ready to break. Samaria has not yet fallen, but is threatened and shall fall soon. The first part of chap. xxviii. can only refer to the year, in which Salmanassar advanced upon Samaria--726 or 725. There is nothing in the rest of it to corroborate this date; but the fact, that there are several turns of thought and speech very similar to turns of thought and speech in x. 5-34, makes us the bolder to take away xxviii. from its present connection with xxix.-xxxii., and place it just before x. 5-34.

Here then is our next group of prophecies, all dating from the first seven years of the reign of Hezekiah: xxviii., a warning addressed to the politicians of Jerusalem from the impending fate of those of Samaria (date 725); x. 5-34, a woe upon the Assyrian (date about 720), describing his boasts and his progress in conquest till his sudden crash by the walls of Jerusalem; xi., of date uncertain, for it reflects no historical circumstance, but standing in such artistic contrast to x. that the two must be treated together; and xii., a hymn of salvation, which forms a fitting conclusion to xi. With these we shall take the few fragments of the book of Isaiah which belong to the fifteen years 720-705, and are as straws to show how Judah all that time was drifting down to alliance with Egypt--xx., xxi. 1-10, and xxxviii.-xxxix. This will bring us to 705, and the beginning of a new series of prophecies, the richest of Isaiah's life, and the subject of our third book.

Footnotes:

27. Delitzsch, who fancies that the fall of Samaria is a completed affair only in the vision of the prophet, not in reality.
28. 2 Kings xvii. 5.

CHAPTER VIII

GOD'S COMMONPLACE.

Isaiah xxviii. (ABOUT 725 B.C.)

The twenty-eighth chapter of the Book of Isaiah is one of the greatest of his prophecies. It is distinguished by that regal versatility of style, which places its author at the head of Hebrew writers. Keen analyses of character, realistic contrasts between sin and judgement, clever retorts and epigrams, rapids of scorn, and "a spate" of judgement, but for final issue a placid stream of argument banked by sweet parable--such are the literary charms of the chapter, which derives its moral grandeur from the force with which its currents set towards faith and reason, as together the salvation of states, politicians and private men. The style mirrors life about ourselves, and still tastes fresh to thirsty men. The truths are relevant to every day in which luxury and intemperance abound, in which there are eyes too fevered by sin to see beauty in simple purity, and minds so surfeited with knowledge or intoxicated with their own cleverness, that they call the maxims of moral reason commonplace and scorn religious instruction as food for babes.

Some time when the big, black cloud was gathering again on the north, Isaiah raised his voice to the magnates of Jerusalem: "Lift your heads from your wine-bowls; look north. The sunshine is still on Samaria, and your fellow-drinkers there are revelling in security. But the storm creeps up behind. They shall certainty perish soon; even you cannot help seeing that. Let it scare you, for their sin is yours, and that storm will not exhaust itself on Samaria. Do not think that your clever policies, alliance with Egypt or the treaty with Assyria herself, shall save you. Men are never saved from death and hell by making covenants with them. Scorners of religion and righteousness, except ye cease being sceptical and drunken, and come back from your diplomacy to faith and reason, ye shall not be saved! This destruction that looms is going to cover the whole earth. So stop your running to and fro across it in search of alliances. He that believeth shall not make haste. Stay at home and trust in the God of Zion, for Zion is the one thing that shall survive." In the parable, which closes the prophecy, Isaiah offers some relief to this dark prospect: "Do not think of God as a mere disaster-monger, maker of terrors for men. He has a plan, even in catastrophe, and this deluge, which looks like destruction for all of us, has its method, term and fruits, just as much as the husbandman's harrowing of the earth or threshing of the corn."

The chapter with this argument falls into four divisions.

I. The Warning from Samaria (vv. 1-6).

They had always been hard drinkers in North Israel. Fifty years before, Amos flashed judgement on those who trusted in the mount of Samaria, lolling upon their couches and gulping their wine out of basons, women as well as men. Upon these same drunkards of Ephraim, now soaked and stunned with wine, Isaiah fastens his Woe. Sunny the sky and balmy the air in which they lie, stretched upon flowers by the heads of their fat valleys--a land that tempts its inhabitants with the security of perpetual summer. But God's swift storm drives up the valley--hail, rain and violent streams from every gorge. Flowers, wreaths and pampered bodies are trampled in the mire. The glory of sunny Ephraim is as the first ripe fig a man findeth, and while it is yet in his hand, he eateth it up. But while drunken magnates and the flowers of a rich land are swept away, there is a residue who can and do abide even that storm, to whom the Lord Himself shall be for a crown, a spirit of justice to him that sitteth for justice, and for strength to them that turn back the battle at the gate.

Isaiah's intention is manifest, and his effort a great one. It is to rob passion of its magic and change men's temptations to their disgusts, by exhibiting how squalid passion shows beneath disaster, and how gloriously purity shines surviving it. It is to strip luxury and indulgence of their attractiveness by drenching them with the storm of judgement, and then not to leave them stunned, but to rouse in them a moral admiration and envy by the presentation of certain grand survivals of the storm--unstained justice and victorious valour. Isaiah first sweeps the atmosphere, hot from infective passion, with the cold tempest from the north. Then in the clear shining after rain he points to two figures, which have preserved through temptation and disaster, and now lift against a smiling sky, the ideal that those corrupt judges and drunken warriors have dragged into the mire--him that sitteth for justice and him that turneth back the battle at the gate. The escape from sensuality, this passage suggests, is two-fold. There is the exposure to nature where God's judgements sweep their irresistible way; and then from the despair, which the unrelieved spectacle of judgement produces, there is the recovery to moral effort through the admiration of those purities and heroisms, that by God's Spirit have survived.

When God has put a conscience into the art or literature of any generation, they have followed this method of Isaiah, but not always to the healthy end which he reaches. To show the slaves of Circe the physical disaster impending--which you must begin by doing if you are to impress their brutalized minds--is not enough. The lesson of Tennyson's "Vision of Sin" and of Arnold's "New Sirens," that night and frost, decay and death, come down at last on pampered sense, is necessary, but not enough. Who stops there remains a defective and morbid moralist. When you have made the sensual shiver before the disease that inevitably awaits them, you must go on to show that there are men who have the secret of surviving the most terrible judgements of God, and lift their figures calm and victorious against the storm-washed sky. Preach the depravity of men, but never apart from the possibilities that remain in them. It is Isaiah's health as a moralist that he combines the two. No prophet ever threatened judgement more inexorable and complete than he. Yet he never failed to tell the sinner, how possible it was for him to be different. If it were necessary to crush men in the mud, Isaiah would not leave them there with the hearts of swine. But he put conscience in them, and the envy of what was pure, and the admiration of what was victorious. Even as they wallowed, he pointed them to the figures of men like themselves, who had survived and overcome by the Spirit of God. Here we perceive the ethical possibilities, that lay in his fundamental doctrine of a remnant. Isaiah never crushed men beneath the fear of judgement, without revealing to them the possibility and beauty of victorious virtue. Had we lived in those great days, what a help he had been to us--what a help he may be still!--not only firm to declare that the wages of sin is death, but careful to effect that our humiliation shall not be despair, and that even when we feel our shame and irretrievableness the most, we shall have the opportunity to behold our humanity crowned and seated on the throne from which we had fallen, our humanity driving back the battle from the gate against which we had been hopelessly driven! That seventh verse sounds like a trumpet in the ears of enervated and despairing men.

II. God's Commonplace (vv. 7-13).

But Isaiah has cast his pearls before swine. The men of Jerusalem, whom he addresses, are too deep in sensuality to be roused by his noble words. Even priest and prophet stagger through strong drink; and the class that should have been the conscience of the city, responding immediately to the word of God, reel in vision and stumble in judgement. They turn upon Isaiah's earnest message with tipsy men's insolence. Verses 9 and 10 should be within inverted commas, for they are the mocking reply of drunkards over their cups. Whom is he going to teach knowledge, and upon whom is he trying to force "the Message," as he calls it? Them that are weaned from the milk and drawn from the breasts? Are we school-children, that he treats us with his endless platitudes and repetitions--precept upon precept and precept upon precept, line upon line and line upon line, here a little and there a little? So did these bibulous prophets, priests and politicians mock Isaiah's messages of judgement, wagging their heads in mimicry of his simple, earnest tones. "We must conceive the abrupt, intentionally short, reiterated and almost childish words of verse 10 as spoken in mimicry, with a mocking motion of the head, and in a childish, stammering, taunting tone." [29]

But Isaiah turns upon them with their own words: "You call me, Stammerer! I tell you that God, Who speaks through me, and Whom in me you mock, will one day speak again to you in a tongue that shall indeed sound stammering to you. When those far-off barbarians have reached your walls, and over them taunt you in uncouth tones, then shall you hear how God can stammer. For these shall be the very voice of Him, and as He threatens you with captivity it shall be your bitterness to remember how by me He once offered you a rest and refreshing, which you refused. I tell you more. God will not only speak in words, but in deeds, and then truly your nickname for His message shall be fulfilled to you. Then shall the word of the Lord be unto you precept upon precept, precept upon precept, line upon line, line upon line, here a little and there a little. For God shall speak with the terrible simplicity and slowness of deeds, with the gradual growth of fate, with the monotonous stages of decay, till step by step you go, and stumble backward, and be broken, and snared, and taken. You have scorned my instruction as monosyllables fit for children! By irritating monosyllables of gradual penalty shall God instruct you the second time."

This is not only a very clever and cynical retort, but the statement of a moral principle. We gather from Isaiah that God speaks twice to men, first in words and then by deeds, but both times very simply and plainly. And if men deride and abuse the simplicity of the former, if they ignore moral and religious truths because they are elementary, and rebel against the quiet reiteration of simple voices, with which God sees it most healthy to conduct their education, then they shall be stunned by the commonplace pertinacity, with which the effects of their insolence work themselves out in life. God's ways with men are mostly commonplace; that is the hardest lesson we have to learn. The tongue of conscience speaks like the tongue of time, prevailingly by ticks and moments; not in undue excitement of soul and body, not in the stirring up of our passions nor by enlisting our ambitions, not in thunder nor in startling visions, but by everyday precepts of faithfulness, honour and purity, to which conscience has to rise unwinged by fancy or ambition, and dreadfully weighted with the dreariness of life. If we, carried away upon the rushing interests of the world, and with our appetite spoiled by the wealth and piquancy of intellectual knowledge, despise the simple monitions of conscience and Scripture, as uninteresting and childish, this is the risk we run,--that God will speak to us in another, and this time unshirkable, kind of commonplace. What that is we shall understand, when a career of dissipation or unscrupulous ambition has bereft life of all interest and joy, when one enthusiasm after another grows dull, and one pleasure after another tasteless, when all the little things of life preach to us of judgement, and the grasshopper becometh a burden, and we, slowly descending through the drab and monotony of decay, suffer the last great commonplace, death. There can be no greater irony than for the soul, which has sinned by too greedily seeking for sensation, to find sensation absent even from the judgements she has brought upon herself. Poor Heine's Confessions acknowledge, at once with the appreciation of an artist and the pain of a victim, the satire, with which the Almighty inflicts, in the way that Isaiah describes, His penalties upon sins of sense.

III. Covenants with Death and Hell (vv. 14-22).

To Isaiah's threats of destruction, the politicians of Jerusalem replied, We have bought destruction off! They meant some treaty with a foreign power. Diplomacy is always obscure, and at that distance its details are buried for us in impenetrable darkness. But we may safely conclude that it was either the treaty of Ahaz with Assyria, or some counter-treaty executed with Egypt since this power began again to rise into pretentiousness, or more probably still it was a secret agreement with the southern power, while the open treaty with the northern was yet in force. Isaiah, from the way in which he speaks, seems to have been in ignorance of all, except that the politician's boast was an unhallowed, underhand intrigue, accomplished by much swindling and false conceit of cleverness. This wretched subterfuge Isaiah exposes in some of the most powerful sentences he ever uttered. A faithless diplomacy was never more thoroughly laid bare, in its miserable mixture of political pedantry and falsehood.

Therefore hear the word of Jehovah, ye men of scorn, rulers of this people, which is in Jerusalem!

Because ye have said, We have entered into a covenant with Death, and with Hell have we made a bargain; the "Overflowing Scourge," a current phrase of Isaiah's which they fling back in his teeth, when it passeth along, shall not come unto us, for we have set lies as our refuge, and in falsehood have we hidden ourselves [the prophet's penetrating scorn drags up into their boast the secret conscience of their hearts, that after all lies did form the basis of this political arrangement], therefore thus saith the Lord Jehovah: Behold, I lay in Zion for foundation a stone, a tried stone, a precious corner-stone of sure foundation; he that believeth shall not make haste. No need of swift couriers to Egypt, and fret and fever of poor political brains in Jerusalem! The word make haste is onomatopoetic, like our fuss, and, if fuss may be applied to the conduct of high affairs of state, its exact equivalent in meaning.

And I will set justice for a line, and righteousness for a plummet, and hail shall sweep away the subterfuge of lies, and the secrecy shall waters overflow. And cancelled shall be your covenant with Death, and your bargain with Hell shall not stand.

"The Overflowing Scourge," indeed! When it passeth over, then ye shall be unto it for trampling. As often as it passeth over, it shall take you away, for morning by morning shall it pass over, by day and by night. Then shall it be sheer terror to realize "the Message"! Too late then for anything else. Had you realized "the Message" now, what rest and refreshing! But then only terror.

For the bed is shorter than that a man can stretch himself upon it, and the covering narrower than that he can wrap himself in it. This proverb seems to be struck out of the prophet by the belief of the politicians, that they are creating a stable and restful policy for Judah. It flashes an aspect of hopeless uneasiness over the whole political situation. However they make their bed, with Egypt's or Assyria's help, they shall not find it comfortable. No cleverness of theirs can create a satisfactory condition of affairs, no political arrangement, nothing short of faith, of absolute reliance on that bare foundation-stone laid in Zion,--God's assurance that Jerusalem is inviolable.

For Jehovah shall arise as on Mount Peratsim; He shall be stirred as in the valley of Gibeon, to do His deed--strange is this deed of His, and to bring to pass His act--strange is His act.

Now, therefore, play no more the scorner, lest your bands be made tight, for a consumption, and that determined, have I heard from the Lord, Jehovah of hosts, upon the whole earth. This finishes the matter. Possibility of alliance there is for sane men nowhere in this world of Western Asia, so evidently near convulsion. Only the foundation-stone in Zion shall be left. Cling to that!

When the pedantic members of the General Assembly of the Kirk of Scotland, in the year 1650, were clinging with all the grip of their hard logic, but with very little heart, to the "Divine right of kings," and attempting an impossible state, whose statute-book was to be the Westminster Confession, and its chief executive officer King Charles II., Cromwell, then encamped at Musselburgh, sent them that letter in which the famous sentence occurs: "I beseech you in the bowels of Christ, think it possible you may be mistaken. Precept may be upon precept, line may be upon line," he goes on to say, "and yet the Word of the Lord may be to some a word of Judgement; that they may fall backward, and be broken, and be snared, and be taken! There may be a spiritual fulness, which the world may call drunkenness; as in the second Chapter of the Acts. There may be, as well, a carnal confidence upon misunderstood and misapplied precepts, which may be called spiritual drunkenness. There may be a Covenant made with Death and Hell! I will not say yours was so. But judge if such things have a politic aim: To avoid the overflowing scourge; or, To accomplish worldly interests? And if therein you have confederated with wicked and carnal men, and have respect for them, or otherwise have drawn them in to associate with us, Whether this be a covenant of God and spiritual? Bethink yourselves; we hope we do.

"I pray you read the Twenty-eighth of Isaiah, from the fifth to the fifteenth verse. And do not scorn to know that it is the Spirit that quickens and giveth life." [30]

Cromwell, as we have said, is the best commentator Isaiah has ever had, and that by an instinct born, not only of the same faith, but of experience in tackling similar sorts of character. In this letter he is dealing, like Isaiah, with stubborn pedants, who are endeavouring to fasten the national fortunes upon a Procrustean policy. The diplomacy of Jerusalem was very clever; the Covenanting ecclesiasticism of Edinburgh was logical and consistent. But a Jewish alliance with Assyria and the attempt of Scotsmen to force their covenant upon the whole United Kingdom were equally sheer impossibilities. In either case the bed was shorter than that a man could stretch himself on it, and the covering narrower than that he could wrap himself in it. Both, too, were covenants with Death and Hell; for if the attempt of the Scots to secure Charles II. by the Covenant was free from the falsehood of Jewish diplomacy, it was fatally certain if successful to have led to the subversion of their highest religious interests; and history has proved that Cromwell was no more than just in applying to it the strong expressions, which Isaiah uses of Judah's ominous treaties with the unscrupulous heathen. Over against so pedantic an idea, as that of forcing the life of the three nations into the mould of the one Covenant, and so fatal a folly as the attempt to commit the interests of religion to the keeping of the dissolute and perjured king, Cromwell stands in his great toleration of everything but unrighteousness and his strong conviction of three truths:--that the religious life of Great Britain and Ireland was too rich and varied for the Covenant: that national and religious interests so complicated and precious could be decided only upon the plainest principles of faith and justice: and that, tested by these principles, Charles II. and his crew were as utterly without worth to the nation and as pregnant with destruction, as Isaiah felt Assyria and Egypt to be to Judah. The battle-cries of the two parties at Dunbar are significant of the spiritual difference between them. That of the Scots was "The Covenant!" Cromwell's was Isaiah's own, "The Lord of hosts!" However logical, religious and sincere theirs might be, it was at the best a scheme of men too narrow for events, and fatally compromised by its association with Charles II. But Cromwell's battle-cry required only a moderately sincere faith from those who adopted it, to ensure their victory. For to them it meant just what it had meant to Isaiah, loyalty to a Divine providence, supreme in righteousness, the willingness to be guided by events, interpreting them by no tradition or scheme, but only by conscience. He who understands this will be able to see which side was right in that strange civil war, where both so sincerely claimed to be Scriptural.

It may be wondered why we spend so much argument on comparing the attempt to force Charles II. into the Solemn League and Covenant with the impious treaty of Judah with the heathen. But the argument has not been wasted, if it have shown how even sincere and religious men may make covenants with death, and even Church creeds and constitutions become beds too short that a man may lie upon them, coverings narrower than that he can wrap himself in them. Not once or twice has it happened that an old and hallowed constitution has become, in the providence of God, unfit for the larger life of a people or of a Church, and yet is clung to by parties in that Church or people from motives of theological pedantry or ecclesiastical cowardice. Sooner or later a crisis is sure to arrive, in which the defective creed has to match itself against some interest of justice; and then endless compromises have to be entertained, that discover themselves perilously like bargains with hell. If we of this generation have to make a public application of the twenty-eighth chapter of Isaiah, it lies in this direction. There are few things, to which his famous proverb of the short bed can be applied more aptly, than to the attempt to fasten down the religious life and thought of the present age too rigorously upon a creed of the fashion of two or three hundred years ago.

But Isaiah's words have wider application. Short of faith as he exemplified it, there is no possibility for the spirit of man to be free from uneasiness. It is so all along the scale of human endeavour. No power of patience or of hope is his, who cannot imagine possibilities of truth outside his own opinions, nor trust a justice larger than his private rights. It is here very often that the real test of our faith meets us. If we seek to fit life solely to the conception of our privileges, if in the preaching of our opinions no mystery of higher truth awe us at least into reverence and caution; then, whatever religious creeds we profess, we are not men of faith, but shall surely inherit the bitterness and turmoil that are the portion of unbelievers. If we make it the chief aim of our politics to drive cheap bargains for our trade or to be consistent to party or class interests; if we trim our conscience to popular opinion; if we sell our honesty in business or our love in marriage, that we may be comfortable in the world; then, however firmly we be established in reputation or in welfare, we have given our spiritual nature a support utterly inadequate to its needs, and we shall never find rest. Sooner or later, a man must feel the pinch of having cut his life short of the demands of conscience. Only a generous loyalty to her decrees will leave him freedom of heart and room for his arm to swing. Nor will any philosophy, however comprehensive, nor poetic fancy, however elastic, be able without the complement of faith to arrange, to account for, or to console us for, the actual facts of experience. It is only belief in the God of Isaiah, a true and loving God, omnipotent Ruler of our life, that can bring us peace. There was never a sorrow, that did not find explanation in that, never a tired thought, that would not cling to it. There are no interests so scattered nor energies so far-reaching that there is not return and rest for them under the shadow of His wings. He that believeth shall not make haste. Be still, says a psalm of the same date as Isaiah--Be still, and know that I am God.

IV. The Almighty the All-methodical (vv. 23-29).

The patience of faith, which Isaiah has so nobly preached, he now proceeds to vindicate by reason. But the vindication implies that his audience are already in another mood. From confidence in their clever diplomacy, heedless of the fact that God has His own purposes concerning them, they have swung round to despair before His judgements. Their despair, however, is due to the same fault as their careless confidence--the forgetfulness that God works by counsel and method. Even a calamity, so universal and extreme as that, of whose certainty the prophet has now convinced them, has its measure and its term. To persuade the crushed and superstitious Jews of this, Isaiah employs a parable. "You know," he says, "the husbandman. Have you ever seen him keep on harrowing and breaking the clods of his land for mere sport, and without farther intention? Does not the harrowing time lead to the sowing time? Or again, when he threshes his crops, does he thresh for ever? Is threshing the end he has in view? Look, how he varies the rigour of his instrument by the kind of plant he threshes. For delicate plants, like fitches and cummin, he does not use the threshing sledge with the sharp teeth, or the lumbering roller, but the fitches are beaten out with a staff and the cummin with a rod. And in the case of bread corn, which needs his roller and horses, he does not use these upon it till it is all crushed to dust." The application of this parable is very evident. If the husbandman be so methodical and careful, shall the God who taught him not also be so? If the violent treatment of land and fruits be so measured and adapted for their greater fruitfulness and purity, ought we not to trust God to have the same intentions in His violent treatment of His people? Isaiah here returns to his fundamental gospel: that the Almighty is the All-methodical, too. Men forget this. In their times of activity they think God indifferent; they are too occupied with their own schemes for shaping life, to imagine that He has any. In days of suffering, again, when disaster bursts, they conceive of God only as force and vengeance. Yet, says Isaiah, Jehovah of hosts is wonderful in counsel, and excellent in that sort of wisdom which causes things to succeed. This last word of the chapter is very expressive. It literally means furtherance, help, salvation, and then the true wisdom or insight which ensures these: the wisdom which carries things through. It splendidly sums up Isaiah's gospel to the Jews, cowering like dogs before the coming calamity: God is not mere force or vengeance. His judgements are not chaos. But He is wonderful in counsel, and all His ways have furtherance or salvation for their end.

We have said this is one of the finest prophecies of Isaiah. His political foresight was admirable, when he alone of his countrymen predicted the visitation of Assyria upon Judah. But now, when all are convinced of it, how still more wonderful does he seem facing that novel disaster, with the whole world's force behind it, and declaring its limit. He has not the temptation, so strong in prophets of judgement, to be a mere disaster-monger, and leave judgement on the horizon unrelieved. Nor is he afraid, as other predicters of evil have been, of the monster he has summoned to the land. The secret of this is that from the first he predicted the Assyrian invasion, not out of any private malice nor merely by superior political foresight, but because he knew--and knew, as he tells us, by the inspiration of God's own Spirit--that God required such an instrument to punish the unrighteousness of Judah. If the enemy was summoned by God at the first, surely till the last the enemy shall be in God's hand.

To this enemy we are now to see Isaiah turn with the same message he has delivered to the men of Jerusalem.

Footnotes:

29. Ewald. The original runs thus: "Ki tsav la-tsav, tsav la-tsav qav la-qav, qav la-qav; z'eir sham z'eir sham."

30. Cromwell's Letters and Speeches, Letter cxxxvi.

Rev. George Adam Smith, M.A.

CHAPTER IX

ATHEISM OF FORCE AND ATHEISM OF FEAR.

Isaiah x. 5-34 (ABOUT 721 B.C.).

    In chap. xxviii. Isaiah, speaking in the year 725 when Salmanassar IV. was marching on Samaria, had explained to the politicians of Jerusalem how entirely the Assyrian host was in the hand of Jehovah for the punishment of Samaria and the punishment and purification of Judah. The invasion which in that year loomed so awful was not unbridled force of destruction, implying the utter annihilation of God's people, as Damascus, Arpad and Hamath had been annihilated. It was Jehovah's instrument for purifying His people, with its appointed term and its glorious intentions of fruitfulness and peace.

    In the tenth chapter Isaiah turns with this truth to defy the Assyrian himself. It is four years later. Samaria has fallen. The judgement, which the prophet spoke upon the luxurious capital, has been fulfilled. All Ephraim is an Assyrian province. Judah stands for the first time face to face with Assyria. From Samaria to the borders of Judah is not quite two days' march, to the walls of Jerusalem a little over two. Now shall the Jews be able to put to the test their prophet's promise! What can possibly prevent Sargon from making Zion as Samaria, and carrying her people away in the track of the northern tribes to captivity?

    There was a very fallacious human reason, and there was a very sound Divine one.

    The fallacious human reason was the alliance which Ahaz had made with Assyria. In what state that alliance now was, does not clearly appear, but the most optimist of the Assyrian party at Jerusalem could not, after all that had happened, be feeling quite comfortable about it. The Assyrian was as unscrupulous as themselves. There was too much impetus in the rush of his northern floods to respect a tiny province like Judah, treaty or no treaty. Besides, Sargon had as good reason to suspect Jerusalem of intriguing with Egypt, as he had against Samaria or the Philistine cities; and the Assyrian kings had already shown their meaning of the covenant with Ahaz by stripping Judah of enormous tribute.

    So Isaiah discounts in this prophecy Judah's treaty with Assyria. He speaks as if nothing was likely to prevent the Assyrian's immediate march upon Jerusalem. He puts into Sargon's mouth the intention of this, and makes him boast of the ease with which it can be accomplished (vv. 7-11). In the end of the prophecy he even describes the probable itinerary of the invader from the borders of Judah to his arrival on the heights, over against the Holy City (vv. 27 last clause to 32). [31]

> *Cometh up from the North the Destroyer.*
> *He is come upon Ai; marcheth through Migron; at Michmash musters his baggage.*
> *They have passed through the Pass; "Let Geba be our bivouac."*
> *Terror-struck is Ramah; Gibeah of Saul hath fled.*
> *Make shrill thy voice, O daughter of Gallim! Listen, Laishah! Answer her, Anathoth!*
> *In mad flight is Madmenah; the dwellers in Gebim gather their stuff to flee.*
> *This very day he halteth at Nob; he waveth his hand at the Mount of the Daughter of Zion, the Hill of Jerusalem.*

    This is not actual fact; but it is vision of what may take place to-day or to-morrow. For there is nothing--not even that miserable treaty--to prevent such a violation of Jewish territory, within which, it ought to be kept in mind, lie all the places named by the prophet.

    But the invasion of Judah and the arrival of the Assyrian on the heights over against Jerusalem does not mean that the Holy City and the shrine of Jehovah of hosts are to be destroyed; does not mean that all the prophecies of Isaiah about the security of this rallying-place for the remnant of God's people are to be annulled, and Israel annihilated. For just at the moment of the Assyrian's triumph, when he brandishes his hand over Jerusalem, as if he would harry it like a bird's nest, Isaiah beholds him struck down, and crash like the fall of a whole Lebanon of cedars (vv. 33, 34).

> Behold the Lord, Jehovah of hosts, lopping the topmost boughs with a sudden crash,
> And the high ones of stature hewn down, and the lofty are brought low!
> Yea, He moweth down the thickets of the forest with iron, and Lebanon by a Mighty One falleth.

All this is poetry. We are not to suppose that the prophet actually expected the Assyrian to take the route, which he has laid down for him with so much detail. As a matter of fact, Sargon did not advance across the Jewish frontier, but turned away by the coast-land of Philistia to meet his enemy of Egypt, whom he defeated at Rafia, and then went home to Nineveh, leaving Judah alone. And, although some twenty years later the Assyrian did appear before Jerusalem, as threatening as Isaiah describes, and was cut down in as sudden and miraculous a manner, yet it was not by the itinerary Isaiah here marked for him that he came, but in quite another direction: from the south-west. What Isaiah merely insists upon is that there is nothing in that wretched treaty of Ahaz--that fallacious human reason--to keep Sargon from overrunning Judah to the very walls of Jerusalem, but that, even though he does so, there is a most sure Divine reason for the Holy City remaining inviolate.

The Assyrian expected to take Jerusalem. But he is not his own master. Though he knows it not, and his only instinct is that of destruction (ver. 7), he is the rod in God's hand. And when God shall have used him for the needed punishment of Judah, then will God visit upon him his arrogance and brutality. This man, who says he will exploit the whole earth as he harries a bird's nest (ver. 14), who believes in nothing but himself, saying, By the strength of my hand I have done it, and by my wisdom, for I am prudent, is but the instrument of God, and all his boasting is that of the axe against him that heweth therewith and of the saw against him that wieldeth it. As if, says the prophet, with a scorn still fresh for those who make material force the ultimate power in the universe--As if a rod should shake them that lift it up, or as if a staff should lift up him that is not wood. By the way, Isaiah has a word for his countrymen. What folly is theirs, who now put all their trust in this world-force, and at another time cower in abject fear before it! Must he again bid them look higher, and see that Assyria is only the agent in God's work of first punishing the whole land, but afterwards redeeming His people! In the midst of denunciation the prophet's stern voice breaks into the promise of this later hope (vv. 24-27a); and at last the crash of the fallen Assyrian is scarcely still, before Isaiah has begun to declare a most glorious future of grace for Israel. But this carries us over into the eleventh chapter, and we had better first of all gather up the lessons of the tenth.

This prophecy of Isaiah contains a great Gospel and two great Protests, which the prophet was enabled to make in the strength of it: one against the Atheism of Force, and one against the Atheism of Fear.

The Gospel of the chapter is just that which we have already emphasized as the gospel par excellence of Isaiah: the Lord exalted in righteousness, God supreme over the supremest men and forces of the world. But we now see it carried to a height of daring not reached before. This was the first time that any man faced the sovereign force of the world in the full sweep of victory, and told himself and his fellow-men: "This is not travelling in the greatness of its own strength, but is simply a dead, unconscious instrument in the hand of God." Let us, at the cost of a little repetition, get at the heart of this. We shall find it wonderfully modern.

Belief in God had hitherto been local and circumscribed. Each nation, as Isaiah tells us, had walked in the name of its god, and limited his power and prevision to its own life and territory. We do not blame the peoples for this. Their conception of God was narrow, because their life was narrow, and they confined the power of their deity to their own borders because, in fact, their thoughts seldom strayed beyond. But now the barriers, that had so long enclosed mankind in narrow circles, were being broken down. Men's thoughts travelled through the breaches, and learned that outside their fatherland there lay the world. Their lives thereupon widened immensely, but their theologies stood still. They felt the great forces which shook the world, but their gods remained the same petty, provincial deities. Then came this great Assyrian power, hurtling through the nations, laughing at their gods as idols, boasting that it was by his own strength he overcame them, and to simple eyes making good his boast as he harried the whole earth like a bird's nest. No wonder that men's hearts were drawn from the unseen spiritualities to this very visible brutality! No wonder all real faith in the gods seemed to be dying out, and that men made it the business of their lives to seek peace with this world-force, that was carrying everything, including the gods themselves, before it! Mankind was in danger of practical atheism: of placing, as Isaiah tells us, the ultimate faith which belongs to a righteous God in this brute force: of substituting embassies for prayers, tribute for sacrifice, and the tricks and compromises of diplomacy for the endeavour to live a holy and righteous life. Behold, what questions were at issue: questions that have come up again and again in the history of human thought, and that are tugging at us to-day harder than ever!--whether the visible, sensible forces of the universe, that break so rudely in upon our primitive theologies, are what we men have to make our peace with, or whether there is behind them a Being, who wields them for purposes, far transcending them, of justice and of love; whether, in short, we are to be materialists or believers in God. It is the same old, ever-new debate. The factors of it have only changed a little as we have become more learned. Where Isaiah felt the Assyrians, we are confronted by the evolution of nature and history, and the material forces into which it sometimes looks ominously like as if these could be analysed. Everything that has come forcibly and gloriously to the front of things, every drift that appears to dominate history, all that asserts its claim on our wonder, and offers its own simple and strong solution of our life--is our Assyria. It is precisely now, as then, a rush of new powers across the horizon of our knowledge, which makes the God, who was sufficient for the narrower knowledge of yesterday, seem petty and old-fashioned to-day. This problem no generation can escape, whose vision of the world has become wider than that of its predecessors. But Isaiah's greatness lay in this: that it was given to him to attack the problem the first time it presented itself to humanity with any serious force, and that he applied to it the only sure solution--a more lofty and spiritual view of God than the one which it had found wanting. We may thus paraphrase his argument: "Give me a God who is more than a national patron, give me a God who cares only for righteousness, and I say that every material force the world exhibits is nothing but subordinate to Him. Brute force cannot be anything but an instrument, an axe, a saw, something essentially mechanical and in need of an arm to lift it. Postulate a supreme and righteous Ruler of the world, and you not only have all its movements explained, but may rest assured, that it shall only be permitted to execute justice and purify men. The world cannot prevent their salvation, if God have willed this."

Isaiah's problem was thus the fundamental one between faith and atheism; but we must notice that it did not arise theoretically, nor did he meet it by an abstract proposition. This fundamental religious question--whether men are to trust in the visible forces of the world or in the invisible God--came up as a bit of practical politics. It was not to Isaiah a philosophical or theological question. It was an affair in the foreign policy of Judah.

Except to a few thinkers, the question between materialism and faith never does present itself as one of abstract argument. To the mass of men it is always a question of practical life. Statesmen meet it in their policies, private persons in the conduct of their fortunes. Few of us trouble our heads about an intellectual atheism, but the temptations to practical atheism abound unto us all day by day. Materialism never presents itself as a mere ism; it always takes some concrete form. Our Assyria may be the world in Christ's sense, that flood of successful, heartless, unscrupulous, scornful forces which burst on our innocence, with their challenge to make terms and pay tribute, or go down straightway in the struggle for existence. Beside their frank and forceful demands, how commonplace and irrelevant do the simple precepts of religion often seem; and how the great brazen laugh of the world seems to bleach the beauty out of purity and honour! According to our temper, we either cower before its insolence, whining that character and energy of struggle and religious peace are impossible against it; and that is the Atheism of Fear, with which Isaiah charged the men of Jerusalem, when they were paralysed before Assyria. Or we seek to ensure ourselves against disaster by alliance with the world. We make ourselves one with it, its subjects and imitators. We absorb the world's temper, get to believe in nothing but success, regard men only as they can be useful to us, and think so exclusively of ourselves as to lose the faculty of imagining about us any other right or need or pity. And all that is the Atheism of Force, with which Isaiah charged the Assyrian. It is useless to think, that we common men cannot possibly sin after the grand manner of this imperial monster. In our measure we fatally can. In this commercial age private persons very easily rise to a position of influence, which gives almost as vast a stage for egotism to display itself as the Assyrian boasted. But after all the human Ego needs very little room to develop the possibilities of atheism that are in it. An idol is an idol, whether you put it on a small or a large pedestal. A little man with a little work may as easily stand between himself and God, as an emperor with the world at his feet. Forgetfulness that he is a servant, a trader on graciously entrusted capital--and then at the best an unprofitable one--is not less sinful in a small egoist than in a great one; it is only very much more ridiculous, than Isaiah, with his scorn, has made it to appear in the Assyrian.

Or our Assyria may be the forces of nature, which have swept upon the knowledge of this generation with the novelty and impetus, with which the northern hosts burst across the horizon of Israel. Men to-day, in the course of their education, become acquainted with laws and forces, which dwarf the simpler theologies of their boyhood, pretty much as the primitive beliefs of Israel dwindled before the arrogant face of Assyria. The alternative confronts them either to retain, with a narrowed and fearful heart, their old conceptions of God, or to find their enthusiasm in studying, and their duty in relating themselves to, the forces of nature alone. If this be the only alternative, there can be no doubt but that most men will take the latter course. We ought as little to wonder at men of to-day abandoning certain theologies and forms of religion for a downright naturalism--for the study of powers that appeal so much to the curiosity and reverence of man--as we wonder at the poor Jews of the eighth century before Christ forsaking their provincial conceptions of God as a tribal Deity for homage to this great Assyrian, who handled the nations and their gods as his playthings. But is such the only alternative? Is there no higher and sovereign conception of God, in which even these natural forces may find their explanation and term? Isaiah found such a conception for his problem, and his problem was very similar to ours. Beneath his idea of God, exalted and spiritual, even the imperial Assyrian, in all his arrogance, fell subordinate and serviceable. The prophet's faith never wavered, and in the end was vindicated by history. Shall we not at least attempt his method of solution? We could not do better than by taking his factors. Isaiah got a God more powerful than Assyria, by simply exalting the old God of his nation in righteousness. This Hebrew was saved from the terrible conclusion, that the selfish, cruel force which in his day carried all before it was the highest power in life, simply by believing righteousness to be more exalted still. But have twenty-five centuries made any change upon this power, by which Isaiah interpreted history and overcame the world? Is righteousness less sovereign now than then, or was conscience more imperative when it spoke in Hebrew than when it speaks in English? Among the decrees of nature, at last interpreted for us in all their scope and reiterated upon our imaginations by the ablest men of the age, truth, purity and civic justice as confidently assert their ultimate victory, as when they were threatened merely by the arrogance of a human despot. The discipline of science and the glories of the worship of nature are indeed justly vaunted over the childish and narrow-minded ideas of God, that prevail in much of our average Christianity. But more glorious than anything in earth or heaven is character, and the adoration of a holy and loving will makes more for "victory and law" than the discipline or the enthusiasm of science. Therefore, if our conceptions of God are overwhelmed by what we know of nature, let us seek to enlarge and spiritualize them. Let us insist, as Isaiah did, upon His righteousness, until our God once more appear indubitably supreme.

Otherwise we are left with the intolerable paradox, that truth and honesty, patience and the love of man to man, are after all but the playthings and victims of force; that, to adapt the words of Isaiah, the rod really shakes him who lifts it up, and the staff is wielding that which is not wood.

Footnote:

31. It will be noticed that in the above version a different reading is adopted from the meaningless clause at the end of verse 27 in the English version, out of which a proper heading for the subsequent itinerary has been obtained by Robertson Smith (Journal of Philology, 1884, p. 62).

Rev. George Adam Smith, M.A.

CHAPTER X

THE SPIRIT OF GOD IN MAN AND THE ANIMALS.

Isaiah xi., xii. (ABOUT 720 B.C.?)

Beneath the crash of the Assyrian with which the tenth chapter closes, we pass out into the eleventh upon a glorious prospect of Israel's future. The Assyrian when he falls shall fall for ever like the cedars of Lebanon, that send no fresh sprout forth from their broken stumps. But out of the trunk of the Judæan oak, also brought down by these terrible storms, Isaiah sees springing a fair and powerful Branch. Assyria, he would tell us, has no future. Judah has a future, and at first the prophet sees it in a scion of her royal house. The nation shall be almost exterminated, the dynasty of David hewn to a stump; yet there shall spring a shoot from the stock of Jesse, and a branch from his roots shall bear fruit.

The picture of this future, which fills the eleventh chapter, is one of the most extensive that Isaiah has drawn. Three great prospects are unfolded in it: a prospect of mind, a prospect of nature and a prospect of history. To begin with, there is (vv. 2-5) the geography of a royal mind in its stretches of character, knowledge and achievement. We have next (vv. 5-9) a vision of the restitution of nature, Paradise regained. And, thirdly (vv. 9-16), there is the geography of Israel's redemption, the coasts and highways along which the hosts of the dispersion sweep up from captivity to a station of supremacy over the world. To this third prospect chapter xii. forms a fitting conclusion, a hymn of praise in the mouth of returning exiles. [32] The human mind, nature and history are the three dimensions of life, and across them all the prophet tells us that the Spirit of the Lord will fill the future with His marvels of righteousness, wisdom and peace. He presents to us three great ideals: the perfect indwelling of our humanity by the Spirit of God; the peace and communion of all nature, covered with the knowledge of God; the traversing of all history by the Divine purposes of redemption.

I. The Messiah and the Spirit of the Lord (xi. 1-5).

The first form, in which Isaiah sees Israel's longed-for future realised, is that which he so often exalts and makes glistering upon the threshold of the future--the form of a king. It is a peculiarity, which we cannot fail to remark about Isaiah's scattered representations of this brilliant figure, that they have no connecting link. They do not allude to one another, nor employ a common terminology, even the word king dropping out of some of them. The earliest of the series bestows a name on the Messiah, which none of the others repeat, nor does Isaiah say in any of them, This is He of whom I have spoken before. Perhaps the disconnectedness of these oracles is as strong a proof as is necessary of the view we have formed that throughout his ministry our prophet had before him no distinct, identical individual, but rather an ideal of virtue and kinghood, whose features varied according to the conditions of the time. In this chapter Isaiah recalls nothing of Immanuel, or of the Prince-of-the-Four-Names. Nevertheless (besides for the first time deriving the Messiah from the house of David), he carries his description forward to a stage which lies beyond and to some extent implies his two previous portraits. Immanuel was only a Sufferer with His people in the day of their oppression. The Prince-of-the-Four-Names was the Redeemer of his people from their captivity, and stepped to his throne not only after victory, but with the promise of a long and just government shining from the titles by which He was proclaimed. But now Isaiah not only speaks at length of this peaceful reign--a chronological advance--but describes his hero so inwardly that we also feel a certain spiritual advance. The Messiah is no more a mere experience, as Immanuel was, nor only outward deed and promise, like the Prince-of-the-Four-Names, but at last, and very strongly, a character. The second verse is the definition of this character; the third describes the atmosphere in which it lives. *And there shall rest upon him the Spirit of Jehovah, the spirit of wisdom and understanding, the spirit of counsel and might, the spirit of knowledge and the fear of Jehovah; and he shall draw breath in the fear of Jehovah*--in other words, ripeness but also sharpness of mind; moral decision and heroic energy; piety in its two forms of knowing the will of God and feeling the constraint to perform it. We could not have a more concise summary of the strong elements of a ruling mind. But it is only as Judge and Ruler that Isaiah cares here to think of his hero. Nothing is said of the tender virtues, and we feel that the prophet still stands in the days of the need of inflexible government and purgation in Judah.

Dean Plumptre has plausibly suggested, that these verses may represent the programme which

Isaiah set before his pupil Hezekiah on his accession to the charge of a nation, whom his weak predecessor had suffered to lapse into such abuse of justice and laxity of morals. [33] The acts of government described are all of a punitive and repressive character. The hero speaks only to make the land tremble: And He shall smite the land [34] with the rod of His mouth [what need, after the whispering, indecisive Ahaz!], and with the breath of His lips shall He slay the wicked.

This, though a fuller and more ethical picture of the Messiah than even the ninth chapter, is evidently wanting in many of the traits of a perfect man. Isaiah has to grow in his conception of his Hero, and will grow as the years go on, in tenderness. His thirty-second chapter is a much richer, a more gracious and humane picture of the Messiah. There the Victor of the ninth and righteous Judge of the eleventh chapters is represented as a Man, who shall not only punish but protect, and not only reign but inspire, who shall be life as well as victory and justice to His people--an hiding-place from the wind and a covert from the tempest, as rivers of water in a dry place, as the shadow of a great rock in a weary land.

A conception so limited to the qualifications of an earthly monarch, as this of chap. xi., gives us no ground for departing from our previous conclusion, that Isaiah had not a "supernatural" personality in his view. The Christian Church, however, has not confined the application of the passage to earthly kings and magistrates, but has seen its perfect fulfilment in the indwelling of Christ's human nature by the Holy Ghost. But it is remarkable, that for this exegesis she has not made use of the most "supernatural" of the details of character here portrayed. If the Old Testament has a phrase for sinlessness, that phrase occurs here, in the beginning of the third verse. In the authorized English version it is translated, and shall make him of quick understanding in the fear of the Lord, and in the Revised Version, His delight shall be in the fear of the Lord, and on the margin the literal meaning of delight is given as scent. But the phrase may as well mean, He shall draw his breath in the fear of the Lord; and it is a great pity, that our revisers have not even on the margin given to English readers any suggestion of so picturesque, and probably so correct, a rendering. It is a most expressive definition of sinlessness--sinlessness which was the attribute of Christ alone. We, however purely intentioned we be, are compassed about by an atmosphere of sin. We cannot help breathing what now inflames our passions, now chills our warmest feelings, and makes our throats incapable of honest testimony or glorious praise. As oxygen to a dying fire, so the worldliness we breathe is to the sin within us. We cannot help it; it is the atmosphere into which we are born. But from this Christ alone of men was free. He was His own atmosphere, drawing breath in the fear of the Lord. Of Him alone is it recorded, that, though living in the world, He was never infected with the world's sin. The blast of no man's cruelty ever kindled unholy wrath within His breast; nor did men's unbelief carry to His soul its deadly chill. Not even when He was led of the devil into the atmosphere of temptation, did His heart throb with one rebellious ambition. Christ drew breath in the fear of the Lord.

But draughts of this atmosphere are possible to us also, to whom the Holy Spirit is granted. We too, who sicken with the tainted breath of society, and see the characters of children about us fall away and the hidden evil within leap to swift flame before the blasts of the world--we too may, by Christ's grace, draw breath, like Him, in the fear of the Lord. Recall some day when, leaving your close room and the smoky city, you breasted the hills of God, and into opened lungs drew deep draughts of the fresh air of heaven. What strength it gave your body, and with what a glow of happiness your mind was filled! What that is physically, Christ has made possible for us men morally. He has revealed stretches and eminences of life, where, following in His footsteps, we also shall draw for our breath the fear of God. This air is inspired up every steep hill of effort, and upon all summits of worship. In the most passion-haunted air, prayer will immediately bring this atmosphere about a man, and on the wings of praise the poorest soul may rise from the miasma of temptation, and sing forth her song into the azure with as clear a throat as the lark's.

And what else is heaven to be, if not this? God, we are told, shall be its Sun; but its atmosphere shall be His fear, which is clean and endureth for ever. Heaven seems most real as a moral open-air, where every breath is an inspiration, and every pulse a healthy joy, where no thoughts from within us find breath but those of obedience and praise, and all our passions and aspirations are of the will of God. He that lives near to Christ, and by Christ often seeks God in prayer, may create for himself even on earth such a heaven, perfecting holiness in the fear of God.

II. The Seven Spirits of God (xi. 2, 3).

This passage, which suggests so much of Christ, is also for Christian Theology and Art a classical passage on the Third Person of the Trinity. If the texts in the book of Revelation (chaps. i. 4; iii. 1; iv. 5; v. 6) upon the Seven Spirits of God were not themselves founded on this text of Isaiah, it is certain that the Church immediately began to interpret them by its details. While there are only six spirits of God named here--three pairs--yet, in order to complete the perfect number, the exegesis of early Christianity sometimes added the Spirit of the Lord at the beginning of verse 2 as the central branch of a seven-branched candlestick; or sometimes the quick understanding in the fear of the Lord in the beginning of verse 3 was attached as the seventh branch. (Compare Zech. iv. 6.)

It is remarkable that there is almost no single text of Scripture, which has more impressed itself upon Christian doctrine and symbol than this second verse of the eleventh chapter, interpreted as a definition of the Seven Spirits of God. In the theology, art and worship of the Middle Ages it dominated the expression of the work of the Holy Ghost. First, and most native to its origin, arose the employment of this text at the coronation of kings and the fencing of tribunals of justice. What Isaiah wrote for Hezekiah of Judah became the official prayer, song or ensemple of the earliest Christian kings in Europe. It is evidently the model of that royal hymn--not by Charlemagne, as usually supposed, but by his grandson Charles the Bald--the Veni Creator Spiritus. In a Greek miniature of the tenth century, the Holy Spirit, as a dove, is seen hovering over King David, who displays the prayer: Give the king Thy judgements, O God, and Thy righteousness to the king's son, while there stand on either side of him the figures of Wisdom and Prophecy. [35] Henry III.'s order of knighthood, "Du Saint Esprit," was restricted to political men, and particularly to magistrates. But perhaps the most interesting identification of the Holy Spirit with the rigorous virtues of our passage occurs in a story of St. Dunstan, who, just before mass on the day of Pentecost, discovered that three coiners, who had been sentenced to death, were being respited till the Festival of the Holy Ghost should be over. "It shall not be thus," cried the indignant saint, and gave orders for their immediate execution. There was remonstrance, but he, no doubt with the eleventh of Isaiah in mind, insisted, and was obeyed. "I now hope," he said, resuming the mass, "that God will be pleased to accept the sacrifice I am about to offer." "Whereupon," says the veracious Acts of the Saints, "a snow-white dove did, in the vision of many, descend from heaven, and until the sacrifice was completed remain above his head in silence, with wings extended and motionless." Which may be as much legend as we have the heart to make it, but nevertheless remains a sure proof of the association, by discerning mediævals who could read their Scriptures, of the Holy Spirit with the decisiveness and rigorous justice of Isaiah's "mirror for magistrates." [36]

But the influence of our passage may be followed to that wider definition of the Spirit's work, which made Him the Fountain of all intelligence. The Spirits of the Lord mentioned by Isaiah are prevailingly intellectual; and the mediæval Church, using the details of this passage to interpret Christ's own intimation of the Paraclete as the Spirit of truth,--remembering also the story of Pentecost, when the Spirit bestowed the gifts of tongues, and the case of Stephen, who, in the triumph of his eloquence and learning, was said to be full of the Holy Ghost,--did regard, as Gregory of Tours expressly declared, the Holy Spirit as the "God of the intellect more than of the heart." All Councils were opened by a mass to the Holy Ghost, and few, who have examined with care the windows of mediæval churches, will have failed to be struck with the frequency with which the Dove is seen descending upon the heads of miraculously learned persons, or presiding at discussions, or hovering over groups of figures representing the sciences. [37] To the mediæval Church, then, the Holy Spirit was the Author of the intellect, more especially of the governing and political intellect; and there can be little doubt, after a study of the variations of this doctrine, that the first five verses of the eleventh of Isaiah formed upon it the classical text of appeal. To Christians, who have been accustomed by the use of the word Comforter to associate the Spirit only with the gentle and consoling influences of heaven, it may seem strange to find His energy identified with the stern rigour of the magistrate. But in its practical, intelligent and reasonable uses the mediæval doctrine is greatly to be preferred, on grounds both of Scripture and common-sense, to those two comparatively modern corruptions of it, one of which emphasizes the Spirit's influence in the exclusive operation of the grace of orders, and the other, driving to an opposite extreme, dissipates it into the vaguest religiosity. It is one of the curiosities of Christian theology, that a Divine influence, asserted by Scripture and believed by the early Church to manifest itself in the successful conduct of civil offices and the fulness of intellectual learning, should in these latter days be so often set up in a sort of "supernatural" opposition to practical wisdom and the results of science. But we may go back to Isaiah for the same kind of correction on this doctrine, as he has given us on the doctrine of faith; and while we do not forget the richer meaning the New Testament bestows on the operation of the Divine Spirit, we may learn from the Hebrew prophet to seek the inspiration of the Holy Ghost in all the endeavours of science, and not to forget that it is His guidance alone which enables us to succeed in the conduct of our offices and fortunes.

III. The Redemption of Nature (xi. 6-9).

But Isaiah will not be satisfied with the establishment of a strong government in the land and the redemption of human society from chaos. He prophesies the redemption of all nature as well. It is one of those errors, which distort both the poetry and truth of the Bible, to suppose that by the bears, lions and reptiles which the prophet now sees tamed in the time of the regeneration, he intends the violent human characters which he so often attacks. When Isaiah here talks of the beasts, he means the beasts. The passage is not allegorical, but direct, and forms a parallel to the well-known passage in the eighth of Romans. Isaiah and Paul, chief apostles of the two covenants, both interrupt their magnificent odes upon the outpouring of the Spirit, to remind us that the benefits of this will be shared by the brute and unintelligent creation. And, perhaps, there is no finer contrast in the Scriptures than here, where beside so majestic a description of the intellectual faculties of humanity Isaiah places so charming a picture of the docility and sportfulness of wild animals,--And a little child shall lead them.

We, who live in countries, from which wild beasts have been exterminated, cannot understand the insecurity and terror, that they cause in regions where they abound. A modern seer of the times of regeneration would leave the wild animals out of his vision. They do not impress any more the human conscience or imagination. But they once did so most terribly. The hostility between man and the beasts not only formed once upon a time the chief material obstacle in the progress of the race, but remains still to the religious thinker the most pathetic portion of that groaning and travailing of all creation, which is so heavy a burden on his heart. Isaiah, from his ancient point of view, is in thorough accord with the order of civilisation, when he represents the subjugation of wild animals as the first problem of man, after he has established a strong government in the land. So far from rhetorizing or allegorizing-- above which literary forms it would appear to be impossible for the appreciation of some of his commentators to follow him--Isaiah is earnestly celebrating a very real moment in the laborious progress of mankind. Isaiah stands where Hercules stood, and Theseus, and Arthur when

> *"There grew great tracts of wilderness,*
> *Wherein the beast was ever more and more,*
> *But man was less and less till Arthur came.*
> *And he drave*
> *The heathen, and he slew the beast, and felled*
> *The forest, and let in the sun, and made*
> *Broad pathways for the hunter and the knight,*
> *And so returned."*

But Isaiah would solve the grim problem of the warfare between man and his lower fellow-creatures in a very different way from that, of which these heroes have set the example to humanity. Isaiah would not have the wild beasts exterminated, but tamed. There our Western and modern imagination may fail to follow him, especially when he includes reptiles in the regeneration, and prophesies of adders and lizards as the playthings of children. But surely there is no genial man, who has watched the varied forms of life that sport in the Southern sunshine, who will not sympathize with the prophet in his joyous vision. Upon a warm spring day in Palestine, to sit upon the grass, beside some old dyke or ruin with its face to the south, is indeed to obtain a rapturous view of the wealth of life, with which the bountiful God has blessed and made merry man's dwelling-place. How the lizards come and go among the grey stones, and flash like jewels in the dust! And the timid snake rippling quickly past through the grass, and the leisurely tortoise, with his shiny back, and the chameleon, shivering into new colour as he passes from twig to stone and stone to straw,--all the air the while alive with the music of the cricket and the bee! You feel that the ideal is not to destroy these pretty things as vermin. What a loss of colour the lizards alone would imply! But, as Isaiah declares,--whom we may imagine walking with his children up the steep vineyard paths, to watch the creatures come and go upon the dry dykes on either hand,--the ideal is to bring them into sympathy with ourselves, make pets of them and playthings for children, who indeed stretch out their hands in joy to the pretty toys. Why should we need to fight with, or destroy, any of the happy life the Lord has created? Why have we this loathing to it, and need to defend ourselves from it, when there is so much suffering we could cure, and so much childlikeness we could amuse and be amused by, and yet it will not let us near? To these questions there is not another answer but the answer of the Bible: that this curse of conflict and distrust between man and his fellow-creatures is due to man's sin, and shall only be done away by man's redemption.

Nor is this Bible answer,--of which the book of Genesis gives us the one end, and this text of Isaiah the other,--a mere pious opinion, which the true history of man's dealing with wild beasts by extermination proves to be impracticable. We may take on scientific authority a few facts as hints from nature, that after all man is to blame for the wildness of the beasts, and that through his sanctification they may be restored to sympathy with himself. Charles Darwin says: "It deserves notice, that at an extremely ancient period, when man first entered any country the animals living there would have felt no instinctive or inherited fear of him, and would consequently have been tamed far more easily than at present." And he gives some very instructive facts in proof of this with regard to dogs, antelopes, manatees and hawks. "Quadrupeds and birds which have seldom been disturbed by man dread him no more than do our English birds the cows or horses grazing in the fields." [38] Darwin's details are peculiarly pathetic in their revelation of the brutes' utter trustfulness in man, before they get to know him. Persons, who have had to do with individual animals of a species that has never been thoroughly tamed, are aware that the difficulty of training them lies in convincing them of our sincerity and good-heartedness, and that when this is got over they will learn almost any trick or habit. The well-known lines of Burns to the field-mouse gather up the cause of all this in a fashion very similar to the Bible's.

Rev. George Adam Smith, M.A.

> "I'm truly sorry man's dominion
> Has broken nature's social union,
> And justifies that ill opinion,
> Which makes thee startle
> At me, thy poor earth-born companion
> And fellow-mortal."

How much the appeal of suffering animals to man--the look of a wounded horse or dog with a meaning which speech would only spoil, the tales of beasts of prey that in pain have turned to man as their physician, the approach of the wildest birds in winter to our feet as their Providence--how much all these prove Paul's saying that the earnest expectation of the creature waiteth for the manifestation of the sons of God. And we have other signals, than those afforded by the pain and pressure of the beasts themselves, of the time when they and man shall sympathize. The natural history of many of our breeds of domesticated animals teaches us the lesson that their growth in skill and character--no one who has enjoyed the friendship of several dogs will dispute the possibility of character in the lower animals--has been proportionate to man's own. Though savages are fond of keeping and taming animals, they fail to advance them to the stages of cunning and discipline, which animals reach under the influence of civilised man. [39] "No instance is on record," says Darwin, "of such dogs as bloodhounds, spaniels or true greyhounds having been kept by savages; they are the products of long-continued civilisation."

These facts, if few, certainly bear in the direction of Isaiah's prophecy, that not by extermination of the beasts, but by the influence upon them of man's greater force of character, may that warfare be brought to an end, of which man's sin, according to the Bible, is the original cause.

The practical "uses" of such a passage of Scripture as this are plain. Some of them are the awful responsibility of man's position as the keystone of creation, the material effects of sin, and especially the religiousness of our relation to the lower animals. More than once do the Hebrew prophets liken the Almighty's dealings with man to merciful man's dealings with his beasts. [40] Both Isaiah and Paul virtually declare that man discharges to the lower creatures a mediatorial office. To say so will of course seem an exaggeration to some people, but not to those who, besides being grateful to remember what help in labour and cheer in dreariness we owe our humble fellow-creatures, have been fortunate enough to enjoy the affection and trust of a dumb friend. Men who abuse the lower animals sin very grievously against God; men who neglect them lose some of the religious possibilities of life. If it is our business in life to have the charge of animals, we should magnify our calling. Every coachman and carter ought to feel something of the priest about him; he should think no amount of skill and patience too heavy if it enables him to gain insight into the nature of creatures of God, all of whose hope, by Scripture and his own experience, is towards himself.

Our relation to the lower animals is one of the three great relations of our nature. For God our worship; for man our service; for the beasts our providence, and according both to Isaiah and Paul, the mediation of our holiness.

IV. The Return and Sovereignty of Israel (xi. 10-16).

In passing from the second to the third part of this prophecy, we cannot but feel that we descend to a lower point of view and a less pure atmosphere of spiritual ambition. Isaiah, who has just declared peace between man and beast, finds that Judah must clear off certain scores against her neighbours before there can be peace between man and man. It is an interesting psychological study. The prophet, who has been able to shake off man's primeval distrust and loathing of wild animals, cannot divest himself of the political tempers of his age. He admits, indeed, the reconciliation of Ephraim and Judah; but the first act of the reconciled brethren, he prophesies with exultation, will be to swoop down upon their cousins Edom, Moab and Ammon, and their neighbours the Philistines. We need not longer dwell on this remarkable limitation of the prophet's spirit, except to point out that while Isaiah clearly saw that Israel's own purity would not be perfected except by her political debasement, he could not as yet perceive any way for the conversion of the rest of the world except through Israel's political supremacy.

The prophet, however, is more occupied with an event preliminary to Israel's sovereignty, namely the return from exile. His large and emphatic assertions remind the not yet captive Judah through how much captivity she has to pass before she can see the margin of the blessed future which he has been describing to her. Isaiah's words imply a much more general captivity than had taken place by the time he spoke them, and we see that he is still keeping steadily in view that thorough reduction of his people, to the prospect of which he was forced in his inaugural vision. Judah has to be dispersed, even as Ephraim has been, before the glories of this chapter shall be realized.

We postpone further treatment of this prophecy, along with the hymn (chap. xii.), which is attached to it, to a separate chapter, dealing with all the representations, which the first half of the book of Isaiah contains, of the return from exile.

Footnotes:

32. The authenticity of this hymn has been called in question.
33. Dean Plumptre notes the identity of the ethical terminology of this passage with that of the book of Proverbs, and conjectures that the additions to the original nucleus, chaps. x.-xxiv., and therefore the whole form, of the book of Proverbs, may be due to the editorship of Isaiah, and perhaps was the manual of ethics, on which he sought to mould the character of Hezekiah (Expositor, series ii., v., p. 213).
34. Perhaps for land--'arets--we ought, with Lagarde, to read tyrant--'arits.
35. Didron, Christian Iconography, Engl. trans., i., 432.
36. Didron, Christian Iconography, Engl. trans., i., 426.
37. See Didron for numerous interesting instances of this.
38. Darwin, Variation of Animals and Plants under Domestication, pp. 20, 21.
39. Galton, quoted by Darwin.
40. Isa. lxiii. 13, 14; Hos. xi. 4.

Rev. George Adam Smith, M.A.

CHAPTER XI

DRIFTING TO EGYPT.

Isaiah xx.; xxi. 1-10; xxxviii.; xxxix. (720-705 B.C.).

From 720, when chap. xi. may have been published, to 705--or, by rough reckoning, from the fortieth to the fifty-fifth year of Isaiah's life--we cannot be sure that we have more than one prophecy from him; but two narratives have found a place in his book which relate events that must have taken place between 712 and 705. These narratives are chap. xx.: How Isaiah Walked Stripped and Barefoot for a Sign against Egypt, and chaps. xxxviii. and xxxix.: The Sickness of Hezekiah, with the Hymn he wrote, and his Behaviour before the Envoys from Babylon. The single prophecy belonging to this period is chap. xxi. 1-10, Oracle of the Wilderness of the Sea, which announces the fall of Babylon. There has been considerable debate about the authorship of this oracle, but Cheyne, mainly following Dr. Kleinert, gives substantial reasons for leaving it with Isaiah. We postpone the full exposition of chaps. xxxviii., xxxix., to a later stage, as here it would only interrupt the history. But we will make use of chaps. xx. and xxi. 1-10 in the course of the following historical sketch, which is intended to connect the first great period of Isaiah's prophesying, 740-720, with the second, 705-701.

All these fifteen years, 720-705, Jerusalem was drifting to the refuge into which she plunged at the end of them--drifting to Egypt. Ahaz had firmly bound his people to Assyria, and in his reign there was no talk of an Egyptian alliance. But in 725, when the overflowing scourge of Assyrian invasion threatened to sweep into Judah as well as Samaria, Isaiah's words give us some hint of a recoil in the politics of Jerusalem towards the southern power. The covenants with death and hell, which the men of scorn flaunted in his face as he harped on the danger from Assyria, may only have been the old treaties with Assyria herself, but the falsehood and lies that went with them were most probably intrigues with Egypt. Any Egyptian policy, however, that may have formed in Jerusalem before 719, was entirely discredited by the crushing defeat, which in that year Sargon inflicted upon the empire of the Nile, almost on her own borders, at Rafia.

Years of quietness for Palestine followed this decisive battle. Sargon, whose annals engraved on the great halls of Khorsabad enable us to read the history of the period year by year, tells us that his next campaigns were to the north of his empire, and till 711 he alludes to Palestine only to say that tribute was coming in regularly, or to mention the deportation to Hamath or Samaria of some tribe he had conquered far away. Egypt, however, was everywhere busy among his feudatories. Intrigue was Egypt's forte. She is always represented in Isaiah's pages as the talkative power of many promises. Her fair speech was very sweet to men groaning beneath the military pressure of Assyria. Her splendid past, in conjunction with the largeness of her promise, excited the popular imagination. Centres of her influence gathered in every state. An Egyptian party formed in Jerusalem. Their intrigue pushed mines in all directions, and before the century was out the Assyrian peace in Western Asia was broken by two great Explosions. The first of these, in 711, was local and abortive; the second, in 705, was universal, and for a time entirely destroyed the Assyrian supremacy.

The centre of the Explosion of 711 was Ashdod, a city of the Philistines. The king had suddenly refused to continue the Assyrian tribute, and Sargon had put another king in his place. But the people--in Ashdod, as everywhere else, it was the people who were fascinated by Egypt--pulled down the Assyrian puppet and elevated Iaman, a friend to Pharaoh. The other cities of the Philistines, with Moab, Edom and Judah, were prepared by Egyptian promise to throw in their lot with the rebels. Sargon gave them no time. "In the wrath of my heart, I did not divide my army, and I did not diminish the ranks, but I marched against Asdod with my warriors, who did not separate themselves from the traces of my sandals. I besieged, I took, Asdod and Gunt-Asdodim.... I then made again these towns. I placed the people whom my arm had conquered. I put over them my lieutenant as governor. I considered them like Assyrians, and they practised obedience." [41] It is upon this campaign of Sargon that Mr. Cheyne argues for the invasion of Judah, to which he assigns so many of Isaiah's prophecies, as, e.g., chaps. i. and x. 5-34. Some day Assyriology may give us proof of this supposition. We are without it just now. Sargon speaks no word of invading Judah, and the only part of the book of Isaiah that unmistakably refers to this time is the picturesque narrative of chap. xx.

In this we are told that in the year the Tartan, the Assyrian commander-in-chief, came to Ashdod when Sargon king of Assyria sent him [that is to be supposed the year of the first revolt in Ashdod, to which Sargon himself did not come], and he fought against Ashdod and took it:--in that time Jehovah had spoken by the hand of Isaiah the son of Amoz, saying, Go and loose the sackcloth, the prophet's robe, from off thy loins, and thy sandal strip from off thy foot; and he did so, walking naked, that is unfrocked, and barefoot. For Egyptian intrigue was already busy; the temporary success of the Tartan at Ashdod did not discourage it, and it needed a protest. And Jehovah said, As My servant Isaiah hath walked unfrocked and barefoot three years for a sign and a portent against Egypt and against Ethiopia [note the double name, for the country was now divided between two rulers, the secret of her impotence to interfere forcibly in Palestine] so shall the king of Assyria lead away the captives of Egypt and exiles of Ethiopia, young and old, stripped and barefoot, and with buttocks uncovered, to the shame of Egypt. And they shall be dismayed and ashamed, because of Ethiopia their expectation and because of Egypt their boast. And the inhabitant of this coastland [that is, all Palestine, and a name for it remarkably similar to the phrase used by Sargon, "the people of Philistia, Judah, Edom and Moab, dwelling by the sea" [42]] shall say in that day, Behold, such is our expectation, whither we had fled for help to deliver ourselves from the king of Assyria, and how shall we escape--we?

This parade of Isaiah for three years, unfrocked and barefoot, is another instance of that habit on which we remarked in connection with chap. viii. 1: the habit of finally carrying everything committed to him before the bar of the whole nation. It was to the mass of the people God said, Come and let us reason together. Let us not despise Isaiah in his shirt any more than we do Diogenes in his tub, or with a lantern in his hand, seeking for a man by its rays at noonday. He was bent on startling the popular conscience, because he held it true that a people's own morals have greater influence on their destinies than the policies of their statesmen. But especially anxious was Isaiah, as we shall again see from chap. xxxi., to bring this Egyptian policy home to the popular conscience. Egypt was a big-mouthed, blustering power, believed in by the mob: to expose her required public, picturesque and persistent advertisement. So Isaiah continued his walk for three years. The fall of Ashdod, left by Egypt to itself, did not disillusion the Jews, and the rapid disappearance of Sargon to another part of his empire where there was trouble, gave the Egyptians audacity to continue their intrigues against him. [43]

Sargon's new trouble had broken out in Babylon, and was much more serious than any revolt in Syria. Merodach Baladan, king of Chaldea, was no ordinary vassal, but as dangerous a rival as Egypt. When he rose, it meant a contest between Babylon and Nineveh for the sovereignty of the world. He had long been preparing for war. He had an alliance with Elam, and the tribes of Mesopotamia were prepared for his signal of revolt. Among the charges brought against him by Sargon is that, "against the will of the gods of Babylon, he had sent during twelve years ambassadors." One of these embassies may have been that which came to Hezekiah after his great sickness (chap. xxxix.). And Hezekiah was glad of them, and showed them the house of his spicery, the silver, and the gold, and the spices, and the precious oil, and all the house of his armour and all that was found in his treasures; there was nothing in his house nor in all his dominion that Hezekiah showed them not. Isaiah was indignant. He had hitherto kept the king from formally closing with Egypt; now he found him eager for an alliance with another of the powers of man. But instead of predicting the captivity of Babylon, as he predicted the captivity of Egypt, by the hand of Assyria, Isaiah declared, according to chap. xxxix., that Babylon would some day take Israel captive; and Hezekiah had to content himself with the prospect that this calamity was not to happen in his time.

Isaiah's prediction of the exile of Israel to Babylon is a matter of difficulty. The difficulty, however, is not that of conceiving how he could have foreseen an event which took place more than a century later. Even in 711 Babylon was not an unlikely competitor for the supremacy of the nations. Sargon himself felt that it was a crisis to meet her. Very little might have transferred the seat of power from the Tigris to the Euphrates. What, therefore, more probable than that when Hezekiah disclosed to these envoys the whole state of his resources, and excused himself by saying that they were come from a far country, even Babylon, Isaiah, seized by a strong sense of how near Babylon stood to the throne of the nations, should laugh to scorn the excuse of distance, and tell the king that his anxiety to secure an alliance had only led him to place the temptation to rob him in the face of a power that was certainly on the way to be able to do it? No, the difficulty is not that the prophet foretold a captivity of the Jews in Babylon, but that we cannot reconcile what he says of that captivity with his intimation of the immediate destruction of Babylon, which has come down to us in chap. xxi. 1-10.

In this prophecy Isaiah regards Babylon as he has been regarding Egypt--certain to go down before Assyria, and therefore wholly unprofitable to Judah. If the Jews still thought of returning to Egypt when Sargon hurried back from completing her discomfiture in order to beset Babylon, Isaiah would tell them it was no use. Assyria has brought her full power to bear on the Babylonians; Elam and Media are with her. He travails with pain for the result. Babylon is not expecting a siege; but preparing the table, eating and drinking, when suddenly the cry rings through her, "Arise, ye princes; anoint the shield. The enemy is upon us." So terrible and so sudden a warrior is this Sargon! At his words nations move; when he saith, Go up, O Elam! Besiege, O Media! it is done. And he falls upon his foes before their weapons are ready. Then the prophet shrinks back from the result of his imagination of how it happened--for that is too painful--upon the simple certainty, which God revealed to him, that it must happen. As surely as Sargon's columns went against Babylon, so surely must the message return that Babylon has fallen. Isaiah puts it this way. The Lord bade him get on his watchtower--that is his phrase for observing the signs of the times--and speak whatever he saw. And he saw a military column on the march: a troop of horsemen by pairs, a troop of asses, a troop of camels. It passed him out of sight, and he hearkened very diligently for news. But none came. It was a long campaign. And he cried like a lion for impatience, O my Lord, I stand continually upon the watchtower by day, and am set in my ward every night. Till at last, behold, there came a troop of men, horsemen in pairs, and now one answered and said, Fallen, fallen is Babylon, and all the images of her gods he hath broken to the ground. The meaning of this very elliptical passage is just this: as surely as the prophet saw Sargon's columns go out against Babylon, so sure was he of her fall. Turning to his Jerusalem, he says, My own threshed one, son of my floor, that which I have heard from Jehovah of hosts, the God of Israel, have I declared unto you. How gladly would I have told you otherwise! But this is His message and His will. Everything must go down before this Assyrian.

Sargon entered Babylon before the year was out, and with her conquest established his fear once more down to the borders of Egypt. In his lifetime neither Judah nor her neighbours attempted again to revolt. But Egypt's intrigue did not cease. Her mines were once more laid, and the feudatories of Assyria only waited for their favourite opportunity, a change of tyrants on the throne at Nineveh. This came very soon. In the fifteenth year of his reign, having finally established his empire, Sargon inscribed on the palace at Khorsabad the following prayer to Assur: "May it be that I, Sargon, who inhabit this palace, may be preserved by destiny during long years for a long life, for the happiness of my body, for the satisfaction of my heart, and may I arrive to my end! May I accumulate in this palace immense treasures, the booties of all countries, the products of mountains and valleys!" The god did not hear. A few months later, in 705, Sargon was murdered; and before Sennacherib, his successor, sat down on the throne, the whole of Assyrian supremacy in the south-west of Asia went up in the air. It was the second of the great Explosions we spoke of, and the rest of Isaiah's prophecies are concerned with its results.

Footnotes:

41. Records of the Past, vii., 40.
42. Cheyne.
43. W. R. Smith, Prophets of Israel, p. 282.

BOOK III

ORATIONS ON THE EGYPTIAN INTRIGUES AND ORACLES ON FOREIGN NATIONS, 705-702 B.C.

Isaiah:-- xxix. About 703. xxx. A little later. xxxi."" xxxii. 1-8. xxxii. 9-20. Date uncertain. ---------- xiv. 28-xxi. 736-702. xxiii. About 703.

We now enter the prophecies of Isaiah's old age, those which he published after 705, when his ministry had lasted for at least thirty-five years. They cover the years between 705, the date of Sennacherib's accession to the Assyrian throne, and 701, when his army suddenly disappeared from before Jerusalem.

They fall into three groups:--

1. Chaps. xxix.-xxxii., dealing with Jewish politics while Sennacherib is still far from Palestine, 704-702, and having Egypt for their chief interest, Assyria lowering in the background.

2. Chaps. xiv. 28-xxi. and xxiii., a group of oracles on foreign nations, threatened, like Judah, by Assyria.

3. Chaps. i., xxii., and xxxiii., and the historical narrative in xxxvi., and xxxvii., dealing with Sennacherib's invasion of Judah and siege of Jerusalem in 701; Egypt and every foreign nation now fallen out of sight, and the storm about the Holy City too thick for the prophet to see beyond his immediate neighbourhood.

The first and second of these groups--orations on the intrigues with Egypt and oracles on the foreign nations--delivered while Sennacherib was still far from Syria, form the subject of this Third Book of our exposition.

The prophecies on the siege of Jerusalem are sufficiently numerous and distinctive to be put by themselves, along with their appendix (xxxviii., xxxix.), in our Fourth Book.

Rev. George Adam Smith, M.A.

CHAPTER XII

ARIEL, ARIEL.

Isaiah xxix. (about 703 B.C.).

In 705 Sargon, King of Assyria, was murdered, and Sennacherib, his second son, succeeded him. Before the new ruler mounted the throne, the vast empire, which his father had consolidated, broke into rebellion, and down to the borders of Egypt cities and tribes declared themselves again independent. Sennacherib attacked his problem with Assyrian promptitude. There were two forces, to subdue which at the beginning made the reduction of the rest certain: Assyria's vassal kingdom and future rival for the supremacy of the world, Babylon; and her present rival, Egypt. Sennacherib marched on Babylon first.

While he did so the smaller States prepared to resist him. Too small to rely on their own resources, they looked to Egypt, and among others who sought help in that quarter was Judah. There had always been, as we have seen, an Egyptian party among the politicians of Jerusalem; and Assyria's difficulties now naturally increased its influence. Most of the prophecies in chaps. xxix.-xxxii. are forward to condemn the alliance with Egypt and the irreligious politics of which it was the fruit.

At the beginning, however, other facts claim Isaiah's attention. After the first excitement, consequent on the threats of Sennacherib, the politicians do not seem to have been specially active. Sennacherib found the reduction of Babylon a harder task than he expected, and in the end it turned out to be three years before he was free to march upon Syria. As one winter after another left the work of the Assyrian army in Mesopotamia still unfinished, the political tension in Judah must have relaxed. The Government--for King Hezekiah seems at last to have been brought round to believe in Egypt--pursued their negotiations no longer with that decision and real patriotism, which the sense of near danger rouses in even the most selfish and mistaken of politicians, but rather with the heedlessness of principle, the desire to show their own cleverness and the passion for intrigue which run riot among statesmen, when danger is near enough to give an excuse for doing something, but too far away to oblige anything to be done in earnest. Into this false ease, and the meaningless, faithless politics, which swarmed in it, Isaiah hurled his strong prophecy of chap. xxix. Before he exposes in chaps. xxx., xxxi., the folly of trusting to Egypt in the hour of danger, he has here the prior task of proving that hour to be near and very terrible. It is but one instance of the ignorance and fickleness of the people, that their prophet has first to rouse them to a sense of their peril, and then to restrain their excitement under it from rushing headlong for help to Egypt.

Chap. xxix. is an obscure oracle, but its obscurity is designed. Isaiah was dealing with a people, in whom political security and religious formalism had stifled both reason and conscience. He sought to rouse them by a startling message in a mysterious form. He addressed the city by an enigma:--

Ho! Ari-El, Ari-El! City David beleaguered! Add a year to a year, let the feasts run their round, then will I bring straitness upon Ari-El, and there shall be moaning and bemoaning, [44] and yet she shall be unto Me as an Ari-El.

The general bearing of this enigma became plain enough after the sore siege and sudden deliverance of Jerusalem in 701. But we are unable to make out one or two of its points. Ari-El may mean either The Lion of God (2 Sam. xxiii. 20), or The Hearth of God (Ezek. xliii. 15, 16). If the same sense is to be given to the four utterances of the name, then God's-Lion suits better the description of ver. 4; but God's-Hearth seems suggested by the feminine pronoun in ver. 1, and is a conception to which Isaiah returns in this same group of prophecies (xxxi. 9). It is possible that this ambiguity was part of the prophet's design; but if he uses the name in both senses, some of the force of his enigma is lost to us. In any case, however, we get a picturesque form for a plain meaning. In a year after the present year is out, says Isaiah, God Himself will straiten the city, whose inhabitants are now so careless, and she shall be full of mourning and lamentation. Nevertheless in the end she shall be a true Ari-El: be it a true God's-Lion, victor and hero; or a true God's-Hearth, His own inviolate shrine and sanctuary.

The next few verses (3-8) expand this warning. In plain words, Jerusalem is to undergo a siege. God Himself shall encamp against thee--round about reads our English version, but more probably, as with the change of a letter, the Septuagint reads it--like David. If we take this second reading, the reference to David in the enigma itself (ver. 1) becomes clear. The prophet has a very startling message to deliver: that God will besiege His own city, the city of David! Before God can make her in truth His own, make her verify her name, He will have to beleaguer and reduce her. For so novel and startling an intimation the prophet pleads a precedent: "City which David himself beleaguered! Once before in thy history, ere the first time thou wast made God's own hearth, thou hadst to be besieged. As then, so now. Before thou canst again be a true Ari-El I must beleaguer thee like David." This reading and interpretation gives to the enigma a reason and a force which it does not otherwise possess.

Jerusalem, then, shall be reduced to the very dust, and whine and whimper in it (like a sick lion, if this be the figure the prophet is pursuing), when suddenly it is the surge of her foes--literally thy strangers--whom the prophet sees as small dust, and as passing chaff shall the surge of tyrants be; yea, it shall be in the twinkling of an eye, suddenly. From Jehovah of hosts shall she be visited with thunder and with earthquake and a great noise,--storm-wind, and tempest and the flame of fire devouring. And it shall be as a dream, a vision of the night, the surge of all the nations that war against Ariel, yea all that war against her and her stronghold, and they that press in upon her. And it shall be as if the hungry had been dreaming, and lo! he was eating; but he hath awaked, and his soul is empty: and as if the thirsty had been dreaming, and lo! he was drinking; but he hath awaked, and lo! he is faint, and his soul is ravenous: thus shall be the surge of all the nations that war against Mount Zion. Now that is a very definite prediction, and in its essentials was fulfilled. In the end Jerusalem was invested by Sennacherib, and reduced to sore straits, when very suddenly--it would appear from other records, in a single night-- the beleaguering force disappeared. This actually happened; and although the main business of a prophet, as we now clearly understand, was not to predict definite events, yet, since the result here predicted was one on which Isaiah staked his prophetic reputation and pledged the honour of Jehovah and the continuance of the true religion among men, it will be profitable for us to look at it for a little.

Isaiah foretells a great event and some details. The event is a double one: the reduction of Jerusalem to the direst straits by siege and her deliverance by the sudden disappearance of the besieging army. The details are that the siege will take place after a year (though the prophet's statement of time is perhaps too vague to be treated as a prediction), and that the deliverance will come as a great natural convulsion--thunder, earthquake and fire--which it certainly did not do. The double event, however, stripped of these details, did essentially happen.

Now it is plain that any one with a considerable knowledge of the world at that day must easily have been able to assert the probability of a siege of Jerusalem by the mixed nations who composed Sennacherib's armies. Isaiah's orations are full of proofs of his close acquaintance with the peoples of the world, and Assyria, who was above them. Moreover, his political advice, given at certain crises of Judah's history, was conspicuous not only for its religiousness, but for what we should call its "worldly-wisdom:" it was vindicated by events. Isaiah, however, would not have understood the distinction we have just made. To him political prudence was part of religion. The Lord of hosts is for a spirit of judgement to him that sitteth in judgement, and for strength to them that turn back the battle to the gate. Knowledge of men, experience of nations, the mental strength which never forgets history, and is quick to mark new movements as they rise, Isaiah would have called the direct inspiration of God. And it was certainly these qualities in this Hebrew, which provided him with the materials for his prediction of the siege of Jerusalem.

But it has not been found that such talents by themselves enable statesmen calmly to face the future, or clearly to predict it. Such knowledge of the past, such vigilance for the present, by themselves only embarrass, and often deceive. They are the materials for prediction, but a ruling principle is required to arrange them. A general may have a strong and well-drilled force under him, and a miserably weak foe in front; but if the sun is not going to rise to-morrow, if the laws of nature are not going to hold, his familiarity with his soldiers and expertness in handling them will not give him confidence to offer battle. He takes certain principles for granted, and on these his soldiers become of use to him, and he makes his venture. Even so Isaiah handled his mass of information by the grasp which he had of certain principles, and his facts fell clear into order before his confident eyes. He believed in the real government of God. I also saw the Lord sitting, high and lifted up. He felt that God had even this Assyria in His hands. He knew that all God's ends were righteousness, and he was still of the conviction that Judah for her wickedness required punishment at the Lord's hands. Grant these convictions to him in the superhuman strength in which he tells us he was conscious of receiving them from God, and it is easy to see how Isaiah could not help predicting a speedy siege of Jerusalem, how he already beheld the valleys around her bristling with barbarian spears.

The prediction of the sudden raising of this siege was the equally natural corollary to another religious conviction, which held the prophet with as much intensity, as that which possessed him with the need of Judah's punishment. Isaiah never slacked his hold on the truth that in the end God would save Zion, and keep her for Himself. Through whatever destruction, a root and remnant of the Jewish people must survive. Zion is impregnable because God is in her, and because her inviolateness is necessary for the continuance of true religion in the world. Therefore as confident as his prediction of the siege of Jerusalem is Isaiah's prediction of her delivery. And while the prophet wraps the fact in vague circumstance, while he masks, as it were, his ignorance of how in detail it will actually take place by calling up a great natural convulsion, yet he makes it abundantly clear--as, with his religious convictions and his knowledge of the Assyrian power, he cannot help doing--that the deliverance will be unexpected and unexplainable by the natural circumstances of the Jews themselves, that it will be evident as the immediate deed of God.

It is well for us to understand this. We shall get rid of the mechanical idea of prophecy, according to which prophets made exact predictions of fact by some particular and purely official endowment. We shall feel that prediction of this kind was due to the most unmistakeable inspiration, the influence upon the prophet's knowledge of affairs of two powerful religious convictions, for which he himself was strongly sure that he had the warrant of the Spirit of God.

Into the easy, selfish politics of Jerusalem, then, Isaiah sent this thunderbolt, this definite prediction: that in a year or more Jerusalem would be besieged and reduced to the direst straits. He tells us that it simply dazed the people. They were like men suddenly startled from sleep, who are too stupid to read a message pushed into their hands (vv. 9-12).

Then Isaiah gives God's own explanation of this stupidity. The cause of it is simply religious formalism. This people draw nigh unto Me with their mouth, and with their lips do they honour Me, but their heart is far from Me, and their fear of Me is a mere commandment of men, a thing learned by rote. This was what Israel called religion--bare ritual and doctrine, a round of sacrifices and prayers in adherence to the tradition of the fathers. But in life they never thought of God. It did not occur to these citizens of Jerusalem that He cared about their politics, their conduct of justice, or their discussions and bargains with one another. Of these they said, taking their own way, Who seeth us, and who knoweth us? Only in the Temple did they feel God's fear, and there merely in imitation of one another. None had an original vision of God in real life; they learned other men's thoughts about Him, and took other men's words upon their lips, while their heart was far away. In fact, speaking words and listening to words had wearied the spirit and stifled the conscience of them.

For such a disposition Isaiah says there is only one cure. It is a new edition of his old gospel, that God speaks to us in facts, not forms. Worship and a lifeless doctrine have demoralized this people. God shall make Himself so felt in real life that even their dull senses shall not be able to mistake Him. Therefore, behold, I am proceeding to work marvellously upon this people, a marvellous work and a wonder! and the wisdom of their wise men shall perish, and the cleverness of their clever ones shall be obscured. This is not the promise of what we call a miracle. It is a historical event on the same theatre as the politicians are showing their cleverness, but it shall put them all to shame, and by its force make the dullest feel that God's own hand is in it. What the people had ceased to attribute to Jehovah was ordinary intelligence; they had virtually said, He hath no understanding. The marvellous work, therefore, which He threatens shall be a work of wisdom, not some convulsion of nature to cow their spirits, but a wonderful political result, that shall shame their conceit of cleverness, and teach them reverence for the will and skill of God. Are the politicians trying to change the surface of the world, thinking that they are turning things upside down, and supposing that they can keep God out of account: Who seeth us, and who knoweth us? God Himself is the real Arranger and Politician. He will turn things upside down! Compared with their attempt, how vast His results shall be! As if the whole surface of the earth were altered, Lebanon changed into garden-land, and garden-land counted as forest! But this, of course, is metaphor. The intent of the miracle is to show that God hath understanding; therefore it must be a work, the prudence and intellectual force of which politicians can appreciate, and it shall take place in their politics. But not for mere astonishment's sake is the wonder to be done. For blessing and morality shall it be: to cure the deaf and blind; to give to the meek and the poor a new joy; to confound the tyrant and the scorner; to make Israel worthy of God and her own great fathers. Therefore thus saith Jehovah to the house of Jacob, He that redeemed Abraham: Not now ashamed shall Jacob be, and not now shall his countenance blanch. So unworthy hitherto have this stupid people been of so great ancestors! But now when his (Jacob's) children behold the work of My hand in the midst of him, they shall hallow My name, yea, they shall hallow the Holy One of Jacob, and the God of Israel shall they make their fear. They also that err in spirit shall know understanding, and they that are unsettled shall learn to accept doctrine.

Such is the meaning of this strong chapter. It is instructive in two ways.

First, it very clearly declares Isaiah's view of the method of God's revelation. Isaiah says nothing of the Temple, the Shechinah, the Altar, or the Scripture; but he points out how much the exclusive confinement of religion to forms and texts has deadened the hearts of his countrymen towards God. In your real life, he says to them, you are to seek, and you shall find, Him. There He is evident in miracles,--not physical interruptions and convulsions, but social mercies and moral providences. The quickening of conscience, the dispersion of ignorance, poor men awakening to the fact that God is with them, the overthrow of the social tyrant, history's plain refutation of the atheist, the growth of civic justice and charity--In these, said the Hebrew prophet to the Old Testament believer, Behold your God!

Wherefore, secondly, we also are to look for God in events and deeds. We are to know that nothing can compensate us for the loss of the open vision of God's working in history and in life about us,--not ecstasy of worship nor orthodoxy of doctrine. To confine our religion to these latter things is to become dull towards God even in them, and to forget Him everywhere else. And this is a fault of our day, just as it was of Isaiah's. So much of our fear of God is conventional, orthodox and not original, a trick caught from men's words or fashions, not a part of ourselves, nor won, like all that is real in us, from contact with real life. In our politics, in our conduct with men, in the struggle of our own hearts for knowledge and for temperance, and in service--there we are to learn to fear God. But there, and wherever else we are busy, self comes too much in the way; we are fascinated with our own cleverness; we ignore God, saying, Who seeth us? who knoweth us? We get to expect Him only in the Temple and on the Sabbath, and then only to influence our emotions. But it is in deeds, and where we feel life most real, that we are to look for Him. He makes Himself evident to us by wonderful works.

For these He has given us three theatres--the Bible, our country's history, and for each man his own life.

We have to take the Bible, and especially the life of Christ, and to tell ourselves that these wonderful events did really take place. In Christ God did dwell; by Christ He spoke to man; man was converted, redeemed, sanctified, beyond all doubt. These were real events. To be convinced of their reality were worth a hundred prayers.

Then let us follow the example of the Hebrew prophets, and search the history of our own people for the realities of God. Carlyle says in a note to Cromwell's fourth speech to Parliament, that "the Bible of every nation is its own history." This note is drawn from Carlyle by Cromwell's frequent insistence, that we must ever be turning from forms and rituals to study God's will and ways in history. And that speech of Cromwell is perhaps the best sermon ever delivered on the subject of this chapter. For he said: "What are all our histories but God manifesting Himself, that He hath shaken, and tumbled down and trampled upon everything that He hath not planted!" And again, speaking of our own history, he said to the House of Commons: "We are a people with the stamp of God upon us, ... whose appearances and providences among us were not to be outmatched by any story." Truly this is national religion:--the reverential acknowledgment of God's hand in history; the admiration and effort of moral progress; the stirring of conscience when we see wrong; the expectation, when evil abounds, that God will bring justice and purity to us if we labour with Him for them.

But for each man there is the final duty of turning to himself.

> *"My soul repairs its fault*
> *When, sharpening sense's hebetude,*
> *She turns on my own life! So viewed,*
> *No mere mote's breadth but teems immense*
> *With witnessings of providence:*
> *And woe to me if when I look*
> *Upon that record, the sole book*
> *Unsealed to me, I take no heed*
> *Of any warning that I read!"* [45]

Footnotes:

44. Cheyne.
45. Browning's Christmas Eve.

Rev. George Adam Smith, M.A.

CHAPTER XIII

POLITICS AND FAITH.

Isaiah xxx. (ABOUT 702 B.C.).

This prophecy of Isaiah rises out of circumstances a little more developed than those in which chap. xxix. was composed. Sennacherib is still engaged with Babylon, and it seems that it will yet be long before he marches his armies upon Syria. But Isaiah's warning has at last roused the politicians of Judah from their carelessness. We need not suppose that they believed all that Isaiah predicted about the dire siege which Jerusalem should shortly undergo and her sudden deliverance at the hand of the Lord. Without the two strong religious convictions, in the strength of which, as we have seen, he made the prediction, it was impossible to believe that this siege and deliverance must certainly happen. But the politicians were at least startled into doing something. They did not betake themselves to God, to whom it had been the purpose of Isaiah's last oration to shut them up. They only flung themselves with more haste into their intrigues with Egypt. But in truth haste and business were all that was in their politics: these were devoid both of intelligence and faith. Where the sole motive of conduct is fear, whether uneasiness or panic, force may be displayed, but neither sagacity nor any moral quality. This was the case with Judah's Egyptian policy, and Isaiah now spends two chapters in denouncing it. His condemnation is twofold. The negotiations with Egypt, he says, are bad politics and bad religion; but the bad religion is the root and source of the other. Yet while he vents all his scorn on the politics, he uses pity and sweet persuasiveness when he comes to speak of the eternal significance of the religion. The two chapters are also instructive, beyond most others of the Old Testament, in the light they cast on revelation--its scope and methods.

Isaiah begins with the bad politics. In order to understand how bad they were, we must turn for a little to this Egypt, with whom Judah was now seeking an alliance.

In our late campaign on the Upper Nile we heard a great deal of the Mudir of Dongola. His province covers part of the ancient kingdom of Ethiopia; and in Meirawi, the village whose name appeared in so many telegrams, we can still discover Meroe, the capital of Ethiopia. Now in Isaiah's day the king of Ethiopia was, what the Mudir of Dongola was at the time of our war, an ambitious person of no small energy; and the ruler of Egypt proper was, what the Khedive was, a person of little influence or resource. Consequently there happened what might have happened a few years ago but for the presence of the British army in Egypt. The Ethiopian came down the Nile, defeated Pharaoh and burned him alive. But he died, and his son died after him; and before their successor could also come down the Nile, the legitimate heir to Pharaoh had regained part of his power. Some years ensued of uncertainty as to who was the real ruler of Egypt.

It was in this time of unsettlement that Judah sought Egypt's help. The ignorance of the policy was manifest to all who were not blinded by fear of Assyria or party feeling. To Isaiah the Egyptian alliance is a folly and fatality that deserve all his scorn (vv. 1-8).

Woe to the rebellious children, saith the Lord, executing a policy, but it is not from Me; and weaving a web, but not of My spirit, that they may heap sin upon sin; who set themselves on the way to go down to Egypt, and at My mouth they have not inquired, to flee to the refuge of Pharaoh, and to hide themselves in the shadow of Egypt. But the refuge of Pharaoh shall be unto you for shame, and the hiding in the shadow of Egypt for confusion! How can a broken Egypt help you? When his princes are at Zoan, and his ambassadors are come to Hanes, they shall all be ashamed of a people that cannot profit them, that are not for help nor for profit, but for shame, and also for reproach.

Then Isaiah pictures the useless caravan which Judah has sent with tribute to Egypt, strings of asses and camels struggling through the desert, land of trouble and anguish, amid lions and serpents, and all for a people that shall not profit them (ver. 6).

What tempted Judah to this profitless expenditure of time and money? Egypt had a great reputation, and was a mighty promiser. Her brilliant antiquity had given her a habit of generous promise, and dazzled other nations into trusting her. Indeed, so full were Egyptian politics of bluster and big language, that the Hebrews had a nickname for Egypt. They called her Rahab--Stormy-speech, Blusterer, Braggart. It was the term also for the crocodile, as being a monster, so that there was a picturesqueness as well as moral aptness in the name. Ay, says Isaiah, catching at the old name and putting to it another which describes Egyptian helplessness and inactivity, I call her Rahab Sit-still, Braggart-that-sitteth-still, Stormy-speech Stay-at-home. Blustering and inactivity, blustering and sitting still, that is her character; for Egypt helpeth in vain and to no purpose.

Knowing how sometimes the fate of a Government is affected by a happy speech or epigram, we can understand the effect of this cry upon the politicians of Jerusalem. But that he might impress it on the popular imagination and memory as well, Isaiah wrote his epigram on a tablet, and put it in a book. We must remind ourselves here of chap. xx., and remember how it tells us that Isaiah had already some years before this endeavoured to impress the popular imagination with the folly of an Egyptian alliance, walking unfrocked and barefoot three years for a sign and a portent upon Egypt and upon Ethiopia (see p. 199).

So that already Isaiah had appealed from politicians to people on this Egyptian question, just as he appealed thirty years ago from court to market-place on the question of Ephraim and Damascus. [46] It is another instance of that prophetic habit of his, on which we remarked in expounding chap. viii.; and we must again emphasize the habit, for chap. xxx. here swings round upon it. Whatever be the matter committed to him, Isaiah is not allowed to rest till he brings it home to the popular conscience; and however much he may be able to charge national disaster upon the folly of politicians or the obduracy of a king, it is the people whom he holds ultimately responsible. To Isaiah a nation's politics are not arbitrary; they are not dependent on the will of kings or the management of parties. They are the natural outcome of the nation's character. What the people are, that will their politics be. If you wish to reform the politics, you must first regenerate the people; and it is no use to inveigh against a senseless policy, like this Egyptian one, unless you go farther and expose the national temper which has made it possible. A people's own morals have greater influence on their destinies than their despots or legislators. Statesmen are what the State makes them. No Government will attempt a policy for which the nation behind it has not a conscience; and for the greater number of errors committed by their rulers, the blame must be laid on the people's own want of character or intelligence.

This is what Isaiah now drives home (xxx. 9 ff.). He tracks the bad politics to their source in bad religion, the Egyptian policy to its roots in the prevailing tempers of the people. The Egyptian policy was doubly stamped. It was disobedience to the word of God; it was satisfaction with falsehood. The statesmen of Judah shut their ears to God's spoken word; they allowed themselves to be duped by the Egyptian Pretence. But these, says Isaiah, are precisely the characteristics of the whole Jewish people. For it is a rebellious people, lying children, children that will not hear the revelation of the Lord. It was these national failings--the want of virtues which are the very substance of a nation: truth and reverence or obedience--that had culminated in the senseless and suicidal alliance with Egypt. Isaiah fastens on their falsehood first: Which say to the seers, Ye shall not see, and to the prophets, Ye shall not prophesy unto us right things; speak to us smooth things: prophesy deceits. No wonder such a character had been fascinated by "Rahab"! It was a natural Nemesis, that a people who desired from their teachers fair speech rather than true vision should be betrayed by the confidence their statesmen placed in the Blusterer, that blustered and sat still. Truth is what this people first require, and therefore the revelation of the Lord will in the first instance be the revealing of the truth. Men who will strip pretence off the reality of things; men who will call things by their right names, as Isaiah had set himself to do; honest satirists and epigrammatists--these are the bearers of God's revelation. For it is one of the means of Divine salvation to call things by their right names, and here in God's revelation also epigrams have their place. So much for truth.

But reverence is truth's other self, for reverence is simply loyalty to the supremest truth. And it is against the truth that the Jews have chiefly sinned. They had shut their eyes to Egypt's real character, but that was a small sin beside this: that they turned their backs on the greatest reality of all--God Himself. Get you out of the way, they said to the prophets, turn out of the path; keep quiet in our presence about the Holy One of Israel. Isaiah's effort rises to its culmination when he seeks to restore the sense of this Reality to his people. His spirit is kindled at the words the Holy One of Israel, and to the end of chap. xxxi. leaps up in a series of brilliant and sometimes scorching descriptions of the name, the majesty and the love of God. Isaiah is not content to have used his power of revelation to unveil the political truth about Egypt. He will make God Himself visible to this people. Passionately does he proceed to enforce upon the Jews what God thinks about their own condition (vv. 12-14), then to persuade them to rely upon Him alone, and wait for the working of His reasonable laws (vv. 15-18). Rising higher, he purges with pity their eyes to see God's very presence, their ears to hear His voice, their wounds to feel His touch (vv. 19-26). Then he remembers the cloud of invasion on the horizon, and bids them spell, in its uncouth masses, the articulate name of the Lord (vv. 27-33). And he closes with another series of figures by which God's wisdom, and His jealousy and His tenderness are made very bright to them (chap. xxxi.).

These brilliant prophecies may not have been given all at the same time: each is complete in itself. They do not all mention the negotiations with Egypt, but they are all dark with the shadow of Assyria. Chap. xxx. vv. 19-26 almost seem to have been written in a time of actual siege; but vv. 27-33 represent

Assyria still upon the horizon. In this, however, these passages are fitly strung together: that they equally strain to impress a blind and hardened people with the will, the majesty and the love of God their Saviour.

I. The Bulging Wall (vv. 12-14).

Starting from their unwillingness to listen to the voice of the Lord in their Egyptian policy, Isaiah tells the people that if they refused to hear His word for guidance, they must now listen to it for judgement. Wherefore thus saith the Holy One of Israel: Because ye look down on this word, and trust in perverseness and crookedness, and lean thereon, therefore this iniquity shall be to you as a breach ready to fall, bulging out in a high wall, whose breaking cometh suddenly at an instant. This iniquity, of course, is the embassy to Egypt. But that, as we have seen, is only the people's own evil character coming to a head; and by the breaking of the wall, we are therefore to suppose that the prophet means the collapse not only of this Egyptian policy, but of the whole estate and substance of the Jewish people. It will not be your enemy that will cause a breach in the nation, but your teeming iniquity shall cause the breach--to wit, this Egyptian folly. Judah will burst her bulwarks from the inside. You may build the strongest form of government round a people, you may buttress it with foreign alliances, but these shall simply prove occasions for the internal wickedness to break forth. Your supposed buttresses will prove real breaches; and of all your social structure there will not be left as much as will make the fragments of a single home, not a sherd big enough to carry fire from the hearth, or to hold water from the cistern.

II. Not Alliances, but Reliance (vv. 15-18).

At this point, either Isaiah was stung by the demands of the politicians for an alternative to their restless Egyptian policy which he condemned, or more likely he rose, unaided by external influence, on the prophet's native instinct to find some purely religious ground on which to base his political advice. The result is one of the grandest of all his oracles. For thus saith the Lord Jehovah, the Holy One of Israel: In returning and rest shall ye be saved; in quietness and in confidence shall be your strength; and ye would not. But ye said, No, for upon horses will we flee; wherefore ye shall flee: and upon the swift will we ride; wherefore swift shall be they that pursue you! One thousand at the rebuke of one--at the rebuke of five shall ye flee: till ye be left as a bare pole on the top of a mountain, and as a standard on an hill. And therefore will the Lord wait that He may be gracious unto you, and therefore will He hold aloof that He may have mercy upon you, for a God of judgement is the Lord; blessed are all they that wait for Him. The words of this passage are their own interpretation and enforcement, all but one; and as this one is obscure in its English guise, and the passage really swings from it, we may devote a paragraph to its meaning.

A God of judgement is the Lord is an unfortunately ambiguous translation. We must not take judgement here in our familiar sense of the word. It is not a sudden deed of doom, but a long process of law. It means manner, method, design, order, system, the ideas, in short, which we sum up under the word "law." Just as we say of a man, He is a man of judgement, and mean thereby not that by office he is a doomster, but that by character he is a man of discernment and prudence, so simply does Isaiah say here that Jehovah is a God of judgement, and mean thereby not that He is One, whose habit is sudden and awful deeds of penalty or salvation, but, on the contrary, that, having laid down His lines according to righteousness and established His laws in wisdom, He remains in His dealings with men consistent with these.

Now it is a great truth that the All-mighty and All-merciful is the All-methodical too; and no religion is complete in its creed or healthy in its influence, which does not insist equally on all these. It was just the want of this third article of faith which perverted the souls of the Jews in Isaiah's day, which (as we have seen under Chapter I.) allowed them to make their worship so mechanical and material--for how could they have been satisfied with mere forms if they had but once conceived of God as having even ordinary intelligence?--and which turned their political life into such a mass of intrigue, conceit and falsehood, for how could they have dared to suppose that they would get their own way, or have been so sure of their own cleverness, if only they had had a glimpse of the perception, that God, the Ruler of the world, had also His policy regarding them? They believed He was the Mighty, they believed He was the Merciful, but because they forgot that He was the Wise and the Worker by law, their faith in His might too often turned into superstitious terror, their faith in His mercy oscillated between the sleepy satisfaction that He was an indulgent God and the fretful impatience that He was an indifferent one. Therefore Isaiah persisted from first to last in this: that God worked by law; that He had His plan for Judah, as well as these politicians; and, as we shall shortly find him reminding them when intoxicated with their own cleverness, that He also is wise (xxxi. 2). Here by the same thought he bids them be at peace, and upon the rushing tides of politics, drawing them to that or the other mad venture, to swing by this anchor: that God has His own law and time for everything. No man could bring the charge of fatalism against such a policy of quietness. For it thrilled with intelligent appreciation of the Divine method. When Isaiah said, In returning and rest shall ye be saved; in quietness and confidence shall be your strength, he did not ask his restless countrymen to yield sullenly to an infinite force or to bow in stupidity beneath the inscrutable will of an arbitrary despot, but to bring their conduct into harmony with a reasonable and gracious plan, which might be read in the historical events of the time, and was vindicated by the loftiest religious convictions. Isaiah preached no submission to fate, but reverence for an all-wise Ruler, whose method was plain to every clear-sighted observer of the fortunes of the nations of the world, and whose purpose could only be love and peace to His own people (cf. p. 110).

III. God's Table in the Midst of the Enemies (vv. 19-26).

This patient purpose of God Isaiah now proceeds to describe in its details. Every line of his description has its loveliness, and is to be separately appreciated. There is perhaps no fairer prospect from our prophet's many windows. It is not argument nor a programme, but a series of rapid glimpses, struck out by language, which often wants logical connection, but never fails to make us see.

To begin with, one thing is sure: the continuance of the national existence. Isaiah is true to his original vision--the survival of a remnant. For a people in Zion--there shall be abiding in Jerusalem. So the brief essential is flashed forth. Thou shalt surely weep no more; surely He will be gracious unto thee at the voice of thy crying; with His hearing of thee He will answer thee. Thus much of general promise had been already given. Now upon the vagueness of the Lord's delay Isaiah paints realistic details, only, however, that he may make more vivid the real presence of the Lord. The siege shall surely come, with its sorely concrete privations, but the Lord will be there, equally distinct. And though the Lord give you the bread of penury and the water of tribulation--perhaps the technical name for siege rations--yet shall not thy Teacher hide Himself any more, but thine eyes shall ever be seeing thy Teacher; and thine ears shall hear a word behind thee, saying, This is the way: walk ye in it, when ye turn to the right hand or when ye turn to the left. Real, concrete sorrows, these are they that make the heavenly Teacher real! It is linguistically possible, and more in harmony with the rest of the passage, to turn teachers, as the English version has it, into the singular, and to render it by Revealer. The word is an active participle, "Moreh," from the same verb as the noun "Torah," which is constantly translated "Law" in our version, but is, in the Prophets at least, more nearly equivalent to "instruction," or to our modern term "revelation" (cf. ver. 9). Looking thus to the One Revealer, and hearkening to the One Voice, the lying and rebellious children shall at last be restored to that capacity for truth and obedience the loss of which has been their ruin. Devoted to the Holy One of Israel, they shall scatter their idols as loathsome (ver. 22). But thereupon a wonder is to happen. As the besieged people, conscious of the One Great Presence in the midst of their encompassed city, cast their idols through the gates and over the walls, a marvellous vision of space and light and fulness of fresh food bursts upon their starved and straitened souls (ver. 23). Promise more sympathetic was never uttered to a besieged and famished city. Mark that all down the passage there is no mention of the noise or instruments of battle. The prophet has not spoken of the besiegers, who they may be, how they may come, nor of the fashion of their war, but only of the effects of the siege on those within: confinement, scant and bitter rations. And now he is almost wholly silent about the breaking up of the investing army and the trail of their slaughter. No battle breaks this siege, but a vision of openness and plenty dawns noiselessly over its famine and closeness. It is not vengeance or blood that an exhausted and penitent people thirst after. But as they have been caged in a fortress, narrow, dark and stony, so they thirst for the sight of the sower, and the drop of the rain on the broken, brown earth, and the juicy corn, and the meadow for their cribbed cattle, and the noise of brooks and waterfalls, and above and about it all fulness of light. And He shall give the rain of thy seed, that thou shalt sow the ground withal, and bread, even the increase of the ground, and it shall be juicy and fat; thy cattle shall feed that day in a broad meadow. And the oxen and the young asses that till the ground shall eat savoury provender, winnowed with the shovel and with the fan. And there shall be upon every lofty mountain and upon every lifted hill rivers, streams of water, in the day of the great slaughter, when the towers fall. And the light of the moon shall be as the light of the sun, and the light of the sun shall be sevenfold, as the light of seven days, in the day that the Lord bindeth up the hurt of His people and healeth the stroke of their wound. It is one of Isaiah's fairest visions, and he is very much to be blamed who forces its beauty of nature into an allegory of spiritual things. Here literally God spreads His people a table in the midst of their enemies.

IV. The Name of the Lord (vv. 27-33).

But Isaiah lays down "the oaten pipe" and lifts again a brazen trumpet to his lips. Between him and that sunny landscape of the future, of whose pastoral details he has so sweetly sung, roll up now the uncouth masses of the Assyrian invasion, not yet fully gathered, far less broken. We are back in the present again, and the whole horizon is clouded.

The passage does not look like one from which comfort or edification can be derived, but it is of extreme interest. The first two verses, for instance, only require a little analysis to open a most instructive glimpse into the prophet's inner thoughts about the Assyrian progress, and show us how they

Rev. George Adam Smith, M.A.

work towards the expression of its full meaning. Behold, the Name of Jehovah cometh from afar--burning His anger and awful the uplifting smoke; His lips are full of wrath, and His tongue as fire that devoureth; and His breath is as an overflowing torrent--even unto the neck it reacheth--to shake the nations in a sieve of destruction, and a bridle that leadeth astray on the jaws of the peoples.

The Name of Jehovah is the phrase the prophets use when they wish to tell us of the personal presence of God. When we hear a name cried out, we understand immediately that a person is there. So when the prophet calls, Behold, the Name of Jehovah, in face of the prodigious advance of Assyria, we understand that he has caught some intuition of God's presence in that uplifting of the nations of the north at the word of the great King and their resistless sweep southward upon Palestine. In that movement God is personally present. The Divine presence Isaiah then describes in curiously mingled metaphor, which proves how gradually it was that he struggled to a knowledge of its purpose there. First of all he describes the advance of Assyria as a thunderstorm, heavy clouds and darting, devouring fire. His imagination pictures a great face of wrath. The thick curtains of cloud as they roll over one another suggest the heavy lips, and the lightnings the fiery tongue. Then the figure passes from heaven to earth. The thunderstorm has burst, and becomes the mountain torrent, which speedily reaches the necks of those who are caught in its bed. But then the prophet's conscience suggests something more than sudden and sheer force in this invasion, and the tossing of the torrent naturally leads him to express this new element in the figure of a sieve. His thought about the Assyrian flood thus passes from one of simple force and rush to one of judgement and being well kept in hand. He sees its ultimate check at Jerusalem, and so his last figure of it is the figure of a bridle, or lasso, such as is thrown upon the jaws of a wild animal when you wish to catch and tame him.

This gradual progress from the sense of sheer wild force, through that of personal wrath, to discipline and sparing is very interesting. Vague and chaotic that disaster rolled up the horizon upon Judah. It cometh from afar. The politicians fled from it to their refuge behind the Egyptian Pretence. But Isaiah bids them face it. The longer they look, the more will conscience tell them that the unavoidable wrath of God is in it; no blustering Rahab will be able to hide them from the anger of the Face that lowers there. But let them look longer still, and the unrelieved features of destruction will change to a hand that sifts and checks, the torrent will become a sieve, and the disaster show itself well held in by the power of their own God.

So wildly and impersonally still do the storms of sorrow and disaster roll up the horizon on men's eyes, and we fly in vague terror from them to our Egyptian refuges. So still does conscience tell us it is futile to flee from the anger of God, and we crouch hopeless beneath the rush of imaginations of unchecked wrath, blackening the heavens and turning every path of life to a tossing torrent. May it then be granted us to have some prophet at our side to bid us face our disaster once more, and see the discipline and judgement of the Lord, the tossing only of His careful sieve, in the wild and cruel waves! We may not be poets like Isaiah nor able to put the processes of our faith into such splendid metaphors as he, but faith is given us to follow the same course as his thoughts did, and to struggle till she arrives at the consciousness of God in the most uncouth judgements that darken her horizon--the consciousness of God present not only to smite, but to sift, and in the end to spare.

Of the angel who led Israel to the land of promise, God said, My Name is in him. Our faith is not perfect till we can, like Isaiah, feel the same of the blackest angel, the heaviest disaster, God can send us, and be able to spell it out articulately: The Lord, the Lord, a God merciful and gracious, long-suffering and abundant in goodness and truth.

For delivery, says Isaiah, shall come to the people of God in the crisis, as sudden and as startling into song as the delivery from Egypt was. Ye shall have a song as in the night when a holy feast is kept, and gladness of heart, as when one goeth with a pipe to come into the mountain of the Lord, to the Rock of Israel.

After this interval of solemn gladness, the storm and fire break out afresh, and rage again through the passage. But their direction is reversed, and whereas they had been shown rolling up the horizon as towards Judah, they are now shown rolling down the horizon in pursuit of the baffled Assyrian. The music of the verses is crashing. And the Lord shall cause the peal [47] of His voice to be heard, and the lighting down of His arm to be seen in the fury of anger, yea flame of devouring fire--bursting and torrent and hailstones. For from the voice of the Lord shall the Assyrian be scattered when He shall smite with the rod. And every passage of the rod of fate which the Lord bringeth down upon him shall be with tabrets and harps, and in battles of waving shall he be fought against. The meaning is obscure, but palpable. Probably the verse describes the ritual of the sacrifice to Moloch, to which there is no doubt the next verse alludes. To sympathize with the prophet's figure, we need of course an amount of information about the details of that ritual which we are very far from possessing. But Isaiah's meaning is evidently this. The destruction of the Assyrian host will be liker a holocaust than a battle, like one of those fatal sacrifices to Moloch which are directed by the solemn waving of a staff, and accompanied by the music, not of war, but of festival. Battles of waving is a very obscure phrase, but the word translated waving is the technical term for the waving of the victim before the sacrifice to signify its dedication to the deity; "and these battles of waving may perhaps have taken place in the fashion in which single victims were thrown from one spear to another till death ensued." [48] At all events, it is evident that Isaiah means to suggest that the Assyrian dispersion is a religious act, a solemn holocaust rather than one of this earth's ordinary battles, and directed by Jehovah Himself from heaven. This becomes clear enough in the next verse: For a Topheth hath been set in order beforehand; yea, for Moloch is it arranged; He hath made it deep and broad; the pile thereof is fire and much wood; the breath of the Lord, like a torrent of brimstone, shall kindle it. So the Assyrian power was in the end to go up in flame.

We postpone remarks on Isaiah's sense of the fierceness of the Divine righteousness till we reach his even finer expression of it in chap. xxxiii.

Footnotes:

46. Chap. viii. 1 (p. 119).
47. So Dr. B. Davis, quoted by Cheyne.
48. So Bredenkamp in his recent commentary on Isaiah.

Rev. George Adam Smith, M.A.

CHAPTER XIV

THREE TRUTHS ABOUT GOD.

Isaiah xxxi. (ABOUT 702 B.C.).

Chap. xxxi., which forms an appendage to chaps. xxix. and xxx., can scarcely be reckoned among the more important prophecies of Isaiah. It is a repetition of the principles which the prophet has already proclaimed in connection with the faithless intrigues of Judah for an alliance with Egypt, and it was published at a time when the statesmen of Judah were further involved in these intrigues, when events were moving faster, and the prophet had to speak with more hurried words. Truths now familiar to us are expressed in less powerful language. But the chapter has its own value; it is remarkable for three very unusual descriptions of God, which govern the following exposition of it. They rise in climax, enforcing three truths:--that in the government of life we must take into account God's wisdom; we must be prepared to find many of His providences grim and savage-looking; but we must also believe that He is most tender and jealous for His people.

I. Yet He also is Wise (vv. 1-3).

We must suppose the negotiations with Egypt to have taken for the moment a favourable turn, and the statesmen who advocated them to be congratulating themselves upon some consequent addition to the fighting strength of Judah. They could point to many chariots and a strong body of cavalry in proof of their own wisdom and refutation of the prophet's maxim, In quietness and in confidence shall be your strength; in returning and rest shall ye be saved.

Isaiah simply answers their self-congratulation with the utterance of a new Woe, and it is in this that the first of the three extraordinary descriptions of God is placed. Woe unto them that go down to Egypt for help; upon horses do they stay, and trust in chariots because they are many, and in horsemen because they are very strong: but they look not unto the Holy One of Israel, and Jehovah they do not seek. Yet He also is wise. You have been clever and successful, but have you forgotten that God also is wise, that He too has His policy, and acts reasonably and consistently? You think you have been making history; but God also works in history, and surely, to put it on the lowest ground, with as much cleverness and persistence as you do. Yet He also is wise, and will bring evil, and will not call back His words, but will arise against the house of the evil-doers, and against the help of them that work iniquity.

This satire was the shaft best fitted to pierce the folly of the rulers of Judah. Wisdom, a reasonable plan for their aims and prudence in carrying it out, was the last thing they thought of associating with God, whom they relegated to what they called their religion--their temples, worship and poetry. When their emotions were stirred by solemn services, or under great disaster, or in the hour of death, they remembered God and it seemed natural to them that in these great exceptions of life He should interfere; but in their politics and their trade, in the common course and conduct of life, they ignored Him and put their trust in their own wisdom. They limited God to the ceremonies and exceptional occasions of life, when they looked for His glory or miraculous assistance, but they never thought that in their ordinary ways He had any interest or design.

The forgetfulness, against which Isaiah directs this shaft of satire, is the besetting sin of very religious people, of very successful people, and of very clever people.

It is the temptation of an ordinary Christian, church-going people, like ourselves, with a religion so full of marvellous mercies, and so blessed with regular opportunities of worship, to think of God only in connection with these, and practically to ignore that along the far greater stretches of life He has any interest or purpose regarding us. Formally-religious people treat God as if He were simply a constitutional sovereign, to step in at emergencies, and for the rest to play a nominal and ceremonial part in the conduct of their lives. Ignoring the Divine wisdom and ceaseless providence of God, and couching their hearts upon easy views of His benevolence, they have no other thought of Him, than as a philanthropic magician, whose power is reserved to extricate men when they have got past helping themselves. From the earliest times that way of regarding God has been prevalent, and religious teachers have never failed to stigmatize it with the hardest name for folly. Fools, says the Psalmist, are afflicted when they draw near unto the gates of death; then, only then, do they cry unto the Lord in their trouble. Thou fool! says Christ of the man who kept God out of the account of his life. God is not mocked, although we ignore half His being and confine our religion to such facile views of His nature. With this sarcasm, Isaiah reminds us that it is not a Fool who is on the throne of the universe; yet is the Being whom the imaginations of some men place there any better? O wise men, God also is wise. Not by fits and starts of a benevolence similar to that of our own foolish and inconsistent hearts does He work. Consistency, reason and law are the methods of His action; and they apply closely, irretrievably, to all of our life. Hath He promised evil? Then evil will proceed. Let us believe that God keeps His word; that He is thoroughly attentive to all we do; that His will concerns the whole of our life.

But the temptation to refuse to God even ordinary wisdom is also the temptation of very successful and very clever people, such as these Jewish politicians fancied themselves to be, or such as the Rich Fool in the parable. They have overcome all they have matched themselves against, and feel as if they were to be masters of their own future. Now the Bible and the testimony of men invariably declare that God has one way of meeting such fools--the way Isaiah suggests here. God meets them with their own weapons; He outmatches them in their own fashion. In the eighteenth Psalm it is written, With the pure Thou wilt show Thyself pure, and with the perverse Thou wilt show Thyself froward. The Rich Fool congratulates himself that his soul is his own; says God, This night thy soul shall be required of thee. The Jewish politicians pride themselves on their wisdom; Yet God also is wise, says Isaiah significantly. After Moscow Napoleon is reported to have exclaimed, "The Almighty is too strong for me." But perhaps the most striking analogy to this satire of Isaiah is to be found in the "Confessions" of that Jew, from whose living sepulchre we are so often startled with weird echoes of the laughter of the ancient prophets of his race. When Heine, Germany's greatest satirist, lay upon a bed to which his evil living had brought him before his time, and the pride of art, which had been, as he says, his god, was at last crushed, he tells us what it was that crushed him. They were singing his songs in every street of his native land, and his fame had gone out through the world, while he lay an exile and paralysed upon his "mattress-grave." "Alas!" he cries, "the irony of Heaven weighs heavily upon me. The great Author of the universe, the celestial Aristophanes, wished to show me, the petty, earthly, German Aristophanes, how my most trenchant satires are only clumsy patchwork compared with His, and how immeasurably He excels me in humour and colossal wit." That is just a soul writing in its own heart's blood this terrible warning of Isaiah: Yet God also is wise.

Yea, the Egyptians are men, and not God, and their horses flesh, and not spirit; and when Jehovah shall stretch out His hand, both he that helpeth shall stumble, and he that is holpen shall fall, and they all shall perish together.

II. The Lion and his Prey (ver. 4).

But notwithstanding what he has said about God destroying men who trust in their own cleverness, Isaiah goes on to assert that God is always ready to save what is worth saving. The people, the city, His own city--God will save that. To express God's persistent grace towards Jerusalem, Isaiah uses two figures borrowed from the beasts. Both of them are truly Homeric, and fire the imagination at once; but the first is not one we should have expected to find as a figure of the saving grace of God. Yet Isaiah knows it is not enough for men to remember how wise God always is. They need also to be reminded how grim and cruel He must sometimes appear, even in His saving providences.

For thus saith Jehovah unto me: Like as when the lion growleth, and the young lion over his prey, if a mob of shepherds be called forth against him, from their voice he will not shrink in dismay, nor for their noise abase himself; so shall Jehovah of hosts come down to fight for Mount Zion and the hill thereof. A lion with a lamb in his claws, growling over it, while a crowd of shepherds come up against him; afraid to go near enough to kill him, they try to frighten him away by shouting at him. But he holds his prey unshrinking.

It is a figure that startles at first. To liken God with a saving hold upon His own to a wild lion with his claws in the prey! But horror plays the part of a good emphasis; while if we look into the figure, we shall feel our horror change to appreciation. There is something majestic in that picture of the lion with the shouting shepherds, too afraid to strike him. He will not be dismayed at their voice, nor abase himself for the noise of them. Is it, after all, an unworthy figure of the Divine Claimant for this city, who kept unceasing hold upon her after His own manner, mysterious and lionlike to men, undisturbed by the screams, formulas, and prayers of her mob of politicians and treaty-mongers? For these are the shepherds Isaiah means--sham shepherds, the shrieking crew of politicians, with their treaties and military display. God will save and carry Jerusalem His own way, paying no heed to such. He will not be dismayed at their voice, nor abase Himself for the noise of them.

There is more than the unyielding persistency of Divine grace taught here. There is that to begin with. God will never let go what He has made His own: the souls He has redeemed from sin, the societies He has redeemed from barbarism, the characters He has hold of, the lives He has laid His hand upon. Persistency of saving grace--let us learn that confidently in the parable. But that is only half of what it is meant to teach. Look at the shepherds: shepherds shouting round a lion; why does Isaiah put it that way, and not as David did--lions growling round a brave shepherd, with the lamb in his arms?

Because it so appeared then in the life Isaiah was picturing, because it often looks the same in real life still. These politicians--they seemed, they played the part of, shepherds; and Jehovah, who persistently frustrated their plans for the salvation of the State--He looked the lion, delivering Jerusalem to destruction. And very often to men does this arrangement of the parts repeat itself; and while human friends are anxious and energetic about them, God Himself appears in providences more lionlike than shepherdly. He grasps with the savage paw of death some one as dear to us as that city was to Isaiah. He rends our body or soul or estate. And friends and our own thoughts gather round the cruel bereavement or disaster with remonstrance and complaint. Our hearts cry out, doing, like shepherds, their best to scare by prayer and cries the foe they are too weak to kill. We all know the scene, and how shabby and mean that mob of human remonstrances looks in face of the great Foe, majestic though inarticulate, that with sullen persistence carries off its prey. All we can say in such times is that if it is God who is the lion, then it is for the best. For though He slay me, yet will I trust Him; and, after all, it is safer to rely on the mercies of God, lionlike though they be, than on the weak benevolences and officious pities of the best of human advisers. "Thy will be done"--let perfect reverence teach us to feel that, even when providence seems as savage as men that day thought God's will towards Jerusalem.

In addition then to remembering, when men seem by their cleverness and success to rule life, that God is wiser and His plans more powerful than theirs, we are not to forget, when men seem more anxious and merciful than His dark providence, that for all their argument and action His will shall not alter. But now we are to hear that this will, so hard and mysterious, is as merciful and tender as a mother's.

III. The Mother-bird and her Nest (ver. 5).

As birds hovering, so will Jehovah of hosts cover Jerusalem, He will cover and deliver it: He will pass over and preserve it. At last we are through dark providence, to the very heart of the Almighty. The meaning is familiar from its natural simplicity and frequent use in Scripture. Two features of it our version has not reproduced. The word birds means the smaller kind of feathered creatures, and the word hovering is feminine in the original: As little mother-birds hovering, so will Jehovah of hosts protect Jerusalem. We have been watching in spring the hedge where we know is a nest. Suddenly the mother-bird, who has been sitting on a branch close by, flutters off her perch, passes backwards and forwards, with flapping wings that droop nervously towards the nest over her young. A hawk is in the sky, and till he disappears she will hover--the incarnation of motherly anxiety. This is Isaiah's figure. His native city, on which he poured so much of his heart in lyrics and parables, was again in danger. Sennacherib was descending upon her; and the pity of Isaiah's own heart for her, evil though she was, suggested to him a motherhood of pity in the breast of God. The suggestion God Himself approved. Centuries after, when He assumed our flesh and spoke our language, when He put His love into parables lowly and familiar to our affections, there were none of them more beautiful than that which He uttered of this same city, weeping as He spake: O Jerusalem, Jerusalem, how often would I have gathered thy children together, as a hen gathereth her brood under her wings, and ye would not!

With such fountains in Scripture, we need not, as some have done, exalt the Virgin, or virtually make a fourth person in the Godhead, and that a woman, in order to satisfy those natural longings of the heart which the widespread worship of the mother of Jesus tells us are so peremptory. For all fulness dwelleth in God Himself. Not only may we rejoice in that pity and wise provision for our wants, in that pardon and generosity, which we associate with the name of father, but also in the wakefulness, the patience, the love, lovelier with fear, which make a mother's heart so dear and indispensable. We cannot tell along what wakened nerve the grace of God may reach our hearts; but Scripture has a medicine for every pain. And if any feel their weakness as little children feel it, let them know that the Spirit of God broods over them, as a mother over her babe; and if any are in pain or anxiety, and there is no human heart to suffer with them, let them know that as closely as a mother may come to suffer with her child, and as sensitive as she is to its danger, so sensitive is God Almighty to theirs, and that He gives them proof of their preciousness to Him by suffering with them.

***

How these three descriptions meet the three failings of our faith! We forget that God is ceaselessly at work in wisdom in our lives. We forget that God must sometimes, even when He is saving us, seem lionlike and cruel. We forget that "the heart of the Eternal is most wonderfully kind."

Having thus made vivid the presence of their Lord to the purged eyes of His people, patient, powerful in order, wise in counsel, persistent in grace, and, last of all, very tender, Isaiah concludes with a cry to the people to turn to this Lord, from whom they have so deeply revolted. Let them cast away their idols, and there shall be no fear of the result of the Assyrian invasion. The Assyrian shall fall, not by the sword of man, but the immediate stroke of God. And his rock shall pass away by reason of terror, and his princes shall be dismayed at the ensign, saith the Lord, whose fire is in Zion, and His furnace in

Jerusalem. And so Isaiah closes this series of prophecies on the keynote with which it opened in the first verse of chap. xxix.: that Jerusalem is Ariel--the hearth and altar, the dwelling-place and sanctuary, of God.

Rev. George Adam Smith, M.A.

CHAPTER XV

A MAN: CHARACTER AND THE CAPACITY TO DISCRIMINATE CHARACTER.

Isaiah xxxii. 1-8 (ABOUT 702 B.C.?).

The Assyrians being thus disposed of, Isaiah turns to a prospect, on which we have scarcely heard him speak these twenty years, since Assyria appeared on the frontier of Judah--the religious future and social progress of his own people. This he paints in a small prophecy of eight verses, the first eight of chap. xxxii.--verses 9-20 of that chapter apparently springing from somewhat different conditions.

The first eight verses of chap. xxxii. belong to a class of prophecies which we may call Isaiah's "escapes." Like St. Paul, Isaiah, when he has finished some exposition of God's dealings with His people or argument with the sinners among them, bursts upon an unencumbered vision of the future, and with roused conscience, and voice resonant from long debate, takes his loftiest flights of eloquence. In Isaiah's book we have several of these visions, and each bears a character of its own according to the sort of sinners from whom the prophet shook himself loose to describe it and the kind of indignation that filled his heart at the time. We have already seen, how in some of Isaiah's visions the Messiah has the chief place, while from others He is altogether absent. But here we come upon another inconsistency. Sometimes, as in chap. xi., Isaiah is content with nothing but a new dispensation--the entire transformation of nature, when there shall be no more desert or storm, but to the wild animals docility shall come, and among men an end to sorrow, fraud and war. But again he limits his prophetic soul and promises less. As if, overcome by the spectacle of the more clamant needs and horrible vices of society, he had said, we must first get rid of these, we must supply those, before we can begin to dream of heaven. Such is Isaiah's feeling here. This prophecy is not a vision of society glorified, but of society established and reformed, with its foundation firmly settled (ver. 1), with its fountain forces in full operation (ver. 2), and with an absolute check laid upon its worst habits, as, for instance, the moral grossness, lying and pretence which the prophet has been denouncing for several chapters (vv. 3-8). This moderation of the prophecy brings it within the range of practical morals; while the humanity of it, its freedom from Jewish or Oriental peculiarities, renders it thoroughly modern. If every unfulfilled prophecy ought to be an accusing conscience in the breast of the Christian Church, there will be none more clamant and practical than this one. Its demands are essential to the social interests of to-day.

In ver. 1 we have the presupposition of the whole prophecy: *Behold, in righteousness shall a king reign, and princes--according to justice shall they rule.* A just government is always the basis of Isaiah's vision of the future. Here he defines it with greater abstractness than he has been wont to do. It is remarkable, that a writer, whose pen has already described the figure of the coming King so concretely and with so much detail, should here content himself with a general promise of a righteous government, regarding, as he seems to do, rather the office of kinghood, than any single eminent occupier of it. That the prophet of Immanuel, and still more the prophet of the Prince-of-the-Four-Names (chap. ix. 7), and of the Son of Jesse (chap. xi. 1), should be able to paint the ideal future, and speak of the just government that was to prevail in it, without at the same time referring to his previous very explicit promises of a royal Individual, is a fact which we cannot overlook in support of the opinion we have expressed on pp. 180 and 181 concerning the object of Isaiah's Messianic hopes.

Nor is the vagueness of the first verse corrected by the terms of the second: *And a man shall be as an hiding-place from the wind*, etc. We have already spoken of this verse as an ethical advance upon Isaiah's previous picture of the Messiah (see p. 182). But while, of course, the Messiah was to Isaiah the ideal of human character, and therefore shared whatsoever features he might foresee in its perfect development, it is evident that in this verse Isaiah is not thinking of the Messiah alone or particularly. When he says with such simplicity *a man*, he means any man, he means the ideal for every man. Having in ver. 1 laid down the foundation for social life, he tells us in ver. 2 what the shelter and fountain force of society are to be: not science nor material wealth, but personal influence, the strength and freshness of the human personality. *A man shall be as an hiding-place from the wind and a covert from the tempest, as rivers of water in a dry place, as the shadow of a great rock in a weary land.* After just government (ver. 1) great characters are the prophet's first demand (ver. 2), and then (vv. 3-8) he will ask for the capacity to discriminate character. "Character and the capacity to discriminate character" indeed summarizes this prophecy.

I. A Man (ver. 2).
Isaiah has described personal influence on so grand a scale that it is not surprising that the Church has leapt to his words as a direct prophecy of Jesus Christ. They are indeed a description of Him, out of whose shadow advancing time has not been able to carry the children of men, who has been the shelter and fertility of every generation since He was lifted up, and to whom the affections of individual hearts never rise higher than when they sing--

"Rock of ages, cleft for me,
Let me hide myself in Thee."

Such a rock was Christ indeed; but, in accordance with what we have said above, the prophet here has no individual specially in his view, but is rather laying down a general description of the influence of individual character, of which Christ Jesus was the highest instance. Taken in this sense, his famous words present us, first, with a philosophy of history, at the heart of which there is, secondly, a great gospel, and in the application of which there is, thirdly, a great ideal and duty for ourselves.

1. Isaiah gives us in this verse a Philosophy of History. Great men are not the whole of life, but they are the condition of all the rest; if it were not for the big men, the little ones could scarcely live. The first requisites of religion and civilisation are outstanding characters.

In the East the following phenomenon is often observed. Where the desert touches a river-valley or oasis, the sand is in a continual state of drift from the wind, and it is this drift which is the real cause of the barrenness of such portions of the desert at least as abut upon the fertile land. For under the rain, or by infiltration of the river, plants often spring up through the sand, and there is sometimes promise of considerable fertility. It never lasts. Down comes the periodic drift, and life is stunted or choked out. But set down a rock on the sand, and see the difference its presence makes. After a few showers, to the leeward side of this some blades will spring up; if you have patience, you will see in time a garden. How has the boulder produced this? Simply by arresting the drift.

Now that is exactly how great men benefit human life. A great man serves his generation, serves the whole race, by arresting the drift. Deadly forces, blind and fatal as the desert wind, sweep down human history. In the beginning it was the dread of Nature, the cold blast which blows from every quarter on the barbarian, and might have stunted men to animals. But into some soul God breathed a great breath of freedom, and the man defied Nature. Nature has had her revenge by burying the rebel in oblivion. On the distant horizon of history we can see, merely in some old legend, the evidence of his audacity. But the drift was arrested; behind the event men took shelter, in the shelter grew free, and learned to think out what the first great resister felt.

When history had left this rock behind, and the drift had again space to grow, the same thing happened; and the hero this time was Abraham. He laid his back to the practice of his forefathers, and lifting his brow to heaven, was the first to worship the One Unseen God. Abraham believed; and in the shadow of his faith, and sheltered by his example, his descendants learned to believe too. To-day from within the three great spiritual religions men look back to him as the father of the faithful.

When Isaiah, while all his countrymen were rushing down the mad, steep ways of politics, carried off by the only powers that were as yet known in these ways, fear of death and greed to be on the side of the strongest--when Isaiah stood still amid that panic rush, and uttered the memorable words, In quietness and in confidence shall be your strength; in returning and rest shall ye be saved, he stopped one of the most dangerous drifts in history, and created in its despite a shelter for those spiritual graces, which have always been the beauty of the State, and are now coming to be recognized as its strength.

When, in the early critical days of the Church, which had overflown the barriers set to the old dispensation, threatened to spread its barrenness upon the fields of the Gentile world, already white to the harvest of Christ, and Peter and Barnabas and all the Apostles were carried away by it, what was it that saved Christianity? Under God, it was this: that Paul got up and, as he tells us, withstood Peter to the face.

And, again, when the powers of the Roman Church and the Roman Empire, checked for a little by the efforts which began the Reformation, gathered themselves together and rose in one awful front of emperor, cardinals, and princes at the Diet of Worms, what was it that stood fast against that drift of centuries, and proved the rock, under whose shelter men dared to read God's pure word again, and preach His Gospel? It was the word of a lonely monk: "Here stand I. I cannot otherwise. So help me, God."

So that Isaiah is right. A single man has been as an hiding-place from the wind and a covert from the tempest. History is swept by drifts: superstition, error, poisonous custom, dust-laden controversy. What has saved humanity has been the uprising of some great man to resist those drifts, to set his will, strong through faith, against the prevailing tendency, and be the shelter of the weaker, but not less

Rev. George Adam Smith, M.A.

desirous, souls of his brethren. "The history of what man has accomplished in the world is at bottom the history of the great men who have worked there." Under God, personal human power is the highest force, and God has ever used it as His chief instrument.

2. But in this philosophy of history there is a GOSPEL. Isaiah's words are not only man's ideal; they are God's promise, and that promise has been fulfilled in Jesus Christ. Jesus Christ is the most conspicuous example--none others are near Him--of this personal influence in which Isaiah places all the shelter and revival of society. God has set His seal to the truth, that the greatest power in shaping human destiny is man himself, by becoming one with man, by using a human soul to be the Saviour of the race. A man, says Isaiah, shall be as an hiding-place from the wind, as the shadow of a great rock in a weary land; and the Rock of ages was a Man. The world indeed knew that personal character could go higher than all else in the world, but they never knew how high till they saw Jesus Christ, or how often till they numbered His followers.

This figure of a rock, a rock resisting drift, gives us some idea, not only of the commanding influence of Christ's person, but of that special office from which all the glory of His person and of His name arises: that He saves His people from their sins.

For what is sin? Sin is simply the longest, heaviest drift in human history. It arose in the beginning, and has carried everything before it since. "The oldest custom of the race," it is the most powerful habit of the individual. Men have reared against it government, education, philosophy, system after system of religion. But sin overwhelmed them all.

Only Christ resisted, and His resistance saves the world. Alone among human lives presented to our view, that of Christ is sinless. What is so prevalent in human nature that we cannot think of a human individual without it never stained Christ's life. Sin was about Him; it was not that He belonged to another sphere of things which lay above it. Sin was about Him. He rose from its midst with the same frailty as other men, encompassed by the same temptations; but where they rose to fall, He rose to stand, and standing, became the world's Saviour. The great tradition was broken; the drift was arrested. Sin never could be the same again after the sinless manhood of Christ. The old world's sins and cruel customs were shut out from the world that came after. Some of them ceased so absolutely as scarcely to be afterwards named; and the rest were so curbed that no civilised society suffered them to pass from its constraint, and no public conscience tolerated them as natural or necessary evils.

What the surface of the world's life bears so deeply, that does every individual, who puts his trust in Jesus, feel to the core. Of Jesus the believer can truly say that life on this side of Him is very different from life on that. Temptations keep far away from the heart that keeps near to Christ. Under the shadow of our Rock, for us the evil of the present loses all its suggestiveness, the evil of the past its awful surge of habit and guilty fear.

3. But there is not only a philosophy of history and a gospel in this promise of a man. There is a great DUTY and IDEAL for every one. If this prophecy distinctly reaches forward to Jesus Christ as its only perfect fulfilment, the vagueness of its expression permits of its application to all, and through Him its fulfilment by all becomes a possibility. Now each of us may be a rock, a shelter and a source of fertility to the life around him in three modes of constant influence. We can be like Christ, the Rock, in shutting out from our neighbours the knowledge and infection of sin, in keeping our conversation so unsuggestive and unprovocative of evil, that, though sin drift upon us, it shall never drift through us. And we may be like Christ, the Rock, in shutting out blame from other men; in sheltering them from the east wind of pitiless prejudice, quarrel or controversy; in stopping the unclean and bitter drifts of scandal and gossip. How many lives have lost their fertility for the want of a little silence and a little shadow! Some righteous people have a terribly north-eastern exposure; children do not play about their doors, nor the prodigal stop there. And again, as there are a number of men and women who fall in struggling for virtue simply because they never see it successful in others, and the spectacle of one pure, heroic character would be their salvation, here is another way in which each servant of God may be a rock. Of the late Clerk Maxwell it was said, "He made faith in goodness easy to other men." A man shall be as streams of water in a desert place.

II. Capacity to Distinguish Character (vv. 3-8).

But after the coming of this ideal, it is not paradise that is regained. Paradise is farther off. We must have truth to begin with: truth and the capacity to discriminate character. The sternness with which Isaiah thus postpones his earlier vision shows us how sore his heart was about the lying temper of his people. We have heard him deploring the fascination of their false minds by the Egyptian Pretence. Their falseness, however, had not only shown itself in their foreign politics, but in their treatment of one another, in their social fashions, judgements and worships. In society there prevailed a want of moral insight and of moral courage. At home also the Jews had failed to call things by their right names (cf. p. 226). Therefore next in their future Isaiah desires the cure of moral blindness, haste and cowardice (vv. 3, 4), with the explosion of all social lies (ver. 5). Men shall stand out for what they are, whether they be bad--for the bad shall not be wanting (vv. 6, 7)--or good (ver. 8). On righteous government (ver. 1) and influence of strong men (ver. 2) must follow social truthfulness (vv. 3-8). Such is the line of the prophet's demands. The details of vv. 3-8 are exceedingly interesting.

And not closed shall be the eyes of them that see, and the ears of them that hear shall be pricked up. The context makes it clear that this is spoken, not of intellectual, but of moral, insight and alertness. And the heart of the hasty shall learn how to know, and the tongue of the stammerer be quick (the verb is the same as the hasty of the previous clause) to speak plain things. Startlingly plain things--for the word literally means blinding-white, and is so used of the sun--startlingly plain, like that scorching epigram upon Egypt. The morally rash and the morally timid are equal fathers of lies.

In illustration Isaiah takes the conventional abuse of certain moral terms, exposes it and declares it shall cease: The vile person shall no more be called liberal, nor the churl said to be bountiful. Liberal and bountiful were conventional names. The Hebrew word for liberal originally meant exactly that-- open-hearted, generous, magnanimous. In the East it is the character which above all they call princely. So like our words "noble" and "nobility," it became a term of rank, lord or prince, and was often applied to men who were not at all great-hearted, but the very opposite--even to the vile person. Vile person is literally the faded or the exhausted, whether mentally or morally--the last kind of character that could be princely. The other conventional term used by Isaiah refers to wealth rather than rank. The Hebrew for bountiful literally means abundant, a man blessed with plenty, and is used in the Old Testament both for the rich and the fortunate. Its nearest English equivalent is perhaps the successful man. To this Isaiah fitly opposes a name, wrongly rendered in our version churl, but corrected in the margin to crafty--the fraudulent, the knave. When moral discrimination comes, says Isaiah, men will not apply the term princely to worn-out characters, nor grant them the social respect implied by the term. They will not call the fraudulent the fortunate, nor canonise him as successful, who has gotten his wealth by underhand means. The worthless character shall no more be called princely, nor the knave hailed as the successful. But men's characters shall stand out true in their actions, and by their fruits ye shall know them. In those magic days the heart shall come to the lips, and its effects be unmistakeable. For the worthless person, worthlessness shall he speak--what else can he?--and his heart shall do iniquity, to practise profaneness and to utter against the Lord rank error, to make empty the soul of the hungry, and he will cause the drink of the thirsty to fail. The tools, too, of the knave (a play upon words here--"Keli Kelav," the knave his knives) are evil; he! low tricks he deviseth to destroy the poor with words of falsehood, even when the poor speaks justice (that is, has justice as well as poverty to plead for him). But the princely things deviseth, and he upon princely things shall stand--not upon conventional titles or rank, or the respect of insincere hearts, but upon actual deeds of generosity and sacrifice.

After great characters, then, what society needs is capacity to discern character, and the chief obstacle in the way of this discernment is the substitution of a conventional morality for a true morality, and of some distinctions of man's making for the eternal difference which God has set between right and wrong.

Human progress consists, according to Isaiah, of getting rid of these conventions; and in this history bears him out. The abolition of slavery, the recognition of the essential nobility of labour, the abolition of infanticide, the emancipation of woman--all these are due to the release of men's minds from purely conventional notions, and the courageous application in their place of the fundamental laws of righteousness and love. If progress is still to continue, it must be by the same method. In many directions it is still a false conventionalism,--sometimes the relic of barbarism, sometimes the fruit of civilisation,--that blocks the way. The savage notions which obstruct the enforcement of masculine purity have to be exposed. Nor shall we ever get true commercial prosperity, or the sense of security which is indispensable to that, till men begin to cease calling transactions all right merely because they are the custom of the trade and the means to which its members look for profits.

But, above all, as Isaiah tells us, we need to look to our use of language. It is one of the standing necessities of pure science to revise the terminology, to reserve for each object a special name, and see that all men understand the same object by the same name. Otherwise confusion comes in, and science is impossible. The necessity, though not so faithfully recognized, is as imperative in morals. If we consider the disgraceful mistakes in popular morals which have been produced by the transference and degradation of names, we shall feel it to be a religious duty to preserve for these their proper meaning. In the interests of morality, we must not be careless in our use of moral terms. As Socrates says in the Phædo: "To use words wrongly and indefinitely is not merely an error in itself; it also creates evil in the soul." [49] What noxious misconceptions, what mistaken ideals of life, are due to the abuse of these four words alone: "noble," "gentleman," "honour" and "Christian"! By applying these, in flattery or deceit, to persons unworthy of them, men have not only deprived them of the virtue which originally the mere utterance of them was enough to instil into the heart, but have sent forth to the world under their attractiveness second-rate types of character and ideals. The word "gentleman"! How the heart sickens as it thinks what a number of people have been satisfied to aim at a shoddy and superficial life because it was labelled with this gracious name. Conventionalism has deprived the English language of some of its most powerful sermons by devoting terms of singular moral expressiveness to do duty as mere labels upon characters that are dead, or on ranks and offices, for the designation of which mere cyphers might have sufficed.

We must not forget, however, Isaiah's chief means for the abolition of this conventionalism and the substitution of a true moral vision and terminology. These results are to follow from the presence of the great character, A Man, whom he has already lifted up. Conventionalism is another of the drifts which that Rock has to arrest. Setting ourselves to revise our dictionaries or to restore to our words their original meanings out of our memories is never enough. The rising of a conspicuous character alone can dissipate the moral haze; the sense of his influence will alone fill emptied forms with meaning. So Christ Jesus judged and judges the world by His simple presence; men fall to His right hand and to His left. He calls things by their right names, and restores to each term of religion and morals its original ideal, which the vulgar use of the world had worn away. [50]

Footnotes:

49. Cf. further with this passage F. J. Church, Trial and Death of Socrates, Introd. xli. ff.

50. Cf. with the fifth and sixth verses of chap. xxxii. the forcible passage in the introduction to Carlyle's Cromwell's Letters, beginning, "Sure enough, in the Heroic Century, as in the Unheroic, knaves and cowards ... were not wanting. But the question always remains, Did they lie chained?" etc.

CHAPTER XVI

ISAIAH TO WOMEN.

Isaiah xxxii. 9-20 (DATE UNCERTAIN).

The date of this prophecy, which has been appended to those spoken by Isaiah during the Egyptian intrigues (704-702), is not certain. It is addressed to women, and there is no reason why the prophet, when he was upbraiding the men of Judah for their false optimism, should not also have sought to awaken the conscience of their wives and daughters on what is the besetting sin rather of women than of men. The chief evidence for dissociating the prophecy from its immediate predecessors is that it predicts, or apparently predicts (vv. 13-14), the ruin of Jerusalem, whereas in these years Isaiah was careful to exempt the Holy City from the fate which he saw falling on the rest of the land. But otherwise the argument of the prophecy is almost exactly that of chaps. xxix.-xxx. By using the same words when he blames the women for ease and carelessness in vv. 9-11, as he does when he promises confidence and quiet resting-places in vv. 17, 18, Isaiah makes clear that his purpose is to contrast the false optimism of society during the postponement of the Assyrian invasion with that confidence and stability upon righteousness which the Spirit of God can alone create. The prophecy, too, has the usual three stages: sin in the present, judgement in the immediate future, and a state of blessedness in the latter days. The near date at which judgement is threatened--days beyond a year--ought to be compared with chap. xxix. 1: Add ye a year to a year; let the feasts come round.

The new points are--that it is the women who are threatened, that Jerusalem itself is pictured in ruin, and that the pouring out of the Spirit is promised as the cause of the blessed future.

I. The Charge to the Women (vv. 9-12)

is especially interesting, not merely for its own terms, but because it is only part of a treatment of women which runs through the whole of Scripture.

Isaiah had already delivered against the women of Jerusalem a severe diatribe (chap. iii.), the burden of which was their vanity and haughtiness. With the satiric temper, which distinguishes his earlier prophecies, he had mimicked their ogling and mincing gait, and described pin by pin their fashions and ornaments, promising them instead of these things rottenness and baldness, and a girdle of sackcloth and branding for beauty. But he has grown older, and penetrating below their outward fashion and gait, he charges them with thoughtlessness as the besetting sin of their sex. Ye women that are at ease, rise up, and hear my voice; ye careless daughters, give ear to my speech. For days beyond a year shall ye be troubled, O careless women, for the vintage shall fail; the ingathering shall not come. Tremble, ye women that are at ease; be troubled, ye careless ones. By a pair of epithets he describes their fault; and almost thrice does he repeat the pair, as if he would emphasize it past all doubt. The besetting sin of women, as he dins into them, is ease; an ignorant and unthinking contentment with things as they are; thoughtlessness with regard to the deeper mysteries of life; disbelief in the possibility of change.

But Isaiah more than hints that these besetting sins of women are but the defects of their virtues. The literal meaning of the two adjectives he uses, at ease and careless, is restful and trustful. Scripture throughout employs these words both in a good and a bad sense. Isaiah does so himself in this very chapter (compare these verses with vv. 17, 18). In the next chapter he describes the state of Jerusalem after redemption as a state of ease or restfulness, and we know that he never ceased urging the people to trustfulness. For such truly religious conditions he uses exactly the same names as for the shallow optimism with which he now charges his countrywomen. And so doing, he reminds us of an important law of character. The besetting sins of either sex are its virtues prostituted. A man's greatest temptations proceed from his strength; but the glory of the feminine nature is repose, and trust is the strength of the feminine character, in which very things, however, lies all the possibility of woman's degradation. Woman's faith amounts at times to real intuition; but what risks are attached to this prophetic power--of impatience, of contentment with the first glance at things, "the inclination," as a great moralist has put it, "to take too easily the knowledge of the problems of life, and to rest content with what lies nearest her, instead of penetrating to a deeper foundation." Women are full of indulgence and hope; but what possibilities lie there of deception, false optimism, and want of that anxiety which alone makes progress possible. Women are more inclined than men to believe all things; but how certain is such a temper to sacrifice the claims of truth and honour. Women are full of tact, the just favourites of success, with infinite power to plead and please; but if they are aware of this, how certain is such a self-consciousness to produce negligence and the fatal sleep of the foolish virgins.

Scripture insists repeatedly on this truth of Isaiah's about the besetting sin of women. The prophet Amos has engraved it in one of his sharpest epigrams, declaring that thoughtlessness is capable of turning women into very brutes, and their homes into desolate ruins: Hear this word, ye kine of Bashan, that are in the mountain of Samaria, which oppress the poor, which crush the needy, which say unto their lords, Bring and let us drink. The Lord Jehovah hath sworn by His holiness that, lo, the days shall come upon you that they shall take you away with hooks, and your residue with fish-hooks, and ye shall go out at the breaches, every one straight before her, and ye shall cast yourselves into Harmon, saith Jehovah. It is a cowherd's picture of women: a troop of cows, heavy, heedless animals, trampling in their anxiety for food upon every frail and lowly object in the way. There is a cowherd's coarseness in it, but a prophet's insight into character. Not of Jezebels, or Messalinas, or Lady-Macbeths is it spoken, but of the ordinary matrons of Samaria. Thoughtlessness is able to make brutes out of women of gentle nurture, with homes and a religion. For thoughtlessness when joined to luxury or beauty plays with cruel weapons. It means greed, arrogance, indifference to suffering, wantonness, pride of conquest, dissimulation in love, and revenge for little slights; and there is no waste, unkind sport, insolence, brutality, or hysterical violence to which it will not lead. Such women are known, as Amos pictured them, through many degrees of this thoughtlessness: interrupters of conversation, an offence to the wise; devourers of many of the little ones of God's creation for the sake of their own ornament; tormentors of servants and subordinates for the sake of their own ease; out of the enjoyment of power or for admiration's sake breakers of hearts. And are not all such victims of thoughtlessness best compared, with Amos, to a cow--an animal that rushes at its grass careless of the many daisies and ferns it tramples, that will destroy the beauty of a whole country lane for a few mouthfuls of herbage? Thoughtlessness, says Amos--and the Lord GOD hath sworn it by His holiness--is the very negation of womanhood, the ruin of homes.

But when we turn from the degradation of woman as thus exposed by the prophets to her glory as lifted up in the New Testament, we find that the same note is struck. Woman in the New Testament is gracious according as she is thoughtful; she offends even when otherwise beautiful by her feeling overpowering her thought. Martha spoils a most estimable character by one moment of unthinking passion, in which she accuses the Master of carelessness. Mary chooses the better part in close attention to her Master's words. The Ten Virgins are divided into five wise and five foolish. Paul seems to have been struck, as Isaiah was, with the natural tendency of the female character, for the first duty he lays upon the old women is to teach the young women to think discreetly, and he repeats the injunction, putting it before chastity and industry--Teach them, he says, teach them discretion (Titus ii. 4, 5). In Mary herself, the mother of our Lord, we see two graces of character, to the honour of which Scripture gives equal place--faith and thoughtfulness. The few sentences, which are all that he devotes to Mary's character, the Evangelist divides equally between these two. She was called blessed because she believed the word of the Lord. But trustfulness did not mean in her, as in other women, neglect to think. Twice, at an interval of twelve years, we are shown thoughtfulness and carefulness of memory as the habitual grace of this first among women. Mary kept all these things and pondered them in her heart. His mother kept all these sayings in her heart. [51] What was Mary's glory was other women's salvation. By her own logic the sufferer of Capernaum, whom many physicians failed to benefit, found her cure; by her persistent argument the Syrophenician woman received her daughter to health again. And when our Lord met that flippant descendant of the kine of Bashan, that are in the mount of Samaria, how did He treat her that He might save her but by giving her matter to think about, by speaking to her in riddles, by exploding her superficial knowledge, and scattering her easy optimism?

So does all Scripture declare, in harmony with the oracle of Isaiah, that thoughtlessness and easy contentment with things as they be, are the besetting sins of woman. But her glory is discretion.

II. The next new point in this prophecy is the Destruction of Jerusalem (vv. 13-15).

Upon the land of my people shall come up thorns and briers; yea, upon all the houses of joy in the joyous city: for the palace shall be forsaken; the populous city shall be deserted; Ophel and the Watch-tower shall be for dens for ever, a joy of wild asses, a pasture of flocks. The attempt has been made to confine this reference to the outskirts of the sacred city, but it is hardly a just one. The prophet, though he does not name the city, evidently means Jerusalem, and means the whole of it. Some therefore deny the authenticity of the prophecy. Certainly it is almost impossible to suppose, that so definite a sentence of ruin can have been published at the same time as the assurances of Jerusalem's inviolability in the preceding orations. But that does not prevent the hypothesis that it was uttered by Isaiah at an earlier period, when, as in chaps. ii. and iii., he did say extreme things about the destruction of his city. It must be noticed, however, that Isaiah speaks with some vagueness; that at the present moment he is not concerned with any religious truth or will of the Almighty, but simply desires to contrast the careless gaiety of the women of Jerusalem with the fate hanging over them. How could he do this more forcibly than by turning the streets and gardens of their delights into ruins and the haunts of the wild ass, even though it should seem inconsistent with his declaration that Zion was inviolable? Licence for a certain amount of inconsistency is absolutely necessary in the case of a prophet who had so many divers truths to utter to so many opposite interests and tempers. Besides, at this time he had already reduced Jerusalem very low (xxix. 4).

III. The Spirit Outpoured (vv. 15-20).

The rest of the prophecy is luminous rather than lucid, full of suffused rather than distinct meanings. The date of the future regeneration is indefinite--another feature more in harmony with Isaiah's earlier prophecies than his later. The cause of the blessing is the outpouring of the Spirit of God (ver. 15). Righteousness and peace are to come to earth by a distinct creative act of God. Isaiah adds his voice to the invariable testimony of prophets and apostles, who, whether they speak of society or the heart of individual man, place their hope in new life from above by the Spirit of the living God. Victor Hugo says, "There are no weeds in society, only bad cultivators;" and places all hope of progress towards perfection in proper methods of social culture. These are needed, as much as the corn, which will not spring from the sunshine alone, requires the hand of the sower, and the harrow. And Isaiah, too, speaks here of human conduct and effort as required to fill up the blessedness of the future: righteousness and labour. But first, and indispensably, he, with all the prophets, places the Spirit of God.

It appears that Isaiah looked for the fruits of the Spirit both as material and moral. He bases the quiet resting-places and regular labours of the future not on righteousness only, but on fertility and righteousness. The wilderness shall become a fruitful field, and what is to-day a fruitful field shall be counted as a forest. That this proverb, used by Isaiah more than once, is not merely a metaphor for the moral revolution he describes in the next verse, is proved by his having already declared the unfruitfulness of their soil as part of his people's punishment. Fertility is promised for itself, and as the accompaniment of moral bountifulness. And there shall dwell in the wilderness justice, and righteousness shall abide in the fruitful field. And the work of righteousness shall be peace, and the effect, or service, of righteousness, quietness and confidence for ever. And my people shall abide in a peaceable habitation, and in sure dwellings, and in quiet resting-places.... Blessed are ye that sow beside all waters, that send forth the feet of the ox and the ass!

There is not a prophecy more characteristic of Isaiah. It unfolds what for him were the two essential and equal contents of the will of God: a secure land and a righteous people, the fertility of nature and the purity of society. But in those years (705-702) he did not forget that something must come between him and that paradise. Across the very middle of his vision of felicity there dashes a cruel storm. In the gap indicated above Isaiah wrote, But it shall hail in the downfall of the forest, and the city shall be utterly laid low. A hailstorm between the promise and fulfilment of summer! Isaiah could only mean the Assyrian invasion, which was now lowering so dark. Before it bursts we must follow him to the survey which he made, during these years before the siege of Jerusalem, of the foreign nations on whom, equally with Jerusalem, that storm was to sweep.

Footnote:

51. Cf. Newman, Oxford University Sermons, xv.

Rev. George Adam Smith, M.A.

CHAPTER XVII

ISAIAH TO THE FOREIGN NATIONS.

Isaiah xiv. 24-32, xv.-xxi., and xxiii. (736-702 B.C.).

The centre of the Book of Isaiah (chaps. xiii. to xxiii.) is occupied by a number of long and short prophecies which are a fertile source of perplexity to the conscientious reader of the Bible. With the exhilaration of one who traverses plain roads and beholds vast prospects, he has passed through the opening chapters of the book as far as the end of the twelfth; and he may look forward to enjoying a similar experience when he reaches those other clear stretches of vision from the twenty-fourth to the twenty-seventh and from the thirtieth to the thirty-second. But here he loses himself among a series of prophecies obscure in themselves and without obvious relation to one another. The subjects of them are the nations, tribes and cities with which in Isaiah's day, by war or treaty or common fear in face of the Assyrian conquest, Judah was being brought into contact. There are none of the familiar names of the land and tribes of Israel which meet the reader in other obscure prophecies and lighten their darkness with the face of a friend. The names and allusions are foreign, some of them the names of tribes long since extinct, and of places which it is no more possible to identify. It is a very jungle of prophecy, in which, without much Gospel or geographical light, we have to grope our way, thankful for an occasional gleam of the picturesque--a sandstorm in the desert, the forsaken ruins of Babylon haunted by wild beasts, a view of Egypt's canals or Phoenicia's harbours, a glimpse of an Arab raid or of a grave Ethiopian embassy.

But in order to understand the Book of Isaiah, in order to understand Isaiah himself in some of the largest of his activities and hopes, we must traverse this thicket. It would be tedious and unprofitable to search every corner of it. We propose, therefore, to give a list of the various oracles, with their dates and titles, for the guidance of Bible-readers, then to take three representative texts and gather the meaning of all the oracles round them.

First, however, two of the prophecies must be put aside. The twenty-second chapter does not refer to a foreign State, but to Jerusalem itself; and the large prophecy which opens the series (chaps. xiii.-xiv. 23) deals with the overthrow of Babylon in circumstances that did not arise till long after Isaiah's time, and so falls to be considered by us along with similar prophecies at the close of this volume. (See Book V.)

All the rest of these chapters--xiv.-xxi. and xxiii.--refer to Isaiah's own day. They were delivered by the prophet at various times throughout his career; but the most of them evidently date from immediately after the year 705, when, on the death of Sargon, there was a general rebellion of the Assyrian vassals.

1. xiv. 24-27. Oath Of Jehovah that the Assyrian shall be broken. Probable date, towards 701.

2. xiv. 28-32. Oracle For Philistia. Warning to Philistia not to rejoice because one Assyrian king is dead, for a worse one shall arise: *Out of the serpent's root shall come forth a basilisk*. Philistia shall be melted away, but Zion shall stand. The inscription to this oracle (ver. 28) is not genuine. The oracle plainly speaks of the death and accession of Assyrian, not Judæan, kings. It may be ascribed to 705, the date of the death of Sargon and accession of Sennacherib. But some hold that it refers to the previous change on the Assyrian throne--the death of Salmanassar and the accession of Sargon.

3. xv.-xvi. 12. Oracle for Moab. A long prophecy against Moab. This oracle, whether originally by himself at an earlier period of his life, or more probably by an older prophet, Isaiah adopts and ratifies, and intimates its immediate fulfilment, in xvi. 13, 14. *This is the word which Jehovah spake concerning Moab long ago. But now Jehovah hath spoken, saying, Within three years, as the years of an hireling, and the glory of Moab shall be brought into contempt with all the great multitude, and the remnant shall be very small and of no account.* The dates both of the original publication of this prophecy and of its reissue with the appendix are quite uncertain. The latter may fall about 711, when Moab was threatened by Sargon for complicity in the Ashdod conspiracy (p. 198), or in 704, when, with other States, Moab came under the cloud of Sennacherib's invasion. The main prophecy is remarkable for its vivid picture of the disaster that has overtaken Moab and for the sympathy with her which the Jewish prophet expresses; for the mention of a remnant of Moab; for the exhortation to her to send tribute in her adversity to the mount of the daughter of Zion (xvi. 1); for an appeal to Zion to shelter the outcasts of Moab and to take up her cause: *Bring counsel, make a decision, make thy shadow as the night in the*

midst of the noonday; hide the outcasts, bewray not the wanderer; for a statement of the Messiah similar to those in chaps. ix. and xi.; and for the offer to the oppressed Moabites of the security of Judah in Messianic times (vv. 4, 5). But there is one great obstacle to this prospect of Moab lying down in the shadow of Judah--Moab's arrogance. We have heard of the pride of Moab, that he is very proud (ver. 6, cf. Jer. xlviii. 29, 42; Zeph. ii. 10), which pride shall not only keep this country in ruin, but prevent the Moabites prevailing in prayer at their own sanctuary (ver. 12)--a very remarkable admission about the worship of another god than Jehovah.

4. xvii. 1-11. Oracle for Damascus. One of the earliest and most crisp of Isaiah's prophecies. Of the time of Syria's and Ephraim's league against Judah, somewhere between 736 and 732.

5. xvii. 12-14. Untitled. The crash of the peoples upon Jerusalem and their dispersion. This magnificent piece of sound, which we analyse below, is usually understood of Sennacherib's rush upon Jerusalem. Verse 14 is an accurate summary of the sudden break-up and "retreat from Moscow" of his army. The Assyrian hosts are described as nations, as they are elsewhere more than once by Isaiah (xxii. 6, xxix. 7). But in all this there is no final reason for referring the oracle to Sennacherib's invasion, and it may just as well be interpreted of Isaiah's confidence of the defeat of Syria and Ephraim (734-723). Its proximity to the oracle against Damascus would then be very natural, and it would stand as a parallel prophecy to viii. 9: Make an uproar, O ye peoples, and ye shall be broken in pieces; and give ear, all ye of the distances of the earth: gird yourselves, and ye shall be broken in pieces; gird yourselves, and ye shall be broken in pieces--a prophecy which we know belongs to the period of the Syro-Ephraimitic league.

6. xviii. Untitled. An address to Ethiopia, land of a rustling of wings, land of many sails, whose messengers dart to and fro upon the rivers in their skiffs of reed. The prophet tells Ethiopia, cast into excitement by the news of the Assyrian advance, how Jehovah is resting quietly till the Assyrian be ripe for destruction. When the Ethiopians shall see His sudden miracle, they shall send their tribute to Jehovah, to the place of the name of Jehovah of hosts, Mount Zion. It is difficult to know to which southward march of Assyria to ascribe this prophecy--Sargon's or Sennacherib's? For at the time of both of these an Ethiopian ruled Egypt.

7. xix. Oracle for Egypt. The first fifteen verses describe judgement as ready to fall on the land of the Pharaohs. The last ten speak of the religious results to Egypt of that judgement, and they form the most universal and "missionary" of all Isaiah's prophecies. Although doubts have been expressed of the Isaian authorship of the second half of this chapter on the score of its universalism, as well as of its literary style, which is judged to be "a pale reflection" of Isaiah's own, there is no final reason for declining the credit of it to Isaiah, while there are insuperable difficulties against relegating it to the late date which is sometimes demanded for it. On the date and authenticity of this prophecy, which are of great importance for the question of Isaiah's "missionary" opinions, see Cheyne's introduction to the chapter and Robertson Smith's notes in The Prophets of Israel (p. 433). The latter puts it in 703, during Sennacherib's advance upon the south. The former suggests that the second half may have been written by the prophet much later than the first, and justly says, "We can hardly imagine a more 'swan-like end' for the dying prophet."

8. xx. Untitled. Also upon Egypt, but in narrative and of an earlier date than at least the latter half of xix. Tells how Isaiah walked naked and barefoot in the streets of Jerusalem for a sign against Egypt and against the help Judah hoped to get from her in the years 711-709, when the Tartan, or Assyrian commander-in-chief, came south to subdue Ashdod. See pp. 198-200.

9. xxi. 1-10. Oracle for the Wilderness of the Sea, announcing but lamenting the fall of Babylon. Probably 709. See pp. 202, 203.

10. xxi. 11, 12. Oracle for Dumah. Dumah, or Silence--in Ps. xciv. 17, cxv. 17, the land of the silence of death, the grave--is probably used as an anagram for Edom and an enigmatic sign to the wise Edomites, in their own fashion, of the kind of silence their land is lying under--the silence of rapid decay. The prophet hears this silence at last broken by a cry. Edom cannot bear the darkness any more. Unto me one is calling from Seir, Watchman, how much off the night? how much off the night? [52] Said the watchman, Cometh the morning, and also the night: if ye will inquire, inquire, come back again. What other answer is possible for a land on which the silence of decay seems to have settled down? He may, however, give them an answer later on, if they will come back. Date uncertain, perhaps between 704 and 701.

11. xxi. 13-17. Oracle For Arabia. From Edom the prophet passes to their neighbours the Dedanites, travelling merchants. And as he saw night upon Edom, so, by a play upon words, he speaks of evening upon Arabia: in the forest, in Arabia, or with the same consonants, in the evening. In the time of the insecurity of the Assyrian invasion the travelling merchants have to go aside from their great trading roads in the evening to lodge in the thickets. There they entertain fugitives, or (for the sense is not quite clear) are themselves as fugitives entertained. It is a picture of the grievousness of war, which was now upon the world, flowing down even those distant, desert roads. But things have not yet reached the worst. The fugitives are but the heralds of armies, that within a year shall waste the children of

Kedar, for Jehovah, the God of Israel, hath spoken it. So did the prophet of little Jerusalem take possession of even the far deserts in the name of his nation's God.

12. xxiii. Oracle For Tyre. Elegy over its fall, probably as Sennacherib came south upon it in 703 or 702. To be further considered by us (pp. 288 ff.).

***

These then are Isaiah's oracles for the Nations, who tremble, intrigue and go down before the might of Assyria.

We have promised to gather the circumstances and meaning of these prophecies round three representative texts. These are--

1. Ah! the booming of the peoples, the multitudes, like the booming of the seas they boom; and the rushing of the nations, like the rushing of mighty waters they rush; nations, like the rushing of many waters they rush. But He rebuketh it, and it fleeth afar off, and is chased like the chaff on the mountains before the wind and like whirling dust before the whirlwind (xvii. 12, 13).

2. What then shall one answer the messengers of a nation? That Jehovah hath founded Zion, and in her shall find refuge the afflicted of His people (xiv. 32).

3. In that day shall Israel be a third to Egypt and to Assyria, a blessing in the midst of the earth, for that Jehovah of hosts hath blessed them, saying, Blessed be My people Egypt, and the work of My hands Assyria, and Mine inheritance Israel (xix. 24, 25).

1. The first of these texts shows all the prophet's prospect filled with storm, the second of them the solitary rock and lighthouse in the midst of the storm: Zion, his own watchtower and his people's refuge; while the third of them, looking far into the future, tells us, as it were, of the firm continent which shall rise out of the waters--Israel no longer a solitary lighthouse, but in that day shall Israel be a third to Egypt and to Assyria, a blessing in the midst of the earth. These three texts give us a summary of the meaning of all Isaiah's obscure prophecies to the foreign nations--a stormy ocean, a solitary rock in the midst of it, and the new continent that shall rise out of the waters about the rock.

The restlessness of Western Asia beneath the Assyrian rule (from 719, when Sargon's victory at Rafia extended that rule to the borders of Egypt) found vent, as we saw (p. 198), in two great Explosions, for both of which the mine was laid by Egyptian intrigue. The first Explosion happened in 711, and was confined to Ashdod. The second took place on Sargon's death in 705, and was universal. Till Sennacherib marched south on Palestine in 701, there were all over Western Asia hurryings to and fro, consultations and intrigues, embassies and engineerings from Babylon to Meroe in far Ethiopia, and from the tents of Kedar to the cities of the Philistines. For these Jerusalem the one inviolate capital from the Euphrates to the river of Egypt, was the natural centre. And the one far-seeing, steady-hearted man in Jerusalem was Isaiah. We have already seen that there was enough within the city to occupy Isaiah's attention, especially from 705 onward; but for Isaiah the walls of Jerusalem, dear as they were and thronged with duty, neither limited his sympathies nor marked the scope of the gospel he had to preach. Jerusalem is simply his watchtower. His field--and this is the peculiar glory of the prophet's later life--his field is the world.

How well fitted Jerusalem then was to be the world's watchtower, the traveller may see to this day. The city lies upon the great central ridge of Palestine, at an elevation of two thousand five hundred feet above the level of the sea. If you ascend the hill behind the city, you stand upon one of the great view-points of the earth. It is a forepost of Asia. To the east rise the red hills of Moab and the uplands of Gilead and Bashan, on to which wandering tribes of the Arabian deserts beyond still push their foremost camps. Just beyond the horizon lie the immemorial paths from Northern Syria into Arabia. Within a few hours' walk along the same central ridge, and still within the territory of Judah, you may see to the north, over a wilderness of blue hills, Hermon's snowy crest; you know that Damascus is lying just beyond, and that through it and round the base of Hermon swings one of the longest of the old world's highways--the main caravan road from the Euphrates to the Nile. Stand at gaze for a little, while down that road there sweep into your mind thoughts of the great empire, whose troops and commerce it used to carry. Then, bearing these thoughts with you, follow the line of the road across the hills to the western coastland, and so out upon the great Egyptian desert, where you may wait till it has brought you imagination of the southern empire to which it travels. Then, lifting your eyes a little further, let them sweep back again from south to north, and you have the whole of the west, the new world, open to you, across the fringe of yellow haze that marks the sands of the Mediterranean. It is even now one of the most comprehensive prospects in the world. But in Isaiah's day, when the world was smaller, the high places of Judah either revealed or suggested the whole of it.

But Isaiah was more than a spectator of this vast theatre. He was an actor upon it. The court of Judah, of which during Hezekiah's reign he was the most prominent member, stood in more or less close connection with the courts of all the kingdoms of Western Asia; and in those days when the nations were busy with intrigue against their common enemy this little highland town and fortress became a gathering place of peoples. From Babylon, from far-off Ethiopia, from Edom, from Philistia, and no doubt from many other places also, embassies came to King Hezekiah, or to inquire of his prophet. The appearance of some of them lives for us still in Isaiah's descriptions: tall and shiny figures of Ethiopians (xviii. 2), with whom we are able to identify the lithe, silky-skinned, shining-black bodies of the present tribes of the Upper Nile. Now the prophet must have talked much with these strangers, for he displays a knowledge of their several countries and ways of life that is full and accurate. The agricultural conditions of Egypt; her social ranks and her industries (xix.); the harbours and markets of Tyre (xxiii.); the caravans of the Arab nomads as in times of war they shun the open desert and seek the thickets (xxi. 14)--Isaiah paints these for us with a vivid realism. We see how this statesman of the least of States, this prophet of a religion which was confessed over only a few square miles, was aware of the wide world, and how he loved the life that filled it. They are no mere geographical terms with which Isaiah thickly studs these prophecies. He looks out upon, and paints for us, lands and cities surging with men--their trades, their castes, their religions, their besetting tempers and sins, their social structures and national policies, all quick and bending to the breeze and the shadow of the coming storm from the north.

We have said that in nothing is the regal power of our prophet's style so manifest as in the vast horizons, which, by the use of a few words, he calls up before us. Some of the finest of these revelations are made in this part of his book, so obscure and unknown to most. Who can ever forget those descriptions of Ethiopia in the eighteenth chapter?--"Ah! the land of the rustling of wings, which borders on the rivers of Cush, which sendeth heralds on the sea, and in vessels of reed on the face of the waters! Travel, fleet messengers, to a people lithe and shining, to a nation feared from ever it began to be, a people strong, strong and trampling, whose land the rivers divide; or of Tyre in chapter xxiii.?-- "And on great waters the seed of Shihor, the harvest of the Nile, was her revenue; and she was the mart of nations. What expanses of sea! what fleets of ships! what floating loads of grain! what concourse of merchants moving on stately wharves beneath high warehouses!"

Yet these are only segments of horizons, and perhaps the prophet reaches the height of his power of expression in the first of the three texts, which we have given as representative of his prophecies on foreign nations (p. 278). Here three or four lines of marvellous sound repeat the effect of the rage of the restless world as it rises, storms and breaks upon the steadfast will of God. The phonetics of the passage are wonderful. The general impression is that of a stormy ocean booming in to the shore and then crashing itself out into one long hiss of spray and foam upon its barriers. The details are noteworthy. In ver. 12 we have thirteen heavy M-sounds, besides two heavy B's, to five N's, five H's, and four sibilants. But in ver. 13 the sibilants predominate; and before the sharp rebuke of the Lord the great, booming sound of ver. 12 scatters out into a long yish-sha 'oon. The occasional use of a prolonged vowel amid so many hurrying consonants produces exactly the effect now of the lift of a storm swell out at sea and now of the pause of a great wave before it crashes on the shore. "Ah, the booming of the peoples, the multitudes, like the booming of the seas they boom; and the rushing of the nations, like the rushing of the mighty waters they rush: nations, like the rushing of many waters they rush. But He checketh it--a short, sharp word with a choke and a snort in it--and it fleeth far away, and is chased like chaff on mountains before wind, and like swirling dust before a whirlwind."

So did the rage of the world sound to Isaiah as it crashed into pieces upon the steadfast providence of God. To those who can feel the force of such language nothing need be added upon the prophet's view of the politics of the outside world these twenty years, whether portions of it threatened Judah in their own strength, or the whole power of storm that was in it rose with the Assyrian, as in all his flood he rushed upon Zion in the year 701.

2. But amid this storm Zion stands immovable. It is upon Zion that the storm crashes itself into impotence. This becomes explicit in the second of our representative texts: What then shall one answer the messengers of a nation? That Jehovah hath founded Zion, and in her shall find a refuge the afflicted of His people (xiv. 32). This oracle was drawn from Isaiah by an embassy of the Philistines. Stricken with panic at the Assyrian advance, they had sent messengers to Jerusalem, as other tribes did, with questions and proposals of defences, escapes and alliances. They got their answer. Alliances are useless. Everything human is going down. Here, here alone, is safety, because the Lord hath decreed it.

With what light and peace do Isaiah's words break out across that unquiet, hungry sea! How they tell the world for the first time, and have been telling it ever since, that, apart from all the struggle and strife of history, there is a refuge and security of men, which God Himself has assured. The troubled surface of life, nations heaving uneasily, kings of Assyria and their armies carrying the world before them--these are not all. The world and her powers are not all. Religion, in the very teeth of life, builds her refuge for the afflicted.

The world seems wholly divided between force and fear. Isaiah says, It is not true. Faith has her abiding citadel in the midst, a house of God, which neither force can harm nor fear enter.

This then was Isaiah's Interim-Answer to the Nations--Zion at least is secure for the people of Jehovah.

3. Isaiah could not remain content, however, with so narrow an interim-answer: Zion at least is

secure, whatever happens to the rest of you. The world was there, and had to be dealt with and accounted for--had even to be saved. As we have already seen, this was the problem of Isaiah's generation; and to have shirked it would have meant the failure of his faith to rank as universal.

Isaiah did not shirk it. He said boldly to his people, and to the nations: "The faith we have covers this vaster life. Jehovah is not only God of Israel. He rules the world." These prophecies to the foreign nations are full of revelations of the sovereignty and providence of God. The Assyrian may seem to be growing in glory; but Jehovah is watching from the heavens, till he be ripe for cutting down (xviii. 4). Egypt's statesmen may be perverse and wilful; but Jehovah of hosts swingeth His hand against the land: they shall tremble and shudder (xix. 16). Egypt shall obey His purposes (17). Confusion may reign for a time, but a signal and a centre shall be lifted up, and the world gather itself in order round the revealed will of God. The audacity of such a claim for his God becomes more striking when we remember that Isaiah's faith was not the faith of a majestic or a conquering people. When he made his claim, Judah was still tributary to Assyria, a petty highland principality, that could not hope to stand by material means against the forces which had thrown down her more powerful neighbours. It was no experience of success, no mere instinct of being on the side of fate, which led Isaiah so resolutely to pronounce that not only should his people be secure, but that his God would vindicate His purposes upon empires like Egypt and Assyria. It was simply his sense that Jehovah was exalted in righteousness. Therefore, while inside Judah only the remnant that took the side of righteousness would be saved, outside Judah wherever there was unrighteousness, it would be rebuked, and wherever righteousness, it would be vindicated. This is the supremacy which Isaiah proclaimed for Jehovah over the whole world.

How spiritual this faith of Isaiah was, is seen from the next step the prophet took. Looking out on the troubled world, he did not merely assert that his God ruled it, but he emphatically said, what was a far more difficult thing to say, that it would all be consciously and willingly God's. God rules this, not to restrain it only, but to make it His own. The knowledge of Him, which is to-day our privilege, shall be to-morrow the blessing of the whole world.

When we point to the Jewish desire, so often expressed in the Old Testament, of making the whole world subject to Jehovah, we are told that it is simply a proof of religious ambition and jealousy. We are told that this wish to convert the world no more stamps the Jewish religion as being universal, and therefore presumably a Divine, religion than the Mohammedans' zeal to force their tenets on men at the point of the sword is a proof of the truth of Islam.

Now we need not be concerned to defend the Jewish religion in its every particular, even as propounded by an Isaiah. It is an article of the Christian creed that Judaism was a minor and imperfect dispensation, where truth was only half revealed and virtue half developed. But at least let us do the Jewish religion justice; and we shall never do it justice till we pay attention to what its greatest prophets thought of the outside world, how they sympathized with this, and in what way they proposed to make it subject to their own faith.

Firstly then, there is something in the very manner of Isaiah's treatment of foreign nations, which causes the old charges of religious exclusiveness to sink in our throats. Isaiah treats these foreigners at least as men. Take his prophecies on Egypt or on Tyre or on Babylon--nations which were the hereditary enemies of his nation--and you find him speaking of their natural misfortunes, their social decays, their national follies and disasters, with the same pity and with the same purely moral considerations, with which he has treated his own land. When news of those far-away sorrows comes to Jerusalem, it moves this large-hearted prophet to mourning and tears. He breathes out to distant lands elegies as beautiful as he has poured upon Jerusalem. He shows as intelligent an interest in their social evolutions as he does in those of the Jewish State. He gives a picture of the industry and politics of Egypt as careful as his pictures of the fashions and statecraft of Judah. In short, as you read his prophecies upon foreign nations, you perceive that before the eyes of this man humanity, broken and scattered in his days as it was, rose up one great whole, every part of which was subject to the same laws of righteousness, and deserved from the prophet of God the same love and pity. To some few tribes he says decisively that they shall certainly be wiped out, but even them he does not address in contempt or in hatred. The large empire of Egypt, the great commercial power of Tyre, he speaks of in language of respect and admiration; but that does not prevent him from putting the plain issue to them which he put to his own countrymen: If you are unrighteous, intemperate, impure--lying diplomats and dishonest rulers, you shall certainly perish before Assyria. If you are righteous, temperate, pure, if you do trust in truth and God, nothing can move you.

But, secondly, he, who thus treated all nations with the same strict measures of justice and the same fulness of pity with which he treated his own, was surely not far from extending to the world the religious privileges, which he has so frequently identified with Jerusalem. In his old age, at least Isaiah looked forward to the time when the particular religious opportunities of the Jew should be the inheritance of humanity. For their old oppressor Egypt, for their new enemy Assyria, he anticipates the same experience and education, which has made Israel the firstborn of God. Speaking to Egypt, Isaiah concludes a missionary sermon, fit to take its place beside that which Paul uttered on the Areopagus to

The Expositor's Bible: The Book of Isaiah Volumes I & II

the younger Greek civilisation, with the words, In that day shall Israel be a third to Egypt and to Assyria, a blessing in the midst of the earth, for that Jehovah of hosts hath blessed them, saying, Blessed be Egypt My people, and Assyria the work of My hands and Israel Mine inheritance.

Footnote:

52. Our translation, though picturesque, is misleading. The voice does not inquire, "What of the night?" i.e., whether it be fair or foul weather, but "How much of the night is passed?" literally "What from off the night?" This brings out a pathos that our English version has disguised. Edom feels that her night is lasting terribly long.

Rev. George Adam Smith, M.A.

CHAPTER XVIII

TYRE; OR, THE MERCENARY SPIRIT.

Isaiah xxiii. (702 B.C.).

The task, which was laid upon the religion of Israel while Isaiah was its prophet, was the task, as we have often told ourselves, of facing the world's forces, and of explaining how they were to be led captive and contributory to the religion of the true God. And we have already seen Isaiah accounting for the largest of these forces: the Assyrian. But besides Assyria, that military empire, there was another power in the world, also novel to Israel's experience and also in Isaiah's day grown large enough to demand from Israel's faith explanation and criticism. This was Commerce, represented by the Phoenicians, with their chief seats at Tyre and Sidon, and their colonies across the seas. Not even Egypt exercised such influence on Isaiah's generation as Phoenicia did; and Phoenician influence, though less visible and painful than Assyrian, was just as much more subtle and penetrating as in these respects the influence of trade exceeds that of war. Assyria herself was fascinated by the glories of Phoenician commerce. The ambition of her kings, who had in that century pushed south to the Mediterranean, was to found a commercial empire. The mercenary spirit, as we learn from prophets earlier than Isaiah, had begun also to leaven the life of the agricultural and shepherd tribes of Western Asia. For good or for evil commerce had established itself as a moral force in the world. Isaiah's chapter on Tyre is, therefore, of the greatest interest. It contains the prophet's vision of commerce the first time commerce had grown vast enough to impress his people's imagination, as well as a criticism of the temper of commerce from the standpoint of the religion of the God of righteousness. Whether as a historical study or a message addressed to the mercantile tempers of our own day, the chapter is worthy of close attention.

But we must first impress ourselves with the utter contrast between Phoenicia and Judah in the matter of commercial experience, or we shall not feel the full force of this excursion which the prophet of a high, inland tribe of shepherds makes among the wharves and warehouses of the great merchant city on the sea.

The Phoenician empire, it has often been remarked, presents a very close analogy to that of Great Britain; but even more entirely than in the case of Great Britain the glory of that empire was the wealth of its trade, and the character of the people was the result of their mercantile habits. A little strip of land, one hundred and forty miles long, and never more than fifteen broad, with the sea upon one side and the mountains upon the other, compelled its inhabitants to become miners and seamen. The hills shut off the narrow coast from the continent to which it belongs, and drove the increasing populations to seek their destiny by way of the sea. These took to it kindly, for they had the Semite's born instinct for trading. Planting their colonies all round the Mediterranean, exploiting every mine within reach of the coastland, establishing great trading depôts both on the Nile and the Euphrates, with fleets that passed the Straits of Gibraltar into the Atlantic and the Straits of Bab-el-Mandeb into the Indian Ocean, the Phoenicians constructed a system of trade, which was not exceeded in range or influence till, more than two thousand years later, Portugal made the discovery of America and accomplished the passage of the Cape of Good Hope. From the coasts of Britain to those of Northwest India, and probably to Madagascar, was the extent of Phoenician credit and currency. Their trade tapped river basins so far apart as those of the Indus, the Euphrates, probably the Zambesi, the Nile, the Rhone, the Guadalquivir. They built ships and harbours for the Pharaohs and for Solomon. They carried Egyptian art and Babylonian knowledge to the Grecian archipelago, and brought back the metals of Spain and Britain. No wonder the prophet breaks into enthusiasm as he surveys Phoenician enterprise! And on great waters the seed of Shihor, the harvest of the Nile, was her revenue; and she was the mart of nations.

But upon trade the Phoenicians had built an empire. At home their political life enjoyed the freedom, energy and resources which are supplied by long habits of an extended commerce with other peoples. The constitution of the different Phoenician cities was not, as is sometimes supposed, republican, but monarchical; and the land belonged to the king. Yet the large number of wealthy families at once limited the power of the throne, and saved the commonwealth from being dependent upon the fortunes of a single dynasty. The colonies in close relation with the mother country assured an empire with its life in better circulation and with more reserve of power than either Egypt or Assyria. Tyre and Sidon were frequently overthrown, but they rose again oftener than the other great cities of antiquity, and were still places of importance when Babylon and Nineveh lay in irreparable ruin.

Besides their native families of royal wealth and influence and their flourishing colonies, each with its prince, these commercial States kept foreign monarchs in their pay, and sometimes determined the fate of a dynasty. Isaiah entitles Tyre the giver of crowns, the maker of kings, whose merchants are princes, and her traffickers are the honourable of the earth.

But trade with political results so splendid had an evil effect upon the character and spiritual temper of the people. By the indiscriminating ancients the Phoenicians were praised as inventors; the rudiments of most of the arts and sciences, of the alphabet and of money have been ascribed to them. But modern research has proved that of none of the many elements of civilisation which they introduced to the West were they the actual authors. The Phoenicians were simply carriers and middlemen. In all time there is no instance of a nation so wholly given over to buying and selling, who frequented even the battlefields of the world that they might strip the dead and purchase the captive. Phoenician history--though we must always do the people the justice to remember that we have their history only in fragments--affords few signs of the consciousness that there are things which a nation may strive after for their own sake, and not for the money they bring in. The world, which other peoples, still in the reverence of the religious youth of the race, regarded as a house of prayer, the Phoenicians had already turned into a den of thieves. They trafficked even with the mysteries and intelligences; and their own religion is largely a mixture of the religions of the other peoples, with whom they came into contact. The national spirit was venal and mercenary--the heart of an hireling, or, as Isaiah by a baser name describes it, the heart of an harlot. There is not throughout history a more perfect incarnation of the mercenary spirit than the Phoenician nation.

Now let us turn to the experience of the Jews, whose faith had to face and account for this world-force.

The history of the Jews in Europe has so identified them with trade that it is difficult for us to imagine a Jew free from its spirit or ignorant of its methods. But the fact is that in the time of Isaiah Israel was as little acquainted with commerce as it is possible for a civilised nation to be. Israel's was an inland territory. Till Solomon's reign the people had neither navy nor harbour. Their land was not abundant in materials for trade--it contained almost no minerals, and did not produce a greater supply of food than was necessary for the consumption of its inhabitants. It is true that the ambition of Solomon had brought the people within the temptations of commerce. He established trading cities, annexed harbours and hired a navy. But even then, and again in the reign of Uzziah, which reflects much of Solomon's commercial glory, Israel traded by deputies, and the mass of the people remained innocent of mercantile habits. Perhaps to moderns the most impressive proof of how little Israel had to do with trade is to be found in their laws of money-lending and of interest. The absolute prohibition which Moses placed upon the charging of interest could only have been possible among a people with the most insignificant commerce. To Isaiah himself commerce must have appeared alien. Human life, as he pictures it, is composed of war, politics and agriculture; his ideals for society are those of the shepherd and the farmer. We moderns cannot dissociate the future welfare of humanity from the triumphs of trade.

> *"For I dipt into the future, far as human eye could see,*
> *Saw the vision of the world and all the wonder that would be;*
> *Saw the heavens fill with commerce, argosies of magic sails,*
> *Pilots of the purple twilight, dropping down with costly bales."*

But all Isaiah's future is full of gardens and busy fields, of irrigating rivers and canals:--

Until the Spirit be poured upon us from on high, and the wilderness become a fruitful field, and the fruitful field be counted for a forest.... Blessed are ye, that sow beside all waters, that send forth the feet of the ox and the ass.

And He shall give the rain of thy seed, that thou shalt sow the ground withal, and bread-corn, the increase of the ground; and it shall be juicy and fat: in that day shall thy cattle feed in large pastures.

Conceive how trade looked to eyes which dwelt with enthusiasm upon scenes like these! It must have seemed to blast the future, to disturb the regularity of life with such violence as to shake religion herself! With all our convictions of the benefits of trade, even we feel no greater regret or alarm than when we observe the invasion by the rude forces of trade of some scene of rural felicity; blackening of sky and earth and stream; increasing complexity and entanglement of life; enormous growth of new problems and temptations; strange knowledge, ambitions and passions, that throb through life and strain the tissue of its simple constitution, like novel engines, which shake the ground and the strong walls, accustomed once to re-echo only the simple music of the mill-wheel and the weaver's shuttle. Isaiah did not fear an invasion of Judah by the habits and the machines of trade. There is no foreboding in this chapter of the day when his own people were to take the place of the Phoenicians as the commercial harlots of the world, and a Jew was to be synonymous with usurer and publican. Yet we may employ our feelings to imagine his, and understand what this prophet--seated in the sanctuary of a pastoral and

Rev. George Adam Smith, M.A.

agricultural tribe, with its simple offerings of doves, and lambs and sheaves of corn, telling how their homes, and fields and whole rustic manner of life were subject to God--thought, and feared, and hoped of the vast commerce of Phoenicia, wondering how it also should be sanctified to Jehovah.

First of all, Isaiah, as we might have expected from his large faith and broad sympathies, accepts and acknowledges this great world-force. His noble spirit shows neither timidity nor jealousy before it. Before his view what an unblemished prospect of it spreads! His descriptions tell more of his appreciation than long laudations would have done. He grows enthusiastic upon the grandeur of Tyre; and even when he prophesies that Assyria shall destroy it, it is with the feeling that such a destruction is really a desecration, and as if there lived essential glory in great commercial enterprise. Certainly from such a spirit we have much to learn. How often has religion, when brought face to face with the new forces of a generation--commerce, democracy or science--shown either a base timidity or baser jealousy, and met the innovations with cries of detraction or despair! Isaiah reads a lesson to the modern Church in the preliminary spirit with which she should meet the novel experiences of Providence. Whatever judgement may afterwards have to be passed, there is the immediate duty of frankly recognising greatness wherever it may occur. This is an essential principle, from the forgetfulness of which modern religion has suffered much. Nothing is gained by attempting to minimise new departures in the world's history; but everything is lost if we sit down in fear of them. It is a duty we owe to ourselves, and a worship which Providence demands from us, that we ungrudgingly appreciate every magnitude of which history brings us the knowledge.

It is almost an unnecessary task to apply Isaiah's meaning to the commerce of our own day. But let us not miss his example in this: that the right to criticise the habits of trade and the ability to criticise them healthily are alone won by a just appreciation of trade's world-wide glory and serviceableness. There is no use preaching against the venal spirit and manifold temptations and degradations of trade, until we have realised the indispensableness of trade and its capacity for disciplining and exalting its ministers. The only way to correct the abuses of "the commercial spirit," against which many in our day are loud with indiscriminate rebuke, is to impress its victims, having first impressed yourself, with the opportunities and the ideals of commerce. A thing is great partly by its traditions and partly by its opportunities--partly by what it has accomplished and partly by the doors of serviceableness of which it holds the key. By either of these standards the magnitude of commerce is simply overwhelming. Having discovered the world-forces, commerce has built thereon the most powerful of our modern empires. Its exigencies compel peace; its resources are the sinews of war. If it has not always preceded religion and science in the conquest of the globe, it has shared with them their triumphs. Commerce has recast the modern world, so that we hardly think of the old national divisions in the greater social classes which have been its direct creation. Commerce determines national policies; its markets are among the schools of statesmen; its merchants are still princes, and its traffickers the honourable of the earth.

Therefore let all merchants and their apprentices believe, "Here is something worth putting our manhood into, worth living for, not with our brains only or our appetites, but with our conscience, with our imagination, with every curiosity and sympathy of our nature. Here is a calling with a healthy discipline, with a free spirit, with unrivalled opportunities of service, with an ancient and essential dignity." The reproach which is so largely imagined upon trade is the relic of a barbarous age. Do not tolerate it, for under its shadow, as under other artificial and unhealthy contempts of society, there are apt to grow up those sordid and slavish tempers, which soon make men deserve the reproach that was at first unjustly cast upon them. Dissipate the base influence of this reproach by lifting the imagination upon the antiquity and world-wide opportunities of trade--trade, whose origin, as Isaiah so finely puts it, is of ancient days; and her feet carry her afar off to sojourn.

So generous an appreciation of the grandeur of commerce does not prevent Isaiah from exposing its besetting sin and degradation.

The vocation of a merchant differs from others in this, that there is no inherent nor instinctive obligation in it to ends higher than those of financial profit--emphasized in our days into the more dangerous constraint of immediate financial profit. No profession is of course absolutely free from the risk of this servitude; but other professions offer escapes, or at least mitigations, which are not possible to nearly the same extent in trade. Artist, artisan, preacher and statesman have ideals which generally act contrary to the compulsion of profit and tend to create a nobility of mind strong enough to defy it. They have given, so to speak, hostages to heaven--ideals of beauty, of accurate scholarship or of moral influence, which they dare not risk by abandoning themselves to the hunt for gain. But the calling of a merchant is not thus safeguarded. It does not afford those visions, those occasions of being caught away to the heavens, which are the inherent glories of other lives. The habits of trade make this the first thought--not what things of beauty are in themselves, not what men are as brothers, not what life is as God's discipline, but what things of beauty, and men and opportunities are worth to us--and in these times what they are immediately worth--as measured by money. In such an absorption art, humanity, morals and religion become matters of growing indifference.

To this spirit, which treats all things and men, high or low, as matters simply of profit, Isaiah gives a very ugly name. We call it the mercenary or venal spirit. Isaiah says it is the spirit of the harlot.

The history of Phoenicia justified his words. To-day we remember her by nothing that is great, by nothing that is original. She left no art nor literature, and her once brave and skilful populations degenerated till we know them only as the slave-dealers, panders and prostitutes of the Roman empire. If we desire to find Phoenicia's influence on the religion of the world, we have to seek for it among the most sensual of Greek myths and the abominable practices of Corinthian worship. With such terrible literalness was Isaiah's harlot-curse fulfilled.

What is true of Phoenicia may become true of Britain, and what has been seen on the large scale of a nation is exemplified every day in individual lives. The man who is entirely eaten up with the zeal of gain is no better than what Isaiah called Tyre. He has prostituted himself to covetousness. If day and night our thoughts are of profit, and the habit, so easily engendered in these times, of asking only, "What can I make of this?" is allowed to grow upon us, it shall surely come to pass that we are found sacrificing, like the poor unfortunate, the most sacred of our endowments and affections for gain, demeaning our natures at the feet of the world for the sake of the world's gold. A woman sacrifices her purity for coin, and the world casts her out. But some who would not touch her have sacrificed honour and love and pity for the same base wage, and in God's sight are no better than she. Ah, how much need is there for these bold, brutal standards of the Hebrew prophet to correct our own social misappreciations!

Now for a very vain delusion upon this subject! It is often imagined in our day that if a man seek atonement for the venal spirit through the study of art, through the practice of philanthropy or through the cultivation of religion, he shall surely find it. This is false--plausible and often practised but utterly false. Unless a man see and reverence beauty in the very workshop and office of his business, unless he feel those whom he meets there, his employés and customers, as his brethren, unless he keep his business methods free from fraud, and honestly recognise his gains as a trust from the Lord, then no amount of devotion elsewhere to the fine arts, nor perseverance in philanthropy, nor fondness for the Church evinced by ever so large subscriptions, will deliver him from the devil of mercenariness. That is a plea of alibi that shall not prevail on the judgement day. He is only living a double life, whereof his art, philanthropy or religion is the occasional and dilettante portion, with not nearly so much influence on his character as the other, his calling and business, in which he still sacrifices love to gain. His real world--the world in which God set him, to buy and sell indeed, but also to serve and glorify his God--he is treating only as a big warehouse and exchange. And so much is this the case at the present day, in spite of all the worship of art and religion which is fashionable in mercantile circles, that we do not go too far when we say that if Jesus were now to visit our large markets and manufactories, in which the close intercourse of numbers of human persons renders the opportunities of service and testimony to God so frequent, He would scourge men from them, as He scourged the traffickers of the Temple, for that they had forgotten that here was their Father's house, where their brethren had to be owned and helped, and their Father's glory revealed to the world.

A nation with such a spirit was of course foredoomed to destruction. Isaiah predicts the absolute disappearance of Tyre from the attention of the world. Tyre shall be forgotten seventy years. Then, like some poor unfortunate whose day of beauty is past, she shall in vain practise her old advertisements on men. After the end of seventy years it shall be unto Tyre as in the song of the harlot: Take an harp, go about the city, thou harlot that hast been forgotten; make sweet melody, sing many songs, that thou mayest be remembered.

But Commerce is essential to the world. Tyre must revive; and the prophet sees her revive as the minister of Religion, the purveyor of the food of the servants of the Lord, and of the accessories of their worship. It must be confessed, that we are not a little shocked when we find Isaiah continuing to apply to Commerce his metaphor of a harlot, even after Commerce has entered the service of the true religion. He speaks of her wages being devoted to Jehovah, just in the same manner as those of certain notorious women of heathen temples were devoted to the idol of the temple. This is even against the directions of the Mosaic law. Isaiah, however, was a poet; and in his flights we must not expect him to carry the whole Law on his back. He was a poet, and probably no analogy would have more vividly appealed to his Oriental audience. It will be foolish to allow our natural prejudice against what we may feel to be the unhealthiness of the metaphor to blind us to the magnificence of the thought which he clothes in it.

All this is another proof of the sanity and far sight of our prophet. Again we find that his conviction that judgement is coming does not render his spirit morbid, nor disturb his eye for things of beauty and profit in the world. Commerce, with all her faults, is essential, and must endure, nay shall prove in the days to come Religion's most profitable minister. The generosity and wisdom of this passage are the more striking when we remember the extremity of unrelieved denunciation to which other great teachers of religion have allowed themselves to be hurled by their rage against the sins of trade. But Isaiah, in the largest sense of the expression, is a man of the world--a man of the world because God made the world and rules it. Yet even from his far sight was hidden the length to which in the last days Commerce would carry her services to man and God, proving as she has done, under the

Rev. George Adam Smith, M.A.

flag of another Phoenicia, to all the extent of Isaiah's longing, one of Religion's most sincere and profitable handmaids.

BOOK IV

JERUSALEM AND SENNACHERIB, 701 B.C.

*Isaiah:-- xxxvi. 1. Early in 701. i. " " xxii. " " xxxiii. A little later. xxxvi. 2-xxxvii." " --------
xxxviii.-xxxix. Date uncertain.*

Into this fourth book we put all the rest of the prophecies of the Book of Isaiah, that have to do with the prophet's own time: chaps. i., xxii. and xxxiii., with the narrative in xxxvi., xxxvii. All these refer to the only Assyrian invasion of Judah and siege of Jerusalem: that undertaken by Sennacherib in 701.

It is, however, right to remember once more, that many authorities maintain that there were two Assyrian invasions of Judah--one by Sargon in 711, the other by Sennacherib in 701--and that chaps. i. and xxii. (as well as x. 5-34) belong to the former of these. The theory is ingenious and tempting; but, in the silence of the Assyrian annals about any invasion of Judah by Sargon, it is impossible to adopt it. And although chaps. i. and xxii. differ very greatly in tone from chap. xxxiii., yet to account for the difference it is not necessary to suppose two different invasions, with a considerable period between them. Virtually, as will appear in the course of our exposition, Sennacherib's invasion of Judah was a double one.

1. The first time Sennacherib's army invaded Judah they took all the fenced cities, and probably invested Jerusalem, but withdrew on payment of tribute and the surrender of the casus belli, the Assyrian vassal Padi, whom the Ekronites had deposed and given over to the keeping of Hezekiah. To this invasion refer Isa. i., xxii. and the first verse of xxxvi.: Now it came to pass in the fourteenth [53] year of King Hezekiah that Sennacherib, King of Assyria, came up against all the fenced cities of Judah and took them. This verse is the same as 2 Kings xviii. 13, to which, however, there is added in vv. 14-16 an account of the tribute sent by Hezekiah to Sennacherib at Lachish, that is not included in the narrative in Isaiah. Compare 2 Chron. xxxii. 1.

2. But scarcely had the tribute been paid when Sennacherib, himself advancing to meet Egypt, sent back upon Jerusalem a second army of investment, with which was the Rabshakeh; and this was the army that so mysteriously disappeared from the eyes of the besieged. To the treacherous return of the Assyrians and the sudden deliverance of Jerusalem from their grasp refer Isa. xxxiii., xxxvi. 2-xxxvii., with the fuller and evidently original narrative in 2 Kings xviii. 17-xix. Compare 2 Chron. xxxii. 9-23.

To the history of this double attempt upon Jerusalem in 701--xxxvi. and xxxvii.--there has been appended in xxxviii. and xxxix. an account of Hezekiah's illness and of an embassy to him from Babylon. These events probably happened some years before Sennacherib's invasion. But it will be most convenient for us to take them in the order in which they stand in the canon. They will naturally lead us up to a question that it is necessary we should discuss before taking leave of Isaiah--whether this great prophet of the endurance of the kingdom of God upon earth had any gospel for the individual who dropped away from it into death.

Footnote:

53. It is confusing to find this date attached to Sennacherib's invasion of 701, unless, with one or two critics, we place Hezekiah's accession in 715. But Hezekiah acceded in 728 or 727, and 701 would therefore be his twenty-sixth or twenty-seventh year. Mr. Cheyne, who takes 727 as the year of Hezekiah's accession, gets out of the difficulty by reading "Sargon" for "Sennacherib" in this verse and in 2 Kings xiii., and thus secures another reference to that invasion of Judah, which he supposes to have taken place under Sargon between 712 and 710. By the change of a letter some would read twenty-fourth for fourteenth. But in any case this date is confusing.

Rev. George Adam Smith, M.A.

CHAPTER XIX

AT THE LOWEST EBB.

Isaiah i. and xxii. (701 B.C.).

In the drama of Isaiah's life we have now arrived at the final act--a short and sharp one of a few months. The time is 701 B.C., the fortieth year of Isaiah's ministry, and about the twenty-sixth of Hezekiah's reign. The background is the invasion of Palestine by Sennacherib. The stage itself is the city of Jerusalem. In the clear atmosphere before the bursting of the storm Isaiah has looked round the whole world--his world--uttering oracles on the nations from Tyre to Egypt and from Ethiopia to Babylon. But now the Assyrian storm has burst, and all except the immediate neighbourhood of the prophet is obscured. From Jerusalem Isaiah will not again lift his eyes.

The stage is thus narrow and the time short, but the action one of the most critical in the history of Israel, taking rank with the Exodus from Egypt and the Return from Babylon. To Isaiah himself it marks the summit of his career. For half a century Zion has been preparing for, forgetting and again preparing for, her first and final struggle with the Assyrian. Now she is to meet her foe, face to face across her own walls. For forty years Isaiah has predicted for the Assyrian an uninterrupted path of conquest to the very gates of Jerusalem, but certain check and confusion there. Sennacherib has overrun the world, and leaps upon Zion. The Jewish nation await their fate, Isaiah his vindication, and the credit of Israel's religion, one of the most extraordinary tests to which a spiritual faith was ever subjected.

In the end, by the mysterious disappearance of the Assyrian, Jerusalem was saved, the prophet was left with his remnant and the future still open for Israel. But at the beginning of the end such an issue was by no means probable. Jewish panic and profligacy almost prevented the Divine purpose, and Isaiah went near to breaking his heart over the city, for whose redemption he had travailed for a lifetime. He was as sure as ever that this redemption must come, but a collapse of the people's faith and patriotism at the eleventh hour made its coming seem worthless. Jerusalem appeared bent on forestalling her deliverance by moral suicide. Despair, not of God but of the city, settled on Isaiah's heart; and in such a mood he wrote chap. xxii. We may entitle it therefore, though written at a time when the tide should have been running to the full, "At the Lowest Ebb."

We have thus stated at the outset the motive of this chapter, because it is one of the most unexpected and startling of all Isaiah's prophecies. In it "we can discern precipices." Beneath our eyes, long lifted by the prophet to behold a future stretching very far forth, this chapter suddenly yawns, a pit of blackness. For utterness of despair and the absolute sentence which it passes on the citizens of Zion we have had nothing like it from Isaiah since the evil days of Ahaz. The historical portions of the Bible which cover this period are not cleft by such a crevasse, and of course the official Assyrian annals, full as they are of the details of Sennacherib's campaign in Palestine, know nothing of the moral condition of Jerusalem. [54] Yet if we put the Hebrew and Assyrian narratives together, and compare them with chaps. i. and xxii. of Isaiah, we may be sure that the following was something like the course of events which led down to this woeful depth in Judah's experience.

In a Syrian campaign Sennacherib's path was plain--to begin with the Phoenician cities, march quickly south by the level coastland, subduing the petty chieftains upon it, meet Egypt at its southern end, and then, when he had rid himself of his only formidable foe, turn to the more delicate task of warfare among the hills of Judah--a campaign which he could scarcely undertake with a hostile force like Egypt on his flank. This course, he tells us, he followed. "In my third campaign, to the land of Syria I went. Luliah (Elulæus), King of Sidon--for the fearful splendour of my majesty overwhelmed him--fled to a distant spot in the midst of the sea. His land I entered." City after city fell to the invader. The princes of Aradus, Byblus and Ashdod, by the coast, and even Moab and Edom, far inland, sent him their submission. He attacked Ascalon, and captured its king. He went on, and took the Philistine cities of Beth-dagon, Joppa, Barka and Azor, all of them within forty miles of Jerusalem, and some even visible from her neighbourhood. South of this group, and a little over twenty-five miles from Jerusalem, lay Ekron; and here Sennacherib had so good a reason for anger, that the inhabitants, expecting no mercy at his hands, prepared a stubborn defence.

Ten years before this Sargon had set Padi, a vassal of his own, as king over Ekron; but the Ekronites had risen against Padi, put him in chains, and sent him to their ally Hezekiah, who now held him in Jerusalem. "These men," says Sennacherib, "were now terrified in their hearts; the shadows of death overwhelmed them." [55] Before Ekron was reduced, however, the Egyptian army arrived in Philistia, and Sennacherib had to abandon the siege for these arch-enemies. He defeated them in the neighbourhood, at Eltekeh, returned to Ekron, and completed its siege. Then, while he himself advanced southwards in pursuit of the Egyptians, he detached a corps, which, marching eastwards through the mountain passes, overran all Judah and threatened Jerusalem. "And Hezekiah, King of Judah, who had not bowed down at my feet, forty-six of his strong cities, his castles and the smaller towns in their neighbourhood beyond number, by casting down ramparts and by open attack, by battle--zuk, of the feet; nisi, hewing to pieces and casting down (?)--I besieged, I captured.... He himself, like a bird in a cage, inside Jerusalem, his royal city, I shut him up; siege-towers against him I constructed, for he had given command to renew the bulwarks of the great gate of his city." [56] But Sennacherib does not say that he took Jerusalem, and simply closes the narrative of his campaign with the account of large tribute which Hezekiah sent after him to Nineveh.

Here, then, we have material for a graphic picture of Jerusalem and her populace, when chaps. i. and xxii. were uttered by Isaiah.

At Jerusalem we are within a day's journey of any part of the territory of Judah. We feel the kingdom throb to its centre at Assyria's first footfall on the border. The nation's life is shuddering in upon its capital, couriers dashing up with the first news; fugitives hard upon them; palace, arsenal, market and temple thrown into commotion; the politicians busy; the engineers hard at work completing the fortifications, leading the suburban wells to a reservoir within the walls, levelling every house and tree outside which could give shelter to the besiegers, and heaping up the material on the ramparts, till there lies nothing but a great, bare, waterless circle round a high-banked fortress. Across this bareness the lines of fugitives streaming to the gates; provincial officials and their retinues; soldiers whom Hezekiah had sent out to meet the foe, returning without even the dignity of defeat upon them; husbandmen, with cattle and remnants of grain in disorder; women and children; the knaves, cowards and helpless of the whole kingdom pouring their fear, dissoluteness and disease into the already-unsettled populace of Jerusalem. Inside the walls opposing political factions and a weak king; idle crowds, swaying to every rumour and intrigue; the ordinary restraints and regularities of life suspended, even patriotism gone with counsel and courage, but in their place fear and shame and greed of life. Such was the state in which Jerusalem faced the hour of her visitation.

Gradually the Visitant came near over the thirty miles which lay between the capital and the border. Signs of the Assyrian advance were given in the sky, and night after night the watchers on Mount Zion, seeing the glare in the west, must have speculated which of the cities of Judah was being burned. Clouds of smoke across the heavens from prairie and forest fires told how war, even if it passed, would leave a trail of famine; and men thought with breaking hearts of the villages and fields, heritage of the tribes of old, that were now bare to the foot and the fire of the foreigner. Your country is desolate; your cities are burned with fire; your land, strangers devour it in your presence, and it is desolate as the overthrow of strangers. And the daughter of Zion is left as a booth in a vineyard, as a lodge in a garden of cucumbers. Except Jehovah of hosts had left unto us a very small remnant, we should have been as Sodom, we should have been like unto Gomorrah. [57] Then came touch of the enemy, the appearance of armed bands, vistas down Jerusalem's favourite valleys of chariots, squadrons of horsemen emerging upon the plateaus to north and west of the city, heavy siege-towers and swarms of men innumerable. And Elam bare the quiver, with troops of men and horsemen; and Kir uncovered the shield. At last they saw their fears of fifty years face to face! Far-away names were standing by their gates, actual bowmen and flashing shields! As Jerusalem gazed upon the terrible Assyrian armaments, how many of her inhabitants remembered Isaiah's words delivered a generation before!--Behold, they shall come with speed swiftly; none shall be weary or stumble among them; neither shall the string of their loins be lax nor the latchet of their shoes be broken; whose arrows are sharp, and all their bows bent; their horses' hoofs shall be counted like flint, and their wheels like a whirlwind; their roaring shall be like a lion: they shall roar like young lions. For all this His anger is not turned away, but His hand is stretched out still.

There were, however, two supports, on which that distracted populace within the walls still steadied themselves. The one was the Temple-worship, the other the Egyptian alliance.

History has many remarkable instances of peoples betaking themselves in the hour of calamity to the energetic discharge of the public rites of religion. But such a resort is seldom, if ever, a real moral conversion. It is merely physical nervousness, apprehension for life, clutching at the one thing within reach that feels solid, which it abandons as soon as panic has passed. When the crowds in Jerusalem betook themselves to the Temple, with unwonted wealth of sacrifice, Isaiah denounced this as hypocrisy and futility. To what purpose is the multitude of your sacrifices unto Me? saith Jehovah.... I am weary to bear them. And when ye spread forth your hands, I will hide Mine eyes from you; yea, when ye make many prayers, I will not hear (i. 11-15).

Isaiah might have spared his scornful orders to the people to desist from worship. Soon afterwards they abandoned it of their own will, but from motives very different from those urged by him. The second support to which Jerusalem clung was the Egyptian alliance--the pet project of the party then in

Rev. George Adam Smith, M.A.

power. They had carried it to a successful issue, taunting Isaiah with their success. [58] He had continued to denounce it, and now the hour was approaching when their cleverness and confidence were to be put to the test. It was known in Jerusalem that an Egyptian army was advancing to Sennacherib, and politicians and people awaited the encounter with anxiety.

We are aware what happened. Egypt was beaten at Eltekeh; the alliance was stamped a failure; Jerusalem's last worldly hope was taken from her. When the news reached the city, something took place, of which our moral judgement tells us more than any actual record of facts. The Government of Hezekiah gave way; the rulers, whose courage and patriotism had been identified with the Egyptian alliance, lost all hope for their country, and fled, as Isaiah puts it, en masse (xxii. 3). There was no battle, no defeat at arms (id. 2, 3); but the Jewish State collapsed.

Then, when the last material hope of Judah fell, fell her religion too. The Egyptian disappointment, while it drove the rulers out of their false policies, drove the people out of their unreal worship. What had been a city of devotees became in a moment a city of revellers. Formerly all had been sacrifices and worship, but now feasting and blasphemy. Behold, joy and gladness, slaying oxen and killing sheep, eating flesh and drinking wine: Let us eat and drink, for to-morrow we die (id. 13. The reference of ver. 12 is probably to chap. i.).

Now all Isaiah's ministry had been directed just against these two things: the Egyptian alliance and the purely formal observance of religion--trust in the world and trust in religiousness. And together both of these had given way, and the Assyrian was at the gates. Truly it was the hour of Isaiah's vindication. Yet--and this is the tragedy--it had come too late. The prophet could not use it. The two things he said would collapse had collapsed, but for the people there seemed now no help to be justified from the thing which he said would remain. What was the use of the city's deliverance, when the people themselves had failed! The feelings of triumph, which the prophet might have expressed, were swallowed up in unselfish grief over the fate of his wayward and abandoned Jerusalem.

What aileth thee now--and in these words we can hear the old man addressing his fickle child, whose changefulness by this time he knew so well--what aileth thee now that thou art wholly gone up to the housetops--we see him standing at his door watching this ghastly holiday--O thou that art full of shoutings, a tumultuous city, a joyous town? What are you rejoicing at in such an hour as this, when you have not even the bravery of your soldiers to celebrate, when you are without that pride which has brought songs from the lips of a defeated people as they learned that their sons had fallen with their faces to the foe, and has made even the wounds of the dead borne through the gate lips of triumph, calling to festival! For thy slain are not slain with the sword, neither are they dead in battle.

All thy chiefs fled in heaps;
Without bow they were taken:
All thine that were found were taken in heaps;
From far had they run.
Wherefore I say, Look away from me;
Let me make bitterness bitterer by weeping.
Press not to comfort me
For the ruin of the daughter of my people.

Urge not your mad holiday upon me! For a day of discomfiture and of breaking and of perplexity hath the Lord, Jehovah of hosts, in the valley of vision, a breaking down of the wall and a crying to the mountain. These few words of prose, which follow the pathetic elegy, have a finer pathos still. The cumulative force of the successive clauses is very impressive: disappointment at the eleventh hour; the sense of a being trampled and overborne by sheer brute force; the counsels, courage, hope and faith of fifty years crushed to blank perplexity, and all this from Himself--the Lord, Jehovah of hosts--in the very valley of vision, the home of prophecy; as if He had meant of purpose to destroy these long confidences of the past on the floor where they had been wrestled for and asserted, and not by the force of the foe, but by the folly of His own people, to make them ashamed. The last clause crashes out the effect of it all; every spiritual rampart and refuge torn down, there is nothing left but an appeal to the hills to fall and cover us--a breaking down of the wall and a crying to the mountain.

On the brink of the precipice, Isaiah draws back for a moment, to describe with some of his old fire the appearance of the besiegers (vv. 6-8a). And this suggests what kind of preparation Jerusalem had made for her foe--every kind, says Isaiah, but the supreme one. The arsenal, Solomon's forest-house, with its cedar pillars, had been looked to (ver. 8), the fortifications inspected and increased, and the suburban waters brought within them (vv. 9-11a). But ye looked not unto Him that had done this, who had brought this providence upon you; neither had ye respect unto Him that fashioned it long ago, whose own plan it had been. To your alliances and fortifications you fled in the hour of calamity, but not to Him in whose guidance the course of calamity lay. And therefore, when your engineering and diplomacy failed you, your religion vanished with them. In that day did the Lord, Jehovah of hosts, call to weeping, and to mourning, and to baldness, and to girding with sackcloth; but, behold, joy and gladness, slaying oxen and killing sheep, eating flesh and drinking wine: Let us eat and drink, for to-morrow we shall die. It was the dropping of the mask. For half a century this people had worshipped God, but they had never trusted Him beyond the limits of their treaties and their bulwarks. And so when their allies were defeated, and their walls began to tremble, their religion, bound up with these things, collapsed also; they ceased even to be men, crying like beasts, Let us eat and drink, for to-morrow we die. For such a state of mind Isaiah will hold out no promise; it is the sin against the Holy Ghost, and for it there is no forgiveness. And Jehovah of hosts revealed Himself in mine ears. Surely this iniquity shall not be purged from you till ye die, saith the Lord, Jehovah of hosts.

Back forty years the word had been, Go and tell this people, Hear ye indeed, but understand not; and see ye indeed, but perceive not. Make the heart of this people fat, and make their ears heavy, and shut their eyes, lest they see with their eyes, and hear with their ears, and understand with their heart, and turn again and be healed. What happened now was only what was foretold then: And if there be yet a tenth in it, it shall again be for consumption. That radical revision of judgement was now being literally fulfilled, when Isaiah, sure at last of his remnant within the walls of Jerusalem, was forced for their sin to condemn even them to death.

***

Nevertheless, Isaiah had still respect to the ultimate survival of a remnant. How firmly he believed in it could not be more clearly illustrated than by the fact that when he had so absolutely devoted his fellow-citizens to destruction he also took the most practical means for securing a better political future. If there is any reason, it can only be this, for putting the second section of chap. xxii., which advocates a change of ministry in the city (vv. 15-22), so close to the first, which sees ahead nothing but destruction for the State (vv. 1-14).

The mayor of the palace at this time was one Shebna, also called minister or deputy (lit. friend of the king). That his father is not named implies perhaps that Shebna was a foreigner; his own name betrays a Syrian origin; and he has been justly supposed to be the leader of the party then in power, whose policy was the Egyptian alliance, and whom in these latter years Isaiah had so frequently denounced as the root of Judah's bitterness. To this unfamilied intruder, who had sought to establish himself in Jerusalem, after the manner of those days, by hewing himself a great sepulchre, Isaiah brought sentence of violent banishment: Behold, Jehovah will be hurling, hurling thee away, thou big man, and crumpling, crumpling thee together. He will roll, roll thee on, thou rolling-stone, like a ball thrown out on broad level ground; there shall thou die, and there shall be the chariots of thy glory, thou shame of the house of thy lord. And I thrust thee from thy post, and from thy station do they pull thee down. This vagabond was not to die in his bed, nor to be gathered in his big tomb to the people on whom he had foisted himself. He should continue a rolling-stone. For him, like Cain, there was a land of Nod; and upon it he was to find a vagabond's death.

To fill this upstart's place, Isaiah solemnly designated a man with a father: Eliakim, the son of Hilkiah. The formulas he uses are perhaps the official ones customary upon induction to an office. But it may be also, that Isaiah has woven into these some expressions of even greater promise than usual. For this change of office-bearers was critical, and the overthrow of the "party of action" meant to Isaiah the beginning of the blessed future. And it shall come to pass that in that day I will call My servant Eliakim, the son of Hilkiah; and I will clothe him with thy robe, and with thy girdle will I strengthen him, and thine administration will I give into his hand, and he shall be for a father to the inhabitant of Jerusalem and to the house of Judah. And I will set the key of the house of David upon his shoulder; and he shall open, and none shut: and he shall shut, and none open. And I will hammer him in, a nail in a firm place, and he shall be for a throne of glory to his father's house. Thus to the last Isaiah will not allow Shebna to forget that he is without root among the people of God, that he has neither father nor family.

But a family is a temptation, and the weight of it may drag even the man of the Lord's own hammering out of his place. This very year we find Eliakim in Shebna's post, [59] and Shebna reduced to be secretary; but Eliakim's family seem to have taken advantage of their relative's position, and either at the time he was designated, or more probably later, Isaiah wrote two sentences of warning upon the dangers of nepotism. Catching at the figure, with which his designation of Eliakim closed, that Eliakim would be a peg in a solid wall, a throne on which the glory of his father's house might settle, Isaiah reminds the much-encumbered statesman that the firmest peg will give way if you hang too much on it, the strongest man be pulled down by his dependent and indolent family. They shall hang upon him all the weight of his father's house, the scions and the offspring (terms contrasted as degrees of worth), all the little vessels, from the vessels of cups to all the vessels of flagons. In that day, saith Jehovah of hosts, shall the peg that was knocked into a firm place give way, and it shall be knocked out and fall, and down shall be cut the burden that was upon it, for Jehovah hath spoken.

So we have not one, but a couple of tragedies. Eliakim, the son of Hilkiah, follows Shebna, the son

Rev. George Adam Smith, M.A.

of Nobody. The fate of the overburdened nail is as grievous as that of the rolling stone. It is easy to pass this prophecy over as a trivial incident; but when we have carefully analysed each verse, restored to the words their exact shade of signification, and set them in their proper contrasts, we perceive the outlines of two social dramas, which it requires very little imagination to invest with engrossing moral interest.

Footnotes:

54. Records of the Past, i. 33 ff. vii.; Schrader's Cuneiform Inscriptions and the Old Testament (Whitehouse's translation).
55. Records of the Past, i. 38; vii. 62.
56. Ibid., i., 40; Schrader, i., 286.
57. Chap. i. 7-9.
58. See p. 238.
59. Isa. xxxvi. 3.

CHAPTER XX

THE TURN OF THE TIDE: MORAL EFFECTS OF FORGIVENESS.

Isaiah xxii., contrasted with xxxiii. (701 B.C.).

The collapse of Jewish faith and patriotism in the face of the enemy was complete. Final and absolute did Isaiah's sentence ring out: Surely this iniquity shall not be purged from you till ye die, saith Jehovah of hosts. So we learn from chap. xxii., written, as we conceive, in 701, when the Assyrian armies had at last invested Jerusalem. But in chap. xxxiii., which critics unite in placing a few months later in the same year, Isaiah's tone is entirely changed. He hurls the woe of the Lord upon the Assyrians; confidently announces their immediate destruction; turns, while the whole city's faith hangs upon him, in supplication to the Lord; and announces the stability of Jerusalem, her peace, her glory and the forgiveness of all her sins. It is this great moral difference between chaps. xxii. and xxxiii.-- prophecies that must have been delivered within a few months of each other--which this chapter seeks to expound.

In spite of her collapse, as pictured in chap. xxii., Jerusalem was not taken. Her rulers fled; her people, as if death were certain, betook themselves to dissipation; and yet the city did not fall into the hands of the Assyrian. Sennacherib himself does not pretend to have taken Jerusalem. He tells us how closely he invested Jerusalem, but he does not add that he took it, a silence which is the more significant that he records the capture of every other town which his armies attempted. He says that Hezekiah offered him tribute, and details the amount he received. He adds that the tribute was not paid at Jerusalem (as it would have been had Jerusalem been conquered), but that for "the payment of the tribute and the performance of homage" Hezekiah "despatched his envoy" [60] to him when he was at some distance from Jerusalem. All this agrees with the Bible narrative. In the book of Kings we are told how Hezekiah sent to the King of Assyria at Lachish, saying, I have offended; return from me; that which thou puttest upon me I will bear. And the King of Assyria appointed unto Hezekiah, King of Judah, three hundred talents of silver and thirty talents of gold. And Hezekiah gave him all the silver that was found in the house of Jehovah and in the treasures of the king's house. At the same time did Hezekiah cut off the gold from the doors of the temple of Jehovah, and from the pillars which Hezekiah, King of Judah, had overlaid, and gave it to the King of Assyria. [61] It was indeed a sore submission, when even the Temple of the Lord had to be stripped of its gold. But it purchased the relief of the city; and no price was too high to pay for that at such a moment as the present, when the populace was demoralised. We may even see Isaiah's hand in the submission. The integrity of Jerusalem was the one fact on which the word of the Lord had been pledged, on which the promised remnant could be rallied. The Assyrian must not be able to say that he has made Zion's God like the gods of the heathen, and her people must see that even when they have given her up Jehovah can hold her for Himself, though in holding He tear and wound (xxxi. 4). The Temple is greater than the gold of the Temple; let even the latter be stripped off and sold to the heathen if it can purchase the integrity of the former. So Jerusalem remained inviolate; she was still the virgin, the daughter of Zion.

And now upon the redeemed city Isaiah could proceed to rebuild the shattered faith and morals of her people. He could say to them, "Everything has turned out as, by the word of the Lord, I said it should. The Assyrian has come down; Egypt has failed you. Your politicians, with their scorn of religion and their confidence in their cleverness, have deserted you. I told you that your numberless sacrifices and pomp of unreal religion would avail you nothing in your day of disaster, and lo! when this came, your religion collapsed. Your abounding wickedness, I said, could only close in your ruin and desertion by God. But one promise I kept steadfast: that Jerusalem would not fall; and to your penitence, whenever it should be real, I assured forgiveness. Jerusalem stands to-day, according to my word; and I repeat my gospel. History has vindicated my word, but Come now, let us bring our reasoning to a close, saith the Lord; though your sins be as scarlet, they shall be white as snow: though they be red like crimson, they shall be as wool. I call upon you to build again on your redeemed city, and by the grace of this pardon, the fallen ruins of your life."

Some such sermon--if indeed not actually part of chap. i.--we must conceive Isaiah to have delivered to the people when Hezekiah had bought off Sennacherib, for we find the state of Jerusalem suddenly altered. Instead of the panic, which imagined the daily capture of the city, and rushed in hectic holiday to the housetops, crying, Let us eat and drink, for to-morrow we die, we see the citizens back upon the walls, trembling yet trusting. Instead of sweeping past Isaiah in their revelry and leaving him to feel that after forty years of travail he had lost all his influence with them, we see them gathering round about him as their single hope and confidence (xxxvii.). King and people look to Isaiah as their counsellor, and cannot answer the enemy without consulting him. What a change from the days of the Egyptian alliance, embassies sent off against his remonstrance, and intrigues developed without his knowledge; when Ahaz insulted him, and the drunken magnates mimicked him, and, in order to rouse an indolent people, he had to walk about the streets of Jerusalem for three years, stripped like a captive! Truly this was the day of Isaiah's triumph, when God by events vindicated his prophecy, and all the people acknowledged his leadership.

It was the hour of the prophet's triumph, but the nation had as yet only trials before it. God has not done with nations or men when He has forgiven them. This people, whom of His grace, and in spite of themselves, God had saved from destruction, stood on the brink of another trial. God had given them a new lease of life, but it was immediately to pass through the furnace. They had bought off Sennacherib, but Sennacherib came back.

When Sennacherib got the tribute, he repented of the treaty he had made with Hezekiah. He may have felt that it was a mistake to leave in his rear so powerful a fortress, while he had still to complete the overthrow of the Egyptians. So, in spite of the tribute, he sent a force back to Jerusalem to demand her surrender. We can imagine the moral effect upon King Hezekiah and his people. It was enough to sting the most demoralised into courage. Sennacherib had doubtless expected so pliant a king and so crushed a people to yield at once. But we may confidently picture the joy of Isaiah, as he felt the return of the Assyrians to be the very thing required to restore spirit to his demoralised countrymen. Here was a foe, whom they could face with a sense of justice, and not, as they had met him before, in carnal confidence and the pride of their own cleverness. Now was to be a war not, like former wars, undertaken merely for party glory, but with the purest feelings of patriotism and the firmest sanctions of religion, a campaign to be entered upon, not with Pharaoh's support and the strength of Egyptian chariots, but with God Himself as an ally--of which it could be said to Judah, Thy righteousness shall go before thee, and the glory of the Lord shall be thy rereward.

On what free, exultant wings the spirit of Isaiah must have risen to the sublime occasion! We know him as by nature an ardent patriot and passionate lover of his city, but through circumstance her pitiless critic and unsparing judge. In all the literature of patriotism there are no finer odes and orations than those which it owes to him; from no lips came stronger songs of war, and no heart rejoiced more in the valour that turns the battle from the gate. But till now Isaiah's patriotism had been chiefly a conscience of his country's sins, his passionate love for Jerusalem repressed by as stern a loyalty to righteousness, and all his eloquence and courage spent in holding his people from war and persuading them to returning and rest. At last this conflict is at an end. The stubbornness of Judah, which has divided like some rock the current of her prophet's energies, and forced it back writhing and eddying upon itself, is removed. Isaiah's faith and his patriotism run free with the force of twin-tides in one channel, and we hear the fulness of their roar as they leap together upon the enemies of God and the fatherland. Woe to thee, thou spoiler, and thou wast not spoiled, thou treacherous dealer, and they did not deal treacherously with thee! Whenever thou ceasest to spoil, thou shall be spoiled; and whenever thou hast made an end to deal treacherously, they shall deal treacherously with thee. O Jehovah, be gracious unto us; for Thee have we waited: be Thou their arm every morning, our salvation also in the time of trouble. From the noise of a surging the peoples have fled; from the lifting up of Thyself the nations are scattered. And gathered is your spoil, the gathering of the caterpillar; like the leaping of locusts, they are leaping upon it. Exalted is Jehovah; yea, He dwelleth on high: He hath filled Zion with justice and righteousness. And there shall be stability of thy times, wealth of salvation, wisdom and knowledge; the fear of Jehovah, it shall be his treasure (xxxiii. 1-6).

Thus, then, do we propose to bridge the gulf which lies between chaps. i. and xxii. on the one hand and chap. xxxiii. on the other. If they are all to be dated from the year 701, some such bridge is necessary. And the one we have traced is both morally sufficient and in harmony with what we know to have been the course of events.

What do we learn from it all? We learn a great deal upon that truth which chap. xxxiii. closes by announcing--the truth of Divine forgiveness.

The forgiveness of God is the foundation of every bridge from a hopeless past to a courageous present. That God can make the past be for guilt as though it had not been is always to Isaiah the assurance of the future. An old Greek miniature [62] represents him with Night behind him, veiled and sullen and holding a reversed torch. But before him stands Dawn and Innocence, a little child, with bright face and forward step and torch erect and burning. From above a hand pours light upon the face of the prophet, turned upwards. It is the message of a Divine pardon. Never did prophet more wearily feel the moral continuity of the generations, the lingering and ineradicable effects of crime. Only faith in a pardoning God could have enabled him, with such conviction of the inseparableness of yesterday and to-morrow, to make divorce between them, and turning his back on the past, as this miniature represents, hail the future as Immanuel, a child of infinite promise. From exposing and scourging the past, from proving it corrupt and pregnant with poison for all the future, Isaiah will turn on a single verse, and give us a future without war, sorrow or fraud. His pivot is ever the pardon of God. But nowhere is his faith in this so powerful, his turning upon it so swift, as at this period of Jerusalem's collapse, when, having sentenced the people to death for their iniquity--It was revealed in mine ears by Jehovah of hosts, Surely this iniquity shall not be purged from you till ye die, saith the Lord, Jehovah of hosts (xxii. 14)--he swings round on his promise of a little before--Though your sins be as scarlet, they shall be white as snow--and to the people's penitence pronounces in the last verse of chap. xxxiii. a final absolution: The inhabitant shall not say, I am sick; the people that dwell therein are forgiven their iniquity. If chap. xxxiii. be, as many think, Isaiah's latest oracle, then we have the literal crown of all his prophesying in these two words: forgiven iniquity. It is as he put it early that same year: Come now and let us bring our reasoning to a close; though your sins be as scarlet, they shall be as white as snow: though they be red like crimson, they shall be as wool. If man is to have a future, this must be the conclusion of all his past.

But the absoluteness of God's pardon, making the past as though it had not been, is not the only lesson which the spiritual experience of Jerusalem in that awful year of 701 has for us. Isaiah's gospel of forgiveness is nothing less than this: that when God gives pardon He gives Himself. The name of the blessed future, which is entered through pardon--as in that miniature, a child--is Immanuel: God-with-us. And if it be correct that we owe the forty-sixth Psalm to these months when the Assyrian came back upon Jerusalem, then we see how the city, that had abandoned God, is yet able to sing when she is pardoned, God is our refuge and our strength, a very present help in the midst of troubles. And this gospel of forgiveness is not only Isaiah's. According to the whole Bible, there is but one thing which separates man from God--that is sin, and when sin is done away with, God cannot be kept from man. In giving pardon to man, God gives back to man Himself. How gloriously evident this truth becomes in the New Testament! Christ, who is set before us as the Lamb of God, who beareth the sins of the world, is also Immanuel--God-with-us. The Sacrament, which most plainly seals to the believer the value of the One Sacrifice for sin, is the Sacrament in which the believer feeds upon Christ and appropriates Him. The sinner, who comes to Christ, not only receives pardon for Christ's sake, but receives Christ. Forgiveness means nothing less than this: that in giving pardon God gives Himself.

But if forgiveness mean all this, then the objections frequently brought against a conveyance of it so unconditioned as that of Isaiah fall to the ground. Forgiveness of such a kind cannot be either unjust or demoralising. On the contrary, we see Jerusalem permoralised by it. At first, it is true, the sense of weakness and fear abounds, as we learn from the narrative in chaps. xxxvi. and xxxvii. But where there was vanity, recklessness and despair, giving way to dissipation, there is now humility, discipline and a leaning upon God, that are led up to confidence and exultation. Jerusalem's experience is just another proof that any moral results are possible to so great a process as the return of God to the soul. Awful is the responsibility of them who receive such a Gift and such a Guest; but the sense of that awfulness is the atmosphere, in which obedience and holiness and the courage that is born of both love best to grow. One can understand men scoffing at messages of pardon so unconditioned as Isaiah's, who think they "mean no more than a clean slate." Taken in this sense, the gospel of forgiveness must prove a savour of death unto death. But just as Jerusalem interpreted the message of her pardon to mean that God is in the midst of her; she shall not be moved, and straightway obedience was in all her hearts, and courage upon all her walls, so neither to us can be futile the New Testament form of the same gospel, which makes our pardoned soul the friend of God, accepted in the Beloved, and our body His holy temple.

Upon one other point connected with the forgiveness of sins we get instruction from the experience of Jerusalem. A man has difficulty in squaring his sense of forgiveness with the return on the back of it of his old temptations and trials, with the hostility of fortune and with the inexorableness of nature. Grace has spoken to his heart, but Providence bears more hard upon him than ever. Pardon does not change the outside of life; it does not immediately modify the movements of history, or suspend the laws of nature. Although God has forgiven Jerusalem, Assyria comes back to besiege her. Although the penitent be truly reconciled to God, the constitutional results of his fall remain: the frequency of temptation, the power of habit, the bias and facility downwards, the physical and social consequences. Pardon changes none of these things. It does not keep off the Assyrians.

But if pardon means the return of God to the soul, then in this we have the secret of the return of the foe. Men could not try nor develop a sense of the former except by their experience of the latter. We have seen why Isaiah must have welcomed the perfidious reappearance of the Assyrians after he had helped to buy them off. Nothing could better test the sincerity of Jerusalem's repentance, or rally her dissipated forces. Had the Assyrians not returned, the Jews would have had no experimental proof of God's restored presence, and the great miracle would never have happened that rang through human history for evermore--a trumpet-call to faith in the God of Israel. And so still the Lord scourgeth every son whom He receiveth, because He would put our penitence to the test; because He would discipline our disorganised affections, and give conscience and will a chance of wiping out defeat by victory;

because He would baptize us with the most powerful baptism possible--the sense of being trusted once more to face the enemy upon the fields of our disgrace.

That is why the Assyrians came back to Jerusalem, and that is why temptations and penalties still pursue the penitent and forgiven.

Footnotes:

60. Schrader, Cuneiform Inscriptions, O.T., i., p. 286.

61. 2 Kings xviii. 13-16. Here closes a paragraph. Ver. 17 begins to describe what Sennacherib did, in spite of Hezekiah's submission. He had withdrawn the army that had invested Jerusalem, for Hezekiah purchased its withdrawal by the tribute he sent. But Sennacherib, in spite of this, sent another corps of war against Jerusalem, which second attack is described in ver. 17 and onwards.

62. Didron Christian Iconography, fig. 52.

CHAPTER XXI

OUR GOD A CONSUMING FIRE.

Isaiah xxxiii. (701 B.C.).

We have seen how the sense of forgiveness and the exultant confidence, which fill chap. xxxiii., were brought about within a few months after the sentence of death, that cast so deep a gloom on chap. xxii. We have expounded some of the contents of chap. xxxiii., but have not exhausted the chapter; and in particular we have not touched one of Isaiah's principles, which there finds perhaps its finest expression: the consuming righteousness of God.

There is no doubt that chap. xxxiii. refers to the sudden disappearance of the Assyrian from the walls of Jerusalem. It was written, part perhaps on the eve of that deliverance, part immediately after morning broke upon the vanished host. Before those verses which picture the disappearance of the investing army, we ought in strict chronological order to take the narrative in chaps. xxxvi. and xxxvii.--the return of the besiegers, the insolence of the Rabshakeh, the prostration of Hezekiah, Isaiah's solitary faith, and the sudden disappearance of the Assyrian. It will be more convenient, however, since we have already entered chap. xxxiii., to finish it, and then to take the narrative of the events which led up to it.

The opening verses of chap. xxxiii. fit the very moment of the crisis, as if Isaiah had flung them across the walls in the teeth of the Rabshakeh and the second embassy from Sennacherib, who had returned to demand the surrender of the city in spite of Hezekiah's tribute for her integrity: Woe to thee, thou spoiler, and thou wast not spoiled, thou treacherous dealer, and they did not deal treacherously with thee! When thou ceasest to spoil, thou shalt be spoiled; and when thou makest an end to deal treacherously, they shall deal treacherously with thee. Then follows the prayer, as already quoted, and the confidence in the security of Jerusalem (ver. 2). A new paragraph (vv. 7-12) describes Rabshakeh and his company demanding the surrender of the city; the disappointment of the ambassadors who had been sent to treat with Sennacherib (ver. 7); the perfidy of the great king, who had broken the covenant they had made with him and swept his armies back upon Judah (ver. 8); the disheartening of the land under this new shock (ver. 9); and the resolution of the Lord now to rise and scatter the invaders: Now will I arise, saith Jehovah; now will I lift up Myself; now will I be exalted. Ye shall conceive chaff; ye shall bring forth stubble; your breath is a fire, that shall devour you. And the peoples shall be as the burnings of lime, as thorns cut down that are burned in the fire (vv. 10-12).

After an application of this same fire of God's righteousness to the sinners within Jerusalem, to which we shall presently return, the rest of the chapter pictures the stunned populace awaking to the fact that they are free. Is the Assyrian really gone, or do the Jews dream as they crowd the walls, and see no trace of him? Have they all vanished--the Rabshakeh, by the conduit of the upper pool, with his loud voice and insults; the scribes to whom they handed the tribute, and who prolonged the agony by counting it under their eyes; the scouts and engineers insolently walking about Zion and mapping out her walls for the assault; the close investment of barbarian hordes, with their awesome speech and uncouth looks! Where is he that counted? where is he that weighed the tribute? where is he that counted the towers? Thou shall not see the fierce people, a people of a deep speech that thou canst not perceive, of a strange tongue that thou canst not understand. They have vanished. Hezekiah may lift his head again. O people--sore at heart to see thy king in sackcloth and ashes [63] as the enemy devoured province after province of thy land and cooped thee up within the narrow walls, thou scarcely didst dare to peep across--take courage, the terror is gone! A king in his beauty thine eyes shall see; they shall behold the land spreading very far forth (ver. 17). We had thought to die in the restlessness and horror of war, never again to know what stable life and regular worship were, our Temple services interrupted, our home a battlefield. But look upon Zion; behold again she is the city of our solemn diets; thine eyes shall see Jerusalem a quiet habitation, a tent that shall not be removed, the stakes whereof shall never be plucked up, neither shall the cords thereof be broken. But there Jehovah, whom we have known only for affliction, shall be in majesty for us. Other peoples have their natural defences, Assyria and Egypt their Euphrates and Nile; but God Himself shall be for us a place of rivers, streams, broad on both hands, on which never a galley shall go, nor gallant ship shall pass upon it. Without sign of battle, God shall be our refuge and our strength. It was that marvellous deliverance of Jerusalem by the hand of God, with no effort of human war, which caused Isaiah to invest with such majesty the meagre rock, its squalid surroundings and paltry defences. The insignificant and waterless city was glorious to the prophet because God was in her. One of the richest imaginations which patriot ever poured upon his fatherland was inspired by the simplest faith saint ever breathed. Isaiah strikes again the old keynote (chap. viii.) about the waterlessness of Jerusalem. We have to keep in mind the Jews' complaints of this, in order to understand what the forty-sixth Psalm means when it says, There is a river the streams whereof make glad the city of our God, the holy place of the tabernacles of the Most High--or what Isaiah means when he says, Glorious shall Jehovah be unto us, a place of broad rivers and streams. Yea, he adds, Jehovah is everything to us: Jehovah is our Judge; Jehovah is our Lawgiver; Jehovah is our King: He will save us.

***

Such were the feelings aroused in Jerusalem by the sudden relief of the city. Some of the verses, which we have scarcely touched, we will now consider more fully as the expression of a doctrine which runs throughout Isaiah, and indeed is one of his two or three fundamental truths--that the righteousness of God is an all-pervading atmosphere, an atmosphere that wears and burns.

For forty years the prophet had been preaching to the Jews his gospel, God-with-us; but they never awakened to the reality of the Divine presence till they saw it in the dispersion of the Assyrian army. Then God became real to them (ver. 14). The justice of God, preached so long by Isaiah, had always seemed something abstract. Now they saw how concrete it was. It was not only a doctrine: it was a fact. It was a fact that was a fire. Isaiah had often called it a fire; they thought this was rhetoric. But now they saw the actual burning--the peoples as the burning of lime, as thorns cut down that are burned in the fire. And when they felt the fire so near, each sinner of them awoke to the fact that he had something burnable in himself, something which could as little stand the fire as the Assyrians could. There was no difference in this fire outside and inside the walls. What it burned there it would burn here. Nay, was not Jerusalem the dwelling-place of God, and Ariel the very hearth and furnace of the fire which they saw consume the Assyrians? Who, they cried in their terror--Who among us shall dwell with the devouring fire? Who among us shall dwell with everlasting burnings?

We are familiar with Isaiah's fundamental God-with-us, and how it was spoken not for mercy only, but for judgement (chap. viii.). If God-with-us meant love with us, salvation with us, it meant also holiness with us, judgement with us, the jealousy of God breathing upon what is impure, false and proud. Isaiah felt this so hotly, that his sense of it has broken out into some of the fieriest words in all prophecy. In his younger days he told the citizens not to provoke the eyes of God's glory, as if Heaven had fastened on their life two gleaming orbs, not only to pierce them with its vision, but to consume them with its wrath. Again, in the lowering cloud of calamity he had seen lips of indignation, a tongue as a devouring fire, and in the overflowing stream which finally issued from it the hot breath of the Almighty. These are unforgettable descriptions of the ceaseless activity of Divine righteousness in the life of man. They set our imaginations on fire with the prophet's burning belief in this. But they are excelled by another, more frequently used by Isaiah, wherein he likens the holiness of God to an universal and constant fire. To Isaiah life was so penetrated by the active justice of God, that he described it as bathed in fire, as blown through with fire. Righteousness was no mere doctrine to this prophet: it was the most real thing in history; it was the presence which pervaded and explained all phenomena. We shall understand the difference between Isaiah and his people if we have ever for our eyes' sake looked at a great conflagration through a coloured glass which allowed us to see the solid materials--stone, wood and iron--but prevented us from perceiving the flames and shimmering heat. To look thus is to see pillars, lintels and cross-beams twist and fall, crumble and fade; but how inexplicable the process seems! Take away the glass, and everything is clear. The fiery element is filling all the interstices, that were blank to us before, and beating upon the solid material. The heat becomes visible, shimmering even where there is no flame. Just so had it been with the sinners in Judah these forty years. Their society and politics, individual fortunes and careers, personal and national habits--the home, the Church, the State--common outlines and shapes of life--were patent to every eye, but no man could explain the constant decay and diminution, because all were looking at life through a glass darkly. Isaiah alone faced life with open vision, which filled up for him the interstices of experience and gave terrible explanation to fate. It was a vision that nearly scorched the eyes out of him. Life as he saw it was steeped in flame--the glowing righteousness of God. Jerusalem was full of the spirit of justice, the spirit of burning. The light of Israel is for a fire, and his Holy One for a flame. The Assyrian empire, that vast erection which the strong hands of kings had reared, was simply their pyre, made ready for the burning. For a Topheth is prepared of old; yea, for the king is made ready; He hath made it deep and large; the pile thereof is fire and much wood; the breath of Jehovah, like a stream of brimstone, doth kindle it. [64] So Isaiah saw life, and flashed it on his countrymen. At last the glass fell from their eyes also, and they cried aloud, Who among us shall dwell with the devouring fire? Who among us shall dwell with everlasting burnings? Isaiah replied that there is one thing which can survive the universal flame, and that is character: He that walketh righteously and speaketh uprightly; he that despiseth the gain of fraud, that shaketh his hands from the holding of bribes, that stoppeth his ears from the hearing of blood, and shutteth his eyes from looking on evil, he shall dwell on high: his place of defence shall be the munitions of rocks: his bread shall be given him: his water shall be sure.

***

Isaiah's Vision of Fire suggests two thoughts to us.

1. Have we done well to confine our horror of the consuming fires of righteousness to the next life? If we would but use the eyes which Scripture lends us, the rifts of prophetic vision and awakened conscience by which the fogs of this world and of our own hearts are rent, we should see fires as fierce, a consumption as pitiless, about us here as ever the conscience of a startled sinner fearfully looked for across the grave. Nay, have not the fires, with which the darkness of eternity has been made lurid, themselves been kindled at the burnings of this life? Is it not because men have felt how hot this world was being made for sin that they have had a certain fearful expectation of judgement and the fierceness of fire? We shudder at the horrible pictures of hell which some older theologians and poets have painted for us; but it was not morbid fancy, nor the barbarism of their age nor their own heart's cruelty that inspired these men. It was their hot honour for the Divine holiness; it was their experience of how pitiless to sin Providence is already in this life; it was their own scorched senses and affections--brands, as many honest men among them felt themselves, plucked from the burning. Our God is a consuming fire--here as well as yonder. Hell has borrowed her glare from the imagination of men aflame with the real fieriness of life, and may be--more truly than of old--pictured as the dead and hollow cinder left by those fires, of which, as every true man's conscience is aware, this life is full. It was not hell that created conscience; it was conscience that created hell, and conscience was fired by the vision which fired Isaiah--of all life aglow with the righteousness of God--God with us, as He was with Jerusalem, a spirit of burning and a spirit of justice. This is the pantheism of conscience, and it stands to reason. God is the one power of life. What can exist beside Him except what is like Him? Nothing--sooner or later nothing but what is like Him. The will that is as His will, the heart that is pure, the character that is transparent-- only these dwell with the everlasting fire, and burning with God, as the bush which Moses saw, are nevertheless not consumed. Let us lay it to heart--Isaiah has nothing to tell us about hell-fire, but a great deal about the pitiless justice of God in this life.

2. The second thought suggested by Isaiah's Vision of Life is a comparison of it with the theory of life which is fashionable to-day. Isaiah's figure for life was a burning. Ours is a battle, and at first sight ours looks the truer. Seen through a formula which has become everywhere fashionable, life is a fierce and fascinating warfare. Civilised thought, when asked to describe any form of life or to account for a death or survival, most monotonously replies, "The struggle for existence." The sociologist has borrowed the phrase from the biologist, and it is on everybody's lips to describe their idea of human life. It is uttered by the historian when he would explain the disappearance of this national type, the prevalence of that one. The economist traces depression and failures, the fatal fevers of speculation, the cruelties and bad humours of commercial life, to the same source. A merchant with profits lessening and failure before him relieves his despair and apologizes to his pride with the words, "It is all due to competition." Even character and the spiritual graces are sometimes set down as results of the same material process. Some have sought to deduce from it all intelligence, others more audaciously all ethics; and it is certain that in the silence of men's hearts after a moral defeat there is no excuse more frequently offered to conscience by will than that the battle was too hot.

But fascinating as life is when seen through this formula, does not the formula act on our vision precisely as the glass we supposed, which when we look through it on a conflagration shows us the solid matter and the changes through which this passes, but hides from us the real agent? One need not deny the reality of the struggle for existence, or that its results are enormous. We struggle with each other, and affect each other for good and for evil, sometimes past all calculation. But we do not fight in a vacuum. Let Isaiah's vision be the complement of our own feeling. We fight in an atmosphere that affects every one of us far more powerfully than the opposing wits or wills of our fellow-men. Around us and through us, within and without as we fight, is the all-pervading righteousness of God; and it is far oftener the effects of this which we see in the falls and the changes of life than the effects of our struggle with each other, enormous though these may be. On this point there is an exact parallel between our days and the days of Isaiah. Then the politicians of Judah, looking through their darkened glass at life, said, Life is simply a war in which the strongest prevail, a game which the most cunning win. So they made fast their alliances, and were ready to meet the Assyrian, or they fled in panic before him, according as Egypt or he seemed the stronger. Isaiah saw that with Assyrian and Jew another Power was present--the real reason of every change in politics, collapse or crash in either of the empires--the active righteousness of God. Assyrian and Jew had not only to contend with each other. They were at strife with Him. We now see plainly that Isaiah was right. Far more operative than the intrigues of politicians or the pride of Assyria, because it used these simply as its mines and its fuel, was the law of righteousness, the spiritual force which is as impalpable as the atmosphere, yet strong to burn and try as a furnace seven times heated. And Isaiah is equally right for to-day. As we look at life through our fashionable formula it does seem a mass of struggle, in which we catch only now and then a glimpse of the decisions of righteousness, but the prevailing lawlessness of which we do not hesitate to make the reason of all that happens, and in particular the excuse of our own defeats. We are wrong. Righteousness is not an occasional spark; righteousness is the atmosphere. Though our dull eyes see it only now and then strike into flame in the battle of life, and take for granted that it is but the flash of meeting wits or of steel on steel, God's justice is everywhere, pervasive and pitiless, affecting the combatants far more than they have power to affect one another.

We shall best learn the truth of this in the way the sinners in Jerusalem learned it--each man first looking into himself. Who among us shall dwell with the everlasting burnings? Can we attribute all our defeats to the opposition that was upon us at the moment they occurred? When our temper failed, when our charity relaxed, when our resoluteness gave way, was it the hotness of debate, was it the pressure of the crowd, was it the sneer of the scorner, that was to blame? We all know that these were only the occasions of our defeats. Conscience tells us that the cause lay in a slothful or self-indulgent heart, which the corrosive atmosphere of Divine righteousness had been consuming, and which, sapped and hollow by its effect, gave way at every material shock.

With the knowledge that conscience gives us, let us now look at a kind of figure which must be within the horizon of all of us. Once it was the most commanding stature among its fellows, the straight back and broad brow of a king of men. But now what is the last sight of him that will remain with us, flung out there against the evening skies of his life? A bent back (we speak of character), a stooping face, the shrinking outlines of a man ready to collapse. It was not the struggle for existence that killed him, for he was born to prevail in it. It was the atmosphere that told on him. He carried in him that on which the atmosphere could not but tell. A low selfishness or passion inhabited him, and became the predominant part of him, so that his outward life was only its shell; and when the fire of God at last pierced this, he was as thorns cut down, that are burned in the fire.

We can explain much with the outward eye, but the most of the explanation lies beyond. Where our knowledge of a man's life ends, the great meaning of it often only begins. All the vacancy beyond the outline we see is full of that meaning. God is there, and God is a consuming fire. Let us not seek to explain lives only by what we see of them, the visible strife of man with man and nature. It is the invisible that contains the secret of what is seen. We see the shoulders stoop, but not the burden upon them; the face darken, but look in vain for what casts the shadow; the light sparkle in the eye, but cannot tell what star of hope its glance has caught. And even so when we behold fortune and character go down in the warfare of this world, we ought to remember that it is not always the things we see that are to blame for the fall, but that awful flame which, unseen by common man, has been revealed to the prophets of God.

Righteousness and retribution, then, are an atmosphere--not lines or laws that we may happen to stumble upon, not explosives, that, being touched, burst out on us, but the atmosphere--always about us and always at work, invisible and yet more mighty than aught we see. God, in whom we live and move and have our being, is a consuming fire.

Footnotes:

    63. Chap. xxxvii.
    64. Chaps. iv. 4; xxx. 33.

CHAPTER XXII

THE RABSHAKEH; OR, LAST TEMPTATIONS OF FAITH.

Isaiah xxxvi. (701 B.C.).

It remains for us now to follow in chaps. xxxvi., xxxvii., the historical narrative of the events, the moral results of which we have seen so vivid in chap. xxxiii.--the perfidious return of the Assyrians to Jerusalem after Hezekiah had bought them off and their final disappearance from the Holy Land.

This historical narrative has also its moral. It is not annals, but drama. The whole moral of Isaiah's prophesying is here flung into a duel between champions of the two tempers, which we have seen in perpetual conflict throughout his book. The two tempers are--on Isaiah's side an absolute and unselfish faith in God, Sovereign of the world and Saviour of His people; on the side of the Assyrians a bare, brutal confidence in themselves, in human cleverness and success, a vaunting contempt of righteousness and of pity. The main interest of Isaiah's book has consisted in the way these tempers oppose each other, and alternately influence the feeling of the Jewish community. That interest is now to culminate in the scene which brings near such thorough representatives of the two tempers as Isaiah and the Rabshakeh, with the crowd of wavering Jews between. Most strikingly, Assyria's last assault is not of force, but of speech, delivering upon faith the subtle arguments of the worldly temper; and as strikingly, while all official religion and power of State stand helpless against them, these arguments are met by the bare word of God. In this mere statement of the situation, however, we perceive that much more than the quarrel of a single generation is being decided. This scene is a parable of the everlasting struggle between faith and force, with doubt and despair between them. In the clever, self-confident, persuasive personage with two languages on his tongue and an army at his back; in the fluttered representatives of official religion who meet him and are afraid of the effect of his speech on the common people; in the ranks of dispirited men who hear the dialogue from the wall; in the sensitive king so aware of faith, and yet so helpless to bring faith forth to peace and triumph; and, in the background of the whole situation, the serene prophet of God, grasping only God's word, and by his own steadfastness carrying the city over the crisis and proving that faith indeed can be the substance of things hoped for--we have a phase of the struggle ordained unto every generation of men, and which is as fresh to-day as when Rabshakeh played the cynic and the scribes and elders filled the part of nervous defenders of the faith, under the walls of faith's fortress, two thousand five hundred years ago.

The Rabshakeh.

This word is a Hebrew transliteration of the Assyrian Rab-sak, chief of the officers. Though there is some doubt on the point, we may naturally presume from the duties he here discharges that the Rabshakeh was a civilian--probably the civil commissioner or political officer attached to the Assyrian army, which was commanded, according to 2 Kings xviii. 16, by the Tartan or commander-in-chief himself.

In all the Bible there is not a personage more clever than this Rabshakeh, nor more typical. He was an able deputy of the king who sent him, but he represented still more thoroughly the temper of the civilisation to which he belonged. There is no word of this man which is not characteristic. A clever, fluent diplomatist, with the traveller's knowledge of men and the conqueror's contempt for them, the Rabshakeh is the product of a victorious empire like the Assyrian, or, say, like the British. Our services sometimes turn out the like of him--a creature able to speak to natives in their own language, full and ready of information, mastering the surface of affairs at a glance, but always baffled by the deeper tides which sway nations; a deft player upon party interests and the superficial human passions, but unfit to touch the deep springs of men's religion and patriotism. Let us speak, however, with respect of the Rabshakeh. From his rank (Sayce calls him the Vizier), as well as from the cleverness with which he explains what we know to have been the policy of Sennacherib towards the populations of Syria, he may well have been the inspiring mind at this time of the great Assyrian empire--Sennacherib's Bismarck.

The Rabshakeh had strutted down from the great centre of civilisation, with its temper upon him, and all its great resources at his back, confident to twist these poor provincial tribes round his little finger. How petty he conceived them we infer from his never styling Hezekiah the king. This was to be an occasion for the Rabshakeh's own glorification. Jerusalem was to fall to his clever speeches. He had indeed the army behind him, but the work to be done was not the rough work of soldiers. All was to be managed by him, the civilian and orator. This fellow, with his two languages and clever address, was to step out in front of the army and finish the whole business.

The Rabshakeh spoke extremely well. With his first words he touched the sore point of Judah's policy: her trust in Egypt. On this he spoke like a very Isaiah. But he showed a deeper knowledge of Judah's internal affairs, and a subtler deftness in using it, when he referred to the matter of the altars. Hezekiah had abolished the high places in all parts of the land, and gathered the people to the central sanctuary in Jerusalem. The Assyrian knew that a number of Jews must look upon this disestablishment of religion in the provinces as likely to incur Jehovah's displeasure and turn Him against them. Therefore he said, But if thou say unto me, We trust in Jehovah our God, is not that He whose high places and whose altars Hezekiah hath taken away, and hath said to Judah and to Jerusalem, Ye shall worship before this altar? And then, having shaken their religious confidence, he made sport of their military strength. And finally he boldly asserted, Jehovah said unto me, Go up against this land and destroy it. All this shows a master in diplomacy, a most clever demagogue. The scribes and elders felt the edge, and begged him to sheathe it in a language unknown to the common people. But he, conscious of his power, spoke the more boldly, addressing himself directly to the poorer sort of the garrison, on whom the siege would press most heavily. His second speech to them is a good illustration of the policy pursued by Assyria at this time towards the cities of Palestine. We know from the annals of Sennacherib that his customary policy, to seduce the populations of a hostile State from allegiance to their rulers, had succeeded in other cases; and it was so plausibly uttered in this case, that it seemed likely to succeed again. To the common soldiers on the walls, with the prospect of being reduced to the foul rations of a prolonged siege (ver. 12), Sennacherib's ambassador offers rich and equal property and enjoyment. Make a treaty with me, and come out to me, and eat every one of his vine and every one of his fig tree, and drink ye every one of the water of his cistern, until I come and take you away to a land like your own land, a land of corn and grapes, a land of bread-corn and orchards. Every one!--it is a most subtle assault upon the discipline, comradeship and patriotism of the common soldiers by the promises of a selfish, sensuous equality and individualism. But then the speaker's native cynicism gets the better of him--it is not possible for an Assyrian long to play the part of clemency--and, with a flash of scorn, he asks the sad men upon the walls whether they really believe that Jehovah can save them: Hath any of the gods of the nations delivered his land out of the hand of the King of Assyria, ... that Jehovah should deliver Jerusalem out of my hand? All the range of their feelings does he thus run through, seeking with sharp words to snap each cord of faith in God, of honour to the king and love of country. Had the Jews heart to answer him, they might point out the inconsistency between his claim to have been sent by Jehovah and the contempt he now pours upon their God. But the inconsistency is characteristic. The Assyrian has some acquaintance with the Jewish faith; he makes use of its articles when they serve his purpose, but his ultimatum is to tear them to shreds in their believers' faces. He treats the Jews as men of culture still sometimes treat barbarians, first scornfully humouring their faith and then savagely trampling it under foot.

So clever were the speeches of the Rabshakeh. We see why he was appointed to this mission. He was an expert both in the language and religion of this tribe, perched on its rock in the remote Judæan highlands. For a foreigner he showed marvellous familiarity with the temper and internal jealousies of the Jewish religion. He turned these on each other almost as adroitly as Paul himself did in the disputes between Sadducees and Pharisees. How the fellow knew his cleverness, strutting there betwixt army and town! He would show his soldier friends the proper way of dealing with stubborn barbarians. He would astonish those faith-proud highlanders by exhibiting how much he was aware of the life behind their thick walls and silent faces, for the king's commandment was, Answer him not.

And yet did the Rabshakeh, with all his raking, know the heart of Judah? No, truly. The whole interest of this man is the incongruity of the expertness and surface-knowledge, which he spattered on Jerusalem's walls, with the deep secret of God, that, as some inexhaustible well, the fortress of the faith carried within her. Ah, Assyrian, there is more in starved Jerusalem than thou canst put in thy speeches! Suppose Heaven were to give those sharp eyes of thine power to look through the next thousand years, and see this race and this religion thou puffest at, the highest-honoured, hottest-hated of the world, centre of mankind's regard and debate, but thou, and thy king and all the glory of your empire wrapped deep in oblivion. To this little fortress of highland men shall the heart of great peoples turn: kings for its nursing-fathers and queens for its nursing-mothers, the forces of the Gentiles shall come to it, and from it new civilisations take their laws; while thou and all thy paraphernalia disappear into blackness, haunted only by the antiquary, the world taking an interest in thee just in so far as thou didst once hopelessly attempt to understand Jerusalem and capture her faith by thine own interpretation of it. Curious pigmy, very grand thou thinkest thyself, and surely with some right as delegate of the king of kings, parading thy cleverness and thy bribes before these poor barbarians; but the world, called to look upon you both from this eminence of history, grants thee to be a very good head of an intelligence department, with a couple of languages on thy glib tongue's end, but adjudges that with the starved and speechless men before thee lies the secret of all that is worth living and dying for in this world.

The Rabshakeh's plausible futility and Jerusalem's faith, greatly distressed before him, are typical. Still as men hang moodily over the bulwarks of Zion, doubtful whether life is worth living within the narrow limits which religion prescribes, or righteousness worth fighting for with such privations and hope deferred, comes upon them some elegant and plausible temptation, loudly calling to give the whole thing up. Disregarding the official arguments and evidences that push forward to parley, it speaks home in practical tones to men's real selves--their appetites and selfishnesses. "You are foolish fellows," it says, "to confine yourselves to such narrowness of life and self-denial! The fall of your faith is only a matter of time: other creeds have gone; yours must follow. And why fight the world for the sake of an idea, or from the habits of a discipline? Such things only starve the human spirit; and the world is so generous, so free to every one, so tolerant of each enjoying his own, unhampered by authority or religion."

In our day what has the greatest effect on the faith of many men is just this mixture, that pervades the Rabshakeh's address,--of a superior culture pretending to expose religion, with the easy generosity, which offers to the individual a selfish life, unchecked by any discipline or religious fear. That modern Rabshakeh, Ernest Rénan, with the forces of historical criticism at his back, but confident rather in his own skill of address, speaking to us believers as poor picturesque provincials, patronising our Deity, and telling us that he knows His intentions better than we do ourselves, is a very good representative of the enemies of the Faith, who owe their impressiveness upon common men to the familiarity they display with the contents of the Faith, and the independent, easy life they offer to the man who throws his strict faith off. Superior knowledge, with the offer on its lips of a life on good terms with the rich and tolerant world--pretence of science promising selfishness--that is to-day, as then under the walls of Jerusalem, the typical enemy of the Faith. But if faith be held simply as the silent garrison of Jerusalem held it, faith in a Lord God of righteousness, who has given us a conscience to serve Him, and has spoken to us in plain explanation of this by those whom we can see, understand and trust--not only by an Isaiah, but by a Jesus--then neither mere cleverness nor the ability to promise comfort can avail against our faith. A simple conscience of God and of duty may not be able to answer subtle arguments word for word, but she can feel the incongruity of their cleverness with her own precious secret; she can at least expose the fallacy of their sensuous promises of an untroubled life. No man, who tempts us from a good conscience with God in the discipline of our religion and the comradeship of His people, can ensure that there will be no starvation in the pride of life, no captivity in the easy tolerance of the world. To the heart of man there will always be captivity in selfishness; there will always be exile in unbelief. Even where the romance and sentiment of faith are retained, after the manner of Rénan, it is only to mock us with mirage. As in a dry and thirsty land, where no water is, our heart and flesh shall cry out for the living God, as we have aforetime seen Him in the sanctuary. The land, in which the tempter promises a life undisturbed by religious restraints, is not our home, neither is it freedom. By the conscience that is in us, God has set us on the walls of faith, with His law to observe, with His people to stand by; and against us are the world and its tempters, with all their wiles to be defied. If we go down from the charge and shelter of so simple a religion, then, whatever enjoyment we have, we shall enjoy it only with the fears of the deserter and the greed of the slave.

In spite of scorn and sensuous promise from Rabshakeh to Rénan, let us lift the hymn which these silent Jews at last lifted from the walls of their delivered city: Walk about Zion and go round about her; tell ye the towers thereof. Mark ye well her bulwarks, and consider her palaces, that ye may tell it to the generation to come. For this God is our God for ever and ever. He will be our Guide even unto death.

Rev. George Adam Smith, M.A.

CHAPTER XXIII

THIS IS THE VICTORY.... OUR FAITH.

Isaiah xxxvii. (701 B.C.).
    Within the fortress of the faith there is only silence and embarrassment. We pass from the Rabshakeh, posing outside the walls of Zion, to Hezekiah, prostrate within them. We pass with the distracted councillors, by the walls crowded with moody and silent soldiers, many of them--if this be the meaning of the king's command that they should not parley--only too ready to yield to the plausible infidel. We are astonished. Has faith nothing to say for herself? Have this people of so long Divine inspiration no habit of self-possession, no argument in answer to the irrelevant attacks of their enemy? Where are the traditions of Moses and Joshua, the songs of Deborah and David? Can men walk about Zion, and their very footsteps on her walls ring out no defiance?
    Hezekiah's complaint reminds us that in this silence and distress we have no occasional perplexity of faith, but her perpetual burden. Faith is inarticulate because of her greatness. Faith is courageous and imaginative; but can she convert her confidence and visions into fact? Said Hezekiah, This is a day of trouble, and rebuke and contumely, for the children are come to the birth, and there is not strength to bring them forth. These words are not a mere metaphor for anguish. They are the definition of a real miscarriage. In Isaiah's contemporaries faith has at last engendered courage, zeal for God's house and strong assurance of victory; but she, that has proved fertile to conceive and carry these confidences, is powerless to bring them forth into real life, to transform them to actual fact. Faith, complains Hezekiah, is not the substance of things hoped for. At the moment when her subjective assurances ought to be realized as facts, she is powerless to bring them to the birth.
    It is a miscarriage we are always deploring. Wordsworth has said, "Through love, through hope, through faith's transcendent dower, we feel that we are greater than we know." Yes, greater than we can articulate, greater than we can tell to men like the Rabshakeh, even though he talk the language of the Jews; and therefore, on the whole, it is best to be silent in face of his argument. But greater also, we sometimes fear, than we can realise to ourselves in actual character and victory. All life thrills with the pangs of inability to bring the children of faith to the birth of experience. The man, who has lost his faith or who takes his faith easily, never knows, of course, this anguish of Hezekiah. But the more we have fed on the promises of the Bible, the more that the Spirit of God has engendered in our pure hearts assurances of justice and of peace, the more we shall sometimes tremble with the fear that in outward fact there is no life for these beautiful conceptions of the soul. Do we really believe in the Fatherhood of God--believe in it till it has changed us inwardly, and we carry a new sense of destiny, a new conscience of justice, a new disgust of sin, a new pity for pain? Then how full of the anguish of impotence must our souls feel when they consciously survey one day of common life about us, or when we honestly look back on a year of our own conduct! Does it not seem as if upon one or two hideous streets in some centre of our civilisation all Christianity, with its eighteen hundred years of promise and impetus, had gone to wreck? Is God only for the imagination of man? Is there no God outwardly to control and grant victory? Is He only a Voice, and not the Creator? Is Christ only a Prophet, and not the King?
    And then over these disappointments there faces us all the great miscarriage itself--black, inevitable death. Hezekiah cried from despair that the Divine assurance of the permanence of God's people in the world was about to be wrecked on fact. But often by a deathbed we utter the same lament about the individual's immortality. There is everything to prove a future life except the fact of it within human experience. This life is big with hopes, instincts, convictions of immortality; and yet where within our sight have these ever passed to the birth of fact? [65] Death is a great miscarriage. The children have come to the birth, and there is not strength to bring them forth.
    And yet within the horizon of this life at least--the latter part of the difficulty we postpone to another chapter--faith is the substance of things hoped for, as Isaiah did now most brilliantly prove. For the miracle of Jerusalem's deliverance, to which the narrative proceeds, was not that by faith the prophet foretold it, but that by faith he did actually himself succeed in bringing it to pass. The miracle, we say, was not that Isaiah made accurate prediction of the city's speedy relief from the Assyrian, but far more that upon his solitary steadfastness, without aid of battle, he did carry her disheartened citizens through this crisis of temptation, and kept them, though silent, to their walls till the futile Assyrian drifted away. The prediction, indeed, was not, although its terms appear exact, so very marvellous for a prophet to

make, who had Isaiah's religious conviction that Jerusalem must survive and Isaiah's practical acquaintance with the politics of the day. Behold, I am setting in him a spirit; and he shall hear a rumour, and shall return into his own land. We may recall the parallel case of Charlemagne in his campaign against the Moors in Spain, from which he was suddenly and unseasonably hastened north on a disastrous retreat by news of the revolt of the Saxons. [66] In the vast Assyrian territories rebellions were constantly occurring, that demanded the swift appearance of the king himself; and God's Spirit, to whose inspiration Isaiah traced all political perception, suggested to him the possibility of one of these. In the end, the Bible story implies that it was not a rumour from some far-away quarter so much as a disaster here in Syria, which compelled Sennacherib's "retreat from Moscow." But it is possible that both causes were at work, and that as Napoleon offered the receipt of news from Paris as his reason for hurriedly abandoning the unfortunate Spanish campaign of 1808, so Sennacherib made the rumour of some news from his capital or the north the occasion for turning his troops from a theatre of war, where they had not met with unequivocal success, and had at last been half destroyed by the plague. Isaiah's further prediction of Sennacherib's death must also be taken in a general sense, for it was not till twenty years later that the Assyrian tyrant met this violent end: I will cause him to fall by the sword in his own land. But do not let us waste our attention on the altogether minor point of the prediction of Jerusalem's deliverance, when the great wonder, of which the prediction is but an episode, lies lengthened and manifest before us--that Isaiah, when all the defenders of Jerusalem were distracted and her king prostrate, did by the single steadfastness of his spirit sustain her inviolate, and procure for her people a safe and glorious future.

The baffled Rabshakeh returned to his master, whom he found at Libnah, for he had heard that he had broken up from Lachish. Sennacherib, the narrative would seem to imply, did not trouble himself further about Jerusalem till he learned that Tirhakah, the Ethiopian ruler of Egypt, was marching to meet him with probably a stronger force than that which Sennacherib had defeated at Eltekeh. Then, feeling the danger of leaving so strong a fortress as Jerusalem in his rear, Sennacherib sent to Hezekiah one more demand for surrender. Hezekiah spread his enemy's letter before the Lord. His prayer that follows is remarkable for two features, which enable us to see how pure and elevated a monotheism God's Spirit had at last developed from the national faith of Israel. The Being whom the king now seeks he addresses by the familiar name Jehovah of hosts, God of Israel, and describes by the physical figure--who art enthroned upon the cherubim. But he conceives of this God with the utmost loftiness and purity, ascribing to Him not only sovereignty and creatorship, but absolute singularity of Godhead. We have but to compare Hezekiah's prayer with the utterances of his predecessor Ahaz, to whom many gods were real, and none absolutely sovereign, or with the utterances of Israelites far purer than Ahaz, to whom the gods of the nations, though inferior to Jehovah, were yet real existences, in order to mark the spiritual advance made by Israel under Isaiah. It is a tribute to the prophet's force, which speaks volumes, when the deputation from Hezekiah talk to him of thy God (ver. 4). For Isaiah by his ministry had made Israel's God to be new in Israel's eyes.

Hezekiah's lofty prayer drew forth through the prophet an answer from Jehovah (vv. 21-32). This is one of the most brilliant of Isaiah's oracles. It is full of much, with which we are now familiar: the triumph of the inviolable fortress, the virgin daughter of Zion, and her scorn of the arrogant foe; the prophet's appreciation of Asshur's power and impetus, which only heightens his conviction that Asshur is but an instrument in the hand of God; the old figure of the enemy's sudden check as of a wild animal by hook and bridle; his inevitable retreat to the north. But these familiar ideas are flung off with a terseness and vivacity, which bear out the opinion that here we have a prophecy of Isaiah, not revised and elaborated for subsequent publication, like the rest of his book, but in its original form, struck quickly forth to meet the city's sudden and urgent prayer.

The new feature of this prophecy is the sign added to it (ver. 30). This sign reminds us of that which in opposite terms described to Ahaz the devastation of Judah by the approaching Assyrians (chap. vii.). The wave of Assyrian war is about to roll away again, and Judah to resume her neglected agriculture, but not quite immediately. During this year of 701 it has been impossible, with the Assyrians in the land, to sow the seed, and the Jews have been dependent on the precarious crop of what had fallen from the harvest of the previous year and sown itself--saphîah, or aftergrowth. Next year, it being now too late to sow for next year's harvest, they must be content with the shahîs--wild corn, that which springs of itself. But the third year sow ye, and reap, and plant vineyards and eat the fruit thereof. Perhaps we ought not to interpret these numbers literally. The use of three gives the statement a formal and general aspect, as if the prophet only meant, It may be not quite at once that we get rid of the Assyrians; but when they do go, then they go for good, and you may till your land again without fear of their return. Then rings out the old promise, so soon now to be accomplished, about the escaped and the remnant; and the great pledge of the promise is once more repeated: The zeal of Jehovah of hosts will perform this. With this exclamation, as in ix. 7, the prophecy reaches a natural conclusion; and vv. 33-35 may have been uttered by Isaiah a little later, when he was quite sure that the Assyrian would not even attempt to repeat his abandoned blockade of Jerusalem.

*** Rev. George Adam Smith, M.A.

At last in a single night the deliverance miraculously came. It is implied by the scattered accounts of those days of salvation, that an Assyrian corps continued to sit before Jerusalem even after the Rabshakeh had returned to the headquarters of Sennacherib. The thirty-third of Isaiah, as well as those Psalms which celebrate the Assyrian's disappearance from Judah, describe it as having taken place from under the walls of Jerusalem and the astonished eyes of her guardians. It was not, however, upon this force--perhaps little more than a brigade of observation (xxxiii. 18)--that the calamity fell which drove Sennacherib so suddenly from Syria. And there went forth (that night, adds the book of Kings) the angel of Jehovah; and he smote in the camp of Assyria one hundred and eighty-five thousand; and when the camp arose in the morning, behold all of them were corpses, dead men. And Sennacherib, King of Assyria, broke up, and returned and dwelt in Nineveh. Had this pestilence dispersed the camp that lay before Jerusalem, and left beneath the walls so considerable a number of corpses, the exclamations of surprise at the sudden disappearance of Assyria, which occur in Isa. xxxiii. and in Psalms xlviii. and lxxvi., could hardly have failed to betray the fact. But these simply speak of vague trouble coming upon them that were assembled about Zion, and of their swift decampment. The trouble was the news of the calamity, whose victims were the main body of the Assyrian army, who had been making for the borders of Egypt, but were now scattered northwards like chaff.

For details of this disaster we look in vain, of course, to the Assyrian annals, which only record Sennacherib's abrupt return to Nineveh. But it is remarkable that the histories of both of his chief rivals in this campaign, Judah and Egypt, should contain independent reminiscences of so sudden and miraculous a disaster to his host. From Egyptian sources there has come down through Herodotus (ii. 14), a story that a king of Egypt, being deserted by the military caste, when "Sennacherib King of the Arabs and Assyrians" invaded his country, entered his sanctuary and appealed with weeping to his god; that the god appeared and cheered him, that he raised an army of artisans and marched to meet Sennacherib in Pelusium; that by night a multitude of field-mice ate up the quivers, bow-strings and shield-straps of the Assyrians; and that, as these fled on the morrow, very many of them fell. A stone statue of the king, adds Herodotus, stood in the temple of Hephæstus, having a mouse in the hand. Now, since the mouse was a symbol of sudden destruction, and even of the plague, this story of Herodotus seems to be merely a picturesque form of a tradition that pestilence broke out in the Assyrian camp. The parallel with the Bible narrative is close. In both accounts it is a prayer of the king that prevails. In both the Deity sends His agent--in the grotesque Egyptian an army of mice, in the sublime Jewish His angel. In both the effects are sudden, happening in a single night. From the Assyrian side we have this corroboration: that Sennacherib did abruptly return to Nineveh without taking Jerusalem or meeting with Tirhakah, and that, though he reigned for twenty years more, he never again made a Syrian campaign. Sennacherib's convenient story of his return may be compared to the ambiguous account which Cæsar gives of his first withdrawal from Britain, laying emphasis on the submission of the tribes as his reason for a swift return to France--a return which was rather due to the destruction of his fleet by storm and the consequent uneasiness of his army. Or, as we have already said, Sennacherib's account may be compared to Napoleon's professed reason for his sudden abandonment of his Spanish campaign and his quick return to Paris in 1808.

The neighbourhood in which the Assyrian army suffered this great disaster [67] was notorious in antiquity for its power of pestilence. Making every allowance for the untutored imagination of the ancients, we must admit the Serbonian bog, between Syria and Egypt, to have been a place terrible for filth and miasma. The noxious vapours travelled far; but the plagues, with which this swamp several times desolated the world, were first engendered among the diseased and demoralised populations, whose villages festered upon its margin. A Persian army was decimated here in the middle of the fourth century before Christ. "The fatal disease which depopulated the earth in the time of Justinian and his successors first appeared in the neighbourhood of Pelusium, between the Serbonian bog and the eastern channel of the Nile." [68] To the north of the bog the Crusaders also suffered from the infection. It is, therefore, very probable that the moral terror of this notorious neighbourhood, as well as its malaria, acting upon an exhausted and disappointed army in a devastated land, was the secondary cause in the great disaster, by which the Almighty humbled the arrogance of Asshur. The swiftness, with which Sennacherib's retreat is said to have begun, has been equalled by the turning-points of other historical campaigns. Alexander the Great's decision to withdraw from India was, after victories as many as Sennacherib's, made in three days. Attila vanished out of Italy as suddenly as Sennacherib, and from a motive less evident. In the famous War of the Fosse the Meccan army broke off from their siege of Mohammed in a single stormy night. Napoleon's career went back upon itself with just as sharp a bend no less than thrice--in 1799, on Sennacherib's own ground in Syria; in 1808, in Spain; and in 1812, when he turned from Moscow upon "one memorable night of frost, in which twenty thousand horses perished, and the strength of the French army was utterly broken." [69]

The amount of the Assyrian loss is enormous, and implies of course a much higher figure for the army which was vast enough to suffer it; but here are some instances for comparison. In the early German invasions of Italy whole armies and camps were swept away by the pestilential climate. The losses of the First Crusade were over three hundred thousand. The soldiers of the Third Crusade, upon the scene of Sennacherib's war, were reckoned at more than half a million, and their losses by disease alone at over one hundred thousand. [70] The Grand Army of Napoleon entered Russia two hundred and fifty thousand, but came out, having suffered no decisive defeat, only twelve thousand; on the retreat from Moscow alone ninety thousand perished.

What we are concerned with, however, is neither the immediate occasion nor the exact amount of Sennacherib's loss, but the bare fact, so certainly established, that, having devastated Judah to the very walls of Jerusalem, the Assyrian was compelled by some calamity apart from human war to withdraw before the sacred city itself was taken. For this was the essential part of Isaiah's prediction; upon this he had staked the credit of the pure monotheism, whose prophet he was to the world. If we keep before us these two simple certainties about the great Deliverance: first, that it had been foretold by Jehovah's word, and second, that it had been now achieved, despite all human probability, by Jehovah's own arm, we shall understand the enormous spiritual impression which it left upon Israel. The religion of the one supreme God, supreme in might because supreme in righteousness, received a most emphatic historical vindication, a signal and glorious triumph. Well might Isaiah exclaim, on the morning of the night during which that Assyrian host had drifted away from Jerusalem, Jehovah is our Judge; Jehovah is our Lawgiver; Jehovah is our King: He saveth us. No other god for the present had any chance in Judah. Idolatry was discredited, not by the political victory of a puritan faction, not even by the distinctive genius or valour of a nation, but by an evident act of Providence, to which no human aid had been contributory. It was nothing less than the baptism of Israel in spiritual religion, the grace of which was never wholly undone.

Nevertheless, the story of Jehovah's triumph cannot be justly recounted without including the reaction which followed upon it within the same generation. Before twenty years had passed from the day, on which Jerusalem, with the forty-sixth Psalm on her lips, sought with all her heart the God of Isaiah, she relapsed into an idolatry, that wore only this sign of the uncompromising puritanism it had displaced: that it was gloomy, and filled with a sense of sin unknown to Israel's idolatries previous to the age of Isaiah. The change would be almost incomprehensible to us, who have realized the spiritual effects of Sennacherib's disappearance, if we had not within our own history a somewhat analogous experience. Puritanism was as gloriously accredited by event and seemed to be as generally accepted by England under Cromwell as faith in the spiritual religion of Isaiah was vindicated by the deliverance of Jerusalem and the peace of Judah under Hezekiah. But swiftly as the ruling temper in England changed after Cromwell's death, and Puritanism was laid under the ban, and persecution and licentiousness broke out, so quickly when Hezekiah died did Manasseh his son--no change of dynasty here--do evil in the sight of Jehovah, and make Judah to sin, building again the high places and rearing up altars for Baal and altars in the house of Jehovah, whereof Jehovah had said, In Jerusalem will I put My name. Idolatry was never so rampant in Judah. Moreover, Manasseh shed innocent blood till he filled Jerusalem from one end to another. It is in this carnage that tradition has placed the death of Isaiah. He, who had been Judah's best counsellor through five reigns, on whom the whole nation had gathered in the day of her distress, and by whose faith her long-hoped-for salvation had at last become substantive, was violently put to death by the son of Hezekiah. It is said that he was sawn asunder. [71]

The parallel, which we are pursuing, does not, however, close here. "As soon," says an English historian, "as the wild orgy of the Restoration was over, men began to see that nothing that was really worthy in the work of Puritanism had been undone. The whole history of English progress since the Restoration, on its moral and spiritual sides, has been the history of Puritanism."

For the principles of Isaiah and their victory we may make a claim as much larger than this claim, as Israel's influence on the world has been greater than England's. Israel never wholly lost the grace of the baptism wherewith she was baptized in 701. Even in her history there was no event in which the unaided interposition of God was more conspicuous. It is from an appreciation of the meaning of such a Providence that Israel derives her character--that character which marks her off so distinctively from her great rival in the education of the human race, and endows her ministry with its peculiar value to the world. If we are asked for the characteristics of the Hellenic genius, we point to the august temples and images of beauty in which the wealth and art of man have evolved in human features most glorious suggestions of divinity, or we point to Thermopylæ, where human valour and devotion seem grander even in unavailing sacrifice than the almighty Fate, that renders them the prey of the barbarian. In Greece the human is greater than the divine. But if we are asked to define the spirit of Israel, we remember the worship which Isaiah has enjoined in his opening chapter, a worship that dispenses even with temple and with sacrifice, but, from the first strivings of conscience to the most certain enjoyment of peace, ascribes all man's experience to the word of God. In contrast with Thermopylæ, we recall Jerusalem's Deliverance, effected apart from human war by the direct stroke of Heaven. In Judah man is great simply as he rests on God. The rocks of Thermopylæ, how imperishably beautiful do they shine to latest ages with the comradeship, the valour, the sacrificial blood of human heroes! It is another beauty which Isaiah saw upon the bare, dry rocks of Zion, and which has drawn to them the admiration of the world. There, he said, Jehovah is glory for us, a place of broad rivers and streams.

***

In returning and rest shall ye be saved; in quietness and in confidence is your strength. How divine Isaiah's message is, may be proved by the length of time mankind is taking to learn it. The remarkable thing is, that he staked so lofty a principle, and the pure religion of which it was the temper, upon a political result, that he staked them upon, and vindicated them by, a purely local and material success-- the relief of Jerusalem from the infidel. Centuries passed, and Christ came. He did not--for even He could not--preach a more spiritual religion than that which He had committed to His greatest forerunner, but He released this religion, and the temper of faith which Isaiah had so divinely expressed, from the local associations and merely national victories, with which even Isaiah had been forced to identify them. The destruction of Jerusalem by the heathen formed a large part of Christ's prediction of the immediate future; and He comforted the remnant of faith with these words, to some of which Isaiah's lips had first given their meaning: Ye shall neither in this mountain nor yet in Jerusalem worship the Father. God is a Spirit, and they that worship Him must worship Him in spirit and in truth.

Again centuries passed--no less than eighteen from Isaiah--and we find Christendom, though Christ had come between, returning to Isaiah's superseded problem, and, while reviving its material conditions, unable to apply to them the prophet's spiritual temper. The Christianity of the Crusades fell back upon Isaiah's position without his spirit. Like him, it staked the credit of religion upon the relief of the holy city from the grasp of the infidel; but, in ghastly contrast to that pure faith and serene confidence with which a single Jew maintained the inviolateness of Mount Zion in the face of Assyria, with what pride and fraud, with what blood and cruelty, with what impious invention of miracle and parody of Divine testimony, did countless armies of Christendom, excited by their most fervent prophets and blessed by their high-priest, attempt in vain the recovery of Jerusalem from the Saracen! The Crusades are a gigantic proof of how easy it is to adopt the external forms of heroic ages, how difficult to repeat their inward temper. We could not have more impressive witness borne to the fact that humanity--though obedient to the orthodox Church, though led by the strongest spirits of the age, though hallowed by the presence of its greatest saints, though enduring all trials, though exhibiting an unrivalled power of self-sacrifice and enthusiasm, though beautified by courtesy and chivalry, and though doing and suffering all for Christ's sake--may yet fail to understand the old precept that in returning and rest men are saved, in quietness and in confidence is their strength. Nothing could more emphatically prove the loftiness of Isaiah's teaching than this failure of Christendom even to come within sight of it.

Have we learned this lesson yet? O God of Israel, God of Isaiah, in returning to whom and resting upon whom alone we are saved, purge us of self and of the pride of life, of the fever and the falsehood they breed. Teach us that in quietness and in confidence is our strength. Help us to be still and know that Thou art God.

Footnotes:

65. Cf. Browning's La Saisiaz.
66. A still more striking analogy may be found in the case of Napoleon I. when in the East in 1799. He had just achieved a small victory which partly masked the previous failure of his campaign, when "Sir Sydney Smith now contrived that he should receive a packet of journals, by which he was informed of all that had passed recently in Europe and the disasters that France had suffered. His resolution was immediately taken. On August 22nd he wrote to Kleber announcing that he transferred to him the command of the expedition, and that he himself would return to Europe.... After carefully spreading false accounts of his intentions, he set sail on the night of the same day" (Professor Seeley, article "Napoleon" in the Ency. Brit.).
67. The statement of the Egyptian legend, that it was from a point in the neighbourhood of Pelusium that Sennacherib's army commenced its retreat, is not contradicted by anything in the Jewish records, which leave the locality of the disaster very vague, but, on the contrary, receives some support from what Isaiah expresses as at least the intention of Sennacherib (chap. xxxvii. 25).
68. Gibbon, Decline and Fall, xliii.
69. Arnold, Lectures on Modern History, 177, quoted by Stanley.
70. Gibbon, xlii.; lix.
71. Heb. xi.

CHAPTER XXIV

A REVIEW OF ISAIAH'S PREDICTIONS CONCERNING THE DELIVERANCE OF JERUSALEM.

As we have gathered together all that Isaiah prophesied concerning the Messiah, so it may be useful for closer students of his book if we now summarise (even at the risk of a little repetition) the facts of his marvellous prediction of the siege and delivery of Jerusalem. Such a review, besides being historically interesting, ought to prove of edification in so far as it instructs us in the kind of faith by which the Holy Ghost inspired a prophet to foretell the future.

1. The primary conviction with which Isaiah felt himself inspired by the Spirit of Jehovah was a purely moral one--that a devastation of Judah was necessary for her people's sin, to which he shortly added a religious one: that a remnant would be saved. He had this double conviction as early as 740 B.C. (vi. 11-13).

2. Looking round the horizon for some phenomenon with which to identify this promised judgement, Isaiah described the latter at first without naming any single people as the invaders of Judah (v. 26 ff.). It may have been that for a moment he hesitated between Assyria and Egypt. Once he named them together as equally the Lord's instruments upon Judah (vii. 18), but only once. When Ahaz resolved to call Assyria into the Syrian quarrels, Isaiah exclusively designated the northern power as the scourge he had predicted; and when in 732 the Assyrian armies had overrun Samaria, he graphically described their necessary overflow into Judah also (viii.). This invasion did not spread to Judah, but Isaiah's combined moral and political conviction, for both elements of which he claimed the inspiration of God's Spirit, seized him with renewed strength in 725, when Salmanassar marched south upon Israel (xxviii.); and in 721, when Sargon captured Samaria, Isaiah uttered a vivid description of his speedy arrival before Jerusalem (x. 28 ff.). This prediction was again disappointed. But Sargon's departure without invading Judah, and her second escape from him on his return to Syria in 711, did not in the least induce Isaiah to relax either of his two convictions. Judah he proclaimed to be as much in need of punishment as ever (xxix.-xxxii.); and, though on Sargon's death all Palestine revolted from Assyria to Egypt, he persisted that this would not save her from Sennacherib (xiv. 29 ff.; xxix.-xxx.). The "dourness" with which his countrymen believed in Egypt naturally caused the prophet to fill his orations at this time with the political side of his conviction that Assyria was stronger than Egypt; but because Jerusalem's Egyptian policy springs from a deceitful temper (xxx. 1, 9, 10) he is as earnest as ever with his moral conviction that judgement is coming. After 705 his pictures of a siege of Jerusalem grow more definite (xxix.; xxx.). He seems scorched by the nearness of the Assyrian conflagration (xxx. 27 ff.). At last in 701, when Sennacherib comes to Palestine, the siege is pictured as immediate--chaps. i. and xx., which also show at its height the prophet's moral conviction of the necessity of the siege for punishing his people.

3. But over against this moral conviction, that Judah must be devastated for her sin, and this political, that Assyria is to be the instrument, even to the extreme of a siege of Jerusalem, the prophet still holds strongly to the religious assurance that God cannot allow His shrine to be violated or His people to be exterminated. At first it is only of the people that Isaiah speaks--the remnant (vi.; viii. 18). Jerusalem is not mentioned in the verses that describe the overflowing of all Judah by Assyria (viii. 7). It is only when at last, in 721, the prophet realizes how near a siege of Jerusalem may be (x. 11, 28-32), that he also pictures the sudden destruction of the Assyrian on his arrival within sight of her walls (x. 33). In 705, when the siege of the sacred city once more becomes imminent, the prophet again reiterates to the heathen that Zion alone shall stand among the cities of Syria (xiv. 32). To herself he says that, though she shall be besieged and brought very low, she shall finally be delivered (xxix. 1-8; xxx. 19-26; xxxi. 1, 4, 5). It is true, this conviction seems to be broken--once by a prophecy of uncertain date (xxxii. 14), which indicates a desolation of the buildings of Jerusalem, and once by the prophet's sentence of death upon the inhabitants in the hour of their profligacy (xxii.)--but when the city has repented, and the enemy have perfidiously come back to demand her surrender, Isaiah again asseverates, though all are hopeless, that she shall not fall (xxxvii.).

4. Now, with regard to the method of Jerusalem's deliverance, Isaiah has uniformly described this as happening not by human battle. From the beginning he said that Israel should be delivered in the last extremity of their weakness (vi. 13). On the Assyrian's arrival over against the city, Jehovah is to lop

Rev. George Adam Smith, M.A.

him off (x. 33). When her enemies have invested Jerusalem, Jehovah is to come down in thunder and a hurricane and sweep them away (after 705, xxix. 5-8). They are to be suddenly disappointed, like a hungry man waking from a dream of food. A beautiful promise is given of the raising of the siege without mention of struggle or any weapon (xxx. 20-26). The Assyrian is to be checked as a wild bull is checked with a lasso, is to be slain by the lighting down of the Lord's arm, by the voice of the Lord, through a judgement that shall be like a solemn holocaust to God than a human battle (xxx. 30-33). When the Assyrian comes back, and Hezekiah is crushed by the new demand for surrender, Isaiah says that, by a Divinely inspired impulse, Sennacherib, hearing bad news, shall suddenly return to his own land (xxxviii. 7).

It is only in very little details that these predictions differ. The thunderstorm and torrents of fire are, of course, but poetic variations. In 721, however, the prophet hardly anticipates the very close siege, which he pictures after 705; and while from 705 to 702 he identifies the relief of Jerusalem with a great calamity to the Assyrian army about to invade Judah, yet in 701, when the Assyrians are actually on the spot, he suggests that nothing but a rumour shall cause their retreat and so leave Jerusalem free of them.

5. In all this we see a certain FIXITY and a certain FREEDOM. The freedom, the changes and inconsistencies in the prediction, are entirely limited to those of Isaiah's convictions which we have called political, and which the prophet evidently gathered from his observation of political circumstances as these developed before his eyes from year to year. But what was fixed and unalterable to Isaiah, he drew from the moral and religious convictions to which his political observation was subservient; viz., Judah's very sore punishment for sin, the survival of a people of God in the world, and their deliverance by His own act.

6. This "Bible-reading" in Isaiah's predictive prophecies reveals very clearly the nature of inspiration under the old covenant. To Isaiah inspiration was nothing more nor less than the possession of certain strong moral and religious convictions, which he felt he owed to the communication of the Spirit of God, and according to which he interpreted, and even dared to foretell, the history of his people and the world. Our study completely dispels, on the evidence of the Bible itself, that view of inspiration and prediction, so long held in the Church, which it is difficult to define, but which means something like this: that the prophet beheld a vision of the future in its actual detail and read this off as a man may read the history of the past out of a book or a clear memory. This is a very simple view, but too simple either to meet the facts of the Bible, or to afford to men any of that intellectual and spiritual satisfaction which the discovery of the Divine methods is sure to afford. The literal view of inspiration is too simple to be true, and too simple to be edifying. On the other hand, how profitable, how edifying, is the Bible's own account of its inspiration! To know that men interpreted, predicted and controlled history in the power of the purest moral and religious convictions--in the knowledge of, and the loyalty to, certain fundamental laws of God--is to receive an account of inspiration, which is not only as satisfying to the reason as it is true to the facts of the Bible, but is spiritually very helpful by the lofty example and reward it sets before our own faith. By faith differing in degree, but not in kind, from ours, faith which is the substance of things hoped for, these men became prophets of God, and received the testimony of history that they spoke from Him. Isaiah prophesied and predicted all he did from loyalty to two simple truths, which he tells us he received from God Himself: that sin must be punished, and that the people of God must be saved. This simple faith, acting along with a wonderful knowledge of human nature and ceaseless vigilance of affairs, constituted inspiration for Isaiah.

There is thus, with great modifications, an analogy between the prophet and the scientific observer of the present day. Men of science are able to affirm the certainty of natural phenomena by their knowledge of the laws and principles of nature. Certain forces being present, certain results must come to pass. The Old Testament prophets, working in history, a sphere where the problems were infinitely more complicated by the presence and powerful operation of man's free-will, seized hold of principles as conspicuous and certain to them as the laws of nature are to the scientist; and out of their conviction of these they proclaimed the necessity of certain events. God is inflexibly righteous, He cannot utterly destroy His people or the witness of Himself among men: these were the laws. Judah shall be punished, Israel shall continue to exist: these were the certainties deduced from the laws. But for the exact conditions and forms both of the punishment and its relief the prophets depended upon their knowledge of the world, of which, as these pages testify, they were the keenest and largest-hearted observers that ever appeared.

This account of prophecy may be offered with advantage to those who are prejudiced against prophecy as full of materials, which are inexplicable to minds accustomed to find a law and reason for everything. Grant the truths of the spiritual doctrines, which the prophets made their premises, and you must admit that their predictions are neither arbitrary nor bewildering. Or begin at the other end: verify that these facts took place, and that the prophets actually predicted them; and if you are true to your own scientific methods, you will not be able to resist the conclusion that the spiritual laws and principles, by which the predictions were made, are as real as those by which in the realm of nature you proclaim the necessity of certain physical phenomena--and all this in spite of there being at work in the prophets'

The Expositor's Bible: The Book of Isaiah Volumes I & II
sphere a force, the free-will of man, which cannot interfere with the laws you work by, as it can with those on which they depend.

But, to turn from the apologetic value of this account of prophecy to the experimental, we maintain that it brings out a new sacredness upon common life. If it be true that Isaiah had no magical means for foretelling the future, but simply his own spiritual convictions and his observation of history, that may, of course, deprive some eyes of a light which they fancied they saw bursting from heaven. But, on the other hand, does it not cast a greater glory upon daily life and history, to have seen in Isaiah this close connection between spiritual conviction and political event? Does it not teach us that life is governed by faith; that the truths we profess are the things that make history; that we carry the future in our hearts; that not an event happens but is to be used by us as meaning the effect of some law of God, and not a fact appears but is the symbol and sacrament of His truth?

Rev. George Adam Smith, M.A.

CHAPTER XXV

AN OLD TESTAMENT BELIEVER'S SICK-BED; OR, THE DIFFERENCE CHRIST HAS MADE.

Isaiah xxxviii.; xxxix. (DATE UNCERTAIN).

To the great national drama of Jerusalem's deliverance, there have been added two scenes of a personal kind, relating to her king. Chaps. xxxviii. and xxxix. are the narrative of the sore sickness and recovery of King Hezekiah, and of the embassy which Merodach-baladan sent him, and how he received the embassy. The date of these events is difficult to determine. If, with Canon Cheyne, we believe in an invasion of Judah by Sargon in 711, we shall be tempted to refer them, as he does, to that date--the more so that the promise of fifteen additional years made to Hezekiah in 711, the fifteenth year of his reign, would bring it up to the twenty-nine, at which it is set in 2 Kings xviii. 2. That, however, would flatly contradict the statement both of Isaiah xxxviii. 1 and 2 Kings xx. 1 that Hezekiah's sickness fell in the days of the invasion of Judah by Sennacherib; that is, after 705. But to place the promise of fifteen additional years to Hezekiah after 705, when we know he had been reigning for at least twenty years, would be to contradict the verse, just cited, which sums up the years of his reign as twenty-nine. This is, in fact, one of the instances, in which we must admit our present inability to elucidate the chronology of this portion of the book of Isaiah. Mr. Cheyne thinks the editor mistook the siege by Sennacherib for the siege by Sargon. But as the fact of a siege by Sargon has never been satisfactorily established, it seems safer to trust the statement that Hezekiah's sickness occurred in the reign of Sennacherib, and to allow that there has been an error somewhere in the numbering of the years. It is remarkable that the name of Merodach-baladan does not help us to decide between the two dates. There was a Merodach-baladan in rebellion against Sargon in 710, and there was one in rebellion against Sennacherib in 705. It has not yet been put past doubt as to whether these two are the same. The essential is that there was a Merodach-baladan alive, real or only claimant king of Babylon, about 705, and that he was likely at that date to treat with Hezekiah, being himself in revolt against Assyria. Unable to come to any decision about the conflicting numbers, we leave uncertain the date of the events recounted in chaps. xxxviii., xxxix. The original form of the narrative, but wanting Hezekiah's hymn, is given in 2 Kings xx. [72]

***

We have given to this chapter the title "An Old Testament Believer's Deathbed; or, The Difference Christ has made," not because this is the only spiritual suggestion of the story, but because it seems to the present expositor as if this were the predominant feeling left in Christian minds after reading for us the story. In Hezekiah's conduct there is much of courage for us to admire, as there are other elements to warn us; but when we have read the whole story, we find ourselves saying, What a difference Christ has made to me! Take Hezekiah from two points of view, and then let the narrative itself bring out this difference.

Here is a man, who, although he lived more than twenty-five centuries ago is brought quite close to our side. Death, who herds all men into his narrow fold, has crushed this Hebrew king so close to us that we can feel his very heart-beat. Hezekiah's hymn gives us entrance into the fellowship of his sufferings. By the figures he so skilfully uses he makes us feel that pain, the shortness of life, the suddenness of death and the utter blackness beyond were to him just what they are to us. And yet this kinship in pain, and fear and ignorance only makes us the more aware of something else which we have and he has not.

Again, here is a man to whom religion gave all it could give without the help of Christ; a believer in the religion out of which Christianity sprang, perhaps the most representative Old Testament believer we could find, for Hezekiah was at once the collector of what was best in its literature and the reformer of what was worst in its worship; a man permeated by the past piety of his Church, and enjoying as his guide and philosopher the boldest prophet who ever preached the future developments of its spirit. Yet when we put Hezekiah and all that Isaiah can give him on one side, we shall again feel for ourselves on the other what a difference Christ has made.

This difference a simple study of the narrative will make clear.

I.

In those days Hezekiah became sick unto death. They were critical days for Judah--no son born to the king (2 Kings xxi. 1), the work of reformation in Judah not yet consolidated, the big world tossing in revolution all around. Under God, everything depended on an experienced ruler; and this one, without a son to succeed him, was drawing near to death. We will therefore judge Hezekiah's strong passion for life to have been patriotic as well as selfish. He stood in the midtime of his days, with a faithfully executed work behind him and so good an example of kinghood that for years Isaiah had not expressed his old longing for the Messiah. The Lord had counted Hezekiah righteous; that twin-sign had been given him which more than any other assured an Israelite of Jehovah's favour--a good conscience and success in his work. Well, therefore, might he cry when Isaiah brought him the sentence of death, Ah, now, Jehovah, remember, I beseech Thee, how I have walked before Thee in truth and with a perfect heart, and have done that which is good in Thine eyes. And Hezekiah wept with a great weeping.

There is difficulty in the strange story which follows. The dial was probably a pyramid of steps on the top of which stood a short pillar or obelisk. When the sun rose in the morning, the shadow cast by the pillar would fall right down the western side of the pyramid to the bottom of the lowest step. As the sun ascended the shadow would shorten, and creep up inch by inch to the foot of the pillar. After noon, as the sun began to descend to the west, the shadow would creep down the eastern steps; and the steps were so measured that each one marked a certain degree of time. It was probably afternoon when Isaiah visited the king. The shadow was going down according to the regular law; the sign consisted in causing the shadow to shrink up the steps again. Such a reversal of the ordinary progress of the shadow may have been caused in either of two ways: by the whole earth being thrown back on its axis, which we may dismiss as impossible, or by the occurrence of the phenomenon known as refraction. Refraction is a disturbance in the atmosphere by which the rays of the sun are bent or deflected from their natural course into an angular one. In this case, instead of shooting straight over the top of the obelisk, the rays of the sun had been bent down and inward, so that the shadow fled up to the foot of the obelisk. There are many things in the air which might cause this; it is a phenomenon often observed; and the Scriptural narratives imply that on this occasion it was purely local (2 Chron. xxxii. 31). Had we only the narrative in the book of Isaiah, the explanation would have been easy. Isaiah, having given the sentence of death, passed the dial in the palace courtyard, and saw the shadow lying ten degrees farther up than it should have done, the sight of which coincided with the inspiration that the king would not die; and Isaiah went back to announce to Hezekiah his reprieve, and naturally call his attention to this as a sign, to which a weak and desponding man would be glad to cling. But the original narrative in the book of Kings tells us that Isaiah offered Hezekiah a choice of signs: that the shadow should either advance or retreat, and that the king chose the latter. The sign came in answer to Isaiah's prayer, and is narrated to us as a special Divine interposition. But a medicine accompanied it, and Hezekiah recovered through a poultice of figs laid on the boil from which he suffered.

While recognising for our own faith the uselessness of a discussion on this sign offered to a sick man, let us not miss the moral lessons of so touching a narrative, nor the sympathy with the sick king which it is fitted to produce, and which is our best introduction to the study of his hymn.

Isaiah had performed that most awful duty of doctor or minister the telling of a friend that he must die. Few men have not in their personal experience a key to the prophet's feelings on this occasion. The leaving of a dear friend for the last time; the coming out into the sunlight which he will nevermore share with us; the passing by the dial; the observation of the creeping shadow; the feeling that it is only a question of time, the passion of prayer into which that feeling throws us that God may be pleased to put off the hour and spare our friend; the invention, that is born, like prayer, of necessity: a cure we suddenly remember; the confidence which prayer and invention bring between them; the return with the joyful news; the giving of the order about the remedy--cannot many in their degree rejoice with Isaiah in such an experience? But he has, too, a conscience of God and God's work to which none of us may pretend: he knows how indispensable to that work his royal pupil is, and out of this inspiration he prophesies the will of the Lord that Hezekiah shall recover.

Then the king, with a sick man's sacramental longing, asks a sign. Out through the window the courtyard is visible; there stands the same step-dial of Ahaz, the long pillar on the top of the steps, the shadow creeping down them through the warm afternoon sunshine. To the sick man it must have been like the finger of death coming nearer. Shall the shadow, asks the prophet, go forward ten steps or go back ten steps? It is easy, says the king, alarmed, for the shadow to go down ten steps. Easy for it to go down! Has he not been feeling that all the afternoon? "Do not," we can fancy him saying, with the gasp of a man who has been watching its irresistible descent--"do not let that black thing come farther; but let the shadow go backward ten steps."

The shadow returned, and Hezekiah got his sign. But when he was well, he used it for more than a sign. He read a great spiritual lesson in it. The time, which upon the dial had been apparently thrown back, had in his life been really thrown back; and God had given him his years to live over again. The past was to be as if it had never been, its guilt and weakness wiped out. Thou hast cast behind Thy back all my sins. As a newborn child Hezekiah felt himself uncommitted by the past, not a sin's-doubt nor a sin's-cowardice in him, with the heart of a little child, but yet with the strength and dignity of a grown man, for it is the magic of tribulation to bring innocence with experience. I shall go softly, or literally, with dignity or caution, as in a procession, all my years because of the bitterness of my soul. O Lord, upon such things do men live; and altogether in them is the life of my spirit.... Behold, for perfection was it bitter to me, so bitter. And through it all there breaks a new impression of God. What shall I say? He hath both spoken with me, and Himself hath done it. As if afraid to impute his profits to the mere experience itself, In them is the life of my spirit, he breaks in with Yea, Thou hast recovered me; yea, Thou hast made me to live. And then, by a very pregnant construction, he adds, Thou hast loved my soul out of the pit of destruction; that is, of course, loved, and by Thy love lifted, but he uses the one word loved, and gives it the active force of drawing or lifting. In this lay the head and glory of Hezekiah's experience. He was a religious man, an enthusiast for the Temple services, and had all his days as his friend the prophet whose heart was with the heart of God; but it was not through any of these means God came near him, not till he lay sick and had turned his face to the wall. Then indeed he cried, What shall I say? He hath both spoken with me, and Himself hath done it!

Forgiveness, a new peace, a new dignity and a visit from the living God! Well might Hezekiah exclaim that it was only through a near sense of death that men rightly learned to live. Ah, Lord, it is upon these things that men live; and wholly therein is the life of my spirit. It is by these things men live, and therein I have learned for the first time what life is!

In all this at least we cannot go beyond Hezekiah, and he stands an example to the best Christian among us. Never did a man bring richer harvest from the fields of death. Everything that renders life really life--peace, dignity, a new sense of God and of His forgiveness--these were the spoils which Hezekiah won in his struggle with the grim enemy. He had snatched from death a new meaning for life; he had robbed death of its awful pomp, and bestowed this on careless life. Hereafter he should walk with the step and the mien of a conqueror--I shall go in solemn procession all my years because of the bitterness of my soul--or with the carefulness of a worshipper, who sees at the end of his course the throne of the Most High God, and makes all his life an ascent thither.

This is the effect which every great sorrow and struggle has upon a noble soul. Come to the streets of the living. Who are these, whom we can so easily distinguish from the crowd by their firmness of step and look of peace, walking softly where some spurt and some halt, holding, without rest or haste, the tenor of their way, as if they marched to music heard by their ears alone? These are they which have come out of great tribulation. They have brought back into time the sense of eternity. They know how near the invisible worlds lie to this one, and the sense of the vast silences stills all idle laughter in their hearts. The life that is to other men chance or sport, strife or hurried flight, has for them its allotted distance; is for them a measured march, a constant worship. For the bitterness of their soul they go in procession all their years. Sorrow's subjects, they are our kings; wrestlers with death, our veterans: and to the rabble armies of society they set the step of a nobler life.

Count especially the young man blessed, who has looked into the grave before he has faced the great temptations of the world, and has not entered the race of life till he has learned his stride in the race with death. They tell us that on the outside of civilisation, where men carry their lives in their hands, a most thorough politeness and dignity are bred, in spite of the want of settled habits, by the sense of danger alone; and we know how battle and a deadly climate, pestilence or the perils of the sea have sent back to us the most careless of our youth with a self-possession and regularity of mind, that it would have been hopeless to expect them to develop amid the trivial trials of village life.

But the greatest duty of us men is not to seek nor to pray for such combats with death. It is when God has found these for us to remain true to our memories of them. The hardest duty of life is to remain true to our psalms of deliverance, as it is certainly life's greatest temptation to fall away from the sanctity of sorrow, and suffer the stately style of one who knows how near death hovers to his line of march to degenerate into the broken step of a wanton life. This was Hezekiah's temptation, and this is why the story of his fall in the thirty-ninth chapter is placed beside his vows in the thirty-eighth--to warn us how easy it is for those who have come conquerors out of a struggle with death to fall a prey to common life. He had said, I will walk softly all my years; but how arrogantly and rashly he carried himself when Merodach-baladan sent the embassy to congratulate him on his recovery. It was not with the dignity of the veteran, but with a childish love of display, perhaps also with the too restless desire to secure an alliance, that he showed the envoys his storehouse, the silver, and the gold, and the spices, and the precious oil, and all the house of his armour and all that was found in his treasures. There was nothing which Hezekiah did not show them in his house nor in all his dominion. In this behaviour there was neither caution nor sobriety, and we cannot doubt but that Hezekiah felt the shame of it when Isaiah sternly rebuked him and threw upon all his house the dark shadow of captivity.

It is easier to win spoils from death than to keep them untarnished by life. Shame burns warm in a soldier's heart when he sees the arms he risked life to win rusting for want of a little care. Ours will not burn less if we discover that the strength of character we brought with us out of some great tribulation has been slowly weakened by subsequent self-indulgence of vanity. How awful to have fought for character with death only to squander it upon life! It is well to keep praying, "My God, suffer me not to forget my bonds and my bitterness. In my hours of wealth and ease, and health and peace, by the memory of Thy judgements deliver me, good Lord."

II.

So far then Hezekiah is an example and warning to us all. With all our faith in Christ, none of us, in the things mentioned, may hope to excel this Old Testament believer. But notice very particularly that Hezekiah's faith and fortitude are profitable only for this life. It is when we begin to think, What of the life to come? that we perceive the infinite difference Christ has made.

We know what Hezekiah felt when his back was turned on death, and he came up to life again. But what did he feel when he faced the other way, and his back was to life? With his back to life and facing deathwards, Hezekiah saw nothing, that was worth hoping for. To him to die was to leave God behind him, to leave the face of God as surely as he was leaving the face of man. I said, I shall not see Jah, Jah in the land of the living; I shall gaze upon man no more with the inhabitants of the world. The beyond was not to Hezekiah absolute nothingness, for he had his conceptions, the popular conceptions of his time, of a sort of existence that was passed by those who had been men upon earth. The imagination of his people figured the gloomy portals of a nether world--Sheol, the Hollow (Dante's "hollow realm"), or perhaps the Craving--into which death herds the shades of men, bloodless, voiceless, without love or hope or aught that makes life worth living. With such an existence beyond, to die to life here was to Hezekiah like as when a weaver rolls up the finished web. My life may be a pattern for others to copy, a banner for others to fight under, but for me it is finished. Death has cut it from the loom. Or it was like going into captivity. Mine age is removed and is carried away from me into exile, like a shepherd's tent--exile which to a Jew was the extreme of despair, implying as it did absence from God, and salvation and the possibility of worship. Sheol cannot praise Thee; death cannot celebrate Thee: they that go down into the pit cannot hope for Thy faithfulness.

Of this then at the best Hezekiah was sure: a respite of fifteen years--nothing beyond. Then the shadow would not return upon the dial; and as the king's eyes closed upon the dear faces of his friends, his sense of the countenance of God would die too, and his soul slip into the abyss, hopeless of God's faithfulness.

It is this awful anticlimax, which makes us feel the difference Christ has made. This saint stood in almost the clearest light that revelation cast before Jesus. He was able to perceive in suffering a meaning and derive from it a strength not to be exceeded by any Christian. Yet his faith is profitable for this life alone. For him character may wrestle with death over and over again, and grow the stronger for every grapple, but death wins the last throw.

It may be said that Hezekiah's despair of the future is simply the morbid thoughts of a sick man or the exaggerated fancies of a poet. "We must not," it is urged, "define a poet's language with the strictness of a theology." True, and we must also make some allowance for a man dying prematurely in the midst of his days. But if this hymn is only poetry, it would have been as easy to poetise on the opposite possibilities across the grave. So quick an imagination as Hezekiah's could not have failed to take advantage of the slightest scintilla of glory that pierced the cloud. It must be that his eye saw none, for all his poetry droops the other way. We seek in heaven for praise in its fulness; there we know God's servants shall see Him face to face. But of this Hezekiah had not the slightest imagination; he anxiously prayed that he might recover to strike the stringed instruments all the days of his life in the house of Jehovah. *The living, the living, he praiseth thee, as I do this day; the father to the children shall make known Thy truth.* But *they that go down into the pit cannot hope for Thy faithfulness.*

Now compare all this with the Psalms of Christian hope; with the faith that fills Paul; with his ardour who says, To me to depart is far better; with the glory which John beholds with open face: the hosts of the redeemed praising God and walking in the light of His face, all the geography of that country laid down, and the plan of the new Jerusalem declared to the very fashion of her stones; with the audacity since of Christian art and song: the rapture of Watts' hymns and the exhilaration of Wesley's praise as they contemplate death; and with the joyful and exact anticipations of so many millions of common men as they turn their faces to the wall. In all these, in even the Book of the Revelation, there is of course a great deal of pure fancy. But imagination never bursts in anywhither till fact has preceded. And it is just because there is a great fact standing between us and Hezekiah that the pureness of our faith and the richness of our imagination of immortality differ so much from his. That fact is Jesus Christ, His resurrection and ascension. It is He who has made all the difference and brought life and immortality to light.

And we shall know the difference if we lose our faith in that fact. For except Christ be risen from the dead and gone before to a country which derives all its reality and light for our imagination from that Presence, which once walked with us in the flesh, there remains for us only Hezekiah's courage to make the best of a short reprieve, only Hezekiah's outlook into Hades when at last we turn our faces to the wall. But to be stronger and purer for having met with death, as he was, only that we must afterwards succumb, with our purity and our strength, to death--this is surely to be, as Paul said, of all men the most miserable.

Better far to own the power of an endless life, which Christ has sealed to us, and translate Hezekiah's experience into the new calculus of immortality. If to have faced death as he did was to inherit dignity and peace and sense of power, what glory of kingship and queenship must sit upon those faces in the other world who have been at closer quarters still with the King of terrors, and through Christ their strength have spoiled him of his sting and victory! To have felt the worst of death and to have triumphed--this is the secret of the peaceful hearts, unfaltering looks and faces of glory, which pass in solemn procession of worship through all eternity before the throne of God.

We shall consider the Old Testament views of a future life and resurrection more fully in chaps. xxvii. and xxx. of this volume.

Footnote:

72. Isa. xxxviii., xxxix., has evidently been abridged from 2 Kings xx. and in some points has to be corrected by the latter. Chap. xxxviii. 21, 22, of course, must be brought forward before ver. 7.

CHAPTER XXVI

HAD ISAIAH A GOSPEL FOR THE INDIVIDUAL?

The two narratives, in which Isaiah's career culminates--that of the Deliverance of Jerusalem (xxxvi.; xxxvii.) and that of the Recovery of Hezekiah (xxxviii.; xxxix.)--cannot fail, coming together as they do, to suggest to thoughtful readers a striking contrast between Isaiah's treatment of the community and his treatment of the individual, between his treatment of the Church and his treatment of single members. For in the first of these narratives we are told how an illimitable future, elsewhere so gloriously described by the prophet, was secured for the Church upon earth; but the whole result of the second is the gain for a representative member of the Church of a respite of fifteen years. Nothing, as we have seen, is promised to the dying Hezekiah of a future life; no scintilla of the light of eternity sparkles either in Isaiah's promise or in Hezekiah's prayer. The net result of the incident is a reprieve of fifteen years: fifteen years of a character strengthened, indeed, by having met with death, but, it would sadly seem, only in order to become again the prey of the vanities of this world (chap. xxxix.). So meagre a result for the individual stands strangely out against the perpetual glory and peace assured to the community. And it suggests this question: Had Isaiah any real gospel for the individual? If so, what was it?

First of all, we must remember that God in His providence seldom gives to one prophet or generation more than a single main problem for solution. In Isaiah's day undoubtedly the most urgent problem--and Divine problems are ever practical, not philosophical--was the continuance of the Church upon earth. It had really got to be a matter of doubt whether a body of people possessing the knowledge of the true God, and able to transfuse and transmit it, could possibly survive among the political convulsions of the world, and in consequence of its own sin. Isaiah's problem was the reformation and survival of the Church. In accordance with this, we notice how many of his terms are collective, and how he almost never addresses the individual. It is the people, upon whom he calls--the nation, Israel, the house of Jacob My vineyard, the men of Judah His pleasant plantation. To these we may add the apostrophes to the city of Jerusalem, under many personifications: Ariel, Ariel, inhabitress of Zion, daughter of Zion. When Isaiah denounces sin, the sinner is either the whole community or a class in the community, very seldom an individual, though there are some instances of the latter, as Ahaz and Shebna. It is This people hath rejected, or The people would not. When Jerusalem collapsed, although there must have been many righteous men still within her, Isaiah said, What aileth thee that all belonging to thee have gone up to the housetops? (xxii. 1). His language is wholesale. When he is not attacking society, he attacks classes or groups: the rulers, the land-grabbers, the drunkards, the sinners, the judges, the house of David, the priests and the prophets, the women. And the sins of these he describes in their social effects, or in their results upon the fate of the whole people; but he never, except in two cases, gives us their individual results. He does not make evident, like Jesus or Paul, the eternal damage a man's sin inflicts on his own soul.

Similarly when Isaiah speaks of God's grace and salvation the objects of these are again collective--the remnant; the escaped (also a collective noun); a holy seed; a stock or stump. It is a restored nation whom he sees under the Messiah, the perpetuity and glory of a city and a State. What we consider to be a most personal and particularly individual matter--the forgiveness of sin--he promises, with two exceptions, only to the community: This people that dwelleth therein hath its iniquity forgiven. We can understand all this social, collective and wholesale character of his language only if we keep in mind his Divinely appointed work--the substance and perpetuity of a purified and secure Church of God.

Had Isaiah then no gospel for the individual? This will indeed seem impossible to us if we keep in view the following considerations:--

1. Isaiah himself had passed through a powerfully individual experience. He had not only felt the solidarity of the people's sin--I dwell among a people of unclean lips--he had first felt his own particular guilt: I am a man of unclean lips. One who suffered the private experiences which are recounted in chap. vi.; whose own eyes had seen the King, Jehovah of hosts; who had gathered on his own lips his guilt and felt the fire come from heaven's altar by an angelic messenger specially to purify him; who had further devoted himself to God's service with so thrilling a sense of his own responsibility, and had so thereby felt his solitary and individual mission--he surely was not behind the very greatest of Christian saints in the experience of guilt, of personal obligation to grace and of personal responsibility. Though

the record of Isaiah's ministry contains no narratives, such as fill the ministries of Jesus and Paul, of anxious care for individuals, could he who wrote of himself that sixth chapter have failed to deal with men as Jesus dealt with Nicodemus, or Paul with the Philippian gaoler? It is not picturesque fancy, nor merely a reflection of the New Testament temper, if we realize Isaiah's intervals of relief from political labour and religious reform occupied with an attention to individual interests, which necessarily would not obtain the permanent record of his public ministry. But whether this be so or not, the sixth chapter teaches that for Isaiah all public conscience and public labour found its necessary preparation in personal religion.

2. But, again, Isaiah had an Individual for his ideal. To him the future was not only an established State; it was equally, it was first, a glorious king. Isaiah was an Oriental. We moderns of the West place our reliance upon institutions; we go forward upon ideas. In the East it is personal influence that tells, persons who are expected, followed and fought for. The history of the West is the history of the advance of thought, of the rise and decay of institutions, to which the greatest individuals are more or less subordinate. The history of the East is the annals of personalities; justice and energy in a ruler, not political principles, are what impress the Oriental imagination. Isaiah has carried this Oriental hope to a distinct and lofty pitch. The Hero whom he exalts on the margin of the future, as its Author, is not only a person of great majesty, but a character of considerable decision. At first only the rigorous virtues of the ruler are attributed to Him (chap. xi. 1 ff.), but afterwards the graces and influence of a much broader and sweeter humanity (xxxii. 2). Indeed, in this latter oracle we saw that Isaiah spoke not so much of his great Hero, as of what any individual might become. A man, he says, shall be as an hiding-place from the wind. Personal influence is the spring of social progress, the shelter and fountain force of the community. In the following verses the effect of so pure and inspiring a presence is traced in the discrimination of individual character--each man standing out for what he is--which Isaiah defines as his second requisite for social progress. In all this there is much for the individual to ponder, much to inspire him with a sense of the value and responsibility of his own character, and with the certainty that by himself he shall be judged and by himself stand or fall. The worthless person shall be no more called princely, nor the knave said to be bountiful.

3. If any details of character are wanting in the picture of Isaiah's Hero, they are supplied by Hezekiah's Self-analysis (chap. xxxviii.). We need not repeat what we have said in the previous chapter of the king's appreciation of what is the strength of a man's character, and particularly of how character grows by grappling with death. In this matter the most experienced Christian saints may learn from Isaiah's pupil.

Isaiah had then, without doubt, a gospel for the individual; and to this day the individual may plainly read it in his book, may truly, strongly, joyfully live by it--so deeply does it begin, so much does it help to self-knowledge and self-analysis, so lofty are the ideals and responsibilities which it presents. But is it true that Isaiah's gospel is for this life only?

Was Isaiah's silence on the immortality of the individual due wholly to the cause we have suggested in the beginning of this chapter--that God gives to each prophet his single problem, and that the problem of Isaiah was the endurance of the Church upon earth? There is no doubt that this is only partly the explanation.

The Hebrew belonged to a branch of humanity--the Semitic--which, as its history proves, was unable to develop any strong imagination of, or practical interest in, a future life apart from foreign influence or Divine revelation. The pagan Arabs laughed at Mahommed when he preached to them of the Resurrection; and even to-day, after twelve centuries of Moslem influence, their descendants in the centre of Arabia, according to the most recent authority, [73] fail to form a clear conception of, or indeed to take almost any practical interest in, another world. The northern branch of the race, to which the Hebrews belonged, derived from an older civilisation a prospect of Hades, that their own fancy developed with great elaboration. This prospect, however, which we shall describe fully in connection with chaps. xiv. and xxvi., was one absolutely hostile to the interests of character in this life. It brought all men, whatever their life had been on earth, at last to a dead level of unsubstantial and hopeless existence. Good and evil, strong and weak, pious and infidel, alike became shades, joyless and hopeless, without even the power to praise God. We have seen in Hezekiah's case how such a prospect unnerved the most pious souls, and that revelation, even though represented at his bedside by an Isaiah, offered him no hope of an issue from it. The strength of character, however, which Hezekiah professes to have won in grappling with death, added to the closeness of communion with God which he enjoyed in this life, only brings out the absurdity of such a conclusion to life as the prospect of Sheol offered to the individual. If he was a pious man, if he was a man who had never felt himself deserted by God in this life, he was bound to revolt from so God-forsaken an existence after death. This was actually the line along which the Hebrew spirit went out to victory over those gloomy conceptions of death, that were yet unbroken by a risen Christ. Thou wilt not, the saint triumphantly cried, leave my soul in Sheol, nor wilt Thou suffer Thine holy one to see corruption. It was faith in the almightiness and reasonableness of God's ways, it was conviction of personal righteousness, it was the sense that the Lord would not desert

His own in death, which sustained the believer in face of that awful shadow through which no light of revelation had yet broken.

If these, then, were the wings by which a believing soul under the Old Testament soared over the grave, Isaiah may be said to have contributed to the hope of personal immortality just in so far as he strengthened them. By enhancing as he did the value and beauty of individual character, by emphasizing the indwelling of God's Spirit, he was bringing life and immortality to light, even though he spoke no word to the dying about the fact of a glorious life beyond the grave. By assisting to create in the individual that character and sense of God, which alone could assure him he would never die, but pass from the praise of the Lord in this life to a nearer enjoyment of His presence beyond, Isaiah was working along the only line by which the Spirit of God seems to have assisted the Hebrew mind to an assurance of heaven.

But further in his favourite gospel of the Reasonableness of God--that God does not work fruitlessly, nor create and cultivate with a view to judgement and destruction--Isaiah was furnishing an argument for personal immortality, the force of which has not been exhausted. In a recent work on The Destiny of Man [74] the philosophic author maintains the reasonableness of the Divine methods as a ground of belief both in the continued progress of the race upon earth and in the immortality of the individual. "From the first dawning of life we see all things working together towards one mighty goal-- the evolution of the most exalted and spiritual faculties which characterize humanity. Has all this work been done for nothing? Is it all ephemeral, all a bubble that bursts, a vision that fades? On such a view the riddle of the universe becomes a riddle without a meaning. The more thoroughly we comprehend the process of evolution by which things have come to be what they are, the more we are likely to feel that to deny the everlasting persistence of the spiritual element in man is to rob the whole process of its meaning. It goes far towards putting us to permanent intellectual confusion. For my own part, I believe in the immortality of the soul, not in the sense in which I accept demonstrable truths of science, but as a supreme act of faith in the reasonableness of God's work."

From the same argument Isaiah drew only the former of these two conclusions. To him the certainty that God's people would survive the impending deluge of Assyria's brute force was based on his faith that the Lord is a God of judgement, of reasonable law and method, and could not have created or fostered so spiritual a people only to destroy them. The progress of religion upon earth was certain. But does not Isaiah's method equally make for the immortality of the individual? He did not draw this conclusion, but he laid down its premises with a confidence and richness of illustration that have never been excelled.

We, therefore, answer the question we put at the beginning of the chapter thus:--Isaiah had a gospel for the individual for this life, and all the necessary premises of a gospel for the individual for the life to come.

Footnotes:

73. Doughty's Arabia Deserta: Travels in Northern Arabia, 1876-1878.
74. By Professor Fiske.

Rev. George Adam Smith, M.A.

BOOK V

PROPHECIES NOT RELATING TO ISAIAH'S TIME.

Isaiah:-- xiii.-xiv. 23 xxiv.-xxvii. xxxiv. xxxv.

In the first thirty-nine chapters of the Book of Isaiah--the half which refers to the prophet's own career and the politics contemporary with that--we find four or five prophecies containing no reference to Isaiah himself nor to any Jewish king under whom he laboured, and painting both Israel and the foreign world in quite a different state from that in which they lay during his lifetime. These prophecies are chap. xiii., an Oracle announcing the Fall of Babylon, with its appendix, chap. xiv. 1-23, the Promise of Israel's Deliverance and an Ode upon the Fall of the Babylonian Tyrant; chaps. xxiv.-xxvii., a series of Visions of the breaking up of the universe, of restoration from exile, and even of resurrection from the dead; chap. xxxiv., the Vengeance of the Lord upon Edom; and chap. xxxv., a Song of Return from Exile.

In these prophecies Assyria is no longer the dominant world-force, nor Jerusalem the inviolate fortress of God and His people. If Assyria or Egypt is mentioned, it is but as one of the three classical enemies of Israel; and Babylon is represented as the head and front of the hostile world. The Jews are no longer in political freedom and possession of their own land; they are either in exile or just returned from it to a depopulated country. With these altered circumstances come another temper and new doctrine. The horizon is different, and the hopes that flush in dawn upon it are not quite the same as those which we have contemplated with Isaiah in his immediate future. It is no longer the repulse of the heathen invader; the inviolateness of the sacred city; the recovery of the people from the shock of attack, and of the land from the trampling of armies. But it is the people in exile, the overthrow of the tyrant in his own home, the opening of prison doors, the laying down of a highway through the wilderness, the triumph of return and the resumption of worship. There is, besides, a promise of the resurrection, which we have not found in the prophecies we have considered.

With such differences, it is not wonderful that many have denied the authorship of these few prophecies to Isaiah. This is a question that can be looked at calmly. It touches no dogma of the Christian faith. Especially it does not involve the other question, so often--and, we venture to say, so unjustly--started on this point, Could not the Spirit of God have inspired Isaiah to foresee all that the prophecies in question foretell, even though he lived more than a century before the people were in circumstances to understand them? Certainly, God is almighty. The question is not, Could He have done this? but one somewhat different: Did He do it? and to this an answer can be had only from the prophecies themselves. If these mark the Babylonian hostility or captivity as already upon Israel, this is a testimony of Scripture itself, which we cannot overlook, and beside which even unquestionable traces of similarity to Isaiah's style or the fact that these oracles are bound up with Isaiah's own undoubted prophecies have little weight. "Facts" of style will be regarded with suspicion by any one who knows how they are employed by both sides in such a question as this; while the certainty that the Book of Isaiah was put into its present form subsequently to his life will permit of,--and the evident purpose of Scripture to secure moral impressiveness rather than historical consecutiveness will account for,--later oracles being bound up with unquestioned utterances of Isaiah.

Only one of the prophecies in question confirms the tradition that it is by Isaiah, viz., chap. xiii., which bears the title Oracle of Babylon which Isaiah, son of Amoz, did see; but titles are themselves so much the report of tradition, being of a later date than the rest of the text, that it is best to argue the question apart from them.

On the other hand, Isaiah's authorship of these prophecies, or at least the possibility of his having written them, is usually defended by appealing to his promise of the return from exile in chap. xi. and his threat of a Babylonish captivity in chap. xxxix. This is an argument that has not been fairly met by those who deny the Isaianic authorship of chaps. xiii.-xiv. 23, xxiv.-xxvii., and xxxv. It is a strong argument, for while, as we have seen (p. 201), there are good grounds for believing Isaiah to have been likely to make such a prediction of a Babylonish captivity as is attributed to him in chap. xxxix. 6, almost all the critics agree in leaving chap. xi. to him. But if chap. xi. is Isaiah's, then he undoubtedly spoke of an exile much more extensive than had taken place by his own day. Nevertheless, even this ability in xi. to foretell an exile so vast does not account for passages in xiii.-xiv. 23, xxiv.-xxvii., which represent the Exile either as present or as actually over. No one who reads these chapters without prejudice can fail to feel the force of such passages in leading him to decide for an exilic or post-exilic authorship (see pp. 429 ff.)

Another argument against attributing these prophecies to Isaiah is that their visions of the last things, representing as they do a judgement on the whole world, and even the destruction of the whole material universe, are incompatible with Isaiah's loftiest and final hope of an inviolate Zion at last relieved and secure, of a land freed from invasion and wondrously fertile, with all the converted world, Assyria and Egypt, gathered round it as a centre. This question, however, is seriously complicated by the fact that in his youth Isaiah did undoubtedly prophesy a shaking of the whole world and the destruction of its inhabitants, and by the probability that his old age survived into a period, whose abounding sin would again make natural such wholesale predictions of judgement as we find in chap. xxiv.

Still, let the question of the eschatology be as obscure as we have shown, there remains this clear issue. In some chapters of the Book of Isaiah, which, from our knowledge of the circumstances of his times, we know must have been published while he was alive, we learn that the Jewish people has never left its land, nor lost its independence under Jehovah's anointed, and that the inviolateness of Zion and the retreat of the Assyrian invaders of Judah, without effecting the captivity of the Jews, are absolutely essential to the endurance of God's kingdom on earth. In other chapters we find that the Jews have left their land, have been long in exile (or from other passages have just returned), and that the religious essential is no more the independence of the Jewish State under a theocratic king, but only the resumption of the Temple worship. Is it possible for one man to have written both these sets of chapters? Is it possible for one age to have produced them? That is the whole question.

Rev. George Adam Smith, M.A.

CHAPTER XXVII

BABYLON AND LUCIFER.

Isaiah xiii. 2-xiv. 23 (DATE UNCERTAIN).
This double oracle is against the City (xiii. 2-xiv. 2) and the Tyrant (xiv. 3-23) of Babylon.

I. The Wicked City (xiii. 2-xiv. 23).
The first part is a series of hurried and vanishing scenes--glimpses of ruin and deliverance caught through the smoke and turmoil of a Divine war. The drama opens with the erection of a gathering standard upon a bare mountain (ver. 2). He who gives the order explains it (ver. 3), but is immediately interrupted by Hark! a tumult on the mountains, like a great people. Hark! the surge of the kingdoms of nations gathering together. Jehovah of hosts is mustering the host of war. It is the day of Jehovah that is near, the day of His war and of His judgement upon the world.

This Old Testament expression, the day of the Lord, starts so many ideas that it is difficult to seize any one of them and say this is just what is meant. For day with a possessive pronoun suggests what has been appointed aforehand, or what must come round in its turn; means also opportunity and triumph, and also swift performance after long delay. All these thoughts are excited when we couple a day with any person's name. And therefore as with every dawn some one awakes saying, This is my day; as with every dawn comes some one's chance, some soul gets its wish, some will shows what it can do, some passion or principle issues into fact: so God also shall have His day, on which His justice and power shall find their full scope and triumph. Suddenly and simply, like any dawn that takes its turn on the round of time, the great decision and victory of Divine justice shall at last break out of the long delay of ages. Howl ye, for the day of Jehovah is near; as destruction from the Destructive does it come. Very savage and quite universal is its punishment. Every human heart melteth. Countless faces, white with terror, light up its darkness like flames. Sinners are to be exterminated out of the earth; the world is to be punished for its iniquity. Heaven, the stars, sun and moon aid the horror and the darkness, heaven shivering above, the earth quaking beneath; and between, the peoples like shepherdless sheep drive to and fro through awful carnage.

From ver. 17 the mist lifts a little. The vague turmoil clears up into a siege of Babylon by the Medians, and then settles down into Babylon's ruin and abandonment to wild beasts. Finally (xiv. 1) comes the religious reason of so much convulsion: For Jehovah will have compassion upon Jacob, and choose again Israel, and settle them upon their own ground; and the foreign sojourner shall join himself to them, and they shall associate themselves to the house of Jacob.

This prophecy evidently came to a people already in captivity--a very different circumstance of the Church of God from that in which we have seen her under Isaiah. But upon this new stage it is still the same old conquest. Assyria has fallen, but Babylon has taken her place. The old spirit of cruelty and covetousness has entered a new body; the only change is that it has become wealth and luxury instead of brute force and military glory. It is still selfishness and pride and atheism. At this, our first introduction to Babylon, it might have been proper to explain why throughout the Bible from Genesis to Revelation this one city should remain in fact or symbol the enemy of God and the stronghold of darkness. But we postpone what may be said of her singular reputation, till we come to the second part of the Book of Isaiah where Babylon plays a larger and more distinct role. Here her destruction is simply the most striking episode of the Divine judgement upon the whole earth. Babylon represents civilisation; she is the brow of the world's pride and enmity to God. One distinctively Babylonian characteristic, however, must not be passed over. With a ring of irony in his voice, the prophet declares, Behold, I stir up the Medes against thee, who regard not silver and take no pleasure in gold. The worst terror that can assail us is the terror of forces, whose character we cannot fathom, who will not stop to parley, who do not understand our language nor our bribes. It was such a power, with which the resourceful and luxurious Babylon was threatened. With money the Babylonians did all they wished to do, and believed everything else to be possible. They had subsidised kings, bought over enemies, seduced the peoples of the earth. The foe whom God now sent them was impervious to this influence. From their pure highlands came down upon corrupt civilisation a simple people, whose banner was a leathern apron, whose goal was not booty nor ease but power and mastery, who came not to rob but to displace.

The lessons of the passage are two: that the people of God are something distinct from civilisation, though this be universal and absorbent as a very Babylon; and that the resources of civilisation are not even in material strength the highest in the universe, but God has in His armoury weapons heedless of men's cunning, and in His armies agents impervious to men's bribes. Every civilisation needs to be told, according to its temper, one of these two things. Is it hypocritical? Then it needs to be told that civilisation is not one with the people of God. Is it arrogant? Then it needs to be told that the resources of civilisation are not the strongest forces in God's universe. Man talks of the triumph of mind over matter, of the power of culture, of the elasticity of civilisation; but God has natural forces, to which all these are as the worm beneath the hoof of the horse: and if moral need arise, He will call His brute forces into requisition. Howl ye, for the day of Jehovah is near; as destruction from the Destructive does it come. There may be periods in man's history when, in opposition to man's unholy art and godless civilisation, God can reveal Himself only as destruction.

II. The Tyrant (xiv. 3-23).

To the prophecy of the overthrow of Babylon there is annexed, in order to be sung by Israel in the hour of her deliverance, a satiric ode or taunt-song (Heb. mashal, Eng. ver. parable) upon the King of Babylon. A translation of this spirited poem in the form of its verse (in which, it is to be regretted, it has not been rendered by the English revisers) will be more instructive than a full commentary. But the following remarks of introduction are necessary. The word mashal, by which this ode is entitled, means comparison, similitude or parable, and was applicable to every sentence composed of at least two members that compared or contrasted their subjects. As the great bulk of Hebrew poetry is sententious, and largely depends for rhythm upon its parallelism, mashal received a general application; and while another term--shîr--more properly denotes lyric poetry, mashal is applied to rhythmical passages in the Old Testament of almost all tempers: to mere predictions, proverbs, orations, satires or taunt-songs, as here, and to didactic pieces. The parallelism of the verses in our ode is too evident to need an index. But the parallel verses are next grouped into strophes. In Hebrew poetry this division is frequently effected by the use of a refrain. In our ode there is no refrain, but the strophes are easily distinguished by difference of subject-matter. Hebrew poetry does not employ rhyme, but makes use of assonance, and to a much less extent of alliteration--a form which is more frequent in Hebrew prose. In our ode there is not much either of assonance or alliteration. But, on the other hand, the ode has but to be read to break into a certain rough and swinging rhythm. This is produced by long verses rising alternate with short ones falling. Hebrew verse at no time relied for a metrical effect upon the modern device of an equal or proportionate number of syllables. The longer verses of this ode are sometimes too short, the shorter too long, variations to which a rude chant could readily adapt itself. But the alternation of long and short is sustained throughout, except for a break at ver. 10 by the introduction of the formula And they answered and said, which evidently ought to stand for a long and a short verse if the number of double verses in the second strophe is to be the same as it is--seven--in the first and in the third.

The scene of the poem, the Underworld and abode of the shades of the dead, is one on which some of the most splendid imagination and music of humanity has been expended. But we must not be disappointed if we do not here find the rich detail and glowing fancy of Virgil's or of Dante's vision. This simple and even rude piece of metre, liker ballad than epic, ought to excite our wonder not so much for what it has failed to imagine as for what, being at its disposal, it has resolutely stinted itself in employing. For it is evident that the author of these lines had within his reach the rich, fantastic materials of Semitic mythology, which are familiar to us in the Babylonian remains. With an austerity, that must strike every one who is acquainted with these, he uses only so much of them as to enable him to render with dramatic force his simple theme--the vanity of human arrogance. [75]

For this purpose he employs the idea of the Underworld which was prevalent among the northern Semitic peoples. Sheol--the gaping or craving place--which we shall have occasion to describe in detail when we come to speak of belief in the resurrection, [76] is the state after death that craves and swallows all living. There dwell the shades of men amid some unsubstantial reflection of their earthly state (ver. 9), and with consciousness and passion only sufficient to greet the arrival of the new-comer and express satiric wonder at his fall (ver. 9). With the arrogance of the Babylonian kings, this tyrant thought to scale the heavens to set his throne in the mount of assembly of the immortals, to match the Most High. [77] But his fate is the fate of all mortals--to go down to the weakness and emptiness of Sheol. Here, let us carefully observe, there is no trace of a judgement for reward or punishment. The new victim of death simply passes to his place among his equals. There was enough of contrast between the arrogance of a tyrant claiming Divinity and his fall into the common receptacle of mortality to point the prophet's moral without the addition of infernal torment. Do we wish to know the actual punishment of his pride and cruelty? It is visible above ground (strophe 4); not with his spirit, but with his corpse; not with himself, but with his wretched family. His corpse is unburied, his family exterminated; his name disappears from the earth. [78]

Thus, by the help of only a few fragments from the popular mythology, the sacred satirist achieves his purpose. His severe monotheism is remarkable in its contrast to Babylonian poems upon similar subjects. He will know none of the gods of the underworld. In place of the great goddess, whom a Babylonian would certainly have seen presiding, with her minions, over the shades, he personifies--it is a frequent figure of Hebrew poetry--the abyss itself. Sheol shuddereth at thee. It is the same when he speaks (ver. 13) of the deep's great opposite, that mount of assembly of the gods, which the northern Semites believed to soar to a silver sky in the recesses of the north (ver. 14), upon the great range which in that direction bounded the Babylonian plain. This Hebrew knows of no gods there but One, whose are the stars, who is the Most High. Man's arrogance and cruelty are attempts upon His majesty. He inevitably overwhelms them. Death is their penalty: blood and squalor on earth, the concourse of shuddering ghosts below.

> *The kings of the earth set themselves,*
> *And the rulers take counsel together,*
> *Against the Lord and against His Anointed.*
> *He that sitteth in the heavens shall laugh;*
> *The Lord shall have them in derision.*

He who has heard that laughter sees no comedy in aught else. This is the one unfailing subject of Hebrew satire, and it forms the irony and the rigour of the following ode. [79]

The only other remarks necessary are these. In ver. 9 the Authorized Version has not attempted to reproduce the humour of the original satire, which styles them that were chief men on earth chief-goats of the herd, bell-wethers. The phrase they that go down to the stones of the pit should be transferred from ver. 19 to ver. 20.

And thou shalt lift up this proverb upon the King of Babylon, and shalt say,--

I.

> *Ah! stilled is the tyrant,*
> *And stilled is the fury!*
> *Broke hath Jehovah the rod of the wicked,*
> *Sceptre of despots:*
> *Stroke of (the) peoples with passion,*
> *Stroke unremitting,*
> *Treading in wrath (the) nations,*
> *Trampling unceasing.*
> *Quiet, at rest, is the whole earth,*
> *They break into singing;*
> *Even the pines are jubilant for thee,*
> *Lebanon's cedars!*
> *"Since thou liest low, cometh not up*
> *Feller against us."*

II.

> *Sheol from under shuddereth at thee*
> *To meet thine arrival,*
> *Stirring up for thee the shades,*
> *All great-goats of earth!*
> *Lifteth erect from their thrones*
> *All kings of peoples.*
> *10. All of them answer and say to thee,--*
> *"Thou, too, made flaccid like us,*
> *To us hast been levelled!*
> *Hurled to Sheol is the pride of thee,*
> *Clang of the harps of thee;*
> *Under thee strewn are (the) maggots*
> *Thy coverlet worms."*

III.

    How art thou fallen from heaven
    Daystar, son of the dawn
    (How) art thou hewn down to earth,
    Hurtler at nations.
    And thou, thou didst say in thine heart,
    "The heavens will I scale,
    Far up to the stars of God
    Lift high my throne,
    And sit on the mount of assembly,
    Far back of the north,
    I will climb on the heights of (the) cloud,
    I will match the Most High!"
    Ah! to Sheol thou art hurled,
    Far back of the pit!

IV.

    Who see thee at thee are gazing;
    Upon thee they muse:
    Is this the man that staggered the earth,
    Shaker of kingdoms?
    Setting the world like the desert,
    Its cities he tore down;
    Its prisoners he loosed not
    (Each of them) homeward.
    All kings of peoples, yes all,
    Are lying in their state;
    But thou! thou art flung from thy grave,
    Like a stick that is loathsome.
    Beshrouded with slain, the pierced of the sword,
    Like a corpse that is trampled.
    They that go down to the stones of a crypt,
    Shalt not be with them in burial.
    For thy land thou hast ruined,
    Thy people hast slaughtered.
    Shall not be mentioned for aye
    Seed of the wicked!
    Set for his children a shambles,
    For guilt of their fathers!
    They shall not rise, nor inherit (the) earth,
    Nor fill the face of the world with cities.

V.

    But I will arise upon them,
    Sayeth Jehovah of hosts;
    And I will cut off from Babel
    Record and remnant,
    And scion and seed,
    Saith Jehovah:
    Yea, I will make it the bittern's heritage,
    Marshes of water!
    And I will sweep it with sweeps of destruction,
    Sayeth Jehovah of hosts.

Footnotes:

75. "Those principles of natural philosophy which smothered the religions of the East with their rank and injurious growth are almost entirely absent from the religion of the Hebrews. Here the motive-power of development is to be found in ethical ideas, which, though not indeed alien to the life of other nations, were not the source from which their religious notions were derived."--(Lotze's Microcosmos, Eng. Transl., il., 466.)

76. P. 447 ff.

77. It is, however, only just to add that, as Mr. Sayce has pointed out in the Hibbert Lectures for 1887 (p. 365), the claims of Babylonian kings and heroes for a seat on the mountain of the gods were not always mere arrogance, but the first efforts of the Babylonian mind to emancipate itself from the gloomy conceptions of Hades and provide a worthy immortality for virtue. Still most of the kings who pray for an entrance among the gods do so on the plea that they have been successful tyrants--a considerable difference from such an assurance as that of the sixteenth Psalm.

78. The popular Semitic conception of Hades contained within it neither grades of condition, according to the merits of men, nor any trace of an infernal torment in aggravation of the unsubstantial state to which all are equally reduced. This statement is true of the Old Testament till at least the Book of Daniel. Sheol is lit by no lurid fires, such as made the later Christian hell intolerable to the lost. That life is unsubstantial; that darkness and dust abound; above all, that God is not there, and that it is impossible to praise Him, is all the punishment which is given in Sheol. Extraordinary vice is punished above ground, in the name and family of the sinner. Sheol, with its monotony, is for average men; but extraordinary piety can break away from it (Ps. xvi.).

79. Readers will remember a parallel to this ode in Carlyle's famous chapter on Louis the Unforgotten. No modern has rivalled Carlyle in his inheritance of this satire, except it be he whom Carlyle called "that Jew blackguard Heine."

CHAPTER XXVIII

THE EFFECT OF SIN ON OUR MATERIAL CIRCUMSTANCE.

Isaiah xxiv. (DATE UNCERTAIN).

The twenty-fourth of Isaiah is one of those chapters, which almost convince the most persevering reader of Scripture that a consecutive reading of the Authorized Version is an impossibility. For what does he get from it but a weary and unintelligent impression of destruction, from which he gladly escapes to the nearest clear utterance of gospel or judgement? Criticism affords little help. It cannot clearly identify the chapter with any historical situation. For a moment there is a gleam of a company standing outside the convulsion, and to the west of the prophet, while the prophet himself suffers captivity. [80] But even this fades before we make it out; and all the rest of the chapter has too universal an application--the language is too imaginative, enigmatic and even paradoxical--to be applied to an actual historical situation, or to its development in the immediate future. This is an ideal description, the apocalyptic vision of a last, great day of judgement upon the whole world; and perhaps the moral truths are all the more impressive that the reader is not distracted by temporary or local references.

With the very first verse the prophecy leaps far beyond all particular or national conditions: Behold, Jehovah shall be emptying the earth and rifling it; and He shall turn it upside down and scatter its inhabitants. This is expressive and thorough; the words are those which were used for cleaning a dirty dish. To the completeness of this opening verse there is really nothing in the chapter to add. All the rest of the verses only illustrate this upturning and scouring of the material universe. For it is with the material universe that the chapter is concerned. Nothing is said of the spiritual nature of man--little, indeed, about man at all. He is simply called the inhabitant of the earth, and the structure of society (ver. 2) is introduced only to make more complete the effect of the convulsion of the earth itself. Man cannot escape those judgements which shatter his material habitation. It is like one of Dante's visions. Terror, and Pit and Snare upon thee, O inhabitant of the earth! And it shall come to pass that he who fleeth from the noise of the Terror shall fall into the Pit, and he who cometh up out of the midst of the Pit shall be taken in the Snare. For the windows on high are opened, and the foundations of the earth do shake. Broken, utterly broken, is the earth; shattered, utterly shattered, the earth; staggering, very staggering, the earth; reeling, the earth reeleth like a drunken man: she swingeth to and fro like a hammock. And so through the rest of the chapter it is the material life of man that is cursed: the new wine, the vine, the tabrets, the harp, the song, and the merriness in men's hearts which these call forth. Nor does the chapter confine itself to the earth. The closing verses carry the effect of judgement to the heavens and far limits of the material universe. The host of the high ones on high (ver. 21) are not spiritual beings, the angels. They are material bodies, the stars. Then, too, shall the moon be confounded, and the stars ashamed, when the Lord's kingdom is established and His righteousness made gloriously clear.

What awful truth is this for illustration of which we see not man, but his habitation, the world and all its surroundings, lifted up by the hand of the Lord, broken open, wiped out and shaken, while man himself, as if only to heighten the effect, staggers hopelessly like some broken insect on the quaking ruins? What judgement is this, in which not only one city or one kingdom is concerned, as in the last prophecy of which we treated, but the whole earth is convulsed, and moon and sun confounded?

The judgement is the visitation of man's sins on his material surroundings--The earth's transgression shall be heavy upon it; and it shall rise, and not fall. The truth on which this judgement rests is that between man and his material circumstance--the earth he inhabits, the seasons which bear him company through time and the stars to which he looks high up in heaven--there is a moral sympathy. The earth also is profaned under the inhabitants thereof, because they have transgressed the laws, changed the ordinance, broken the everlasting covenant.

The Bible gives no support to the theory that matter itself is evil. God created all things; and God saw everything that He had made; and, behold, it was very good. When, therefore, we read in the Bible that the earth is cursed, we read that it is cursed for man's sake; when we read of its desolation, it is as the effect of man's crime. The Flood, the destruction of Sodom and Gomorrah, the plagues of Egypt and other great physical catastrophes happened because men were stubborn or men were foul. We cannot help noticing, however, that matter was thus convulsed or destroyed, not only for the purpose of punishing the moral agent, but because of some poison which had passed from him into the unconscious instruments, stage and circumstance of his crime. According to the Bible, there would appear to be some mysterious sympathy between man and Nature. Man not only governs Nature; he infects and informs her. As the moral life of the soul expresses itself in the physical life of the body for the latter's health or corruption, so the conduct of the human race affects the physical life of the universe to its farthest limits in space. When man is reconciled to God, the wilderness blossoms like a rose; but the guilt of man sullies, infects and corrupts the place he inhabits and the articles he employs; and their destruction becomes necessary, not for his punishment so much as because of the infection and pollution that is in them.

The Old Testament is not contented with a general statement of this great principle, but pursues it to all sorts of particular and private applications. The curses of the Lord fell, not only on the sinner, but on his dwelling, on his property and even on the bit of ground these occupied. This was especially the case with regard to idolatry. When Israel put a pagan population to the sword, they were commanded to raze the city, gather its wealth together, burn all that was burnable and put the rest into the temple of the Lord as a thing devoted or accursed, which it would harm themselves to share (Deut. vii. 25, 26; xiii. 7). The very site of Jericho was cursed, and men were forbidden to build upon its horrid waste. The story of Achan illustrates the same principle.

It is just this principle which chap. xxiv. extends to the whole universe. What happened in Jericho because of its inhabitants' idolatry is now to happen to the whole earth because of man's sin. The earth also is profane under her inhabitants, because they have transgressed the laws, changed the ordinance, broken the everlasting covenant. In these words the prophet takes us away back to the covenant with Noah, which he properly emphasizes as a covenant with all mankind. With a noble universalism, for which his race and their literature get too little credit, this Hebrew recognises that once all mankind were holy unto God, who had included them under His grace, that promised the fixedness and fertility of nature. But that covenant, though of grace, had its conditions for man. These had been broken. The race had grown wicked, as it was before the Flood; and therefore, in terms which vividly recall that former judgement of God--the windows on high are opened--the prophet foretells a new and more awful catastrophe. One word which he employs betrays how close he feels the moral sympathy to be between man and his world. The earth, he says, is profane. This is a word, whose root meaning is that which has fallen away or separated itself, which is delinquent. Sometimes, perhaps, it has a purely moral significance, like our word "abandoned" in the common acceptance: he who has fallen far and utterly into sin, the reckless sinner. But mostly it has rather the religious meaning of one who has fallen out of the covenant relation with God and the relevant benefits and privileges. Into this covenant not only Israel and their land, but humanity and the whole world, have been brought. Is man under covenant grace? The world is also. Does man fall? So does the world, becoming with him profane. The consequence of breaking the covenant oath was expressed in Hebrew by a technical word; and it is this word which, translated curse, is applied in ver. 6 to the earth.

The whole earth is to be broken up and dissolved. What then is to become of the people of God--the indestructible remnant? Where are they to settle? In this new deluge is there a new ark? For answer the prophet presents us with an old paradise (ver. 23). He has wrecked the universe; but he says now, Jehovah of hosts shall dwell in Mount Zion and in Jerusalem. It would be impossible to find a better instance of the limitations of Old Testament prophecy than this return to the old dispensation after the old dispensation has been committed to the flames. At such a crisis as the conflagration of the universe for the sin of man, the hope of the New Testament looks for the creation of a new heaven and a new earth, but there is no scintilla of such a hope in this prediction. The imagination of the Hebrew seer is beaten back upon the theatre his conscience has abandoned. He knows "the old is out of date," but for him "the new is not yet born;" and, therefore, convinced as he is that the old must pass away, he is forced to borrow from its ruins a provisional abode for God's people, a figure for the truth which grips him so firmly, that, in spite of the death of all the universe for man's sin, there must be a visibleness and locality of the Divine majesty, a place where the people of God may gather to bless His holy name.

In this contrast of the power of spiritual imagination possessed respectively by the Old and New Testaments we must not, however, lose the ethical interest which the main lesson of this chapter has for the individual conscience. A breaking universe, the great day of judgement, may be too large and too far off to impress our conscience. But each of us has his own world--body, property and environment--which is as much and as evidently affected by his own sins as our chapter represents the universe to be by the sins of the race.

To grant that the moral and physical universes are from the same hand is to affirm a sympathy and mutual reaction between them. This affirmation is confirmed by experience, and this experience is of two kinds. To the guilty man Nature seems aware, and flashes back from her larger surfaces the magnified reflection of his own self-contempt and terror. But, besides, men are also unable to escape attributing to the material instruments or surroundings of their sin a certain infection, a certain power of recommunicating to their imaginations and memories the desire for sin, as well as of inflicting upon them the pain and penalty of the disorder it has produced among themselves. Sin, though born, as Christ said, in the heart, has immediately a material expression; and we may follow this outwards through man's mind, body and estate, not only to find it "hindering, disturbing, complicating all," but reinfecting with the lust and odour of sin the will which gave it birth. As sin is put forth by the will, or is cherished in the heart, so we find error cloud the mind, impurity the imagination, misery the feelings, and pain and weariness infect the flesh and bone. God, who modelled it, alone knows how far man's physical form has been degraded by the sinful thoughts and habits of which for ages it has been the tool and expression; but even our eyes may sometimes trace the despoiler, and that not only in the case of what are preferably named sins of the flesh, but even with lusts that do not require for their gratification the abuse of the body. Pride, as one might think the least fleshly of all the vices, leaves yet in time her damning signature, and will mark the strongest faces with the sad symptoms of that mental break-down, for which unrestrained pride is so often to blame. If sin thus disfigures the body, we know that sin also infects the body. The habituated flesh becomes the suggester of crime to the will which first constrained it to sin, and now wearily, but in vain, rebels against the habits of its instrument. But we recall all this about the body only to say that what is true of the body is true of the soul's greater material surroundings. With the sentence Thou shalt surely die, God connects this other: Cursed is the ground for thy sake.

When we pass from a man's body, the wrapping we find next nearest to his soul is his property. It has always been an instinct of the race, that there is nothing a man may so infect with the sin of his heart as his handiwork and the gains of his toil. And that is a true instinct, for, in the first place, the making of property perpetuates a man's own habits. If he is successful in business, then every bit of wealth he gathers is a confirmation of the motives and tempers in which he conducted his business. A man deceives himself as to this, saying, Wait till I have made enough; then I will put away the meanness, the harshness and the dishonesty with which I made it. He shall not be able. Just because he has been successful, he will continue in his habit without thinking; just because there has been no break-down to convict of folly and suggest penitence, so he becomes hardened. Property is a bridge on which our passions cross from one part of our life to another. The Germans have an ironical proverb: "The man who has stolen a hundred thousand dollars can afford to live honestly." The emphasis of the irony falls on the words in italics: he can afford, but never does. His property hardens his heart, and keeps him from repentance.

But the instinct of humanity has also been quick to this: that the curse of ill-gotten wealth passes like bad blood from father to child. What is the truth in this matter? A glance at history will tell us. The accumulation of property is the result of certain customs, habits and laws. In its own powerful interest property perpetuates these down the ages, and infects the fresh air of each new generation with their temper. How often in the history of mankind has it been property gained under unjust laws or cruel monopolies which has prevented the abolition of these, and carried into gentler, freer times the pride and exclusiveness of the age, by whose rude habits it was gathered. This moral transference, which we see on so large a scale in public history, is repeated to some extent in every private bequest. A curse does not necessarily follow an estate from the sinful producer of it to his heir; but the latter is, by the bequest itself generally brought into so close a contact with his predecessor as to share his conscience and be in sympathy with his temper. And the case is common where an heir, though absolutely up to the date of his succession separate from him who made and has left the property, nevertheless finds himself unable to alter the methods, or to escape the temper, in which the property has been managed. In nine cases out of ten property carries conscience and transfers habit; if the guilt does not descend, the infection does.

When we pass from the effect of sin upon property to its effect upon circumstance, we pass to what we can affirm with even greater conscience. Man has the power of permanently soaking and staining his surroundings with the effect of sins in themselves momentary and transient. Sin increases terribly by the mental law of association. It is not the gin-shop and the face of wanton beauty that alone tempt men to sin. Far more subtle seductions are about every one of us. That we have the power of inflicting our character upon the scenes of our conduct is proved by some of the dreariest experiences of life. A failure in duty renders the place of it distasteful and enervating. Are we irritable and selfish at home? Then home is certain to be depressing, and little helpful to our spiritual growth. Are we selfish and niggardly in the interest we take in others? Then the congregation we go to, the suburb we dwell in, will appear insipid and unprofitable; we shall be past the possibility of gaining character or happiness from the ground where God planted us and meant us to grow. Students have been idle in their studies till every time they enter them a reflex languor comes down like stale smoke, and the room they desecrated takes its revenge on them. We have it in our power to make our workshops, our laboratories and our studies places of magnificent inspiration, to enter which is to receive a baptism of industry and hope; and we have power to make it impossible ever to work in them again at full pitch. The pulpit, the pew, the very communion-table, come under this law. If a minister of God have made up his mind to say nothing from his accustomed place, which has not cost him toil, to feel nothing but a dependence on God and a desire for souls, then he will never set foot there but the power of the Lord shall be upon him.

But there are men who would rather set foot anywhere than in their pulpit--men who out of it are full of fellowship, information, and infective health, but there they are paralysed with the curse of their idle past. How history shows us that the most sacred shelters and institutions of man become tainted with sin, and are destroyed in revolution or abandoned to decay by the intolerant conscience of younger generations! How the hidden life of each man feels his past sins possessing his home and hearth, his pew, and even his place at the Sacrament, till it is sometimes better for his soul's health to avoid these!

Such considerations give a great moral force to the doctrine of the Old Testament that man's sin has rendered necessary the destruction of his material circumstances, and that the Divine judgement includes a broken and a rifled universe.

The New Testament has borrowed this vision from the Old, but added, as we have seen, with greater distinctness, the hope of new heavens and a new earth. We have not concluded the subject, however, when we have pointed this out, for the New Testament has another gospel. The grace of God affects even the material results of sin; the Divine pardon that converts the sinner converts his circumstance also; Christ Jesus sanctifies even the flesh, and is the Physician of the body as well as the Saviour of the soul. To Him physical evil abounds only that He may show forth His glory in curing it. Neither did this man sin nor his parents, but that the works of God should be made manifest in him. To Paul the whole creation groaneth and travaileth with the sinner till now, the hour of the sinner's redemption. The Gospel bestows an evangelic liberty which permits the strong Christian to partake of meats offered to idols. And, finally, all things work together for good to them that love God, for although to the converted and forgiven sinner the material pains which his sins have brought on him may continue into his new life, they are experienced by him no more as the just penalties of an angry God, but as the loving, sanctifying chastisements of his Father in heaven.

Footnote:

80. vv. 14-16, which are very perplexing. In 14 a company is introduced to us very vaguely as those or yonder ones, who are represented as seeing the bright side of the convulsion which is the subject of the chapter. They cry aloud from the sea; that is, from the west of the prophet. He is therefore in the east, and in captivity, in the centre of the convulsion. The problem is to find any actual historical situation, in which part of Israel was in the east in captivity, and part in the west free and full of reasons for praising God for the calamity, out of which their brethren saw no escape for themselves.

CHAPTER XXIX.

GOD'S POOR.

Isaiah xxv.-xxvii. (DATE UNCERTAIN).

We have seen that no more than the faintest gleam of historical reflection brightens the obscurity of chap. xxiv., and that the disaster which lowers there is upon too world-wide a scale to be forced within the conditions of any single period in the fortunes of Israel. In chaps. xxv.-xxvii., which may naturally be held to be a continuation of chap. xxiv., the historical allusions are more numerous. Indeed, it might be said they are too numerous, for they contradict one another to the perplexity of the most acute critics. They imply historical circumstances for the prophecy both before and after the exile. On the one hand, the blame of idolatry in Judah (xxvii. 9), the mention of Assyria and Egypt (xxvii. 12, 13), and the absence of the name of Babylon are indicative of a pre-exilic date. [81] Arguments from style are always precarious; but it is striking that some critics, who deny that chaps. xxiv.-xxvii. can have come as a whole from Isaiah's time, profess to see his hand in certain passages. [82] Then, secondly, through these verses which point to a pre-exilic date there are woven, almost inextricably, phrases of actual exile: expressions of the sense of living on a level and in contact with the heathen (xxvi. 9, 10); a request to God's people to withdraw from the midst of a heathen public to the privacy of their chambers (20, 21); prayers and promises of deliverance from the oppressor (passim); hopes of the establishment of Zion, and of the repopulation of the Holy Land. And, thirdly, some verses imply that the speaker has already returned to Zion itself: he says more than once, in this mountain; there are hymns celebrating a deliverance actually achieved, as--God has done a marvel. For Thou hast made a citadel into a heap, a fortified city into a ruin, a castle of strangers to be no city, not to be built again. Such phrases do not read as if the prophet were creating for the lips of his people a psalm of triumph against a far future deliverance; they have in them the ring of what has already happened.

This bare statement of the allusions of the prophecy will give the ordinary reader some idea of the difficulties of Biblical criticism. What is to be made of a prophecy uttering the catch-words and breathing the experience of three distinct periods? One solution of the difficulty may be that we have here the composition of a Jew already returned from exile to a desecrated sanctuary and depopulated land, who has woven through his original utterances of complaint and hope the experience of earlier oppressions and deliverances, using even the names of earlier tyrants. In his immediate past a great city that oppressed the Jews has fallen, though, if this is Babylon, it is strange that he nowhere names it. But his intention is rather religious than historical; he seeks to give a general representation of the attitude of the world to the people of God, and of the judgement which God brings on the world. This view of the composition is supported by either of two possible interpretations of that difficult verse xxvii. 1: In that day Jehovah with His sword, the hard and the great and the strong, shall perform visitation upon Leviathan, Serpent Elusive, and upon Leviathan, Serpent Tortuous; and He shall slay the Dragon that is in the sea. Cheyne treats these monsters as mythic personifications of the clouds, the darkness and the powers of the air, so that the verse means that, just as Jehovah is supreme in the physical world, He shall be in the moral. But it is more probable that the two Leviathans mean Assyria and Babylon--the Elusive one, Assyria on the swift-shooting Tigris; the Tortuous one, Babylon on the winding Euphrates--while the Dragon that is in the sea or the west is Egypt. But if the prophet speaks of a victory over Israel's three great enemies all at once, that means that he is talking universally or ideally; and this impression is further heightened by the mythic names he gives them. Such arguments, along with the undoubted post-exilic fragments in the prophecy, point to a late date, so that even a very conservative critic, who is satisfied that Isaiah is the author, admits that "the possibility of exilic authorship does not allow itself to be denied."

If this character which we attribute to the prophecy be correct--viz., that it is a summary or ideal account of the attitude of the alien world to Israel, and of the judgement God has ready for the world--then, though itself be exilic, its place in the Book of Isaiah is intelligible. Chaps. xxiv.-xxvii. fitly crown the long list of Isaiah's oracles upon the foreign nations; they finally formulate the purposes of God towards the nations and towards Israel, whom the nations have oppressed. Our opinions must not be final or dogmatic about this matter of authorship; the obscurities are not nearly cleared up. But if it be ultimately found certain that this prophecy, which lies in the heart of the Book of Isaiah, is not by Isaiah himself, that need neither startle nor unsettle us. No doctrinal question is stirred by such a discovery, not even that of the accuracy of the Scriptures. For that a book is entitled by Isaiah's name does not necessarily mean that it is all by Isaiah; and we shall feel still less compelled to believe that these chapters are his when we find other chapters called by his name while these are not said to be by him. In truth there is a difficulty here, only because it is supposed that a book entitled by Isaiah's name must necessarily contain nothing but what is Isaiah's own. Tradition may have come to say so; but the Scripture itself, bearing as it does unmistakable marks of another age than Isaiah's, tells us that tradition

Rev. George Adam Smith, M.A.

is wrong: and the testimony of Scripture is surely to be preferred, especially when it betrays, as we have seen, sufficient reasons why a prophecy, though not Isaiah's, was attached to his genuine and undoubted oracles. In any case, however, as even the conservative critic whom we have quoted admits, "for the religious value" of the prophecy "the question" of the authorship "is thoroughly irrelevant."

We shall perceive this at once as we now turn to see what is the religious value of our prophecy. Chaps. xxv.-xxvii. stand in the front rank of evangelical prophecy. In their experience of religion, their characterisations of God's people, their expressions of faith, their missionary hopes and hopes of immortality, they are very rich and edifying. Perhaps their most signal feature is their designation of the people of God. In this collection of prayers and hymns the people of God are not regarded as a political body. They are only once called the nation and spoken of in connection with a territory (xxvi. 15). Only twice are they named with the national names of Israel and Jacob (xxvii. 6, 9, 12). We miss Isaiah's promised king, his pictures of righteous government, his emphasis upon social justice and purity, his interest in the foreign politics of his State, his hopes of national grandeur and agricultural felicity. In these chapters God's people are described by adjectives signifying spiritual qualities. Their nationality is no more pleaded, only their suffering estate and their hunger and thirst after God. The ideals that are presented for the future are neither political nor social, but ecclesiastical. We saw how closely Isaiah's prophesying was connected with the history of his time. The people of this prophecy seem to have done with history, and to be interested only in worship. And along with the assurance of the continued establishment of Zion as the centre for a secure and holy people, filling a secure and fertile land,--with which, as we have seen, the undoubted visions of Isaiah content themselves, while silent as to the fate of the individuals who drop from this future through death,--we have the most abrupt and thrilling hopes expressed for the resurrection of these latter to share in the glory of the redeemed and restored community.

Among the names applied to God's people there are three which were destined to play an enormous part in the history of religion. In the English version these appear as two: poor and needy; but in the original they are three. In chap. xxv. 4: Thou hast been a stronghold to the poor and a stronghold to the needy, poor renders a Hebrew word, "dal," literally wavering, tottering, infirm, then slender or lean, then poor in fortune and estate; needy literally renders the Hebrew "'ebhyôn," Latin egenus. In chap. xxvi. 6: the foot of the poor and the steps of the needy, needy renders "dal," while poor renders "'anî," a passive form--forced, afflicted, oppressed, then wretched, whether under persecution, poverty, loneliness or exile, and so tamed, mild, meek. These three words, in their root ideas of infirmity, need and positive affliction, cover among them every aspect of physical poverty and distress. Let us see how they came also to be the expression of the highest moral and evangelical virtues.

If there is one thing which distinguishes the people of the revelation from other historical nations, it is the evidence afforded by their dictionaries of the power to transmute the most afflicting experiences of life into virtuous disposition and effectual desire for God. We see this most clearly if we contrast the Hebrews' use of their words for poor with that of the first language which was employed to translate these words--the Greek in the Septuagint version of the Old Testament. In the Greek temper there was a noble pity for the unfortunate; the earliest Greeks regarded beggars as the peculiar protegés of Heaven. Greek philosophy developed a capacity for enriching the soul in misfortune; Stoicism gave imperishable proof of how bravely a man could hold poverty and pain to be things indifferent, and how much gain from such indifference he could bring to his soul. But in the vulgar opinion of Greece penury and sickness were always disgraceful; and Greek dictionaries mark the degradation of terms, which at first merely noted physical disadvantage, into epithets of contempt or hopelessness. It is very striking that it was not till they were employed to translate the Old Testament ideas of poverty that the Greek words for "poor" and "lowly" came to bear an honourable significance. And in the case of the Stoic, who endured poverty or pain with such indifference, was it not just this indifference that prevented him from discovering in his tribulations the rich evangelical experience which, as we shall see, fell to the quick conscience and sensitive nerves of the Hebrew?

Let us see how this conscience was developed. In the East poverty scarcely ever means physical disadvantage alone: in its train there follow higher disabilities. A poor Eastern cannot be certain of fair play in the courts of the land. He is very often a wronged man, with a fire of righteous anger burning in his breast. Again, and more important, misfortune is to the quick religious instinct of the Oriental a sign of God's estrangement. With us misfortune is so often only the cruelty, sometimes real sometimes imagined, of the rich; the unemployed vents his wrath at the capitalist, the tramp shakes his fist after the carriage on the highway. In the East they do not forget to curse the rich, but they remember as well to humble themselves beneath the hand of God. With an unfortunate Oriental the conviction is supreme, God is angry with me; I have lost His favour. His soul eagerly longs for God.

A poor man in the East has, therefore, not only a hunger for food: he has the hotter hunger for justice, the deeper hunger for God. Poverty in itself, without extraneous teaching, develops nobler appetites. The physical, becomes the moral, pauper; poor in substance, he grows poor in spirit. It was by developing, with the aid of God's Spirit, this quick conscience and this deep desire for God, which in the

East are the very soul of physical poverty, that the Jews advanced to that sense of evangelical poverty of heart, blessed by Jesus in the first of His Beatitudes as the possession of the kingdom of heaven.

Till the Exile, however, the poor were only a portion of the people. In the Exile the whole nation became poor, and henceforth "God's poor" might become synonymous with "God's people." This was the time when the words received their spiritual baptism. Israel felt the physical curse of poverty to its extreme of famine. The pains, privations and terrors, which the glib tongues of our comfortable middle classes, as they sing the psalms of Israel, roll off so easily for symbols of their own spiritual experience, were felt by the captive Hebrews in all their concrete physical effects. The noble and the saintly, the gentle and the cultured, priest, soldier and citizen, woman, youth and child, were torn from home and estate, were deprived of civil standing, were imprisoned, fettered, flogged and starved to death. We learn something of what it must have been from the words which Jeremiah addressed to Baruch, a youth of good family and fine culture: Seekest thou great things for thyself? Seek them not, for, behold, I will bring evil upon all flesh, saith the Lord; only thy life will I give unto thee for a prey in all places whither thou goest. Imagine a whole nation plunged into poverty of this degree--not born into it having known no better things, nor stunted into it with sensibility and the power of expression sapped out of them, but plunged into it, with the unimpaired culture, conscience and memories of the flower of the people. When God's own hand sent fresh from Himself a poet's soul into "the clay biggin'" of an Ayrshire ploughman, what a revelation we received of the distress, the discipline and the graces of poverty! But in the Jewish nation as it passed into exile there were a score of hearts with as unimpaired an appetite for life as Robert Burns; and, worse than he, they went to feel its pangs away from home. Genius, conscience and pride drank to the dregs in a foreign land the bitter cup of the poor. The Psalms and Lamentations show us how they bore their poison. A Greek Stoic might sneer at the complaint and sobbing, the self-abasement so strangely mixed with fierce cries for vengeance. But the Jew had within him the conscience that will not allow a man to be a Stoic. He never forgot that it was for his sin he suffered, and therefore to him suffering could not be a thing indifferent. With this, his native hunger for justice reached in captivity a famine pitch; his sense of guilt was equalled by as sincere an indignation at the tyrant who held him in his brutal grasp. The feeling of estrangement from God increased to a degree that only the exile of a Jew could excite: the longing for God's house and the worship lawful only there; the longing for the relief which only the sacrifices of the Temple could bestow; the longing for God's own presence and the light of His face. My soul thirsteth for Thee, my flesh longeth after Thee, in a dry and thirsty land, where no water is, as I have looked upon Thee in the sanctuary, to see Thy power and Thy glory. For Thy lovingkindness is better than life!

Thy lovingkindness is better than life!--is the secret of it all. There is that which excites a deeper hunger in the soul than the hunger for life, and for the food and money that give life. This spiritual poverty is most richly bred in physical penury, it is strong enough to displace what feeds it. The physical poverty of Israel which had awakened these other hungers of the soul--hunger for forgiveness, hunger for justice, hunger for God--was absorbed by them; and when Israel came out of exile, to be poor meant, not so much to be indigent in this world's substance as to feel the need of pardon, the absence of righteousness, the want of God.

It is at this time, as we have seen, that Isa. xxiv.-xxvii. was written; and it is in the temper of this time that the three Hebrew words for "poor" and "needy" are used in chaps. xxv. and xxvi. The returned exiles were still politically dependent and abjectly poor. Their discipline therefore continued, and did not allow them to forget their new lessons. In fact, they developed the results of these further, till in this prophecy we find no fewer than five different aspects of spiritual poverty.

1. We have already seen how strong the sense of sin is in chap. xxiv. This POVERTY of PEACE is not so fully expressed in the following chapters, and indeed seems crowded out by the sense of the iniquity of the inhabitants of the earth and the desire for their judgement (xxvi. 21).

2. The feeling of the POVERTY of JUSTICE is very strong in this prophecy. But it is to be satisfied; in part it has been satisfied (xxv. 1-4). A strong city, probably Babylon, has fallen. Moab shall be trodden down in his place, even as straw is trodden down in the water of the dunghill. The complete judgement is to come when the Lord shall destroy the two Leviathans and the great Dragon of the west (xxvii. 1). It is followed by the restoration of Israel to the state in which Isaiah (chap. v. 1) sang so sweetly of her. A pleasant vineyard, sing ye of her. I, Jehovah, her Keeper, moment by moment do I water her; lest any make a raid upon her, night and day will I keep her. The Hebrew text then reads, Fury is not in Me; but probably the Septuagint version has preserved the original meaning: I have no walls. If this be correct, then Jehovah is describing the present state of Jerusalem, the fulfilment of Isaiah's threat, chap. v. 6: Walls I have not; let there but be briers and thorns before me! With war will I stride against them; I will burn them together. But then there breaks the softer alternative of the reconciliation of Judah's enemies: Or else let him seize hold of My strength; let him make peace with Me--peace let him make with Me. In such a peace Israel shall spread, and his fulness become the riches of the Gentiles. In that by-and-bye Jacob shall take root, Israel blossom and bud, and fill the face of the world with fruit.

Rev. George Adam Smith, M.A.

    Perhaps the wildest cries that rose from Israel's famine of justice were those which found expression in chap. xxxiv. This chapter is so largely a repetition of feelings we have already met with elsewhere in the Book of Isaiah, that it is necessary now only to mention its original features. The subject is, as in chap. xiii., the Lord's judgement upon all the nations; and as chap. xiii. singled out Babylon for special doom, so chap. xxxiv. singles out Edom. The reason of this distinction will be very plain to the reader of the Old Testament. From the day the twins struggled in their mother Rebekah's womb, Israel and Edom were either at open war or burned towards each other with a hate, which was the more intense for wanting opportunities of gratification. It is an Eastern edition of the worst chapters in the history of England and Ireland. No bloodier massacres stained Jewish hands than those which attended their invasions of Edom, and Jewish psalms of vengeance are never more flagrant than when they touch the name of the children of Esau. The only gentle utterance of the Old Testament upon Israel's hereditary foe is a comfortless enigma. Isaiah's Oracle for Dumah (xxii. 11 f.), shows that even that large-hearted prophet, in face of his people's age-long resentment at Edom's total want of appreciation of Israel's spiritual superiority, could offer Edom, though for the moment submissive and inquiring, nothing but a sad, ambiguous answer. Edom and Israel, each after his fashion, exulted in the other's misfortunes: Israel by bitter satire when Edom's impregnable mountain-range was treacherously seized and overrun by his allies (Obadiah 4-9); Edom, with the harassing, pillaging habits of a highland tribe, hanging on to the skirts of Judah's great enemies, and cutting off Jewish fugitives, or selling them into slavery, or malignantly completing the ruin of Jerusalem's walls after her overthrow by the Chaldeans (Obadiah 10-14; Ezek. xxxv. 10-15; Ps. cxxxi. 7). In the quarrel of Zion with the nations of the world Edom had taken the wrong side,--his profane, earthy nature incapable of understanding his brother's spiritual claims, and therefore envious of him, with the brutal malice of ignorance, and spitefully glad to assist in disappointing such claims. This is what we must remember when we read the indignant verses of chap. xxxiv. Israel, conscious of his spiritual calling in the world, felt bitter resentment that his own brother should be so vulgarly hostile to his attempts to carry it out. It is not our wish to defend the temper of Israel towards Edom. The silence of Christ before the Edomite Herod and his men of war has taught the spiritual servants of God what is their proper attitude towards the malignant and obscene treatment of their claims by vulgar men. But at least let us remember that chap. xxxiv., for all its fierceness, is inspired by Israel's conviction of a spiritual destiny and service for God, and by the natural resentment that his own kith and kin should be doing their best to render these futile. That a famine of bread makes its victims delirious does not tempt us to doubt the genuineness of their need and suffering. As little ought we to doubt or to ignore the reality or the purity of those spiritual convictions, the prolonged starvation of which bred in Israel such feverish hate against his twin-brother Esau. Chap. xxxiv., with all its proud prophecy of judgement, is, therefore, also a symptom of that aspect of Israel's poverty of heart, which we have called a hunger for the Divine justice.

    3. Poverty of the Exile. But as fair flowers bloom upon rough stalks, so from Israel's stern challenges of justice there break sweet prayers for home. Chap. xxxiv., the effusion of vengeance on Edom, is followed by chap. xxxv., the going forth of hope to the return from exile and the establishment of the ransomed of the Lord in Zion. [83] Chap. xxxv. opens with a prospect beyond the return, but after the first two verses addresses itself to the people still in a foreign captivity, speaking of their salvation (vv. 3, 4), of the miracles that will take place in themselves (vv. 5, 6) and in the desert between them and their home (vv. 6, 7), of the highway which God shall build, evident and secure (vv. 8, 9), and of the final arrival in Zion (ver. 10). In that march the usual disappointments and illusions of desert life shall disappear. The mirage shall become a pool; and the clump of vegetation which afar off the hasty traveller hails for a sign of water, but which on his approach he discovers to be the withered grass of a jackal's lair, shall indeed be reeds and rushes, standing green in fresh water. Out of this exuberant fertility there emerges in the prophet's thoughts a great highway, on which the poetry of the chapter gathers and reaches its climax. Have we of this nineteenth century, with our more rapid means of passage, not forgotten the poetry of the road? Are we able to appreciate either the intrinsic usefulness or the gracious symbolism of the king's highway? How can we know it as the Bible-writers or our forefathers knew it when they made the road the main line of their allegories and parables of life? Let us listen to these verses as they strike the three great notes in the music of the road: And an highway shall be there, and a way; yea, The Way of Holiness shall it be called, for the unclean shall not pass over it-- that is what is to distinguish this road from all other roads. But here is what it is as being a road. First, it shall be unmistakably plain: The wayfaring man, yea fools, shall not err therein. Second, it shall be perfectly secure: No lion shall be there, nor shall any ravenous beast go up thereon; they shall not be met with there. Third, it shall bring to a safe arrival and ensure a complete overtaking: And the ransomed of the Lord shall return and come with singing unto Zion, and everlasting joy shall be upon their heads; they shall overtake gladness and joy, and sorrow and sighing shall flee away.

    4. So Israel was to come home. But to Israel home meant the Temple, and the Temple meant God. The poverty of the Exile was, in the essence of it, Poverty of God, Poverty of love. The prayers which express this are very beautiful,--that trail like wounded animals to the feet of their master, and look up

in His face with large eyes of pain. And they shall say in that day, Lo, this is our God: we have waited for Him, that He should save us; this is the LORD: we have waited for Him; we will rejoice and be glad in His salvation.... Yea, in the way of Thy ordinances, O LORD, have we waited for Thee; to Thy name and to Thy Memorial was the desire of our soul. With my soul have I desired Thee in the night; yea, by my spirit within me do I seek Thee with dawn (chaps. xxv. 9; xxvi. 8).

An Arctic explorer was once asked, whether during eight months of slow starvation which he and his comrades endured they suffered much from the pangs of hunger. No, he answered, we lost them in the sense of abandonment, in the feeling that our countrymen had forgotten us and were not coming to the rescue. It was not till we were rescued and looked in human faces that we felt how hungry we were. So is it ever with God's poor. They forget all other need, as Israel did, in their need of God. Their outward poverty is only the weeds of their heart's widowhood. But Jehovah of hosts shall make to all the peoples in this mountain a banquet of fat things, a banquet of wines on the lees, fat things bemarrowed, wines on the lees refined.

We need only note here--for it will come up for detailed treatment in connection with the second half of Isaiah--that the centre of Israel's restored life is to be the Temple, not, as in Isaiah's day, the king; that her dispersed are to gather from all parts of the world at the sound of the Temple trumpet; and that her national life is to consist in worship (cf. xxvii. 13).

***

These then were four aspects of Israel's poverty of heart: a hunger for pardon, a hunger for justice, a hunger for home, and a hunger for God. For the returning Jews these wants were satisfied only to reveal a deeper poverty still, the complaint and comfort of which we must reserve to another chapter.

Footnotes:

81. The mention of Moab (xxv. 10, 11) is also consistent with a pre-exilic date, but does not necessarily imply it.

82. E.g., xxv. 6-8, 10, 11; xxvii. 10, 11, 9, 12, 13.

83. Even at the risk of incurring Canon Cheyne's charge of "ineradicable error," I feel I must keep to the older view of chap. xxxv. which makes it refer to the return from exile. No doubt the chapter covers more than the mere return, and includes "the glorious condition of Israel after the return;" but vv. 4 and 10 are undoubtedly addressed to Jews still in exile and undelivered.

Rev. George Adam Smith, M.A.

CHAPTER XXX

THE RESURRECTION.

Isaiah xxvi. 14-19; xxv. 6-9.

Granted the pardon, the justice, the Temple and the God, which the returning exiles now enjoyed, the possession of these only makes more painful the shortness of life itself. This life is too shallow and too frail a vessel to hold peace and righteousness and worship and the love of God. St. Paul has said, If in this life only we have hope in Christ, we are of all men most miserable. What avails it to have been pardoned, to have regained the Holy Land and the face of God, if the dear dead are left behind in graves of exile, and all the living must soon pass into that captivity, [84] from which there is no return?

It must have been thoughts like these, which led to the expression of one of the most abrupt and powerful of the few hopes of the resurrection which the Old Testament contains. This hope, which lightens chap. xxv. 7, 8, bursts through again--without logical connection with the context--in vv. 14-19 of chap. xxvi.

The English version makes ver. 14 to continue the reference to the lords, whom in ver. 13 Israel confesses to have served instead of Jehovah. "They are dead; they shall not live: they are deceased; they shall not rise." Our translators have thus intruded into their version the verb "they are," of which the original is without a trace. In the original, dead and deceased (literally shades) are themselves the subject of the sentence--a new subject and without logical connection with what has gone before. The literal translation of ver. 14 therefore runs: Dead men do not live; shades do not rise: wherefore Thou visitest them and destroyest them, and perisheth all memory of them. The prophet states a fact, and draws an inference. The fact is, that no one has ever returned from the dead; the inference, that it is God's own visitation or sentence which has gone forth upon them, and they have really ceased to exist. But how intolerable a thought is this in presence of the other fact that God has here on earth above gloriously enlarged and established His people (ver. 15). Thou hast increased the nation, Jehovah; Thou hast increased the nation. Thou hast covered Thyself with glory; Thou hast expanded all the boundaries of the land. To this follows a verse (16), the sense of which is obscure, but palpable. It "feels" to mean that the contrast which the prophet has just painted between the absolute perishing of the dead and the glory of the Church above ground is the cause of great despair and groaning: O Jehovah, in The Trouble they supplicate Thee; they pour out incantations when Thy discipline is upon them. [85] In face of The Trouble and The Discipline par excellence of God, what else can man do but betake himself to God? God sent death; in death He is the only resource. Israel's feelings in presence of The Trouble are now expressed in ver. 17: Like as a woman with child that draweth near the time of her delivery writheth and crieth out in her pangs, so have we been before Thee, O Jehovah. Thy Church on earth is pregnant with a life, which death does not allow to come to the birth. We have been with child; we have been in the pangs, as it were; we have brought forth wind; we make not the earth, in spite of all we have really accomplished upon it in our return, our restoration and our enjoyment of Thy presence--we make not the earth salvation, neither are the inhabitants of the world born. [86]

The figures are bold. Israel achieves, through God's grace, everything but the recovery of her dead; this, which alone is worth calling salvation, remains wanting to her great record of deliverances. The living Israel is restored, but how meagre a proportion of the people it is! The graves of home and of exile do not give up their dead. These are not born again to be inhabitants of the upper world.

The figures are bold, but bolder is the hope that breaks from them. Like as when the Trumpet shall sound, ver. 19 peals forth the promise of the resurrection--peals the promise forth, in spite of all experience, unsupported by any argument, and upon the strength of its own inherent music. Thy dead shall live! my dead bodies shall arise! The change of the personal pronoun is singularly dramatic. Returned Israel is the speaker, first speaking to herself: thy dead, as if upon the depopulated land, in face of all its homes in ruin, and only the sepulchres of ages standing grim and steadfast, she addressed some despairing double of herself; and secondly speaking of herself: my dead bodies, as if all the inhabitants of these tombs, though dead, were still her own, still part of her, the living Israel, and able to arise and bless with their numbers their bereaved mother. These she now addresses: Awake and sing, ye dwellers in the dust, for a dew of lights is Thy dew, and the land bringeth forth the dead. [87]

If one has seen a place of graves in the East, he will appreciate the elements of this figure, which takes dust for death and dew for life. With our damp graveyards mould has become the traditional trappings of death; but where under the hot Eastern sun things do not rot into lower forms of life, but crumble into sapless powder, that will not keep a worm in life, dust is the natural symbol of death. When they die, men go not to feed fat the mould, but down into the dust; and there the foot of the living falls silent, and his voice is choked, and the light is thickened and in retreat, as if it were creeping away to die. The only creatures the visitor starts are timid, unclean bats, that flutter and whisper about him like the ghosts of the dead. There are no flowers in an Eastern cemetery; and the withered branches and other ornaments are thickly powdered with the same dust that chokes, and silences and darkens all.

Hence the Semitic conception of the underworld was dominated by dust. It was not water nor fire nor frost nor altogether darkness, which made the infernal prison horrible, but that upon its floor and rafters, hewn from the roots and ribs of the primeval mountains, dust lay deep and choking. Amid all the horrors he imagined for the dead, Dante did not include one more awful than the horror of dust. The picture which the northern Semites had before them when they turned their faces to the wall was of this kind. [88]

> *The house of darkness....*
> *The house men enter, but cannot depart from.*
> *The road men go, but cannot return.*
> *The house from whose dwellers the light is withdrawn.*
> *The place where dust is their food, their nourishment clay.*
> *The light they behold not; in darkness they dwell.*
> *They are clothed like birds, all fluttering wings.*
> *On the door and the gateposts, the dust lieth deep.*

Either, then, an Eastern sepulchre, or this its infernal double, was gaping before the prophet's eyes. What more final and hopeless than the dust and the dark of it?

But for dust there is dew, and even to graveyards the morning comes that brings dew and light together. The wonder of dew is that it is given from a clear heaven, and that it comes to sight with the dawn. If the Oriental looks up when dew is falling, he sees nothing to thank for it between him and the stars. If he sees dew in the morning, it is equal liquid and lustre; it seems to distil from the beams of the sun--the sun, which riseth with healing under his wings. The dew is thus doubly "dew of light." But our prophet ascribes the dew of God, that is to raise the dead, neither to stars nor dawn, but, because of its Divine power, to that higher supernal glory which the Hebrews conceived to have existed before the sun, and which they styled, as they styled their God, by the plural of majesty: A dew of lights is Thy dew. [89] As, when the dawn comes, the drooping flowers of yesterday are seen erect and lustrous with the dew, every spike a crown of glory, so also shall be the resurrection of the dead. There is no shadow of a reason for limiting this promise to that to which some other passages of resurrection in the Old Testament have to be limited: a corporate restoration of the holy State or Church. This is the resurrection of its individual members to a community which is already restored, the recovery by Israel of her dead men and women from their separate graves, each with his own freshness and beauty, in that glorious morning when the Sun of righteousness shall arise, with healing under His wings--Thy dew, O Jehovah!

Attempts are so often made to trace the hopes of resurrection, which break the prevailing silence of the Old Testament on a future life, to foreign influences experienced in the Exile, that it is well to emphasize the origin and occasion of the hopes that utter themselves so abruptly in this passage. Surely nothing could be more inextricably woven with the national fortunes of Israel, as nothing could be more native and original to Israel's temper, than the verses just expounded. We need not deny that their residence among a people, accustomed as the Babylonians were to belief in the resurrection, may have thawed in the Jews that reserve which the Old Testament clearly shows that they exhibited towards a future life. The Babylonians themselves had received most of their suggestions of the next world from a non-Semitic race; and therefore it would not be to imagine anything alien to the ascertained methods of Providence if we were to suppose that the Hebrews, who showed what we have already called the Semitic want of interest in a future life, were intellectually tempered by their foreign associations to a readiness to receive any suggestions of immortality, which the Spirit of God might offer them through their own religious experience. That it was this last, which was the effective cause of Israel's hopes for the resurrection of her dead, our passage puts beyond doubt. Chap. xxvi. shows us that the occasion of these hopes was what is not often noticed: the returned exiles' disappointment with the meagre repopulation of the holy territory. A restoration of the State or community was not enough: the heart of Israel wanted back in their numbers her dead sons and daughters.

If the occasion of these hopes was thus an event in Israel's own national history, and if the impulse to them was given by so natural an instinct of her own heart, Israel was equally indebted to herself for the convictions that the instinct was not in vain. Nothing is more clear in our passage than that Israel's first ground of hope in a future life was her simple, untaught reflection upon the power of her God.

Death was His chastening. Death came from Him, and remained in His power. Surely He would deliver from it. This was a very old belief in Israel. The Lord killeth and maketh alive; He bringeth down to Sheol and bringeth up. Such words, of course, might be only an extreme figure for recovery from disease, and the silence of so great a saint as Hezekiah about any other issue into life than by convalescence from mortal sickness staggers us into doubt whether an Israelite ever did think of a resurrection. But still there was Jehovah's almightiness; a man could rest his future on that, even if he had not light to think out what sort of a future it would be. So mark in our passage, how confidence is chiefly derived from the simple utterance of the name of Jehovah, and how He is hailed as our God. It seems enough to the prophet to connect life with Him and to say merely, Thy dew. As death is God's own discipline, so life, Thy dew, is with Him also.

Thus in its foundation the Old Testament doctrine of the resurrection is but the conviction of the sufficiency of God Himself, a conviction which Christ turned upon Himself when He said, I am the Resurrection and the Life. Because I live, ye shall live also.

If any object that in this picture of a resurrection we have no real persuasion of immortality, but simply the natural, though impossible, wish of a bereaved people that their dead should to-day rise from their graves to share to-day's return and glory--a revival as special and extraordinary as that appearing of the dead in the streets of Jerusalem when the Atonement was accomplished, but by no means that general resurrection at the last day which is an article of the Christian faith--if any one should bring this objection, then let him be referred to the previous promise of immortality in chap. xxv. The universal and final character of the promise made there is as evident as of that for which Paul borrowed its terms in order to utter the absolute consequences of the resurrection of the Son of God: Death is swallowed up in victory. For the prophet, having in ver. 6 described the restoration of the people, whom exile had starved with a famine of ordinances, to a feast in Zion of fat things and wines on the lees well refined, intimates that as certainly as exile has been abolished, with its dearth of spiritual intercourse, so certainly shall God Himself destroy death: And He shall swallow up in this mountain--perhaps it is imagined, as the sun devours the morning mist on the hills--the mask of the veil, the veil that is upon all the peoples, and the film spun upon all the nations. He hath swallowed up death for ever, and the Lord Jehovah shall wipe away tears from off all faces, and the reproach of His people shall He remove from off all the earth, for Jehovah hath spoken it. And they shall say in that day, Behold, this is our God: we have waited for Him, and He shall save us; this is Jehovah: we have waited for Him; we will rejoice and be glad in His salvation. Thus over all doubts, and in spite of universal human experience, the prophet depends for immortality on God Himself. In chap. xxvi. 3 our version beautifully renders, Thou wilt keep him in perfect peace whose mind is stayed on Thee, because he trusteth in Thee. This is a confidence valid for the next life as well as for this. Therefore trust ye in the Lord for ever. Amen.

Almighty God, we praise Thee that, in the weakness of all our love and the darkness of all our knowledge before death, Thou hast placed assurance of eternal life in simple faith upon Thyself. Let this faith be richly ours. By Thine omnipotence, by Thy righteousness, by the love Thou hast vouchsafed, we lift ourselves and rest upon Thy word. Because I live, ye shall live also. Oh keep us steadfast in union with Thyself, through Jesus Christ our Lord. Amen.

Footnotes:

84. Hezekiah's expression for death, xxxviii. 12.

85. I think this must be the meaning of ver. 16, if we are to allow that it has any sympathy with vv. 14 and 15. Bredenkamp suggests that the persons meant are themselves the dead. Jehovah has glorified the Church on earth; but the dead below are still in trouble, and pour out prayers (Virgil's "preces fundunt," Æneid, vi., 55), beneath this punishment which God causes to pass on all men (ver. 14). Bredenkamp bases this exegesis chiefly on the word for "prayer," which means chirping or whispering, a kind of voice imputed to the shades by the Hebrews and other ancient peoples. But while this word does originally mean whispering, it is never in Scripture applied to the dead, but, on the other hand, is a frequent name for divining or incantation. I therefore have felt compelled to understand it as used in this passage of the living, whose only resource in face of death--Goa's discipline par excellence--is to pour out incantations. If it be objected that the prophet would scarcely parallel the ordinary incantations on behalf of the dead with supplications to Jehovah, the answer is that he is talking poetically or popularly.

86. English version, fallen; i.e., like our expression for the birth of animals, dropped.

87. Technical Hebrew word for the inhabitants of the underworld--the shades.

88. Extracted from the Assyrian Descent of Istar to Hades (Dr. Jeremias' German translation, p. 11, and Records of the Past, i., 145).

89. Cf. James i. 17.

Volume II

TABLE OF DATES.

b.c.
721. Fall of Samaria. Captivity of Northern Israel.
701. Deliverance of Jerusalem from Sennacherib.
696?-641.Reign of Manasseh. Supposed time of Isaiah's death.
630. Josiah's Reformation begun.
629 or 628. Jeremiah called to be a prophet.
621. The Book of Deuteronomy discovered.
607. Fall of Nineveh and Assyria. Babylon supreme.

THE EXILE.

599-598. Siege of Jerusalem by Nebuchadrezzar. First Captivity of the Jews.
594. Ezekiel begins to prophesy in Chaldea.
587. Destruction of Jerusalem by Nebuchadrezzar. Second Captivity of the Jews. Flight of many Jews with Jeremiah to Egypt.
585. Battle of the Eclipse. Triple League: Babylon, Media, Lydia.
561. Nebuchadrezzar dies. Evil-Merodach succeeds.
559. Neriglissar succeeds Evil-Merodach.
554. Nabunahid or Nabonidos usurps the throne of Babylon. Harder times for the Jews.
549. Fall of Median monarchy before Cyrus.
545. Cyrus attacks Babylonia from the north, and is repulsed. Invades Lydia, and takes Sardis and King Croesus.
538. Cyrus captures Babylon. Permission to the Jews to return and rebuild Jerusalem. Zerubbabel, Joshua.
529. Cyrus dies. Cambyses sole king.
522. Cambyses dies.
521. Babylon revolts. Retaken by Darius
486. Xerxes succeeds Darius.
466. Artaxerxes Longimanus.
458. Second great return of Jews. Ezra.
401. Revolt and defeat of Cyrus. The Anabasis.

Rev. George Adam Smith, M.A.

INTRODUCTION

This volume upon Isaiah xl.-lxvi. carries on the exposition of the Book of Isaiah from the point reached by the author's previous volume in the same series. But as it accepts these twenty-seven chapters, upon their own testimony, as a separate prophecy from a century and a half later than Isaiah himself, in a style and on subjects not altogether the same as his, and as it accordingly pursues a somewhat different method of exposition from the previous volume, a few words of introduction are again necessary.

The greater part of Isaiah i.-xxxix. was addressed to a nation upon their own soil,--with their temple, their king, their statesmen, their tribunals and their markets,--responsible for the discharge of justice and social reform, for the conduct of foreign policies and the defence of the fatherland. But chs. xl.-lxvi. came to a people wholly in exile, and partly in servitude, with no civic life and few social responsibilities: a people in the passive state, with occasion for the exercise of almost no qualities save those of penitence and patience, of memory and hope. This difference between the two parts of the Book is summed up in their respective uses of the word Righteousness. In Isaiah i.-xxxix., or at least in such of these chapters as refer to Isaiah's own day, righteousness is man's moral and religious duty, in its contents of piety, purity, justice and social service. In Isaiah xl.-lxvi. righteousness (except in a very few cases) is something which the people expect from God--their historical vindication by His restoral and reinstatement of them as His people.

It is, therefore, evident that what rendered Isaiah's own prophecies of so much charm and of so much meaning to the modern conscience--their treatment of those political and social questions which we have always with us--cannot form the chief interest of chapters xl.-lxvi. But the empty place is taken by a series of historical and religious questions of supreme importance. Into the vacuum created in Israel's life by the Exile, there comes rushing the meaning of the nation's whole history--all the conscience of their past, all the destiny with which their future is charged. It is not with the fortunes and duties of a single generation that this great prophecy has to do: it is with a people in their entire significance and promise. The standpoint of the prophet may be the Exile, but his vision ranges from Abraham to Christ. Besides the business of the hour,--the deliverance of Israel from Babylon,--the prophet addresses himself to these questions: What is Israel? What is Israel's God? How is Jehovah different from other gods? How is Israel different from other peoples? He recalls the making of the nation, God's treatment of them from the beginning, all that they and Jehovah have been to each other and to the world, and especially the meaning of this latest judgement of Exile. But the instruction and the impetus of that marvellous past he uses in order to interpret and proclaim the still more glorious future,--the ideal, which God has set before His people, and in the realisation of which their history shall culminate. It is here that the Spirit of God lifts the prophet to the highest station in prophecy--to the richest consciousness of spiritual religion--to the clearest vision of Christ.

Accordingly, to expound Isaiah xl.-lxvi. is really to write the religious history of Israel. A prophet whose vision includes both Abraham and Christ, whose subject is the whole meaning and promise of Israel, cannot be adequately interpreted within the limits of his own text or of his own time. Excursions are necessary both to the history that is behind him, and to the history that is still in front of him. This is the reason of the appearance in this volume of chapters whose titles seem at first beyond its scope--such as From Isaiah to the Fall of Jerusalem: What Israel took into Exile: One God, One People: The Servant of the Lord in the New Testament. Moreover, much of this historical matter has an interest that is only historical. If in Isaiah's own prophecies it is his generation's likeness to ourselves, which appeals to our conscience, in chs. xl.-lxvi. of the Book called by his name it is Israel's unique meaning and office for God in the world, which we have to study. We are called to follow an experience and a discipline unshared by any other generation of men; and to interest ourselves in matters that then happened once for all, such as the victory of the One God over the idols, or His choice of a single people through whom to reveal Himself to the world. We are called to watch work, which that representative and priestly people did for humanity, rather than, as in Isaiah's own prophecies, work which has to be repeated by each new generation in its turn, and to-day also by ourselves. This is the reason why in an exposition of Isaiah xl.-lxvi., like the present volume, there should be a good deal more of historical recital, and a good deal less of practical application, than in the exposition of Isaiah i.-xxxix.

At the same time we must not suppose that there is not very much in Isaiah xl.-lxvi. with which to stir our own consciences and instruct our own lives. For, to mention no more, there is that sense of sin with which Israel entered exile, and which has made the literature of Israel's Exile the confessional of the world; there is that great unexhausted programme of the Service of God and Man, which our prophet lays down as Israel's duty and example to humanity; and there is that prophecy of the virtue and glory of vicarious suffering for sin, which is the gospel of Jesus Christ and His Cross.

I have found it necessary to devote more space to critical questions than in the previous volume. Chs. xl.-lxvi. approach more nearly to a unity than chs. i.-xxxix.: with very few exceptions they lie in chronological order. But they are not nearly so clearly divided and grouped: their connection cannot be so briefly or so lucidly explained. The form of the prophecy is dramatic, but the scenes and the speakers are not definitely marked off. In spite of the chronological advance, which we shall be able to trace, there are no clear stages--not even, as we shall see, at those points at which most expositors divide the prophecy, the end of ch. xlix. and of ch. lviii. The prophet pursues simultaneously several lines of thought; and though the close of some of these and the rise of others may be marked to a verse, his frequent passages from one to another are often almost imperceptible. He everywhere requires a more continuous translation, a closer and more elaborate exegesis, than were necessary for Isaiah i.-xxxix.

In order to effect some general arrangement and division of Isa. xl.-lxvi. it is necessary to keep in view that the immediate problem which the prophet had before him was twofold. It was political, and it was spiritual. There was, first of all, the deliverance of Israel from Babylon, according to the ancient promises of Jehovah: to this were attached such questions as Jehovah's omnipotence, faithfulness and grace; the meaning of Cyrus; the condition of the Babylonian Empire. But after their political deliverance from Babylon was assured, there remained the really larger problem of Israel's spiritual readiness for the freedom and the destiny to which God was to lead them through the opened gates of their prison-house: to this were attached such questions as the original calling and mission of Israel; the mixed and paradoxical character of the people; their need of a Servant from the Lord, since they themselves had failed to be His Servant; the coming of this Servant, his methods and results.

This twofold division of the prophet's problem will not, it is true, strike his prophecy into separate and distinct groups of chapters. He who attempts such a division simply does not understand "Second Isaiah." But it will make clear to us the different currents of the sacred argument, which flow sometimes through and through one another, and sometimes singly and in succession; and it will give us a plan for grouping the twenty-seven chapters very nearly, if not quite, in the order in which they lie.

On these principles, the following exposition is divided into Four Books. The First is called The Exile: it contains an argument for placing the date of the prophecy about 550 b.c., and brings the history of Israel down to that date from the time of Isaiah; it states the political and spiritual sides of the double problem to which the prophecy is God's answer; it describes what Israel took with them into exile, and what they learned and suffered there, till, after half a century, the herald voices of our prophecy broke upon their waiting ears. The Second Book, The Lord's Deliverance, discusses the political redemption from Babylon, with the questions attached to it about God's nature and character, about Cyrus and Babylon, or all of chs. xl.-xlviii., except the passages about the Servant, which are easily detached from the rest, and refer rather to the spiritual side of Israel's great problem. The Third Book, The Servant of the Lord, expounds all the passages on that subject, both in chs. xl.-xlviii. and in chs. xlix.-liii., with the development of the subject in the New Testament, and its application to our life to-day. The Servant and his work are the solution of all the spiritual difficulties in the way of the people's Return and Restoration. To these latter and their practical details the rest of the prophecy is devoted; that is, all chs. xlix.-lxvi., except the passages on the Servant, and these chapters are treated in the Fourth Book of this volume, The Restoration.

As much as possible of the merely critical discussion has been put in Chapter [1]I., or in the opening paragraphs of the other chapters, or in foot-notes. A new translation from the original (except where a few verses have been taken from the Revised English Version) has been provided for nearly the whole prophecy. Where the rhythm of the original is at all discernible, the translation has been made in it. But it must be kept in mind that this reproduction of the original rhythm is only approximate, and that in it no attempt has been made to elegance; its chief aim being to make clear the order and the emphases of the original. The translation is almost quite literal.

Having felt the want of a clear account of the prophet's use of his great key-word Righteousness, I have inserted for students, at the end of Book [2]II., a chapter on this term. Summaries of our prophet's use of such cardinal terms as Mishpat, R'ishonoth, The Isles, etc., will be found in notes. For want of space I have had to exclude some sections on the Style of Isaiah, xl.-lxvi., on the Influence of Monotheism on the Imagination, and on What Isaiah xl.-lxvi. owes to Jeremiah. This debt, as we shall be able to trace, is so great that "Second Jeremiah" would be a title no less proper for the prophecy than "Second Isaiah."

I had also wished to append a chapter on Commentaries on the Book of Isaiah. No Scripture has been so nobly served by its commentaries. To begin with there was Calvin, and there is Calvin,--still as valuable as ever for his strong spiritual power, his sanity, his moderation, his sensitiveness to the changes and shades of the prophet's meaning. After him Vitringa, Gesenius, Hitzig, Ewald, Delitzsch, all the great names of the past in Old Testament criticism, are connected with Isaiah. In recent years (besides Nägelsbach in Lange's Bibelwerk) we have had Cheyne's two volumes, too well known both here and in Germany to need more than mention; Bredenkamp's clear and concise exposition, the characteristic of which is an attempt--not, however, successful--to distinguish authentic prophecies of Isaiah in the disputed chapters; Orelli's handy volume (in Strack and Zöckler's compendious Commentary, and translated into English by Professor Banks in Messrs. Clarks' Foreign Theological Library), from the conservative side, but accepting, as Delitzsch does in his last edition, the dual authorship; and this year Dillmann's great work, replacing Knobel's in the "Kurzgefasstes Exegetisches Handbuch" series. I regret that I did not receive Dillmann's work till more than half of this volume was written. English students will have all they can possibly need if they can add Dillmann to Delitzsch and Cheyne, though Calvin and Ewald must never be forgotten. Professor Driver's Isaiah: His Life and Times is a complete handbook to the prophet. On the theology, besides the relevant portions of Schultz's Alt-Testamentliche Theologie (4th ed., 1889), and Duhm's Theologie der Propheten, the student will find invaluable Professor Robertson Smith's Prophets of Israel for Isaiah i.-xxxix., and Professor A. B. Davidson's papers in the Expositor for 1884 on the theology of Isaiah xl.-lxvi. There are also Krüger's able and lucid Essai sur la Théologie d'Isaïe xl.-lxvi. (Paris, 1882), and Guthe's Das Zukunftsbild Jesaias, and Barth's and Giesebrecht's respective Beiträge zur Jesaiakritik, the latter published this year.

In conclusion, I have to express my thanks for the very great assistance which I have derived in the composition of both volumes from my friend the Rev. Charles Anderson Scott, B.A., who has sought out facts, read nearly all the proofs and helped to prepare the Index.

BOOK I

THE EXILE.

Rev. George Adam Smith, M.A.

CHAPTER I

THE DATE OF ISAIAH XL.-LXVI.

The problem of the date of Isaiah xl.-lxvi. is this: In a book called by the name of the prophet Isaiah, who flourished between 740 and 700 b.c., the last twenty-seven chapters deal with the captivity suffered by the Jews in Babylonia from 598 to 538, and more particularly with the advent, about 550, of Cyrus, whom they name. Are we to take for granted that Isaiah himself prophetically wrote these chapters, or must we assign them to a nameless author or authors of the period of which they treat?

Till the end of last century it was the almost universally accepted tradition, and even still is an opinion retained by many, that Isaiah was carried forward by the Spirit, out of his own age to the standpoint of one hundred and fifty years later; that he was inspired to utter the warning and comfort required by a generation so very different from his own, and was even enabled to hail by name their redeemer, Cyrus. This theory, involving as it does a phenomenon without parallel in the history of Holy Scripture, is based on these two grounds: first, that the chapters in question form a considerable part-- nearly nine-twentieths--of the "Book of Isaiah;" and second, that portions of them are quoted in the New Testament by the prophet's name. The theory is also supported by arguments drawn from resemblances of style and vocabulary between these twenty-seven chapters and the undisputed oracles of Isaiah; but, as the opponents of the Isaian authorship also appeal to vocabulary and style, it will be better to leave this kind of evidence aside for the present, and to discuss the problem upon other and less ambiguous grounds.

The first argument, then, for the Isaian authorship of chapters xl.-lxvi. is that they form part of a book called by Isaiah's name. But, to be worth anything, this argument must rest on the following facts: that everything in a book called by a prophet's name is necessarily by that prophet, and that the compilers of the book intended to hand it down as altogether from his pen. Now there is no evidence for either of these conclusions. On the contrary, there is considerable testimony in the opposite direction. The Book of Isaiah is not one continuous prophecy. It consists of a number of separate orations, with a few intervening pieces of narrative. Some of these orations claim to be Isaiah's own: they possess such titles as The vision of Isaiah the son of Amoz. [1] But such titles describe only the individual prophecies they head, and other portions of the book, upon other subjects and in very different styles, do not possess titles at all. It seems to me, that those, who maintain the Isaian authorship of the whole book, have the responsibility cast upon them of explaining why some chapters in it should be distinctly said to be by Isaiah, while others should not be so entitled. Surely this difference affords us sufficient ground for understanding, that the whole book is not necessarily by Isaiah, nor intentionally handed down by its compilers as the work of that prophet. [2]

Now, when we come to chs. xl.-lxvi., we find that, occurring in a book which we have just seen no reason for supposing to be in every part of it by Isaiah, these chapters nowhere claim to be his. They are separated from that portion of the book, in which his undisputed oracles are placed, by a historical narrative of considerable length. And there is not anywhere upon them nor in them a title nor other statement that they are by the prophet, nor any allusion which could give the faintest support to the opinion, that they offer themselves to posterity as dating from his time. It is safe to say, that, if they had come to us by themselves, no one would have dreamt for an instant of ascribing them to Isaiah; for the alleged resemblances, which their language and style bear to his language and style, are far more than overborne by the undoubted differences, and have never been employed, even by the defenders of the Isaian authorship, except in additional and confessedly slight support of their main argument, viz. that the chapters must be Isaiah's because they are included in a book called by his name.

Let us understand, therefore, at this very outset, that in discussing the question of the authorship of "Second Isaiah," we are not discussing a question, upon which the text itself makes any statement, or into which the credibility of the text enters. No claim is made by the Book of Isaiah itself for the Isaian authorship of chs. xl.-lxvi.

A second fact in Scripture, which seems at first sight to make strongly for the unity of the Book of Isaiah, is that in the New Testament, portions of the disputed chapters are quoted by Isaiah's name, just as are portions of his admitted prophecies. These citations are nine in number. [3] None is by our Lord Himself. They occur in the Gospels, Acts and Paul. Now if any of these quotations were given in answer to the question, Did Isaiah write chs. xl.-lxvi. of the book called by his name? or if the use of his name along with them were involved in the arguments which they are borrowed to illustrate (as, for instance, is the case with David's name in the quotation made by our Lord from Psalm cx.), then those who deny the unity of the Book of Isaiah would be face to face with a very serious problem indeed. But in none of the nine cases is the authorship of the Book of Isaiah in question. In none of the nine cases is there anything in the argument, for the purpose of which the quotation has been made, that depends on the quoted words being by Isaiah. For the purposes, for which the Evangelists and Paul borrow the texts, these might as well be unnamed, or attributed to any other canonical writer. Nothing in them requires us to suppose that Isaiah's name is mentioned with them for any other end than that of reference, viz., to point out that they lie in the part of prophecy usually known by his name. But, if there is nothing in these citations to prove that Isaiah's name is being used for any other purpose than that of reference, then it is plain--and this is all that we ask assent to at the present time--that they do not offer the authority of Scripture as a bar to our examining the evidence of the chapters in question.

It is hardly necessary to add that neither is there any other question of doctrine in our way. There is none about the nature of prophecy, for, to take an example, ch. liii., as a prophecy of Jesus Christ, is surely as great a marvel if you date it from the Exile as if you date it from the age of Isaiah. And, in particular, let us understand that no question need be started about the ability of God's Spirit to inspire a prophet to mention Cyrus by name one hundred and fifty years before Cyrus appeared. The question is not, Could a prophet have been so inspired?--to which question, were it put, our answer might only be, God is great!--but the question is, Was our prophet so inspired? does he himself offer evidence of the fact? Or, on the contrary, in naming Cyrus does he give himself out as a contemporary of Cyrus, who already saw the great Persian above the horizon? To this question only the writings under discussion can give us an answer. Let us see what they have to say.

Apart from the question of the date, no chapters in the Bible are interpreted with such complete unanimity as Isa. xl.-xlviii. They plainly set forth certain things as having already taken place--the Exile and Captivity, the ruin of Jerusalem, and the devastation of the Holy Land. Israel is addressed as having exhausted the time of her penalty, and is proclaimed to be ready for deliverance. Some of the people are comforted as being in despair because redemption does not draw near; others are exhorted to leave the city of their bondage, as if they were growing too familiar with its idolatrous life. Cyrus is named as their deliverer, and is pointed out as already called upon his career, and as blessed with success by Jehovah. It is also promised that he will immediately add Babylon to his conquests, and so set God's people free.

Now all this is not predicted, as if from the standpoint of a previous century. It is nowhere said--as we should expect it to be said, if the prophecy had been uttered by Isaiah--that Assyria, the dominant world-power of Isaiah's day, was to disappear and Babylon to take her place; that then the Babylonians should lead the Jews into an exile which they had escaped at the hands of Assyria; and that after nearly seventy years of suffering God would raise up Cyrus as a deliverer. There is none of this prediction, which we might fairly have expected had the prophecy been Isaiah's; because, however far Isaiah carries us into the future, he never fails to start from the circumstances of his own day. Still more significant, however--there is not even the kind of prediction that we find in Jeremiah's prophecies of the Exile, with which indeed it is most instructive to compare Isa. xl.-lxvi. Jeremiah also spoke of exile and deliverance, but it was always with the grammar of the future. He fairly and openly predicted both; and, let us especially remember, he did so with a meagreness of description, a reserve and reticence about details, which are simply unintelligible if Isa. xl.-lxvi. was written before his day, and by so well-known a prophet as Isaiah. No: in the statements, which our chapters make concerning the Exile and the condition of Israel under it, there is no prediction, not the slightest trace of that grammar of the future in which Jeremiah's prophecies are constantly uttered. But there is a direct appeal to the conscience of a people already long under the discipline of God; their circumstance of exile is taken for granted; there is a most vivid and delicate appreciation of their present fears and doubts, and to these the deliverer Cyrus is not only named, but introduced as an actual and notorious personage already upon the midway of his irresistible career.

These facts are more broadly based than just at first sight appears. You cannot turn their flank by the argument that Hebrew prophets were in the habit of employing in their predictions what is called "the prophetic perfect"--that is, that in the ardour of their conviction that certain things would take place they talked of these, as the flexibility of the Hebrew tenses allowed them to do, in the past or perfect as if the things had actually taken place. No such argument is possible in the case of the introduction of Cyrus. For it is not only that the prophecy, with what might be the mere ardour of vision, represents the Persian as already above the horizon and upon the flowing tide of victory; but that, in the course of a sober argument for the unique divinity of the God of Israel, which takes place throughout chs. xli.-xlviii., Cyrus, alive and irresistible, already accredited by success, and with Babylonia at his feet, is pointed out as the unmistakable proof that former prophecies of a deliverance for Israel are at last coming to pass. Cyrus, in short, is not presented as a prediction, but as the proof that a prediction is being fulfilled. Unless he had already appeared in flesh and blood, and was on the point of striking at

Rev. George Adam Smith, M.A.

Babylon, with all the prestige of unbroken victory, a great part of Isa. xli.-xlviii. would be utterly unintelligible.

This argument is so conclusive for the date of Second Isaiah, that it may be well to state it a little more in detail, even at the risk of anticipating some of the exposition of the text.

Among the Jews at the close of the Exile there appear to have been two classes. One class was hopeless of deliverance, and to their hearts is addressed such a prophecy as ch. xl.: Comfort ye, comfort ye My people. But there was another class, of opposite temperament, who had only too strong opinions on the subject of deliverance. In bondage to the letter of Scripture and to the great precedents of their history, these Jews appear to have insisted that the Deliverer to come must be a Jew, and a descendant of David. And the bent of much of the prophet's urgency in ch. xlv. is to persuade those pedants, that the Gentile Cyrus, who had appeared to be not only the biggest man of his age, but the very likely means of Israel's redemption, was of Jehovah's own creation and calling. Does not such an argument necessarily imply that Cyrus was already present, an object of doubt and debate to earnest minds in Israel? Or are we to suppose that all this doubt and debate were foreseen, rehearsed and answered one hundred and fifty years before the time by so famous a prophet as Isaiah, and that, in spite of his prediction and answer, the doubt and debate nevertheless took place in the minds of the very Israelites, who were most earnest students of ancient prophecy? The thing has only to be stated to be felt to be impossible.

But besides the pedants in Israel, there is apparent through these prophecies another body of men, against whom also Jehovah claims the actual Cyrus for His own. They are the priests and worshippers of the heathen idols. It is well known that the advent of Cyrus cast the Gentile religions of the time and their counsellors into confusion. The wisest priests were perplexed; the oracles of Greece and Asia Minor either were dumb when consulted about the Persian, or gave more than usually ambiguous answers. Over against this perplexity and despair of the heathen religions, our prophet confidently claims Cyrus for Jehovah's own. In a debate in ch. xli., in which he seeks to establish Jehovah's righteousness--that is, Jehovah's faithfulness to His word, and power to carry out His predictions--the prophet speaks of ancient prophecies which have come from Jehovah, and points to Cyrus as their fulfilment. It does not matter to us in the meantime what those prophecies were. They may have been certain of Jeremiah's predictions; we may be sure that they cannot have contained anything so definite as Cyrus' name, or such a proof of Divine foresight must certainly have formed part of the prophet's plea. It is enough that they could be quoted; our business is rather with the evidence which the prophet offers of their fulfilment. That evidence is Cyrus. Would it have been possible to refer the heathen to Cyrus as proof that those ancient prophecies were being fulfilled, unless Cyrus had been visible to the heathen,--unless the heathen had been beginning already to feel this Persian "from the sunrise" in all his weight of war? It is no esoteric doctrine which the prophet is unfolding to initiated Israelites about Cyrus. He is making an appeal to men of the world to face facts. Could he possibly have made such an appeal unless the facts had been there, unless Cyrus had been within the ken of "the natural man"? Unless Cyrus and his conquests were already historically present, the argument in xli.-xlviii. is unintelligible.

If this evidence for the exilic date of Isa. xl.-xlviii.--for all these chapters hang together--required any additional support, it would find it in the fact that the prophet does not wholly treat of what is past and over, but makes some predictions as well. Cyrus is on the way of triumph, but Babylon has still to fall by his hand. Babylon has still to fall, before the exiles can go free. Now, if our prophet were predicting from the standpoint of one hundred and forty years before, why did he make this sharp distinction between two events which appeared so closely together? If he had both the advent of Cyrus and the fall of Babylon in his long perspective, why did he not use "the prophetic perfect" for both? That he speaks of the first as past and of the second as still to come, would most surely, if there had been no tradition the other way, have been accepted by all as sufficient evidence, that the advent of Cyrus was behind him and the fall of Babylon still in front of him, when he wrote these chapters.

Thus the earlier part, at least, of Isa. xl.-lxvi.--that is, chs. xl.-xlviii.--compels us to date it between 555, Cyrus' advent, and 538, Babylon's fall. But some think that we may still further narrow the limits. In ch. xli. 25, Cyrus, whose own kingdom lay east of Babylonia, is described as invading Babylonia from the north. This, it has been thought, must refer to his union with the Medes in 549, and his threatened descent upon Mesopotamia from their quarter of the prophet's horizon. [4] If it be so, the possible years of our prophecy are reduced to eleven, 549-538. But even if we take the wider and more certain limit, 555 to 538, we may well say that there are very few chapters in the whole of the Old Testament whose date can be fixed so precisely as the date of chs. xl.-xlviii.

If what has been unfolded in the preceding paragraphs is recognised as the statement of the chapters themselves, it will be felt that further evidence of an exilic date is scarcely needed. And those, who are acquainted with the controversy upon the evidence furnished by the style and language of the prophecies, will admit how far short in decisiveness it falls of the arguments offered above. But we may fairly ask whether there is anything opposed to the conclusion we have reached, either, first, in the local colour of the prophecies; or, second, in their language; or, third, in their thought--anything which shows that they are more likely to have been Isaiah's than of exilic origin.

1. It has often been urged against the exilic date of these prophecies, that they wear so very little local colour, and one of the greatest of critics, Ewald, has felt himself, therefore, permitted to place their home, not in Babylonia, but in Egypt, while he maintains the exilic date. But, as we shall see in surveying the condition of the exiles, it was natural for the best among them, their psalmists and prophets, to have no eyes for the colours of Babylon. They lived inwardly; they were much more the inhabitants of their own broken hearts than of that gorgeous foreign land; when their thoughts rose out of themselves it was to seek immediately the far-away Zion. How little local colour is there in the writings of Ezekiel! Isa. xl.-lxvi. has even more to show; for indeed the absence of local colour from our prophecy has been greatly exaggerated. We shall find as we follow the exposition, break after break of Babylonian light and shadow falling across our path,--the temples, the idol-manufactories, the processions of images, the diviners and astrologers, the gods and altars especially cultivated by the characteristic mercantile spirit of the place; the shipping of that mart of nations, the crowds of her merchants; the glitter of many waters, and even that intolerable glare, which so frequently curses the skies of Mesopotamia (xlix. 10). The prophet speaks of the hills of his native land with just the same longing, that Ezekiel and a probable psalmist of the Exile [5] betray,--the homesickness of a highland-born man whose prison is on a flat, monotonous plain. The beasts he mentions have for the most part been recognised as familiar in Babylonia; and while the same cannot be said of the trees and plants he names, it has been observed that the passages, into which he brings them, are passages where his thoughts are fixed on the restoration to Palestine. [6] Besides these, there are many delicate symptoms of the presence, before the prophet, of a people in a foreign land, engaged in commerce, but without political responsibilities, each of which, taken by itself, may be insufficient to convince, but the reiterated expression of which has even betrayed commentators, who lived too early for the theory of a second Isaiah, into the involuntary admission of an exilic authorship. It will perhaps startle some to hear John Calvin quoted on behalf of the exilic date of these prophecies. But let us read and consider this statement of his: "Some regard must be had to the time when this prophecy was uttered; for since the rank of the kingdom had been obliterated, and the name of the royal family had become mean and contemptible, during the captivity in Babylon, it might seem as if through the ruin of that family the truth of God had fallen into decay; and therefore he bids them contemplate by faith the throne of David, which had been cast down." [7]

2. What we have seen to be true of the local colour of our prophecy, holds good also of its style and language. There is nothing in either of these to commit us to an Isaian authorship, or to make an exilic date improbable; on the contrary, the language and style, while containing no stronger nor more frequent resemblances to the language and style of Isaiah than may be accounted for by the natural influence of so great a prophet upon his successors, are signalised by differences from his undisputed oracles, too constant, too subtle, and sometimes too sharp, to make it at all probable that the whole book came from the same man. On this point it is enough to refer our readers to the recent exhaustive and very able reviews of the evidence by Canon Cheyne in the second volume of his Commentary, and by Canon Driver in the last chapter of Isaiah: His Life and Times, and to quote the following words of so great an authority as Professor A. B. Davidson. After remarking on the difference in vocabulary of the two parts of the Book of Isaiah, he adds that it is not so much words in themselves as the peculiar uses and combinations of them, and especially "the peculiar articulation of sentences and the movement of the whole discourse, by which an impression is produced so unlike the impression produced by the earlier parts of the book." [8]

3. It is the same with the thought and doctrine of our prophecy. In this there is nothing to make the Isaian authorship probable, or an exilic date impossible. But, on the contrary, whether we regard the needs of the people or the analogies of the development of their religion, we find that, while everything suits the Exile, nearly everything is foreign both to the subjects and to the methods of Isaiah. We shall observe the items of this as we go along, but one of them may be mentioned here (it will afterwards require a chapter to itself), our prophet's use of the terms righteous and righteousness. No one, who has carefully studied the meaning which these terms bear in the authentic oracles of Isaiah, and the use to which they are put in the prophecies under discussion, can fail to find in the difference a striking corroboration of our argument--that the latter were composed by a different mind than Isaiah's, speaking to a different generation. [9]

***

To sum up this whole argument. We have seen that there is no evidence in the Book of Isaiah to prove that it was all by himself, but much testimony which points to a plurality of authors; that chs. xl.-lxvi. nowhere assert themselves to be by Isaiah; and that there is no other well-grounded claim of Scripture or of doctrine on behalf of his authorship. We have then shown that chs. xl.-xlviii. do not only present the Exile as if nearly finished and Cyrus as if already come, while the fall of Babylon is still future; but that it is essential to one of their main arguments that Cyrus should be standing before Israel and the world, as a successful warrior, on his way to attack Babylon. That led us to date these chapters between 555 and 538. Turning then to other evidence,--the local colour they show, their language and style, and their theology,--we have found nothing which conflicts with that date, but, on the contrary, a very great deal, which much more agrees with it than with the date, or with the authorship, of Isaiah.

It will be observed, however, that the question has been limited to the earlier chapters of the twenty-seven under discussion, viz., to xl.-xlviii. Does the same conclusion hold good of xlix. to lxvi.? This can be properly discovered only as we closely follow their exposition; it is enough in the meantime to have got firm footing on the Exile. We can feel our way bit by bit from this standpoint onwards. Let us now merely anticipate the main features of the rest of the prophecy.

A new section has been marked by many as beginning with ch. xlix. This is because ch. xlviii. concludes with a refrain: There is no peace, saith Jehovah, to the wicked, which occurs again at the end of ch. lvii., and because with ch. xlviii. Babylon and Cyrus drop out of sight. But the circumstances are still those of exile, and, as Professor Davidson remarks, ch. xlix. is parallel in thought to ch. xlii., and also takes for granted the restoration of Israel in ch. xlviii., proceeding naturally from that to the statement of Israel's world-mission. Apart from the alternation of passages dealing with the Servant of the Lord, and passages whose subject is Zion--an alternation which begins pretty early in the prophecy, and has suggested to some its composition out of two different writings [10] --the first real break in the sequence occurs at ch. lii. 13, where the prophecy of the sin-bearing Servant is introduced. By most critics this is held to be an insertion, for ch. liv. 1 follows naturally upon ch. lii. 12, though it is undeniable that there is also some association between chs. lii. 13-liii., and ch. liv. [11] In chs. liv.-lv. we are evidently still in exile. It is in commenting on a verse of these chapters that Calvin makes the admission of exilic origin which has been quoted above.

A number of short prophecies now follow, till the end of ch. lix. is reached. These, as we shall see, make it extremely difficult to believe in the original unity of "Second Isaiah." Some of them, it is true, lie in evident circumstance of exile; but others are undoubtedly of earlier date, reflecting the scenery of Palestine, and the habits of the people in their political independence, with Jehovah's judgement-cloud still unburst, but lowering. Such is ch. lvi. 9-lvii., which regards the Exile as still to come, quotes the natural features of Palestine, and charges the Jews with unbelieving diplomacy--a charge not possible against them when they were in captivity. But others of these short prophecies are, in the opinion of some critics, post-exilic. Cheyne assigns ch. lvi. to after the Return, when the temple was standing, and the duty of holding fasts and sabbaths could be enforced, as it was enforced by Nehemiah. I shall give, when we reach the passage, my reasons for doubting his conclusion. The chapter seems to me as likely to have been written upon the eve of the Return as after the Return had taken place.

Ch. lvii., the eighteenth of our twenty-seven chapters, closes with the same refrain as ch. xlviii., the ninth of the series: There is no peace, saith Jehovah, to the wicked. Ch. lviii. has, therefore, been regarded as beginning the third great division of the prophecy. But here again, while there is certainly an advance in the treatment of the subject, and the prophet talks less of the redemption of the Jews and more of the glory of the restoration of Zion, the point of transition is very difficult to mark. Some critics [12] regard ch. lviii. as post-exilic; but when we come to it we shall find a number of reasons for supposing it to belong, just as much as Ezekiel, to the Exile. Ch. lix. is perhaps the most difficult portion of all, because it makes the Jews responsible for civic justice in a way they could hardly be conceived to be in exile, and yet speaks, in the language of other portions of "Second Isaiah," of a deliverance that cannot well be other than the deliverance from exile. We shall find in this chapter likely marks of the fusion of two distinct addresses, making the conclusion probable that it is Israel's earlier conscience which we catch here, following her into the days of exile, and reciting her former guilt just before pardon is assured. Chs. lx., lxi., and lxii. are certainly exilic. The inimitable prophecy, ch. lxiii. 1-6, complete within itself, and unique in its beauty, is either a promise given just before the deliverance from a long captivity of Israel under heathen nations (ver. 4), or an exultant song of triumph immediately after such a deliverance has taken place. Ch. lxiii. 7-lxiv. implies a ruined temple (ver. 10), but bears no traces of the writer being in exile. It has been assigned to the period of the first attempts to rebuild Jerusalem after the Return. Ch. lxv. has been assigned to the same date, and its local colour interpreted as that of Palestine. But we shall find the colour to be just as probably that of Babylon, and again I do not see any certain proofs of a post-exilic date. Ch. lxvi., however, betrays more evidence of being written after the Return. It divides into two parts. In verses 1 to 4 the temple is still unbuilt, but the building would seem to be already begun. In verses 5 to 24, the arrival of the Jews in Palestine, the resumption of the life of the sacred community, and the disappointments of the returned at the first meagre results, seem to be implied. And the music of the book dies out in tones of warning, that sin still hinders the Lord's work with His people.

***

This rapid survey has made two things sufficiently clear. First, that while the bulk of chs. xl.-lxvi. was composed in Babylonia during the Exile of the Jews, there are considerable portions which date from before the Exile, and betray a Palestinian origin; and one or two smaller pieces that seem--rather less evidently, however--to take for granted the Return from the Exile. But, secondly, all these pieces, which it seems necessary to assign to different epochs and authors, have been arranged so as to exhibit a certain order and progress--an order, more or less observed, of date, and a progress very apparent (as we shall see in the course of exposition) of thought and of clearness in definition. The largest portion, of whose unity we are assured and whose date we can fix, is found at the beginning. Chs. xl.-xlviii. are certainly by one hand, and may be dated, as we have seen, between 555 and 538--the period of Cyrus' approach to take Babylon. There the interest in Cyrus ceases, and the thought of the redemption from Babylon is mainly replaced by that of the subsequent Return. Along with these lines, we shall discover a development in the prophecy's great doctrine of the Servant of Jehovah. But even this dies away, as if the experience of suffering and discipline were being replaced by that of return and restoration; and it is Zion in her glory, and the spiritual mission of the people, and the vengeance of the Lord, and the building of the temple, and a number of practical details in the life and worship of the restored community, which fill up the remainder of the book, along with a few echoes from pre-exilic times. Can we escape feeling in all this a definite design and arrangement, which fails to be absolutely perfect, probably, from the nature of the materials at the arranger's disposal?

We are, therefore, justified in coming to the provisional conclusion, that Second Isaiah is not a unity, in so far as it consists of a number of pieces by different men, whom God raised up at various times before, during, and after the Exile, to comfort and exhort amid the shifting circumstance and tempers of His people; but that it is a unity, in so far as these pieces have been gathered together by an editor very soon after the Return from the Exile, in an order as regular both in point of time and subject as the somewhat mixed material would permit. It is in this sense that throughout this volume we shall talk of "our prophet," or "the prophet;" up to ch. xlix., at least, we shall feel that the expression is literally true; after that it is rather an editorial than an original unity which is apparent. In this question of unity the dramatic style of the prophecy forms, no doubt, the greatest difficulty. Who shall dare to determine of the many soliloquies, apostrophes, lyrics and other pieces that are here gathered, often in want of any connection save that of dramatic grouping and a certain sympathy of temper, whether they are by the same author or have been collected from several origins? We must be content to leave the matter uncertain. One great reason, which we have not yet quoted, for supposing that the whole prophecy is not by one man, is that if it had been his name would certainly have come down with it.

Do not let it be thought that such a conclusion, as we have been led to, is merely a dogma of modern criticism. Here, if anywhere, the critic is but the patient student of Scripture, searching for the testimony of the sacred text about itself, and formulating that. If it be found that such a testimony conflicts with ecclesiastical tradition, however ancient and universal, so much the worse for tradition. In Protestant circles, at least, we have no choice. Litera Scripta manet. When we know that the only evidence for the Isaian authorship of chs. xl.-lxvi. is tradition, supported by an unthinking interpretation of New Testament citations, while the whole testimony of these Scriptures themselves denies them to be Isaiah's, we cannot help making our choice, and accepting the testimony of Scripture. Do we find them any the less wonderful or Divine? Do they comfort less? Do they speak with less power to the conscience? Do they testify with more uncertain voice to our Lord and Saviour? It will be the task of the following pages to show that, interpreted in connection with the history out of which they themselves say that God's Spirit drew them, these twenty-seven chapters become only more prophetic of Christ, and more comforting and instructive to men, than they were before.

But the remarkable fact is, that anciently tradition itself appears to have agreed with the results of modern scholarship. The original place of the Book of Isaiah in the Jewish canon seems to have been after both Jeremiah and Ezekiel, [13] a fact which goes to prove that it did not reach completion till a later date than the works of these two prophets of the Exile.

If now it be asked, Why should a series of prophecies written in the Exile be attached to the authentic works of Isaiah? that is a fair question, and one which the supporters of the exilic authorship have the duty laid upon them of endeavouring to answer. Fortunately they are not under the necessity of falling back, for want of other reasons, on the supposition that this attachment was due to the error of some scribe, or to the custom which ancient writers practised of filling up any part of a volume, that remained blank when one book was finished, with the writing of any other that would fit the place. [14] The first of these reasons is too accidental, the second too artificial, in face of the undoubted sympathy which exists among all parts of the Book of Isaiah. Isaiah himself plainly prophesied of an exile longer than his own generation experienced, and prophesied of a return from it (ch. xi.). We saw no reason to dispute his claims to the predictions about Babylon in chs. xxi. and xxxix. Isaiah's, too, more than any other prophet's, were those great and final hopes of the Old Testament--the survival of Israel and the gathering of the Gentiles to the worship of Jehovah at Jerusalem. But it is for the express purpose of emphasizing the immediate fulfilment of such ancient predictions, that Isa. xl.-lxvi. were published.

Although our prophet has new things to publish, his first business is to show that the former things have come to pass, especially the Exile, the survival of a Remnant, the sending of a Deliverer, the doom of Babylon. What more natural than to attach to his utterances those prophecies, of which the events he pointed to were the vindication and fulfilment? The attachment was the more easy to arrange that the authentic prophecies had not passed from Isaiah's hand in a fixed form. They do not bear those marks of their author's own editing, which are borne by the prophecies both of Jeremiah and Ezekiel. It is impossible to be dogmatic on the point. But these facts--that our chapters are concerned, as no other Scriptures are, with the fulfilment of previous prophecies; that it is the prophecies of Isaiah which are the original and fullest prediction of the events they are busy with; and that the form, in which Isaiah's prophecies are handed down, did not preclude additions of this kind to them--contribute very evident reasons why Isa. xl.-lxvi., though written in the Exile, should be attached to Isa. i.-xxxix. [15]

***

Thus we present a theory of the exilic authorship of Isa. xl.-lxvi. within itself complete and consistent, suited to all parts of the evidence, and not opposed by the authority of any part of Scripture. In consequence of its conclusion, our duty, before proceeding to the exposition of the chapters, is twofold: first, to connect the time of Isaiah with the period of the Captivity, and then to sketch the condition of Israel in Exile. This we shall undertake in the next three chapters.

Note to Chapter I.
Readers may wish to have a reference to other passages of this volume, in which the questions of the date, authorship and structure of Isaiah xl.-lxvi. are discussed. See pp. [3]65-[4]68, [5]112, [6]146 f., [7]212, [8]223; Introduction to Book [9]III.; opening paragraphs of ch. [10]xviii. and of ch. [11]xix., etc.

Footnotes:

1. Chs. i., ii., etc. The only title that could be offered as covering the whole book is that in ch. i., ver. 1: The vision of Isaiah the son of Amoz, which he saw concerning Judah and Jerusalem, in the days of Uzziah, Jotham, Ahaz, and Hezekiah, kings of Judah. But this manifestly cannot apply to any but the earlier chapters, of which Judah and Jerusalem are indeed the subjects.
2. There are, it will be remembered, certain narratives in the Book of Isaiah, which are not by the prophet. They speak of him in the third person (chs. vii., xxxvi.-xxxix.), while in other narratives (chs. vi. and viii.) he speaks of himself in the first person. Their presence is sufficient proof that the Book of Isaiah, in its extant shape, did not come from Isaiah's hands, but was compiled by others.
3. Matt. iii. 3, viii. 17, xii. 17; Luke iii. 4, iv. 17; John i. 23, xii. 38; Acts viii. 28; Rom. x. 16-20.
4. Driver's Isaiah, pp. 137, 139.
5. Psalm cxxi.
6. Driver's Isaiah: His Life and Times, p. 191.
7. Calvin on Isa. lv. 3.
8. So quoted by Driver (Isaiah, etc., p. 200), from the British and Foreign Evangelical Review, 1879, p. 339.
9. See p. [12]223.
10. Professor Briggs' Messianic Prophecy, 339 ff.
11. Ewald is very strong on this.
12. Including Professor Cheyne, Encyc. Britann., article "Isaiah."
13. According to the arrangement given in the Talmud (Baba bathra, f. 14, col. 2): "Jeremiah, Ezekiel, Isaiah, the Twelve." Cf. Bleek, Introduction to Old Testament, on Isaiah; Orelli's Isaiah, Eng. ed., p. 214.
14. Robertson Smith, The Old Testament in Jewish Church, 109.
15. It is the theory of some, that although Isa. xl.-lxvi. dates as a whole from the Exile, there are passages in it by Isaiah himself, or in his style by pupils of his (Klostermann in Herzog's Encyclopædia and Bredenkamp in his Commentary). But this, while possible, is beyond proof.

CHAPTER II

FROM ISAIAH TO THE FALL OF JERUSALEM.

701-587 b.c.

At first sight, the circumstances of Judah in the last ten years of the seventh century present a strong resemblance to her fortunes in the last ten years of the eighth. The empire of the world, to which she belongs, is again divided between Egypt and a Mesopotamian power. Syria is again the field of their doubtful battle, and the question, to which of the two shall homage be paid, still forms the politics of all her states. Judah still vacillates, intrigues and draws down on herself the wrath of the North by her treaties with Egypt. Again there is a great prophet and statesman, whose concern is righteousness, who exposes both the immorality of his people and the folly of their politics, and who summons the evil from the North as God's scourge upon Israel: Isaiah has been succeeded by Jeremiah. And, as if to complete the analogy, the nation has once more passed through a puritan reformation. Josiah has, even more thoroughly than Hezekiah, effected the disestablishment of idols.

Beneath this circumstantial resemblance, however, there is one fundamental difference. The strength of Isaiah's preaching was bent, especially during the closing years of the century, to establish the inviolableness of Jerusalem. Against the threats of the Assyrian siege, and in spite of his own more formidable conscience of his people's corruption, Isaiah persisted that Zion should not be taken, and that the people, though cut down to their roots, should remain planted in the land,--the stock of an imperial nation in the latter days. This prophecy was vindicated by the marvellous relief of Jerusalem on the apparent eve of her capture in 701. But its echoes had not yet died away, when Jeremiah to his generation delivered the very opposite message. Round him the popular prophets babbled by rote Isaiah's ancient assurances about Zion. Their soft, monotonous repetitions lapped pleasantly upon the immovable self-confidence of the people. But Jeremiah called down the storm. Even while prosperity seemed to give him the lie, he predicted the speedy ruin of Temple and City, and summoned Judah's enemies against her in the name of the God, on whose former word she relied for peace. The contrast between the two great prophets grows most dramatic in their conduct during the respective sieges, of which each was the central figure. Isaiah, alone steadfast in a city of despair, defying the taunts of the heathen, rekindling within the dispirited defenders, whom the enemy sought to bribe to desertion, the passions of patriotism and religion, proclaiming always, as with the voice of a trumpet, that Zion must stand inviolate; Jeremiah, on the contrary, declaring the futility of resistance, counselling each citizen to save his own life from the ruin of the state, in treaty with the enemy, and even arrested as a deserter,--these two contrasting figures and attitudes gather up the difference which the century had wrought in the fortunes of the City of God. And so, while in 701 Jerusalem triumphed in the Lord by the sudden raising of the Assyrian siege, three years after the next century was out she twice succumbed to the Assyrian's successor, and nine years later was totally destroyed.

What is the reason of this difference, which a century sufficed to work? Why was the sacredness of Judah's shrine not as much an article of Jeremiah's as of Isaiah's creed,--as much an element of Divine providence in 600 as in 700 b.c.? This is not a very hard question to answer, if we keep in our regard two things--firstly, the moral condition of the people, and, secondly, the necessities of the spiritual religion, which was identified for the time with their fortunes.

The Israel, which was delivered into captivity at the word of Jeremiah, was a people at once more hardened and more exhausted than the Israel, which, in spite of its sin, Isaiah's efforts had succeeded in preserving upon its own land. A century had come and gone of further grace and opportunity, but the grace had been resisted, the opportunity abused, and the people stood more guilty and more wilful than ever before God. Even clearer, however, than the deserts of the people was the need of their religion. That local and temporary victory--after all, only the relief of a mountain fortress and a tribal shrine--with which Isaiah had identified the will and honour of Almighty God, could not be the climax of the history of a spiritual religion. It was impossible for Monotheism to rest on so narrow and material a security as that. The faith, which was to overcome the world, could not be satisfied with a merely national triumph. The time must arrive--were it only by the ordinary progress of the years and unhastened by human guilt--for faith and piety to be weaned from the forms of an earthly temple, however sacred; for the individual--after all, the real unit of religion--to be rendered independent of the community and cast upon his God alone; and for this people, to whom the oracles of the living God had been entrusted, to be led out from the selfish pride of guarding these for their own honour--to be led out, were it through the breaches of their hitherto inviolate walls, and amid the smoke of all that was most sacred to them, so that in level contact with mankind they might learn to communicate their glorious trust. Therefore, while the Exile was undoubtedly the penance, which an often-spared but ever more obdurate people had to pay for their accumulated sins, it was also for the meek and the pure-hearted in Israel a step upwards even from the faith and the results of Isaiah--perhaps the most effectual step which Israel's religion ever took. Schultz has finely said: "The proper Tragedy of History--doom required by long-gathering guilt, and launched upon a generation which for itself is really turning towards good--is most strikingly consummated in the Exile." Yes: but this is only half the truth. The accomplishment of the moral tragedy is really but one incident in a religious epic--the development of a spiritual faith. Long-delaying Nemesis overtakes at last the sinners, but the shock of the blows, which beat the guilty nation into captivity, releases their religion from its material bonds. Israel on the way to Exile is on the way to become Israel after the Spirit.

With these principles to guide us, let us now, for a little, thread our way through the crowded details of the decline and fall of the Jewish state.

Isaiah's own age had foreboded the necessity of exile for Judah. There was the great precedent of Samaria, and Judah's sin was not less than her sister's. When the authorities at Jerusalem wished to put Jeremiah to death for the heresy of predicting the ruin of the sacred city, it was pointed out in his defence that a similar prediction had been made by Micah, the contemporary of Isaiah. And how much had happened since then! The triumph of Jehovah in 701, the stronger faith and purer practice, which had followed as long as Hezekiah reigned, gave way to an idolatrous reaction under his successor Manasseh. This reaction, while it increased the guilt of the people, by no means diminished their religious fear. They carried into it the conscience of their former puritanism--diseased, we might say delirious, but not dead. Men felt their sin and feared Heaven's wrath, and rushed headlong into the gross and fanatic exercises of idolatry, in order to wipe away the one and avert the other. It availed nothing. After an absence of thirty years the Assyrian arms returned in full strength, and Manasseh himself was carried captive across the Euphrates. But penitence revived, and for a time it appeared as if it were to be at last valid for salvation. Israel made huge strides towards their ideal life of a good conscience and outward prosperity. Josiah, the pious, came to the throne. The Book of the Law was discovered in 621, and king and people rallied to its summons with the utmost loyalty. All the nation stood to the covenant. The single sanctuary was vindicated, the high places destroyed, the land purged of idols. There were no great military triumphs, but Assyria, so long the accepted scourge of God, gave signs of breaking up; and we can feel the vigour and self-confidence, induced by years of prosperity, in Josiah's ambition to extend his borders, and especially in his daring assault upon Necho of Egypt at Megiddo, when Necho passed north to the invasion of Assyria. Altogether, it was a people that imagined itself righteous, and counted upon a righteous God. In such days who could dream of exile?

But in 608 the ideal was shivered. Israel was threshed at Megiddo, and Josiah, the king after God's own heart, was slain on the field. And then happened, what happened at other times in Israel's history when disillusion of this kind came down. The nation fell asunder into the elements of which it was ever so strange a composition. The masses, whose conscience did not rise beyond the mere performance of the Law, nor their view of God higher than that of a Patron of the state, bound by His covenant to reward with material success the loyalty of His clients, were disappointed with the results of their service and of His providence. Being a new generation from Manasseh's time, they thought to give the strange gods another turn. The idols were brought back, and after the discredit which righteousness received at Megiddo, it would appear that social injustice and crime of many kinds dared to be very bold. Jehoahaz, who reigned for three months after Josiah, and Jehoiakim, who succeeded him, were idolaters. The loftier few, like Jeremiah, had never been deceived by the people's outward allegiance to the Temple or the Law, nor considered it valid either to atone for the past or now to fulfil the holy demands of Jehovah; and were confirmed by the disaster at Megiddo, and the consequent reaction to idolatry, in the stern and hopeless views of the people which they had always entertained. They kept reiterating a speedy captivity. Between these parties stood the formal successors of earlier prophets, so much the slaves of tradition that they had neither conscience for their people's sins nor understanding of the world around them, but could only affirm in the strength of ancient oracles that Zion should not be destroyed. Strange is it to see how this party, building upon the promises of Jehovah through a prophet like Isaiah, should be taken advantage of by the idolaters, but scouted by Jehovah's own servants. Thus they mingle and conflict. Who indeed can distinguish all the elements of so ancient and so rich a life, as they chase, overtake and wrestle with each other, hurrying down the rapids to the final cataract? Let us leave them for a moment, while we mark the catastrophe itself. They will be more easily distinguished in the calm below.

It was from the North that Jeremiah summoned the vengeance of God upon Judah. In his earlier threats he might have meant the Scythians; but by 605, when Nebuchadrezzar, Nabopolassar of Babylon's son, the rising general of the age, defeated Pharaoh at Carchemish, all men accepted

Jeremiah's nomination for this successor of Assyria in the lordship of Western Asia. From Carchemish Nebuchadrezzar overran Syria. Jehoiakim paid tribute to him, and Judah at last felt the grip of the hand that was to drag her into exile. Jehoiakim attempted to throw it off in 602; but, after harassing him for four years by means of some allies, Nebuchadrezzar took his capital, executed him, suffered Jehoiachin, his successor, to reign only three months, took Jerusalem a second time, and carried off to Babylon the first great portion of the people. This was in 598, only ten years from the death of Josiah, and twenty-one from the discovery of the Book of the Law.

The exact numbers of this first captivity of the Jews it is impossible to determine. The annalist sets the soldiers at seven thousand, the smiths and craftsmen at one thousand; so that, making allowance for other classes whom he mentions, the grown men must alone have been over ten thousand; [16] but how many women went, and how many children--the most important factor for the period of the Exile with which we have to deal--it is impossible to estimate. The total number of persons can scarcely have been less than twenty-five thousand. More important, however, than their number was the quality of these exiles, and this we can easily appreciate. The royal family and the court were taken, a large number of influential persons, the mighty men of the land, or what must have been nearly all the fighting men, with the necessary artificers; priests also went, Ezekiel among them, and probably representatives of other classes not mentioned by the annalist. That this was the virtue and flower of the nation is proved by a double witness. Not only did the citizens, for the remaining ten years of Jerusalem's life, look to these exiles for her deliverance, but Jeremiah himself counted them the sound half of Israel--a basket of good figs, as he expressed it, beside a basket of bad ones. They were at least under discipline, but the remnant of Jerusalem persisted in the wilfulness of the past.

For although Jeremiah remained in the city, and the house of David and a considerable population, and although Jeremiah himself held a higher position in public esteem since the vindication of his word by the events of 598, yet he could not be blind to the unchanged character of the people, and the thorough doom which their last respite had only more evidently proved to be inevitable. Gangs of false prophets, both at home and among the exiles, might predict a speedy return. All the Jewish ability of intrigue, with the lavish promises of Egypt and frequent embassies from other nations, might work for the overthrow of Babylon. But Jeremiah and Ezekiel knew better. Across the distance which now separated them they chanted, as it were in antiphon, the alternate strophes of Judah's dirge. Jeremiah bade the exiles not to remember Zion, but "let them settle down," he said, "into the life of the land they are in, building houses, planting gardens, and begetting children, and seek the peace of the city whither I have caused you to be carried away captives, and pray unto Jehovah for it, for in the peace thereof ye shall have peace--the Exile shall last seventy years." And as Jeremiah in Zion blessed Babylon, so Ezekiel in Babylon cursed Zion, thundering back that Jerusalem must be utterly wasted through siege and famine, pestilence and captivity. There is no rush of hope through Ezekiel. His expectations are all distant. He lives either in memory or in cold fancy. His pictures of restoration are too elaborate to mean speedy fulfilment. They are the work of a man with time on his hands; one does not build so colossally for to-morrow. Thus reinforced from abroad, Jeremiah proclaimed Nebuchadrezzar as the servant of Jehovah, and summoned him to work Jehovah's doom upon the city. The predicted blockade came in the ninth year of Zedekiah. The false hopes which still sustained the people, their trust in Egypt, the arrival of an Egyptian army in result of their intrigue, as well as all their piteous bravery, only afforded time for the fulfilment of the terrible details of their penalty. For nearly eighteen months the siege closed in--months of famine and pestilence, of faction and quarrel and falling away to the enemy. Then Jerusalem broke up. The besiegers gained the northern suburb and stormed the middle gate. Zedekiah and the army burst their lines only to be captured on an aimless flight at Jericho. A few weeks more, and a forlorn defence by civilians of the interior parts of the city was at last overwhelmed. The exasperated besiegers gave her up to fire--the house of Jehovah, the king's house, and every great house--and tore to the stones the stout walls that resisted the conflagration. As the city was levelled, so the citizens were dispersed. A great number--and among them the king's family--were put to death. The king himself was blinded, and, along with a host of his subjects, impossible for us to estimate, and with all the temple furniture, was carried to Babylon. A few peasants were left to cultivate the land; a few superior personages--perhaps such as, with Jeremiah, had favoured the Babylonians, and Jeremiah was among them--were left at Mizpah under a Jewish viceroy. It was a poor apparition of a state; but, as if the very ghost of Israel must be chased from the land, even this small community was broken up, and almost every one of its members fled to Egypt. The Exile was complete.

Footnote:

[16] The figure actually mentioned in 2 Kings xxiv. 14, but, as Stade points out (Geschichte, p. 680), vv. 14, 15 interrupt the narrative, and may have been intruded here from the account of the later captivity.

Rev. George Adam Smith, M.A.

CHAPTER III

WHAT ISRAEL TOOK INTO EXILE.

Before we follow the captives along the roads that lead to exile, we may take account of the spiritual goods which they carried with them, and were to realise in their retirement. Never in all history did paupers of this world go forth more richly laden with the treasures of heaven.

1. First of all, we must emphasize and define their Monotheism. We must emphasize it as against those who would fain persuade us that Israel's monotheism was for the most part the product of the Exile; we must analyse its contents and define its limits among the people, if we would appreciate the extent to which it spread and the peculiar temper which it assumed, as set forth in the prophecy we are about to study.

Idolatry was by no means dead in Israel at the fall of Jerusalem. On the contrary, during the last years which the nation spent within those sacred walls, that had been so miraculously preserved in the sight of the world by Jehovah, idolatry increased, and to the end remained as determined and fanatic as the people's defence of Jehovah's own temple. The Jews who fled to Egypt applied themselves to the worship of the Queen of Heaven, in spite of all the remonstrances of Jeremiah and him they carried with them, not because they listened to him as the prophet of the One True God, but superstitiously, as if he were a pledge of the favour of one of the many gods, whom they were anxious to propitiate. And the earliest effort, upon which we shall have to follow our own prophet, is the effort to crush the worship of images among the Babylonian exiles. Yet when Israel returned from Babylon the people were wholly monotheist; when Jerusalem was rebuilt no idol came back to her.

That this great change was mainly the result of the residence in Babylon and of truths learned there, must be denied by all who remember the creed and doctrine about God, which in their literature the people carried with them into exile. The law was already written, and the whole nation had sworn to it: Hear, O Israel, Jehovah our God; Jehovah is One, and thou shalt worship Jehovah thy God with all thine heart, and with all thy soul, and with all thy strength. These words, it is true, may be so strictly interpreted as to mean no more than that there was one God for Israel: other gods might exist, but Jehovah was Sole Deity for His people. It is maintained that such a view receives some support from the custom of prophets, who, while they affirmed Jehovah's supremacy, talked of other gods as if they were real existences. But argument from this habit of the prophets is precarious: such a mode of speech may have been a mere accommodation to a popular point of view. And, surely, we have only to recall what Isaiah and Jeremiah had uttered concerning Jehovah's Godhead, to be persuaded that Israel's monotheism, before the beginning of the Exile, was a far more broad and spiritual faith than the mere belief that Jehovah was the Sovereign Deity of the nation, or the satisfaction of the desires of Jewish hearts alone. Righteousness was not coincident with Israel's life and interest; righteousness was universally supreme, and it was in righteousness that Isaiah saw Jehovah exalted. [17] There is no more prevailing witness to the unity of God than the conscience, which in this matter takes far precedence of the intellect; and it was on the testimony of conscience that the prophets based Israel's monotheism. Yet they did not omit to enlist the reason as well. Isaiah and Jeremiah delight to draw deductions from the reasonableness of Jehovah's working in nature to the reasonableness of His processes in history,-- analogies which could not fail to impress both intellect and imagination with the fact that men inhabit a universe, that One is the will and mind which works in all things. But to this training of conscience and reason, the Jews, at the beginning of the Exile, felt the addition of another considerable influence. Their history lay at last complete, and their conscience was at leisure from the making of its details to survey it as a whole. That long past, seen now by undazzled eyes from under the shadow of exile, presented through all its changing fortunes a single and a definite course. One was the intention of it, one its judgement from first to last. The Jew saw in it nothing but righteousness, the quality of a God, who spake the same word from the beginning, who never broke His word, and who at last had summoned to its fulfilment the greatest of the world-powers. In those historical books, which were collected and edited during the Exile, we observe each of the kings and generations of Israel, in their turn, confronted with the same high standard of fidelity to the One True God and His holy Law. The regularity and rigour, with which they are thus judged, have been condemned by some critics as an arbitrary and unfair application of the standard of a later faith to the conduct of ruder and less responsible ages. But, apart from the question of historical accuracy, we cannot fail to remark that this method of writing history is at least instinct with the Oneness of God, and the unvarying validity of His Law from generation to generation. Israel's God was the same, their conscience told them, down all their history; but now as He summoned one after another of the great world-powers to do His bidding,--Assyria, Babylon, Persia,-- how universal did He prove His dominion to be! Unchanging through all time, He was surely omnipotent through all space.

This short review--in which, for the sake of getting a complete view of our subject, we have anticipated a little--has shown that Israel had enough within themselves, in the teaching of their prophets and in the lessons of their own history, to account for that consummate expression of Jehovah's Godhead, which is contained in our prophet, and to which every one allows the character of an absolute monotheism. We shall find this, it is true, to be higher and more comprehensive than anything which is said about God in pre-exilic Scriptures. The prophet argues the claims of Jehovah, not only with the ardour that is born of faith, but often with the scorn which indicates the intellect at work. It is monotheism, treated not only as a practical belief or a religious duty, but as a necessary truth of reason; not only as the secret of faith and the special experience of Israel, but also as an essential conviction of human nature, so that not to believe in One God is a thing irrational and absurd for Gentiles as well as Jews. God's infinitude in the works of creation, His universal providence in history, are preached with greater power than ever before; and the gods of the nations are treated as things, in whose existence no reasonable person can possibly believe. In short, our great prophet of the Exile has already learned to obey the law of Deuteronomy as it was expounded by Christ. Deuteronomy says, Thou shalt love Jehovah thy God with all thine heart, with all thy soul, and with all thy strength. Christ added, and with all thy mind. This was what our prophet did. He held his monotheism with all his mind. We shall find him conscious of it, not only as a religious affection, but as a necessary intellectual conviction; which if a man has not, he is less than a man. Hence the scorn, which he pours upon the idols and mythologies of his conquerors. Beside his tyrants, though in physical strength he was but a worm to them, the Jew felt that he walked, by virtue of his faith in One God, their intellectual master.

We shall see all this illustrated later on. Meantime, what we are concerned to show is, that there is enough to account for this high faith within Israel themselves--in their prophecy and in the lessons of their history. And where indeed are we to be expected to go in search of the sources of Israel's monotheism, if not to themselves? To the Babylonians? The Babylonians had nothing spiritual to teach to Israel; our prophet regards them with scorn. To the Persians, who broke across Israel's horizon with Cyrus? Our prophet's high statement of monotheism is of earlier date than the advent of Cyrus to Babylon. Nor did Cyrus, when he came, give any help to the faith, for in his public edicts he owned the gods of Babylon and the God of Israel with equal care and equal policy. It was not because Cyrus and his Persians were monotheists, that our prophet saw the sovereignty of Jehovah vindicated, but it was because Jehovah was sovereign that the prophet knew the Persians would serve His holy purposes.

2. But if in Deuteronomy the exiles carried with them the Law of the One God, they preserved in Jeremiah's writings what may be called the charter of the Individual Man. Jeremiah had found religion in Judah a public and a national affair. The individual derived his spiritual value only from being a member of the nation, and through the public exercises of the national faith. But, partly by his own religious experience, and partly by the course of events, Jeremiah was enabled to accomplish what may be justly described as the vindication of the individual. Of his own separate value before God, and of his right of access to his Maker apart from the nation, Jeremiah himself was conscious, having belonged to God before he belonged to his mother, his family, or his nation. Before I found thee in the belly I knew thee, and before thou camest out of the womb I consecrated thee. His whole life was but the lesson of how one man can be for God and all the nation on the other side. And it was in the strength of this solitary experience, that he insisted, in his famous thirty-first chapter, on the individual responsibility of man and on every man's immediate communication with God's Spirit; and that, when the ruin of the state was imminent, he advised each of his friends to take his own life out of it for a prey. [18] But Jeremiah's doctrine of the religious value and independence of the individual had a complement. Though the prophet felt so keenly his separate responsibility and right of access to God, and his religious independence of the people, he nevertheless clave to the people with all his heart. He was not, like some other prophets, outside the doom he preached. He might have saved himself, for he had many offers from the Babylonians. But he chose to suffer with his people--he, the saint of God, with the idolaters. More than that, it may be said that Jeremiah suffered for the people. It was not they, with their dead conscience and careless mind, but he, with his tender conscience and breaking heart, who bore the reproach of their sins, the anger of the Lord, and all the agonizing knowledge of his country's inevitable doom. In Jeremiah one man did suffer for the people.

In our prophecy, which is absorbed with the deliverance of the nation as a whole, there was, of course, no occasion to develop Jeremiah's remarkable suggestions about each individual soul of man. In fact, these suggestions were germs, which remained uncultivated in Israel till Christ's time. Jeremiah himself uttered them, not as demands for the moment, but as ideals that would only be realised when the New Covenant was made. [19] Our prophecy has nothing to say about them. But that figure, which

Rev. George Adam Smith, M.A.

Jeremiah's life presented, of One Individual--of One Individual standing in moral solitude over against the whole nation, and in a sense suffering for the nation, can hardly have been absent from the influences, which moulded the marvellous confession of the people in the fifty-third chapter of Isaiah, where they see the solitary servant of God on one side and themselves on the other, and Jehovah made to light on him the iniquities of us all. It is true that the exiles themselves had some consciousness of suffering for others. Our fathers, cried a voice in their midst, when Jerusalem broke up, Our fathers have sinned, and we have borne their iniquities. But Jeremiah had been a willing sufferer for his people; and the fifty-third chapter is, as we shall see, more like his way of bearing his generation's guilt for love's sake than their way of bearing their fathers' guilt in the inevitable entail of sin. [20]

3. To these beliefs in the unity of God, the religious worth of the individual and the virtue of his self-sacrifice, we must add some experiences of scarcely less value rising out of the destruction of the material and political forms--the temple, the city, the monarchy--with which the faith of Israel had been so long identified.

Without this destruction, it is safe to say, those beliefs could not have assumed their purest form. Take, for instance, the belief in the unity of God. There is no doubt that this belief was immensely helped in Israel by the abolition of all the provincial sanctuaries under Josiah, by the limitation of Divine worship to one temple and of valid sacrifice to one altar. But yet it was well that this temple should enjoy its singular rights for only thirty years and then be destroyed. For a monotheism, however lofty, which depended upon the existence of any shrine, however gloriously vindicated by Divine providence, was not a purely spiritual faith. Or, again, take the individual. The individual could not realise how truly he himself was the highest temple of God, and God's most pleasing sacrifice a broken and a contrite heart, till the routine of legal sacrifice was interrupted and the ancient altar torn down. Or, once more, take that high, ultimate doctrine of sacrifice, that the most inspiring thing for men, the most effectual propitiation before God, is the self-devotion and offering up of a free and reasonable soul, the righteous for the unrighteous--how could common Jews have adequately learned that truth, in days when, according to immemorial practice, the bodies of bulls and goats bled daily on the one valid altar? The city and temple, therefore, went up in flames that Israel might learn that God is a Spirit, and dwelleth not in a house made with hands; that men are His temple, and their hearts the sacrifices well-pleasing in His sight; and that beyond the bodies and blood of beasts, with their daily necessity of being offered, He was preparing for them another Sacrifice, of perpetual and universal power, in the voluntary sufferings of His own holy Servant. It was for this Servant, too, that the monarchy, as it were, abdicated, yielding up to Him all its title to represent Jehovah and to save and rule Jehovah's people.

4. Again, as we have already hinted, the fall of the state and city of Jerusalem gave scope to Israel's missionary career. The conviction, that had inspired many of Isaiah's assertions of the inviolableness of Zion, was the conviction that, if Zion were overthrown and the last remnant of Israel uprooted from the land, there must necessarily follow the extinction of the only true testimony to the living God which the world contained. But by a century later that testimony was firmly secured in the hearts and consciences of the people, wheresoever they might be scattered; and what was now needed was exactly such a dispersion,--in order that Israel might become aware of the world for whom the testimony was meant, and grow expert in the methods by which it was to be proclaimed. Priesthood has its human as well as its Godward side. The latter was already sufficiently secured for Israel by Jehovah's age-long seclusion of them in their remote highlands--a people peculiar to Himself. But now the same Providence completed its purpose by casting them upon the world. They mixed with men face to face, or, still more valuably to themselves, on a level with the most downtrodden and despised of the peoples. With no advantage but the truth, they met the other religions of the world in argument, debating with them upon the principles of a common reason and the facts of a common history. They learned sympathy with the weak things of earth. They discovered that their religion could be taught. But, above all, they became conscious of martyrdom, the indispensable experience of a religion that is to prevail; and they realised the supreme influence upon men of a love which sacrifices itself. In a word, Israel, in going into exile, put on humanity with all its consequences. How real and thorough the process was, how successful in perfecting their priesthood, may be seen not only from the hopes and obligations towards all mankind, which burst in our prophecy to an urgency and splendour unmatched elsewhere in their history, but still more from the fact that when the Son of God Himself took flesh and became man, there were no words oftener upon His lips to describe His experience and commission, there are no passages which more clearly mirror His work for the world, than the words and the passages in which these Jews of the Exile, stripped to their bare humanity, relate their sufferings or exult in their destiny that should follow.

5. But with their temple in ruins, and all the world before them for the service of God, the Jews go forth to exile upon the distinct promise of return. The material form of their religion is suspended, not abolished. Let them feel religion in purely spiritual aspects, unassisted by sanctuary or ritual; let them look upon the world and the oneness of men; let them learn all God's scope for the truth He has entrusted to them,--and then let them gather back again and cherish their new experience and ideas for

yet awhile in the old seclusion. Jehovah's discipline of them as a nation is not yet exhausted. They are no mere band of pilgrims or missionaries, with the world for their home; they are still a people, with their own bit of the earth. If we keep this in mind, it will explain certain apparent anomalies in our prophecy. In all the writings of the Exile the reader is confused by a strange mingling of the spiritual and the material, the universal and the local. The moral restoration of the people to pardon and righteousness is identified with their political restoration to Judah and Jerusalem. They have been separated from ritual in order to cultivate a more spiritual religion, but it is to this that a restoration to ritual is promised for a reward. While Jeremiah insists upon the free and immediate communication of every believer with Jehovah, Ezekiel builds a more exclusive priesthood, a more elaborate system of worship. Within our prophecy, while one voice deprecates a house for God built with hands, affirming that Jehovah dwells with every one who is of a poor and contrite spirit, other voices dwell fondly on the prospect of the new temple and exult in its material glory. This double line of feeling is not merely due to the presence in Israel of those two opposite tempers of mind, which so naturally appear in every national literature. But a special purpose of God is in it. Dispersed to obtain more spiritual ideas of God and man and the world, Israel must be gathered back again to get these by heart, to enshrine them in literature, and to transmit them to posterity, as they could alone be securely transmitted, in the memories of a nation, in the liturgies and canons of a living Church.

Therefore the Jews, though torn for their discipline from Jerusalem, continued to identify themselves more passionately than ever with their desecrated city. A prayer of the period exclaims: Thy saints take pleasure in her stones, and her dust is dear to them. [21] The exiles proved this by taking her name. Their prophets addressed them as Zion and Jerusalem. Scattered and leaderless groups of captives in a far-off land, they were still that City of God. She had not ceased to be; ruined and forsaken as she lay, she was yet graven on the palms of Jehovah's hands; and her walls were continually before Him.[22] The exiles kept up the register of her families; they prayed towards her; they looked to return to build her bulwarks; they spent long hours of their captivity in tracing upon the dust of that foreign land the groundplan of her restored temple.

***

With such beliefs in God and man and sacrifice, with such hopes and opportunities for their world-mission, but also with such a bias back to the material Jerusalem, did Israel pass into exile.

Footnotes:

17. See vol. i., p. 100 f.
18. Jer. xlv.
19. This is especially clear from ch. xxxi.
20. Having read through the Book of Jeremiah once again since I wrote the above paragraph, I am more than ever impressed with the influence of his life upon Isa. xl.-lxvi.
21. Psalm cii. 14.
22. Isa. xlix. 16.

Rev. George Adam Smith, M.A.

CHAPTER IV

ISRAEL IN EXILE.

From 589 till about 550 b.c.

It is remarkable how completely the sound of the march from Jerusalem to Babylon has died out of Jewish history. It was an enormous movement: twice over within ten years, ten thousand Jews, at the very least, must have trodden the highway to the Euphrates; and yet, except for a doubtful verse or two in the Psalter, they have left no echo of their passage. The sufferings of the siege before, the remorse and lamentation of the Exile after, still pierce our ears through the Book of Lamentations and the Psalms by the rivers of Babylon. We know exactly how the end was fulfilled. We see most vividly the shifting panorama of the siege,--the city in famine, under the assault, and in smoke; upon the streets the pining children, the stricken princes, the groups of men with sullen, famine-black faces, the heaps of slain, mothers feeding on the bodies of the infants whom their sapless breasts could not keep alive; by the walls the hanging and crucifixion of multitudes, with all the fashion of Chaldean cruelty, the delicate and the children stumbling under heavy loads, no survivor free from the pollution of blood. Upon the hills around, the neighbouring tribes are gathered to jeer at the day of Jerusalem, and to cut off her fugitives, we even see the departing captives turn, as the worm turns, to curse those children of Edom. But there the vision closes. Was it this hot hate which blinded them to the sights of the way, or that weariness and depression among strange scenes, that falls upon all unaccustomed caravans, and has stifled the memory of nearly every other great historical march? The roads which the exiles traversed were of immemorial use in the history of their fathers; almost every day they must have passed names which, for at least two centuries, had rung in the market-place of Jerusalem--the Way of the Sea, across Jordan, Galilee of the Gentiles, round Hermon, and past Damascus; between the two Lebanons, past Hamath, and past Arpad; or less probably by Tadmor-in-the-Wilderness and Rezeph,--till they reached the river on which the national ambition had lighted as the frontier of the Messianic Empire, and whose rolling greatness had so often proved the fascination and despair of a people of uncertain brooks and trickling aqueducts. Crossing the Euphrates by one of its numerous passages--either at Carchemish, if they struck the river so high, or at the more usual Thapsacus, Tiphsah, the passage, where Xenophon crossed with his Greeks, or at some other place--the caravans must have turned south across the Habor, on whose upper banks the captives of Northern Israel had been scattered, and then have traversed the picturesque country of Aram-Naharaim, past Circesium and Rehoboth-of-the-River, and many another ancient place mentioned in the story of the Patriarchs, till through dwindling hills they reached His--that marvellous site which travellers praise as one of the great view-points of the world--and looked out at last upon the land of their captivity, the boundless, almost level tracts of Chaldea, the first home of the race, the traditional Garden of Eden. But of all that we are told nothing. Every eye in the huge caravans seems to have been as the eyes of the blinded king whom they carried with them,--able to weep, but not to see.

One fact, however, was too large to be missed by these sad, wayworn men; and it has left traces on their literature. In passing from home to exile, the Jews passed from the hills to the plain. They were highlanders. Jerusalem lies four thousand feet above the sea. From its roofs the skyline is mostly a line of hills. To leave the city on almost any side you have to descend. The last monuments of their fatherland, on which the emigrants' eyes could have lingered, were the high crests of Lebanon; the first prospect of their captivity was a monotonous level. The change was the more impressive, that to the hearts of Hebrews it could not fail to be sacramental. From the mountains came the dew to their native crofts--the dew which, of all earthly blessings, was likest God's grace. For their prophets, the ancient hills had been the symbols of Jehovah's faithfulness. In leaving their highlands, therefore, the Jews not only left the kind of country to which their habits were most adapted and all their natural affections clung; they left the chosen abode of God, the most evident types of His grace, the perpetual witnesses to His covenant. Ezekiel constantly employs the mountains to describe his fatherland. But it is far more with a sacramental longing than a mere homesickness that a psalmist of the Exile cries out, I will lift up mine eyes to the hills: from whence cometh mine help? or that our prophet exclaims: How beautiful upon the mountains are the feet of him that bringeth good tidings, that publisheth peace; that saith unto Zion, Thy God reigneth.

By the route sketched above, it is at least seven hundred miles from Jerusalem to Babylon--a distance which, when we take into account that many of the captives walked in fetters, cannot have occupied them less than three months. We may form some conception of the aspect of the caravans from the transportations of captives which are figured on the Assyrian monuments, as in the Assyrian basement in the British Museum. From these it appears as if families were not separated, but marched together. Mules, asses, camels, ox-waggons, and the captives themselves carried goods. Children and women suckling infants were allowed to ride on the waggons. At intervals fully-armed soldiers walked in pairs. [23]

I.

Mesopotamia, the land "in the middle of the rivers," Euphrates and Tigris, consists of two divisions, an upper and a lower. The dividing line crosses from near Hit or His on the Euphrates to below Samarah on the Tigris. Above this line the country is a gently undulating plain of secondary formation at some elevation above the sea. But Lower Mesopotamia is absolutely flat land, an unbroken stretch of alluvial soil, scarcely higher than the Persian Gulf, upon which it steadily encroaches. Chaldea was confined to this Lower Mesopotamia, and was not larger, Rawlinson estimates, than the kingdom of Denmark. [24] It is the monotonous level which first impresses the traveller; but if the season be favourable, he sees this only as the theatre of vast and varied displays of colour, which all visitors vie with one another in describing: "It is like a rich carpet;" "emerald green, enamelled with flowers of every hue;" "tall wild grasses and broad extents of waving reeds;" "acres of water-lilies;" "acres of pansies." There was no such country in ancient times for wheat, barley, millet, and sesame; [25] tamarisks, poplars, and palms; here and there heavy jungle; with flashing streams and canals thickly athwart the whole, and all shining the more brilliantly for the interrupting patches of scurvy, nitrous soil, and the grey sandy setting of the desert with its dry scrub. The possible fertility of Chaldea is incalculable. But there are drawbacks. Bounded to the north by so high a tableland, to the south and south-west by a superheated gulf and broad desert, Mesopotamia is the scene of violent changes of atmosphere. The languor of the flat country, the stagnancy and sultriness of the air, of which not only foreigners but the natives themselves complain, is suddenly invaded by southerly winds, of tremendous force and laden with clouds of fine sand, which render the air so dense as to be suffocating, and "produce a lurid red haze intolerable to the eyes." Thunderstorms are frequent, and there are very heavy rains. But the winds are the most tremendous. In such an atmosphere we may perhaps discover the original shapes and sounds of Ezekiel's turbulent visions--the fiery wheels; the great cloud with a fire infolding itself; the colour of amber, with sapphire, or lapis lazuli, breaking through; the sound of a great rushing. Also the Mesopotamian floods are colossal. The increase of both Tigris and Euphrates is naturally more violent and irregular than that of the Nile. [26] Frequent risings of these rivers spread desolation with inconceivable rapidity, and they ebb only to leave pestilence behind them. If civilisation is to continue, there is need of vast and incessant operations on the part of man.

Thus, both by its fertility and by its violence, this climate--before the curse of God fell on those parts of the world--tended to develop a numerous and industrious race of men, whose numbers were swollen from time to time both by forced and by voluntary immigration. The population must have been very dense. The triumphal lists of Assyrian conquerors of the land, as well as the rubbish mounds which to-day cover its surface, testify to innumerable villages and towns; while the connecting canals and fortifications, by the making of them and the watching of them, must have filled even the rural districts with the hum and activity of men. Chaldea, however, did not draw all her greatness from herself. There was immense traffic with East and West, between which Babylon lay, for the greater part of antiquity, the world's central market and exchange. The city was practically a port on the Persian Gulf, by canals from which vessels reached her wharves direct from Arabia, India and Africa. Down the Tigris and Euphrates rafts brought the produce of Armenia and the Caucasus; but of greater importance than even these rivers were the roads, which ran from Sardis to Shushan, traversed Media, penetrated Bactria and India, and may be said to have connected the Jaxartes and the Ganges with the Nile and the harbours of the Ægean Sea. These roads all crossed Chaldea and met at Babylon. Together with the rivers and ocean highways, they poured upon her markets the traffic of the whole ancient world.

It was, in short, the very centre of the world--the most populous and busy region of His earth--to which God sent His people for their exile. The monarch, who transplanted them, was the genius of Babylonia incarnate. The chief soldier of his generation, Nebuchadrezzar will live in history as one of the greatest builders of all time. But he fought as he built--that he might traffic. His ambition was to turn the trade with India from the Red Sea to the Persian Gulf, and he thought to effect this by the destruction of Tyre, by the transportation of Arab and Nabathean merchants to Babylon, and by the deepening and regulation of the river between Babylon and the sea.

There is no doubt that Nebuchadrezzar carried the Jews to Babylon not only for political reasons, but in order to employ them upon those large works of irrigation and the building of cities, for which his ambition required hosts of labourers. Thus the exiles were planted, neither in military prisons nor in the comparative isolation of agricultural colonies, but just where Babylonian life was most busy, where they were forced to share and contribute to it, and could not help feeling the daily infection of their captors' habits. Do not let us forget this. It will explain much in what we have to study. It will explain how the captivity, which God inflicted upon the Jews as a punishment, might become in time a new sin to them, and why, when the day of redemption arrived, so many forgot that their citizenship was in Zion, and clung to the traffic and the offices of Babylon.

The majority of the exiles appear to have been settled within the city, or, as it has been more correctly called, "the fortified district," of Babylon itself. Their mistress was thus constantly before them, at once their despair and their temptation. Lady of Kingdoms she lifted herself to heaven from broad wharves and ramparts, by wide flights of stairs and terraces, high walls and hanging gardens, pyramids and towers--so colossal in her buildings, so imperially lavish of space between! No wonder that upon that vast, far-spreading architecture, upon its great squares and between its high portals guarded by giant bulls, the Jew felt himself, as he expressed it, but a poor worm. If, even as they stand in our museums, captured and catalogued, one feels as if one crawled in the presence of the fragments of these striding monsters, with how much more of the feeling of the worm must the abject members of that captive nation have writhed before the face of the city, which carried these monsters as the mere ornaments of her skirts, and rose above all kingdoms with her strong feet upon the poor and the meek of the earth?

Ah, the despair of it! To see her every day so glorious, to be forced to help her ceaseless growth,-- and to think how Jerusalem, the daughter of Zion, lay forsaken in ruins! Yet the despair sometimes gave way to temptation. There was not an outline or horizon visible to the captive Jew, not a figure in the motley crowds in which he moved, but must have fascinated him with the genius of his conquerors. In that level land no mountain, with its witness of God, broke the skyline; but the work of man was everywhere: curbed and scattered rivers, artificial mounds, buildings of brick, gardens torn from their natural beds and hung high in air by cunning hands to please the taste of a queen; lavish wealth and force and cleverness, all at the command of one human will. The signature ran across the whole, "I have done this, and with mine own hand have I gotten me my wealth;" and all the nations of the earth came and acknowledged the signature, and worshipped the great city. It was fascinating merely to look on such cleverness, success and self-confidence; and who was the poor Jew that he, too, should not be drawn with the intoxicated nations to the worship of this glory that filled his horizon? If his eyes rose higher, and from these enchantments of men sought refuge in the heavens above, were not even they also a Babylonian realm? Did not the Chaldean claim the great lights there for his patron gods? were not the movements of sun, moon, and planets the secret of his science? did not the tyrant believe that the very stars in their courses fought for him? And he was vindicated; he was successful; he did actually rule the world. There seemed to be no escape from the enchantments of this sorceress city, as the prophets called her, and it is not wonderful that so many Jews fell victims to her worldliness and idolatry.

II.

The social condition of the Jews in Exile is somewhat obscure, and yet, both in connection with the date and with the exposition of some portions of "Second Isaiah," it is an element of the greatest importance, of which we ought to have as definite an idea as possible.

What are the facts? By far the most significant is that which faces us at the end of the Exile. There, some sixty years after the earlier, and some fifty years after the later, of Nebuchadrezzar's two deportations, we find the Jews a largely multiplied and still regularly organised nation, with considerable property and decided political influence. Not more than forty thousand can have gone into exile, but forty-two thousand returned, and yet left a large portion of the nation behind them. The old families and clans survived; the social ranks were respected; the rich still held slaves; and the former menials of the temple could again be gathered together. Large subscriptions were raised for the pilgrimage, and for the restoration of the temple; a great host of cattle was taken. To such a state of affairs do we see any traces leading up through the Exile itself? We do.

The first host of exiles, the captives of 598, comprised, as we have seen, the better classes of the nation, and appear to have enjoyed considerable independence. They were not scattered, like the slaves in North America, as domestic bondsmen over the surface of the land. Their condition must have much more closely resembled that of the better-treated exiles in Siberia; though of course, as we have seen, it was not a Siberia, but the centre of civilisation, to which they were banished. They remained in communities, with their own official heads, and at liberty to consult their prophets. They were sufficiently in touch with one another, and sufficiently numerous, for the enemies of Babylon to regard them as a considerable political influence, and to treat with them for a revolution against their captors. But Ezekiel's strong condemnation of this intrigue exhibits their leaders on good terms with the government. Jeremiah bade them throw themselves into the life of the land; buy and sell, and increase their families and property. At the same time, we cannot but observe that it is only religious sins, with which Ezekiel upbraids them. When he speaks of civic duty or social charity, he either refers to their past or to the life of the remnant still in Jerusalem. There is every reason to believe, therefore, that this captivity was an honourable and an easy one. The captives may have brought some property with them; they had leisure for the pursuit of business and for the study and practice of their religion. Some of them suffered, of course, from the usual barbarity of Oriental conquerors, and were made eunuchs; some, by their learning and abstinence, rose to high positions in the court. [27] Probably to the end of the Exile they remained the good figs, as Jeremiah had called them. Theirs was, perhaps, the literary work of the Exile; and theirs, too, may have been the wealth which rebuilt Jerusalem.

But it was different with the second captivity, of 589. After the famine, the burning of the city, and the prolonged march, this second host of exiles must have reached Babylonia in an impoverished condition. They were a lower class of men. They had exasperated their conquerors, who, before the march began, subjected many of them to mutilation and cruel death; and it is, doubtless, echoes of their experience which we find in the more bitter complaints of our prophet. This is a people robbed and spoiled; all of them snared in holes, and hid in prison-houses: they are for a prey, and for a spoil. Thou, that is, Babylon, didst show them no mercy; upon the aged hast thou very heavily laid thy yoke. [28] Nebuchadrezzar used them for his building, as Pharaoh had used their forefathers. Some of them, or of their countrymen who had reached Babylonia before them, became the domestic slaves and chattels of their conquerors. Among the contracts and bills of sale of this period we find the cases of slaves with apparently Jewish names. [29]

In short, the state of the Jews in Babylonia resembled what seems to have been their fortune wherever they have settled in a foreign land. Part of them despised and abused, forced to labour or overtaxed; part left alone to cultivate literature or to gather wealth. Some treated with unusual rigour-- and perhaps a few of these with reason, as dangerous to the government of the land--but some also, by the versatile genius of their race, advancing to a high place in the political confidence of their captors.

Their application to literature, to their religion, and to commerce must be specially noted.

1. Nothing is more striking in the writings of Ezekiel than the air of large leisure which invests them. Ezekiel lies passive; he broods, gazes and builds his visions up, in a fashion like none of his terser predecessors; for he had time on his hands, not available to them in days when the history of the nation was still running. Ezekiel's style swells to a greater fulness of rhetoric; his pictures of the future are elaborated with the most minute detail. Prophets before him were speakers, but he is a writer. Many in Israel besides Ezekiel took advantage of the leisure of the Exile to the great increase and arrangement of the national literature. Some Assyriologists have lately written, as if the schools of Jewish scribes owed their origin entirely to the Exile. [30] But there were scribes in Israel before this. What the Exile did for these, was to provide them not only with the leisure from national business which we have noted, but with a powerful example of their craft as well. Babylonia at this time was a land full of scribes and makers of libraries. They wrote a language not very different from the Jewish, and cannot but have powerfully infected their Jewish fellows with the spirit of their toil and of their methods. To the Exile we certainly owe a large part of the historical books of the Old Testament, the arrangement of some of the prophetic writings, as well as--though the amount of this is very uncertain--part of the codification of the Law.

2. If the Exile was opportunity to the scribes, it can only have been despair to the priests. In this foreign land the nation was unclean; none of the old sacrifice or ritual was valid, and the people were reduced to the simplest elements of religion--prayer, fasting and the reading of religious books. We shall find our prophecy noting the clamour of the exiles to God for ordinances of righteousness--that is, for the institution of legal and valid rites. [31] But the great lesson, which prophecy brings to the people of the Exile, is that pardon and restoration to God's favour are won only by waiting upon Him with all the heart. It was possible, of course, to observe some forms; to gather at intervals to inquire of the Lord, to keep the Sabbath, and to keep fasts. The first of these practices, out of which the synagogue probably took its rise, is noted by our prophet, [32] and he enforces Sabbath-keeping with words, that add the blessing of prophecy to the law's ancient sanction of that institution. Four annual fasts were instituted in memory of the dark days of Jerusalem--the day of the beginning of Nebuchadrezzar's siege in the tenth month, the day of the capture in the fourth month, the day of the destruction in the fifth month, and the day of Gedaliah's murder in the tenth month. It might have been thought, that solemn anniversaries of a disaster so recent and still unrepaired would be kept with sincerity; but our prophet illustrates how soon even the most outraged feelings may grow formal, and how on their days of special humiliation, while their captivity was still real, the exiles could oppress their own bondsmen and debtors. But there is no religious practice of this epoch more apparent through our prophecies than the reading of Scripture. Israel's hope was neither in sacrifice, nor in temple, nor in vision nor in lot, but in God's written Word; and when a new prophet arose like the one we are about to study, he did not appeal for his authorisation, as previous prophets had done, to the fact of his call or inspiration, but it was enough for him to point to some former word of God, and cry, "See! at last the day has dawned for the fulfilment of that." Throughout Second Isaiah this is what the anonymous prophet cares to establish--that the facts of to-day fit the promise of yesterday. We shall not understand our great prophecy unless we realise a people

rising from fifty years' close study of Scripture, in strained expectation of its immediate fulfilment.

3. The third special feature of the people in exile is their application to commerce. At home the Jews had not been a commercial people. [33] But the opportunities of their Babylonian residence seem to have started them upon those habits, for which, through their longer exile in our era, the name of Jew has become a synonym. If that be so, Jeremiah's advice to build and plant [34] is historic, for it means no less than that the Jews should throw themselves into the life of the most trafficking nation of the time. Their increasing wealth proves how they followed this advice,--as well as perhaps such passages as Isa. lv. 2, in which the commercial spirit is reproached for overwhelming the nobler desires of religion. The chief danger, incurred by the Jews from an intimate connection with the commerce of Babylonia, lay in the close relations of Babylonian commerce with Babylonian idolatry. The merchants of Mesopotamia had their own patron gods. In completing business contracts, a man had to swear by the idols, [35] and might have to enter their temples. In Isa. lxv. 11, Jews are blamed for forsaking Jehovah, and forgetting My holy mountain; preparing a table for Luck, and filling up mixed wine to Fortune. Here it is more probable that mercantile speculation, rather than any other form of gambling, is intended.

III.

But while all this is certain and needing to be noted about the habits of the mass of the people, what little trace it has left in the best literature of the period! We have already noticed in that the great absence of local colour. The truth is that what we have been trying to describe as Jewish life in Babylon was only a surface over deeps in which the true life of the nation was at work--was volcanically at work. Throughout the Exile the true Jew lived inwardly. Out of the depths do I cry to Thee, O Lord. He was the inhabitant not so much of a foreign prison as of his own broken heart. He sat by the rivers of Babylon; but he thought upon Zion. Is it not a proof of what depths in human nature were being stirred, that so little comes to the surface to tell us of the external conditions of those days? There are no fossils in the strata of the earth, which have been cast forth from her inner fires; and if we find few traces of contemporary life in these deposits of Israel's history now before us, it is because they date from an age in which the nation was shaken and boiling to its centre.

For if we take the writings of this period--the Book of Lamentations, the Psalms of the Exile, and parts of other books--and put them together, the result is the impression of one of the strangest decompositions of human nature into its elements which the world has ever seen. Suffering and sin, recollection, remorse and revenge, fear and shame and hate--over the confusion of these the Spirit of God broods as over a second chaos, and draws each of them forth in turn upon some articulate prayer. Now it is the crimson flush of shame: our soul is exceedingly filled with contempt. Now it is the black rush of hate; for if we would see how hate can rage, we must go to the Psalms of the Exile, which call on the God of vengeance and curse the enemy and dash the little ones against the stones. But the deepest surge of all in that whirlpool of misery was the surge of sin. To change the figure, we see Israel's spirit writhing upward from some pain it but partly understands, crying out, "What is this that keeps God from hearing and saving me?" turning like a wounded beast from the face of its master to its sore again, understanding as no brute could the reason of its plague, till confession after confession breaks away and the penalty is accepted, and acknowledged guilt seems almost to act as an anodyne to the penalty it explains. Wherefore doth a living man complain, a man for the punishment of his sins? If thou, Jehovah, shouldest mark iniquity, who shall stand? No wonder, that with such a conscience the Jews occupied the Exile in writing the moral of their delinquent history, or that the rest of their literature which dates from that time should have remained ever since the world's confessional.

But in this awful experience, there is still another strain, as painful as the rest, but pure and very eloquent of hope--the sense of innocent suffering. We cannot tell the sources, from which this considerable feeling may have gathered during the Exile, any more than we can trace from how many of the upper folds of a valley the tiny rivulets start, which form the stream that issues from its lower end. One of these sources may have been, as we have already suggested, the experience of Jeremiah; another very probably sprang with every individual conscience in the new generation. Children come even to exiles, and although they bear the same pain with the same nerves as their fathers, they do so with a different conscience. The writings of the time dwell much on the sufferings of the children. The consciousness is apparent in them, that souls are born into the wrath of God, as well as banished there. Our fathers have sinned and are not, and we bear their iniquities. This experience developed with great force, till Israel felt that she suffered not under God's wrath, but for His sake; and so passed from the conscience of the felon to that of the martyr. But if we are to understand the prophecy we are about to study, we must remember how near akin these two consciences must have been in exiled Israel, and how easy it was for a prophet to speak--as our prophet does, sometimes with confusing rapidity of exchange--now in the voice of the older and more guilty generation, and now in the voice of the younger and less deservedly punished.

***

Our survey of the external as well as the internal conditions of Israel in Exile is now finished. It has, I think, included every known feature of their experience in Babylonia, which could possibly illustrate our prophecy--dated, as we have felt ourselves compelled to date this, from the close of the Exile. Thus, as we have striven to trace, did Israel suffer, learn, grow and hope for fifty years--under Nebuchadrezzar till 561, under his successor Evil-merodach till 559, under Neriglassar till 554, and then under the usurper Nabunahid. The last named probably oppressed the Jews more grievously than their previous tyrants, but with the aggravation of their yoke there grew evident, at the same time, the certainty of their deliverance. In 549, Cyrus overthrew the Medes, and became lord of Asia from the Indus to the Halys. From that event his conquest of Babylonia, however much delayed, could only be a matter of time.

It is at this juncture that our prophecy breaks in. Taking for granted Cyrus' sovereignty of the Medes, it still looks forward to his capture of Babylon. Let us, before advancing to its exposition, once more cast a rapid glance over the people, to whom it is addressed, and whom in their half century of waiting for it we have been endeavouring to describe.

First and most manifest, they are a People with a Conscience--a people with the most awful and most articulate conscience that ever before or since exposed a nation's history or tormented a generation with the curse of their own sin and the sin of their fathers. Behind them, ages of delinquent life, from the perusal of the record of which, with its regularly recurring moral, they have just risen: the Books of Kings appear to have been finished after the accession of Evil-merodach in 561. Behind them also nearly fifty years of sore punishment for their sins--punishment, which, as their Psalms confess, they at last understand and accept as deserved.

But, secondly, they are a People with a Great Hope. With their awful consciousness of guilt, they have the assurance that their punishment has its limits; that, to quote ch. xl., ver. 2, it is a set period of service: a former word of God having fixed it at not more than seventy years, and having promised the return of the nation thereafter to their own land.

And, thirdly, they are a People with a Great Opportunity. History is at last beginning to set towards the vindication of their hope: Cyrus, the master of the age, is moving rapidly, irresistibly, down upon their tyrants.

But, fourthly, in face of all their hope and opportunity, they are a People Disorganised, Distracted, and very Impotent--worms and not men, as they describe themselves. The generation of the tried and responsible leaders of the days of their independence are all dead, for flesh is like grass; no public institutions remain in their midst such as ever in the most hopeless periods of the past proved a rallying-point of their scattered forces. There is no king, temple, nor city; nor is there any great personality visible to draw their little groups together, marshal them, and lead them forth behind him. Their one hope is in the Word of God, for which they wait more than they that watch for the morning; and the one duty of their nameless prophets is to persuade them, that this Word has at last come to pass, and, in the absence of king, Messiah, priest, and great prophet, is able to lift them to the opportunity that God's hand has opened before them, and to the accomplishment of their redemption.

Upon Israel, with such a Conscience, such a Hope, such an Opportunity, and such an unaided Reliance on God's bare Word, that Word at last broke in a chorus of voices.

Of these the first, as was most meet, spoke pardon to the people's conscience and the proclamation that their set period of warfare was accomplished; the second announced that circumstances and the politics of the world, hitherto adverse, would be made easy to their return; the third bade them, in their bereavement of earthly leaders, and their own impotence, find their eternal confidence in God's Word; while the fourth lifted them, as with one heart and voice, to herald the certain return of Jehovah, at the head of His people, to His own City, and His quiet, shepherdly rule of them on their own land.

These herald voices form the prologue to our prophecy, ch. xl. 1-11, to which we will now turn.

Footnotes:

23. If we would construct for ourselves some more definite idea of that long march from Judah to Babylon, we might assist our imagination by the details of the only other instance on so great a scale of "exile by administrative process"--the transportation to Siberia which the Russian Government effects (it is said, on good authority) to the extent of eighteen thousand persons a year. Every week throughout the year marching parties, three to four hundred strong, leave Tomsk for Irkutsk, doing twelve to twenty miles daily in fetters, with twenty-four hours' rest every third day, or three hundred and thirty miles in a month (Century Magazine, Nov. 1888).

24. For the above details, see Rawlinson's Five Great Monarchies of the Ancient Eastern World, vol. i.

25. Herodotus, Bk. I.; "Memoirs by Commander James Felix Jones, I. N.," in Selections from the Records of the Bombay Government, No. XLIII., New Series, 1857; Ainsworth's Euphrates Valley Expedition; Layard's Nineveh.

26. Perrot and Chipiez, Histoire de l'Art d'Antiquité, vol. ii.; Assyrie p. 9.
27. The Book of Daniel.
28. Isa. xlii. 22, xlvii. 6.
29. Records of the Past, second series, vol. i., M. Oppert's Translations.
30. Mr. St. Chad Boscawen's recent lectures, of which I have been able to see only the reports in the Manchester Guardian.
31. Ch. lviii. 2.
32. Ch. lviii. 13, 14.
33. See vol. i., p. 292 ff.
34. Jer. xxix.
35. Records of the Past, first series, ix., 95 seq.

BOOK II

THE LORD'S DELIVERANCE.

Rev. George Adam Smith, M.A.

CHAPTER V

THE PROLOGUE: THE FOUR HERALD VOICES.

Isaiah xl. 1-11.

It is only Voices which we hear in this Prologue. No forms can be discerned, whether of men or angels, and it is even difficult to make out the direction from which the Voices come. Only one thing is certain--that they break the night, that they proclaim the end of a long but fixed period, during which God has punished and forsaken His people. At first, the persons addressed are the prophets, that they may speak to the people (vv. 1, 2); but afterwards Jerusalem as a whole is summoned to publish the good tidings (ver. 9). This interchange between a part of the people and the whole--this commission to prophesy, made with one breath to some of the nation for the sake of the rest, and with the next breath to the entire nation--is a habit of our prophet to which we shall soon get accustomed. How natural and characteristic it is, is proved by its appearance in these very first verses.

The beginning of the good tidings is Israel's pardon; yet it seems not to be the people's return to Palestine which is announced in consequence of this, so much as their God's return to them. *Prepare ye the way of Jehovah, make straight a highway for our God. Behold the Lord Jehovah will come.* We may, however, take the way of Jehovah in the wilderness to mean what it means in the sixty-eighth Psalm,--His going forth before His people and leading of them back; while the promise that He will come to shepherd His flock (ver. 11) is, of course, the promise that He will resume the government of Israel upon their own land. There can be no doubt, therefore, that this chapter was meant for the people at the close of their captivity in Babylon. But do not let us miss the pathetic fact, that Israel is addressed not in her actual shape of a captive people in a foreign land, but under the name and aspect of her far-away, desolate country. In these verses Israel is Jerusalem, Zion, the cities of Judah. Such designations do not prove, as a few critics have rather pedantically supposed, that the writer of the verses lived in Judah and addressed himself to what was under his eyes. It is not the vision of a Jew at home that has determined the choice of these names, but the desire and the dream of a Jew abroad: that extraordinary passion, which, however distant might be the land of his exile, ever filled the Jew's eyes with Zion, caused him to feel the ruin and forsakenness of his Mother more than his own servitude, and swept his patriotic hopes, across his own deliverance and return, to the greater glory of her restoration. [36] There is nothing, therefore, to prevent us taking for granted, as we did in the previous chapter, that the speaker or speakers of these verses stood among the exiles themselves; but who they were--men or angels, prophets or scribes--is lost in the darkness out of which their music breaks. [37]

Nevertheless the prophecy is not anonymous. By these impersonal voices a personal revelation is made. The prophets may be nameless, but the Deity who speaks through them speaks as already known and acknowledged: *My people,* saith your God.

This is a point, which, though it takes for its expression no more than these two little pronouns, we must not hurriedly pass over. All the prophecy we are about to study may be said to hang from these pronouns. They are the hinges, on which the door of this new temple of revelation swings open before the long-expectant people. And, in fact, such a conscience and sympathy as these little words express form the necessary premise of all revelation. Revelation implies a previous knowledge of God, and cannot work upon men, except there already exist in them the sense that they and God somehow belong to each other. This sense need be neither pure, nor strong, nor articulate. It may be the most selfish and cowardly of guilty fears,--Jacob's dread as he drew near Esau, whom he had treacherously supplanted,--the vaguest of ignorant desires, the Athenians' worship of the Unknown God. But, whatever it is, the angel comes to wrestle with it, the apostle is sent to declare it; revelation in some form takes it as its premise and starting-point. This previous sense of God may also be fuller than in the cases just cited. Take our Lord's own illustration. Upon the prodigal in the strange country there surged again the far-ebbed memory of his home and childhood, of his years of familiarity with a Father; and it was this tide which carried back his penitent heart within the hearing of his Father's voice, and the revelation of the love that became his new life. Now Israel, also in a far-off land, were borne upon the recollection of home and of life in the favour of their God. We have seen with what knowledge of Him and from what relations with Him they were banished. To the men of the Exile God was already a Name and an Experience, and because that Name was The Righteous, and that Experience was all grace and promise, these men waited for His Word more than they that wait for the morning; and when at length the Word broke from the long darkness and silence, they received it, though its bearers might be unseen and unaccredited, because they recognised and acknowledged in it Himself. He who spoke was their God, and they were His people. This conscience and sympathy was all the title or credential which the revelation required. It is, therefore, not too much to say, as we have said, that the two pronouns in ch. xl., ver. 1, are the necessary premise of the whole prophecy which that verse introduces.

***

With this introduction we may now take up the four herald voices of the Prologue. Whatever may have been their original relation to one another, whether or not they came to Israel by different messengers, they are arranged (as we saw at the close of the previous chapter) in manifest order and progress of thought, and they meet in due succession the experiences of Israel at the close of the Exile. For the first of them (vv. 1 and 2) gives the subjective assurance of the coming redemption: it is the Voice of Grace. The second (vv. 3-5) proclaims the objective reality of that redemption: it may be called the Voice of Providence, or--to use the name by which our prophecy loves to entitle the just and victorious providence of God--the Voice of Righteousness. The third (vv. 6-8) uncovers the pledge and earnest of the redemption: in the weakness of men this shall be the Word of God. While the fourth (vv. 9-11) is the Proclamation of Jehovah's restored kingdom, when He cometh as a shepherd to shepherd His people. To this progress and climax the music of the passage forms a perfect accompaniment. It would be difficult to find in any language lips that first more softly woo the heart, and then take to themselves so brave a trumpet of challenge and assurance. The opening is upon a few short pulses of music, which steal from heaven as gently as the first ripples of light in a cloudless dawn--

Nahamu, nahamu ammi;
- Comfort ye, comfort ye my people;
DabbEru `al-lev Yerushalaim.
- Speak upon the heart of Jerusalem. [38]

But then the trumpet-tone breaks forth, Call unto her; and on that high key the music stays, sweeping with the second voice across hill and dale like a company of swift horsemen, stooping with the third for a while to the elegy upon the withered grass, but then recovering itself, braced by all the strength of the Word of God, to peal from tower to tower with the fourth, upon the cry, Behold, the Lord cometh, till it sinks almost from sound to sight, and yields us, as from the surface of still waters, that sweet reflection of the twenty-third Psalm with which the Prologue concludes.

1. Comfort ye, comfort ye My people, saith your God. Speak ye home to the heart of Jerusalem, and call unto her, That accomplished is her warfare, that absolved is her iniquity; That she hath received of Jehovah's hand double for all her sins.

This first voice, with the music of which our hearts have been thrilled ever since we can remember, speaks twice: first in a whisper, then in a call--the whisper of the Lover and the call of the Lord. Speak ye home to the heart of Jerusalem, and call unto her.

Now Jerusalem lay in ruins, a city through whose breached walls all the winds of heaven blew mournfully across her forsaken floors. And the heart of Jerusalem, which was with her people in exile, was like the city--broken and defenceless. In that far-off, unsympathetic land it lay open to the alien; tyrants forced their idols upon it, the peoples tortured it with their jests.

For they that led us captive required of us songs,
And they that wasted us required of us mirth.

But observe how gently the Divine Beleaguerer approaches, how softly He bids His heralds plead by the gaps, through which the oppressor has forced his idols and his insults. Of all human language they might use, God bids His messengers take and plead with the words with which a man will plead at a maiden's heart, knowing that he has nothing but love to offer as right of entrance, and waiting until love and trust come out to welcome him. Speak ye, says the original literally, on to, or up against, or up round the heart of Jerusalem,--a forcible expression, like the German "An das Herz," or the sweet Scottish, "It cam' up roond my heart," and perhaps best rendered into English by the phrase, Speak home to the heart. It is the ordinary Hebrew expression for wooing. As from man to woman when he wins her, the Old Testament uses it several times. To speak home to the heart is to use language in which authority and argument are both ignored, and love works her own inspiration. While the haughty Babylonian planted by force his idols, while the folly and temptations of heathendom surged recklessly in, God Himself, the Creator of this broken heart, its Husband and Inhabitant of old, [39] stood lowly by its breaches, pleading in love the right to enter. But when entrance has been granted, see how He bids His heralds change their voice and disposition. The suppliant lover, being received, assumes possession and defence, and they, who were first bid whisper as beggars by each unguarded breach, now leap upon the walls to call from the accepted Lord of the city: Fulfilled is thy time of service, absolved thine iniquity, received hast thou of Jehovah's hand double for all thy sins.

Now this is no mere rhetorical figure. This is the abiding attitude and aim of the Almighty towards men. God's target is our heart. His revelation, whatever of law or threat it send before, is, in its own superlative clearness and urgency, Grace. It comes to man by way of the heart; not at first by argument addressed to the intellect, nor by appeal to experience, but by the sheer strength of a love laid on to the heart. It is, to begin with, a subjective thing. Is revelation, then, entirely a subjective assurance? Do the pardon and peace which it proclaims remain only feelings of the heart, without anything to correspond to them in real fact? By no means; for these Jews the revelation now whispered to their heart will actually take shape in providences of the most concrete kind. A voice will immediately call, Prepare ye the way of the Lord, and the way will be prepared. Babylon will fall; Cyrus will let Israel go; their release will appear--most concrete of things!--in "black and white" on a Persian state-parchment. Yet, before these events happen and become part of His people's experience, God desires first to convince His people by the sheer urgency of His love. Before He displays His Providence, He will speak in the power and evidence of His Grace. Afterwards, His prophets shall appeal to outward facts; we shall find them in succeeding chapters arguing both with Israel and the heathen on grounds of reason and the facts of history. But, in the meantime, let them only feel that in His Grace they have something for the heart of men, which, striking home, shall be its own evidence and force.

Thus God adventures His Word forth by nameless and unaccredited men upon no other authority than the Grace, with which it is fraught for the heart of His people. The illustration, which this affords of the method and evidence of Divine revelation, is obvious. Let us, with all the strength of which we are capable, emphasize the fact that our prophecy--which is full of the materials for an elaborate theology, which contains the most detailed apologetic in the whole Bible, and displays the most glorious prospect of man's service and destiny--takes its source and origin from a simple revelation of Grace and the subjective assurance of this in the heart of those to whom it is addressed. This proclamation of Grace is as characteristic and dominant in Second Isaiah, as we saw the proclamation of conscience in ch. i. to be characteristic of the First Isaiah.

Before we pass on, let us look for a moment at the contents of this Grace, in the three clauses of the prophet's cry: Fulfilled is her warfare, absolved her guilt, received hath she of Jehovah's hand double for all her sins. The very grammar here is eloquent of grace. The emphasis lies on the three predicates, which ought to stand in translation, as they do in the original, at the beginning of each clause. Prominence is given, not to the warfare, nor to the guilt, nor to the sins, but to this, that accomplished is the warfare, absolved the guilt, sufficiently expiated the sins. It is a great At Last which these clauses peal forth; but an At Last whose tone is not so much inevitableness as undeserved grace. The term translated warfare means period of military service, appointed term of conscription; and the application is apparent when we remember that the Exile had been fixed, by the Word of God through Jeremiah, to a definite number of years. Absolved is the passive of a verb meaning to pay off what is due. [40] But the third clause is especially gracious. It declares that Israel has suffered of punishment more than double enough to atone for her sins. This is not a way of regarding either sin or atonement, which, theologically speaking, is accurate. What of its relation to our Articles, that man cannot give satisfaction for his sins by the work of his hands or the pains of his flesh? No: it would scarcely pass some of our creeds to-day. But all the more, that it thus bursts forth from strict terms of dealing, does it reveal the generosity of Him who utters it. How full of pity God is, to take so much account of the sufferings sinners have brought upon themselves! How full of grace to reckon those sufferings double the sins that had earned them! It is, as when we have seen gracious men make us a free gift, and in their courtesy insist that we have worked for it. It is grace masked by grace. As the height of art is to conceal art, so the height of grace is to conceal grace, which it does in this verse.

Such is the Voice of Grace. But,

2. Hark, One calling! In the wilderness prepare the way of Jehovah! Make straight in the desert an highway for our God! Every valley shall be exalted, And every mountain and hill be made low: And the crooked grow straight, And rough places a plain: And the glory of Jehovah be revealed, And see it shall all flesh together; For the mouth of Jehovah hath spoken.

The relation of this Voice to the previous one has already been indicated. This is the witness of Providence following upon the witness of Grace. Religion is a matter in the first place between God and the heart; but religion does not, as many mock, remain an inward feeling. The secret relation between God and His people issues into substantial fact, visible to all men. History vindicates faith; Providence executes Promise; Righteousness follows Grace. So, as the first Voice was spoken to the heart, this second is for the hands and feet and active will. Prepare ye the way of the Lord. If you, poor captives as you are, begin to act upon the grace whispered in your trembling hearts, the world will show the result. All things will come round to your side. A levelled empire, an altered world--across those your way shall lie clear to Jerusalem. You shall go forth in the sight of all men, and future generations looking back shall praise this manifest wonder of your God. The glory of Jehovah shall be revealed, and see it shall all flesh together.

On which word, how can our hearts help rising from the comfort of grace to the sense of mastery over this world, to the assurance of heaven itself? History must come round to the side of faith--as it has come round not in the case of Jewish exiles only, but wheresoever such a faith as theirs has been repeated. History must come round to the side of faith, if men will only obey the second as well as the first of these herald voices. But we are too ready to listen to the Word of the Lord, without seeking to prepare His way. We are satisfied with the personal comfort of our God; we are contented to be forgiven and--oh mockery!--left alone. But the word of God will not leave us alone, and not for comfort only is it spoken. On the back of the voice, which sets our heart right with God, comes the voice to set the world right, and no man is godly who has not heard both. Are we timid and afraid that facts will not correspond to our faith? Nay, but as God reigneth they shall, if only we put to our hands and make them; all flesh shall see it, if we will but prepare the way of the Lord.

Have we only ancient proofs of this? On the contrary, God has done like wonders within the lives of those of us who are yet young. During our generation, a people has appealed from the convictions of her heart to the arbitrament of history, and appealed not in vain. When the citizens of the Northern States of the American Republic, not content as they might have been with their protests against slavery, rose to vindicate these by the sword, they faced, humanly speaking, a risk as great as that to which Jew was ever called by the word of God. Their own brethren were against them; the world stood aloof. But even so, unaided by united patriotism and as much dismayed as encouraged by the opinions of civilisation, they rose to the issue on the strength of conscience and their hearts. They rose and they conquered. Slavery was abolished. What had been but the conviction of a few men, became the surprise, the admiration, the consent of the whole world. The glory of the Lord was revealed, and all flesh saw it together.

3. But the shadow of death falls on everything, even on the way of the Lord. By 550 b.c.--that is, after thirty-eight years of exile--nearly all the strong men of Israel's days of independence must have been taken away. Death had been busy with the exiles for more than a generation. There was no longer any human representative of Jehovah to rally the people's trust; the monarchy, each possible Messiah who in turn held it, the priesthood, and the prophethood--whose great personalities so often took the place of Israel's official leaders--had all alike disappeared. It was little wonder, then, that a nation accustomed to be led, not by ideas like us Westerns, but by personages, who were to it the embodiment of Jehovah's will and guidance, should have been cast into despair by the call, Prepare ye the way of the Lord. What sort of a call was this for a people, whose strong men were like things uprooted and withered! How could one be, with any heart, a herald of the Lord to such a people!

> Hark one saying "Call." [41]
> And I said:
> "What can I call?
> All flesh is grass,
> And all its beauty like a wild-flower!
> Withers grass, fades flower,
> When the breath of Jehovah blows on it.
> Surely grass is the people."

Back comes a voice like the east wind's for pitilessness to the flowers, but of the east wind's own strength and clearness, to proclaim Israel's everlasting hope.

> Withers grass, fades flower,
> But the word of our God endureth for ever.

Everything human may perish; the day may be past of the great prophets, of the priests--of the King in his beauty, who was vicegerent of God. But the people have God's word; when all their leaders have fallen, and every visible authority for God is taken away, this shall be their rally and their confidence.

All this is too like the actual experience of Israel in Exile not to be the true interpretation of this third, stern Voice. Their political and religious institutions, which had so often proved the initiative of a new movement, or served as a bridge to carry the nation across disaster to a larger future, were not in existence. Nor does any Moses, as in Egypt of old, rise to visibleness from among his obscure people, impose his authority upon them, marshal them, and lead them out behind him to freedom. But what we see is a scattered and a leaderless people, stirred in their shadow, as a ripe cornfield is stirred by the breeze before dawn--stirred in their shadow by the ancient promises of God, and everywhere breaking out at the touch of these into psalms and prophecies of hope. We see them expectant of redemption, we see them resolved to return, we see them carried across the desert to Zion, and from first to last it is the word of God that is their inspiration and assurance.

They, who formerly had rallied round the Ark or the Temple, or who had risen to the hope of a glorious Messiah, do not now speak of all these, but their hope, they tell us, is in His word; it is the instrument of their salvation, and their destiny is to be its evangelists.

4. To this high destiny the fourth Voice now summons them, by a vivid figure.

Up on a high mountain, get thee up,
Heraldess of good news, O Zion!
Lift up with strength thy voice,
Heraldess of good news, Jerusalem!
Lift up, fear not, say to the cities of Judah:--
Behold, your God.
Behold, my Lord Jehovah, with power He cometh,
And His arm rules for Him.
Behold, His reward with Him,
And His recompense before Him.
As a shepherd His flock He shepherds;
With His right arm gathers the lambs,
And in His bosom bears them.
Ewe-mothers He tenderly leads.

The title which I have somewhat awkwardly translated heraldess--but in English there is really no better word for it--is the feminine participle of a verb meaning to thrill, or give joy, by means of good news. It is used generally to tell such happy news as the birth of a child, but mostly in the special sense of carrying tidings of victory or peace home from the field to the people. The feminine participle would seem from Psalm lxviii., the women who publish victory to the great host, to have been the usual term for the members of those female choirs, who, like Miriam and her maidens, celebrated a triumph in face of the army, or came forth from the city to hail the returning conqueror, as the daughters of Jerusalem hailed Saul and David. As such a chorister, Zion is now summoned to proclaim Jehovah's arrival at the gates of the cities of Judah.

The verses from Behold, your God, to the end of the Prologue are the song of the heraldess. Do not their mingled martial and pastoral strains exactly suit the case of the Return? For this is an expedition, on which the nation's champion has gone forth, not to lead His enemies captive to His gates, but that He may gather His people home. Not mailed men, in the pride of a victory they have helped to win, march in behind Him,--armour and tumult and the garment rolled in blood,--but a herd of mixed and feeble folk, with babes and women, in need of carriage and gentle leading, wander wearily back. And, therefore, in the mouth of the heraldess the figure changes from a warrior-king to the Good Shepherd. With His right arm He gathers the lambs, and in His bosom bears them. Ewe-mothers He gently leads. How true a picture, and how much it recalls! Fifty years before, the exiles left their home (as we can see to this day upon Assyrian sculptures) in closely-driven companies, fettered, and with the urgency upon them of grim soldiers, who marched at intervals in their ranks to keep up the pace, and who tossed the weaklings impatiently aside. But now, see the slow and loosely-gathered bands wander back, just as quickly as the weakest feel strength to travel, and without any force or any guidance save that of their Almighty, Unseen Shepherd.

We are now able to appreciate the dramatic unity of this Prologue. How perfectly it gathers into its four Voices the whole course of Israel's redemption: the first assurance of Grace whispered to the heart, co-operation with Providence, confidence in God's bare Word, the full Return and the Restoration of the City.

But its climax is undoubtedly the honour it lays upon the whole people to be publishers of the good news of God. Of this it speaks with trumpet tones. All Jerusalem must be a herald-people. And how could Israel help owning the constraint and inspiration to so high an office, after so heartfelt an experience of grace, so evident a redemption, so glorious a proof of the power of the Word of God? To have the heart thus filled with grace, to have the will enlisted in so Divine a work, to have known the almightiness of the Divine Word when everything else failed--after such an experience, who would not be able to preach the good news of God, to foretell, as our prophet bids Israel foretell, the coming of the Kingdom and Presence of God--the day when the Lord's flock shall be perfect and none wanting, when society, though still weary and weak and mortal, shall have no stragglers nor outcasts nor reprobates.

O God, so fill us with Thy grace and enlist us in Thy work, so manifest the might of Thy word to us, that the ideal of Thy perfect kingdom may shine as bright and near to us as to Thy prophet of old, and that we may become its inspired preachers and ever labour in its hope. Amen.

Footnotes:

36. See p. 1347.
37. From the sequence of the voices, it would seem that we had in ch. xl. not a mere collection of anonymous prophecies arranged by an editor, but one complete prophecy by the author of most of Isa. xl.-lxvi., set in the dramatic form which obtains through the other chapters.
38. Every one who appreciates the music of the original will agree how incomparably Handel has interpreted it in those pulses of music with which his Messiah opens.
39. See ch. liv., where this figure is developed with great beauty.
40. Lev. xxvii.
41. The technical word to preach or proclaim.

Rev. George Adam Smith, M.A.

CHAPTER VI

GOD: A SACRAMENT.

Isaiah xl. 12-31.

Such are the Four Voices which herald the day of Israel's redemption. They are scarcely silent, before the Sun Himself uprises, and horizon after horizon of His empire is displayed to the eyes of His starved and waiting people. From the prologue of the prophecy, in ch. xl. 1-11, we advance to the presentation, in chs. xl. 12-xli., of its primary and governing truth--the sovereignty and omnipotence of God, the God of Israel.

We may well call this truth the sun of the new day which Israel is about to enter. For as it is the sun which makes the day, and not the day which reveals the sun; so it is God, supreme and almighty, who interprets, predicts and controls His people's history, and not their history, which, in its gradual evolution, is to make God's sovereignty and omnipotence manifest to their experience. Let us clearly understand this. The prophecy, which we are about to follow, is an argument not so much from history to God as from God to history. Israel already have their God; and it is because He is what He is, and what they ought to know Him to be, [42] that they are bidden believe that their future shall take a certain course. The prophet begins with God, and everything follows from God. All that in these chapters lends light or force, all that interprets the history of to-day and fills to-morrow with hope, fact and promise alike, the captivity of Israel, the appearance of Cyrus, the fall of Babylon, Israel's redemption, the extension of their mission to the ends of the earth, the conversion of the Gentiles, the equipment, discipline and triumph of the Servant Himself,--we may even say the expanded geography of our prophet, the countries which for the first time emerge from the distant west within the vision of a Hebrew seer,--all are due to that primary truth about God with which we are now presented. It is God's sovereignty which brings such far-off things into the interest of Israel; it is God's omnipotence which renders such impossible things practical. And as with the subjects, so with the style of the following chapters. The prophet's style is throughout the effect of his perfect and brilliant monotheism. It is the thought of God which everywhere kindles his imagination. His most splendid passages are those, in which he soars to some lofty vision of the Divine glory in creation or history; while his frequent sarcasm and ridicule owe their effectiveness to the sudden scorn, with which, from such a view, scattering epigrams the while, he sweeps down upon the heathen's poor images, or Israel's grudging thoughts of his God. The breadth and the force of his imagination, the sweep of his rhetoric, the intensity of his scorn, may all be traced to his sense of God's sovereignty, and are the signs to us of how absolutely he was possessed by this as his main and governing truth.

This, then, being the sun of Israel's coming day, we may call what we find in ch. xl. 11-xli. the sunrise--the full revelation and uprising on our sight of this original gospel of the prophet. It is addressed to two classes of men; in ch. xl. 12-31 to Israel, but in ch. xli. (for the greater part, at least) to the Gentiles. In dealing with these two classes the prophet makes a great difference. To Israel he presents their God, as it were, in sacrament; but to the Gentiles he urges God's claims in challenge and argument. It is to the past that he summons Israel, and to what they ought to know already about their God; it is to the future, to history yet unmade, that he proposes to the Gentiles they should together appeal, in order to see whether his God or their gods are the true Deity. In this chapter we shall deal with the first of these--God in sacrament.

***

The fact is familiar to all, that the Old Testament nowhere feels the necessity of proving the existence of God. That would have been a proof unintelligible to those to whom its prophets addressed themselves. In the time when the Old Testament came to him, man as little doubted the existence of God as he doubted his own life. But as life sometimes burned low, needing replenishment, so faith would grow despondent and morbid, needing to be led away from objects which only starved it, or produced, as idolatry did, the veriest delirium of a religion. A man had to get his faith lifted from the thoughts of his own mind and the works of his own hand, to be borne upon and nourished by the works of God,--to kindle with the sunrise, to broaden out by the sight of the firmament, to deepen as he faced the spaces of night,--and win calmness and strength to think life into order as he looked forth upon the marshalled hosts of heaven, having all the time no doubt that the God who created and guided these was his God. Therefore, when psalmist or prophet calls Israel to lift their eyes to the hills, or to behold how the heavens declare the glory of God, or to listen to that unbroken tradition, which day passes to day and night to night, of the knowledge of the Creator, it is not proofs to doubting minds which he offers: it is spiritual nourishment to hungry souls. These are not arguments--they are sacraments. When we Christians go to the Lord's Supper, we go not to have the Lord proved to us, but to feed upon a life and a love of whose existence we are past all doubt. Our sacrament fills all the mouths by which needy faith is fed--such as outward sight, and imagination, and memory, and wonder, and love. Now very much what the Lord's Supper is to us for fellowship with God and feeding upon Him, that were the glory of the heavens, and the everlasting hills, and the depth of the sea, and the vision of the stars to the Hebrews. They were the sacraments of God. By them faith was fed, and the spirit of man entered into the enjoyment of God, whose existence indeed he had never doubted, but whom he had lost, forgotten, or misunderstood.

Now it is as such a minister of sacrament to God's starved and disheartened people that our prophet appears in ch. xl. 12-31.

There were three elements in Israel's starvation. Firstly, for nearly fifty years they had been deprived of the accustomed ordinances of religion. Temple and altar had perished; the common praise and the national religious fellowship were impossible; the traditional symbols of the faith lay far out of sight; there was at best only a precarious ministry of the Word. But, in the second place, this famine of the Word and of Sacraments was aggravated by the fact that history had gone against the people. To the baser minds among them, always ready to grant their allegiance to success, this could only mean that the gods of the heathen had triumphed over Jehovah. It is little wonder that such experience, assisted by the presentation, at every turn in their ways, of idols and a splendid idol-worship, the fashion and delight of the populations through whom they were mixed, should have tempted many Jews to feed their starved hearts at the shrines of their conquerors' gods. But the result could only be the further atrophy of their religious nature. It has been held as a reason for the worship of idols that they excite the affection and imagination of the worshipper. They do no such thing: they starve and they stunt these. The image reacts upon the imagination, infects it with its own narrowness and poverty, till man's noblest creative faculty becomes the slave of its own poor toy. But, thirdly, if the loftier spirits in Israel refused to believe that Jehovah, exalted in righteousness, could be less than the brutal deities whom Babylon vaunted over Him, they were flung back upon the sorrowful conviction that their God had cast them off; that He had retreated from the patronage of so unworthy a people into the veiled depths of His own nature. Then upon that heaven, from which no answer came to those who were once its favourites, they cast we can scarcely tell what reflection of their own weary and spiritless estate. As, standing over a city by night, you will see the majestic darkness above stained and distorted into shapes of pain or wrath by the upcast of the city's broken, murky lights, so many of the nobler exiles saw upon the blank, unanswering heaven a horrible mirage of their own trouble and fear. Their weariness said, He is weary; the ruin of their national life reflected itself as the frustration of His purposes; their accusing conscience saw the darkness of His counsel relieved only by streaks of wrath.

But none of these tendencies in Israel went so far as to deny that there was a God, or even to doubt His existence. This, as we have said, was nowhere yet the temptation of mankind. When the Jew lapsed from that true faith, which we have seen his nation carry into exile, he fell into one of the two tempers just described--devotion to false gods in the shape of idols, or despondency consequent upon false notions of the true God. It is against these tempers, one after another, that ch. xl. 12-31 is directed. And so we understand why, though the prophet is here declaring the basis and spring of all his subsequent prophecy, he does not adopt the method of abstract argument. He is not treating with men, who have had no true knowledge of God in the past, or whose intellect questions God's reality. He is treating with men, who have a national heritage of truth about God, but they have forgotten it; who have hearts full of religious affection, but it has been betrayed; who have a devout imagination, but it has been starved; who have hopes, but they are faint unto death. He will recall to them their heritage, rally their shrinking convictions by the courage of his own faith, feed their hunger after righteousness [43] by a new hope set to noble music, and display to the imagination that has been stunted by so long looking upon the face of idols the wide horizons of Divine glory in earth and heaven.

His style corresponds to his purpose. He does not syllogize; he exhorts, recalls and convicts by assertion. The passage is a series of questions, rallies and promises. Have ye not known? have ye not heard? is his chief note. Instead of arranging facts in history or nature as in themselves a proof for God, he mentions them only by way of provoking inward recollections. His sharp questions are as hooks to draw from his hearers' hearts their timid and starved convictions, that he may nourish these upon the sacramental glories of nature and of history.

Such a purpose and style trust little to method, and it would be useless to search for any strict division of strophes in the passage. [44] The following, however, is a manifest division of subject, according to the two tempers to which the prophet had to appeal. Verses 12 to 25, and perhaps 26, are addressed to the idolatrous Jews. But in 26 there is a transition to the despair of the nobler hearts in Israel, who, though they continued to believe in the One True God, imagined that He had abandoned them; and to such vv. 27 to 31 are undoubtedly addressed. The different treatment accorded to the two classes is striking. The former of these the prophet does not call by any title of the people of God; with the latter he pleads by a dear double name that he may win them through every recollection of their gracious past, Jacob and Israel (ver. 27). Challenge and sarcasm are his style with the idolaters, his language clashing out in bursts too loud and rapid sometimes for the grammar, as in ver. 24; but with the despondent his way is gentle persuasiveness, with music that swells and brightens steadily, passing without a break from the minor key of pleading to the major of glorious promise.

1. Against the Idolaters. A couple of sarcastic sentences upon idols and their manufacture (vv. 19, 20) stand between two majestic declarations of God's glory in nature and in history (vv. 12-17 and 21-24). It is an appeal from the worshippers' images to their imagination. Who hath measured in his hollow hand the waters, and heaven ruled off with a span? Or caught in a tierce the dust of the earth, and weighed in scales mountains, and hills in a balance? Who hath directed the spirit of Jehovah, and as man of His counsel hath helped Him to know? With whom took He counsel, that such an one informed Him and taught Him in the orthodox path, and taught Him knowledge and helped Him to know the way of intelligence? The term translated orthodox path is literally path of ordinance or judgement, the regular path, and is doubtless to be taken along with its parallel, way of intelligence, as a conventional phrase of education, which the prophet employed to make his sarcasm the stronger. Lo nations! as a drop from a bucket, and like dust in a balance, are they reckoned. Lo the Isles! [45] as a trifle He lifteth. And Lebanon is by no means enough for burning, nor its brute-life enough for an offering. All the nations are as nothing before Him, as spent and as waste are they reckoned for Him.

When he has thus soared enough, as on an archangel's wings, he swoops with one rapid question down from the height of his imagination upon the images.

To whom then will ye liken God, and what likeness will ye range by Him?

The image! A smith cast it, and a smelter plates it with gold, and smelts silver chains. He that is straitened for an offering--he chooseth a tree that does not rot, seeks to him a cunning carver to set up an image that will not totter. [46]

The image shrivels up in face of that imagination; the idol is abolished by laughter. There is here, and for almost the first time in history, the same intellectual intolerance of images, the same burning sense of the unreasonableness of their worship, which has marked all monotheists, and turned even the meekest of their kind into fierce scorners and satirists--Elijah, Mohammed, Luther, and Knox. [47] We hear this laughter from them all. Sometimes it may sound truculent or even brutal, but let us remember what is behind it. When we hear it condemned--as, in the interests of art and imagination, its puritan outbursts have often been condemned--as a barbarian incapacity to sympathise with the æsthetic instincts of man, or to appreciate the influence of a beautiful and elevating cult, we can reply that it was the imagination itself which often inspired both the laughter at, and the breaking of, images, and that, because the iconoclast had a loftier vision of God than the image-maker, he has, on the whole, more really furthered the progress of art than the artist whose works he has destroyed. It is certain, for instance, that no one would exchange the beauties of the prophecy now before us, with its sublime imaginations of God, for all the beauty of all the idols of Babylonia which it consigned to destruction. And we dare to say the same of two other epochs, when the uncompromising zeal of monotheists crushed to the dust the fruits of centuries of Christian art. The Koran is not often appealed to as a model of poetry, but it contains passages whose imagination of God, broad as the horizon of the desert of its birth, and swift and clear as the desert dawn, may be regarded as infinitely more than compensation--from a purely artistic point of view--for the countless works of Christian ritual and imagery which it inspired the rude cavalry of the desert to trample beneath the hoofs of their horses. And again, if we are to blame the Reformers of Western Christendom for the cruelty with which they lifted their hammers against the carved work of the sanctuary, do not let us forget how much of the spirit of the best modern art is to be traced to their more spiritual and lofty conceptions of God. No one will question how much Milton's imagination owed to his Protestantism, or how much Carlyle's dramatic genius was the result of his Puritan faith. But it is to the spirit of the Reformation, as it liberated the worshipper's soul from bondage to artificial and ecclesiastical symbols of the Deity, that we may also ascribe a large part of the force of that movement towards Nature and the imagination of God in His creation which inspired, for example, Wordsworth's poetry, and those visual sacraments of rainbow, storm, and dawn to which Browning so often lifts our souls from their dissatisfaction with ritual or with argument.

From his sarcasm on the idols our prophet returns to his task of drawing forth Israel's memory and imagination. Have ye not known? Have ye not heard? Hath it not been told you from the beginning? Have ye not understood from the foundations of the earth? He that is enthroned above the circle of the earth, and its dwellers are before Him as grasshoppers; who stretcheth as a fine veil the heavens, and spreadeth them like a dwelling tent--that is, as easily as if they were not even a pavilion or marquee, but only a humble dwelling tent. He who bringeth great men to nothing, the judges of the earth He maketh as waste. Yea, they were not planted; yea, they were not sown; yea, their root had not struck in the earth, but immediately He blew upon them and they withered, and a whirlwind like stubble carried them away. To whom, then, will ye liken Me, that I may match with him? saith the Holy One. But this time it is not necessary to suggest the idols; they were dissolved by that previous burst of laughter. Therefore, the prophet turns to the other class in Israel with whom he has to deal.

2. To the Despairers of the Lord. From history we pass back to nature in ver. 26, which forms a transition, the language growing steadier from the impetuosity of the address to the idolaters to the serene music of the second part. Enough rebuke has the prophet made. As he now lifts his people's vision to the stars, it is not to shame their idols, but to feed their hearts. Lift up on high your eyes and see! Who hath created these? Who leads forth by number their host, and all of them calleth by name, by abundance of might, for He is powerful in strength, not one is amissing. Under such a night, that veils the confusion of earth only to bring forth all the majesty and order of heaven, we feel a moment's pause. Then as the expanding eyes of the exiles gaze upon the infinite power above, the prophet goes on. Why then sayest thou, O Jacob, and speakest, O Israel? Hidden is my way from Jehovah, and from my God my right hath passed.

Why does the prophet point his people to the stars? Because he is among Israel on that vast Babylonian plain, from whose crowded and confused populations, struggling upon one monotonous level, there is no escape for the heart but to the stars. Think of that plain when Nebuchadrezzar was its tyrant; of the countless families of men torn from their far homes and crushed through one another upon its surface; of the ancient liberties that were trampled in that servitude, of the languages that were stifled in that Babel, of the many patriotisms set to sigh themselves out into the tyrant's mud and mortar. Ah heaven! was there a God in thee, that one man could thus crush nations in his vat, as men crushed shell-fish in those days, to dye his imperial purple? Was there any Providence above, that he could tear peoples from the lands and seas, where their various gifts and offices for humanity had been developed, and press them to his selfish and monotonous servitude? In that medley of nations, all upon one level of captivity, Israel was just as lost as the most insignificant tribe; her history severed, her worship impossible, her very language threatened with decay. No wonder, that from the stifling crowd and desperate flatness of it all she cried, Hidden is my way from Jehovah, and from my God my right hath passed.

But from the flatness and the crowd the stars are visible; and it was upon the stars that the prophet bade his people feed their hearts. There were order and unfailing guidance; for the greatness of His might not one is missing. And He is your God. Just as visible as those countless stars are, one by one, in the dark heavens, to your eyes looking up, so your lives and fortunes are to His eyes looking down on this Babel of peoples. He gathereth the outcasts of Israel.... He telleth the number of the stars. [48] And so the prophet goes on earnestly to plead: Hast thou not known? Hast thou not heard? that an everlasting God is Jehovah, Creator of the ends of the earth. He fainteth not, neither is weary. There is no searching of His understanding. Giver to the weary of strength! And upon him that is of no might, He lavisheth power. Even youths may faint and be weary, and young men utterly fall; but they who hope in Jehovah shall renew strength, put forth pinions like eagles, run and not weary, walk and not faint. Listen, ears, not for the sake of yourselves only, though the music is incomparably sweet! Listen for the sake of the starved hearts below, to whom you carry the sacraments of hope, whom you lift to feed upon the clear symbols of God's omnipotence and unfailing grace.

This chapter began with the assurance to the heart of Israel of their God's will to redeem and restore them. It closes with bidding the people take hope in God. Let us again emphasize--for we cannot do so too often, if we are to keep ourselves from certain errors of to-day on the subject of Revelation--the nature of this prophecy. It is not a reading-off of history; it is a call from God. No deed has yet been done pointing towards the certainty of Israel's redemption; it is not from facts writ large on the life of their day, that the prophet bids the captives read their Divine discharge. That discharge he brings from God; he bids them find the promise and the warrant of it in their God's character, in their own convictions of what that character is. In order to revive those convictions, he does, it is true, appeal to certain facts, but these facts are not the facts of contemporary history which might reveal to any clear eye, that the current and the drift of politics was setting towards the redemption of Israel. They are facts of nature and facts of general providence, which, as we have said, like sacraments evidence God's power to the pious heart, feed it with the assurance of His grace, and bid it hope in His word, though history should seem to be working quite the other way.

This instance of the method of revelation does not justify two opinions, which prevail at the present day regarding prophecy. In the first place, it proves to us, that those are wrong who, too much infected by the modern temper to judge accurately writers so unsophisticated, describe prophecy as if it were merely a philosophy of history, by which the prophets deduced from their observation of the course of events their idea of God and their forecast of His purposes. The prophets had indeed to do with history; they argued from it, and they appealed to it. The history that was past was full of God's condescension to men, and shone like Nature's self with sacramental signs of His power and will: the history that was future was to be His supreme tribunal, and to afford the vindication of the word they claimed to have brought from Him. But still all this--their trust in history and their use of it--was something secondary in the prophetic method. With them God Himself was first; they came forth from His presence, as they describe it, with the knowledge of His will gained through the communion of their spirits with His Spirit. If they then appealed to past history, it was to illustrate their message; or to future, it was for vindication of this. But God Himself was the Source and Author of it; and therefore, before they had facts beneath their eyes to corroborate their promises, they appealed to the people, like our prophet in ch. xl., to wait on Jehovah. The day might not yet have dawned so as to let them read the signs of the times. But in the darkness they hoped in Jehovah, and borrowed for their starved hearts from the stars above, or other sacrament, some assurance of His unfailing power.

Jehovah, then, was the source of the prophets' word: His character was its pledge. The prophets were not mere readers from history, but speakers from God.

But the testimony of our chapter to all this enables us also to arrest an opinion about Revelation, which has too hurriedly run off with some Christians, and to qualify it. In the inevitable recoil from the scholastic view of revelation as wholly a series of laws and dogmas and predictions, a number of writers on the subject have of late defined Revelation as a chain of historical acts, through which God uttered His character and will to men. According to this view, Revelation is God manifesting Himself in history, and the Bible is the record of this historical process. Now, while it is true that the Bible is, to a large extent, the annals and interpretation of the great and small events of a nation's history--of its separation from the rest of mankind, its miraculous deliverances, its growth, its defeats and humiliations, its reforms and its institutions; in all of which God manifested His character and will--yet the Bible also records a revelation, which preceded these historical deeds; a revelation the theatre of which was not the national experience, but the consciousness of the individual; which was recognised and welcomed by choice souls in the secret of their own spiritual life, before it was realised and observed in outward fact; which was uttered by the prophet's voice and accepted by the people's trust in the dark and the stillness, before the day of the Lord had dawned or there was light to see His purposes at work. In a word, God's revelation to men was very often made clear in their subjective consciousness, before it became manifest in the history about them.

And, for ourselves, let us remember that to this day true religion is as independent of facts as it was with the prophet. True religion is a conviction of the character of God, and a resting upon that alone for salvation. We need nothing more to begin with; and everything else, in our experience and fortune, helps us only in so far as it makes that primary conviction more clear and certain. Darkness may be over us, and we lonely and starved beneath it. We may be destitute of experience to support our faith; we may be able to discover nothing in life about us making in the direction of our hopes. Still, let us wait on the Lord. It is by bare trust in Him, that we renew our strength, put forth wings like eagles, run and not weary, walk and not faint.

Put forth wings--run--walk! Is the order correct? Hope swerves from the edge of so descending a promise, which seems only to repeat the falling course of nature--that droop, we all know, from short ambitions, through temporary impulsiveness, to the old commonplace and routine. Soaring, running, walking--and is not the next stage, a cynic might ask, standing still?

On the contrary, it is a natural and a true climax, rising from the easier to the more difficult, from the ideal to the real, from dream to duty, from what can only be the rare occasions of life to what must be life's usual and abiding experience. History followed this course. Did the prophet, as he promised, think of what should really prove to be the fortune of his people during the next few years?--the great flight of hope, on which we see them rising in their psalms of redemption as on the wings of an eagle; the zeal and liberality of preparation for departure from Babylon; the first rush at the Return; and then the long tramp, day after day, with the slow caravan, at the pace of its most heavily-laden beasts of burden, when they shall walk and not faint should indeed seem to them the sweetest part of their God's promise.

Or was it the far longer perspective of Israel's history that bade the prophet follow this descending scale? The spirit of prophecy was with himself to soar higher than ever before, reaching by truly eagle-flight to a vision of the immediate consummation of Israel's glory: the Isles waiting for Jehovah, the Holy City radiant in His rising, and open with all her gates to the thronging nations; the true religion flashing from Zion across the world, and the wealth of the world pouring back upon Zion. And some have wondered, and some scoff, that after this vision there should follow centuries of imperceptible progress--five-and-a-half centuries of preparation for the coming of the Promised Servant; and then--Israel, indeed gone forth over the world, but only in small groups, living upon the grudged and fitful tolerance of the great centres of Gentile civilisation. The prophet surely anticipates all this, when he places the walking after the soaring and the running. When he says last, and most impressively, of his people's fortunes, that they shall walk and not faint, he has perhaps just those long centuries in view, when, instead of a nation of enthusiasts taking humanity by storm, we see small bands of pioneers pushing their way from city to city by the slow methods of ancient travel,--Damascus, Antioch, Tarsus,

Iconium, Ephesus, Thessalonica, Athens, Corinth and Rome,--everywhere that Paul and the missionaries of the Cross found a pulpit and a congregation ready for the Gospel; toiling from day to day at their own trades, serving the alien for wages, here and there founding a synagogue, now and then completing a version of their Scriptures, oftentimes achieving martyrdom, but ever living a pure and a testifying life in face of the heathen, with the passion of these prophecies at their hearts. It was certainly for such centuries and such men that the word was written, they shall walk and not faint. This persistence under persecution, this monotonous drilling of themselves in school and synagogue, this slow progress without prize or praise along the common highways of the world and by the world's ordinary means of livelihood, was a greater proof of indomitableness than even the rapture which filled their hearts on the golden eve of the Return, under the full diapason of prophecy.

And so must it ever be. First the ideal, and then the rush at it with passionate eyes, and then the daily trudge onward, when its splendour has faded from the view, but is all the more closely wrapped round the heart. For glorious as it is to rise to some great consummation on wings of dream and song, glorious as it is, also, to bend that impetus a little lower and take some practical crisis of life by storm, an even greater proof of our religion and of the help our God can give us is the lifelong tramp of earth's common surface, without fresh wings of dream, or the excitement of rivalry, or the attraction of reward, but with the head cool, and the face forward, and every footfall upon firm ground. Let hope rejoice in a promise, which does not go off into the air, but leaves us upon solid earth; and let us hold to a religion, which, while it exults in being the secret of enthusiasm and the inspiration of heroism, is daring and Divine enough to find its climax in the commonplace.

Footnotes:

42. See xl. 21, Have ye not known?

43. That is in the sense, in which our prophet uses the word, of salvation. See Ch. [14]XIV. of this volume.

44. Some intention of division undoubtedly appears. Notice the double refrain, To whom will ye liken, etc., of vv. 18 and 25; and then at equal distance from either occurrence of this challenge the appeal, Dost thou not know, etc., vv. 21 and 28. But though these signs of a strict division appear, the rest is submerged by the strong flood of feeling which rushes too deep and rapid for any hard-and-fast embankments.

45. See p. [15]109.

46. If an idol leant over or fell that was the very worst of omens; cf. the case of Dagon.

47. When John Knox was a prisoner in France, "the officers brought to him a painted board, which they called Our Lady, and commanded him to kiss it. They violently thrust it into his face, and put it betwixt his hands, who, seeing the extremity, took the idol, and advisedly looking about, he cast it into the river, and said, 'Let Our Lady now save herself; she is light enough; let her learn to swim!' After that was no Scotsman urged with that idolatry."--Knox, History of the Reformation.

48. Psalm cxlvii.

CHAPTER VII

GOD: AN ARGUMENT FROM HISTORY.

Isaiah xli.
    Having revealed Himself to His own people in ch. xl., Jehovah now turns in ch. xli. to the heathen, but, naturally, with a very different kind of address. Displaying His power to His people in certain sacraments, both of nature and history, He had urged them to wait upon Him alone for the salvation, of which there were as yet no signs in the times. But with the heathen it is evidently to these signs of the times, that He can best appeal. Contemporary history, facts open to every man's memory and reason, is the common ground on which Jehovah and the other gods can meet. Ch. xli. is, therefore, the natural complement to ch. xl. In ch. xl. we have the element in revelation that precedes history: in ch. xli. we have history itself explained as a part of revelation.
    Ch. xli. is loosely cast in the same form of a Trial-at-Law, which we found in ch. i. To use a Scotticism, which exactly translates the Hebrew of ver. 1, Jehovah goes to the law with the idols. His summons to the Trial is given in ver. 1; the ground of the Trial is advanced in vv. 2-7. Then comes a digression, vv. 8-20, in which the Lord turns from controversy with the heathen to comfort His people. In vv. 21-29 Jehovah's plea is resumed, and in the silence of the defendants--a silence, which, as we shall presently see by calling in the witness of a Greek historian, was actual fact--the argument is summed up and the verdict given for the sole divinity of Israel's God.
    The main interest of the Trial lies, of course, in its appeal to contemporary history, and to the central figure Cyrus, although it is to be noted that the prophet as yet refrains from mentioning the hero by name. This appeal to contemporary history lays upon us the duty of briefly indicating, how the course of that history was tending outside Babylon,--outside Babylon, as yet, but fraught with fate both to Babylon and to her captives.

***

    Nebuchadrezzar, although he had virtually succeeded to the throne of the Assyrian, had not been able to repeat from Babylon that almost universal empire, which his predecessors had swayed from Nineveh. Egypt, it is true, was again as thoroughly driven from Asia as in the time of Sargon: to the south the Babylonian supremacy was as unquestioned as ever the Assyrian had been. But to the north Nebuchadrezzar met with an almost equal rival, who had helped him in the overthrow of Nineveh, and had fallen heir to the Assyrian supremacy in that quarter. This was Kastarit or Kyaxares, an Aryan, one of the pioneers of that Aryan invasion from the East, which, though still tardy and sparse, was to be the leading force in Western Asia for the next century. This Kyaxares had united under his control a number of Median tribes, [49] a people of Turanian stock. With these, when Nineveh fell, he established to the north of Nebuchadrezzar's power the empire of Media, with its western boundary at the river Halys, in Asia Minor, and its capital at Ecbatana under Mount Elwand. It is said that the river Indus formed his frontier to the east. West of the Halys, the Mede's progress was stopped by the Lydian Empire, under King Alyattis, whose capital was Sardis, and whose other border was practically the coast of the Ægean. In 585, or two years after the destruction of Jerusalem, Alyattis and Kyaxares met in battle on the Halys. But the terrors of an eclipse took the heart to fight out of both their armies, and, Nebuchadrezzar intervening, the three monarchs struck a treaty among themselves, and strengthened it by intermarriage. Western Asia now virtually consisted of the confederate powers, Babylonia, Media and Lydia. [50]
    Let us realise how far this has brought us. When we stood with Isaiah in Jerusalem, our western horizon lay across the middle of Asia Minor in the longitude of Cyprus. [51] It now rests upon the Ægean; we are almost within sight of Europe. Straight from Babylon to Sardis runs a road, with a regular service of couriers. The court of Sardis holds domestic and political intercourse with the courts of Babylon and Ecbatana; but the court of Sardis also lords it over the Asiatic Greeks, worships at Greek shrines, will shortly be visited by Solon and strike an alliance with Sparta. In the time of the Jewish exile there were without doubt many Greeks in Babylon; men may have spoken there with Daniel, who had spoken at Sardis with Solon.
    This extended horizon makes clear to us what our prophet has in his view, when in this forty-first chapter he summons Isles to the bar of Jehovah: Be silent before me, O Isles, and let Peoples renew

Rev. George Adam Smith, M.A.

their strength,--a vision and appeal which frequently recur in our prophecy. Listen, O Isles, and hearken, O Peoples from afar (xlix. 1); Isles shall wait for His law (xlii. 4); Let them give glory to Jehovah, and publish His praise in the Isles (xlii. 12); Unto me Isles shall hope (li. 5); Surely Isles shall wait for me, ships of Tarshish first. [52] The name is generally taken by scholars--according to the derivation in the note below--to have originally meant habitable land, and so land as opposed to water. In some passages of the Old Testament it is undoubtedly used to describe a land either washed, or surrounded, by the sea.[53]

But by our prophet's use of the word it is not necessarily maritime provinces that are meant. He makes isles parallel to the well-known terms nations, peoples, Gentiles, and in one passage he opposes it, as dry soil, to water. [54] Hence many translators take it in its original sense of countries or lands. This bare rendering, however, does not do justice to the sense of remoteness, which the prophet generally attaches to the word, nor to his occasional association of it with visions of the sea. Indeed, as one reads most of his uses of it, one is quite sure that the island-meaning of the word lingers on in his imagination; and that the feeling possesses him, which has haunted the poetry of all ages, to describe as coasts or isles any land or lighting-place of thought which is far and dim and vague; which floats across the horizon, or emerges from the distance, as strips and promontories of land rise from the sea to him who has reached some new point of view. I have therefore decided to keep the rendering familiar to the English reader, isles, though, perhaps, coasts would be better. If, as is probable, our prophet's thoughts are always towards the new lands of the west as he uses the word, it is doubly suitable; those countries were both maritime and remote; they rose both from the distance and from the sea.

> "The sprinkled isles,
> Lily on lily, that o'erlace the sea
> And laugh their pride, where the light wave lisps, 'Greece.'"

But if Babylonia lay thus open to Lydia, and through Lydia to the isles and coasts of Greece, it was different with her northern frontier. What strikes us here is the immense series of fortifications, which Nebuchadrezzar, in spite of his alliance with Astyages, cast up between his country and Media. Where the Tigris and Euphrates most nearly approach one another, about seventy miles to the north of Babylon, Nebuchadrezzar connected their waters by four canals, above which he built a strong bulwark, called by the Greeks the Median wall. This may have been over sixty miles long; Xenophon tells us it was twenty feet broad by one hundred high. [55] At Sippara this line of defence was completed by the creation of a great bason of water to flood the rivers and canals on the approach of an enemy, and of a large fortress to protect the bason. Alas for the vanity of human purposes! It is said to have been this very bason which caused the easy fall of Babylon. By turning the Euphrates into it, the enemy entered the capital through the emptied river-bed.

The triple alliance--Lydia, Media, Babylonia--stood firm after its founders passed away. In 555, Croesus and Astyages, who had succeeded their fathers at Sardis and Ecbatana respectively, and Nabunahid, who had usurped the throne at Babylon, were still at peace, and contented with the partition of 585. But outside them and to the east, in a narrow nook of land at the head of the Persian Gulf, the man was already crowned, who was destined to bring Western Asia again under one sceptre. This was Kurush or Cyrus II. of Anzan, but known to history as Cyrus the Great or Cyrus the Persian. Cyrus was a prince of the Akhæmenian house of Persia, and therefore, like the Mede, an Aryan, but independent of his Persian cousins, and ruling in his own right the little kingdom of Anzan or Anshan, which, with its capital of Susan, lay on the rivers Choaspes and Eulæus, between the head of the Persian Gulf and the Zagros Mountains. [56]

Cyrus the Great is one of those mortals whom the muse of history, as if despairing to do justice to him by herself, has called in her sisters to aid her in describing to posterity. Early legend and later and more elaborate romance; the schoolmaster, the historian, the tragedian and the prophet, all vie in presenting to us this hero "le plus sympathique de l'antiquité" [57] --this king on whom we see so deeply stamped the double signature of God, character and success. We shall afterwards have a better opportunity to speak of his character. Here we are only concerned to trace his rapid path of conquest.

He sprang, then, from Anshan, the immediate neighbour of Babylonia to the east. This is the direction indicated in the second verse of this forty-first chapter: Who hath raised up one from the east? But the twenty-fifth verse veers round with him to the north: I have raised up one from the north, and he is come. This was actually the curve, from east to north, which his career almost immediately took.

For in 549 Astyages, king of Media, attacked Cyrus, [58] king of Anshan; which means that Cyrus was already a considerable and an aggressive prince. Probably he had united by this time the two domains of his house, Persia and Anshan, under his own sceptre, and secured as his lieutenant Hystaspes, his cousin, the lineal king of Persia. The Mede, looking south and east from Ecbatana, saw a solid front opposed to him, and resolved to crush it before it grew more formidable. But the Aryans among the Medes, dissatisfied with so indolent a leader as Astyages, revolted to Cyrus, and so the latter, with characteristic good fortune, easily became lord of Media. A lenient lord he made. He spared Astyages, and ranked the Aryan Medes second only to the Persians. But it took him till 546 to complete his conquest. When he had done so he stood master of Asia from the Halys to perhaps as far east as the Indus. He replaced the Medes in the threefold power of Western Asia, and thus looked down on Babylon, as v. 25 says, from the north (xli. 25).

In 545, Cyrus advanced upon Babylonia, and struck at the northern line of fortifications at Sippara. He was opposed by an army under Belshazzar, Bel-shar-uzzur, the son of Nabunahid, and probably by his mother's side grandson of Nebuchadrezzar. Army or fortifications seem to have been too much for Cyrus, and there is no further mention of his name in the Babylonian annals till the year 538. It has been suggested that Cyrus was aware of the discontent of the people with their ruler Nabunahid, and, with that genius which distinguished his whole career for availing himself of the internal politics of his foes, he may have been content to wait till the Babylonian dissatisfaction had grown riper, perhaps in the meantime fostering it by his own emissaries.

In any case, the attention of Cyrus was now urgently demanded on the western boundary of his empire, where Lydia was preparing to invade him. Croesus, king of Lydia, fresh from the subjection of the Ionian Greeks, and possessing an army and a treasure second to none in the world, had lately asked of Solon, whether he was not the most fortunate of men; and Solon had answered, to count no man happy till his death. The applicability of this advice to himself Croesus must have felt with a start, when, almost immediately after it, the news came that his brother-in-law Astyages had fallen before an unknown power, which was moving up rapidly from the east, and already touched the Lydian frontier at the Halys. Croesus was thrown into alarm. He eagerly desired to know Heaven's will about this Persian and himself, who now stood face to face. But, in that heathen world, with its thousand shrines to different gods, who knew the will of Heaven? In a fashion only possible to the richest man in the world, Croesus resolved to discover, by sending a test-question, on a matter of fact within his own knowledge, to every oracle of repute: to the oracles of the Greeks at Miletus, Delphi, Abæ; to that of Trophonius; to the sanctuary of Amphiaraus at Thebes; to Dodona; and even to the far-off temple of Ammon in Libya. The oracles of Delphi and Amphiaraus alone sent an answer, which in the least suggested the truth. "To the gods of Delphi and Amphiaraus, Croesus, therefore, offered great sacrifices,--three thousand victims of every kind; and on a great pile of wood he burned couches plated with gold and silver, golden goblets, purple robes and garments, in the hope that he would thereby gain the favour of the god yet more.... And as the sacrifice left behind an enormous mass of molten gold, Croesus caused bricks to be made, six palms in length, three in breadth and one in depth; in all there were 117 bricks.... In addition there was a golden lion which weighed ten talents. When these were finished, Croesus sent them to Delphi; and he added two very large mixing bowls, one of gold, weighing eight talents and a half and twelve minæ, and one of silver (the work of Theodorus of Samos, as the Delphians say, and I believe it, for it is the work of no ordinary artificer), four silver jars, and two vessels for holy water, one of gold, the other of silver, circular casts of silver, a golden statue of a woman three cubits high, and the necklace and girdles of his queen." [59] We can understand, that for all this Croesus got the best advice consistent with the ignorance and caution of the priests whom he consulted. The oracles told him that if he went against Cyrus he would destroy a great empire; but he forgot to ask, whether it was his own or his rival's. When he inquired a second time, if his reign should be long, they replied: "When a mule became king of the Medes," then he might fly from his throne; but again he forgot to consider that there might be mules among men as among beasts. [60] At the same time, the oracles tempered their ambiguous prophecies with some advice of undoubted sense, for when he asked them who were the most powerful among the Greeks, they replied the Spartans, and to Sparta he sent messengers with presents to conclude an alliance. "The Lacedæmonians were filled with joy; they knew the oracle which had been given Croesus, and made him a friend and ally, as they had previously received many kindnesses at his hands." [61]

This glimpse into the preparations of Croesus, whose embassies compassed the whole civilised world, and whose wealth got him all that politics or religion could, enables us to realise the political and religious excitement into which Cyrus' advent threw that generation. The oracles in doubt and ambiguous; the priests, the idol-manufacturers, and the crowd of artisans, who worked in every city at the furniture of the temple, in a state of unexampled activity, with bustle perhaps most like the bustle of our government dockyards on the eve of war; hammering new idols together, preparing costly oblations, overhauling the whole religious "ordnance," that the gods might be propitiated and the stars secured to fight in their courses against the Persian; rival politicians practising conciliation, and bolstering up one another with costly presents to stand against this strange and fatal force, which indifferently threatened them all. What a commentary Herodotus' story furnishes upon the verses of this chapter, in which Jehovah contrasts the idols with Himself. It may actually have been Croesus and the Greeks whom the prophet had in his mind when he wrote vv. 5-7: The isles have seen, and they fear; the ends of the earth tremble: they draw near and they come. They help every man his neighbour, and to his brother each sayeth, Be strong. So carver encourageth smelter, smoother with hammer, smiter on anvil; one saith of the soldering, It is good: and he fasteneth it with nails lest it totter. The irony is severe, but true to the facts as Herodotus relates them. The statesmen hoped to keep back Cyrus by sending sobbing messages to one another, Be of good courage; the priests "by making a particularly good and strong set of gods."[62]

While the imbecility of the idolatries was thus manifest, and the great religious centres of heathendom were reduced to utter doubt that veiled itself in ambiguity and waited to see how things would issue, there was one religion in the world, whose oracles gave no uncertain sound, whose God stepped boldly forth to claim Cyrus for His own. In the dust of Babylonia lay the scattered members of a nation captive and exiled, a people civilly dead and religiously degraded; yet it was the faith of this worm of a people, which welcomed and understood Cyrus, it was the God of this people who claimed to be his author. The forty-first chapter looks dreary and ancient to the uninstructed eye, but let our imagination realise all these things: the ambiguous priests, oracles that would not speak out, religions that had no articulate counsel nor comfort in face of the conqueror who was crushing up the world before him, but only sobs, solder and nails; and our heart will leap as we hear how God forces them all into judgement before Him, and makes His plea as loud and clear as mortal ear may hear. Clatter of idols, and murmur of muffled oracles, filling all the world; and then, hark how the voice of Jehovah crashes His oracle across it all!

Keep silence towards Me, O Isles, and let the peoples renew their strength: let them approach; then let them speak: to the Law let us come.

Who hath stirred up from the sunrise Righteousness, calleth it to his foot? He giveth to his face peoples, and kings He makes him to trample; giveth them as dust to his sword, as driven stubble to his bow. He pursues them, and passes to peace a road that he comes not with his feet. Who has wrought it and done it? Summoner of generations from the source, [63] I Jehovah the First, and with the Last; I am He.

Croesus would have got a clear answer here, but it is probable that he had never heard of the Hebrews or of their God.

After this follows the satiric picture of the heathen world, which has already been quoted. And then, after an interval during which Jehovah turns to His own people (vv. 8-20),--for whatever be His business or His controversy, the Lord is mindful of His own,--He directs His speech specially against the third class of the leaders of heathendom. He has laughed the foolish statesmen and imagemakers out of court (vv. 5-7); He now challenges, in ver. 21, the oracles and their priests.

We have seen what these were, which this vast heathen world--heathen but human, convinced as we are that at the back of the world's life there is a secret, a counsel and a governor, and anxious as we are to find them--had to resort to. Timid waiters upon time, whom not even the lavish wealth of a Croesus could tempt from their ambiguity; prophets speechless in face of history; oracles of meaning as dark and shifty as their steamy caves at Delphi, of tune as variable as the whispering oak of Dodona; wily-tongued Greeks, masters of ambiguous phrase, at Miletus, Abæ, and Thebes; Egyptian mystics in the far off temple of "Lybic Hammon,"--these are what the prophet sees standing at the bar of history, where God is Challenger.

Bring here your case, saith Jehovah; apply your strong grounds, saith the King of Jacob. Let them bring out and declare unto us what things are going to happen; the first things [64] announce what they are, that we may set our heart on them, and know the issue of them; or the things that are coming, let us hear them. Announce the things that are to come hereafter, that we may know that ye are gods. Yea, do good or do evil, that we may stare and see it together. Lo! ye are nothing, and your work is of nought; an abomination is he who chooseth you.

Which great challenge just means, Come and be tested by facts. Here is history needing an explanation, and running no one knows whither. Prove your divinity by interpreting or guiding it. Cease your ambiguities, and give us something we can set our minds to work upon. Or do something, effect something in history, be it good or be it evil,--only let it be patent to our senses. For the test of godhead is not ingenuity or mysteriousness, but plain deeds, which the senses can perceive, and plain words, which the reason and conscience can judge. The insistance upon the senses and mental faculties of man is remarkable: Make us hear them, that we may know, stare, see all together, set our mind to them.

But as we have learned from Herodotus, there was nobody in the world to answer such a challenge. Therefore Jehovah Himself answers it. He gives His explanation of history, and claims its events for His doing.

I have stirred up from the north, and he hath come; from the rising of the sun one who calleth upon My Name: and he shall trample satraps like mortar, and as the potter treadeth out clay.

Who hath announced on-ahead [65] that we may know, and beforehand that we may say, "Right!" Yea, there is none that announced, yea, there is none that published, yea, there is none that heareth your words. But a prediction--or predicter, literally a thing or man on-ahead (r'ishôn corresponding to the me-r'osh of ver. 26)--a prediction to Zion, "Behold, behold them," and to Jerusalem a herald of good news-- I am giving. The language here comes forth in jerks, and is very difficult to render. But I look and there is no man even among these, and no counsellor, that I might ask them and they return word. Lo, all of them vanity! and nothingness their works; wind and waste their molten images.

***

Let us look a little more closely at the power of Prediction, on which Jehovah maintains His unique and sovereign Deity against the idols.

Jehovah challenges the idols to face present events, and to give a clear, unambiguous forecast of their issue. It is a debatable question, whether He does not also ask them to produce previous predictions of events happening at the time at which He speaks. This latter demand is one that He makes in subsequent chapters; it is part of His prophet's argument in chs. xlv.-xlvi., that Jehovah intimated the advent of Cyrus by His servants in Israel long before the present time. Whether He makes this same demand for previous predictions in ch. xli. depends on how we render a clause of ver. 22, declare ye the former things. Some scholars take former things in the sense, in which it is used later on in this prophecy, of previous predictions. This is very doubtful. I have explained in a note, why I think them wrong; but even if they are right, and Jehovah be really asking the idols to produce former predictions of Cyrus' career, the demand is so cursory, it proves so small an item in His plea, and we shall afterwards find so many clearer statements of it, that we do better to ignore it now and confine ourselves to emphasizing the other challenge, about which there is no doubt,--the challenge to take present events and predict their issue. [66] Croesus had asked the oracles for a forecast of the future. This is exactly what Jehovah demands in ver. 22, declare unto us what things are going to happen; in ver. 23, declare the things that are to come hereafter, that we may know that ye are gods; in ver. 26 (spoken from the standpoint of the subsequent fulfilment of the prediction), who declared it on-ahead that we may know, and beforehand that we may now say, "Right!" Yea, there is none that declared, yea, there is none that published, yea, there is none that heareth your words. But a prediction unto Zion, "Behold, behold them," and to Jerusalem a herald of good news--I give. I give is emphatically placed at the end,--"I Jehovah alone, through my prophets in Israel, give such a prediction and publisher of good news."

We scarcely require to remind ourselves, that this great challenge and plea are not mere rhetoric or idle boasting. Every word in them we have seen to be true to fact. The heathen religions were, as they are here represented, helpless before Cyrus, and dumb about the issue of the great movements which the Persian had started. On the other hand, Jehovah had uttered to His people all the meaning of the new stir and turmoil in history. We have heard Him do so in ch. xl. There He gives a herald of good news to Jerusalem,--tells them of their approaching deliverance, explains His redemptive purposes, proclaims a gospel. In addition, He has in this chapter accepted Cyrus for His own creation and as part of His purpose, and has promised him victory.

The God of Israel, then, is God, because He alone by His prophets claims facts as they stand for His own deeds, and announces what shall become of them.

Do not let us, however, fall into the easy but vulgar error of supposing, that Jehovah claims to be God simply because He can predict. It is indeed prediction, which He demands from the heathen; for prediction is a minimum of godhead, and in asking it He condescends to the heathen's own ideas of what a god should be able to do. When Croesus, the heathen who of all that time spent most upon religion, sought to decide which of the gods was worthiest to be consulted about the future and propitiated in face of Cyrus, what test did he apply to them? As we have seen, he tested them by their ability to predict a matter of fact: the god who told him what he, Croesus, should be doing on a certain day was to be his god. It is evident, that, to Croesus, divinity meant to be able to divine. But the God, who reveals Himself to Israel, is infinitely greater than this. He is not merely a Being with a far sight into the future; He is not only Omniscience. In the chapter preceding this one His power of prediction is not once expressed; it is lost in the two glories by which alone the prophet seeks to commend His Godhead to Israel,--the glory of His power and the glory of His faithfulness. Jehovah is Omnipotence, Creator of heaven and earth; He leads forth the stars by the greatness of His might; Supreme Director of history, it is He who bringeth princes to nothing. But Jehovah is also unfailing character: the word of the Lord standeth for ever; it is foolishness to say of Him that He has forgotten His people, or that their right has passed from Him; He disappoints none who wait upon Him. Such is the God, who steps down from ch. xl. into the controversy with the heathen in ch. xli. If in the latter He chiefly makes His claim to godhead to rest upon specimens of prediction, it is simply, as we have said, that He may meet the gods of the heathen before a bar and upon a principle, which their worshippers recognise as practical and decisive. What were single predictions, here and there, upon the infinite volume of His working, who by His power could gather all things to serve His own purpose, and in His faithfulness remained true to that purpose from everlasting to everlasting! The unity of history under One Will--this is a far more adequate idea of godhead than the mere power to foretell single events of history. And it is even to this truth that Jehovah seeks to raise the unaccustomed thoughts of the heathen. Past the rude wonder, which is all that fulfilled predictions of fact can excite, He lifts their religious sense to Himself and His purpose, as the one secret and motive of all history. He not only claims Cyrus and Cyrus' career as His own work, but He speaks of Himself as summoner of the generations from aforehand; I Jehovah, the First, and with the Last; I am He. It is a consummate expression of godhead, which lifts us far above the thought of Him as a mere divining power.

Now, it is well for us--were it only for the great historic interest of the thing, though it will also further our argument--to take record here that, although this conception of the unity of life under One Purpose and Will was still utterly foreign, and perhaps even unintelligible, to the heathen world, which the prophecy has in view, the first serious attempt in that world to reach such a conception was contemporary with the forty-first chapter of Isaiah. It is as miners feel, when, tunnelling from opposite sides of a mountain, they begin to hear the noise of each other's picks through the dwindling rock. We, who have come down the history of Israel towards the great consummation of religion in Christianity, may here cease for a moment our labours, to listen to the faint sound from the other side of the wall, still separating Israel from Greece, of a witness to God and an argument against idolatry similar to those with which we have been working. Who is not moved by learning, that, in the very years when Jewish prophecy reached its most perfect statement of monotheism, pouring its scorn upon the idols and their worshippers, and in the very Isles on which its hopes and influence were set, the first Greek should be already singing, who used his song to satirize the mythologies of his people, and to celebrate the unity of God? Among the Ionians, whom Cyrus' invasion of Lydia and of the Ægean coast in 544 drove across the seas, was Xenophanes of Colophon. [67] After some wanderings he settled at Elea in South Italy, and became the founder of the Eleatic school, the first philosophic attempt of the Greek mind to grasp the unity of Being. How far Xenophanes himself succeeded in this attempt is a matter of controversy. The few fragments of his poetry which are extant do not reveal him as a philosophical monotheist, so much as a prophet of "One greatest God." His language (like that of the earlier Hebrew prophets in praising Jehovah) apparently implies the real existence of lesser divinities:--

"One God, 'mongst both gods and men He is greatest,
Neither in shape is He like unto mortals, nor thought." [68]

Xenophanes scorns the anthropomorphism of his countrymen, and the lawless deeds which their poets had attributed to the gods:--
"Mortals think the gods can be born, have their feelings, voice and form; but, could horses or oxen draw like men, they too would make their gods after their own image." [69]

"All things did Homer and Hesiod lay on the gods,
Such as with mortals are full of blame and disgrace,
To steal and debauch and outwit one another." [70]

Our prophet, to whose eyes Gentile religiousness was wholly of the gross Croesus kind, little suspected that he had an ally, with such kindred tempers of faith and scorn, among the very peoples to whom he yearns to convey his truth. But ages after, when Israel and Greece had both issued into Christianity, the service of Xenophanes to the common truth was recounted by two Church writers--by Clement of Alexandria in his Stromata, and by Eusebius the historian in his Præparatio Evangelica.

We find, then, that monotheism had reached its most absolute expression in Israel in the same decade, in which the first efforts towards the conception of the unity of Being were just starting in Greece. But there is something more to be stated. In spite of the splendid progress, which it pursued from such beginnings, Greek philosophy never reached the height on which, with Second Isaiah, Hebrew prophecy already rests; and the reason has to do with two points on which we are now engaged,--the omnipotence and the righteousness of God.

Professor Pfleiderer remarks: "Even in the idealistic philosophy of the Greeks ... matter remains, however sublimated, an irrational something, with which the Divine power can never come to terms. It was only in the consciousness, which the prophets of Israel had of God, that the thought of the Divine omnipotence fully prevailed." [71] We cannot overvalue such high and impartial testimony to the uniqueness of the Hebrew doctrine of God, but it needs to be supplemented. To the prophets' sense of the Divine omnipotence, we must add their unrivalled consciousness of the Divine character. To them Jehovah is not only the Holy, the incomparable God, almighty and sublime; He is also the true, consistent God. He has a great purpose, which He has revealed of old to His people, and to which He remains for ever faithful. To express this the Hebrews had one word,--the word we translate righteous. We should often miss our prophet's meaning, if by righteousness we understood some of the qualities to which the term is often applied by us: if, for instance, we used it in the general sense of morality, or if we gave it the technical meaning, which it bears in Christian theology, of justification from guilt. We shall afterwards devote a chapter to the exposition of its meaning in Second Isaiah, but let us here look at its use in ch. xli. In ver. 26, it is applied to the person whose prediction turns out to be correct: men are to say of him "right" or "righteous." Here it is evident that the Hebrew--ssaddîq--is used in its simplest meaning, like the Latin rectus, and our "right," of what has been shown to be in accordance with truth or fact. In ver. 2, again, though the syntax is obscure, it seems to have the general sense of good faith with the ability to ensure success. Righteousness is here associated with Cyrus, because he has not been called for nothing, but in good faith for a purpose which will be carried through. Jehovah's righteousness, then, will be His trueness, His good faith, His consistency; and indeed this is the sense which it must evidently bear in ver. 10. Take it with the context: But thou, Israel, My servant, Jacob whom I have chosen, seed of Abraham who loved Me, whom I took hold of from the ends of the earth and its corners, I called thee and said unto thee, Thou art My servant. I have chosen thee, and will not cast thee away. Fear not, for I am with thee. Look not round in despair, for I am thy God. I will strengthen thee; yea, I will help thee; yea, I will uphold thee with the right hand of My righteousness. Here righteousness evidently means that Jehovah will act in good faith to the people He has called, that He will act consistently with His anciently revealed purpose towards them. Hitherto Israel has had nothing but the memory that God called them, and the conscience that He chose them. Now Jehovah will vindicate this conscience in outward fact. He will carry through His calling of His people, and perform His promise. How He will do this, He proceeds to relate. Israel's enemies shall become as nothing (vv. 11, 12). Israel himself, though a poor worm of a people, shall be changed to the utmost conceivable opposite of a worm--even a sharp threshing instrument having teeth--a people who shall leave their mark on the world. They shall overcome all difficulties and rejoice in Jehovah. Their redemption shall be accomplished in a series of evident facts. The poor and the needy are seeking water, and there is none, their tongue faileth for thirst; I, Jehovah, will answer them, I the God of Israel will not forsake them. And this shall be done on such a scale, that all the world will wonder and be convinced, vv. 18-19: I will open on the bare heights rivers, and in the midst of the plains fountains. I will make the desert a pool of water, and the dry ground water-springs. I will plant in the wilderness cedars and acacias and myrtles and oil-trees; I will plant in the desert pines, planes and sherbins together. Do not let us spoil the meaning of this passage by taking these verses literally, or even as illustrative of the kind of restoration which Israel was to enjoy. This vast figure of a well-watered and planted desert the prophet uses rather to illustrate the scale on which the Restoration will take place: its evident extent and splendour. That they may see and know and consider and understand together, that Jehovah hath done this, and the Holy One of Israel hath created it. The whole passage, then, tells us what God means by His righteousness. It is His fidelity to His calling of Israel, and to His purpose with His people. It is the quality by which He cannot forsake His own, but carries through and completes His promises to them; by which He vindicates and justifies, in facts so large that they are evident to all mankind, His ancient word by His prophets. [72]

This lengthened exposition will not have been in vain, if it has made clear to us, that Hebrew monotheism owed its unique quality to the emphasis, which the prophets laid upon the two truths of the Power and the Character of God. There was One Supreme Being, infinite in might, and with one purpose running down the ages, which He had plainly revealed, and to which He remained constant. The people, who knew this, did not need to wait for the fulfilment of certain test-predictions before trusting Him as the One God. Test-predictions and their fulfilment might be needful for the heathen, from whose minds the idea of One Supreme Being with such a character had vanished; the heathen might need to be convinced by instances of Jehovah's omniscience, for omniscience was the most Divine attribute of which they had conceived. But Israel's faith rested upon glories in the Divine nature of which omniscience was the mere consequence. Israel knew God was Almighty and All-true, and that was enough.

Note upon Jehovah's Claim to Cyrus.

In ver. 25 a phrase is used of Cyrus which is very obscure, and to which, considering its vagueness even upon the most definite construction, far too much importance has been attached. The meaning of the words, the tenses, the syntax--perhaps even the original text itself--of this verse are uncertain. The English revisers give, I have raised up one from the north, and he is come; from the rising of the sun one that calleth upon My Name. This is probably the true syntax. [73] But in what tense is the verb to call, and what does calling upon My name mean? In the Old Testament the phrase is used in two senses,--to invoke or adore, and to proclaim or celebrate the name of a person. [74] As long as scholars understood that Cyrus was a monotheist, there was a temptation to choose the former of these meanings, and to find in the verse Jehovah's claim upon the Persian, as a worshipper of Himself, the One True God. But this interpretation received a shock from the discovery of a proclamation of Cyrus after his entry into Babylon, in which he invokes the names of Babylonian deities, and calls himself their "servant." [75] Of course his doing so in the year 538 does not necessarily discredit a description of him as a monotheist eight years before. Between 548 and 546--the probable date of ch. xli.--a prophet might in all good faith have hailed as a worshipper of Jehovah a Persian who still stood in the rising of the sun,--who had not yet issued from the east and its radiant repute of a religion purer than the Babylonian; although eight years afterwards, from motives of policy, the same king acknowledged the gods of his new subjects.

This may be; but there is a more natural way out of the difficulty. Is it fair to lay upon the expression, calleth on My name, so precise a meaning as that of a strict monotheism? Some have turned to the other use of the verb, and, taking it in the future tense, have translated, who shall proclaim or celebrate My name,--which Cyrus surely did, when, in the name of Jehovah, he drew up the edict for the return of the Jews to Palestine. [76] But do we need to put even this amount of meaning upon the phrase? In itself it is vague, but it also stands parallel to another vague phrase: I have raised up one from the north, and he is come; from the sunrising one who calleth on My name. Taken in apposition to the phrase he is come, calleth on My name may mean no more than that, answering to the instigation of Jehovah, and owning His impulse, Cyrus by his career proclaimed or celebrated Jehovah's name. In any case, we have said enough to show that, in our comparative ignorance of what Cyrus' faith was, and in face of the elastic use of the phrase to call on the name of, it is quite unwarrantable to maintain that the prophet must have meant a strict monotheist, and therefore absurd to draw the inference that the prophet was incorrect. A way has been attempted out of the difficulty by slightly altering the text, and so obtaining the version, I have raised up one from the north, and he is come; from the sunrise I call him by name. [77] This is a change which is in harmony with ch. xlv. 3, 4, but has otherwise no evidence in its favour.

Footnotes:

49. Media simply means "the country." It is supposed, that of the six Median tribes only one was Aryan, holding the rest, which were Turanian, under its influence.

50. There were, besides, a few small independent powers in Asia Minor, such as Cilicia, whose prince also intervened at the Battle of the Eclipse; and the Ionian cities in the west. But all these, with perhaps the exception of Lycia, were brought into subjection to Lydia by Croesus, son of Alyattis.

51. Vol. i., p. 92.

52. Other passages are: xli. 5, Isles saw and feared, the ends of the earth trembled; xlii. 10, The sea and its fulness, Isles and their dwellers; lix. 18, He will repay, fury to His adversaries, recompence to His enemies: to the Isles He will repay recompence; lxvi. 19, The nations, Tarshish, Pul, Lud, drawers of the bow, Tubal, Javan, the Isles afar off that have not heard my fame. The Hebrew is 'y 'î, and is supposed to be from a root 'vh awah, to inhabit, which sense, however, never attaches to the verb in Hebrew, but is borrowed from the cognate Arabic word.

53. Of the Philistine coast, Isa. xx. 6; of the Tyrian coast, Isa. xxiii. 2, 6; of Greece, Ezek. xxvii. 7; of Crete, Jer. xlvii. 4; of the islands of the sea, Isa. xi. 11 and Esther x. 1.

54. xlii. 15: Eng. version, I will turn rivers into islands.

55. Anabasis 2, 4.

56. There were two branches of the Persian royal family after Teispes, the son of Akhæmenes, the founder. Teispes annexed Anshan on the level land between the north-east corner of the Persian Gulf and the mountains of Persia. Teispes' eldest son, Cyrus I., became king of Anshan; his other, Ariaramnes, king of Persia. These were succeeded by their sons, Kambyses I. and Arsames. Kambyses I. was the father of Cyrus II., the great Cyrus, who rejoined Persia to Anshan, to the exclusion of his second cousin, Hystaspes. Cyrus the Great was succeeded by his son, Kambyses II., with whom the Anshan line closed, and the power was transferred to Darius, son of Hystaspes. Cf. Ragozin's Media, in the "Story of the Nations" series.

57. Halévy, "Cyrus et le Retour de l'Exil," Études Juives, I.

58. Inscription of Nabunahid.

59. Herodotus, Book I.

60. Herodotus explains this by his legend of Cyrus' birth, according to which Cyrus was a hybrid--half Persian, half Mede.

61. Herodotus, Book I.

62. Sir Edward Strachey.

63. Lit. from the head, "da capo." I am not sure, however, that it does not rather mean beforehand, like our on ahead.

64. See p. [16]121.

65. This seems to me to be more likely to be the meaning of the prophet, than the absolute from the beginning. It suits its parallel beforehand, and it is more in line with the general demand of the chapter for anticipation of events. It is literally from the head, "da capo," cf. p. [17]117.

66. r'snvt r'ishonôth is a relative term, meaning head things, things ahead, first things, prior things, whether in rank or time. Here of course the time meaning is undoubted. But ahead of what? prior to what?--this is the difficulty. Ewald, Hitzig, A. B. Davidson, Driver, etc., take it as prior to the standpoint of the speaker; things that happened or were uttered previous to him,--a sense in which the word is used in subsequent chapters. But Delitzsch, Hahn, Cheyne, etc., take it to be things prior to other things that will happen in the later future, early events, as opposed to hv'vt of the next clause, which they take to mean subsequent things, things that are to come afterwards. I think Dr. Davidson's reasons (see

Expositor, second series, vol. vii., p. 256) are quite conclusive against this view of Delitzsch, that in this clause the idols are being asked to predict events in the near future. It is difficult, as he says, to see why the idols should be given a choice between the earlier and the later future: nor does the hv'vt of the contrasted clause at all suggest a later future; it simply means things coming, a term which is as applicable to the near as to the far future. Nevertheless, I am not persuaded that Dr. Davidson's own view of r'ishonôth is the correct one. The rest of the context (see above) is occupied with predictions of the future only. And r'ishonôth does not necessarily mean previous predictions, although used in this sense in the subsequent chapters. It simply means, as we have seen, head things, things ahead, things beforehand, or fountain-things, origins, causes. That we are to understand it here in some such general and absolute sense is suggested, I think, by the word 'chrytn which follows it, their result or issue, and is confirmed by r'sn, r'ishôn (masc. singular) of ver. 27, which is undoubtedly used in a general sense, meaning something or somebody on ahead, an anticipator, predicter, forerunner (as Cheyne gives it), or as I have rendered it above, neuter, a prediction. If r'ishôn in ver. 27 means a thing or a man given beforehand, then r'ishonôth in ver. 22 may also mean things given beforehand, predictions made now, or at least things selected and announced as causes now, whose issue, 'chrytn, may be recognised in the future. In a word, r'ishonôth would mean things not necessarily previous to the speech in which they were allowed, but simply things previous to certain results, or anticipating certain events, either as their prediction or as their cause.

67. Ueberweg, History of Philosophy, English translation, i., 51.

68. Quoted by Clement of Alexandria, Stromata, Bk. V., ch. iv., and by Eusebius, Præp. Evang. xiii., 13.

69. Ibid.

70. Quoted by Ueberweg, as above.

71. Pfleiderer, Philosophy of Religion: Contents of the Religious Consciousness, ch. i. (Eng. trans., vol. iii., p. 291).

72. See further on the subject the chapter on the Righteousness of Israel and of God, Chapter [18]XIV. of this volume.

73. And that which runs: ... he is come, from the rising of the sun he calleth upon My name (Bredenkamp) is wrong.

74. The former of these in ch. lxiv. 7; the latter in xliv. 5.

75. Translation of the Cyrus-cylinder in "Cyrus et le Retour de l'Exil," by Halévy, Revue des Études Juives, No. 1, 1880.

76. Ezra i. 2; 2 Chron. xxxvi. 22, 23.

77. 'qr' vsmv for yqr' vsmy.

CHAPTER VIII

THE PASSION OF GOD.

Isaiah xlii. 13-17.

At the beginning of ch. xlii. we reach one of those distinct stages, the frequent appearance of which in our prophecy assures us, that, for all its mingling and recurrent style, the prophecy is a unity with a distinct, if somewhat involved, progress of thought. For while chs. xl. and xli. establish the sovereignty and declare the character of the One True God before His people and the heathen, ch. xlii. takes what is naturally the next step, of publishing to both these classes His Divine will. This purpose of God is set forth in the first seven verses of the chapter. It is identified with a human Figure, who is to be God's agent upon earth, and who is styled the Servant of Jehovah. Next to Jehovah Himself, the Servant of Jehovah is by far the most important personage within our prophet's gaze. He is named, described, commissioned and encouraged over and over again throughout the prophecy; his character and indispensable work are hung upon with a frequency and a fondness almost equal to the steadfast faith, which the prophet reposes in Jehovah Himself. Were we following our prophecy chapter by chapter, now would be the time to put the question, Who is this Servant, who is suddenly introduced to us? and to look ahead for the various and even conflicting answers, which rise from the subsequent chapters. But we agreed, for clearness' sake, [78] to take all the passages about the Servant, which are easily detached from the rest of the prophecy, and treat by themselves, and to continue in the meantime our prophet's main theme of the Power and Righteousness of God as shown forth in the deliverance of His people from Babylon. Accordingly, at present we pass over xlii. 1-9, keeping this firmly in mind, however, that God has appointed for His work upon earth, including, as it does, the ingathering of His people and the conversion of the Gentiles, a Servant,--a human figure of lofty character and unfailing perseverance, who makes God's work of redemption his own, puts his heart into it, and is upheld by God's hand. God, let us understand, has committed His cause upon earth to a human agent.

God's commission of His Servant is hailed by a hymn. Earth answers the proclamation of the new things which the Almighty has declared (ver. 9) by a new song (vv. 10-13). But this song does not sing of the Servant; its subject is Jehovah Himself.

> *Sing to Jehovah a new song,*
> *His praise from the end of the earth;*
> *Ye that go down to the sea, and its fulness,*
> *Isles, and their dwellers!*
> *Let be loud,--the wilderness and its townships,*
> *Villages that Kedar inhabits!*
> *Let them ring out,--the dwellers of Sela!*
> *From the top of the hills let them shout!*
> *Let them give to Jehovah the glory,*
> *And publish His praise in the Isles!*
> *Jehovah as hero goes forth,*
> *As a man of war stirs up zeal,*
> *Shouts the alarm and battle cry,*
> *Against his foes proves Himself hero.*

The terms of the last four lines are military. Most of them will be found in the historical books, in descriptions of the onset of Israel's battles with the heathen. But it is no human warrior to whom they are here applied. They who sing have forgotten the Servant. Their hearts are warm only with this, that Jehovah Himself will come down to earth to give the alarm, and to bear the brunt of the battle. And to such a hope He now responds, speaking also of Himself and not of the Servant. His words are very intense, and glow and strain with inward travail.

Rev. George Adam Smith, M.A.

> *I have long time kept my peace,*
> *Am dumb and hold myself in:*
> *Like a woman in travail I gasp,*
> *Pant and palpitate together.*

Remember it is God who speaks these words of Himself, and then think what they mean of unshareable thought and pain, of solitary yearning and effort. But from the pain comes forth at last the power.

> *I waste mountains and hills,*
> *And all their herb I parch;*
> *And I have set rivers for islands,*
> *And marshes I parch.*

Yet it is not the passion of a mere physical effort that is in God; not mere excitement of war that thrills Him. But the suffering of men is upon Him, and He has taken their redemption to heart. He had said to His Servant (vv. 6, 7): I give thee ... to open the blind eyes, to bring out from prison the bound, from the house of bondage the dwellers in darkness. But here He Himself puts on the sympathy and strain of that work.

And I will make the blind to walk in a way they know not, By paths they know not I will guide them; Turn darkness before them to light, And serrated land to level. These are the things that I do, and do not remit them. They fall backwards, with shame are they shamed, That put trust in a Carving, That do say to a Cast, Ye are our Gods. [79]

Now this pair of passages, in one of which God lays the work of redemption upon His human agent, and in another Himself puts on its passion and travail, are only one instance of a duality that runs through the whole of the Old Testament. As we repeatedly saw in the prophecies of Isaiah himself, [80] there is a double promise of the future through the Old Testament:--first, that God will achieve the salvation of Israel by an extraordinary human personality, who is figured now as a King, now as a Prophet and now as a Priest; but, second also, that God Himself, in undeputed, unshared power, will come visibly to deliver His people and to reign over them. These two lines of prophecy run parallel, and even entangled, through the Old Testament, but within its bounds no attempt is made to reconcile them. They pass from it still separate, to find their synthesis, as we all know, in One of whom each is the incomplete prophecy. While considering the Messianic prophecies of Isaiah, which run upon the first of these two lines, we pointed out, that, though standing in historical connection with Christ, they were not prophecies of His divinity. Lofty and expansive as were the titles they attributed to the Messiah, these titles did not imply more than an earthly ruler of extraordinary power and dignity. But we added that in the other and concurrent line of prophecy, and especially in those well-developed stages of it which appear in Isa. xl.-lxvi., we should find the true Old Testament promise of the Deity in human form and tabernacling among men. We urged that, if the divinity of Christ was to be seen in the Old Testament, we should more naturally find it in the line of promise, which speaks of God Himself descending to battle and to suffer by the side of men, than in the line that lifts a human ruler almost to the right hand of God. We have now come to a passage, which gives us the opportunity of testing this connection, which we have alleged between the so-called anthropomorphism of the Old Testament, and the Incarnation, which is the glory of the New.

When God presents Himself in the Old Testament as His people's Saviour, it is not always as Isaiah mostly saw Him, in awful power and majesty--a King high and lifted up, or as coming from far, burning and thick-rising smoke, and overflowing streams; causing the peal of His voice to be heard, and the lighting down of His arm to be seen, in the fury of anger and devouring fire--bursting and torrent and hailstones. [81] But in a large number of passages, of which the one before us and the famous first six verses of ch. lxiii. are perhaps the most forcible, the Almighty is clothed with human passion and agony. He is described as loving, hating, showing zeal or jealousy, fear, repentance and scorn. He bides His time, suddenly awakes to effort, and makes that effort in weakness, pain and struggle, so extreme that He likens Himself not only to a solitary man in the ardour of battle, but to a woman in her unshareable hour of travail. To use a technical word, the prophets in their descriptions of God do not hesitate to be anthropopathic--imparting to Deity the passions of men.

In order to appreciate the full effect of this habit of the Jewish religion, we must contrast it with some principles of that religion, with which at first it seems impossible to reconcile it.

No religion more necessarily implies the spirituality of God than does the Jewish. It is true that in the pages of the Old Testament, you will nowhere find this formally expressed. No Jewish prophet ever said in so many words what Jesus said to the woman of Samaria, God is spirit. In our own prophecy, spirit is frequently used, not to define the nature of God, but to express His power and the effectiveness of His will. But the Jewish Scriptures insist throughout upon the sublimity of God, or, to use their own term, His holiness. He is the Most High, Creator, Lord,--the Force and Wisdom that are behind nature and history. It is a sin to make any image of Him; it is an error to liken Him to man. I am God and not man, the Holy One. [82] We have seen how absolutely the Divine omnipotence and sublimity are expressed by our own prophet, and we shall find Him again speaking thus: My thoughts are not your thoughts, neither are your ways My ways, saith the Lord. For as the heavens are higher than the earth, so are My ways higher than your ways, and My thoughts than your thoughts. [83] But perhaps the doctrine of our prophet which most effectively sets forth God's loftiness and spirituality is his doctrine of God's word. God has but to speak and a thing is created or a deed done. He calls and the agent He needs is there; He sets His word upon him and the work is as good as finished. My word that goeth forth out of My mouth, it shall not return unto Me void, but it shall accomplish that which I please, and shall prosper in the thing whereto I sent it. [84] Omnipotence could not farther go. It would seem that all man needed from God was a word,--the giving of a command, that a thing must be.

Yet it is precisely in our prophecy, that we find the most extreme ascriptions to the Deity of personal effort, weakness and pain. The same chapters which celebrate God's sublimity and holiness, which reveal the eternal counsels of God working to their inevitable ends in time, which also insist, as this very chapter does, that for the performance of works of mercy and morality God brings to bear the slow creative forces that are in nature, or which again (as in other chapters) attribute all to the power of His simple word,--these same Scriptures suddenly change their style and, after the most human manner, clothe the Deity in the travail and passion of flesh. Why is it, that instead of aspiring still higher from those sublime conceptions of God to some consummate expression of His unity, as for instance in Islam, or of His spirituality, as in certain modern philosophies, prophecy dashes thus thunderously down upon our hearts with the message, scattered in countless, broken words, that all this omnipotence and all this sublimity are expended and realised for men only in passion and in pain?

It is no answer, which is given by many in our day, that after all the prophets were but frail men, unable to stay upon the high flight to which they sometimes soared, and obliged to sacrifice their logic to the fondness of their hearts and the general habit of man to make his god after his own image. No easy sneer like that can solve so profound a moral paradox. We must seek the solution otherwise, and earnest minds will probably find it along one or other of the two following paths.

1. The highest moral ideal is not, and never can be, the righteousness that is regnant, but that which is militant and agonizing. It is the deficiency of many religions, that while representing God as the Judge and almighty executor of righteousness, they have not revealed Him as its advocate and champion as well. Christ gave us a very plain lesson upon this. As He clearly showed, when He refused the offer of all the kingdoms of the world, the highest perfection is not to be omnipotence upon the side of virtue, but to be there as patience, sympathy and love. To will righteousness, and to rule life from above in favour of righteousness, is indeed Divine; but if these were the highest attributes of divinity, and if they exhausted the Divine interest in our race, then man himself, with his conscience to sacrifice himself on behalf of justice or of truth,--man himself, with his instinct to make the sins of others his burden, and their purity his agonizing endeavour, would indeed be higher than his God. Had Jehovah been nothing but the righteous Judge of all the earth, then His witnesses and martyrs, and His prophets who took to themselves the conscience and reproach of their people's sins, would have been as much more admirable than Himself, as the soldier who serves his country on the battle-field or lays down his life for his people is more deserving of their gratitude and more certain of their devotion, than the king who equips him, sends him forth--and himself stays at home.

The God of the Old Testament is not such a God. In the moral warfare to which He has predestined His creatures, He Himself descends to participate. He is not abstract--that is, withdrawn-- Holiness, nor mere sovereign Justice enthroned in heaven. He is One who arises and comes down for the salvation of men, who makes virtue His Cause and righteousness His Passion. He is no whit behind the chiefest of His servants. No seraph burns as God burns with ardour for justice; no angel of the presence flies more swiftly than Himself to the front rank of the failing battle. The human Servant, who is pictured in our prophecy, is more absolutely identified with suffering and agonizing men than any angel could be; but even he does not stand more closely by their side, nor suffer more on their behalf, than the God who sends him forth. For the Lord stirreth up jealousy like a man of war; in all His people's affliction He is afflicted; against His enemies He beareth Himself as a hero. So much from the side of righteousness.

2. But take the equally Divine attribute of love. When a religion affirms that God is love, it gives immense hostages. What is love without pity and compassion and sympathy? and what are these but self-imposed weakness and pain? Christ has told us of the greatest love. Greater love than this hath no man, that a man lay down his life for his friends; and the cost and sacrifice in which He thus outmatched man is one that the prophets before He came did not hesitate to impute to God. As far as human language is adequate for such a task, they picture God's love for men as costing Him so much. He painfully pleads for His people's loyalty; He travails in pain for their new birth and growth in holiness; in all their affliction He is afflicted; and He meets their stubbornness, not with the swift sentence of

outraged holiness, but with longsuffering and patience, if so in the end He may win them. But the pain, that is thus essentially inseparable from love, reaches its acme, when the beloved are not only in danger but in sin, when not only the future of their holiness is uncertain, but their guilty past bars the way to any future at all. We saw how Jeremiah's love thus took upon itself the conscience and reproach of Israel's sin; how much distress and anguish, how much sympathy and self-sacrificing labour, and at last how much hopeless endurance of the common calamity, that sin cost the noble prophet, though he might so easily have escaped it all. Now even thus does God deal with His people's sins; not only setting them in the light of His awful countenance, but taking them upon His heart; making them not only the object of His hate, but the anguish and the effort of His love. Jeremiah was a weak mortal, and God is the Omnipotent. Therefore, the issue of His agony shall be what His servant's never could effect, the redemption of Israel from sin; but in sympathy and in travail the Deity, though omnipotent, is no whit behind the man.

***

We have said enough to prove our case, that the true Old Testament prophecy of the nature and work of Jesus Christ is found not so much in the long promise of the exalted human ruler, for whom Israel's eyes looked, as in the assurance of God's own descent to battle with His people's foes and to bear their sins. In this God, omnipotent, yet in His zeal and love capable of passion, who before the Incarnation was afflicted in all His people's affliction, and before the Cross made their sin His burden and their salvation His agony, we see the love that was in Jesus Christ. For Jesus, too, is absolute holiness, yet not far off. He, too, is righteousness militant at our side, militant and victorious. He, too, has made our greatest suffering and shame His own problem and endeavour. He is anxious for us just where conscience bids us be most anxious about ourselves. He helps us, because He feels when we feel our helplessness the most. Never before or since in humanity has righteousness been perfectly victorious as in Him. Never before or since, in the whole range of being, has any one felt as He did all the sin of man with all the conscience of God. He claims to forgive, as God forgives; to be able to save, as we know only God can save. And the proof of these claims, apart from the experience of their fulfilment in our own lives, is that the same infinite love was in Him, the same agony and willingness to sacrifice Himself for men, which we have seen made evident in the Passion of God.

Footnotes:

78. See [19]Introduction.
79. So the grammar of the original.
80. Vol. i., pp. 144, 334.
81. Isa. xxxi.
82. Hosea xi. 9.
83. Ch. lv. 8, 9.
84. Ibid. ver. 11.

CHAPTER IX

FOUR POINTS OF A TRUE RELIGION.

Isaiah xliii.-xlviii.

We have now surveyed the governing truths of Isa. xl.-xlviii.: the One God, omnipotent and righteous; the One People, His servants and witnesses to the world; the nothingness of all other gods and idols before Him; the vanity and ignorance of their diviners, compared with His power, who, because He has a purpose working through all history, and is both faithful to it and almighty to bring it to pass, can inspire His prophets to declare beforehand the facts that shall be. He has brought His people into captivity for a set time, the end of which is now near. Cyrus the Persian, already upon the horizon, and threatening Babylon, is to be their deliverer. But whomever He raises up on Israel's behalf, God is always Himself their foremost champion. Not only is His word upon them, but His heart is among them. He bears the brunt of their battle, and their deliverance, political and spiritual, is His own travail and agony. Whomever else He summons on the stage, He remains the true hero of the drama.

Now, chs. xliii.-xlviii. are simply the elaboration and more urgent offer of all these truths, under the sense of the rapid approach of Cyrus upon Babylon. They declare again God's unity, omnipotence and righteousness, they confirm His forgiveness of His people, they repeat the laughter at the idols, they give us nearer views of Cyrus, they answer the doubts that many orthodox Israelites felt about this Gentile Messiah; chs. xlvi. and xlvii. describe Babylon as if on the eve of her fall, and ch. xlviii., after Jehovah more urgently than ever presses upon reluctant Israel to show the results of her discipline in Babylon, closes with a call to leave the accursed city, as if the way were at last open. This call has been taken as the mark of a definite division of our prophecy. But too much must not be put upon it. It is indeed the first call to depart from Babylon; but it is not the last. And although ch. xlix., and the chapters following, speak more of Zion's Restoration and less of the Captivity, yet ch. xlix. is closely connected with ch. xlviii., and we do not finally leave Babylon behind till ch. lii. 12. Nevertheless, in the meantime ch. xlviii. will form a convenient point on which to keep our eyes.

Cyrus, when we last saw him, was upon the banks of the Halys, 546 b.c., startling Croesus and the Lydian Empire into extraordinary efforts, both of a religious and political kind, to avert his attack. He had just come from an unsuccessful attempt upon the northern frontier of Babylon, and at first it appeared as if he were to find no better fortune on the western border of Lydia. In spite of his superior numbers, the Lydian army kept the ground on which he met them in battle. But Croesus, thinking that the war was over for the season, fell back soon afterwards on Sardis, and Cyrus, following him up by forced marches, surprised him under the walls of the city, routed the famous Lydian cavalry by the novel terror of his camels, and after a siege of fourteen days sent a few soldiers to scale a side of the citadel too steep to be guarded by the defenders; and so Sardis, its king and its empire, lay at his feet. This Lydian campaign of Cyrus, which is related by Herodotus, is worth noting here for the light it throws on the character of the man, whom according to our prophecy, God chose to be His chief instrument in that generation. If his turning back from Babylonia, eight years before he was granted an easy entrance to her capital, shows how patiently Cyrus could wait upon fortune, his quick march upon Sardis is the brilliant evidence that when fortune showed the way, she found this Persian an obedient and punctual follower. The Lydian campaign forms as good an illustration as we shall find of these texts of our prophet: He pursueth them, he passeth in safety; by a way he almost treads not with his feet. He cometh upon satraps as on mortar, and as the potter treadeth upon clay (xli. 3, 25). I have holden his right hand to bring down before him nations, and the loins of kings will I loosen,--poor ungirt Croesus, for instance, relaxing so foolishly after his victory!--to open before him doors, and gates shall not be shut,--so was Sardis unready for him,--I go before thee, and will level the ridges; doors of brass I will shiver, and bolts of iron cut in sunder. And I will give to thee treasures of darkness, hidden riches of secret places (xlv. 1-3). Some have found in this an allusion to the immense hoards of Croesus, which fell to Cyrus with Sardis.

With Lydia, the rest of Asia Minor, including the cities of the Greeks, who held the coast of the Ægean, was bound to come into the Persian's hands. But the process of subjection turned out to be a long one. The Greeks got no help from Greece. Sparta sent to Cyrus an embassy with a threat, but the Persian laughed at it and it came to nothing. Indeed, Sparta's message was only a temptation to this irresistible warrior to carry his fortunate arms into Europe. His own presence, however, was required in the East, and his lieutenants found the thorough subjection of Asia Minor a task requiring several years. It cannot have well been concluded before 540, and while it was in progress we understand why Cyrus did not again attack Babylonia. Meantime, he was occupied with lesser tribes to the north of Media.

Cyrus' second campaign against Babylonia opened in 539. This time he avoided the northern wall from which he had been repulsed in 546. Attacking Babylonia from the east, he crossed the Tigris, beat the Babylonian king into Borsippa, laid siege to that fortress and marched on Babylon, which was held by the king's son, Belshazzar, Bil-sar-ussur. All the world knows the supreme generalship by which Cyrus is said to have captured Babylon without assaulting the walls from whose impregnable height their defenders showered ridicule upon him; how he made himself master of Nebuchadrezzar's great bason at Sepharvaim, and turned the Euphrates into it; and how, before the Babylonians had time to notice the dwindling of the waters in their midst, his soldiers waded down the river bed, and by the river gates surprised the careless citizens upon a night of festival. But recent research makes it more probable that her inhabitants themselves surrendered Babylon to Cyrus.

Now it was during the course of the events just sketched, but before their culmination in the fall of Babylon, that chs. xliii.-xlviii. were composed. That, at least, is what they themselves suggest. In three passages, which deal with Cyrus or with Babylon, some of the verbs are in the past, some in the future. Those in the past tense describe the calling and full career of Cyrus or the beginning of preparations against Babylon. Those in the future tense promise Babylon's fall or Cyrus' completion of the liberation of the Jews. Thus, in ch. xliii. 14 it is written: For your sakes I have sent to Babylon, and I will bring down as fugitives all of them, and the Chaldeans in the ships of their rejoicing. Surely these words announce that Babylon's fate was already on the way to her, but not yet arrived. Again, in the verses which deal with Cyrus himself, xlv. 1-6, which we have partly quoted, the Persian is already grasped by his right hand by God, and called; but his career is not over, for God promises to do various things for him. The third passage is ver. 13 of the same chapter, where Jehovah says, I have stirred him up in righteousness, and, changing to the future tense, all his ways will I level; he shall build My city, and My captivity shall he send away. What could be more precise than the tenor of all these passages? If people would only take our prophet at his word; if with all their belief in the inspiration of the text of Scripture, they would only pay attention to its grammar, which surely, on their own theory, is also thoroughly sacred, then there would be to-day no question about the date of Isa. xl.-xlviii. As plainly as grammar can enable it to do, this prophecy speaks of Cyrus' campaign against Babylon as already begun, but of its completion as still future. Ch. xlviii., it is true, assumes events as still farther developed, but we will come to it afterwards.

During Cyrus' preparations, then, for invading Babylonia, and in prospect of her certain fall, chs. xliii.-xlviii. repeat with greater detail and impetuosity the truths, which we have already gathered from chs. xl.-xlii.

1. And first of these comes naturally the omnipotence, righteousness and personal urgency of Jehovah Himself. Everything is again assured by His power and purpose; everything starts from His initiative. To illustrate this we could quote from almost every verse in the chapters under consideration. I, I Jehovah, and there is none beside Me a Saviour. I am God--El. Also from to-day on I am He. [85] I will work, and who shall let it? I am Jehovah. I, I am He that blotteth out thy transgressions. I First, and I Last; and beside Me there is no God--Elohim. Is there a God, Eloah, beside Me? yea, there is no Rock; I know not any. I Jehovah, Maker of all things. I am Jehovah, and there is none else; beside Me there is no God. I am Jehovah, and there is none else. Former of light and Creator of darkness, Maker of peace and Creator of evil, I am Jehovah, Maker of all these. I am Jehovah, and there is none else, God, Elohim, beside Me, God-Righteous, El Ssaddîq, and a Saviour: there is none except Me. Face Me, and be saved all ends of the earth; for I am God, El, and there is none else. Only in Jehovah--of Me shall they say--are righteousnesses and strength. I am God, El, and there is none else; God, Elohim, and there is none like Me. I am He; I am First, yea, I am Last. I, I have spoken. I have declared it.

It is of advantage to gather together so many passages--and they might have been increased--from chs. xliii.-xlviii. They let us see at a glance what a part the first personal pronoun plays in the Divine revelation. Beneath every religious truth is the unity of God. Behind every great movement is the personal initiative and urgency of God. And revelation is, in its essence, not the mere publication of truths about God, but the personal presence and communication to men of God Himself. Three words are used for Deity--El, Eloah, Elohim--exhausting the Divine terminology. But besides these, there is a formula which puts the point even more sharply: I am He. It was the habit of the Hebrew nation, and indeed of all Semitic peoples, who shared their reverent unwillingness to name the Deity, to speak of Him simply by the third personal pronoun. The Book of Job is full of instances of the habit, and it also appears in many proper names, as Eli-hu, "My God-is-He," Abi-hu, "My-Father-is-He." Renan adduces the practice as evidence that the Semites were "naturally monotheistic," [86] --as evidence for what was never the case! But if there was no original Semitic monotheism for this practice to prove, we may yet take the practice as evidence for the personality of the Hebrew God. The God of the prophets is not the it, which Mr. Matthew Arnold so strangely thought he had identified in their writings, and which, in philosophic language, that unsophisticated Orientals would never have understood, he so cumbrously named "a tendency not ourselves that makes for righteousness." Not anything like this is the God, who here urges His self-consciousness upon men. He says, I am He,--the unseen Power, who was too awful and too dark to be named, but about whom, when in their terror and ignorance His worshippers sought to describe Him, they assumed that He was a Person, and called Him, as they would have called one of themselves, by a personal pronoun. By the mouth of His prophet this vague and awful He declares Himself as I, I, I,--no mere tendency, but a living Heart and urgent Will, personal character and force of initiative, from which all tendencies move and take their direction and strength. I am He.

History is strewn with the errors of those, who have sought from God something else than Himself. All the degradation, even of the highest religions, has sprung from this, that their votaries forgot that religion was a communion with God Himself, a life in the power of His character and will, and employed it as the mere communication either of material benefits or of intellectual ideas. It has been the mistake of millions to see in revelation nothing but the telling of fortunes, the recovery of lost things, decision in quarrels, direction in war, or the bestowal of some personal favour. Such are like the person, of whom St. Luke tells us, who saw nothing in Christ but the recoverer of a bad debt: Master, speak unto my brother that he divide the inheritance with me; and their superstition is as far from true faith as the prodigal's old heart, when he said, Give me the portion of goods that falleth unto me, was from the other heart, when, in his poverty and woe, he cast himself utterly upon his Father: I will arise and go to my Father. But no less a mistake do those make, who seek from God not Himself, but only intellectual information. The first Reformers did well, who brought the common soul to the personal grace of God; but many of their successors, in a controversy, whose dust obscured the sun and allowed them to see but the length of their own weapons, used Scripture chiefly as a store of proofs for separate doctrines of the faith, and forgot that God Himself was there at all. And though in these days we seek from the Bible many desirable things, such as history, philosophy, morals, formulas of assurance of salvation, the forgiveness of sins, maxims for conduct, yet all these will avail us little, until we have found behind them the living Character, the Will, the Grace, the Urgency, the Almighty Power, by trust in whom and communion with whom alone they are added unto us.

Now the deity, who claims in these chapters to be the One, Sovereign God, was the deity of a little tribe. I am Jehovah, I Jehovah am God, I Jehovah am He. We cannot too much impress ourselves with the historical wonder of this. In a world, which contained Babylon and Egypt with their large empires, Lydia with all her wealth, and the Medes with all their force; which was already feeling the possibilities of the great Greek life, and had the Persians, the masters of the future, upon its threshold,--it was the god of none of these, but of the obscurest tribe of their bondsmen, who claimed the Divine Sovereignty for Himself; it was the pride of none of these, but the faith of the most despised and, at its heart, most mournful religion of the time, which offered an explanation of history, claimed the future and was assured that the biggest forces of the world were working for its ends. Thus saith Jehovah, King of Israel, and his Redeemer Jehovah of Hosts, I First, and I Last; and beside Me there is no God. Is there a God beside Me? yea, there is no Rock; I know not any.

By itself this were a cheap claim, and might have been made by any idol among them, were it not for the additional proofs by which it is supported. We may summarise these additional proofs as threefold: Laughter, Gospel and Control of History,--three marvels in the experience of exiles. People, mournfullest and most despised, their mouths were to be filled with the laughter of Truth's scorn upon the idols of their conquerors. Men, most tormented by conscience and filled with the sense of sin, they were to hear the gospel of forgiveness. Nation, against whom all fact seemed to be working, their God told them, alone of all nations of the world, that He controlled for their sake the facts of to-day and the issues of to-morrow.

2. A burst of laughter comes very weirdly out of the Exile. But we have already seen the intellectual right to scorn which these crushed captives had. They were monotheists and their enemies were image worshippers. Monotheism, even in its rudest forms, raises men intellectually,--it is difficult to say by how many degrees. Indeed, degrees do not measure the mental difference between an idolater and him who serves with his mind, as well as with all his heart and soul, One God, Maker of heaven and earth: it is a difference that is absolute. Israel in captivity was conscious of this, and therefore, although the souls of those sad men were filled beyond any in the world with the heaviness of sorrow and the humility of guilt, their proud faces carried a scorn they had every right to wear, as the servants of the One God. See how this scorn breaks forth in the following passage. Its text is corrupt, and its rhythm, at this distance from the voices that utter it, is hardly perceptible; but thoroughly evident is its tone of intellectual superiority, and the scorn of it gushes forth in impetuous, unequal verse, the force of which the smoothness and dignity of our Authorised Version has unfortunately disguised.

Rev. George Adam Smith, M.A.

1.
    Formers of an idol are all of them waste,
    And their darlings are utterly worthless!
    And their confessors [87] *--they! they see not and know not*
    Enough to feel shame.
    Who has fashioned a god, or an image has cast?
    'Tis to be utterly worthless.
    Lo! all that depend on't are shamed,
    And the gravers are less than men:
    Let all of them gather and stand.
    They quake and are shamed in the lump.

2.
    Iron-graver--he takes [88] *a chisel,*
    And works with hot coals,
    And with hammers he moulds;
    And has done it with the arm of his strength.
    --Anon hungers, and strength goes;
    Drinks no water, and wearies!

3.
    Wood-graver--he draws a line,
    Marks it with pencil,
    Makes it with planes,
    And with compasses marks it.
    So has made it the build of a man,
    To a grace that is human--
    To inhabit a house, cutting it cedars. [89]

4.
    Or one takes an ilex or oak,
    And picks for himself from the trees of the wood;
    One has planted a pine, and the rain makes it big,
    And 'tis there for a man to burn.
    And one has taken of it, and been warmed;
    Yea, kindles and bakes bread,--
    Yea, works out a god, and has worshipped it!
    Has made it an idol, and bows down before it!
    Part of it burns he with fire,
    Upon part eats flesh,
    Roasts roast and is full;
    Yea, warms him and saith,
    "Aha, I am warm, have seen fire!"
    And the rest of it--to a god he has made--to his image!
    He bows to it, worships it, prays to it,
    And says, "Save me, for my god art thou!"

5.
    They know not and deem not!
    For He hath bedaubed, past seeing, their eyes,
    Past thinking, their hearts.
    And none takes to heart,
    Neither has knowledge nor sense to say,
    "Part of it burned I in fire--
    Yea, have baked bread on its coals,
    Do roast flesh that I eat,--
    And the rest o't, to a Disgust should I make it?

> The trunk of a tree should I worship?"
> Herder of ashes, [90] a duped heart has sent him astray,
> That he cannot deliver his soul, neither say,
> "Is there not a lie in my right hand?"

Is not the prevailing note in these verses surprise at the mental condition of an idol-worshipper? They see not and know not enough to feel shame. None takes it to heart, neither has knowledge nor sense to say, Part of it I have burned in fire ... and the rest, should I make it a god? This intellectual confidence, breaking out into scorn, is the second great token of truth, which distinguishes the religion of this poor slave of a people.

3. The third token is its moral character. The intellectual truth of a religion would go for little, had the religion nothing to say to man's moral sense--did it not concern itself with his sins, had it no redemption for his guilt. Now, the chapters before us are full of judgement and mercy. If they have scorn for the idols, they have doom for sin, and grace for the sinner. They are no mere political manifesto for the occasion, declaring how Israel shall be liberated from Babylon. They are a gospel for sinners in all time. By this they farther accredit themselves as a universal religion.

God is omnipotent, yet He can do nothing for Israel till Israel put away their sins. Those sins, and not the people's captivity, are the Deity's chief concern. Sin has been at the bottom of their whole adversity. This is brought out with all the versatility of conscience itself. Israel and their God have been at variance; their sin has been, what conscience feels the most, a sin against love. Yet not upon Me hast thou called, O Jacob; how hast thou been wearied with Me, O Israel.... I have not made thee to slave with offerings, nor wearied thee with incense ... but thou hast made Me to slave with thy sins, thou hast wearied Me with thine iniquities (xliii. 22-24). So God sets their sins, where men most see the blackness of their guilt, in the face of His love. And now He challenges conscience. Put Me in remembrance; let us come to judgement together; indict, that thou mayest be justified (ver. 26). But it had been agelong and original sin. Thy father, the first had sinned; yea, thy representative men--literally interpreters, mediators--had transgressed against Me. Therefore did I profane consecrated princes, and gave Jacob to the ban, and Israel to reviling (vv. 27, 28). The Exile itself was but an episode in a tragedy, which began far back with Israel's history. And so ch. xlviii. repeats: I knew that thou dost deal very treacherously, and Transgressor-from-the-womb do they call thee (ver. 8). And then there comes the sad note of what might have been. O that thou hadst hearkened to My commandments! then had thy peace been as the river, and thy righteousness as the waves of the sea (ver. 18). As broad Euphrates thou shouldst have lavishly rolled, and flashed to the sun like a summer sea. But now, hear what is left. There is no peace, saith Jehovah, to the wicked (ver. 22).

Ah, it is no dusty stretch of ancient history, no long-extinct volcano upon the far waste of Asian politics, to which we are led by the writings of the Exile. But they treat of man's perennial trouble; and conscience, that never dies, speaks through their old-fashioned letters and figures with words we feel like swords. And therefore, still, whether they be psalms or prophecies, they stand like some ancient minster in the modern world,--where, on each new soiled day, till time ends, the heavy heart of man may be helped to read itself, and lift up its guilt for mercy.

They are the confessional of the world, but they are also its gospel, and the altar where forgiveness is sealed. I, even I, am He that blotteth out thy transgressions for Mine own sake, and will not remember thy sins. O Israel, thou shalt not be forgotten of Me. I have blotted out as a thick cloud thy transgressions, and as a cloud thy sins; turn unto Me, for I have redeemed thee. Israel shall be saved by Jehovah with an everlasting salvation; ye shall not be ashamed nor confounded world without end. [91] Now, when we remember who the God is, who thus speaks,--not merely One who flings the word of pardon from the sublime height of His holiness, but, as we saw, speaks it from the midst of all His own passion and struggle under His people's sins,--then with what assurance does His word come home to the heart. What honour and obligation to righteousness does the pardon of such a God put upon our hearts. One understands why Ambrose sent Augustine, after his conversion, first to these prophecies.

4. The fourth token, which these chapters offer for the religion of Jehovah, is the claim they make for it to interpret and to control history. There are two verbs, which are frequently repeated throughout the chapters, and which are given together in ch. xliii. 12: I have published and I have saved. These are the two acts by which Jehovah proves His solitary divinity over against the idols.

The publishing, of course, is the same prediction, of which ch. xli. spoke. It is publishing in former times things happening now; it is publishing now things that are still to happen. And who, like Me, calls out and publishes it, and sets it in order for Me, since I appointed the ancient people? and the things that are coming, and that shall come, let them publish. Tremble not, nor fear: did I not long ago cause thee to hear? and I published, and ye are My witnesses. Is there a God beside Me? nay, there is no Rock; I know none (xliv. 7, 8).

The two go together, the doing of wonderful and saving acts for His people and the publishing of them before they come to pass. Israel's past is full of such acts. Ch. xliii. instances the delivery from

Rev. George Adam Smith, M.A.

Egypt (vv. 16, 17), but immediately proceeds (vv. 18, 19): Remember ye not the former things--here our old friend ri'shonôth occurs again, but this time means simply previous events--neither consider the things of old. Behold, I am doing a new thing; even now it springs forth. Shall ye not know it? Yea, I will set in the wilderness a way, in the desert rivers. And of this new event of the Return, and of others which will follow from it, like the building of Jerusalem, the chapters insist over and over again, that they are the work of Jehovah, who is therefore a Saviour God. But what better proof can be given, that these saving facts are indeed His own and part of His counsel, than that He foretold them by His messengers and prophets to Israel,--of which previous publication His people are the witnesses. Who among the peoples can publish thus, and let us hear predictions?--again ri'shonôth, things ahead--let them bring their witnesses, that they may be justified, and let them hear and say, Truth. Ye are my witnesses, saith Jehovah, to Israel (xliii. 9, 10). I have published, and I have saved, and I have shewed, and there was no strange god among you; therefore--because Jehovah was notoriously the only God who had to do with them during all this prediction and fulfilment of prediction--ye are witnesses for Me, saith Jehovah, that I am God (id. ver. 12). The meaning of all this is plain. Jehovah is God alone, because He is directly effective in history for the salvation of His people, and because He has published beforehand what He will do. The great instance of this, which the prophecy adduces, is the present movement towards the liberation of the people, of which movement Cyrus is the most conspicuous factor. Of this xlv. 19 ff. says: Not in secret have I spoken, in a place of the land of darkness. I have not said to the seed of Jacob, In vanity seek ye Me. I Jehovah am a speaker of righteousness, [92] a publisher of things that are straight. Be gathered and come in; draw together, ye survivors of the nations: they have no knowledge that carry about the log of their image, and are suppliants to a god that cannot save. Publish, and bring it here; nay, let them advise together; who made this to be heard,--that is, who published this,--of ancient time? Who published this of old? I Jehovah, and there is none God beside Me: a God righteous,--that is, consistent, true to His published word,--and a Saviour, there is none beside Me. Here we have joined together the same ideas as in xliii. 12. There I have declared and saved is equivalent to a God righteous and a Saviour here. Only in Jehovah are righteousnesses, that is, fidelity to His anciently published purposes; and strength, that is, capacity to carry these purposes out in history. God is righteous because, according to another verse in the same prophecy (xliv. 26), He confirmeth the word of His servant, and the advice of His messengers He fulfilleth.

Now the question has been asked, To what predictions does the prophecy allude as being fulfilled in those days when Cyrus was so evidently advancing to the overthrow of Babylon? Before answering this question it is well to note, that, for the most part, the prophet speaks in general terms. He gives no hint to justify that unfounded belief, to which so many think it necessary to cling, that Cyrus was actually named by a prophet of Jehovah years before he appeared. Had such a prediction existed, we can have no doubt that our prophet would now have appealed to it. No: he evidently refers only to those numerous and notorious predictions by Isaiah, and by Jeremiah, of the return of Israel from exile after a certain and fixed period. Those were now coming to pass.

But from this new day Jehovah also predicts for the days to come, and He does this very particularly, xliv. 26, Who is saying of Jerusalem, She shall be inhabited; and of the cities of Judah, They shall be built; and of her waste places, I will raise them up. Who saith to the deep, Be dry, and thy rivers I will dry up. Who saith of Koresh, My Shepherd, and all My pleasure he shall fulfil: even saying of Jerusalem, She shall be built, and the Temple shall be founded.

Thus, backward and forward, yesterday, to-day and for ever, Jehovah's hand is upon history. He controls it: it is the fulfilment of His ancient purpose. By predictions made long ago and fulfilled to-day, by the readiness to predict to-day what will happen to-morrow, He is surely God and God alone. Singular fact, that in that day of great empires, confident in their resources, and with the future so near their grasp, it should be the God of a little people, cut off from their history, servile and seemingly spent, who should take the big things of earth--Egypt, Ethiopia, Seba--and speak of them as counters to be given in exchange for His people; who should speak of such a people as the chief heirs of the future, the indispensable ministers of mankind. The claim has two Divine features. It is unique, and history has vindicated it. It is unique: no other religion, in that or in any other time, has so rationally explained past history or laid out the ages to come upon the lines of a purpose so definite, so rational, so beneficent--a purpose so worthy of the One God and Creator of all. And it has been vindicated: Israel returned to their own land, resumed the development of their calling, and, after the centuries came and went, fulfilled the promise that they should be the religious teachers of mankind. The long delay of this fulfilment surely but testifies the more to the Divine foresight of the promise; to the patience, which nature, as well as history, reveals to be, as much as omnipotence, a mark of Deity.

***

These, then, are the four points, upon which the religion of Israel offers itself. First, it is the force of the character and grace of a personal God; second, it speaks with a high intellectual confidence, whereof its scorn is here the chief mark; third, it is intensely moral, making man's sin its chief concern; and fourth, it claims the control of history, and history has justified the claim.

Footnotes:

85. From to-day on, Ez. xlviii. 35; but others take it Also to-day I am He.

86. Renan's theory of the "natural monotheism" of the Semites was first published in his Histoire des Langues Semitiques some forty years ago. Nearly every Semitic scholar of repute found some occasion or other to refute it. But with Renan's charming genius for neglecting all facts that disturb an artistic arrangement of his subject, the overwhelming evidence against the natural monotheism of the Semite has been ignored by him, and he repeats his theory unmodified in his Histoire du Peuple d'Israel, i., 31, published 1888.

87. Literally witnesses--i.e., of the idols.

88. This word is wanting in the text, which is corrupt here. Some supply the word sharpeneth, imagining that chdd has fallen away from the beginning of the verse, through confusion with the ychd which ends the previous verse; or they bring ychd itself, changing it to chdd. But evidently chrs vrzl begins the verse; cf. the parallel chrs tsym which begins ver. 13.

89. Here, again, the text is uncertain. With some critics I have borrowed for this verse the first three words of the following verse.

90. Perhaps feeder on ashes.

91. Chs. xliii. 25; xliv. 21, 22; xlv. 17.

92. See ch. [20]xiv. of this volume.

Rev. George Adam Smith, M.A.

CHAPTER X

CYRUS.

Isaiah xli. 2, 25; xliv. 28-xlv. 13; xlvi. 11; xlviii. 14, 15.

    Cyrus, the Persian, is the only man outside the covenant and people of Israel, who is yet entitled the Lord's Shepherd, and the Lord's Messiah or Christ. He is, besides, the only great personality, of whom both the Bible and Greek literature treat at length and with sympathy. Did we know nothing more of him than this, the heathen who received the most sacred titles of Revelation, the one man in history who was the cynosure of both Greece and Judah, could not fail to be of the greatest interest to us. But apart from the way, in which he impressed the Greek imagination and was interpreted by the Hebrew conscience, we have an amount of historical evidence about Cyrus, which, if it dissipates the beautiful legends told of his origin and his end, confirms most of what is written of his character by Herodotus and Xenophon, and all of what is described as his career by the prophet whom we are studying. Whether of his own virtue, or as being the leader of a new race of men at the fortunate moment of their call, Cyrus lifted himself, from the lowest of royal stations, to a conquest and an empire achieved by only two or three others in the history of the world. Originally but the prince of Anshan, or Anzan,[93] --a territory of uncertain size at the head of the Persian Gulf,--he brought under his sway, by policy or war, the large and vigorous nations of the Medes and Persians; he overthrew the Lydian kingdom, and subjugated Asia Minor; he so impressed the beginnings of Greek life, that, with all their own great men, the Greeks never ceased to regard this Persian as the ideal king; he captured Babylon, the throne of the ancient East, and thus effected the transfer of empire from the Semitic to the Aryan stock. He also satisfied the peoples, whom he had beaten, with his rule, and organised his realms with a thoroughness unequalled over so vast an extent till the rise of the Roman Empire.

    We have scarcely any contemporary or nearly contemporary evidence about his personality. But his achievements testify to extraordinary genius, and his character was the admiration of all antiquity. To Greek literature Cyrus was the Prince pre-eminent,--set forth as the model for education in childhood, self-restraint in youth, just and powerful government in manhood. Most of what we read of him in Xenophon's Cyropædia is, of course, romance; but the very fact, that, like our own King Arthur, Cyrus was used as a mirror to flash great ideals down the ages, proves that there was with him native brilliance and width of surface as well as fortunate eminence of position. He owed much to the virtue of his race. Rotten as the later Persians have become, the nation in those days impressed its enemies with its truthfulness, purity and vigour. But the man, who not only led such a nation, and was their darling, but combined under his sceptre, in equal discipline and contentment, so many other and diverse peoples, so many powerful and ambitious rulers, cannot have been merely the best specimen of his own nation's virtue, but must have added to this, at least much of the original qualities--humanity, breadth of mind, sweetness, patience and genius for managing men--which his sympathetic biographer imputes to him in so heroic a degree. It is evident that the Cyropædia is ignorant of many facts about Cyrus, and must have taken conscious liberties with many more, but nobody--who, on the one hand, is aware of what Cyrus effected upon the world, and who, on the other, can appreciate that it was possible for a foreigner (who, nevertheless, had travelled through most of the scenes of Cyrus' career) to form this rich conception of him more than a century after his death--can doubt that the Persian's character (due allowance being made for hero-worship) must have been in the main as Xenophon describes it.

    Yet it is very remarkable, that our Scripture states not one moral or religious virtue as the qualification of this Gentile to the title of Jehovah's Messiah. We search here in vain for any gleam of appreciation of that character, which drew the admiring eyes of Greece. In the whole range of our prophecy there is not a single adjective, expressing a moral virtue, applied to Cyrus. The righteousness, which so many passages associate with his name, is attributed, not to him, but to God's calling of him, and does not imply justice or any similar quality, but is, as we shall afterwards see when we examine the remarkable use of this word in Second Isaiah, a mixture of good faith and thoroughness,--all-rightness.[94] The one passage of our prophet, in which it has been supposed by some that Jehovah makes a religious claim to Cyrus, as if the Persian were a monotheist--he calleth on My name--is, as we have seen,[95] too uncertain, both in text and rendering, to have anything built upon it. Indeed, no Hebrew could have justly praised this Persian's faith, who called himself the "servant of Merodach," and in his public proclamations to Babylonia ascribed to the Babylonian gods his power to enter their city.[96] Cyrus was very probably the pious ruler, described by Xenophon, but he was no monotheist. And our prophet denies all religious sympathy between him and Jehovah, in words too strong to be misunderstood: I woo thee, though thou hast not known Me.... I gird thee, though thou hast not known Me (ch. xlv. 4, 5).

On what, then, is the Divine election of Cyrus grounded by our prophet, if not upon his character and his faith? Simply and barely upon God's sovereignty and will. That is the impressive lesson of the passage: I am Jehovah, Maker of everything; that stretch forth the heavens alone, and spread the earth by Myself ... that say of Koresh, My shepherd, and all My pleasure he shall accomplish (xliv. 24, 28). Cyrus is Jehovah's, because all things are Jehovah's; of whatsoever character or faith they be, they are His and for His uses. I am Jehovah, and there is none else: Former of light and Creator of darkness, Maker of peace and Creator of evil; I, Jehovah, Maker of all these. God's sovereignty could not be more broadly stated. All things, irrespective of their character, are from Him and for His ends. But what end is dearer to the Almighty, what has He more plainly declared, than that His people [97] shall be settled again in their own land? For this He will use the fittest force. The return of Israel to Palestine is a political event, requiring political power; and the greatest political power of the day is Cyrus. Therefore, by His prophet, the Almighty declares Cyrus to be His people's deliverer, His own anointed. Thus saith Jehovah to His Messiah, to Koresh: ... That thou mayest know that I am Jehovah, Caller of thee by thy name, God of Israel, for the sake of My servant Jacob and Israel My chosen. And I have called thee by thy name. I have wooed thee, though thou hast not known Me (xlv. 1, 3, 4).

Now to this designation of Cyrus, as the Messiah, great objections rose from Israel. We can understand them. People, who have fallen from a glorious past, cling passionately to its precedents. All the ancient promises of a deliverer for Israel represented him as springing from the house of David. The deliverance, too, was to have come by miracle, or by the impression of the people's own holiness upon their oppressors. The Lord Himself was to have made bare His arm and Israel to go forth in the pride of His favour, as in the days of Egypt and the Red Sea. But this deliverer, who was announced, was alien to the commonwealth of Israel; and not by some miracle was the people's exodus promised, but as the effect of his imperial word--a minor incident in his policy! The precedents and the pride of Israel called out against such a scheme of salvation, and the murmurs of the people rose against the word of God.

Sternly replies the Almighty: Woe to him that striveth with his Moulder, a potsherd among the potsherds of the ground! Saith clay to its moulder, What doest thou? or thy work of thee, No hands hath he? Woe to him that saith to a father, What begettest thou? or to a woman, With what travailest thou? Thus saith Jehovah, Holy of Israel and his Moulder: The things that are coming ask of Me; concerning My sons, and concerning the work of My hands, command ye Me! I have made Earth, [98] and created man upon her: I, My hands, have stretched Heaven, and all its host have I ordered. In that universal providence, this Cyrus is but an incident. I have stirred him up in righteousness, and all his ways shall I make level. He--emphatic--shall build My City, and My Captivity he shall send off--not for price and not for reward, saith Jehovah of Hosts (xlv. 9-13).

To this bare fiat, the passages referring to Cyrus in ch. xlvi. and ch. xlviii. add scarcely anything. I am God, and there is none like Me.... Who say, My counsel shall stand, and all My pleasure will I perform. Who call from the sunrise a Bird-of-prey, from a land far-off the Man of My counsel. Yea, I have spoken, yea, I will bring it to pass. I have formed, yea, will do it (xlvi. 9, 10, 11). Bird-of-prey here has been thought to have reference to the eagle, which was the standard of Cyrus. But it refers to Cyrus himself. What God sees in this man to fulfil His purpose is swift, resistless force. Not his character, but his swoop is useful for the Almighty's end. Again: Be gathered, all of you, and hearken; who among them hath published these things? Jehovah hath loved him: he will do His pleasure on Babel, and his arm shall be on the Chaldeans. I, I have spoken; yea, I have called him: I have brought him, and will cause his way to prosper, or, I will pioneer his way (xlviii. 14, 15). This verb to cause to prosper is one often used by our prophet, but nowhere more appropriately to its original meaning, than here, where it is used of a way. The word signifies to cut through; then to ford a river--there is no word for bridge in Hebrew; then to go on well, prosper. [99]

In all these passages, then, there is no word about character. Cyrus is neither chosen for his character nor said to be endowed with one. But that he is there, and that he does so much, is due simply to this, that God has chosen him. And what he is endowed with is force, push, swiftness, irresistibleness. He is, in short, not a character, but a tool; and God makes no apology for using him but this, that he has the qualities of a tool.

Now we cannot help being struck with the contrast of all this, the Hebrew view of Cyrus, with the well-known Greek views of him. To the Greeks he is first and foremost a character. Xenophon, and Herodotus almost as much as Xenophon, are less concerned with what Cyrus did than with what he was. He is the King, the ideal ruler. It is his simplicity, his purity, his health, his wisdom, his generosity, his moral influence upon men, that attract the Greeks, and they conceive that he cannot be too brightly painted in his virtues, if so he may serve for an example to following generations. But bring Cyrus out of the light of the eyes of this hero-worshipping people, that light that has so gilded his native virtues, into the shadow of the austere Hebrew faith, and the brilliance is quenched. He still moves forcibly, but his character is neutral. Scripture emphasizes only his strength, his serviceableness, his success: Whose right hand I have holden, to subdue nations before him, and I will loosen the loins of kings; to open doors before him, and gates shall not be shut. I will go before thee, and make the rugged places plain. I will shiver doors of brass, and bars of iron will I sunder (xlv. 1, 2). That Cyrus is doing a work in God's hand and for God's end, and therefore forcibly, and sure of success--that is all the interest Scripture takes in Cyrus.

Observe the difference. It is characteristic of the two nations. The Greek views Cyrus as an example; therefore cannot too abundantly multiply his morality. The Hebrew views him as a tool; but with a tool you are not anxious about its moral character, you only desire to be convinced of its force and its fitness. The Greek mind is careful to unfold the noble humanity of the man,--a humanity universally and eternally noble. By the side of that imperishable picture of him, how meagre to Greek eyes would have seemed the temporary occasion, for which the Hebrew claimed that Cyrus had been raised up--to lead the petty Jewish tribe back to their own obscure corner of the earth. Herodotus and Xenophon, had you told them that this was the chief commission of Cyrus from God, to restore the Jews to Palestine, would have laughed. "Identify him, forsooth, with those provincial interests!" they would have said. "He was meant, we lift him up, for mankind!"

What judgement are we to pass on these two characteristic pictures of Cyrus? What lessons are we to draw from their contrast?

They do not contradict, but in many particulars they corroborate one another. Cyrus would not have been the efficient weapon in the Almighty's hand, which our prophet panegyrises, but for that thoughtfulness in preparation and swift readiness to seize the occasion, which Xenophon extols. And nothing is more striking to one familiar with our Scriptures, when reading the Cyropædia, than the frequency with which the writer insists on the success that followed the Persian. If to the Hebrew Cyrus was the called of God, upheld in righteousness, to the Greek he was equally conspicuous as the favourite of fortune. "I have always," Xenophon makes the dying king say, "seemed to feel my strength increase with the advance of time, so that I have not found myself weaker in my old age than in my youth, nor do I know that I have attempted or desired anything in which I have not been successful."[100] And this was said piously, for Xenophon's Cyrus was a devout servant of the gods.

The two views, then, are not hostile, nor are we compelled to choose between them. Still, they make a very suggestive contrast, if we put these two questions about them: Which is the more true to historical fact? Which is the more inspiring example?

Which is the more true to historical fact? There is no difficulty in answering this: undoubtedly, the Hebrew. It has been of far more importance to the world that Cyrus freed the Jews than that he inspired the Cyropædia. That single enactment of his, perhaps only one of a hundred consequences of his capture of Babylon, has had infinitely greater results than his character, or than its magnificent exaggeration by Greek hero-worship. No one who has read the Cyropædia--out of his school-days--would desire to place it in any contrast, in which its peculiar charm would be shadowed, or its own modest and strictly-limited claims would not receive justice. The charm, the truth of the Cyropædia, are eternal; but the significance they borrow from Cyrus--though they are as much due, perhaps, to Xenophon's own pure soul as to Cyrus--is not to be compared for one instant to the significance of that single deed of his, into which the Bible absorbs the meaning of his whole career,--the liberation of the Jews. The Cyropædia has been the instruction and delight of many,--of as many in modern times, perhaps, as in ancient. But the liberation of the Jews meant the assurance of the world's religious education. Cyrus sent this people back to their land solely as a spiritual people. He did not allow them to set up again the house of David, but by his decree the Temple was rebuilt. Israel entered upon their purely religious career, set in order their vast stores of spiritual experience, wrote their histories of grace and providence, developed their worship, handed down their law, and kept themselves holy unto the Lord. Till, in the fulness of the times, from this petty and exclusive tribe, and by the fire, which they kept burning on the altar that Cyrus had empowered them to raise, there was kindled the glory of an universal religion. To change the figure, Christianity sprang from Judaism as the flower from the seed; but it was the hand of Cyrus, which planted the seed in the only soil, in which it could have fructified. Of such an universal destiny for the Faith, Cyrus was not conscious, but the Jews themselves were. Our prophet represents him, indeed, as acting for Jacob My servant's sake, and Israel's My chosen, but the chapter does not close without proclamation to the ends of the earth to look unto Jehovah and be saved, and the promise of a time when every knee shall bow and every tongue swear unto the God of Israel.

Now put all these results, which the Jews, regardless of the character of Cyrus, saw flowing from his policy, as the servant of God on their behalf, side by side with the influence which the Greeks borrowed from Cyrus, and say whether Greek or Jew had the more true and historical conscience of this great power,--whether Greek or Jew had his hand on the pulse of the world's main artery. Surely we see that the main artery of human life runs down the Bible, that here we have a sense of the control of history, which is higher than even the highest hero-worship. Some may say, "True, but what a very unequal contest, into which to thrust the poor Cyropædia!" Precisely; it is from the inequality of the contrast, that we learn the uniqueness of Israel's inspiration. Let us do all justice to the Greek and his appreciation of Cyrus. In that, he seems the perfection of humanity; but with the Jew we rise to the Divine, touching the right hand of the providence of God.

There is a moral lesson for ourselves in these two views about Cyrus. The Greeks regard him as a hero, the Jews as an instrument. The Greeks are interested in him that he is so attractive a figure, so effective an example to rouse men and restrain them. But the Jews stand in wonder of his subjection to the will of God; their Scriptures extol, not his virtues, but his predestination to certain Divine ends.

Now let us say no word against hero-worship. We have need of all the heroes, which the Greek, and every other, literature can raise up for us. We need the communion of the saints. To make us humble in our pride, to make us hopeful in our despair, we need our big brothers, the heroes of humanity. We need them in history, we need them in fiction; we cannot do without them for shame, for courage, for fellowship, for truth. But let us remember that still more indispensable--for strength, as well as for peace, of mind--is the other temper. Neither self nor the world is conquered by admiration of men, but only by the fear and obligation of God. I speak now of applying this temper to ourselves. We shall live fruitful and consistent lives only in so far as we hear God saying to us, I gird thee, and give ourselves into His guidance. Admire heroes if thou wilt, but only admire them and thou remainest a slave. Learn their secret, to commit themselves to God and to obey Him, and thou shalt become a hero too.

God's anointing of Cyrus, the heathen, has yet another lesson to teach us, which religious people especially need to learn.

This passage about Cyrus lifts us to a very absolute and awful faith. I am Jehovah, and none else: Former of light and Creator of darkness, Maker of peace and Creator of mischief; I Jehovah, Maker of all these things. The objection at once rises, "Is it possible to believe this? Are we to lay upon providence everything that happens? Surely we Westerns, with our native scepticism and strong conscience, cannot be expected to hold a faith so Oriental and fatalistic as that."

But notice to whom the passage is addressed. To religious people, who professedly accept God's sovereignty, but wish to make an exception in the one case against which they have a prejudice--that a Gentile should be the deliverer of the holy people. Such narrow and imperfect believers are reminded that they must not substitute for faith in God their own ideas of how God ought to work; that they must not limit His operations to their own conception of His past revelations; that God does not always work even by His own precedents; and that many other forces than conventional and religious ones--yea, even forces as destitute of moral or religious character as Cyrus himself seemed to be--are also in God's hands, and may be used by Him as means of grace. There is frequent charge made in our day against what are called the more advanced schools of theology, of scepticism and irreverence. But this passage reminds us that the most sceptical and irreverent are those old-fashioned believers, who, clinging to precedent and their own stereotyped notions of things, deny that God's hands are in a movement, because it is novel and not orthodox. Woe unto him that striveth with his Moulder; shall the clay say to its moulder, What makest thou? God did not cease moulding when He gave us the canon and our creeds, when He founded the Church and the Sacraments. His hand is still among the clay, and upon time, that great "potter's wheel," which still moves obedient to His impulse. All the large forward movements, the big things of to-day--commerce, science, criticism--however neutral, like Cyrus, their character may be, are, like Cyrus, grasped and anointed by God. Therefore let us show reverence and courage before the great things of to-day. Do not let us scoff at their novelty or grow fearful because they show no orthodox, or even no religious, character. God reigns, and He will use them, for what has been the dearest purpose of His heart, the emancipation of true religion, the confirmation of the faithful, the victory of righteousness. When Cyrus rose and the prophet named him as Israel's deliverer, and the severely orthodox in Israel objected, did God attempt to soothe them by pointing out how admirable a character he was, and how near in religion to the Jews themselves? God did no such thing, but spoke only of the military and political fitness of this great engine, by which He was to batter Babylon. That Cyrus was a quick marcher, a far shooter, an inspirer of fear, a follower up of victory, one who swooped like a bird-of-prey, one whose weight of war burst through every obstruction,--this is what the astonished pedants are told about the Gentile, to whose Gentileness they had objected. No soft words to calm their bristling orthodoxy, but heavy facts,--an appeal to their common-sense, if they had any, that this was the most practical means for the practical end God had in view. For again we learn the old lesson the prophets are ever so anxious to teach us, God is wise. He is concerned, not to be orthodox or true to His own precedent, but to be practical, and effective for salvation.

And so, too, in our own day, though we may not see any religious character whatsoever about certain successful movements--say in science, for instance--which are sure to affect the future of the Church and of Faith, do not let us despair, neither deny that they, too, are in the counsels of God. Let us only be sure that they are permitted for some end--some practical end; and watch, with meekness but with vigilance, to see what that end shall be. Perhaps the endowment of the Church with new weapons of truth; perhaps her emancipation from associations which, however ancient, are unhealthy; perhaps

Rev. George Adam Smith, M.A.

her opportunity to go forth upon new heights of vision, new fields of conquest.

Footnotes:

93. Identified by Delitzsch as East, Halévy as West, and Winckler as North, Elam. Cyrus, though reigning here, was a pure Persian, an Akhæmenid or son of the royal house of Persia.

94. The parallel which Professor Sayce (Fresh Light from the Ancient Monuments, p. 147) draws between the statement of the Cyrus-cylinder, that Cyrus "governed in justice and righteousness, and was righteous in hand and heart," and Isa. xlv. 13, "Jehovah raised him up in righteousness," is therefore utterly unreal. It is very difficult to see how the Deputy-Professor of Comparative Philology at Oxford could have been reminded of the one passage by the other, for in Isa. xlv. 13 righteousness neither is used of Cyrus, nor signifies the moral virtue which it does on the cylinder.

95. See [21]note to ch. vii.

96. The following are extracts from the Cylinder of Cyrus (see Sayce's Fresh Light from the Ancient Monuments, pp. 138-140):--"Cyrus, king of Elam, he (Merodach) proclaimed by name for the sovereignty.... Whom he had conquered with his hand, he governed in justice and righteousness. Merodach, the great lord, the restorer of his people, beheld with joy the deeds of his vicegerent, who was righteous in hand and heart. To Babylon he summoned his march, and he bade him take the road to Babylon; like a friend and a comrade he went at his side. Without fighting or battle he caused him to enter into Babylon, his city of Babylon feared. The god ... has in goodness drawn nigh to him, has made strong his name. I Cyrus ... I entered Babylon in peace.... Merodach the great lord (cheered) the heart of his servant.... My vast armies he marshalled peacefully in the midst of Babylon; throughout Sumer and Accad I had no revilers.... Accad, Marad, etc., I restored the gods who dwelt within them to their places ... all their peoples I assembled and I restored their lands. And the gods of Sumer and Accad whom Nabonidos, to the anger of the lord of gods (Merodach), had brought into Babylon, I settled in peace in their sanctuaries by command of Merodach, the great lord. In the goodness of their hearts may all the gods whom I have brought into their strong places daily intercede before Bel and Nebo, that they should grant me length of days; may they bless my projects with prosperity, and may they say to Merodach my lord, that Cyrus the king, thy worshipper, and Kambyses his son (deserve his favour)."

97. Why so sovereign a God should be in such peculiar relations with one people, we will try to see in ch. [22]xv. of this volume.

98. Earth here without the article, but plainly the earth, and not the land of Judah.

99. Cf. with this Hebrew word tslch the Greek prokoptein, to beat or cut a way through like pioneers; then to forward a work, advance, prosper (Luke ii. 52; Gal. i. 14; 2 Tim. ii. 16).

100. Cyropædia, Book VIII., ch. vii., 6.

CHAPTER XI

BEARING OR BORNE.

Isaiah xlvi.

Chapter xlvi. is a definite prophecy, complete in itself. It repeats many of the truths which we have found in previous chapters, and we have already seen what it says about Cyrus. But it also strikes out a new truth, very relevant then, when men made idols and worshipped the works of their hands, and relevant still, when so many, with equal stupidity, are more concerned about keeping up the forms of their religion than allowing God to sustain themselves.

The great contrast, which previous chapters have been elaborating, is the contrast between the idols and the living God. On the one side we have had pictures of the busy idol-factories, cast into agitation by the advent of Cyrus, turning out with much toil and noise their tawdry, unstable images. Foolish men, instead of letting God undertake for them, go to and try what their own hands and hammers can effect. Over against them, and their cunning and toil, the prophet sees the God of Israel rise alone, taking all responsibility of salvation to Himself--I, I am He: look unto Me, all the ends of the earth, and be ye saved. This contrast comes to a head in ch. xlvi.

It is still the eve of the capture of Babylon; but the prophet pictures to himself what will happen on the morrow of the capture. He sees the conqueror following the old fashion of triumph--rifling the temples of his enemies and carrying away the defeated and discredited gods as trophies to his own. The haughty idols are torn from their pedestals and brought head foremost through the temple doors. Bel crouches--as men have crouched to Bel; Nebo cowers--a stronger verb than crouches, but assonant to it, like cower to crouch. [101] Their idols have fallen to the beast and to the cattle. Beast, "that is, tamed beast, perhaps elephants in contrast to cattle, or domestic animals." [102] The things with which ye burdened yourselves, carrying them shoulder high in religious processions, are things laden, mere baggage-bales, a burden for a hack, or jade. The nouns are mostly feminine--the Hebrew neuter--in order to heighten the dead-weight impression of the idols. So many baggage-bales for beasts' backs-- such are your gods, O Babylonians! They cower, they crouch together (fall limp is the idea, like corpses); neither are they able to recover the burden, and themselves!--literally their soul, any real soul of deity that ever was in them--into captivity are they gone.

This never happened. Cyrus entered Babylon not in spite of the native gods, but under their patronage, and was careful to do homage to them. Nabunahid, the king of Babylon, whom he supplanted, had vexed the priests of Bel or Merodach; and these priests had been among the many conspirators in favour of the Persian. So far, then, from banishing the idols, upon his entry into the city, Cyrus had himself proclaimed as "the servant of Merodach," restored to their own cities the idols that Nabunahid had brought to Babylon, and prayed, "In the goodness of their hearts may all the gods whom I have brought into their strong places daily intercede before Bel and Nebo, that they should grant me length of days. May they bless my projects with prosperity, and may they say to Merodach, my lord, that Cyrus the king, thy worshipper, and Kambyses, his son (deserve thy favour)." [103]

Are we, then, because the idols were not taken into captivity, as our prophet pictures, to begin to believe in him less? We shall be guilty of that error, only when we cease to disallow to a prophet of God what we do allow to any other writer, and praise him when he employs it to bring home a moral truth-- the use of his imagination. What if these idols never were packed off by Cyrus, as our prophet here paints for us? It still remains true that, standing where they did, or carried away, as they may have been later on, by conquerors, who were monotheists indeed, they were still mere ballast, so much dead-weight for weary beasts.

Now, over against this kind of religion, which may be reduced to so many pounds avoirdupois, the prophet sees in contrast the God of Israel. And it is but natural, when contrasted with the dead-weight of the idols, that God should reveal Himself as a living and a lifting God: a strong, unfailing God, who carries and who saves. Hearken unto Me, O House of Jacob, and all the remnant of the House of Israel; burdens from the womb, things carried from the belly. Burdens, things carried, are the exact words used of the idols in ver. 1. Even unto old age I am He, and unto grey hairs I will bear--a grievous word, used only of great burdens. I have made, and I will carry; yea, I will bear, and will recover. Then follow some verses in the familiar style. To whom will ye liken Me, and match Me, and compare Me, that we may be like? They who pour gold from a bag, and silver they measure off with an ellwand--gorgeous, vulgar

Rev. George Adam Smith, M.A.

Babylonians!--they hire a smelter, and he maketh it a god--out of so many ells of silver!--they bow down to it, yea, they worship it! They carry him upon the shoulder, they bear him,--again the grievous word,--to bring him to his station; and he stands; from his place he never moves. Yea, one cries unto him, and he answers not; from his trouble he doth not save him. Remember this, and show yourselves men--the playing with these gilded toys is so unmanly to the monotheist (it will be remembered what we said in ch. iii. about the exiles feeling that to worship idols was to be less than a man [104])--lay it again to heart, ye transgressors. Remember the former things of old: for I am God, El, and there is none else; God, Elohim, and there is none like Me. Publishing from the origin the issue, and from ancient times things not yet done; saying, My counsel shall stand, and all My pleasure shall I perform; calling out of the sunrise a Bird-of-prey, from the land that is far off the Man of My counsel. Yea, I have spoken; yea, I will bring it in. I have purposed; yea, I will do it. Hearken unto Me, ye obdurate of heart--that is, brave, strong, sound, but too sound to adapt their preconceived notions to God's new revelation;--ye that are far from righteousness, in spite of your sound opinions as to how it ought to come. I have brought near My righteousness, in distinction to yours. It shall not be far off, like your impossible ideas, and My salvation shall not tarry, and I will set in Zion salvation, for Israel My glory. It is evident that from the idolaters Jehovah has turned again, in these last verses, to the pedants in Israel, who were opposed to Cyrus because he was a Gentile, and who cherished their own obdurate notions of how salvation and righteousness should come. Ah, their kind of righteousness would never come, they would always be far from it! Let them rather trust to Jehovah's, which He was rapidly bringing near in His own way.

Such is the prophecy. It starts a truth, which bursts free from local and temporal associations, and rushes in strength upon our own day and our own customs. The truth is this: it makes all the difference to a man how he conceives his religion--whether as something that he has to carry, or as something that will carry him. We have too many idolatries and idol manufactories among us to linger longer on those ancient ones. This cleavage is permanent in humanity--between the men that are trying to carry their religion, and the men that are allowing God to carry them.

Now let us see how God does carry. God's carriage of man is no mystery. It may be explained without using one theological term; the Bible gives us the best expression of it. But it may be explained without a word from the Bible. It is broad and varied as man's moral experience.

1. The first requisite for stable and buoyant life is ground, and the faithfulness of law. What sends us about with erect bodies and quick, firm step is the sense that the surface of the earth is sure, that gravitation will not fail, that our eyes and the touch of our feet and our judgement of distance do not deceive us. Now, what the body needs for its world, the soul needs for hers. For her carriage and bearing in life the soul requires the assurance, that the moral laws of the universe are as conscience has interpreted them to her, and will continue to be as in experience she has found them. To this requisite of the soul--this indispensable condition of moral behaviour--God gives His assurance. I have made, He says, and I will bear. [105] These words were in answer to an instinct, that must have often sprung up in our hearts when we have been struggling for at least moral hope--the instinct which will be all that is sometimes left to a man's soul when unbelief lowers, and under its blackness a flood of temptations rushes in, and character and conduct feel impossible to his strength--the instinct that springs from the thought, "Well, here I am, not responsible for being here, but so set by some One else, and the responsibility of the life, which is too great for me, is His." Some such simple faith, which a man can hardly separate from his existence, has been the first rally and turning-point in many a life. In the moral drift and sweep he finds bottom there, and steadies on it, and gets his face round, and gathers strength. And God's Word comes to him to tell him that his instinct is sure. Yea, I have made, and I will bear.

2. The most terrible anguish of the heart, however, is that it carries something, which can shake a man off even that ground. The firmest rock is of no use to the paralytic, or to a man with a broken leg. And the most steadfast moral universe, and most righteous moral governor, is no comfort--but rather the reverse--to the man with a bad conscience, whether that conscience be due to the guilt, or to the habit, of sin. Conscience whispers, "God indeed made thee, but what if thou hast unmade thyself? God reigns; the laws of life are righteousness; creation is guided to peace. But thou art outlaw of this universe, fallen from God of thine own will. Thou must bear thine own guilt, endure thy voluntarily contracted habits. How canst thou believe that God, in this fair world, would bear thee up, so useless, soiled, and infected a thing?" Yet here, according to His blessed Word, God does come down to bear up men. Because man's sunkenness and helplessness are so apparent beneath no other burden or billows, God insists that just here He is most anxious, and just here it is His glory, to lift men and bear them upward. Some may wonder what guilt is or the conviction of sin, because they are selfishly or dishonestly tracing the bitterness and unrest of their lives to some other source than their own wicked wills; but the thing is man's realest burden, and man's realest burden is what God stoops lowest to bear. The grievous word for bear, "sabal," which we emphasized in the above passage, is elsewhere in the writings of the Exile used of the bearing of sins, or of the result of sins. *Our fathers have sinned, and are not, and we bear their iniquities,* [106] says one of the Lamentations. And in the fifty-third of Isaiah it is used twice of the

Servant, that He bore our sorrows, and that He bare their iniquities. [107] Here its application to God--to such a God as we have seen bearing the passion of His people's woes--cannot fail to carry with it the associations of these passages. When it is said, God bears, and this grievous verb is used, we remember at once that He is a God, who does not only set His people's sins in the awful light of His countenance, but takes them upon His heart. Let us learn, then, that God has made this sin and guilt of ours His special care and anguish. We cannot feel it more than He does. It is enough: we may not be able to understand what the sacrifice of Christ meant to the Divine justice, but who can help comprehending from it that in some Divine way the Divine love has made our sin its own business and burden, so that that might be done which we could not do, and that lifted which we could not bear?

3. But this gospel of God's love bearing our sins is of no use to a man unless it goes with another--that God bears him up for victory over temptation and for attainment in holiness. It is said to be a thoroughly Mohammedan fashion, that when a believer is tempted past the common he gives way, and slides into sin with the cry, "God is merciful;" meaning that the Almighty will not be too hard on this poor creature, who has held out so long. If this be Mohammedanism, there is a great deal of Mohammedanism in modern Christianity. It is a most perfidious distortion of God's will. For this is the will of God, even our sanctification; and God never gives a man pardon but to set him free for effort, and to constrain him for duty. And here we come to what is the most essential part of God's bearing of man. God, as we have seen, bears us by giving us ground to walk on. He bears us by lifting those burdens from our hearts that make the firmest ground slippery and impossible to our feet. But He bears us best and longest by being the spirit and the soul and the life of our life. Every metaphor here falls short of the reality. By inspired men the bearing of God has been likened to a father carrying his child, to an eagle taking her young upon her wings, to the shepherd with the lamb in his bosom. But no shepherd, nor mother-bird, nor human father ever bore as the Lord bears. For He bears from within, as the soul lifts and bears the body. The Lord and His own are one. To me, says he who knew it best, To me to live is Christ. It is, indeed, difficult to describe to others what this inward sustainment really is, seating itself at the centre of a man's life, and thence affecting vitally every organ of his nature. The strongest human illustration is not sufficient for it. If in the thick of the battle a leader is able to infuse himself into his followers, so is Christ. If one man's word has lifted thousands of defeated soldiers to an assault and to a victory, even so have Christ's lifted millions: lifted them above the habit and depression of sin, above the weakness of the flesh, above the fear of man, above danger and death and temptation more dangerous and fatal still. And yet it is not the sight of a visible leader, though the Gospels have made that sight imperishable; it is not the sound of Another's Voice, though that Voice shall peal to the end of time, that Christians only feel. It is something within themselves; another self--purer, happier, victorious. Not as a voice or example, futile enough to the dying, but as a new soul, is Christ in men; and whether their exhaustion needs creative forces, or their vices require conquering forces, He gives both, for He is the fountain of life.

4. But God does not carry dead men. His carrying is not mechanical, but natural; not from below, but from within. You dare not be passive in God's carriage; for as in the natural, so in the moral world, whatever dies is thrown aside by the upward pressure of life, to rot and perish. Christ showed this over and over again in His ministry. Those who make no effort--or, if effort be past, feel no pain--God will not stoop to bear. But all in whom there is still a lift and a spring after life: the quick conscience, the pain of their poverty, the hunger and thirst after righteousness, the sacredness of those in their charge, the obligation and honour of their daily duty, some desire for eternal life--these, however weak, He carries forward to perfection.

Again, in His bearing God bears, and does not overbear, using a man, not as a man uses a stick, but as a soul uses a body,--informing, inspiring, recreating his natural faculties. So many distrust religion, as if it were to be an overbearing of their originality, as if it were bound to destroy the individual's peculiar freshness and joy. But God is not by grace going to undo His work by nature. I have made, and I will bear--will bear what I have made. Religion intensifies the natural man.

And now, if that be God's bearing--the gift of the ground, and the lifting of the fallen, and the being a soul and an inspiration of every organ--how wrong those are who, instead of asking God to carry them, are more anxious about how He and His religion are to be sustained by their consistency or efforts!

To young men, who have not got a religion, and are brought face to face with the conventional religion of the day, the question often presents itself in this way: "Is this a thing I can carry?" or "How much of it can I afford to carry? How much of the tradition of the elders can I take upon myself, and feel that it is not mere dead weight?" That is an entirely false attitude. Here you are, weak, by no means master of yourself; with a heart wonderfully full of suggestions to evil; a world before you, hardest where it is clearest, seeming most impossible where duty most loudly calls; yet mainly dark and silent, needing from us patience oftener than effort, and trust as much as the exercise of our own cleverness; with death at last ahead. Look at life whole, and the question you will ask will not be, Can I carry this faith? but, Can this faith carry me? Not, Can I afford to take up such and such and such opinions? but,

Rev. George Adam Smith, M.A.

Can I afford to travel at all without such a God? It is not a creed, but a living and a lifting God, who awaits your decision.

At the opposite end of life, there is another class of men, who are really doing what young men too often suppose that they must do if they take up a religion,--carrying it, instead of allowing it to carry them; men who are in danger of losing their faith in God, through over-anxiety about traditional doctrines concerning Him. A great deal is being said just now in our country of upholding the great articles of the faith. Certainly let us uphold them. But do not let us have in our churches that saddest of all sights, a mere ecclesiastical procession,--men flourishing doctrines, but themselves with their manhood remaining unseen. We know the pity of a show, sometimes seen in countries on the Continent, where they have not given over carrying images about. Idols and banners and texts will fill a street with their tawdry, tottering progress, and you will see nothing human below, but now and then jostling shoulders and a sweaty face. Even so are many of the loud parades of doctrines in our day by men, who, in the words of this chapter, show themselves stout of heart by holding up their religion, but give us no signs in their character or conduct that their religion is holding up them. Let us prize our faith, not by holding it high, but by showing how high it can hold us.

Which is the more inspiring sight,--a banner carried by hands, that must sooner or later weary; or the soldier's face, mantling with the inexhaustible strength of the God who lives at his heart and bears him up?

Footnotes:

101. Crouches, Kara`; cowers, Kores.
102. Bredenkamp.
103. Sayce, Fresh Light, etc., p. 140.
104. See p. [23]39 f.
105. There is a play on the words 'anî `asîthî, wa'anî, 'essa'--I have made, and I will aid.
106. Lam. v. 7.
107. Ver. 4, second clause, and vii.

CHAPTER XII

BABYLON.

Isaiah xlvii.

Throughout the extent of Bible history, from Genesis to Revelation, One City remains, which in fact and symbol is execrated as the enemy of God and the stronghold of evil. In Genesis we are called to see its foundation, as of the first city that wandering men established, and the quick ruin, which fell upon its impious builders. By the prophets we hear it cursed as the oppressor of God's people, the temptress of the nations, full of cruelty and wantonness. And in the Book of Revelation its character and curse are transferred to Rome, and the New Babylon stands over against the New Jerusalem.

The tradition and infection, which have made the name of Babylon as abhorred in Scripture as Satan's own, are represented as the tradition and infection of pride,--the pride, which, in the audacity of youth, proposes to attempt to be equal with God: Go to, let us build us a city and a tower, whose top may touch heaven, and let us make us a name; the pride, which, amid the success and wealth of later years, forgets that there is a God at all: Thou sayest in thine heart, I am, and there is none beside me. Babylon is the Atheist of the Old Testament, as she is the Antichrist of the New.

That a city should have been originally conceived by Israel as the arch-enemy of God is due to historical causes, as intelligible as those which led, in later days, to the reverse conception of a city as God's stronghold, and the refuge of the weak and the wandering. God's earliest people were shepherds, plain men dwelling in tents,--desert nomads, who were never tempted to rear permanent structures of their own except as altars and shrines, but marched and rested, waked and slept, between God's bare earth and God's high heaven; whose spirits were chastened and refined by the hunger and clear air of the desert, and who walked their wide world without jostling or stunting one another. With the dear habits of those early times, the truths of the Bible are therefore, even after Israel has settled in towns, spelt to the end in the images of shepherd life. The Lord is the Shepherd, and men are the sheep of His pasture. He is a Rock and a Strong Tower, such as rise here and there in the desert's wildness for guidance or defence. [108] He is rivers of water in a dry place, and the shadow of a great rock in a weary land. And man's peace is to lie beside still waters, and his glory is, not to have built cities, but to have all these things put under his feet--sheep and oxen and the beasts of the field, the fowls of the air and the fish of the sea.

Over against that lowly shepherd life, the first cities rose, as we can imagine, high, terrible and impious. They were the production of an alien race, [109] a people with no true religion, as it must have appeared to the Semites, arrogant and coarse. But Babylon had a special curse. Babylon was not the earliest city,--Akkad and Erekh were famous long before,--but it is Babylon that the Book of Genesis represents as overthrown and scattered by the judgement of God. What a contrast this picture in Genesis,--and let it be remembered that the only other cities to which that book leads us are Sodom and Gomorrah,--what a contrast it forms to the passages in which classic poets celebrate the beginnings of their great cities! There, the favourable omens, the patronage of the gods, the prophecies of the glories of civil life; the tracing of the temple and the forum; visions of the city as the school of industry, the treasury of wealth, the home of freedom. Here, but a few rapid notes of scorn and doom: man's miserable manufacture, without Divine impulse or omen; his attempt to rise to heaven upon that alone, his motive only to make a name for himself; and the result--not, as in Greek legend, the foundation of a polity, the rise of commerce, the growth of a great language, by which through the lips of one man the whole city may be swayed together to high purposes, but only scattering and confusion of speech. To history, a great city is a multitude of men within reach of one man's voice. Athens is Demosthenes; Rome is Cicero persuading the Senate; Florence is Savonarola putting by his word one conscience within a thousand hearts. But Babylon, from the beginning, gave its name to Babel, confusion of speech, incapacity for union and for progress. And all this came, because the builders of the city, the men who set the temper of its civilisation, did not begin with God, but in their pride deemed everything possible to unaided and unblessed human ambition, and had only the desire to make a name upon earth.

The sin and the curse never left the generations, who in turn succeeded those impious builders. Pride and godlessness infested the city, and prepared it for doom, as soon as it again gathered strength to rise to heaven. The early nomads had watched Babylon's fall from afar; but when their descendants were carried as captives within her in the time of her second glory, [110] they found that the besetting sin, which had once reared its head so fatally high, infected the city to her very heart. We need not again go over the extent and glory of Nebuchadrezzar's architecture, or the greatness of the traffic, from the Levant to India, which his policy had concentrated upon his own wharves and markets. [111] It was stupendous. But neither walls nor wealth make a city, and no observant man, with the Hebrew's faith and conscience, could have lived those fifty years in the centre of Babylon, and especially after Nebuchadrezzar had passed away, without perceiving, that her life was destitute of every principle which ensured union or promised progress. Babylon was but a medley of peoples, without common traditions or a public conscience, and incapable of acting together. Many of her inhabitants had been brought to her, like the Jews, against their own will, and were ever turning from those glorious battlements they were forced to build in their disgust, to scan the horizon for the advent of a deliverer. And many others, who moved in freedom through her busy streets, and shared her riches and her joys, were also foreigners, and bound to her only so long as she ministered to their pleasure or their profit. Her king was an usurper, who had insulted her native gods; her priesthood was against him. And although his army, sheltered by the fortifications of Nebuchadrezzar, had repulsed Cyrus upon the Persian's first invasion from the north, conspiracies were now so rife among his oppressed and insulted subjects, that, on Cyrus' second invasion, Babylon opened her impregnable gates and suffered herself to be taken without a blow. Nor, even if the city's religion had been better served by the king, could it in the long run have availed for her salvation. For, in spite of the science with which it was connected,-- and this "wisdom of the Chaldeans" was contemptible in neither its methods nor its results,--the Babylonian religion was not one to inspire either the common people with those moral principles, which form the true stability of states, or their rulers with a reasonable and consistent policy. Babylon's religion was broken up into a multitude of wearisome and distracting details, whose absurd solemnities, especially when administered by a priesthood hostile to the executive, must have hampered every adventure of war, and rendered futile many opportunities of victory. In fact, Babylon, for all her glory, could not but be short-lived. There was no moral reason why she should endure. The masses, who contributed to her building, were slaves who hated her; the crowds, who fed her business, would stay with her only so long as she was profitable to themselves; her rulers and her priests had quarrelled; her religion was a burden, not an inspiration. Yet she sat proud, and felt herself secure.

It is just these features, which our prophet describes in ch. xlvii., in verses more notable for their moral insight and indignation, than for their beauty as a work of literature. He is certain of Babylon's immediate fall from power and luxury into slavery and dishonour (vv. 1-3). He speaks of her cruelty to her captives (ver. 6), of her haughtiness and her secure pride (vv. 7, 8). He touches twice upon her atheistic self-sufficiency, her "autotheism,"--"I am, and there is none beside me," words which only God can truly use, but words which man's ignorant, proud self is ever ready to repeat (vv. 8-10). He speaks of the wearisomeness and futility of her religious magic (vv. 10-14). And he closes with a vivid touch, that dissolves the reality of that merely commercial grandeur on which she prides herself. Like every association that arises only from the pecuniary profit of its members, Babylon shall surely break up, and none of those, who sought her for their selfish ends, shall wait to help her one moment after she has ceased to be profitable to them.

Here now are his own words, rendered literally except in the case of one or two conjunctions and articles,--rendered, too, in the original order of the words, and, as far as it can be determined, in the rhythm of the original. The rhythm is largely uncertain, but some verses--1, 5, 14, 15--are complete in that measure which we found in the Taunt-song against the king of Babylon in ch. xiii., [112] and nearly every line or clause has the same metrical swing upon it.

> Down! and sit in the dust, O virgin,
> Daughter of Babel!
> Sit on the ground, with no throne,
> Daughter of Khasdim!
> For not again shall they call thee
> Tender and Dainty.
> Take to thee millstones, and grind out the meal,
> Put back thy veil, strip off the garment,
> Make bare the leg, wade through the rivers;
> Bare be thy nakedness, yea, be beholden thy shame!
> Vengeance I take, and strike treaty with none.
> Our Redeemer! Jehovah of Hosts is His Name,
> Holy of Israel!
> Sit thou dumb, and get into darkness,
> Daughter of Khasdim!
> For not again shall they call thee
> Mistress of Kingdoms.

> I was wroth with My people, profaned Mine inheritance,
> Gave them to thy hand:
> Thou didst show them no mercy, on old men thou madest
> Thy yoke very sore.
> And thou saidst, For ever I shall be mistress,
> Till thou hast set not these things to thy heart,
> Nor thought of their issue.
> Therefore now hear this, Voluptuous,
> Sitting self-confident:
> Thou, who saith in her heart, "I am: there is none else.
> I shall not sit a widow, nor know want of children."
> Surely shall come to thee both of these, sudden, the same day,
> Childlessness, widowhood!
> To their full come upon thee, spite of the mass of thy spells,
> Spite of the wealth of thy charms--to the full!
> And thou wast bold in thine evil; thou saidst,
> "None doth see me."
> Thy wisdom and knowledge--they have led thee astray,
> Till thou hast said in thine heart, "I am: there is none else."
> Yet there shall come on thee Evil,
> Thou know'st not to charm it.
> And there shall fall on thee Havoc,
> Thou canst not avert it.
> And there shall come on thee suddenly,
> Unawares, Ruin.
> Stand forth, I pray, with thy charms, with the wealth of thy spells--
> With which thou hast wearied thyself from thy youth up--
> If so thou be able to profit,
> If so to strike terror!
> Thou art sick with the mass of thy counsels--
> Let them stand up and save thee--
> Mappers of heaven, Planet-observers, Tellers at new moons--
> From what must befall thee!
> Behold, they are grown like the straw!
> Fire hath consumed them;
> Nay, they save not their life
> From the hand of the flame!
> --'Tis no fuel for warmth,
> Fire to sit down at!--
> Thus are they grown to thee, they who did weary thee,
> Traders of thine from thy youth up;
> Each as he could pass have they fled;
> None is thy saviour!

We, who remember Isaiah's elegies on Egypt and Tyre, [113] shall be most struck here by the absence of all appreciation of greatness or of beauty about Babylon. Even while prophesying for Tyre as certain a judgement as our prophet here predicts for Babylon, Isaiah spoke as if the ruin of so much enterprise and wealth were a desecration, and he promised that the native strength of Tyre, humbled and purified, would rise again to become the handmaid of religion. But our prophet sees no saving virtue whatever in Babylon, and gives her not the slightest promise of a future. There is pity through his scorn: the way in which he speaks of the futility of the mass of Babylonian science; the way in which he speaks of her ignorance, though served by hosts of counsellors; the way in which, after recalling her countless partners in traffic, he describes their headlong flight, and closes with the words, None is thy saviour,--all this is most pathetic. But upon none of his lines is there one touch of awe or admiration or regret for the fall of what is great. To him Babylon is wholly false, vain, destitute--as Tyre was not destitute--of native vigour and saving virtue. Babylon is sheer pretence and futility. Therefore his scorn and condemnation are thorough; and mocking laughter breaks from him, now with an almost savage coarseness, as he pictures the dishonour of the virgin who was no virgin--Bare thy nakedness, yea, be beholden thy shame; and now in roguish glee, as he interjects about the fire which shall destroy the mass of Babylon's magicians, astrologers and haruspices: No coal this to warm oneself at, fire to sit down before. But withal we are not allowed to forget, that it is one of the Tyrant's poor captives, who thus judges and scorns her. How vividly from the midst of his satire does the prisoner's sigh break forth to God:--

*"Our Redeemer! Jehovah of Hosts is His Name,
Holy of Israel!"*

Not the least interesting feature of this taunt-song is the expression which it gives to the characteristic Hebrew sense of the wearisomeness and immorality of that system of divination, which formed the mass of the Babylonian and many other Gentile religions. The worship of Jehovah had very much in common with the rest of the Semitic cults. Its ritual, its temple-furniture, the division of its sacred year, its terminology, and even many of its titles for the Deity and His relations to men, may be matched in the worship of Phoenician, Syrian and Babylonian gods, or in the ruder Arabian cults. But in one thing the "law of Jehovah" stands by itself, and that is in its intolerance of all augury and divination. It owed this distinction to the unique moral and practical sense which inspired it. Augury and divination, such as the Chaldeans were most proficient in, exerted two most evil influences. They hampered, sometimes paralysed, the industry and politics of a nation, and they more or less confounded the moral sense of a people. They were, therefore, utterly out of harmony with the practical sanity and Divine morality of the Jewish law, which strenuously forbade them; while the prophets, who were practical men as well as preachers of righteousness, constantly exposed the fatigue they laid upon public life, and the way they distracted attention from the simple moral issues of conduct. Augury and divination wearied a people's intellect, stunted their enterprise, distorted their conscience. Thy spells,--the mass of thy charms, with which thou hast wearied thyself from thy youth. Thou art sick with the mass of thy counsels. Thy wisdom and thy knowledge! they have led thee astray. When "the Chaldean astrology" found its way to the New Babylon, Juvenal's strong conscience expressed the same sense of its wearisomeness and waste of time. [114]

Ashes and ruins, a servile and squalid life, a desolate site abandoned by commerce,--what the prophet predicted, that did imperial Babylon become. Not, indeed, at the hand of Cyrus, or of any other single invader; but gradually by the rivalry of healthier peoples, by the inevitable working of the poison at her heart, Babylon, though situated in the most fertile and central part of God's earth, fell into irredeemable decay. Do not let us, however, choke our interest in this prophecy, as so many students of prophecy do, in the ruins and dust, which were its primary fulfilment. The shell of Babylon, the gorgeous city which rose by Euphrates, has indeed sunk into heaps; but Babylon herself is not dead. Babylon never dies. To the conscience of Christ's seer, this mother of harlots, though dead and desert in the East, came to life again in the West. To the city of Rome, in his day, John transferred word by word the phrases of our prophet and of the prophet who wrote the fifty-first chapter of the Book of Jeremiah. Rome was Babylon, in so far as Romans were filled with cruelty, with arrogance, with trust in riches, with credulity in divination, with that waste of mental and moral power which Juvenal exposed in her. I sit a queen, John heard Rome say in her heart, and am no widow, and shall in no wise see mourning. Therefore in one day shall her plagues come, death and mourning and famine, and she shall be utterly burned with fire, for strong is the Lord God which judged her. [115] But we are not to leave the matter even here: we are to use that freedom with John, which John uses with our prophet. We are to pass by the particular fulfilment of his words, in which he and his day were interested, because it can only have a historical and secondary interest to us in face of other Babylons in our own day, with which our consciences, if they are quick, ought to be busy. Why do some honest people continue to confine the reference of those chapters in the Book of Revelation to the city and church of Rome? It is quite true, that John meant the Rome of his day; it is quite true, that many features of his Babylon may be traced upon the successor of the Roman Empire, the Roman Church. But what is that to us, with incarnations of the Babylonian spirit so much nearer ourselves for infection and danger, than the Church of Rome can ever be. John's description, based upon our prophet's, suits better a commercial, than an ecclesiastical state,--though self-worship has been as rife in ecclesiasticism, Roman or Reformed, as among the votaries of Mammon. For every phrase of John's, that may be true of the Church of Rome in certain ages, there are six apt descriptions of the centres of our own British civilisation, and of the selfish, atheistic tempers that prevail in them. Let us ask what are the Babylonian tempers and let us touch our own consciences with them.

Forgetfulness of God, cruelty, vanity of knowledge (which so easily breeds credulity) and vanity of wealth,--but the parent of them all is idolatry of self. Isaiah told us about this in the Assyrian with his war; we see it here in Babylon with her commerce and her science; it was exposed even in the orthodox Jews, [116] for they put their own prejudices before their God's revelation; and it is perhaps as evident in the Christian Church as anywhere else. For selfishness follows a man like his shadow; and religion, like the sun, the stronger it shines, only makes the shadow more apparent. But to worship your shadow is to turn your back on the sun; selfishness is atheism, says our prophet. Man's self takes God's word about Himself and says, I am, and there is none beside me. And he, who forgets God, is sure also to forget his brother; thus self-worship leads to cruelty. A heavy part of the charge against Babylon is her treatment of the Lord's own people. These were God's convicts, and she, for the time, God's minister of justice. But she unnecessarily and cruelly oppressed them. On the aged thou hast very heavily laid thy yoke. God's people were given to her to be reformed, but she sought to crush the life out of them. God's purpose was upon them, but she used them for her aggrandisement. She did not feel that she was responsible to God for her treatment even of the most guilty and contemptible of her subjects.

In all this Babylon acted in accordance with what was the prevailing spirit of antiquity; and here we may safely affirm that our Christian civilisation has at least a superior conscience. The modern world does recognise, in some measure, its responsibility to God for the care even of its vilest and most forfeit lives. No Christian state at the present day would, for instance, allow its felons to be tortured or outraged against their will in the interests either of science or of public amusement. We do not vivisect our murderers nor kill them off by gladiatorial combats. Our statutes do not get rid of worthless or forfeit lives by condemning them to be used up in dangerous labours of public necessity. On the contrary, in prisons we treat our criminals with decency and even with comfort, and outside prisons we protect and cherish even the most tainted and guilty lives. In all our discharge of God's justice, we take care that the inevitable errors of our human fallibility may fall on mercy's side. Now it is true that in the practice of all this we often fail, and are inconsistent. The point at present is that we have at least a conscience about the matter. We do not say, like Babylon, "I am, and there is none beside me. There is no law higher than my own will and desire. I can, therefore, use whatever through its crime or its uselessness falls into my power, for the increase of my wealth or the satisfaction of my passions." We remember God, and that even the criminal and the useless are His. In wielding the power which His Law and Providence put into our hands towards many of His creatures, we remember that we are administering His justice, and not satisfying our own revenge, or feeding our own desire for sensation, or experimenting for the sake of our science. They are His convicts, not our spoil. In our treatment of them we are subject to His laws,--one of which, that fences even His justice, is the law against cruelty; and another, for which His justice leaves room, is that to every man there be granted, with his due penalty, the opportunity of penitence and reform. There are among us Positivists, who deny that these opinions and practices of modern civilisation are correct. Carrying out the essential atheism of their school--I am man, and there is none else: that in the discharge of justice and the discharge of charity men are responsible only to themselves--they dare to recommend that the victims of justice should be made the experiments, however painful, of science, and that charity should be refused to the corrupt and the useless. But all this is simply reversion to the Babylonian type, and the Babylonian type is doomed to decay. For history has writ no surer law upon itself than this--that cruelty is the infallible precursor of ruin.

But while speaking of the state, we should remember individual responsibilities as well. Success, even where it is the righteous success of character, is a most subtle breeder of cruelty. The best of us need most strongly to guard ourselves against censoriousness. If God does put the characters of sinful men and women into our keeping, let us remember that our right of judging them, our right of punishing them, our right even of talking about them, is strictly limited. Religious people too easily forget this, and their cruel censoriousness or selfish gossip warns us that to be a member of the Church of Christ does not always mean that a man's citizenship is in heaven; he may well be a Babylonian and carry the freedom of that city upon his face. To "be hard on those who are down" is Babylonian; to make material out of our neighbours' faults, for our pride, or for love of gossip, or for prurience, is Babylonian. There is one very good practical rule to keep us safe. We may allow ourselves to speak about our erring brothers to men, just as much as we pray for them to God. But if we pray much for a man, he will surely become too sacred to be made the amusement of society or the food of our curiosity or of our pride.

The last curse on Babylon reminds us of the fatal looseness of a society that is built only upon the interests of trade; of the loneliness and uselessness that await, in the end, all lives, which keep themselves alive simply by trafficking with men. If we feed life only by the news of the markets, by the interest of traffic, by the excitement of competition, by the fever of speculation, by the passions of cupidity and pride, we may feel healthy and powerful for a time. But such a life, which is merely a being kept brisk by the sense of gaining something or overreaching some one, is the mere semblance of living; and when the inevitable end comes, when they that have trafficked with us from our youth depart, then each particle of strength with which they fed us shall be withdrawn, and we shall fall into decay. There never was a truer picture of the quick ruin of a merely commercial community, or of the ultimate loneliness of a mercenary and selfish life, than the headlong rush of traders, each as he could find passage, from the city that never had other attractions even for her own citizens than those of gain or of pleasure.

Footnotes:

108. Cf. Doughty, Arabia Deserta.

109. The Turanians, who occupied Mesopotamia before the Semitic invasion, were the first builders of cities.

110. Babylon, as far as we can learn, first rose to power about the time of that Amraphel who fought in the Mesopotamian league against the neighbours and friends of Abraham. Amraphel is supposed to have been the father of Hammurabis, who first made Babylon the capital of Chaldea. It scarcely ever again ceased to be such; but it was not till the fall of Assyria, about 625 b.c., and the rebuilding of Babylon by Nebuchadrezzar (604-561), that the city's second and greatest glory began.

111. See ch. iv., pp. ^{24}53-^{25}56.

112. Vol. i., pp. 409-315.

113. Vol. i., pp. 275, 286, 294.

114. See especially Satires III. and VI., and cf. Bagehot's Physics and Politics.

115. Rev. xvii., xviii.

116. Ch. xlv.

CHAPTER XIII

THE CALL TO GO FORTH.

Isaiah xlviii.

On the substance of ch. xlviii. we have already encroached, and now it is necessary only to summarise its argument, and to give some attention to the call to go forth from Babylon, with which it concludes.

Chapter xlviii. is addressed, as its first verse declares, to the exiles from Judah [117] : Hear this, Oh House of Jacob, that call yourselves by the name of Israel, and from the waters of Judah have come forth: that is, you so-called Israelites, who spring from Judah. But their worship of Jehovah is only nominal and unreal: They who swear by the name of Jehovah, and celebrate the God of Israel, not in truth and not in righteousness; although by the Holy City they name themselves, and upon the God of Israel they lean--Jehovah of Hosts is His Name!

The former things I published long ago; [118] from My mouth they went forth, and I let them be heard--suddenly I did them, and they came to pass. Because I knew how hard thou wert, and a sinew of iron thy neck, and thy brow brass. And I published to thee long ago; before it came to pass I let thee hear it, lest thou shouldest say: Mine idol hath wrought them, and my Image and my Casting hath commanded them. Thou didst hear it: look at it whole,--now that it is fulfilled,--and you! should ye not publish it? All the past lies as a unity, prediction and fulfilment together complete; all of it the doing of Jehovah, and surely enough of it to provide the text of confession of Him by His people. But now,--

I let thee hear new things--in contrast with the former things--from now, and hidden things, and thou knewest them not. Now are they created, and not long ago; and before to-day thou hadst not heard them, lest thou shouldest say, Behold I knew them. Verily, [119] thou hadst not heard, verily, thou hadst not known, verily, long since thine ear was not open; because I knew thou art thoroughly treacherous, and Transgressor-from-the-womb do they call thee.

The meaning of all this is sufficiently clear. It is a reproach addressed to the formal Israelites. It divides into two parts, each containing an explanation Because I knew that, etc.: vv. 3-6a, and vv. 6b-9. In the first part Jehovah treats of history already finished, both in its prediction and fulfilment. Many of the wonderful things of old Jehovah predicted long before they happened, and so left His stubborn people no excuse for an idolatry to which otherwise they would have given themselves (ver. 5). Now that they see that wonderful past complete, and all the predictions fulfilled, they may well publish Jehovah's renown to the world. In the first part of His reproach, then, Jehovah is dealing with stages of Israel's history that were closed before the Exile. The former things are wonderful events, foretold and come to pass before the present generation. But in the second part of His reproach (vv. 6b-9) Jehovah mentions new things. These new things are being created while His prophet speaks, and they have not been foretold (in contradistinction to the former things of ver. 3). What events fulfil these two conditions? Well, Cyrus was on his way, the destruction of Babylon was imminent, Israel's new destiny was beginning to shape itself under God's hands: these are evidently the things that are in process of creation while the prophet speaks. But could it also be said of them, that they had not been foretold? This could be said, at least, of Cyrus, the Gentile Messiah. A Gentile Messiah was something so new to Israel, that many, clinging to the letter of the old prophecies, denied, as we have seen, that Cyrus could possibly be God's instrument for the redemption of Israel. Cyrus, then, as a Gentile, and at the same time the Anointed of Jehovah, is the new thing which is being created while the prophet speaks, and which has not been announced beforehand.

How is it possible, some may now ask, that Cyrus should be one of the unpredicted new things that are happening while the prophet speaks, when the prophet has already pointed to Cyrus and his advance on Babylon as a fulfilment of ancient predictions? The answer to this question is very simple. There were ancient predictions of a deliverance and a deliverer from Babylon. To name no more, there were Jeremiah's [120] and Habakkuk's; and Cyrus, in so far as he accomplished the deliverance, was the fulfilment of these ancient r'ishonôth. But in so far as Cyrus sprang from a quarter of the world, not hinted at in former prophecies of Jehovah--in so far as he was a Gentile and yet the Anointed of the Lord, a combination not provided for by any tradition in Israel--Cyrus and his career were the new things not predicted beforehand, the new things which caused such offence to certain tradition-bound parties in Israel.

Rev. George Adam Smith, M.A.

We cannot overestimate the importance of this passage. It supplies us with the solution of the problem, how the presently-happening deliverance of Israel from Babylon could be both a thing foretold from long ago, and yet so new as to surprise those Israelites who were most devoted to the ancient prophecies. And at the same time such of us as are content to follow our prophet's own evidence, and to place him in the Exile, have an answer put into our mouths, to render to those, who say that we destroy a proof of the Divinity of prophecy by denying to Isaiah or to any other prophet, so long before Cyrus was born, the mention of Cyrus by name. Let such objectors, who imagine that they are more careful of the honour of God and of the Divinity of Scripture, because they maintain that Cyrus was named two hundred years before he was born, look at verse 7. There God Himself says, that there are some things, which, for a very good reason, He does not foretell before they come to pass. We believe, and have shown strong grounds for believing, that the selection of Cyrus, the mention of his name, and the furtherance of his arms against Babylon, were among those new things, which God says He purposely did not reveal till the day of their happening, and which, by their novel and unpredicted character, offended so many of the traditional and stupid party in Israel. Must there always be among God's people, to-day as in the day of our prophet, some who cannot conceive a thing to be Divine unless it has been predicted long before?

In vv. 3-8, then, God claims to have changed His treatment of His people, in order to meet and to prevent the various faults of their character. Some things He told to them, long before, so that they might not attribute the occurrence of these to their idols. But other things He sprang upon them, without predictions, and in an altogether novel shape, so that they might not say of these things, in their familiarity with them, We knew of them ourselves. A people who were at one time so stubborn, and at another so slippery, were evidently a people who deserved nothing at God's hand. Yet He goes on to say, vv. 9-11, that He will treat them with forbearance, if not for their sake, yet for His own: For the sake of My Name I defer Mine anger, and for My praise--or renown, or reputation, as we would say of a man--I will refrain for thee, that I cut thee not off. Behold I have smelted thee, but not as silver: I have tested thee in the furnace of affliction. For Mine own sake, for Mine own sake, I am working;--for how was My Name being profaned! [121] --and My glory to another I will not give.

Then he gathers up the sum of what He has been saying in a final appeal.

Hearken unto Me, O Jacob, and Israel My Called: I am He; I am First, yea, I am Last. Yea, My hand hath founded Earth, [122] and My right hand hath spread Heaven; when I call unto them they stand together.

Be gathered, all of you, and hearken, Who among them--that is, the Gentiles--hath published these things?--that is, such things as the following, the prophecy given in the next clause of the verse: Whom Jehovah loveth shall perform His pleasure on Babylon, and his arm shall be on the Chaldeans. This was the sum of what Jehovah promised long ago; [123] not Cyrus' name, not that a Gentile, a Persian, should deliver God's people, for these are among the new things which were not published beforehand, at which the traditional Israelites were offended,--but this general fiat of God's sovereignty, that whomever Jehovah loves, or likes, he shall perform His pleasure on Babylon. I, even I, have spoken--this, in ver. 14b, was My speaking. Yea, I have called him; I have brought him, and he will make his way to prosper. Again emphasize the change of tense. Cyrus is already called, but, while the prophet speaks, he has not yet reached his goal in the capture of Babylon.

Some ambassador from the Lord, whether the prophet or the Servant of Jehovah, now takes up the parable, and, after presenting himself, addresses a final exhortation to Israel, summing up the moral meaning of the Exile. Draw near to me, hear this; not from aforetime in secret have I spoken; from the time that it was, there am I: and now my Lord, Jehovah, hath sent me with His Spirit. [124]

Thus saith Jehovah, thy Redeemer, Holy of Israel, I am Jehovah thy God, thy Teacher to profit, thy Guide in the way thou shouldest go: Would that thou hadst hearkened to My commandments, then were like the River thy peace, and thy righteousness like the waves of the sea! Then were like the sand thy seed, and the offspring of thy bowels like its grains! [125] He shall not be cut off, nor shall perish his name from before Me.

And now at last it is time to be up. Our salvation is nearer than when first we believed. Day has dawned, the gates are opening, the Word has been sufficiently spoken.

Go forth from Babel, fly from the Chaldeans; With a ringing voice publish and let this be heard, Send ye it out to the end of the earth, Say, Redeemed hath Jehovah His Servant Jacob. And they thirsted not in the deserts He caused them to walk; Waters from a rock He let drop for them, Clave a rock and there flowed forth waters! No peace, saith Jehovah, for the wicked.

We have arrived at the most distinct stage of which our prophecy gives trace. Not that a new start is made with the next passage. Ch. xlix. is the answer of the Servant himself to the appeal made to him in xlviii. 20; and ch. xlix. does not introduce the Servant for the first time, but simply carries further the substance of the opening verses of ch. xlii. Nor is this urgent appeal to Go forth from Babylon, which has come to Israel, the only one, or the last, of its kind. It is renewed in ch. lii. 11-12. So that we cannot think that our prophet has even yet got the Fall of Babylon behind him. Nevertheless, the end of ch.

xlviii. is the end of the first and chief stage of the prophecy. The fundamental truths about God and salvation have been laid down; the idols have been thoroughly exposed; Cyrus has been explained; Babylon is practically done with. Neither Babylon, nor Cyrus, nor, except for a moment, the idols, are mentioned in the rest of the prophecy. The Deliverance of Israel is certain. And what now interests the prophet is first, how the Holy Nation will accomplish the destiny for which it has been set free, and next, how the Holy City shall be prepared for the Nation to inhabit. These are the two themes of chs. xlix. to lxvi. The latter of them, the Restoration of Jerusalem, has scarcely been touched by our prophet as yet. But he has already spoken much of the Nation's Destiny as the Servant of the Lord; and now that we have exhausted the subject of the deliverance from Babylon, we will take up his prophecies on the Servant, both those which we have passed over in chs. xl.-xlviii. and those which still lie ahead of us.

Before we do this, however, let us devote a chapter to a study of our prophet's use of the word righteousness, for which this seems to be as convenient a place as any other.

Footnotes:

117. Bredenkamp will have it, that the prophet here mentions first Northern Israel and then Judah: O House of Jacob, the general term, both those that are called by the name of Israel, and that have come forth from the waters of Judah. But this is entirely opposed to the syntax, and I note the opinion simply to show how precarious the arguments are for the existence of pre-exilic elements in Isa. xl.-xlviii. The point, which Bredenkamp makes by his rendering of this verse, is that it could only be a pre-exilic prophet, who would distinguish between Judah and Northern Israel; and that, therefore, it might be Isaiah himself who wrote the verse!

118. Former things (ri'shonôth). It is impossible to determine whether these mean predictions which Jehovah published long ago, and which have already come to pass, or former events which He foretold long ago, and which have happened as He said they would. The distinction, however, is immaterial.

119. Literally, also. But nm, a cumulative conjunction, when it is introduced to repeat the same thought as preceded it, means yea, truly, profecto, imo.

120. Ch. xxv., which is undoubtedly an authentic prophecy of Jeremiah.

121. The Hebrew has not the words My Name. The LXX. has them.

122. A second time without article though applied to the whole world.

123. Giesebrecht takes this as an actual quotation from some former prophet: a specimen of the ancient prophecies which Jehovah sent to Israel, and which were now being fulfilled. At least it is the sum of what Jehovah's prophets had often predicted.

124. This very difficult verse has been attributed either to Jehovah in the first three clauses and to the Servant in the fourth (Delitzsch); or in the same proportion to Jehovah and the prophet (Cheyne and Bredenkamp); or to the Servant all through (Orelli); or to the prophet all through (Hitzig, Knobel, Giesebrecht. See the latter's Beiträge zur Kritik Jesaia's, p. 136). It is a subtle matter. The present expositor thinks it clear that all four clauses must be understood as the voice of one speaker, but sees nothing in them to decide finally whether that speaker is the Servant, the people Israel, in which case I am there would have reference to Israel's consciousness of every deed done by God since the beginning of their history (cf. ver. 6a); or whether the speaker is the prophet, in which case I am there would mean that he had watched the rise of Cyrus from the first. But cf. Zech. ii. 10-11, Eng. Ver., and iv. 9.

125. Or like its bowels, referring to the sea.

Rev. George Adam Smith, M.A.

CHAPTER XIV

THE RIGHTEOUSNESS OF ISRAEL AND THE RIGHTEOUSNESS OF GOD.

Isaiah xl.-lxvi.

In the chapters which we have been studying we have found some difficulty with one of our prophet's keynotes--right or righteousness. In the chapters to come we shall find this difficulty increase, unless we take some trouble now to define how much the word denotes in Isa. xl.-lxvi. There is no part of Scripture, in which the term righteousness suffers so many developments of meaning. To leave these vague, as readers usually do, or to fasten upon one and all the technical meaning of righteousness in Christian theology, is not only to obscure the historical reference and moral force of single passages,--it is to miss one of the main arguments of the prophecy. We have read enough to see that righteousness was the great question of the Exile. But what was brought into question was not only the righteousness of the people, but the righteousness of their God. In Isa. xl.-lxvi. righteousness is more often claimed as a Divine attribute, than enforced as a human duty or ideal. [126]

I. Righteousness.

Ssedheq, the Hebrew root for righteousness, had, like the Latin "rectus," in its earliest and now almost forgotten uses, a physical meaning. This may have been either straightness, or more probably soundness,--the state in which a thing is all right. [127] Paths of righteousness, in Psalm xxiii., ver. 4, are not necessarily straight paths, but rather sure, genuine, safe paths. [128] Like all physical metaphors, like our own words "straight" and "right," the applicability of the term to moral conduct was exceedingly elastic. It has been attempted to gather most of its meaning under the definition of conformity to norm; [129] and so many are the instances in which the word has a forensic force, [130] as of vindication or justification, that some have claimed this for its original, or, at least, its governing sense. But it is improbable that either of these definitions conveys the simplest or most general sense of the word. Even if conformity or justification were ever the prevailing sense of ssedheq, there are a number of instances in which its meaning far overflows the limits of such definitions. Every one can see how a word, which may generally be used to express an abstract idea, like conformity, or a formal relation towards a law or person, like justification, might come to be applied to the actual virtues, which realise that idea or lift a character into that relation. Thus righteousness might mean justice, or truth, or almsgiving, or religious obedience,--to each of which, in fact, the Hebrew word was at various times specially applied. Or righteousness might mean virtue in general, virtue apart from all consideration of law or duty whatsoever. In the prophet Amos, for instance, righteousness is applied to a goodness so natural and spontaneous that no one could think of it for a moment as conformity to norm or fulfilment of law. [131]

In short, it is impossible to give a definition of the Hebrew word, which our version renders as righteousness, less wide than our English word right. Righteousness is right in all its senses,--natural, legal, personal, religious. It is to be all right, to be right-hearted, to be consistent, to be thorough; but also to be in the right, to be justified, to be vindicated; and, in particular, it may mean to be humane (as with Amos), to be just (as with Isaiah), to be correct or true to fact (as sometimes with our own prophet), to fulfil the ordinances of religion, and especially the command about almsgiving (as with the later Jews).

Let us now keep in mind that righteousness could express a relation, or a general quality of character, or some particular virtue. For we shall find traces of all these meanings in our prophet's application of the term to Israel and to God.

II. The Righteousness of Israel.

One of the simplest forms of the use of righteousness in the Old Testament is when it is employed in the case of ordinary quarrels between two persons; in which for one of them to be righteous means to be right or in the right. [132] Now to the Hebrew all life and religion was based upon covenants between two,--between man and man and between man and God. Righteousness meant fidelity to the terms of those covenants. The positive contents of the word in any single instance of its use would, therefore, depend on the faithfulness and delicacy of conscience by which those terms were interpreted. In early Israel this conscience was not so keen as it afterwards came to be, and accordingly Israel's sense of their righteousness towards God was, to begin with, a comparatively shallow one. When a Psalmist asseverates his righteousness and pleads it as the ground for God rewarding him, it is plain that he is able with sincerity to make a claim, so repellent to a Christian's feeling, just because he has not anything like a Christian's conscience of what God demands from man. As Calvin says on Psalm xviii., ver. 20, "David here represents God as the President of an athletic contest, who had chosen him as one of His champions, and David knows that so long as he keeps to the rules of the contest, so long will God defend him." It is evident that in such an assertion righteousness cannot mean perfect innocence, but simply the good conscience of a man, who, with simple ideas of what is demanded from him, feels that on the whole "he has" (slightly to paraphrase Calvin) "played fair."

Two things, almost simultaneously, shook Israel out of this primitive and naïve self-righteousness. History went against them, and the prophets quickened their conscience. [133] The effect of the former of these two causes will be clear to us, if we recollect the judicial element in the Hebrew righteousness,--that it often meant not so much to be right, as to be vindicated or declared right. History, to Israel, was God's supreme tribunal. It was the faith of the people, expressed over and over again in the Old Testament, that the godly man is vindicated or justified by his prosperity: the way of the ungodly shall perish. And Israel felt themselves to be in the right, just as David, in Psalm xviii., felt himself, because God had accredited them with success and victory. But when the decision of history went against the nation, when they were threatened with expulsion from their land and with extinction as a people, that just meant that the Supreme Judge of men was giving His sentence against them. Israel had broken the terms of the Covenant. They had lost their right; they were no longer righteous. The keener conscience, developed by prophecy, swiftly explained this sentence of history. This declaration, that the people were unrighteous, was due, the prophet said, to the people's sins. Isaiah not only exclaimed, Your country is desolate, your cities are burned with fire; he added, in equal indictment, How is the faithful city become an harlot! it was full of justice, righteousness lodged in it, but now murderers: thy princes are rebellious, they judge not the fatherless, neither doth the cause of the widow come before them. To Isaiah and the earlier prophets Israel was unrighteous because it was so immoral. With their strong social conscience, righteousness meant to these prophets the practice of civic virtues,--truth-telling, honesty between citizens, tenderness to the poor, inflexible justice in high places.

Here then we have two possible meanings for Israel's righteousness in the prophetic writings, allied and necessary to one another, yet logically distinct,--the one becoming righteous through the exercise of virtue, the other a being shown to be righteous by the voice of history. In the one case righteousness is the practical result of the working of the Spirit of God; in the other it is vindication, or justification, by the Providence of God. Isaiah and the earlier prophets, while the sentence of history was still not executed and might through the mercy of God be revoked, incline to employ righteousness predominantly in the former sense. But it will be understood how, after the Exile, it was the latter, which became the prevailing determination of the word. By that great disaster God finally uttered the clear sentence, of which previous history had been but the foreboding. Israel in exile was fully declared to be in the wrong--to be unrighteous. As a church, she lay under the ban; as a nation, she was discredited before the nations of the world. And her one longing, hope and effort during the weary years of Captivity was to have her right vindicated again, was to be restored to right relations to God and to the world, under the Covenant.

This is the predominant meaning of the term, as applied to Israel, in Isa. xl.-lxvi. Israel's unrighteousness is her state of discredit and disgrace under the hands of God; her righteousness, which she hopes for, is her restoral to her station and destiny as the elect people. To our Christian habit of thinking, it is very natural to read the frequent and splendid phrases, in which righteousness is attributed or promised to the people of God in this evangelical prophecy, as if righteousness were that inward assurance and justification from an evil conscience, which, as we are taught by the New Testament, is provided for us through the death of Christ, and inwardly sealed to us by the Holy Ghost, irrespective of the course of our outward fortune. But if we read that meaning into righteousness in Isa. xl.-lxvi., we shall simply not understand some of the grandest passages of the prophecy. We must clearly keep in view, that while the prophet ceaselessly emphasizes the pardon of God spoken home to the heart of the people, as the first step towards their restoral, he does not apply the term righteousness to this inward justification, [134] but to the outward vindication and accrediting of Israel by God before the whole world, in their redemption from Captivity, and their reinstatement as His people. This is very clear from the way in which righteousness is coupled with salvation by the prophet, as (lxii. 1): I will not rest till her righteousness go forth as brightness, and her salvation as a lamp that burneth. Or again from the way in which righteousness and glory are put in parallel (lxii. 2): And the nations shall see thy righteousness, and all kings thy glory. Or again in the way that righteousness and renown are identified (lxi. 11): The Lord Jehovah will cause righteousness and renown to spring forth before all the nations. In each of these promises the idea of an external and manifest splendour is evident; not the inward peace of justification felt only by the conscience to which it has been granted, but the outward historical victory appreciable by the gross sense of the heathen. Of course the outward implies the inward,--this historical triumph is the crown of a religious process, the result of forgiveness and a long purification,--but while in the New Testament it is these which would be most readily called a people's righteousness, it is the former (what the New Testament would rather call the crown of life), which has appropriated the name in Isa. xl.-lxvi. The same is manifest from another text (xlviii. 18): O that thou hadst hearkened to My commandments; then had thy peace been as the River, and thy righteousness like the waves of the sea. Here righteousness is not only not applied to inward morality, but set over against this as its external reward,--the health and splendour which a good conscience produces. It is in the same external sense that the prophet talks of the robe of righteousness with its bridal splendour, and compares it to the appearance of Spring (lxi. 10-11).

For this kind of righteousness, this vindication by God before the world, Israel waited throughout the Exile. God addresses them as they that pursue righteousness, that seek Jehovah (li. 1). And it is a closely allied meaning, though perhaps with a more inward application, when the people are represented as praying God to give them ordinances of righteousness (lviii. 2),--that is, to prescribe such a ritual as will expiate their guilt and bring them into a right relation with Him. They sought in vain. The great lesson of the Exile was that not by works and performances, but through simply waiting upon the Lord, their righteousness should shine forth. Even this outward kind of justification was to be by faith.

The other meaning of righteousness, however,--the sense of social and civic morality, which was its usual sense with the earlier prophets,--is not altogether excluded from the use of the word in Isa. xl.-lxvi. Here are some commands and reproaches which seem to imply it. Keep judgement, and do righteousness,--where, from what follows, righteousness evidently means observing the Sabbath and doing no evil (lvi. 1 ff). And justice is fallen away backward, and righteousness standeth afar off, for truth is fallen in the street, and steadfastness cannot enter (lix. 14). These must be terms for human virtues, for shortly afterwards it is said: Jehovah was displeased because there was no justice. Again, They seek Me as a nation that did righteousness (lviii. 2); Hearken unto Me, ye that know righteousness, a people--My law is in their hearts (li. 7); Thou meetest him that worketh righteousness (lxiv. 5); No one sues in righteousness, and none goeth to law in truth (lix. 4). In all these passages righteousness means something that man can know and do, his conscience and his duty, and is rightly to be distinguished from those others, in which righteousness is equivalent to the salvation, the glory, the peace, which only God's power can bring. If the passages, that employ righteousness in the sense of moral or religious observance, really date from the Exile, then the interesting fact is assured to us that the Jews enjoyed some degree of social independence and responsibility during their Captivity. But it is a very striking fact that these passages all belong to chapters, the exilic origin of which is questioned even by critics, who assign the rest of Isa. xl.-lxvi. to the Exile. Yet, even if these passages have all to be assigned to the Exile, how few they are in number! How they contrast with the frequency, with which, in the earlier part of this book,--in the orations addressed by Isaiah to his own times, when Israel was still an independent state,--righteousness is reiterated as the daily, practical duty of men, as justice, truthfulness and charity between man and man! The extreme rarity of such inculcations in Isa. xl.-lxvi. warns us that we must not expect to find here the same practical and political interest, which formed so much of the charm and the force of Isa. i.-xxxix. The nation has now no politics, almost no social morals. Israel are not citizens working out their own salvation in the market, the camp and the senate; but captives waiting a deliverance in God's time, which no act of theirs can hasten. It is not in the street that the interest of Second Isaiah lies: it is on the horizon. Hence the vague feeling of a distant splendour, which, as the reader passes from ch. xxxix. to ch. xl., replaces in his mind the stir of living in a busy crowd, the close and throbbing sense of the civic conscience, the voice of statesmen, the clash of the weapons of war. There is no opportunity for individuals to reveal themselves. It is a nation waiting, indistinguishable in shadow, whose outlines only we see. It is no longer the thrilling practical cry, which sends men into the arenas of social life with every sinew in them strung: Learn to do well; seek justice, relieve the oppressed, judge the fatherless, plead for the widow. It is rather the cry of one who still waits for his working day to dawn: I will lift up mine eyes to the hills, from whence cometh my help? Righteousness is not the near and daily duty, it is the far-off peace and splendour of skies, that have scarce begun to redden to the day.

III. The Righteousness of God.

But there was another Person, whose righteousness was in question during the Exile, and who Himself argues for it throughout our prophecy. Perhaps the most peculiar feature of the theology of Isa. xl.-lxvi. is its argument for the righteousness of Jehovah.

Some critics maintain that righteousness, when applied to Jehovah, bears always a technical reference to His covenant with Israel. This is scarcely correct. Jehovah's dealings with Israel were no doubt the chief of His dealings, and it is these, which He mainly quotes to illustrate His righteousness; but we have already studied passages, which prove to us that Jehovah's righteousness was an absolute quality of His Godhead, shown to others besides Israel, and in loyalty to obligations different from the terms of His covenant with Israel. In ch. xli. Jehovah calls upon the heathen to match their righteousness with His; righteousness was therefore a quality that might have been attributed to them as well as to Himself. Again, in xlv. 19,--I, Jehovah, speak righteousness, I declare things that are right,-- righteousness evidently bears a general sense, and not one of exclusive application to God's dealing with Israel. It is the same in the passage about Cyrus (xlv. 13): I have raised him up in righteousness, I will make straight all his ways. Though Cyrus was called in connection with God's purpose towards Israel, it is not that purpose which makes his calling righteous, but the fact that God means to carry him through, or, as the parallel verse says, to make straight all his ways. These instances are sufficient to prove that the righteousness, which God attributes to His words, to His actions and to Himself, is a general quality not confined to His dealings with Israel under the covenant,--though, of course, most clearly illustrated by these.

If now we enquire, what this absolute quality of Jehovah's Deity really means, we may conveniently begin with His application of it to His Word. In ch. xli. He summons the other religions to exhibit predictions that are true to fact. Who hath declared it on-ahead that we may know, or from aforetime that we may say, He is ssaddîq. [135] Here ssaddîq simply means right, correct, true to fact. It is much the same meaning in xliii. 9, where the verb is used of heathen predicters, that they may be shown to be right, or correct (English version, justified). But when, in ch. xlvi., the word is applied by Jehovah to His own speech, it has a meaning, of far richer contents, than mere correctness, and proves to us that after all the Hebrew ssedheq was almost as versatile as the English "right." The following passage shows us that the righteousness of Jehovah's speech is its clearness, straightforwardness and practical effectiveness: Not in secret have I spoken, in a place of the land of darkness,--this has been supposed to refer to the remote or subterranean localities in which heathen oracles mysteriously entrenched themselves,--I have not said to the seed of Jacob, In Chaos seek Me. I am Jehovah, a Speaker of righteousness, a Publisher of straight things. Be gathered and come, draw near together, O remnants of the nations. They know not that carry the log of their image, and pray to a god who does not save. Publish and bring near, yea, let them take counsel together. Who caused this to be heard of old? long since hath published it? Is it not I, Jehovah, and there is none else God beside Me; a God righteous and a Saviour, there is none except Me. Turn unto Me and be saved, all ends of Earth, [136] for I am God, and there is none else. By Myself have I sworn, gone forth from My mouth hath righteousness: a word and it shall not turn; for to Me shall bow every knee, shall swear every tongue. Truly in Jehovah, shall they say of Me, are righteousnesses and strength. To Him shall it come, [137] and shamed shall be all that are incensed against Him. In Jehovah shall be righteous and renowned all the seed of Israel (xlv. 19-25).

In this very suggestive passage righteousness means far more than simple correctness of prediction. Indeed, it is difficult to distinguish how much it means, so quickly do its varying echoes throng upon our ear, from the new associations in which it is spoken. A word such as righteousness is like the sensitive tones of the human voice. Spoken in a desert, the voice is itself and nothing more; but utter it where the landscape is crowded with novel obstacles, and the original note is almost lost amid the echoes it startles. So with the righteousness of Jehovah; among the new associations in which the prophet affirms it, it starts novel repetitions of itself. Against the ambiguity of the oracles, it is echoed back as clearness, straightforwardness, good faith (ver. 19); against their opportunism and want of foresight, it is described as equivalent to the capacity for arranging things beforehand and predicting what must come to pass, therefore as purposefulness; while against their futility, it is plainly effectiveness and power to prevail (ver. 23). It is the quality in God, which divides His Godhead with His power, something intellectual as well as moral, the possession of a reasonable purpose as well as fidelity towards it.

This intellectual sense of righteousness, as reasonableness or purposefulness, is clearly illustrated by the way in which the prophet appeals, in order to enforce it, to Jehovah's creation of the world. Thus saith Jehovah, Creator of the heavens--He is the God--Former of the Earth and her Maker, He founded her; not Chaos did He create her, to be dwelt in did He form her (xlv. 18). The word Chaos here is the same as is used in opposition to righteousness in the following verse. The sentence plainly illustrates the truth, that whatever God does, He does not so as to issue in confusion, but with a reasonable purpose and for a practical end. We have here the repetition of that deep, strong note, which Isaiah himself so often sounded to the comfort of men in perplexity or despair, that God is at least reasonable, not working for nothing, nor beginning only to leave off, nor creating in order to destroy. The same God, says our prophet, who formed the earth in order to see it inhabited, must surely be believed to be consistent enough to carry to the end also His spiritual work among men. Our prophet's idea of God's righteousness, therefore, includes the idea of reasonableness; implies rational as well as moral consistency, practical sense as well as good faith; the conscience of a reasonable plan, and, perhaps also, the power to carry it through.

To know that this great and varied meaning belongs to righteousness gives us new insight into those passages, which find in it all the motive and efficiency of the Divine action: It pleased Jehovah for His righteousness' sake (xlii. 21); His righteousness, it upheld Him; and He put on righteousness as a breastplate (lix. 16, 17).

With such a righteousness did Jehovah deal with Israel. To her despair that He has forgotten her He recounts the historical events by which He has made her His own, and affirms that He will carry them on; and you feel the expression both of fidelity and of the consciousness of ability to fulfil, in the words, I will uphold thee with the right hand of My righteousness. Right hand--there is more than the touch of fidelity in this; there is the grasp of power. Again, to the Israel who was conscious of being His Servant, God says, I, Jehovah, have called thee in righteousness; and, taken with the context, the word plainly means good faith and intention to sustain and carry to success.

It was easy to transfer the name righteousness from the character of God's action to its results, but always, of course, in the vindication of His purpose and word. Therefore, just as the salvation of Israel, which was the chief result of the Divine purpose, is called Israel's righteousness, so it is also called Jehovah's righteousness. Thus, in xlvi. 13, I bring near My righteousness; and in li. 5, My righteousness is near, My salvation is gone forth; ver. 6, My salvation shall be for ever, and My righteousness shall not be abolished. It seems to be in the same sense, of finished and visible results, that the skies are called upon to pour down righteousness, and the earth to open that they may be fruitful in salvation, and let her cause righteousness to spring up together (xlv. 8; cf. lxi. 10, My Lord Jehovah will cause righteousness to spring forth).

One passage is of great interest, because in it righteousness is used to play upon itself, in its two meanings of human duty and Divine effect--lvi. 1, Observe judgement--probably religious ordinances-- and do righteousness; for My salvation is near to come, and My righteousness to be revealed.

***

To complete our study of righteousness it is necessary to touch still upon one point. In Isa. xl.-lxvi. both the masculine and feminine forms of the Hebrew word for righteousness are used, and it has been averred that they are used with a difference. This opinion is entirely dispelled by a collation of the passages. I give the particulars in a note, from which it will be seen that both forms are indifferently employed for each of the many shades of meaning which righteousness bears in our prophecies. [138]

That the masculine and feminine forms sometimes occur, with the same or with different meanings, in the same verse, or in the next verse to one another, proves that the selection of them respectively cannot be due to any difference in the authorship of our prophecy. So that we are reduced to say that nothing accounts for their use, except, it might be, the exigencies of the metre. But who is able to prove this?

Footnotes:

126. It is only by confining his review of the word to its applications to God, and overlooking the passages which attribute it to the people, that Krüger, Essai sur la Théologie d'Isaïe xl.-lxvi., can affirm that the prophet holds throughout to a single idea of righteousness (p. 36). On this, as on many other points, it is Calvin's treatment, that is most sympathetic to the variations of the original.

127. In Arabic the cognate word is applied to a lance, but this may mean a sound or fit lance as well as a straight one. "Originem Schult. de defect. hodiernis § 214-224 ponit in rigore, duritia, coll. arabic lancea dura, al. aequabilis" (Gesenii Thesaurus, art. tsdq).

128. It is not certain whether righteousness is here used in a physical sense; and in all other cases in which the root is applied in the Old Testament to material objects, it is plainly employed in some reflection of its moral sense, e.g., just weights, just balance, Lev. xix. 36.

129. "Der Zustand welcher der Norm entspricht." Schultz, Alt. Test. Theologie, 4th ed., p. 540, n. 1.

130. Cf. Robertson Smith, Prophets of Israel, p. 388, and Kautzsch's paper, which is there quoted.

131. "Die Begriffe tsdqh und tsdq ... bedeuten nun wirklich bei Amos mehr als die juristische Gerechtigkeit. Indirect gehen die Forderungen des Amos über die blos rechtliche Sphäre hinaus" (Duhm, Theologie der Propheten, p. 115).

132. Gen. xxxviii. 26. Cf. 2 Sam. xv. 4.

133. The first chapter of Isaiah is a perfect summary of these two.

134. But the verb to make righteous or justify is used in a sense akin to the New Testament sense in liii. 11. See our chapter on that prophecy.

135. At first sight this is remarkably like the cognate Arabic root, which is continually used for truthful. But the Hebrew word never meant truthful in the moral sense of truth, and here is right or correct.

136. Earth again without article, though obviously referring to the world.

137. Sense doubtful here. Bredenkamp translates by a slight change of reading: Only speaking by Jehovah: Fulness of righteousness and might come to Him, and ashamed, etc.

138. tsdq, the masculine, is used sixteen times; tsdqh, twenty-four. Both are used of Jehovah: xlii.

21 tsdqv, and lix. 16 tsdqtv. Both of His speech: masc. in xlv. 19, fem. in xlv. 23 and lxiii. 1. Perhaps the passage in which their identity is most plain is li. 5, 6, where they are both parallel to salvation: ver. 5, My righteousness (m.) is near; ver. 6, My righteousness (f.) shall not be abolished. Both are used of the people's duty: lix. 4, None sueth in righteousness (m.); xlviii. 1, But not in truth nor in righteousness (f.); lvi. 1, Keep justice and do righteousness (f.) And both are used of the people's saved and glorious condition: lviii. 8, Thy righteousness (m.) shall go before thee; lxii. 1, Until her righteousness (m.) go forth as brightness; xlviii. 18, Thy righteousness (f.) as the waves of the sea; liv. 17, Their righteousness (f.) which is of Me. Both are used with prepositions (cf. xlii. 6 with xlviii. 1), and both with possessive pronouns. In fact, there is absolutely no difference made between the two.

Rev. George Adam Smith, M.A.

BOOK III

THE SERVANT OF THE LORD.

Having completed our survey of the fundamental truths of our prophecy, and studied the subject which forms its immediate and most urgent interest, the deliverance of Israel from Babylon, we are now at liberty to turn to consider the great duty and destiny which lie before the delivered people--the Service of Jehovah. The passages of our prophecy which describe this are scattered both among those chapters we have already studied and among those which lie before us. But, as was explained in the Introduction, they are all easily detached from their surroundings; and the continuity and progress, of which their series, though so much interrupted, gives evidence, demand that they should be treated by us together. They will, therefore, form the Third of the Books, into which this volume is divided.

The passages on the Servant of Jehovah, or, as the English reader is more accustomed to hear him called, the Servant of the Lord, are as follows: xli. 8 ff; xlii. 1-7, 18-25; xliii. passim, especially 8-10; xliv. 1, 21; xlviii. 20; xlix. 1-9; l. 4-11; lii. 13-liii. The main passages are those in xli., xlii., xliii., xlix., l., and lii.-liii. The others are incidental allusions to Israel as the Servant of the Lord, and do not develop the character of the Servant or the Service.

Upon the questions relevant to the structure of these prophecies--why they have been so scattered, and whether they were originally from the main author of Isa. xl.-lxvi., or from any other single writer,--questions on which critics have either preserved a discreet silence, or have spoken to convince nobody but themselves,--I have no final opinions to offer. It may be that these passages formed a poem by themselves before their incorporation with our prophecy; but the evidence, which has been offered for this, is very far from adequate. It may be that one or more of them are insertions from other authors, to which our prophet consciously works up with ideas of his own about the Servant; but neither for this is there any evidence worth serious consideration. I think that all we can do is to remember that they occur in a dramatic work, which may, partly at least, account for the interruptions which separate them; that the subject of which they treat is woven through and through other portions of Isa. xl.-liii., and that even those of them which, like ch. xlix., look as if they could stand by themselves, are led up to by the verses before them; and that, finally, the series of them exhibits a continuity and furnishes a distinct development of their subject. See pp. [26]313, [27]314, and [28]336 ff.

It is this development which the following exposition seeks to trace. As the prophet starts from the idea of the Servant as being the whole, historical nation Israel, it will be necessary to devote, first of all, a chapter to Israel's peculiar relation to God. This will be ch. xv., "One God, One People." In ch. xvi. we shall trace the development of the idea through the whole series of the passages; and in ch. xvii. we shall give the New Testament interpretation and fulfilment of the Servant. Then will follow an exposition of the contents of the Service and of the ideal it presents to ourselves, first, as it is given in Isa. xlii. 1-9, as the service of God and man, ch. xviii. of this volume; then as it is realised and owned by the Servant himself, as prophet and martyr, Isa. xlix.-l., ch. xix. of this volume; and finally as it culminates in Isa. lii. 13-liii., ch. [29]xx. of this volume.

CHAPTER XV

ONE GOD, ONE PEOPLE.

Isaiah xli. 8-20, xlii.-xliii.

We have been listening to the proclamation of a Monotheism so absolute, that, as we have seen, modern critical philosophy, in surveying the history of religion, can find for it no rival among the faiths of the world. God has been exalted before us, in character so perfect, in dominion so universal, that neither the conscience nor the imagination of man can add to the general scope of the vision. Jesus and His Cross shall lead the world's heart farther into the secrets of God's love; God's Spirit in science shall more richly instruct us in the secrets of His laws. But these shall thereby only increase the contents and illustrate the details of this revelation of our prophet. They shall in no way enlarge its sweep and outline, for it is already as lofty an idea of the unity and sovereignty of God, as the thoughts of man can follow.

Across this pure light of God, however, a phenomenon thrusts itself, which seems for the moment to affect the absoluteness of the vision and to detract from its sublimity. This is the prominence given before God to a single people, Israel. In these chapters the uniqueness of Israel is as much urged upon us as the unity of God. Is He the One God in heaven? they are His only people on earth, His elect, His own, His witnesses to the end of the earth. His guidance of them is matched with His guidance of the stars, as if, like the stars shining against the night, their tribes alone moved to His hand through an otherwise dark and empty space. His revelation to humanity is given through their little language; the restoration of their petty capital, that hill fort in the barren land of Judah, is exhibited as the end of His processes, which sweep down through history and affect the surface of the whole inhabited world. And His very righteousness turns out to be for the most part His faithfulness to His covenant with Israel.

Now to many in our day it has been a great offence to have "the curved nose of the Jew" thus thrust in between their eyes and the pure light of God. They ask, Can the Judge of all the earth have been thus partial to one people? Did God confine His revelation to men to the literature of a small, unpolished tribe? Even most uncritical souls have trouble to understand why salvation is of the Jews.

The chief point to know is that the election of Israel was an election, not to salvation, but to service. To understand this is to get rid of by far the greater part of the difficulty that attaches to the subject. Israel was a means, and not an end; God chose in him a minister, not a favourite. No prophet in Israel failed to say this; but our prophet makes it the burden of his message to the exiles. Ye are My witnesses, My Servant whom I have chosen. Ye are My witnesses, and I am God. I will also give thee for a light to the nations, to be My salvation to the end of the earth (xliii. 10). Numbers of other verses might be quoted to the same effect, that "there is no God but God, and Israel is His prophet." [139] But if the election of Israel is thus an election to service, it is surely in harmony with God's usual method, whether in nature or history. So far from such a specialisation as Israel's being derogatory to the Divine unity, it is but part of that order and division of labour which the Divine unity demands as its consequence throughout the whole range of Being. The universe is diverse. To every man his own work is the proper corollary of God over all, and Israel's prerogative was but the specialisation of Israel's function for God in the world. In choosing Israel to be His mediator with mankind, God did but do for religion what in the exercise of the same practical discipline He did for philosophy, when He dowered Greece with her gifts of subtle thought and speech, or with Rome when He trained her people to become the legislators of mankind. And how else should work succeed but by specialisation,--the secret as it is of fidelity and expertness? Of fidelity--for the constraint of my duty surely lies in this, that it is due from me and no other; of expertness--for he drives best and deepest who drives along one line. In lighting a fire you begin with a kindled faggot; and in lighting a world it was in harmony with all His law, physical and moral, for God to begin with a particular portion of mankind.

The next question is, Why should this particular portion of mankind be a nation, and not a single prophet, or a school of philosophers, or a church universal? The answer is found in the condition of the ancient world. Amid its diversities of language and of racial feeling, a missionary prophet travelling like Paul from people to people is inconceivable; and almost as inconceivable is the kind of Church which Paul founded among various nations, in no other bonds than the consciousness of a common faith. Of all possible combinations of men the nation was the only form, which in the ancient world stood a chance of surviving in the struggle for existence. The nation furnished the necessary shelter and fellowship for personal religion; it gave to the spiritual a habitation upon earth, enlisted in its behalf the

Rev. George Adam Smith, M.A.

force of heredity, and secured the continuity of its traditions. But the service of the nation to religion was not only conservative, it was missionary as well. It was only through a people that a God became visible and accredited to the world. Their history supplied the drama in which He played the hero's part. At a time when it was impossible to spread a religion, by means of literature, or by the example of personal holiness, the achievements of a considerable nation, their progress and prestige, furnished a universally understood language, through which the God could publish to mankind His power and will; and in choosing, therefore, a single nation to reveal Himself by, God was but employing the means best adapted for His purpose. The nation was the unit of religious progress in the ancient world. In the nation God chose as His witness, not only the most solid and permanent, but the most widely intelligible and impressive. [140]

The next question is, Why Israel should have been this singular and indispensable nation? When God selected Israel to serve His purpose, He did so, we are told, of His sovereign grace. But this strong thought, which forms the foundation of our prophet's assurance about his people, does not prevent him from dwelling also on Israel's natural capacity for religious service. This, too, was of God. Over and over again Israel hears Jehovah say: I have created thee, I have formed thee, I have prepared thee. One passage describes the nation's equipment for the office of a prophet; another their discipline for the life of a saint; and every now and then our prophet shows how far back he feels this preparation to have begun, even when the nation, as he puts it, was still in the womb. How easily these well-worn phrases slip over our lips! Yet they are not mere formulas. Modern research has put a new meaning into them, and taught us that Israel's creation, forming, election, polishing, carriage, and defence were processes as real and measurable as any in natural or political history. For instance, when our prophet says that Israel's preparation began from the womb,--I am thy moulder, saith Jehovah, from the womb,--history takes us back to the pre-natal circumstance of the nation, and there exhibits it to us as already being tempered to a religious disposition and propensity. The Hebrews were of the Semitic stock. The womb from which Israel sprang was a race of wandering shepherds, upon the hungry deserts of Arabia, where man's home is the flitting tent, hunger is his discipline for many months of the year, his only arts are those of speech and war, and in the long irremediable starvation there is nothing to do but to be patient and dream. Born in these deserts, the youth of the Semitic race, like the probation of their greatest prophets, was spent in a long fast, which lent their spirit a wonderful ease of detachment from the world and of religious imagination, and tempered their will to long suffering--though it touched their blood, too, with a rancorous heat that breaks out through the prevailing calm of every Semitic literature. [141] They were trained also in the desert's august style of eloquence. He hath made my mouth like a sharp sword; in the shadow of His hand hath He hid me. [142] A "natural prophecy," as it has been called, is found in all the branches of the Semitic stock. No wonder that from this race there came forth the three great universal religions of mankind--that Moses and the prophets, John, Jesus Himself and Paul, and Mohammed were all of the seed of Shem.

This racial disposition the Hebrew carried with him into his calling as a nation. The ancestor, who gave the people the double name by which they are addressed throughout our prophecy, Jacob-Israel, inherited with all his defects the two great marks of the religious temper. Jacob could dream and he could wait. Remember him by the side of the brother, who could so little think of the future, that he was willing to sell its promise for a mess of pottage; who, though God was as near to him as to Jacob, never saw visions or wrestled with angels; who seemed to have no power of growth about him, but carrying the same character, unchanged through the discipline of life, finally transmitted it in stereotype to his posterity;--remember Jacob by the side of such a brother, and you have a great part of the secret of the emergence of his descendants from the life of wandering cattle-breeders to be God's chief ministers of religion in the world. Their habits, like their father's, might be bad, but they had the tough and malleable constitution, which it was possible to mould to something better. Like their father, they were false, unchivalrous, selfish, "with the herdsman's grossness in their blood," and much of the rancour and cruelty of their ancestors, the desert-warriors, but with it all they had the two most potential of habits-- they could dream and they could wait. In his love and hope for promised Rachel, that were not quenched or soured by the substitution, after seven years' service for her, of her ill-favoured sister, but began another seven years' effort for herself, Jacob was a type of his strange, tenacious people, who, when they were brought face to face with some Leah of a fulfilment of their fondest ideals, as they frequently were in their history, took up again with undiminished ardour the pursuit of their first unforgettable love. It is the wonder of history, how this people passed through the countless disappointments of the prophecies to which they had given their hearts, yet with only a strengthening expectation of the arrival of the promised King and His kingdom. If other peoples have felt a gain in character from such miscarriages of belief, it has generally been at the expense of their faith. But Israel's experience did not take faith away or even impair faith's elasticity. We see their appreciation of God's promises growing only more spiritual with each postponement, and patience performing her perfect work upon their character; yet this never happens at the cost of the original buoyancy and ardour. The glory of it we ascribe, as is most due, to the power of the Word of God; but the people who could stand the strain of the discipline of such a word, its alternate glow and frost, must have been a people of extraordinary fibre and frame. When we think of how they wore for those two thousand years of postponed promise, and how they wear still, after two thousand years more of disillusion and suffering, we cease to wonder why God chose this small tribe to be His instrument on earth. Where we see their bad habits, their Creator knew their sound constitution, and the constitution of Israel is a thing unique among mankind.

From the racial temper of the elect nation we pass to their history, on the singularity of which our prophet dwells with emphasis. Israel's political origin had no other reason than a call to God's service. Other peoples grew, as it were, from the soil; they were the product of a fatherland, a climate, certain physical environments: root them out of these, and, as nations, they ceased to be. But Israel had not been so nursed into nationality on the lap of nature. The captive children of Jacob had sprung into unity and independence as a nation at the special call of God, and to serve His will in the world,--His will that so lay athwart the natural tendencies of the peoples. All down their history it is wonderful to see how it was the conscience of this service, which in periods of progress was the real national genius in Israel, and in times of decay or of political dissolution upheld the assurance of the nation's survival. Whenever a ruler like Ahaz forgot that Israel's imperishableness was bound up with their faithfulness to God's service, and sought to preserve his throne by alliances with the world-powers, then it was that Israel were most in danger of absorption into the world. And, conversely, when disaster came down, and there was no hope in the sky, it was upon the inward sense of their election to the service of God that the prophets rallied the people's faith and assured them of their survival as a nation. They brought to Israel that sovereign message, which renders all who hear it immortal: "God has a service for you to serve upon earth." In the Exile especially, the wonderful survival of the nation, with the subservience of all history to that end, is made to turn on this,--that Israel has a unique purpose to serve. When Jeremiah and Ezekiel seek to assure the captives of their return to the land and of the restoration of the people, they commend so unlikely a promise by reminding them that the nation is the Servant of God. This name, applied by them for the first time to the nation as a whole, they bind up with the national existence. Fear thou not, O My Servant Jacob, saith Jehovah; neither be dismayed, O Israel: for, lo, I will save thee from afar, and thy seed from the land of their captivity. [143] These words plainly say, that Israel as a nation cannot die, for God has a use for them to serve. The singularity of Israel's redemption from Babylon is due to the singularity of the service that God has for the nation to perform. Our prophet speaks in the same strain: Thou, Israel, My Servant, Jacob whom I have chosen, seed of Abraham My lover, whom I took hold of from the ends of the earth and its corners. I have called thee and said unto thee, My Servant art thou, I have chosen thee and have not cast thee away (ch. xli. 8 ff). No one can miss the force of these words. They are the assurance of Israel's miraculous survival, not because he is God's favourite, but because he is God's servant, with a unique work in the world. Many other verses repeat the same truth. [144] They call Israel the Servant, and Jacob the chosen, of God, in order to persuade the people that they are not forgotten of Him, and that their seed shall live and be blessed. Israel survives because he serves--Servus servatur.

Now for this service,--which had been the purpose of the nation's election at first, the mainstay of its unique preservation since, and the reason of all its singular pre-eminence before God,--Israel was equipped by two great experiences. These were Redemption and Revelation.

On the former redemptions of Israel from the power of other nations our prophet does not dwell much. You feel, that they are present to his mind, for he sometimes describes the coming redemption from Babylon in terms of them. And once, in an appeal to the Arm of Jehovah, he calls out: Awake like the days of old, ancient generations! Art thou not it that hewed Rahab in pieces, that pierced the Dragon? Art thou not it which dried up the sea, the waters of the great deep; that made the depths of the sea a way of passage for the redeemed? [145] There is, too, that beautiful passage in ch. lxiii., which makes mention of the lovingkindnesses of Jehovah, according to all that He hath bestowed upon us; which describes the carriage of the people all the days of old, how He brought them out of the sea, caused His glorious arm to go at the right hand of Moses, divided the water before them, led them through the deeps as a horse on the meadow, that they stumbled not. But, on the whole, our prophet is too much engrossed with the immediate prospect of release from Babylon, to remember that past, of which it has been truly said, He hath not dealt so with any people. It is the new glory that is upon him. He counts the deliverance from Babylon as already come; to his rapt eye it is its marvellous power and costliness, which already clothes the people in their unique brilliance and honour. Thus saith Jehovah, your Redeemer, the Holy One of Israel: For your sake have I sent to Babylon, and I will bring down their nobles, all of them, and the Chaldeans, in the ships of their exulting. [146] But it is more than Babylon that is balanced against them. I am Jehovah, thy God, the Holy One of Israel, thy Saviour. I am giving as thy ransom, Egypt, Cush and Seba in exchange for thee, because thou art precious in mine eyes, and hast made thyself valuable (lit., of weight); and I have loved thee, therefore do I give mankind for thee, and peoples for thy life. [147] Mankind for thee, and peoples for thy life,--all the world for this little people? It is intelligible only because this little people are to be for all the world. Ye are My witnesses that I am

God. I will also give thee for a light to nations, to be My salvation to the end of the earth.

But more than on the Redemption, which Israel experienced, our prophet dwells on the Revelation, that has equipped them for their destiny. In a passage, in ch. xliii., to which we shall return, the present stupid and unready character of the mass of the people is contrasted with the instruction which God has lavished upon them. Thou hast seen many things, and wilt not observe; there is opening of the ears, but he heareth not. Jehovah was pleased for His righteousness' sake to magnify the Instruction and make it glorious,--but that--the result and the precipitate of it all--is a people robbed and spoiled. The word Instruction or Revelation is that same technical term, which we have met with before, for Jehovah's special training and illumination of Israel. How special these were, how distinct from the highest doctrine and practice of any other nation in that world to which Israel belonged, is an historical fact that the results of recent research enable us to state in a few sentences.

Recent exploration in the East, and the progress of Semitic philology, have proved that the system of religion, which prevailed among the Hebrews, had a very great deal in common with the systems of the neighbouring and related heathen nations. This common element included not only such things as ritual and temple-furniture, or the details of priestly organization, but even the titles and many of the attributes of God, and especially the forms of the covenant in which He drew near to men. But the discovery of this common element has only thrown into more striking relief the presence at work in the Hebrew religion of an independent and original principle. In the Hebrew religion historians observe a principle of selection operating upon the common Semitic materials for worship,--ignoring some of them, giving prominence to others, and with others again changing the reference and application. Grossly immoral practices are forbidden; forbidden, too, are those superstitions, which, like augury and divination, draw men away from single-minded attention to the moral issues of life; and even religious customs are omitted, such as the employment of women in the sanctuary, which, however innocent in themselves, might lead men into temptations, not desirable in connection with the professional pursuit of religion. [148] In short, a stern and inexorable conscience was at work in the Hebrew religion, which was not at work in any of the religions most akin to it. In our previous volume we saw the same conscience inspiring the prophets. Prophecy was not confined to the Hebrews; it was a general Semitic institution; but no one doubts the absolutely distinct character of the prophecy, which was conscious of having the Spirit of Jehovah. Its religious ideas were original, and in it we have, as all admit, a moral phenomenon unique in history. When we turn to ask the secret of this distinction, we find the answer in the character of the God, whom Israel served. The God explains the people; Israel is the response to Jehovah. Each of the laws of the nation is enforced by the reason, For I am holy. Each of the prophets brings his message from a God, exalted in righteousness. In short, look where you will in the Old Testament,--come to it as a critic or as a worshipper,--you discover the revealed character of Jehovah to be the effective principle at work. It is this Divine character, which draws Israel from among the nations to their destiny, which selects and builds the law to be a wall around them, and which by each revelation of itself discovers to the people both the measure of their delinquency and the new ideals of their service to humanity. Like the pillar of cloud by day and the pillar of fire by night, we see it in front of Israel at every stage of their marvellous progress down the ages.

So that when Jehovah says that He has magnified the Revelation and made it glorious, He speaks of a magnitude of a real, historical kind, that can be tested by exact methods of observation. Israel's election by Jehovah, their formation, their unique preparation for service, are not the mere boasts of an overweening patriotism, but sober names for historical processes as real and evident as any that history contains.

To sum up, then. If Jehovah's sovereignty be absolute, so also is the uniqueness of Israel's calling and equipment for His Service. For, to begin with, Israel had the essential religious temper; they enjoyed a unique moral instruction and discipline; and by the side of this they were conscious of a series of miraculous deliverances from servitude and from dissolution. So singular an experience and career were not, as we have seen, bestowed from any arbitrary motive, which exhausted itself upon Israel, but in accordance with God's universal method of specialisation of function, were granted to fit the nation as an instrument for a practical end. The sovereign unity of God does not mean equality in His creation. The universe is diverse. There is one glory of the sun, and another glory of the moon, and another glory of the stars; and even so in the moral kingdom of Him, who is Lord of the Hosts of both earth and heaven, each nation has its own destiny and function. Israel's was religion; Israel was God's specialist in religion.

For confirmation of this we turn to the supreme witness. Jesus was born a Jew, He confined His ministry to Judæa, and He has told us why. By various passing allusions, as well as by deliberate statements, He revealed His sense of a great religious difference between Jew and Gentile. Use not vain repetitions as the Gentiles do.... For after all these things do the nations of the world seek; but your Father knoweth that you have need of these things. He refused to work except upon Jewish hearts: I am not sent but to the lost sheep of the house of Israel. And He charged His disciples, saying, Go not into any way of the Gentiles, and enter not into any city of the Samaritans; but go rather to the lost sheep of the House of Israel. And again He said to the woman of Samaria: Ye worship ye know not what; we know what we worship, for salvation is of the Jews.

These sayings of our Lord have created as much question as the pre-eminence given in the Old Testament to a single people by a God, who is described as the one God of Heaven and earth. Was He narrower of heart than Paul, His servant, who was debtor to Greek and Barbarian? Or was He ignorant of the universal character of His mission till it was forced upon His reluctant sympathies by the importunity of such heathen as the Syrophenician woman? A little common-sense dispels the perplexity, and leaves the problem, over which volumes have been written, no problem at all. Our Lord limited Himself to Israel, not because He was narrow, but because He was practical; not from ignorance, but from wisdom. He came from heaven to sow the seed of Divine truth; and where in all humanity should He find the soil so ready as within the long-chosen people? He knew of that discipline of the centuries. In the words of His own parable, the Son when He came to earth directed His attention not to a piece of desert, but to the vineyard which His Father's servants had so long cultivated, and where the soil was open. Jesus came to Israel because He expected faith in Israel. That this practical end was the deliberate intention of His will, is proved by the fact that when He found faith elsewhere, either in Syrian or Greek or Roman hearts, He did not hesitate to let His love and power go forth to them.

In short, we shall have no difficulty about these Divine methods with a single, elect people, if we only remember that to be Divine is to be practical. Yet God also is wise, said Isaiah to the Jews when they preferred their own clever policies to Jehovah's guidance. And we need to be told the same, who murmur that to confine Himself to a single nation was not the ideal thing for the One God to do; or who imagine that it was left to one of our Lord's own creatures to suggest to Him the policy of His mission upon earth. We are shortsighted: and the Almighty is past finding out. But this at least it is possible for us to see, that, in choosing one nation to be His agent among men, God chose the type of instrument best fitted at the time for the work for which He designed it, and that in choosing Israel to be that nation, He chose a people of temper singularly suitable to His end.

Israel's election as a nation, therefore, was to Service. To be a nation and to be God's Servant was pretty much one and the same thing for Israel. Israel were to survive the Exile, because they were to serve the world. Let us carry this over to the study of our next chapter--The Servant of Jehovah.

Footnotes:

139. Wellhausen.

140. "Revelation is never revolutionary.... As a rule, revelation accepts the fragments of truth and adopts the methods of religion already existing, uniting the former into a whole, and purifying the latter for its own purposes."... For instance, "in the East each people had its particular god. The god and the people were correlative ideas, that which gave the individuals of a nation unity and made them a people was the unity of its god; as, on the other hand, that which gave a god prestige was the strength and victorious career of his people. The self-consciousness of the nation and its religion re-acted on one another, and rose and fell simultaneously. This conception was not repudiated, but adopted by revelation; and, as occasion demanded, purified from its natural abuses."--Professor A. B. Davidson, Expositor, Second Series, vol. viii., pp. 257-8.

141. Mr. Doughty, in his most interesting account of the nomads of Central Arabia, the unsophisticated Semites on their native soil, furnishes ample material for accounting for the strange mixture of passion and resignation in these prophet-peoples of the world.

142. Ch. xlix. 2.

143. Jer. xxx. 10, cf. xlvi. 27; also Ezek. xxxvii. 25: And they shall dwell in the land that I have given My servant Jacob. Cf. xxviii. 25.

144. xliv. 1, 21; xlviii. 20, etc.

145. Ch. li. 9, 10.

146. Ch. xliii. 14.

147. Ib. 3, 4.

148. Robertson Smith, Burnett Lectures in Aberdeen, 1889-90.

Rev. George Adam Smith, M.A.

CHAPTER XVI

THE SERVANT OF THE LORD.

Isaiah xli. 8-20; xlii. 1-7, 18 ff; xliii. 5-10; xlix. 1-9; l. 4-10; lii. 13-liii.

With chapter xlii. we reach a distinct stage in our prophecy. The preceding chapters have been occupied with the declaration of the great, basal truth, that Jehovah is the One Sovereign God. This has been declared to two classes of hearers in succession--to God's own people, Israel, in ch. xl., and to the heathen in ch. xli. Having established His sovereignty, God now publishes His will, again addressing these two classes according to the purpose which He has for each. Has He vindicated Himself to Israel, the Almighty and Righteous God, Who will give His people freedom and strength: He will now define to them the mission for which that strength and freedom are required. Has He proved to the Gentiles that He is the one true God: He will declare to them now what truth He has for them to learn. In short, to use modern terms, the apologetic of chs. xl.-xli. is succeeded by the missionary programme of ch. xlii. And although, from the necessities of the case, we are frequently brought back, in the course of the prophecy, to its fundamental claims for the Godhead of Jehovah, we are nevertheless sensible that with ver. 1 of ch. xlii. we make a distinct advance. It is one of those logical steps which, along with a certain chronological progress that we have already felt, assures us that Isaiah, whether originally by one or more authors, is in its present form a unity, with a distinct order and principle of development.

The Purpose of God is identified with a Minister or Servant, whom He commissions to carry it out in the world. This Servant is brought before us with all the urgency with which Jehovah has presented Himself, and next to Jehovah he turns out to be the most important figure of the prophecy. Does the prophet insist that God is the only source and sufficiency of His people's salvation: it is with equal emphasis that He introduces the Servant as God's indispensable agent in the work. Cyrus is also acknowledged as an elect instrument. But neither in closeness to God, nor in effect upon the world, is Cyrus to be compared for an instant to the Servant. Cyrus is subservient and incidental: with the overthrow of Babylon, for which he was raised up, he will disappear from the stage of our prophecy. But God's purpose, which uses the gates opened by Cyrus, only to pass through them with the redeemed people to the regeneration of the whole world, is to be carried to this Divine consummation by the Servant: its universal and glorious progress is identified with his career. Cyrus flashes through these pages a well-polished sword: it is only his swift and brilliant usefulness that is allowed to catch our eye. But the Servant is a Character, to delineate whose immortal beauty and example the prophet devotes as much space as he does to Jehovah Himself. As he turns again and again to speak of God's omnipotence and faithfulness and agonising love for His own, so with equal frequency and fondness does he linger on every feature of the Servant's conduct and aspect: His gentleness, His patience, His courage, His purity, His meekness; His daily wakefulness to God's voice, the swiftness and brilliance of His speech for others, His silence under His own torments; His resorts--among the bruised, the prisoners, the forwandered of Israel, the weary, and them that sit in darkness, the far-off heathen; His warfare with the world, His face set like a flint; His unworldly beauty, which men call ugliness; His unnoticed presence in His own generation, yet the effect of His face upon kings; His habit of woe, a man of sorrows and acquainted with sickness; His sore stripes and bruises, His judicial murder, His felon's grave; His exaltation and eternal glory--till we may reverently say that these pictures, by their vividness and charm, have drawn our eyes away from our prophet's visions of God, and have caused the chapters in which they occur to be oftener read among us, and learned by heart, than the chapters in which God Himself is lifted up and adored. Jehovah and Jehovah's Servant--these are the two heroes of the drama.

Now we might naturally expect that so indispensable and fondly imagined a figure would also be defined past all ambiguity, whether as to His time or person or name. But the opposite is the case. About Scripture there are few more intricate questions than those on the Servant of the Lord. Is He a Person or Personification? If the latter, is He a Personification of all Israel? Or of a part of Israel? Or of the ideal Israel? Or of the Order of the Prophets? Or if a Person--is he the prophet himself? Or a martyr who has already lived and suffered, like Jeremiah? Or One still to come, like the promised Messiah? Each of these suggestions has not only been made about the Servant, but derives considerable support from one or another of our prophet's dissolving views of his person and work. A final answer to them can be given only after a comparative study of all the relevant passages; but as these are scattered over the prophecy, and our detailed exposition of them must necessarily be interrupted, it will be of advantage to take here a prospect of them all, and see to what they combine to develop this sublime character and mission. And after we have seen what the prophecies themselves teach concerning the Servant, we shall inquire how they were understood and fulfilled by the New Testament; and that will show us how to expound and apply them with regard to ourselves.

I.

The Hebrew word for Servant means a person at the disposal of another--to carry out his will, do his work, represent his interests. It was thus applied to the representatives of a king or the worshippers of a god. [149] All Israelites were thus in a sense the servants of Jehovah; though in the singular the title was reserved for persons of extraordinary character or usefulness.

But we have seen, as clearly as possible, that God set apart for His chief service upon earth, not an individual nor a group of individuals, but a whole nation in its national capacity. We have seen Israel's political origin and preservation bound up with that service; we have heard the whole nation plainly called, by Jeremiah and Ezekiel, the Servant of Jehovah. [150] Nothing could be more clear than this, that in the earlier years of the Exile the Servant of Jehovah was Israel as a whole, Israel as a body politic.

It is also in this sense that our prophet first uses the title in a passage we have already quoted (xli. 8); Thou Israel, My Servant, Jacob whom I have chosen, seed of Abraham My lover, whom I took hold of from the ends of the earth and its corners! I called thee and said unto thee, My Servant art thou. I have chosen thee, and not cast thee away. Here the Servant is plainly the historical nation, descended from Abraham, and the subject of those national experiences which are traced in the previous chapter. It is the same in the following verses:--xliv. 1 ff: Yet now hear, O Jacob My servant; and Israel, whom I have chosen: thus saith Jehovah thy Maker, and thy Moulder from the womb, He will help thee. Fear not, My servant Jacob; and Jeshurun, whom I have chosen.... I will pour My spirit upon thy seed, and My blessing upon thine offspring. xliv. 21: Remember these things, O Jacob; and Israel, for My servant art thou: I have formed thee; a servant for Myself art thou; O Israel, thou shalt not be forgotten of Me. xlviii. 20: Go ye forth from Babylon; say ye, Jehovah hath redeemed His servant Jacob. In all these verses, which bind up the nation's restoration from exile with the fact that God called it to be His Servant, the title Servant is plainly equivalent to the national name Israel or Jacob. But Israel or Jacob is not a label for the mere national idea, or the bare political framework, without regard to the living individuals included in it. To the eye and heart of Him, Who counts the number of the stars, Israel means no mere outline, but all the individuals of the living generation of the people--thy seed, that is, every born Israelite, however fallen or forwandered. This is made clear in a very beautiful passage in ch. xliii. (vv. 1-7): Thus saith Jehovah, thy Creator, O Jacob; thy Moulder, O Israel.... Fear not, for I am with thee; from the sunrise I will bring thy seed, and from the sunset will I gather thee; ... My sons from far, and My daughters from the end of the earth; every one who is called by My name, and whom for My glory I have created, formed, yea, I have made him. To this Israel--Israel as a whole, yet no mere abstraction or outline of the nation, but the people in mass and bulk--every individual of whom is dear to Jehovah, and in some sense shares His calling and equipment--to this Israel the title Servant of Jehovah is at first applied by our prophet.

2. We say "at first," for very soon the prophet has to make a distinction, and to sketch the Servant as something less than the actual nation. The distinction is obscure; it has given rise to a very great deal of controversy. But it is so natural, where a nation is the subject, and of such frequent occurrence in other literatures, that we may almost state it as a general law.

In all the passages quoted above, Israel has been spoken of in the passive mood, as the object of some affection or action on the part of God: loved, formed, chosen, called, and about to be redeemed by Him. Now, so long as a people thus lie passive, their prophet will naturally think of them as a whole. In their shadow his eye can see them only in the outline of their mass; in their common suffering and servitude his heart will go out to all their individuals, as equally dear and equally in need of redemption. But when the hour comes for the people to work out their own salvation, and they emerge into action, it must needs be different. When they are no more the object of their prophet's affection only, but pass under the test of his experience and judgement, then distinctions naturally appear upon them. Lifted to the light of their destiny, their inequality becomes apparent; tried by its strain, part of them break away. And so, though the prophet continues still to call on the nation by its name to fulfil its calling, what he means by that name is no longer the bulk and the body of the citizenship. A certain ideal of the people fills his mind's eye--an ideal, however, which is no mere spectre floating above his own generation, but is realised in their noble and aspiring portion--although his ignorance as to the exact size of this portion, must always leave his image of them more or less ideal to his eyes. It will be their quality rather than their quantity that is clear to him. In modern history we have two familiar illustrations of this process of winnowing and idealising a people in the light of their destiny, which may prepare us for the more obscure instance of it in our prophecy.

In a well-known passage in the Areopagitica, Milton exclaims, "Methinks I see in my mind a noble and puissant nation rousing herself and shaking her invincible locks; methinks I see her as an eagle mewing her mighty youth, and kindling her undazzled eyes at the full midday beam, ... while the whole noise of timorous and flocking birds, with those also that love the twilight, flutter about, amazed at what she means." In this passage the "nation" is no longer what Milton meant by the term in the earlier part of his treatise, where "England" stands simply for the outline of the whole English people; but the "nation" is the true genius of England realised in her enlightened and aspiring sons, and breaking away from the hindering and debasing members of the body politic--"the timorous and flocking birds with those also that love the twilight"--who are indeed Englishmen after the flesh, but form no part of the nation's better self.

Or, recall Mazzini's bitter experience. To no man was his Italy more really one than to this ardent son of hers, who loved every born Italian because he was an Italian, and counted none of the fragments of his unhappy country too petty or too corrupt to be included in the hope of her restoration. To Mazzini's earliest imagination, it was the whole Italian seed, who were ready for redemption, and would rise to achieve it at his summons. But when his summons came, how few responded, and after the first struggles how fewer still remained,--Mazzini himself has told us with breaking heart. The real Italy was but a handful of born Italians; at times it seemed to shrink to the prophet alone. From such a core the conscience indeed spread again, till the entire people was delivered from tyranny and from schism, and now every peasant and burgher from the Alps to Sicily understands what Italy means, and is proud to be an Italian. But for a time Mazzini and his few comrades stood alone. Others of their blood and speech were Piedmontese, Pope's men, Neapolitans,--merchants, lawyers, scholars,--or merely selfish and sensual. They alone were Italians; they alone were Italy.

It is a similar winnowing process, through which we see our prophet's thoughts pass with regard to Israel. Him, too, experience teaches that the many are called, but the few chosen. So long as his people lie in the shadow of captivity, so long as he has to speak of them in the passive mood, the object of God's call and preparation, it is their seed, the born people in bulk and mass, whom he names Israel, and entitles the Servant of Jehovah. But the moment that he lifts them to their mission in the world, and to the light of their destiny, a difference becomes apparent upon them, and the Servant of Jehovah, though still called Israel, shrinks to something less than the living generation, draws off to something finer than the mass of the people. How, indeed, could it be otherwise with this strange people, than which no nation on earth had a loftier ideal identified with its history, or more frequently turned upon its better self, with a sword in its hand. Israel, though created a nation by God for His service, was always what Paul found it, divided into an Israel after the flesh, and an Israel after the spirit. But it was in the Exile that this distinction gaped most broad. With the fall of Jerusalem, the political framework, which kept the different elements of the nation together, was shattered, and these were left loose to the action of moral forces. The baser elements were quickly absorbed by heathendom; the nobler, that remained loyal to the divine call, were free to assume a new and ideal form. Every year spent in Babylonia made it more apparent that the true and effective Israel of the future would not coincide with all the seed of Jacob, who went into exile. Numbers of the latter were as contented with their Babylonian circumstance as numbers of Mazzini's "Italians" were satisfied to live on as Austrian and Papal subjects. Many, as we have seen, became idolaters; many more settled down into the prosperous habits of Babylonian commerce, while a large multitude besides were scattered far out of sight across the world. It required little insight to perceive that the true, effective Israel--the real Servant of Jehovah--must needs be a much smaller body than the sum of all these: a loyal kernel within Israel, who were still conscious of the national calling, and capable of carrying it out; who stood sensible of their duty to the whole world, but whose first conscience was for their lapsed and lost countrymen. This Israel within Israel was the real Servant of the Lord; to personify it in that character--however vague might be the actual proportion it would assume in his own or in any other generation--would be as natural to our dramatic prophet as to personify the nation as a whole.

All this very natural process--this passing from the historical Israel, the nation originally designed by God to be His Servant, to the conscious and effective Israel, that uncertain quantity within the present and every future generation--takes place in the chapters before us; and it will be sufficiently easy for us to follow if we only remember that our prophet is not a dogmatic theologian, careful to make clear each logical distinction, but a dramatic poet, who delivers his ideas in groups, tableaux, dialogues, interrupted by choruses; and who writes in a language incapable of expressing such delicate differences, except by dramatic contrasts, and by the one other figure of which he is so fond--paradox.

Perhaps the first traces of distinction between the real Servant and the whole nation are to be found in the Programme of his Mission in ch. xlii. 1-7. There it is said that the Servant is to be for a covenant of the people (ver. 6). I have explained below why we are to understand people as here meaning Israel. [151] And in ver. 7 it is said of the Servant that he is to open blind eyes, bring forth from prison the captive, from the house of bondage dwellers in darkness: phrases that are descriptive, of course, of the captive Israel. Already, then, in ch. xlii. the Servant is something distinct from the whole nation, whose Covenant and Redeemer he is to be.

The next references to the Servant are a couple of paradoxes, which are evidently the prophet's attempt to show why it was necessary to draw in the Servant of Jehovah from the whole to a part of the people. The first of these paradoxes is in ch. xlii. ver. 18.

Ye deaf, hearken! and ye blind, look ye to see! Who is blind but My Servant, and deaf as My Messenger whom I send? Who is blind as Meshullam, and blind as the Servant of Jehovah? Vision of many things--and thou dost not observe, Opening of ears and he hears not!

The context shows that the Servant here--or Meshullam, as he is called, the devoted or submissive one, from the same root, and of much the same form as the Arabic Muslim [152] --is the whole people; but they are entitled Servant only in order to show how unfit they are for the task to which they have been designated, and what a paradox their title is beside their real character. God had given them every opportunity by making great His instruction (ver. 21, cf. p. [30]247), and, when that failed, by His sore discipline in exile (vers. 24, 25). For who gave Jacob for spoil and Israel to the robbers? Did not Jehovah? He against whom we sinned, and they would not walk in His ways, neither were obedient to His instruction. So He poured upon him the fury of His anger and the force of war. But even this did not awake the dull nation. Though it set him on fire round about, yet he knew not; and it kindled upon him, yet he laid it not to heart. The nation as a whole had been favoured with God's revelation; as a whole they had been brought into His purifying furnace of the Exile. But as they have benefited by neither the one nor the other, the natural conclusion is that as a whole they are no more fit to be God's Servant. Such is the hint which this paradox is intended to give us.

But a little further on there is an obverse paradox, which plainly says, that although the people are blind and deaf as a whole, still the capacity for service is found among them alone (xliii. 8, 10).

Bring forth the blind people--yet eyes are there! And the deaf, yet ears have they!... Ye are My witnesses, saith Jehovah, and My Servant whom I have chosen.

The preceding verses (vv. 1-7) show us that it is again the whole people, in their bulk and scattered fragments, who are referred to. Blind though they be, yet are there eyes among them; deaf though they be, yet they have ears. And so Jehovah addresses them all, in contradistinction to the heathen peoples (ver. 9), as His Servant.

These two complementary paradoxes together show this: that while Israel as a whole is unfit to be the Servant, it is nevertheless within Israel, alone of all the world's nations, that the true capacities for service are found--eyes are there, ears have they. They prepare us for the Servant's testimony about himself, in which, while he owns himself to be distinct from Israel as a whole, he is nevertheless still called Israel. This is given in ch. xlix. And He said unto me, My Servant art thou; Israel, in whom I will glorify Myself. And now saith Jehovah, my moulder from the womb to be a Servant unto Him, to turn again Jacob to Him, and that Israel might not be destroyed; and I am of value in the eyes of Jehovah, and my God is my strength. And He said, It is too light for thy being My Servant, merely to raise up the tribes of Jacob, and to restore the preserved of Israel; I will also set thee for a light of nations, to be My salvation to the end of the earth (xlix. 3-6). Here the Servant, though still called Israel, is clearly distinct from the nation as a whole, for part of his work is to raise the nation up again. And, moreover, he tells us this as his own testimony about himself. He is no longer spoken of in the third person, he speaks for himself in the first. This is significant. It is more than a mere artistic figure, the effect of our prophet's dramatic style--as if the Servant now stood opposite him, so vivid and near that he heard him speak, and quoted him in the direct form of speech. It is more probably the result of moral sympathy: the prophet speaks out of the heart of the Servant, in the name of that better portion of Israel which was already conscious of the Divine call, and of its distinction in this respect from the mass of the people.

It is futile to inquire what this better portion of Israel actually was, for whom the prophet speaks in the first person. Some have argued, from the stress which the speaker lays upon his gifts of speech and office of preaching, that what is now signified by the Servant is the order of the prophets; but such forget that in these chapters the proclamation of the Kingdom of God is the ideal, not of prophets only, but of the whole people. Zion as a whole is to be heraldess of good news (xl. 9). It is, therefore, not the official function of the prophet-order which the Servant here owns, but the ideal of the prophet-nation. Others have argued from the direct form of speech, that the prophet puts himself forward as the Servant. But no individual would call himself Israel. And as Professor Cheyne remarks, the passage is altogether too self-assertive to be spoken by any man of himself as an individual; although, of course, our prophet could not have spoken of the true Israel with such sympathy, unless he had himself been part of it. The writer of these verses may have been, for the time, as virtually the real Israel as Mazzini was the real Italy. But still he does not speak as an individual. The passage is manifestly a piece of personification. The Servant is Israel--not now the nation as a whole, not the body and bulk of the Israelites, for they are to be the object of his first efforts, but the loyal, conscious and effective Israel, realised in some of her members, and here personified by our prophet, who himself speaks for her out of his heart, in the first person.

By ch. xlix., then, the Servant of Jehovah is a personification of the true, effective Israel as distinguished from the mass of the nation--a Personification, but not yet a Person. Something within Israel has wakened up to find itself conscious of being the Servant of Jehovah, and distinct from the mass of the nation--something that is not yet a Person. And this definition of the Servant may stand (with some modifications) for his next appearance in ch. l. 4-9. In this passage the Servant, still speaking in the first person, continues to illustrate his experience as a prophet, and carries it to its consequence in martyrdom. But let us notice that he now no longer calls himself Israel, and that if it were not for the previous passages it would be natural to suppose that an individual was speaking. This supposition is confirmed by a verse that follows the Servant's speech, and is spoken, as chorus, by the Prophet himself. Who among you is a fearer of Jehovah, obedient to the voice of His Servant, who walketh in darkness, and hath no light. Let him trust in the name of Jehovah, and stay himself upon his God. In this too much neglected verse, which forms a real transition to ch. lii. 13-liii., the prophet is addressing any individual Israelite, on behalf of a personal God. It is very difficult to refrain from concluding that therefore the Servant also is a Person. Let us, however, not go beyond what we have evidence for; and note only that in ch. l. the Servant is no more called Israel, and is represented not as if he were one part of the nation, over against the mass of it, but as if he were one individual over against other individuals; that in fine the Personification of ch. xlix. has become much more difficult to distinguish from an actual Person.

3. This brings us to the culminating passage--ch. lii. 13-liii. Is the Servant still a Personification here, or at last and unmistakably a Person?

It may relieve the air of that electricity, which is apt to charge it at the discussion of so classic a passage as this, and secure us calm weather in which to examine exegetical details, if we at once assert, what none but prejudiced Jews have ever denied, that this great prophecy, known as the fifty-third of Isaiah, was fulfilled in One Person, Jesus of Nazareth, and achieved in all its details by Him alone. But, on the other hand, it requires also to be pointed out that Christ's personal fulfilment of it does not necessarily imply that our prophet wrote it of a Person. The present expositor hopes, indeed, to be able to give strong reasons for the theory usual among us, that the Personification of previous passages is at last in ch. liii. presented as a Person. But he fails to understand, why critics should be regarded as unorthodox or at variance with New Testament teaching on the subject, who, while they acknowledge that only Christ fulfilled ch. liii., are yet unable to believe that the prophet looked upon the Servant as an individual, and who regard ch. liii. as simply a sublimer form of the prophet's previous pictures of the ideal people of God. Surely Christ could and did fulfil prophecies other than personal ones. The types of Him, which the New Testament quotes from the Old Testament, are not exclusively individuals. Christ is sometimes represented as realising in His Person and work statements, which, as they were first spoken, could only refer to Israel, the nation. Matthew, for instance, applies to Jesus a text which Hosea wrote primarily of the whole Jewish people: Out of Egypt have I called My Son.[153] Or, to take an instance from our own prophet--who but Jesus fulfilled ch. xlix., in which, as we have seen, it is not an individual, but the ideal of the prophet people, that is figured? So that, even if it were proved past all doubt--proved from grammar, context, and every prophetic analogy--that in writing ch. liii. our prophet had still in view that aspect of the nation which he has personified in ch. xlix., such a conclusion would not weaken the connection between the prophecy and its unquestioned fulfilment by Jesus Christ, nor render the two less evidently part of one Divine design.

But we are by no means compelled to adopt the impersonal view of ch. liii. On the contrary, while the question is one, to which all experts know the difficulty of finding an absolutely conclusive answer one way or the other, it seems to me that reasons prevail, which make for the personal interpretation. . Let us see what exactly are the objections to taking ch. lii. 13-liii. in a personal sense. First, it is very important to observe, that they do not rise out of the grammar or language of the passage. The reference of both of these is consistently individual. Throughout, the Servant is spoken of in the singular.[154] The name Israel is not once applied to him: nothing--except that the nation has also suffered--suggests that he is playing a national rôle; there is no reflection in his fate of the features of the Exile. The antithesis, which was evident in previous passages, between a better Israel and the mass of the people has disappeared. The Servant is contrasted, not with the nation as a whole, but with His people as individuals. All we like sheep have gone astray; we have turned every one to his own way; and the Lord hath laid on him the iniquity of us all. As far as grammar can, this surely distinguishes a single person. It is true, that one or two phrases suggest so colossal a figure--he shall startle many nations, and kings shall shut their mouths at him--that for a moment we think of the spectacle of a people rather than of a solitary human presence. But even such descriptions are not incompatible with a single person.[155] On the other hand, there are phrases which we can scarcely think are used of any but a historical individual; such as that he was taken from oppression and judgement, that is from a process of law which was tyranny, from a judicial murder, and that he belonged to a particular generation--As for his generation, who considered that he was cut off out of the land of the living. Surely a historical individual is the natural meaning of these words. And, in fact, critics like Ewald and Wellhausen, who interpret the passage, in its present context, of the ideal Israel, find themselves forced to argue, that it has been borrowed for this use from the older story of some actual martyr--so individual do its references seem to them throughout.

If, then, the grammar and language of the passage thus conspire to convey the impression of an individual, what are the objections to supposing that an individual is meant? Critics have felt, in the main, three objections to the discovery of a historical individual in Isa. lii. 13-liii.

The first of these that we take is chronological, and arises from the late date to which we have found it necessary to assign the prophecy. Our prophet, it is averred, associates the work of the Servant with the restoration of the people; but he sees that restoration too close to him to be able to think of the appearance, ministry and martyrdom of a real historic life happening before it. (Our prophet, it will be remembered, wrote about 546, and the Restoration came in 538.) "There is no room for a history like that of the suffering Servant between the prophet's place and the Restoration."[156]

Now, this objection might be turned, even if it were true that the prophet identified the suffering Servant's career with so immediate and so short a process as the political deliverance from Babylon. For, in that case, the prophet would not be leaving less room for the Servant, than, in ch. ix., Isaiah himself leaves for the birth, the growth to manhood, and the victories of the Prince-of-the-Four-Names, before that immediate relief from the Assyrian, which he expects the Prince to effect. But does our prophet identify the suffering Servant's career with the redemption from Babylon and the Return? It is plain that he does not--at least in those portraits of the Servant, which are most personal. Our prophet has really two prospects for Israel--one, the actual deliverance from Babylon, the other, a spiritual redemption and restoration. If, like his fellow prophets, he sometimes runs these two together, and talks of the latter in the terms of the former, he keeps them on the whole distinct, and assigns them to different agents. The burden of the first he lays on Cyrus, though he also connects it with the Servant, while the Servant is still to him an aspect of the nation (see xlix. 8a, 9b). It is temporary, and soon passes from his thoughts, Cyrus being dropped with it. But the other, the spiritual redemption, is confined to no limits of time; and it is with its process--indefinite in date and in length of period--that he associates the most personal portraits of the Servant (ch. l. and lii. 13-liii.). In these the Servant, now spoken of as an individual, has nothing to do with that temporary work of freeing the people from Babylon, which was over in a year or two, and which seems to be now behind the prophet's standpoint. His is the enduring office of prophecy, sympathy, and expiation--an office in which there is all possible "room" for such a historical career as is sketched for him. His relation to Cyrus, before whose departure from connection with Israel's fate the Servant does not appear as a person, is thus most interesting. Perhaps we may best convey it in a homely figure. On the ship of Israel's fortunes--as on every ship and on every voyage--the prophet sees two personages. One is the Pilot through the shallows, Cyrus, who is dropped as soon as the shallows are past; and the other is the Captain of the ship, who remains always identified with it--the Servant. The Captain does not come to the front till the Pilot has gone; but, both alongside the Pilot, and after the Pilot has been dropped, there is every room for his office.

The second main objection to identifying an individual in ch. lii. 13-liii. is, that an individual with such features has no analogy in Hebrew prophecy. It is said that, neither in his humiliation, nor in the kind of exaltation, which is ascribed to him, is there his like in any other individual in the Old Testament, and certainly not in the Messiah. Elsewhere in Scripture (it is averred) the Messiah reigns, and is glorious; it is the people who suffer, and come through suffering to power. Nor is the Messiah's royal splendour at all the same as the very vague influence, evidently of a spiritual kind, which is attributed to the Servant in the end of ch. liii. The Messiah is endowed with the military and political virtues. He is a warrior, a king, a judge. He sits on the throne of David, He establishes David's kingdom. He smites the land with the rod of His mouth, and with the breath of His lips He slays the wicked. But very different phrases are used of the Servant. He is not called king, though kings shut their mouths at him,--he is a prophet and a martyr, and an expiation; and the phrases, I will divide him a portion with the great, and he shall divide the spoil with the strong, are simply metaphors of the immense spiritual success and influence with which His self-sacrifice shall be rewarded; as a spiritual power He shall take His place among the dominions and forces of the world. This is a true prophecy of what Israel, that worm of a people, should be lifted to; but it is quite different from the political throne, from which Isaiah had promised that the Messiah should sway the destinies of Israel and mankind.

But, in answer to this objection to finding the Messiah, or any other influential individual, in ch. liii., we may remember that there were already traces in Hebrew prophecy of a suffering Messiah: we come across them in ch. vii. There Isaiah presents Immanuel, whom we identified with the Prince-of-the-Four-Names in ch. ix., as at first nothing but a sufferer--a sufferer from the sins of His predecessors.[157] And, even though we are wrong in taking the suffering Immanuel for the Messiah, and though Isaiah meant him only as a personification of Israel suffering for the error of Ahaz, had not the two hundred years, which elapsed between Isaiah's prophecy of Israel's glorious Deliverer, been full of room enough, and, what is more, of experience enough, for the ideal champion of the people to be changed to something more spiritual in character and in work? Had the nation been baptized, for most of those two centuries, in vain, in the meaning of suffering, and in vain had they seen exemplified in their noblest spirits the fruits and glory of self-sacrifice?[158] The type of Hero had changed in Israel since Isaiah wrote of his Prince-of-the-Four-Names. The king had been replaced by the prophet; the conqueror by the martyr; the judge who smote the land by the rod of his mouth, and slew the wicked by the breath of his lips,--by the patriot who took his country's sins upon his own conscience. The monarchy had perished; men knew that, even if Israel were set upon their own land again, it would not be under an independent king of their own; nor was a Jewish champion of the martial kind, such as Isaiah had promised for deliverance from the Assyrian, any more required. Cyrus, the Gentile, should do all the campaigning required against Israel's enemies, and Israel's native Saviour be relieved for gentler methods and more spiritual aims. It is all this experience, of nearly two centuries, which explains the omission of the features of warrior and judge from ch. liii., and their replacement by those of a suffering patriot, prophet and priest. The reason of the change is, not because the prophet who wrote the chapter had not, as much as Isaiah, an individual in his view, but because, in the historical circumstance of the Exile, such an individual as Isaiah had promised, seemed no longer probable or required.

So far, then, from the difference between ch. liii. and previous prophecies of the Messiah affording evidence that in ch. liii. it is not the Messiah who is presented, this very change, that has taken place, explicable as it is from the history of the intervening centuries, goes powerfully to prove that it is the Messiah, and therefore an individual, whom the prophet so vividly describes.

The third main objection to our recognising an individual in ch. liii. is concerned only with our prophet himself. Is it not impossible, say some--or at least improbably inconsistent--for the same prophet first to have identified the Servant with the nation, and then to present him to us as an individual? We can understand the transference by the same writer of the name from the whole people to a part of the people; it is a natural transference, and the prophet sufficiently explains it. But how does he get from a part of the nation to a single individual? If in ch. xlix. he personifies, under the name Servant, some aspect of the nation, we are surely bound to understand the same personification when the Servant is again introduced--unless we have an explanation to the contrary. But we have none. The prophet gives no hint, except by dropping the name Israel, that the focus of his vision is altered,--no more paradoxes such as marked his passage from the people as a whole to a portion of them,---no consciousness that any explanation whatever is required. Therefore, however much finer the personification is drawn in ch. liii. than in ch. xlix., it is surely a personification still.

To which objection an obvious answer is, that our prophet is not a systematic theologian, but a dramatic poet, who allows his characters to disclose themselves and their relation without himself intervening to define or relate them. And any one who is familiar with the literature of Israel knows, that no less than the habit of drawing in from the whole people upon a portion of them, was the habit of drawing in from a portion of the people upon one individual. The royal Messiah Himself is a case in point. The original promise to David was of a seed; but soon prophecy concentrated the seed in one glorious Prince. The promise of Israel had always culminated in an individual. Then, again, in the nation's awful sufferings, it had been one man--the prophet Jeremiah--who had stood forth singly and alone, at once the incarnation of Jehovah's word, and the illustration in his own person of all the penalty that Jehovah laid upon the sinful people. With this tendency of his school to focus Israel's hope on a single individual, and especially with the example of Jeremiah before him, it is almost inconceivable that our prophet could have thought of any but an individual when he drew his portrait of the suffering Servant. No doubt the national sufferings were in his heart as he wrote; it was probably a personal share in them that taught him to write so sympathetically about the Man of pains, who was familiar with ailing. But to gather and concentrate all these sufferings upon one noble figure, to describe this figure as thoroughly conscious of their moral meaning, and capable of turning them to his people's salvation, was a process absolutely in harmony with the genius of Israel's prophecy, as well as with the trend of their recent experience; and there is, besides, no word in that great chapter, in which the process culminates, but is in thorough accordance with it. So far, therefore, from its being an impossible or an unlikely thing for our prophet to have at last reached his conception of an individual, it is almost impossible to conceive of him executing so personal a portrait as ch. lii. 13-liii., without thinking of a definite historical personage, such as Hebrew prophecy had ever associated with the redemption of his people.

4. We have now exhausted the passages in Isa. xl.-lxvi. which deal with the Servant of the Lord. We have found that our prophet identifies him at first with the whole nation, and then with some indefinite portion of the nation--indefinite in quantity, but most marked in character; that this personification grows more and more difficult to distinguish from a person; and that in ch. lii. 13-liii. there are very strong reasons, both in the text itself and in the analogy of other prophecy, to suppose that the portrait of an individual is intended. To complete our study of this development of the substance of the Servant, it is necessary to notice that it runs almost stage for stage with a development of his office. Up to ch. xlix., that is to say, while he is still some aspect of the people, the Servant is a prophet. In ch. l., where he is no longer called Israel, and approaches more nearly to an individual, his prophecy passes into martyrdom. And in ch. liii., where at last we recognise him as intended for an actual personage, his martyrdom becomes an expiation for the sins of the people. Is there a natural connection between these two developments? We have seen that it was by a very common process that our prophet transferred the national calling from the mass of the nation to a select few of the people. Is it by any equally natural

tendency that he shrinks from the many to the few, as he passes from prophecy to martyrdom, or from the few to the one, as he passes from martyrdom to expiation? It is a possibility for all God's people to be prophets: few are needed as martyrs. Is it by any moral law equally clear, that only one man should die for the people? These are questions worth thinking about. In Israel's history we have already found the following facts with which to answer them. The whole living generation of Israel felt themselves to be sinbearers: Our fathers have sinned, and we bear their iniquities. This conscience and penalty were more painfully felt by the righteous in Israel. But the keenest and heaviest sense of them was conspicuously that experienced by one man--the prophet Jeremiah. [159] And yet all these cases from the past of Israel's history do not furnish more than an approximation to the figure presented to us in ch. liii. Let us turn, therefore, to the future to see if we can find in it motive or fulfilment for this marvellous prophecy.

Footnotes:

149. A king's courtiers, soldiers, or subjects are called his servants. In this sense Israel was often styled the servants of Jehovah, as in Deut. xxxii. 36; Neh. i. 10, where the phrase is parallel to His people. But Jehovah's servants is a phrase also parallel to His worshippers (Psalm cxxxiv. 1, etc.); to those who trust Him (Psalm xxxiv. 22); and to those who love His name (Psalm lxix. 36). The term is also applied in the plural to the prophets (Amos iii. 7); and in the singular, to eminent individuals--such as Abraham, Joshua, David and Job; also by Jeremiah to the alien Nebuchadrezzar, while engaged on his mission from God against Jerusalem.

150. See p. [31]244.

151. The definite article is not used here with the word people, and hence the phrase has been taken by some in the vaguer sense of a people's covenant, as a general expression, along with its parallel clause, of the kind of influence the Servant was to exert, not on Israel, but on any people in the world; he was to be a people's covenant, and a light for nations. So practically Schultz, A. T. Theologie, 4th ed., p. 284. But the Hebrew word for people m is often used without the article to express the people Israel, just as the Hebrew word for land 'rts is often used without the article to express the land of Judah. (h'rts with the article, is in Isa. xl.-lxvi. the Earth.) And in ch. xlix. the phrase a covenant of the people again occurs, and in a context in which it can only mean a covenant of the people, Israel. Some render vryt m a covenant people. But in xlix. 8 this is plainly an impossible rendering.

152. Meshullam is found as a proper name in the historical books of the Old Testament, especially Nehemiah, e.g., iii. 4, 6, 30.

153. Hosea xi. 1; Matt. ii. 15

154. Of all the expressions used of him the only one which shows a real tendency to a plural reference is in his deaths (ver. 9), and even it (if it is the correct reading) is quite capable of application to an individual who suffered such manifold martyrdom as is set forth in the passage.

155. Not one word in them betrays any sense of a body of men or an ideal people standing behind them, which sense surely some expression would have betrayed, if it had been in the prophet's mind.

156. A. B. D., in a review of the last edition of Delitzsch's Isaiah, in the Theol. Review, iv., p. 276.

157. Isaiah I. i.-xxxix., pp. [32]134, [33]135.

158. See p. [34]42.

159. See ch. [35]ii. of this volume.

Rev. George Adam Smith, M.A.

CHAPTER XVII

THE SERVANT OF THE LORD IN THE NEW TESTAMENT.

In last chapter we confined our study of the Servant of Jehovah to the text of Isa. xl.-lxvi., and to the previous and contemporary history of Israel. Into our interpretation of the remarkable Figure, whom our prophet has drawn for us, we have put nothing which cannot be gathered from those fields and by the light of the prophet's own day. But now we must travel further, and from days far future to our prophet borrow a fuller light to throw back upon his mysterious projections. We take this journey into the future for reasons he himself has taught us. We have learned that his pictures of the Servant are not the creation of his own mind; a work of art complete "through fancy's or through logic's aid." They are the scattered reflections and suggestions of experience. The prophet's eyes have been opened to read them out of the still growing and incomplete history of his people. With that history they are indissolubly bound up. Their plainest forms are but a transcript of its clearest facts; their paradoxes are its paradoxes (reflections now of the confused and changing consciousness of this strange people, or again of the contrast between God's design for them and their real character): their ideals are the suggestion and promise which its course reveals to an inspired eye. Thus, in picturing the Servant, our prophet sometimes confines himself to history that has already happened to Israel; but sometimes, also, upon the purpose and promise of this, he outruns what has happened, and plainly lifts his voice from the future. Now we must remember that he does so, not merely because the history itself has native possibilities of fulfilment in it, but because he believes that it is in the hands of an Almighty and Eternal God, who shall surely guide it to the end of His purpose revealed in it. It is an article of our prophet's creed, that the God who speaks through him controls all history, and by His prophets can publish beforehand what course it will take; so that, when we find in our prophet anything we do not see fully justified or illustrated by the time he wrote, it is only in observance of the conditions he has laid down, that we seek for its explanation in the future.

Let us, then, take our prophet upon his own terms, and follow the history, with which he has so closely bound up the prophecy of the Servant, both in suggestion and fulfilment, in order that we may see whether it will yield to us the secret of what, if we have read his language aright, his eyes perceived in it--the promise of an Individual Servant. And let us do so in his faith, that history is one progressive and harmonious movement under the hand of the God in whose name he speaks. Our exploration will be rewarded, and our faith confirmed. We shall find the nation, as promised, restored to its own land, and pursuing through the centuries its own life. We shall find within the nation what the prophet looked for,--an elect and effective portion, with the conscience of a national service to the world, but looking for the achievement of this to such an Individual Servant, as the prophet seemed ultimately to foreshadow. The world itself we shall find growing more and more open to this service. And at last, from Israel's national conscience of the service we shall see emerge One with the sense that He alone is responsible and able for it. And this One Israelite will not only in His own person exhibit a character and achieve a work, that illustrate and far excel our prophet's highest imaginations, but will also become, to a new Israel infinitely more numerous than the old, the conscience and inspiration of their collective fulfilment of the ideal.

***

1. In the Old Testament we cannot be sure of any further appearance of our prophet's Servant of the Lord. It might be thought, that in a post-exilic promise, Zech. iii. 8, I will bring forth My Servant the Branch, we had an identification of the hero of the first part of the Book of Isaiah, the Branch out of Jesse's roots (xi. 1), with the hero of the second part; but servant here may so easily be meant in the more general sense in which it occurs in the Old Testament, that we are not justified in finding any more particular connection. In Judaism beyond the Old Testament the national and personal interpretations of the Servant were both current. The Targum of Jonathan, and both the Talmud of Jerusalem and the Talmud of Babylon, recognise the personal Messiah in ch. liii.; the Targum also identifies him as early as in ch. xlii. This personal interpretation the Jews abandoned only after they had entered on their controversy with Christian theologians; and in the cruel persecutions, which Christians inflicted upon them throughout the middle ages, they were supplied with only too many reasons for insisting that ch.

liii. was prophetic of suffering Israel--the martyr-people--as a whole. [160] It is a strange history--the history of our race, where the first through their pride and error so frequently become the last, and the last through their sufferings are set in God's regard with the first. But of all its strange reversals none surely was ever more complete than when the followers of Him, who is set forth in this passage, the unresisting and crucified Saviour of men, behaved in His Name with so great a cruelty as to be righteously taken by His enemies for the very tyrants and persecutors whom the passage condemns.

2. But it is in the New Testament that we see the most perfect reflection of the Servant of the Lord, both as People and Person.

In the generation, from which Jesus sprang, there was, amid national circumstances closely resembling those in which the Second Isaiah was written, a counterpart of that Israel within Israel, which our prophet has personified in ch. xlix. The holy nation lay again in bondage to the heathen, partly in its own land, partly scattered across the world; and Israel's righteousness, redemption and ingathering were once more the questions of the day. The thoughts of the masses, as of old in Babylonian days, did not rise beyond a political restoration; and although their popular leaders insisted upon national righteousness as necessary to this, it was a righteousness mainly of a ceremonial kind-- hard, legal, and often more unlovely in its want of enthusiasm and hope than even the political fanaticism of the vulgar. But around the temple, and in quiet recesses of the land, a number of pious and ardent Israelites lived on the true milk of the word, and cherished for the nation hopes of a far more spiritual character. If the Pharisees laid their emphasis on the law, this chosen Israel drew their inspiration rather from prophecy; and of all prophecy it was the Book of Isaiah, and chiefly the latter part of it, on which they lived.

As we enter the Gospel history from the Old Testament, we feel at once that Isaiah is in the air. In this fair opening of the new year of the Lord, the harbinger notes of the book awaken about us on all sides like the voices of birds come back with the spring. In Mary's song, the phrase He hath holpen His Servant Israel; in the description of Simeon, that he waited for the consolation of Israel, a phrase taken from the Comfort ye, comfort ye My people in Isa. xl. 1; such frequent phrases, too, as the redemption of Jerusalem, a light of the Gentiles and the glory of Israel, light to them that sit in darkness, and other echoed promises of light and peace and the remission of sins, are all repeated from our evangelical prophecy. In the fragments of the Baptist's preaching, which are extant, it is remarkable that almost every metaphor and motive may be referred to the Book of Isaiah, and mostly to its exilic half: the generation of vipers, [161] the trees and axe laid to the root, [162] the threshing floor and fan, [163] the fire, [164] the bread and clothes to the poor, [165] and especially the proclamation of Jesus, Behold the Lamb of God that beareth the sin of the world. [166] To John himself were applied the words of Isa. xl.: The voice of one crying in the wilderness, Make ye ready the way of the Lord, make His paths straight; and when Christ sought to rouse again the Baptist's failing faith it was of Isa. lxi. that He reminded him.

Our Lord, then, sprang from a generation of Israel, which had a strong conscience of the national aspect of the Service of God,--a generation with Isa. xl.-lxvi. at its heart. We have seen how He Himself insisted upon the uniqueness of Israel's place among the nations--salvation is of the Jews--and how closely He identified Himself with His people--I am not sent but to the lost sheep of the house of Israel. But all Christ's strong expression of Israel's distinction from the rest of mankind, is weak and dim compared with His expression of His own distinction from the rest of Israel. If they were the one people with whom God worked in the world, He was the one Man, whom God sent to work upon them, and to use them to work upon others. We cannot tell how early the sense of this distinction came to the Son of Mary. Luke reveals it in Him, before He had taken His place as a citizen and was still within the family: Wist ye not that I must be about My Father's business? At His first public appearance He had it fully, and others acknowledged it. In the opening year of His ministry it threatened to be only a Distinction of the First--they took Him by force, and would have made Him King. But as time went on it grew evident that it was to be, not the Distinction of the First, but the Distinction of the Only. The enthusiastic crowds melted away: the small band, whom He had most imbued with His spirit, proved that they could follow Him but a certain length in His consciousness of His Mission. Recognising in Him the supreme prophet- -Lord, to whom shall we go? Thou hast the words of eternal life--they immediately failed to understand, that suffering also must be endured by Him for the people: Be it far from Thee, Lord. This suffering was His conscience and His burden alone. Now, we cannot overlook the fact, that the point at which Christ's way became so solitary was the same point at which we felt our prophet's language cease to oblige us to understand by it a portion of the people, and begin to be applicable to a single individual,--the point, namely, where prophecy passes into martyrdom. But whether our prophet's pictures of the suffering and atoning Servant of the Lord are meant for some aspect of the national experience, or as the portrait of a real individual, it is certain that in His martyrdom and service of ransom Jesus felt Himself to be absolutely alone. He who had begun His Service of God with all the people on His side, consummated the same with the leaders and the masses of the nation against Him, and without a single partner from among His own friends, either in the fate which overtook Him, or in the conscience with which He bore it.

Rev. George Adam Smith, M.A.

Now all this parallel between Jesus of Nazareth and the Servant of the Lord is unmistakable enough, even in this mere outline; but the details of the Gospel narrative and the language of the Evangelists still more emphasize it. Christ's herald hailed Him with words which gather up the essence of Isa. liii.: Behold the Lamb of God. He read His own commission from ch. lxi.: The Spirit of the Lord is upon Me. To describe His first labours among the people, His disciples again used words from ch. liii.: Himself bare our sicknesses. To paint His manner of working in face of opposition they quoted the whole passage from ch. xlii.: Behold My Servant ... He shall not strive. The name Servant was often upon His own lips in presenting Himself: Behold, I am among you as one that serveth. When His office of prophecy passed into martyrdom, He predicted for Himself the treatment which is detailed in ch. l.,-- the smiting, plucking and spitting: and in time, by Jew and Gentile, this treatment was inflicted on Him to the very letter. [167] As to His consciousness in fulfilling something more than a martyrdom, and alone among the martyrs of Israel offering by His death an expiation for His people's sins, His own words are frequent and clear enough to form a counterpart to ch. liii. With them before us, we cannot doubt that He felt Himself to be the One of whom the people in that chapter speak, as standing over against them all, sinless, and yet bearing their sins. But on the night on which He was betrayed, while just upon the threshold of this extreme and unique form of service, into which it has been given to no soul of man, that ever lived, to be conscious of following Him--as if anxious that His disciples should not be so overwhelmed by the awful part in which they could not imitate Him as to forget the countless other ways in which they were called to fulfil His serving spirit--He took a towel and girded Himself, and when He had washed their feet, He said unto them, If I, then, your Lord and Master, have washed your feet, you also ought to wash one another's feet--thereby illustrating what is so plainly set forth in our prophecy, that short of the expiation, of which only One in His sinlessness has felt the obligation, and short of the martyrdom, which it has been given to but few of His people to share with Him, there are a thousand humble forms rising out of the needs of everyday life, in which men are called to employ towards one another the gentle and self-forgetful methods of the true Servant of God.

With the four Gospels in existence, no one doubts or can doubt that Jesus of Nazareth fulfilled the cry, Behold My Servant. With Him it ceased to be a mere ideal, and took its place as the greatest achievement in history.

3. In the earliest discourses of the Apostles, therefore, it is not wonderful that Jesus should be expressly designated by them as the Servant of God,--the Greek word used being that by which the Septuagint specially translates the Hebrew term in Isa. xl.-lxvi. [168] : God hath glorified His Servant Jesus. Unto you first, God, having raised up His Servant, sent Him to bless you, in turning away every one of you from your iniquities.... In this city against Thy holy Servant Jesus, whom Thou didst anoint, both Herod and Pontius Pilate, with the Gentiles and the peoples of Israel, were gathered together to do whatsoever Thy hand and Thy counsel foreordained to pass. Grant that signs and wonders may be done through the name of Thy Holy Servant Jesus. [169] It must also be noticed, that in one of the same addresses, and again by Stephen in his argument before the Sanhedrin, Jesus is called The Righteous One, [170] doubtless an allusion to the same title for the Servant in Isa. liii. 11. Need we recall the interpretation of Isa. liii. by Philip? [171]

It is known to all how Peter develops this parallel in his First Epistle, borrowing the figures but oftener the very words of Isa. liii. to apply to Christ. Like the Servant of the Lord, Jesus is as a lamb: He is a patient sufferer in silence; He is the Righteous--again the classic title--for the unrighteous; in exact quotation from the Greek of Isa. liii.: He did no sin, neither was found guile in His mouth, ye were as sheep gone astray, but He Himself hath borne our sins, with whose stripes ye are healed. [172]

Paul applies two quotations from Isa. lii. 13-liii. to Christ: I have striven to preach the Gospel not where Christ was named; as it is written, To whom He was not spoken of they shall see: and they that have not heard shall understand; and He hath made Him to be sin for us who knew no sin. [173] And none will doubt that when he so often disputed that the Messiah must suffer, or wrote Messiah died for our sins according to the Scriptures, he had Isa. liii. in mind, exactly as we have seen it applied to the Messiah by Jewish scholars a hundred years later than Paul.

4. Paul, however, by no means confines the prophecy of the Servant of the Lord to Jesus the Messiah. In a way which has been too much overlooked by students of the subject, Paul revives and reinforces the collective interpretation of the Servant. He claims the Servant's duties and experience for himself, his fellow-labourers in the gospel, and all believers.

In Antioch of Pisidia, Paul and Barnabas said of themselves to the Jews: For so hath the Lord commanded us saying, I have set thee to be a light of the Gentiles, that thou shouldest be for salvation to the ends of the earth. [174] Again, in the eighth of Romans, Paul takes the Servant's confident words, and speaks them of all God's true people. He is near that justifieth me, who is he that condemneth? cried the Servant in our prophecy, and Paul echoes for all believers: It is God that justifieth, who is he that condemneth? [175] And again, in his second letter to Timothy, he says, speaking of that pastor's work, For the servant of the Lord must not strive, but be gentle towards all; words which were borrowed from, or suggested by, Isa. xlii. 1-3. [176] In these instances, as well as in his constant use of the terms slave, servant, minister, with their cognates, Paul fulfils the intention of Jesus, who so continually, by example, parable, and direct commission, enforced the life of His people as a Service to the Lord.

5. Such, then, is the New Testament reflection of the Prophecy of the Servant of the Lord, both as People and Person. Like all physical reflections, this moral one may be said, on the whole, to stand reverse to its original. In Isa. xl.-lxvi. the Servant is People first, Person second. But in the New Testament--except for a faint and scarcely articulate application to Israel in the beginning of the gospels--the Servant is Person first and People afterwards. The Divine Ideal which our prophet saw narrowing down from the Nation to an Individual, was owned and realised by Christ. But in Him it was not exhausted. With added warmth and light, with a new power of expansion, it passed through Him to fire the hearts and enlist the wills of an infinitely greater people than the Israel for whom it was originally designed. With this witness, then, of history to the prophecies of the Servant, our way in expounding and applying them is clear. Jesus Christ is their perfect fulfilment and illustration. But we who are His Church are to find in them our ideal and duty,--our duty to God and to the world. In this, as in so many other matters, the unfulfilled prophecy of Israel is the conscience of Christianity.

Footnotes:

160. Cf. The Jewish Interpreters on Isa. liii., Driver and Neubauer, Oxford, 1877. Abravanel, who himself takes ch. liii. in a national sense, admits, after giving the Christian interpretation, that "in fact Jonathan ben Uziel, 'the Targumist,' applied it to the Messiah, who was still to come, and this is likewise the opinion of the wise in many of their Midrashim." And R. Moscheh al Shech, of the sixteenth century, says: "See, our masters have with one voice held as established and handed down, that here it is King Messiah who is spoken of." (Both these passages quoted by Bredenkamp in his commentary, p. 307.)

161. Isa. lix. 5.
162. Id. vi. 13; ix. 18; x. 17, 34; xlvii. 14.
163. Id. xxi. 10; xxviii. 27; xl. 24; xli. 15 ff.
164. Id. i. 31; xlvii. 14.
165. Isa. lviii. 7.
166. Undoubtedly taken from Isa. liii.
167. Cf. with the Greek version of Isa. l. 4-7, Luke xviii. 31, 32; Matt. xxvi. 67.
168. In Isa. xl.-lxvi. the Septuagint translates the Hebrew for Servant by one or other of two words--pais and doulos. Pais is used in xli. 8; xlii. 1; xliv. 1 ff.; xliv. 21; xlv. 4; xlix. 6; l. 10; lii. 13. But doulos is used in xlviii. 20; xlix. 3 and 5. In the Acts it is pais that is used of Christ: "An apostle is never called pais (but only doulos) Theou" (Meyer). But David is called pais (Acts iv. 25).

169. Acts iii. 13, 26; iv. 27-30.
170. Acts iii. 14; vii. 52.
171. Acts viii. 30 ff.
172. 1 Peter i. 19; ii. 22, 23; iii. 18.
173. Rom. xv. 20 f.; 2 Cor. v. 21.
174. Acts xiii. 47, after Isa. xlix. 6.
175. Isa. l. 8, and Rom. viii. 33, 34.
176. 2 Tim. ii. 24. We may note, also, how Paul in Eph. vi. takes the armour with which God is clothed in Isa. lix. 17, breastplate and helmet, and equips the individual Christian with them; and how, in the same passage, he takes for the Christian from Isa. xl. the Messiah's girdle of truth and the sword of the Spirit,--he shall smite the land with the rod of his mouth, and with the breath of his lips shall he slay the wicked.

Rev. George Adam Smith, M.A.

CHAPTER XVIII

THE SERVICE OF GOD AND MAN.

Isaiah xlii. 1-7.

We now understand, whom to regard as the Servant of the Lord. The Service of God was a commission to witness and prophesy for God upon earth, made out at first in the name of the entire nation Israel. When their unfitness as a whole became apparent, it was delegated to a portion of them. But as there were added to its duties of prophecy, those of martyrdom and atonement for the sins of the people, our prophet, it would seem, saw it focussed in the person of an individual.

In history Jesus Christ has fulfilled this commission both in its national and in its personal aspects. He realised the ideal of the prophet-people. He sacrificed Himself and made atonement for the sins of men. But having illustrated the service of God in the world, Christ did not exhaust it. He returned it to His people, a more clamant conscience than ever, and He also gave them grace to fulfil its demands. Through Christ the original destination of these prophecies becomes, as Paul saw, their ultimate destination as well. That Israel refused this Service or failed in it only leaves it more clearly to us as duty; that Jesus fulfilled it not only confirms that duty, but adds hope and courage to discharge it.

Although the terms of this Service were published nearly two thousand five hundred years ago, in a petty dialect that is now dead, to a helpless tribe of captives in a world, whose civilisation has long sunk to ruin, yet these terms are so free of all that is provincial or antique, they are so adapted to the lasting needs of humanity, they are so universal in their scope, they are so instinct with that love which never faileth, though prophecies fail and tongues cease, that they come home to heart and conscience to-day with as much tenderness and authority as ever. The first programme of these terms is given in ch. xlii. 1-7. The authorised English version is one of unapproachable beauty, but its emphasis and rhythm are not the emphasis and rhythm of the original, and it has missed one at least of the striking points of the Hebrew. The following version, which makes no attempt at elegance, is almost literal, follows the same order as the original that it may reproduce the same emphasis, and, as far as English can, repeats the original rhythm. The point, which it rescues from the neglect of the Authorised Version, is this, that the verbs used of the Servant in ver. 4, He shall not fade nor break, are the same as are used of the wick and the reed in ver. 3.

> Lo, My Servant! I hold by him;
> My Chosen! Well-pleased is My soul!
> I have set My Spirit upon him;
> Law to the Nations he brings forth.
> He cries not, nor lifts up, [177]
> Nor lets his voice be heard in the street.
> Reed that is broken he breaks not off,
> Wick that is fading he does not quench:
> Faithfully brings he forth Law.
> He shall not fade neither break,
> Till he have set in the Earth [178] Law;
> And for his teaching the Isles are waiting.
> Thus saith the God, Jehovah,
> Creator of the heavens that stretched them forth,
> Spreader of Earth and her produce,
> Giver of breath to the people upon her,
> And of spirit to them that walk therein:
> I, Jehovah, have called thee in righteousness,
> To grasp thee fast by thy hand, and to keep thee,
> And to set thee for a covenant of the People,
> For a light of the Nations:
> To open blind eyes,
> To bring forth from durance the captive,
> From prison the dwellers in darkness.

The Expositor's Bible: The Book of Isaiah Volumes I & II
1. The Conscience of Service.

As several of these lines indicate, this is a Service to Man, but what we must first fasten upon is that before being a Service to Man it is a Service for God. Behold, My Servant, says God's commission very emphatically. And throughout the prophecy the Servant is presented as chosen of God, inspired of God, equipped of God, God's creature, God's instrument; useful only because he is used, influential because he is influenced, victorious because he is obedient; learning the methods of his work by daily wakefulness to God's voice, a good speaker only because he is first a good listener; with no strength or courage but what God lends, and achieving all for God's glory. Notice how strongly it is said that God holds by him, grasps him by the hand. We shall see that his Service is as sympathetic and comprehensive a purpose for humanity as was ever dreamed in any thought or dared in any life. Whether we consider its tenderness for individuals, or the universalism of its hope for the world, or its gentle appreciation of all human effort and aspiration, or its conscience of mankind's chief evil, or the utterness of its self-sacrifice in order to redeem men,--we shall own it to be a programme of human duty, and a prophecy of human destiny, to which the growing experience of our race has been able to add nothing that is essential. But the Service becomes all that to man, because it first takes all that from God. Not only is the Servant's sense of duty to all humanity just the conscience of God's universal sovereignty,--for it is a remarkable and never-to-be-forgotten fact, that Israel recognised their God's right to the whole world, before they felt their own duty to mankind,--but the Servant's character and methods are the reflection of the Divine. Feature by feature the Servant corresponds to His Lord. His patience is but sympathy with Jehovah's righteousness,--I will uphold thee with the right hand of My righteousness. His gentleness with the unprofitable and the unlovely--He breaks not off the broken reed nor quenches the flickering wick--is but the temper of the everlasting God, who giveth power to the faint, and to them that have no might He increaseth strength. His labour and passion and agony, even they have been anticipated in the Divine nature, for the LORD stirreth up zeal like a man of war; He saith, I will cry out like a travailing woman. In no detail is the Servant above his Master. His character is not original, but is the impress of his God's: I have put My spirit upon him.

There are many in our day, who deny this indebtedness of the human character to the Divine, and in the Service of Man would have us turn our backs upon God. Positivists, while admitting that the earliest enthusiasm of the individual for his race did originate in the love of a Divine Being, assert nevertheless that we have grown away from this illusory motive; and that in the example of humanity itself we may find all the requisite impulse to serve it. The philosophy of history, which the extreme Socialists have put forward, is even more explicit. According to them, mankind was disturbed in a primitive, tribal socialism--or service of each other--by the rise of spiritual religion, which drew the individual away from his kind and absorbed him in selfish relations to God. Such a stage, represented by the Hebrew and Christian faiths, and by the individualist political economy which has run concurrent with the later developments of Christianity, was (so these Socialists admit) perhaps necessary for temporary discipline and culture, like the land of Egypt to starved Jacob's children; but like Egypt, when it turned out to be the house of bondage, the individualist economy and religion are now to be abandoned for the original land of promise,--Socialism once more, but universal instead of tribal as of old. Out of this analogy, which is such Socialists' own, Sinai and the Ten Commandments are, of course, omitted. We are to march back to freedom without a God, and settle down to love and serve each other by administration.

But can we turn our backs on God, without hurting man? The natural history of philanthropy would seem to say that we cannot. This prophecy is one of its witnesses. Earliest ideal as it is, of a universal service of mankind, it starts in its obligation from the universal Sovereignty of God; it starts in every one of its affections from some affection of the Divine character. And we have not grown away from the need of its everlasting sources. Cut off God from the Service of man, and the long habit and inherent beauty of that Service may perpetuate its customs for a few generations; but the inevitable call must come to subject conduct to the altered intellectual conditions, and in the absence of God every man's ideal shall surely turn from, How can I serve my neighbour? to, How can I make my neighbour serve me? As our prophet reminds us in his vivid contrast between Israel, the Servant of the Lord, and Babylon, who saith in her heart: I am, and there is none beside me, there are ultimately but two alternative lords of the human will, God and Self. If we revolt from the Authority and Example of the One, we shall surely become subject, in the long run, to the ignorance, the short-sightedness, the pedantry, the cruelty of the other. These words are used advisedly. With no sense of the sacredness of every human life as created in the image of God, and with no example of an Infinite Mercy before them, men would leave to perish all that was weak, or, from the limited point of view of a single community or generation, unprofitable. Some Positivists and those Socialists, who do not include God in the society they seek to establish, admit that they expect something like that to follow from their denial of God. In certain Positivist proposals for the reform of charity, we are told that the ideal scheme of social relief would be the one which limited itself to persons judged to be of use to the community as a whole; that is, that in their succour of the weak, their bounty to the poor, and their care of the young, society should be guided, not by the eternal laws of justice and of mercy, but by the opinions of the representatives of the public for the time being and by their standard of utility to the commonwealth. Your atheist-Socialist is still more frank. In the state, which he sees rising after he has got rid of Christianity, he would suppress, he tells us, all who preached such a thing as the fear of the future life, and he would not repeat the present exceptional legislation for the protection of women and children, for whom, he whines, far too much has been recently done in comparison with what has been enacted for the protection of men. [179] These are, of course, but vain things which the heathen imagine (and some of us have an ideal of socialism very different from the godlessness which has usurped the noble name), but they serve to illustrate what clever men, who have thrown off all belief in God, will bring themselves to hope for: a society utterly Babylonian, without pity or patience,--if it were possible for these eternal graces to die out of any human community,--subject to the opinion of pedants, whose tender mercies would be far more fatal to the weak and poor than the present indifference of the rich; seriously fettering liberty of conscience and destitute of chivalry. It may be that our Positivist critics are right, and that the interests of humanity have suffered in Christian times from the prevalence of too selfish and introspective a religion; but whether our religion has looked too intensely inward or not, we cannot, it is certain, do without a religion that looks steadily up, owning the discipline of Divine Law and the Example of an Infinite Mercy and Longsuffering.

But, though we had never heard of Positivism or of the Socialism that denies God, our age, with its popular and public habits, would still require this example of Service, which our prophecy enforces: it is an age so charged with the instincts of work, with the ambition to be useful, with the fashion of altruism; but so empty of the sense of God, of reverence, discipline and prayer. We do not need to learn philanthropy,--the thing is in the air; but we do need to be taught that philanthropy demands a theology both for its purity and its effectiveness. When philanthropy has become, what it is so much to-day, the contest of rival politicians, the ambition of every demagogue, who can get his head above the crowd, the fitful self-indulgence of weak hearts, the opportunity of vain theorists, and for all a temptation to work with lawless means for selfish ends,--it is time to remember that the Service of Man is first of all a great Service for God. This faith alone can keep us from the wilfulness, the crotchets and the insubordination, which spoil so many well-intentioned to their kind, and so wofully break up the ranks of progress. Humility is the first need of the philanthropist of to-day: humility, discipline and the sense of proportion; and these are qualities, which only faith in God and the conscience of law are known to bestow upon the human heart. It is the fear of God that will best preserve us from making our philanthropy the mere flattery of the popular appetite. To keep us utterly patient with men we need to think of God's patience with ourselves. While to us all there come calls to sacrifice, which our fellow-men may so little deserve from us, and against which our self-culture can plead so many reasons, that unless God's will and example were before us, the calls would never be obeyed. In short, to be most useful in this life it is necessary to feel that we are used. Look at Christ. To Him philanthropy was no mere habit and spontaneous affection; even for that great heart the love of man had to be enforced by the compulsion of the will of God. The busy days of healing and teaching had between them long nights of lonely prayer; and the Son of God did not pass to His supreme self-sacrifice for men till after the struggle with, and the submission to, His Father's will in Gethsemane.

II. The Substance of Service.

The substance of the Servant's work is stated in one word, uttered thrice in emphatic positions. Judgement for the nations shall he bring forth.... According to truth shall he bring forth judgement.... He shall not flag nor break, till he set in the earth [180] judgement.

The English word judgement is a natural but misleading translation of the original, and we must dismiss at once the idea of judicial sentence, which it suggests. The Hebrew is "mishpat," which means, among other things, either a single statute, or the complete body of law which God gave Israel by Moses, at once their creed and their code; or, perhaps, also the abstract quality of justice or right. We rendered it as the latter in Isa. i.-xxxix. But, as will be seen from the note below, [181] when used in Isa. xl.-lxvi. without the article, as here, it is the "mishpat" of Jehovah,--not so much the actual body of statutes given to Israel, as the principles of right or justice which they enforce. In one passage it is given in parallel to the civic virtues righteousness, truth, uprightness, but--as its etymology compared with theirs shows us--it is these viewed not in their character as virtues, but in their obligation as ordained by God. Hence, duty to Jehovah as inseparable from His religion (Ewald), religion as the law of life (Delitzsch), the law (Cheyne, who admirably compares the Arabic ed-Dîn) are all good renderings. Professor Davidson gives the fullest exposition. "It can scarcely," he says, "be rendered 'religion' in the modern sense, it is the equity and civil right which is the result of the true religion of Jehovah; and though comprehended under religion in the Old Testament sense, is rather, according to our conceptions, religion applied in civil life. Of old the religious unit was the state, and the life of the state was the expression of its religion. Morality was law or custom, and both reposed upon God. A condition of thought such as now prevails, where morality is based on independent grounds, whether natural law or the principles inherent in the mind apart from religion, did not then exist. What the prophet means by 'bringing forth right' is explained in another passage, where it is said that Jehovah's 'arms shall judge the peoples,' and that the 'isles shall wait for His arm' (ch. li. 5). 'Judgment' is that pervading of life by the principles of equity and humanity which is the immediate effect of the true religion of Jehovah." [182] In short, "mishpat" is not only the civic righteousness and justice, to which it is made parallel in our prophecy, but it is these with God behind them. On the one hand it is conterminous with national virtue, on the other it is the ordinance and will of God.

This, then, is the burden of the Servant's work, to pervade and instruct every nation's life on earth with the righteousness and piety that are ordained of God. He shall not flag nor break, till he have set in the earth Law,--till in every nation justice, humanity and worship are established as the law of God. We have seen that the Servant is in this passage still some aspect or shape of the people,--the people who are not a people, but scattered among the brickfields of Babylonia, a horde of captives. When we keep that in mind, two or three things come home to us about this task of theirs. First, it is no mere effort at proselytism. It is not an ambition to Judaise the world. The national consciousness and provincial habits, which cling about so many of the prophecies of Israel's relation to the world, have dropped from this one, and the nation's mission is identified with the establishment of law, the diffusion of light, the relief of suffering. I will give thee for a light to the nations: to open blind eyes, to bring out from durance the bound, from the prison the dwellers in darkness. [183] Again, it is no mere office of preaching, to which the Servant's commission is limited, no mere inculcation of articles of belief. But we have here the same rich, broad idea of religion, identifying it with the whole national life, which we found so often illustrated by Isaiah, and which is one of the beneficial results to religion of God's choice for Himself of a nation as a whole. [184] What such a Service has to give the world, is not merely testimony to the truth, nor fresh views of it, nor artistic methods of teaching it; but social life under its obligation, the public conscience of it, the long tradition and habit of it, the breed--what the prophets call the seed--of it. To establish true religion as the constitution, national duty, and regular practice of every people under the sun, in all the details of order, cleanliness, justice, purity and mercy, in which it had been applied to themselves,--such was the Service and the Destiny of Israel. And the marvel of so universal and political an ideal was, that it came not to a people in the front ranks of civilisation or of empire, but to a people that at the time had not even a political shape for themselves,--a mere herd of captives, despised and rejected of men. When we realise this, we understand that they never would have dared to think of it, or to speak of it to one another, unless they had believed it to be the purpose and will of Almighty God for them; unless they had recognised it, not only as a service desirable and true in itself, and, needed also by humanity, but withal as His "mishpat," His judgement or law, who by His bare word can bring all things to pass. But before we see how strongly He impressed them with this, that His creative force was in their mission, let us turn to the methods by which He commanded them to achieve it,-- methods corresponding to its purely spiritual and universal character.

III. *The Temper of Service.*
1. He shall not cry, nor lift up, Nor make his voice to be heard in the street.

There is nothing more characteristic of our prophecy than its belief in the power of speech, its exultation in the music and spell of the human voice. It opens with a chorus of high calls: none are so lovely to it as heralds, or so musical as watchmen when they lift up the voice; it sets the preaching of glad tidings before the people as their national ideal; eloquence it describes as a sharp sword leaping from God's scabbard. The Servant of the Lord is trained in style of speech; his words are as pointed arrows; he has the mouth of the learned, a voice to command obedience. The prophet's own tones are superb: nowhere else does the short sententiousness of Hebrew roll out into such long, sonorous periods. He uses speech in every style: for comfort, for bitter controversy, in clear proclamation, in deep-throated denunciation: Call with the throat, spare not, lift up the voice like a trumpet. His constant key-notes are, speak a word, lift up the voice with strength, sing, publish, declare. In fact, there is no use to which the human voice has ever been put in the Service of Man, for comfort's sake, or for justice, or for liberty, for the diffusion of knowledge or for the scattering of music, which our prophet does not enlist and urge upon his people.

When, then, he says of the Servant that he shall not cry, nor lift up, nor make his voice to be heard in the street, he cannot be referring to the means and art of the Service, but rather to the tone and character of the Servant. Each of the triplet of verbs he uses shows us this. The first one, translated cry, is not the cry or call of the herald voice in ch. xl., the high, clear Kara; it is ssa`a?, a sharper word with a choke in the centre of it meaning to scream, especially under excitement. Then to lift up is the exact equivalent of our "to be loud." And if we were seeking to translate into Hebrew our phrase "to advertise oneself," we could not find a closer expression for it than to make his voice be heard in the street. To be "screamy," to be "loud," to "advertise oneself,"--these modern expressions for vices that were ancient as well as modern render the exact force of the verse. Such the Servant of God will not be nor do. He is at once too strong, too meek and too practical. That God is with him, holding him fast, keeps him calm and unhysterical; that he is but God's instrument keeps him humble and quiet; and that his heart is in his work keeps him from advertising himself at its expense. It is perhaps especially for the last of these reasons that Matthew (in his twelfth chapter) quotes this passage of our Lord. Jesus had been disturbed in His labours of healing by the disputatious Pharisees. He had answered them, and then withdrawn from their neighbourhood. Many sick were brought after Him to His privacy, and He healed them all. But He charged them that they should not make Him known; that it might be fulfilled which was spoken by Isaiah the prophet, saying, Behold, My Servant ... he shall not strive, nor cry aloud, neither shall any one hear his voice in the streets. Now this cannot be, what some carelessly take it for, an example against controversy or debate of all kinds, for Jesus had Himself just been debating; nor can it be meant as an absolute forbidding of all publishing of good works, for Christ has shown us, on other occasions, that such advertisement is good. The difficulty is explained, by what we have seen to explain other perplexing actions of our Lord, His intensely practical spirit. The work to be done determined everything. When it made argument necessary, as that same day it had done in the synagogue, then our Lord entered on argument: He did not only heal the man with the withered hand, but He made him the text of a sermon. But when talking about His work hindered it, provoked the Pharisees to come near with their questions, and took up His time and strength in disputes with them, then for the work's sake He forbade talk about it. We have no trace of evidence that Christ forbade this advertisement also for His own sake,--as a temptation to Himself and fraught with evil effects upon His feelings. We know that it is for this reason we have to shun it. Even though we are quite guiltless of contributing to such publication ourselves, and it is the work of generous and well-meaning friends, it still becomes a very great danger to us. For it is apt to fever us and exhaust our nervous force, even when it does not turn our heads with its praise,--to distract us and to draw us more and more into the enervating habit of paying attention to popular opinion. Therefore, as a man values his efficiency in the Service of Man, he will not make himself to be heard in the street. There is an amount of making to be heard which is absolutely necessary for the work's sake; but there is also an amount which can be indulged in only at the work's expense. Present-day philanthropy, even with the best intentions, suffers from this over-publicity, and its besetting sins are "loudness" and hysteria.

What, then, shall tell us how far we can go? What shall teach us how to be eloquent without screaming, clear without being loud, impressive without wasting our strength in seeking to make an impression? These questions bring us back to what we started with, as the indispensable requisite for Service--some guiding and religious principles behind even the kindliest and steadiest tempers. For many things in the Service of Man no exact rules will avail; neither logic nor bye-laws of administration can teach us to observe the uncertain and constantly varying degree of duty, which they demand. Tact for that is bestowed only by the influence of lofty principles working from above. This is a case in point. What rules of logic or "directions of the superior authority" can, in the Service of Man, distinguish for us between excitement and earnestness, bluster and eloquence, energy and mere self-advertisement; on whose subtle differences the whole success of the service must turn. Only the discipline of faith, only the sense of God, can help us here. The practical temper by itself will not help us. To be busy but gives us too great self-importance; and hard work often serves only to bring out the combative instincts. To know that we are His Servants shall keep us meek; that we are held fast by His hand shall keep us calm; that His great laws are not abrogated shall keep us sane. When for our lowliest and most commonplace kinds of service we think no religion is required, let us remember the solemn introduction of the evangelist to his story of the foot-washing. Jesus knowing that the Father had given all things into His hands, and that He came forth from God and goeth unto God, riseth from supper, and layeth aside His garments; and He took a towel, and girded Himself; then He poureth water into the bason, and began to wash His disciples' feet.

2. But to meekness and discipline the Servant adds gentleness.

Reed that is broken he breaks not off,
Wick that is fading he does not quench;
Faithfully brings he forth law.

The force of the last of these three lines is, of course, qualificative and conditional. It is set as a guard against the abuse of the first two, and means that though the Servant in dealing with men is to be solicitous about their weakness, yet the interests of religion shall in no way suffer. Mercy shall be practised, but so that truth is not compromised.

The original application of the verse is thus finely stated by Professor Davidson: "This is the singularly humane and compassionate view the Prophet takes of the Gentiles,--they are bruised reeds and expiring flames.... What the prophet may refer to is the human virtues, expiring among the nations, but not yet dead; the sense of God, debased by idolatries, but not extinct; the consciousness in the individual soul of its own worth and its capacities, and the glimmering ideal of a true life and a worthy activity almost crushed out by the grinding tyranny of rulers and the miseries entailed by their ambitions--this flickering light the Servant shall feed and blow into a flame. [185] ... It is the future relation of the 'people' Israel to other peoples that he describes. The thought which has now taken possession of statesmen of the higher class, that the point of contact between nation and nation need not be the sword, that the advantage of one people is not the loss of another but the gain of mankind, that the land where freedom has grown to maturity and is worshipped in her virgin serenity and loveliness should nurse the new-born babe in other homes, and that the strange powers of the mind of man and the subtle activities of his hand should not be repressed but fostered in every people, in order that the product may be poured into the general lap of the race--this idea is supposed to be due to Christianity. And, immediately, it is; but it is older than Christianity. It is found in this Prophet. And it is not new in him, for a Prophet, presumably a century and a half his senior, had said: The remnant of Jacob shall be in the midst of many peoples as a dew from the Lord, as showers upon the grass (Micah v. 7)." [186]

But while this national reference may be the one originally meant, the splendid vagueness of the metaphor forbids us to be content with it, or with any solitary application. For the two clauses are as the eyes of the All-Pitiful Father, that rest wherever on this broad earth there is any life, though it be so low as to be conscious only through pain or doubt; they are as the healing palms of Jesus stretched over the multitudes to bless and gather to Himself the weary and the poor in spirit. We contrast our miserable ruin of character, our feeble sparks of desire after holiness, with the life, which Christ demands and has promised, and in despair we tell ourselves, this can never become that. But it is precisely this that Christ has come to lift to that. The first chapter of the Sermon on the Mount closes with the awful command, Be ye perfect, as your Father in Heaven is perfect; but we work our way back through the chapter, and we come to this, Blessed are they that hunger and thirst after righteousness, for they shall be filled; and to this, Blessed are the poor in spirit, for theirs is the kingdom of heaven. Such is Christ's treatment of the bruised reed and the smoking flax. Let us not despair. There is only one kind of men, for whom it has no gospel,--the dead and they who are steeped in worldliness, who have forgotten what the pain of a sore conscience is, and are strangers to humility and aspiration. But for all who know their life, were it only through their pain or their doubt, were it only in the despair of what they feel to be a last struggle with temptation, were it only in contrition for their sin or in shame for their uselessness, this text has hope. Reed that is broken he breaketh not off, wick that is fading he doth not quench.

This objective sense of the Servant's temper must always be the first for us to understand. For more than he was, we are, mortal, ready ourselves to break and to fade. But having experienced the grace, let us show the same in our service to others. Let us understand that we are sent forth like the great Servant of God, that man may have life, and have it more abundantly. We need resolutely and with pious obstinacy to set this temper before us, for it is not natural to our hearts. Even the best of us, in the excitement of our work, forget to think of anything except of making our mark, or of getting the better of what we are at work upon. When work grows hard, the combative instincts waken within us, till we look upon the characters God has given us to mould as enemies to be fought. We are passionate to convince men, to overcome them with an argument, to wring the confession from them that we are right and they wrong. Now Christ our Master must have seen in every man He met a very great deal more to be fought and extirpated than we can possibly see in one another. Yet He largely left that alone, and addressed Himself rather to the sparks of nobility He found, and fostered these to a strong life, which from within overcame the badness of the man,--the badness which opposition from the outside would but have beaten into harder obduracy. We must ever remember that we are not warriors but artists,-- artists after the fashion of Jesus Christ, who came not to condemn life because it was imperfect, but to build life up to the image of God. So He sends us to be artists; as it is written, He gave some apostles, and some prophets, and some pastors and teachers. For what end? For convincing men, for telling them what fools they mostly are, for crushing them in the inquisition of their own conscience, for getting the better of them in argument?--no, not for these combative purposes at all, but for fostering and artistic ones: for the perfecting of the saints, for the building up of the body of Christ; till we all come unto a full grown man, unto the measure of the stature of the fulness of Christ.

He who, in his Service of Man, practises such a temper towards the breaking and the fading, shall never himself break or fade, as this prophecy implies when it uses the same verbs in verses three and four. For he who is loyal to life shall find life generous to him; he who is careful of weakness shall never want for strength.

IV. The Power behind Service.

There only remains now to emphasize the power that is behind Service. It is, say verses five and six, the Creative Power of God.

Thus saith The God, Jehovah,
Creator of the heavens, that stretched them forth,
Spreader of the earth and her produce,
Giver of breath to the people upon her,

Rev. George Adam Smith, M.A.

And of spirit to them that walk thereon,
I Jehovah have called thee in righteousness,
That I may grasp thee by thy hand, and keep thee.

Majestic confirmation of the call to Service! based upon the fundamental granite of this whole prophecy, which here crops out into a noble peak, firm station for the Servant, and point for prospect of all the future. It is our easy fault to read these words of the Creator as the utterance of mere ceremonial commonplace, blast of trumpets at the going forth of a hero, scenery for his stage, the pomp of nature summoned to assist at the presentation of God's elect before the world. Yet not for splendour were they spoken, but for bare faith's sake. God's Servant has been sent forth, weak and gentle, with quiet methods and to very slow effects. He shall not cry, nor lift up, nor make his voice to be heard in the streets. What chance has such, our service, in the ways of the world, where to be forceful and selfish, to bluster and battle, is to survive and overcome! So we speak, and the panic ambition rises to fight the world with its own weapons, and to employ the kinds of debate, advertisement and competition by which the world goes forward. For this, the Creator calls to us, and marshals His powers before our eyes. We thought there were but two things,--our own silence and the world's noise. There are three, and the world's noise is only an interruption between the other two. Across it deep calleth unto deep; the immeasurable processes of creation cry to the feeble convictions of truth in our hearts, We are one. Creation is the certificate that no moral effort is a forlorn hope. When God, after repeating His results in creation, adds, I have called thee in righteousness, He means that there is some consistency between His processes in creation, rational and immense as they are, and those poor efforts He calls on our weakness to make, which look so foolish in face of the world. Behind every moral effort there is, He says, Creative force. Right and Might are ultimately one. Paul sums up the force of the passage, when, after speaking of the success of his ministry, he gives as its reason that the God of Creation and of Grace are the same. Therefore seeing we have received this ministry we faint not. For God, who hath commanded the light to shine out of darkness, hath shined in our hearts, to give the light of the knowledge of God in the face of Jesus Christ.

The spiritual Service of Man, then, has creative forces behind it; work for God upon the hearts and characters of others has creative force behind it. And nature is the seal and the sacrament of this. Let our souls, therefore, dilate with her prospects. Let our impatience study her reasonableness and her laws. Let our weak wills feel the rush of her tides. For the power that is in her, and the faithful pursuance of purposes to their ends, are the power and the character that work behind each witness of our conscience, each effort of our heart for others. Not less strong than she, not less calm, not less certain of success, shall prove the moral Service of Man.

Footnotes:

177. The English equivalent is, nor is loud.
178. This time with the article, so not the land of Judah only, but the Earth.
179. Bax, Religion of Socialism.
180. This time "arets" with the article. So not the land of Judah only but the world.
181. The following are the four main meanings of "mishpat" in Isa. xl.-lxvi.: 1. In a general sense, a legal process, xli. 1, let us come together to the judgement, or the law (with the article), cf. l. 8, man of my judgement, i.e., my fellow-at-law, my adversary; liii. 8, oppression and judgement, i.e., a judgement which was oppressive, a legal injustice. 2. A person's cause or right, xl. 27, xlix. 4. 3. Ordinance instituted by Jehovah for the life and worship of His people, lviii. 2, ordinances of righteousness, i.e., either canonical laws, or ordinances by observing which the people would make themselves righteous. 4. In general, the sum of the laws given by Jehovah to Israel, the Law, lviii. 2, Law of their God; li. 4, Jehovah says My Law (Rev. Ver. judgement), parallel to "Torah" or Revelation (Rev. Ver. law). Then absolutely, without the article or Jehovah's name attached, xlii. 1, 3, 4. In lvi. 1 parallel to righteousness; lix. 14 parallel to righteousness, truth and uprightness. In fact, in this last use, while represented as equivalent to civic morality, it is this, not as viewed in its character, right, upright, but in its obligation as ordained by God: morality as His Law. The absence of the article may either mean what it means in the case of people and land, i.e., the Law, too much of a proper name to need the article, or it may be an attempt to abstract the quality of the Law; and if so mishpat is equal to justice.
182. Expositor, second series, vol. viii., p. 364.
183. This might, of course, only mean what the Servant had to do for his captive countrymen. But coming as it does after the light of nations, it seems natural to take it in its wider and more spiritual sense.
184. See ch. [36]xv. of this volume.
185. Expositor, second series, viii., pp. 364, 365, 366.
186. Ibid., p. 366.

CHAPTER XIX

PROPHET AND MARTYR.

Isaiah xlix. 1-9; l. 4-11.

The second great passage upon the Servant of the Lord is ch. xlix. 1-9, and the third is ch. l. 4-11. In both of these the servant himself speaks; in both he speaks as prophet; while in the second he tells us that his prophecy leads him on to martyrdom. The two passages may, therefore, be taken together.

Before we examine their contents, let us look for a moment at the way in which they are woven into the rest of the text. As we have seen, ch. xlix. begins a new section of the prophecy, in so far that with it the prophet leaves Babylon and Cyrus behind him, and ceases to speak of the contrast between God and the idols. But, still, ch. xlix. is linked to ch. xlviii. In leading up to its climax,--the summons to Israel to depart from Babylon,--ch. xlviii. does not forget that Israel is delivered from Babylon in order to be the Servant of Jehovah: say ye, Jehovah hath redeemed His Servant Jacob. It is this service, which ch. xlix. carries forward from the opportunity, and the call, to go forth from Babylon, with which ch. xlviii. closes. That opportunity, though real, does not at all mean that Israel's redemption is complete. There were many moral reasons which prevented the whole nation from taking full advantage of the political freedom offered them by Cyrus. Although the true Israel, that part of the nation which has the conscience of service, has shaken itself free from the temptation as well as from the tyranny of Babel, and now sees the world before it as the theatre of its operations,--ver. 1, Hearken, ye isles, unto Me; and listen, ye peoples, from far,--it has still, before it can address itself to that universal mission, to exhort, rouse and extricate the rest of its nation, saying to the bounden, Go forth; and to them that are in darkness, Show yourselves (ver. 9). Ch. xlix., therefore, is the natural development of ch. xlviii. There is certainly a little interval of time implied between the two--the time during which it became apparent that the opportunity to leave Babylon would not be taken advantage of by all Israel, and that the nation's redemption must be a moral as well as a political one. But ch. xlix. 1-9 comes out of chs. xl.-xlviii., and it is impossible to believe that in it we are not still under the influence of the same author.

A similar coherence is apparent if we look to the other end of ch. xlix. 1-9. Here it is evident that Jehovah's commission to the Servant concludes with ver. 9a; but then its closing words, Say to the bound, Go forth; to them that are in darkness, Show yourselves, start fresh thoughts about the redeemed on their way back (vv. 9b-13); and these thoughts naturally lead on to a picture of Jerusalem imagining herself forsaken, and amazed by the appearance of so many of her children before her (vv. 14-21). Promises to her and to them follow in due sequence down to ch. l. 3, when the Servant resumes his soliloquy about himself, but abruptly, and in no apparent connection with what immediately precedes. His soliloquy ceases in ver. 9, and another voice, probably that of God Himself, urges obedience to the Servant (ver. 10), and judgement to the sinners in Israel (ver. 11); and ch. li. is an address to the spiritual Israel, and to Jerusalem, with thoughts much the same as those uttered in xlix. 14-l. 3.

In face of these facts, and taking into consideration the dramatic form in which the whole prophecy is cast, we find ourselves unable to say that there is anything which is incompatible with a single authorship, or which makes it impossible for the two passages on the Servant to have originally sprung, each at the place at which it now stands, from the progress of the prophet's thoughts. [187]

***

Babylon is left behind, and the way of the Lord is prepared in the desert. Israel have once more the title-deeds to their own land, and Zion looms in sight. Yet with their face to home, and their heart upon freedom, the voice of this people, or at least of the better half of this people, rises first upon the conscience of their duty to the rest of mankind.

> *Hearken, O Isles, unto Me;*
> *And listen, O Peoples, from far!*
> *From the womb Jehovah hath called me,*
> *From my mother's midst mentioned my name.* [188]
> *And He set my mouth like a sharp sword,*
> *In the shadow of His hand did He hide me;*

Rev. George Adam Smith, M.A.

> *Yea, He made me a pointed arrow,*
> *In His quiver He laid me in store,*
> *And said to me, My Servant art thou,*
> *Israel, in whom I shall break into glory.*
> *And I--I said, In vain have I laboured,*
> *For waste and for wind my strength have I spent!*
> *Surely my right's with Jehovah,*
> *And the meed of my work with my God!*
> *But now, saith Jehovah--*
> *Moulding me from the womb to be His own Servant,*
> *To turn again Jacob towards Him,*
> *And that Israel be not destroyed.* [189]
> *And I am of honour in the eyes of Jehovah,*
> *And my God is my strength!*
> *And He saith,*
> *'Tis too light for thy being My Servant,*
> *To raise up the tribes of Jacob,*
> *Or gather the survivors of Israel.*
> *So I will set thee a light of the Nations,*
> *To be My salvation to the end of the earth.*
> *Thus saith Jehovah,*
> *Israel's Redeemer, his Holy,*
> *To this mockery of a life, abhorrence of a nation, servant of tyrants,* [190]
> *Kings shall behold and shall stand up,*
> *Princes shall also do homage,*
> *For the sake of Jehovah, who shows Himself faithful,*
> *Holy of Israel, and thou art His chosen.*
> *Thus saith Jehovah,*
> *In a favourable time I have given thee answer,*
> *In the day of salvation have helped thee,*
> *To keep thee, to give thee for covenant of the people,*
> *To raise up the land,*
> *To give back the heirs to the desolate heirdoms,*
> *Saying to the bounden, Go forth!*
> *To them that are in darkness, Appear!*

"Who is so blind as not to perceive that the consciousness of the Servant here is only a mirror in which the history of Israel is reflected--first, in its original call and design that Jehovah should be glorified in it; second, in the long delay and apparent failure of the design; and, thirdly, as the design is now in the present juncture of circumstances and concurrence of events about to be realized?" [191] Yes: but it is Israel's calling, native insufficiency, and present duty, as owned by only a part of the people, which, though named by the national name (ver. 3), feels itself standing over against the bulk of the nation, whose redemption it is called to work out (vv. 8 and 9) before it takes up its world-wide service. We have already sufficiently discussed this distinction of the Servant from the whole nation, as well as the distinction of the moral work he has to effect in Israel's redemption from Babylon, from the political enfranchisement of the nation, which is the work of Cyrus. Let us, then, at once address ourselves to the main features of his consciousness of his mission to mankind. We shall find these features to be three. The Servant owns for his chief end the glory of God; and he feels that he has to glorify God in two ways--by Speech, and by Suffering.

I. The Servant glorifies God.

He did say to me, My servant art thou, Israel, in whom I shall break into glory.

The Hebrew verb, which the Authorised Version translates will be glorified, means to burst forth, become visible, break like the dawn into splendour. This is the scriptural sense of Glory. Glory is God become visible. As we put it in Volume I., [192] glory is the expression of holiness, as beauty is the expression of health. But, in order to become visible, the Absolute and Holy God needs mortal man. We have felt something like a paradox in these prophecies. Nowhere else is God lifted up so absolute, and so able to effect all by His mere will and word; yet nowhere else is a human agency and service so strongly asserted as indispensable to the Divine purpose. But this is no more a paradox, than the fact that physical light needs some material in which to become visible. Light is never revealed of itself, but always when shining from, or burning in, something else. To be seen, light requires a surface that will reflect, or a substance that will consume. And so, to break into glory, God requires something outside

Himself. A responsive portion of humanity is indispensable to Him,--a people who will reflect Him and spend itself for Him. Man is the mirror and the wick of the Divine. God is glorified in man's character and witness,--these are His mirror; and in man's sacrifice,--that is His wick.

And so we meet again the central truth of our prophecy, that in order to serve men it is necessary first to be used of God. We must place ourselves at the disposal of the Divine, we must let God shine on us and kindle us, and break into glory through us, before we can hope either to comfort mankind or to set them on fire. It is true that ideas very different from this prevail among the ranks of the servants of humanity in our day. A large part of our most serious literature professes for "its main bearing this conclusion, that the fellowship between man and man, which has been the principle of development, social and moral, is not dependent upon conceptions of what is not man, and that the idea of God, so far as it has been a high spiritual influence, is the ideal of a goodness entirely human." [193] But such theories are possible only so long as the still unexhausted influence of religion upon society continues to supply human nature, directly or indirectly, with a virtue which may be plausibly claimed for human nature's own original product. Let religion be entirely withdrawn, and the question, Whence comes virtue? will be answered by virtue ceasing to come at all. The savage imagines that it is the burning-glass which sets the bush on fire, and as long as the sun is shining it may be impossible to convince him that he is wrong; but a dull day will teach even his mind that the glass can do nothing without the sun upon it. And so, though men may talk glibly against God, while society still shines in the light of His countenance, yet, if they and society resolutely withdraw themselves from that light, they shall certainly lose every heat and lustre of the spirit which is indispensable for social service. [194] On this the ancient Greek was at one with the ancient Hebrew. Enthusiasm is just God breaking into glory through a human life. Here lies the secret of the buoyancy and "freshness of the earlier world," whether pagan or Hebrew, and by this may be understood the depression and pessimism which infects modern society. They had God in their blood, and we are anæmic. But I, I said, I have laboured in vain; for waste and for wind have I spent my strength. We must all say that, if our last word is our strength. But let this not be our last word. Let us remember the sufficient answer: Surely my right is with the Lord, and the meed of my work with my God. We are set, not in our own strength or for our own advantage, but with the hand of God upon us, and that the Divine life may break into glory through our life. Carlyle said, and it was almost his last testimony, "The older I grow, and I am now on the brink of eternity, the more comes back to me the first sentence of the catechism, which I learned when a child, and the fuller does its meaning grow--'What is the chief end of man? Man's chief end is to glorify God and enjoy Him for ever.'"

***

It was said above, that, as light breaks to visibleness either from a mirror or a wick, so God breaks to glory either from the witness of men,--that is His mirror,--or from their sacrifice--that is His wick. Of both of these ways of glorifying God is the Servant conscious. His service is Speech and Sacrifice, Prophecy and Martyrdom.

II. The Servant as Prophet.
Concerning his service of Speech, the Servant speaks in these two passages--ch. xlix. 2 and l. 4-5:

He set my mouth like a sharp sword,
In the shadow of His hand did He hide me,
And made me a pointed arrow;
In His quiver He laid me in store.
My Lord Jehovah hath given me
The tongue of the learners,
To know how to succour the weary with words.
He wakeneth morning by morning, He wakeneth mine ear
To hear as the learners.
My Lord Jehovah hath opened mine ear.
I was not rebellious,
Nor turned away backward.

At the bidding of our latest prophet we have become suspicious of the power of speech, and the goddess of eloquence walks, as it were, under surveillance among us. Carlyle reiterated, "All speech and rumour is short-lived, foolish, untrue. Genuine work alone is eternal. The talent of silence is our fundamental one. The dumb nations are the builders of the world." Under such doctrine some have grown intolerant of words, and the ideal of to-day tends to become the practical man rather than the prophet. Yet, as somebody has said, Carlyle makes us dissatisfied with preaching only by preaching himself; and you have but to read him with attention to discover that his disgust with human speech is consistent with an immense reverence for the voice as an instrument of service to humanity. "The tongue of man," he says, "is a sacred organ. Man himself is definable in philosophy as an 'Incarnate Word;' the Word not there, you have no man there either, but a Phantasm instead."

Let us examine our own experience upon the merits of this debate between Silence and Speech in the service of man. Though beginning low, it will help us quickly to the height of the experience of the Prophet Nation, who, with nought else for the world but the voice that was in them, accomplished the greatest service that the world has ever received from her children.

One thing is certain,--that Speech has not the monopoly of falsehood or of any other presumptuous sin. Silence does not only mean ignorance,--by some supposed to be the heaviest sin of which Silence can be guilty,--but many things far worse than ignorance, like unreadiness, and cowardice, and falsehood, and treason, and base consent to what is evil. No man can look back on his past life, however lowly or limited his sphere may have been, and fail to see that not once or twice his supreme duty was a word, and his guilt was not to have spoken it. We all have known the shame of being straitened in prayer or praise; the shame of being, through our cowardice to bear witness, traitors to the truth; the shame of being too timid to say No to the tempter, and speak out the brave reasons of which the heart was full; the shame of finding ourselves incapable of uttering the word that would have kept a soul from taking the wrong turning in life; the shame, when truth, clearness and authority were required from us, of being able only to stammer or to mince or to rant. To have been dumb before the ignorant or the dying, before a questioning child or before the tempter,--this, the frequent experience of our common life, is enough to justify Carlyle when he said, "If the Word is not there, you have no man there either, but a Phantasm instead."

Now, when we look within ourselves we see the reason of this. We perceive that the one fact, which amid the mystery and chaos of our inner life gives certainty and light, is a fact which is a Voice. Our nature may be wrecked and dissipated, but conscience is always left; or in ignorance and gloom, but conscience is always audible; or with all the faculties strong and assertive, yet conscience is still unquestionably queen,--and conscience is a Voice. It is a still, small voice, which is the surest thing in man, and the noblest; which makes all the difference in his life; which lies at the back and beginning of all his character and conduct. And the most indispensable, and the grandest service, therefore, which a man can do his fellow-men, is to get back to this voice, and make himself its mouthpiece and its prophet. What work is possible till the word be spoken? Did ever order come to social life before there was first uttered the command, in which men felt the articulation and enforcement of the ultimate voice within themselves? Discipline and instruction and energy have not appeared without speech going before them. Knowledge and faith and hope do not dawn of themselves; they travel, as light issued forth in the beginning, upon the pulses of the speaking breath.

It was the greatness of Israel to be conscious of their call as a nation to this fundamental service of humanity. Believing in the Word of God as the original source of all things,--In the beginning God said, Let there be light; and there was light,--they had the conscience, that, as it had been in the physical world, so must it always be in the moral. Men were to be served and their lives to be moulded by the Word. God was to be glorified by letting His Word break through the life and the lips of men. There was in the Old Testament, it is true, a triple ideal of manhood: prophet, priest and king. But the greatest of these was the prophet, for king and priest had to be prophets too. Eloquence was a royal virtue,--with persuasion, the power of command and swift judgement. Among the seven spirits of the Lord which Isaiah sees descending in the King-to-Come is the spirit of counsel, and he afterwards adds of the King: He shall smite the earth with the rod of his mouth, and with the breath of his lips shall he slay the wicked. Similarly, the priests had originally been the ministers, not so much of sacrifice, as of the revealed Word of God. And now the new and high ideal of priesthood, the laying down of one's life a sacrifice for God and for the people, was not the mere imitation of the animal victim required by the priestly law, but was the natural development of the prophetic experience. It was (as we shall presently see) the prophet, who, in his inevitable sufferings on behalf of the truth he uttered, developed that consciousness of sacrifice for others, in which the loftiest priesthood consists. Prophecy, therefore, the Service of Men by the Word of God, was for Israel the highest and most essential of all service. It was the individual's and it was the nation's ideal. As there was no true king and no true priest, so there was no true man, without the Word. Would to God, said Moses, that all the Lord's people were prophets. And in our prophecy Israel exclaims: Listen, O Isles, unto me; and hearken, ye peoples from far. He hath made my mouth like a sharp sword, in the shadow of His hand hath He hid me.

At first it seems a forlorn hope thus to challenge the attention of the world in the dialect of one of its most obscure provinces,--a dialect, too, that was already ceasing to be spoken even there. But the fact only serves more forcibly to emphasize the belief of these prophets, that the word committed to what they must have known to be a dying language was the Word of God Himself,--bound to render immortal the tongue in which it was spoken, bound to re-echo to the ends of the earth, bound to touch the conscience and commend itself to the reason of universal humanity. We have already seen, and will again see, how our prophet insists upon the creative and omnipotent power of God's Word; so we need not dwell longer on this instance of his faith. Let us look rather at what he expresses as Israel's preparation for the teaching of it.

To him the discipline and qualification of the prophet nation--and that means, of every Servant of God--in the high office of the Word, are threefold.

1. First, he lays down the supreme condition of Prophecy, that behind the Voice there must be the Life. Before he speaks of his gifts of Speech, the Servant emphasizes his peculiar and consecrated life. From the womb Jehovah called me, from my mother's midst mentioned my name. Now, as we all know, Israel's message to the world was largely Israel's life. The Old Testament is not a set of dogmas, nor a philosophy, nor a vision; but a history, the record of a providence, the testimony of experience, the utterances called forth by historical occasions from a life conscious of the purpose for which God has called it and set it apart through the ages. But these words, which the prophet nation uses, were first used of an individual prophet. Like so much else in "Second Isaiah," we find a suggestion of them in the call of Jeremiah. Before I formed thee in the belly I knew thee, and before thou camest forth from the womb I consecrated thee: I have appointed thee a prophet unto the nations. [195] A prophet is not a voice only. A prophet is a life behind a voice. He who would speak for God must have lived for God. According to the profound insight of the Old Testament, speech is not the expression of a few thoughts of a man, but the utterance of his whole life. A man blossoms through his lips; [196] and no man is a prophet, whose word is not the virtue and the flower of a gracious and a consecrated life.

2. The second discipline of the prophet is the Art of Speech. He hath made my mouth like a sharp sword, in the shadow of His hand hath He hid me: He hath made me a polished shaft, in His quiver hath He laid me in store. It is very evident, that in these words the Servant does not only recount technical qualifications, but a moral discipline as well. The edge and brilliance of his speech are stated as the effect of solitude, but of a solitude that was at the same time a nearness to God. Now solitude is a great school of eloquence. In speaking of the Semitic race, of which Israel was part, we pointed out that, prophet-race of the world as it has proved, it sprang from the desert, and nearly all its branches have inherited the desert's clear and august style of speech; for, in the leisure and serene air of the desert, men speak as they speak nowhere else. But Israel speaks of a solitude, that was the shadow of God's hand, and the fastness of God's quiver; a seclusion, which, to the desert's art of eloquence, added a special inspiration by God, and a special concentration upon His main purpose in the world. The desert sword felt the grasp of God; He laid the Semitic shaft in store for a unique end. [197]

3. But in ch. l., vv. 4-5, the Servant unfolds the most beautiful and true understanding of the Secret of Prophecy, that ever was unfolded in any literature,--worth quoting again by us, if so we may get it by heart.

> My Lord Jehovah hath given me
> The tongue of the learners,
> To know how to succour the weary with words.
> He wakeneth, morning by morning He wakeneth mine ear
> To hear as the learners.
> My Lord Jehovah hath opened mine ear,
> I was not rebellious,
> Nor turned away backward.

The prophet, say these beautiful lines, learns his speech, as the little child does, by listening. Grace is poured upon the lips through the open ear. It is the lesson of our Lord's Ephphatha. When He took the deaf man with the impediment in his speech aside from the multitude privately, He said unto him, not, Be loosed, but, Be opened; and first his ears were opened, and then the bond of his tongue was loosed, and he spake plain. To speak, then, the prophet must listen; but mark to what he must listen! The secret of his eloquence lies not in the hearing of thunder, nor in the knowledge of mysteries, but in a daily wakefulness to the lessons and experience of common life. Morning by morning He openeth mine ear. This is very characteristic of Hebrew prophecy and Hebrew wisdom, which listened for the truth of God in the voices of each day, drew their parables from things the rising sun lights up to every wakeful eye, and were, in the bulk of their doctrine, the virtues, needed day by day, of justice, temperance and mercy, and in the bulk of their judgements the results of everyday observation and experience. The strength of the Old Testament lies in this its realism, its daily vigilance and experience of life. It is its contact with life--the life, not of the yesterday of its speakers, but of their to-day--that makes its voice so fresh and helpful to the weary. He whose ear is daily open to the music of his current life will always find himself in possession of words that refresh and stimulate.

But serviceable speech needs more than attentiveness and experience. Having gained the truth, the prophet must be obedient and loyal to it. Yet obedience and loyalty to the truth are the beginnings of martyrdom, of which the Servant now goes on to speak as the natural and immediate consequence of his prophecy.

Rev. George Adam Smith, M.A.

III. The Servant as Martyr.

The classes of men, who suffer physical ill-usage at the hands of their fellow-men, may roughly be described as three,--the Military Enemy, the Criminal, and the Prophet; and of these three we have only to read history to know that the Prophet fares by far the worst. However fatal men's treatment of their enemies in war or of their criminals may be, it is, nevertheless, subject to a certain order, code of honour or principle of justice. But in all ages the Prophet has been the target for the most licentious spite and cruelty; for torture, indecency and filth past belief. Although our own civilisation has outlived the system of physical punishment for speech, we even yet see philosophers and statesmen, who have used no weapons but exposition and persuasion, treated by their opponents--who would speak of a foreign enemy with respect--with execration, gross epithets, vile abuse and insults, that the offenders would not pour upon a criminal. If we have this under our own eyes, let us think how the Prophet must have fared before humanity learned to meet speech by speech. Because men attacked it, not with the sword of the invader or with the knife of the assassin, but with words, therefore (till not very long ago) society let loose upon them the foulest indignities and most horrible torments. Socrates' valour as a soldier did not save him from the malicious slander, the false witness, the unjust trial and the poison, with which the Athenians answered his speech against themselves. Even Hypatia's womanhood did not awe the mob from tearing her to pieces for her teaching. This unique and invariable experience of the Prophet is summed up and clenched in the name Martyr. Martyr originally meant a witness or witness-bearer, but now it is the synonym for every shame and suffering which the cruel ingenuity of men's black hearts can devise for those they hate. A Book of Battles is horrible enough, but at least valour and honour have kept down in it the baser passions. A Newgate Chronicle is ugly enough, but there at least is discipline and an hospital. You have got to go to a Book of Martyrs to see to what sourness, wickedness, malignity, pitilessness and ferocity men's hearts can lend themselves. There is something in the mere utterance of truth, that rouses the very devil in the hearts of many men.

Thus it had always been in Israel, nation not only of prophets, but of the slayers of prophets. According to Christ, prophet-slaying was the ineradicable habit of Israel. Ye are the sons of them that slew the prophets.... O Jerusalem, Jerusalem, killer of prophets and stoner of them that are sent unto her! To them who bare it the word of Jehovah had always been a reproach: cause of estrangement, indignities, torments, and sometimes of death. Up to the time of our prophet there had been the following notable sufferers for the Word: Elijah; Micaiah the son of Imlah; Isaiah, if the story be true that he was slain by Manasseh; but nearer, more lonely and more heroic than all, Jeremiah, a laughing-stock and mockery, reviled, smitten, fettered, and condemned to death. In words which recall the experience of so many individual Israelites, and most of which were used by Jeremiah of himself, the Servant of Jehovah describes his martyrdom in immediate consequence from his prophecy.

> And I--I was not rebellious,
> Nor turned away backward.
> My back I have given to the smiters,
> And my cheek to tormenters;
> My face I hid not from insults and spitting.

These are not national sufferings. They are no reflection of the hard usage which the captive Israel suffered from Babylon. They are the reflection of the reproach and pains, which, for the sake of God's word, individual Israelites more than once experienced from their own nation. But if individual experience, and not national, formed the original of this picture of the Servant as Martyr, then surely we have in this another strong reason against the objection to recognise in the Servant at last an individual. It may be, of course, that for the moment our prophet feels that this frequent experience of individuals in Israel is to be realised by the faithful Israel, as a whole, in their treatment by the rest of their cruel and unspiritual countrymen. But the very fact that individuals have previously fulfilled this martyrdom in the history of Israel, surely makes it possible for our prophet to foresee, that the Servant, who is to fulfil it again, shall also be an individual.

But, returning from this slight digression on the person of the Servant to his fate, let us emphasize again, that his sufferings came to him as the result of his prophesying. The Servant's sufferings are not penal, they are not yet felt to be vicarious. They are simply the reward with which obdurate Israel met all her prophets, the inevitable martyrdom which followed on the uttering of God's Word. And in this the Servant's experience forms an exact counterpart to that of our Lord. For to Christ also reproach and agony and death--whatever higher meaning they evolved--came as the result of His Word. The fact that Jesus suffered as our great High Priest must not make us forget, that His sufferings fell upon Him because He was a Prophet. He argued explicitly He must suffer, because so suffered the prophets before Him. He put Himself in the line of the martyrs: as they had killed the servants, He said, so would they kill the Son. Thus it happened. His enemies sought to entangle Him in His talk: it was for His talk they brought Him to trial. Each torment and indignity which the Prophet-Servant relates, Jesus suffered to the letter. They put Him to shame and insulted Him; [198] His helpless hands were bound; they spat in His face and smote Him with their palms; they mocked and they reviled Him; scourged Him again; teased and tormented Him; hung Him between thieves; and to the last the ribald jests went up, not only from the soldiers and the rabble, but from the learned and the religious authorities as well, to whom His fault had been that He preached another word than their own. The literal fulfilments of our prophecy are striking, but the main fulfilment, of which they are only incidents, is, that like the Servant, our Lord suffered directly as a Prophet. He enforced and He submitted to the essential obligation, which lies upon the true Prophet, of suffering for the Word's sake. Let us remember to carry this over with us to our final study of the Suffering Servant as the expiation for sin.

In the meantime, we have to conclude the Servant's appearance as Martyr in ch. l. He has accepted his martyrdom; but he feels it is not the end with him. God will bring him through, and vindicate him in the eyes of the world. For the world, in their usual way, will say that because he gives them a new truth he must be wrong, and because he suffers he is surely guilty and cursed before God. But he will not let himself be confounded, for God is his help and advocate.

But my Lord Jehovah shall help me;
Therefore, I let not myself be rebuffed:
Therefore, I set my face like a flint,
And know that I shall not be shamed.
Near is my Justifier; who will dispute with me?
Let us stand up together!
Who is mine adversary? [199]
Let him draw near me.
Lo! my Lord Jehovah shall help me;
Who is he that condemns me?
Lo! like a garment all of them rot;
The moth doth devour them.

These lines, in which the Holy Servant, the Martyr of the Word, defies the world and asserts that God shall vindicate his innocence, are taken by Paul and used to assert the justification, which every believer enjoys through faith in the sufferings of Him, who was indeed the Holy Servant of God. [200]

The last two verses of ch. l. are somewhat difficult. The first of them still speaks of the Servant,[201] and distinguishes him--a distinction we must note and emphasize--from the God-fearing in Israel.

Who is among you that feareth Jehovah,
That hearkens the voice of His Servant,
That walks in dark places,
And light he has none?
Let him trust in the name of Jehovah,
And lean on his God.

That is, every pious believer in Israel is to take the Servant for an example; for the Servant in distress leans upon his God. And so Paul's application of the Servant's words to the individual believer is a correct one. But if our prophet is able to think of the Servant as an example to the individual Israelite, that surely is a thought not very far from the conception of the Servant himself as an individual.

If ver. 10 is addressed to the pious in Israel, ver. 11 would seem to turn with a last word--as the last words of the discourses in Second Isaiah so often turn--to the wicked in Israel.

Lo! all you, players with fire, [202]
That gird you with firebrands!
Walk in the light of your fire,
In the firebrands ye kindled.
This from my hand shall be yours;
Ye shall lie down in sorrow.

It is very difficult to know, who are meant by this warning. An old and almost forgotten interpretation is, that the prophet meant those exiles who played with the fires of political revolution, instead of abiding the deliverance of the Lord. But there is now current among exegetes the more general interpretation that these incendiaries are the revilers and abusers of the Servant within Israel: for so the Psalms speak of the slingers of burning words at the righteous. We must notice, however, that the metaphor stands over against those in Israel who walk in dark places and have no light. In contrast to that kind of life, this may be the kind that coruscates with vanity, flashes with pride, or burns and scorches with its evil passions. We have a similar name for such a life. We call it a display of fireworks. The prophet tells them, who depend on nothing but their own false fires, how transient these are, how quickly quenched.

But is it not weird, that on our prophet's stage, however brilliantly its centre shines with figures of heroes and deeds of salvation, there should always be this dark, lurid background of evil and accursed men?

Footnotes:

187. This, of course, goes against Prof. Briggs's theory of the composition of Isa. xl.-lxvi. out of two poems (see p. [37]18).

188. This line is full of the letter m.

189. This is as the text is written; but the Massoretic reading gives, that Israel to Him may be gathered.

190. So it seems best to give the sense of this difficult line, but most translators render despised of soul, or thoroughly despised, abhorred by peoples, or by a people, etc. The word for despised is used elsewhere only in ch. liii. 3.

191. Prof. A. B. Davidson, Expositor, Second Series, viii., 441.

192. Page 68.

193. So George Eliot wrote of her own writings shortly before her death. See Life, iii., 245.

194. Lady Ponsonby, to whom George Eliot wrote the letter quoted above, confessed that, with the disappearance of religious faith from her soul, there vanished also the power of interest in, and of pity for, her kind.

195. Jer. i. 5.

196. See vol. i., p. 70.

197. See p. [38]240 f.

198. How all their meanness, how all the sense of shame from which He suffered, breaks forth in these words: Are ye come out as against a robber?

199. Literally, lord of my cause; my adversary or opponent at law.

200. Epistle to the Romans, viii., 31 ff.

201. Though Cheyne takes His Servant in ver. 10 to be, not the Servant, but the prophet.

202. Kindlers of fire is the literal rendering. But the word is not the common word to kindle, and is here used of wanton fireraising.

CHAPTER XX

THE SUFFERING SERVANT.

Isaiah lii. 13-liii.

We are now arrived at the last of the passages on the Servant of the Lord. It is known to Christendom as the Fifty-third of Isaiah, but its verses have, unfortunately, been divided between two chapters, lii. 13-15 and liii. Before we attempt the interpretation of this high and solemn passage of Revelation, let us look at its position in our prophecy, and examine its structure.

The peculiarities of the style and of the vocabulary of ch. lii. 13-liii., along with the fact, that, if it be omitted, the prophecies on either side readily flow together, have led some critics to suppose it to be an insertion, borrowed from an earlier writer. [203] The style--broken, sobbing and recurrent--is certainly a change from the forward, flowing sentences, on which we have been carried up till now, and there are a number of words that we find quite new to us. Yet surely both style and words are fully accounted for by the novel and tragic nature of the subject, to which the prophet has brought us: regret and remorse, though they speak through the same lips as hope and the assurance of salvation, must necessarily do so with a very different accent and set of terms. Criticism surely overreaches itself, when it suggests that a writer, so versatile and dramatic as our prophet, could not have written ch. lii. 13-liii. along with, say, ch. xl. or ch. lii. 1-12 or ch. liv. We might as well be asked to assign to different authors Hamlet's soliloquy, and the King's conversation, in the same play, with the ambassadors from Norway. To aver that if ch. lii. 13-liii. were left out, no one who had not seen it would miss it, so closely does ch. liv. follow on to ch. lii. 12, is to aver what means nothing. In any dramatic work you may leave out the finest passage,--from a Greek tragedy its grandest chorus, or from a play of Shakespeare's the hero's soliloquy,--without seeming, to eyes that have not seen what you have done, to have disturbed the connection of the whole. Observe the juncture in our prophecy at which this last passage on the Servant appears. It is one exactly the same as that at which another great passage on the Servant was inserted (ch. xlix. 1-9), viz., just after a call to the people to seize the redemption achieved for them and to come forth from Babylon. It is the kind of climax or pause in their tale, which dramatic writers of all kinds employ for the solemn utterance of principles lying at the back, or transcending the scope, of the events of which they treat. To say the least, it is surely more probable that our prophet himself employed so natural an opportunity to give expression to his highest truths about the Servant, than that some one else took his work, broke up another already extant work on the Servant and thrust the pieces of the latter into the former. Moreover, we shall find many of the ideas, as well as of the phrases, of ch. lii. 13-liii. to be essentially the same as some we have already encountered in our prophecy. [204]

There is then no evidence that this singular prophecy ever stood apart from its present context, or that it was written by another writer than the prophet, by whom we have hitherto found ourselves conducted. On the contrary, while it has links with what goes before it, we see good reasons, why the prophet should choose just this moment for uttering its unique and transcendent contents, as well as why he should employ in it a style and a vocabulary, so different from his usual.

Turning now to the structure of ch. lii. 13-liii., we observe that, as arranged in the Canon, there are fifteen verses in the prophecy. These fifteen verses fall into five strophes of three verses each, as printed by the Revised English Version. When set in their own original lines, however, the strophes appear, not of equal, but of increasing length. As will be seen from the version given below, the first (ch. lii. 13-15) has nine lines, the second (ch. liii. 1-3) has ten lines, the third (vv. 4-6) has eleven lines, the fourth (vv. 7-9) thirteen lines, the fifth (vv. 10-12) fourteen lines. This increase would be absolutely regular, if, in the fourth strophe, we made either the first two lines one, or the last two one, and if in the fifth again we ran the first two lines together,--changes which the metre allows and some translators have adopted. But, in either case, we perceive a regular increase from strophe to strophe, that is not only one of the many marks with which this most artistic of poems has been elaborated, but gives the reader the very solemn impression of a truth that is ever gathering more of human life into itself, and sweeping forward with fuller and more resistless volume.

Each strophe, it is well to notice, begins with one word or two words which summarise the meaning of the whole strophe and form a title for it. Thus, after the opening exclamation Behold, the words My Servant shall prosper form, as we shall see, not only a summary of the first strophe, in which his ultimate exaltation is described, but the theme of the whole prophecy. Strophe ii. begins Who hath believed, and accordingly in this strophe the unbelief and thoughtlessness of them who saw the Servant without feeling the meaning of his suffering is confessed. Surely our sicknesses fitly entitles strophe iii., in which the people describe how the Servant in his suffering was their substitute. Oppressed yet he humbled himself is the headline of strophe iv., and that strophe deals with the humility and innocence of the Servant in contrast to the injustice accorded him. While the headline of strophe v., But Jehovah had purposed, brings us back to the main theme of the poem, that behind men's treatment of the Servant is God's holy will; which theme is elaborated and brought to its conclusion in strophe v. These opening and entitling words of each strophe are printed, in the following translation, in larger type than the rest.

As in the rest of Hebrew poetry, so here, the measure is neither regular nor smooth, and does not depend on rhyme. Yet there is an amount of assonance, which at times approaches to rhyme. Much of the meaning of the poem depends on the use of the personal pronouns--we and he stand contrasted to each other--and it is these coming in a lengthened form at the end of many of the lines that suggest to the ear something like rhyme. For instance, in liii. 5, 6, the second and third verses of the third strophe, two of the lines run out on the bisyllable -ênu, two on înu, and two on the word lanu, while the third has ênu, not at the end, but in the middle; in each case, the pronominal suffix of the first person plural. We transcribe these lines to show the effect of this.

W^ehu' m^eholal mipp^esha'ênu
M^edhukka' me`awOnOthênu
Mu?ar sh^elOmenu `alaw
Ubhahabhuratho nirpa'-lanu
Kullanu kass-ss'on ta`înu
'ish l^edharko panînu
Wa Jahweh hiphgi`a bô 'eth-`awon kullanu.

This is the strophe in which the assonance comes oftenest to rhyme; but in strophe i. êhu ends two lines, and in strophe ii. it ends three. These and other assonants occur also at the beginning and in the middle of lines. We must remember that in all the cases quoted it is the personal pronouns, which give the assonance,--the personal pronouns on which so much of the meaning of the poem turns; and that, therefore, the parallelism primarily intended by the writer is one rather of meaning than of sound. The pair of lines, parallel in meaning, though not in sound, which forms so large a part of Hebrew poetry, is used throughout this poem; but the use of it is varied and elaborated to a unique degree. The very same words and phrases are repeated, and placed on points, from which they seem to call to each other; as, for instance, the double many in strophe i., the of us all in strophe iii., and nor opened he his mouth in strophe iv. The ideas are very few and very simple; the words he, we, his, ours, see, hear, know, bear, sickness, strike, stroke, and many form, with prepositions and particles, the bulk of the prophecy. It will be evident how singularly suitable this recurrence is for the expression of reproach, and of sorrowful recollection. It is the nature of grief and remorse to harp upon the one dear form, the one most vivid pain. The finest instance of this repetition is verse 6, with its opening keynote "kullanu"--of us all like sheep went astray, with its close on that keynote guilt of us all, "kullanu." But throughout notes are repeated, and bars recur, expressive of what was done to the Servant, or what the Servant did for man, which seem in their recurrence to say, You cannot hear too much of me: I am the very Gospel. A peculiar sadness is lent to the music by the letters h and l in "holie" and "hehelie," the word for sickness or ailing (ailing is the English equivalent in sense and sound), which happens so often in the poem. The new words, which have been brought to vary this recurrence of a few simple features, are mostly of a sombre type. The heavier letters throng the lines: grievous bs and ms are multiplied, and syllables with long vowels before m and w. But the words sob as well as tramp; and here and there one has a wrench and one a cry in it.

Most wonderful and mysterious of all is the spectral fashion in which the prophecy presents its Hero. He is named only in the first line and once again: elsewhere He is spoken of as He. We never hear or see Himself. But all the more solemnly is He there: a shadow upon countless faces, a grievous memory on the hearts of the speakers. He so haunts all we see and all we hear, that we feel it is not Art, but Conscience, that speaks of Him.

Here is now the prophecy itself, rendered into English quite literally, except for a conjunction here and there, and, as far as possible, in the rhythm of the original. A few necessary notes on difficult words and phrases are given.

I.

> lii. 13: Behold, my Servant shall prosper, [205]
> Shall rise, be lift up, be exceedingly high. [206]
> Like as they that were astonied before thee were many,
> --So marred from a man's was his visage,
> And his form from the children of men!--
> So shall the nations he startles [207] be many,
> Before him shall kings shut their mouths.
> For that which had never been told them they see,
> And what they had heard not, they have to consider.

II.

> Who gave believing to that which we heard, [208]
> And the arm of Jehovah to whom was it bared?
> For he sprang like a sapling before Him, [209]
> As a root from the ground that is parched;
> He had no form nor beauty that we should regard him,
> Nor aspect that we should desire him.
> Despised and rejected of men,
> Man of pains and familiar with ailing,
> And as one we do cover the face from,
> Despised, and we did not esteem him.

III.

> Surely our ailments he bore,
> And our pains he did take for his burden. [210]
> But we--we accounted him stricken,
> Smitten of God and degraded. [211]
> Yet he--he was pierced for crimes that were ours, [212]
> He was crushed for guilt that was ours, [213]
> The chastisement of our peace was upon him,
> By his stripes healing is ours. [214]
> Of us all [215] like to sheep went astray,
> Every man to his way we did turn,
> And Jehovah made light upon him
> The guilt of us all.

IV.

> Oppressed, he did humble himself,
> Nor opened his mouth--
> As a lamb to the slaughter is led,
> As a sheep 'fore her shearers is dumb--
> Nor opened his mouth.
> By tyranny and law was he taken; [216]
> And of his age who reflected,
> That he was wrenched [217] from the land of the living,
> For My people's transgressions the stroke was on him?
> So they made with the wicked his grave,
> Yea, with the felon [218] his tomb.
> Though never harm had he done,
> Neither was guile in his mouth.

Rev. George Adam Smith, M.A.

V.

> But Jehovah had purposed to bruise him,
> Had laid on him sickness;
> So [219] if his life should offer guilt offering,
> A seed he should see, he should lengthen his days.
> And the purpose of Jehovah by his hand should prosper,
> From the travail of his soul shall he see, [220]
> By his knowledge be satisfied.
> My Servant, the Righteous, righteousness wins he for many,
> And their guilt he takes for his load.
> Therefore I set him a share with the great, [221]
> Yea, with the strong shall he share the spoil:
> Because that he poured out his life unto death,
> Let himself with transgressors be reckoned;
> Yea, he the sin of the many hath borne,
> And for the transgressors he interposes.

Let us now take up the interpretation strophe by strophe.

I. Ch. lii. 13-15.

When last our eyes were directed to the Servant, he was in suffering unexplained and unvindicated (ch. l. 4-6). His sufferings seemed to have fallen upon him as the consequence of his fidelity to the Word committed to him; the Prophet had inevitably become the Martyr. Further than this his sufferings were not explained, and the Servant was left in them, calling upon God indeed, and sure that God would hear and vindicate him, but as yet unanswered by word of God or word of man.

It is these words, words both of God and of man, which are given in Isaiah ch. lii. 13-liii. The Sufferer is explained and vindicated, first by God in the first strophe, ch. lii. 13-15, and then by the Conscience of Men, His own people, in the second and third (liii. 1-6); and then, as it appears, the Divine Voice, or the Prophet speaking for it, resumes in strophes iv. and v., and concludes in a strain similar to strophe i.

God's explanation and vindication of the Sufferer is, then, given in the first strophe. It is summed up in the first line, and in one very pregnant word. Jeremiah had said of the Messiah, He shall reign as a King and deal wisely or prosper; [222] and so God says here of the Servant, Behold he shall deal wisely or prosper. The Hebrew verb does not get full expression in any English one. In rendering it shall deal wisely or prudently our translators undoubtedly touch the quick of it. For it is originally a mental process or quality: has insight, understands, is farseeing. But then it also includes the effect of this-- understands so as to get on, deals wisely so as to succeed, is practical both in his way of working and in being sure of his end. Ewald has found an almost exact equivalent in German, "hat Geschick;" for Geschick means both skill or address and fate or destiny. The Hebrew verb is the most practical in the whole language, for this is precisely the point which the prophecy seeks to bring out about the Servant's sufferings. They are practical. He is practical in them. He endures them, not for their own sake, but for some practical end of which he is aware and to which they must assuredly bring him. His failure to convince men by his word, the pain and spite which seem to be his only wage, are not the last of him, but the beginning and the way to what is higher. So shall he rise and be lift up and be very high. The suffering, which in ch. l. seemed to be the Servant's misfortune, is here seen as his wisdom which shall issue in his glory.

But of themselves men do not see this, and they need to be convinced. Pain, the blessed means of God, is man's abhorrence and perplexity. All along the history of the world the Sufferer has been the astonishment and stumbling-block of humanity. The barbarian gets rid of him; he is the first difficulty with which every young literature wrestles; to the end he remains the problem of philosophy and the sore test of faith. It is not native to men to see meaning or profit in the Sufferer; they are staggered by him, they see no reason or promise in him. So did men receive this unique Sufferer, this Servant of Jehovah. The many were astonied at him; his visage was so marred more than men, and his form than the children of men. But his life is to teach them the opposite of their impressions, and to bring them out of their perplexity into reverence before the revealed purpose of God in the Sufferer. As they that were astonied at thee were many, so shall the nations he startles be many; kings shall shut their mouths at him, for that which was not told them they see, and that which they have heard not they have to consider,--viz., the triumph and influence to which the Servant was consciously led through suffering. There may be some reflection here of the way in which the Gentiles regarded the Suffering Israel, but the reference is vague, and perhaps purposely so.

The first strophe, then, gives us just the general theme. In contrast to human experience God reveals in His Servant that suffering is fruitful, that sacrifice is practical. Pain, in God's service, shall lead to glory.

II. Ch. liii. 1-3.

God never speaks but in man He wakens conscience, and the second strophe of the prophecy (along with the third) is the answer of conscience to God. Penitent men, looking back from the light of the Servant's exaltation to the time when his humiliation was before their eyes, say, "Yes: what God has said is true of us. We were the deaf and the indifferent. We heard, but who of us believed what we heard, and to whom was the arm of the Lord--His purpose, the hand He had in the Servant's sufferings--revealed?" [223]

Who are these penitent speakers? Some critics have held them to be the heathen, more have said that they are Israel. But none have pointed out that the writer gives himself no trouble to define them, but seems more anxious to impress us with their consciousness of their moral relation to the Servant. On the whole, it would appear that it is Israel, whom the prophet has in mind as the speakers of vv. 1-6. For, besides the fact that the Old Testament knows nothing of a bearing by Israel of the sins of the Gentiles, it is expressly said in ver. 8, that the sins for which the Servant was stricken were the sins of my people; which people must be the same as the speakers, for they own in vv. 4-6 that the Servant bore their sins. For these and other reasons the mass of Christian critics at the present day are probably right when they assume that Israel are the speakers in vv. 1-6; [224] but the reader must beware of allowing his attention to be lost in questions of that kind. The art of the poem seems intentionally to leave vague the national relation of the speakers to the Servant, in order the more impressively to bring out their moral attitude towards him. There is an utter disappearance of all lines of separation between Jew and Gentile,--both in the first strophe, where, although Gentile names are used, Jews may yet be meant to be included, and in the rest of the poem,--as if the writer wished us to feel that all men stood over against that solitary Servant in a common indifference to his suffering and a common conscience of the guilt he bears. In short, it is no historical situation, such as some critics seem anxious to fasten him down upon, that the prophet reflects; but a certain moral situation, ideal in so far as it was not yet realised,--the state of the quickened human conscience over against a certain Human Suffering, in which, having ignored it at the time, that conscience now realises that the purpose of God was at work.

In vv. 2 and 3 the penitent speakers give us the reasons of their disregard of the Servant in the days of his suffering. In these reasons there is nothing peculiar to Israel, and no special experience of Jewish history is reflected by the terms in which they are conveyed. They are the confession, in general language, of an universal human habit,--the habit of letting the eye cheat the heart and conscience, of allowing the aspect of suffering to blind us to its meaning; of forgetting in our sense of the ugliness and helplessness of pain, that it has a motive, a future and a God. It took ages to wean mankind from those native feelings of aversion and resentment, which caused them at first to abandon or destroy their sick. And, even now, scorn for the weak and incredulity in the heroism or in the profitableness of suffering are strong in the best of us. We judge by looks; we are hurried by the physical impression, which the sufferer makes on us, or by our pride that we are not as he is, into peremptory and harsh judgements upon him. Every day we allow the dulness of poverty, the ugliness of disease, the unprofitableness of misfortune, the ludicrousness of failure, to keep back conscience from discovering to us our share of responsibility for them, and to repel our hearts from that sympathy and patience with them, which along with conscience would assuredly discover to us their place in God's Providence and their special significance for ourselves. It is this original sin of man, of which these penitent speakers own themselves guilty.

But no one is ever permitted to rest with a physical or intellectual impression of suffering. The race, the individual, has always been forced by conscience to the task of finding a moral reason for pain; and nothing so marks man's progress as the successive solutions he has attempted to this problem. The speakers, therefore, proceed in the next part of their confession, strophe iii., to tell us what they first falsely accounted the moral reason of the Servant's suffering and what they afterwards found to be the truth.

III. liii. 4-6.

The earliest and most common moral judgement, which men pass upon pain, is that which is implied in its name--that it is penal. A man suffers because God is angry with him and has stricken him. So Job's friends judged him, and so these speakers tell us they had at first judged the Servant. We had accounted him stricken, smitten of God and afflicted,--stricken, that is, with a plague of sickness, as Job was, for the simile of the sick man is still kept up; smitten of God and degraded or humbled, for it seemed to them that God's hand was in the Servant's sickness, to punish and disgrace him for his own sins. But now they know they were wrong. The hand of God was indeed upon the Servant, and the reason was sin; yet the sin was not his, but theirs. Surely our sicknesses he bore, and our pains he took as his burden. He was pierced for iniquities that were ours. He was crushed for crimes that were ours. Strictly interpreted, these verses mean no more than that the Servant was involved in the consequences of his people's sins. The verbs bore and made his burden are indeed taken by some to mean necessarily, removal or expiation; but in themselves, as is clear from their application to Jeremiah, Ezekiel, and the whole of the generation of Exile, they mean no more than implication in the reproach and the punishment of the people's sins. [225] Nevertheless, as we have explained in a note below, it is really impossible to separate the suffering of a Servant, who has been announced as practical and prosperous in his suffering, from the end for which it is endured. We cannot separate the Servant's bearing of the people's guilt from his removal of it. And, indeed, this practical end of his passion springs forth, past all doubt, from the rest of the strophe, which declares that the Servant's sufferings are not only vicarious but redemptive. The discipline of our peace was upon him, and with his stripes we are healed. Translators agree that discipline of our peace must mean discipline which procures our peace. The peace, the healing, is ours, in consequence of the chastisement and the scourging that was his. The next verse gives us the obverse and complement of the same thought. The pain was his in consequence of the sin that was ours. All we like sheep had gone astray, and the Lord laid on him the iniquity of us all,-- literally iniquity, but inclusive of its guilt and consequences. Nothing could be plainer than these words. The speakers confess, that they know that the Servant's suffering was both vicarious and redemptive.[226]

But how did they get this knowledge? They do not describe any special means by which it came to them. They state this high and novel truth simply as the last step in a process of their consciousness. At first they were bewildered by the Servant's suffering; then they thought it contemptible, thus passing upon it an intellectual judgement; then, forced to seek a moral reason for it, they accounted it as penal and due to the Servant for his own sins; then they recognised that its penalty was vicarious, that the Servant was suffering for them; and finally, they knew that it was redemptive, the means of their own healing and peace. This is a natural climax, a logical and moral progress of thought. The last two steps are stated simply as facts of experience following on other facts. Now our prophet usually publishes the truths, with which he is charged, as the very words of God, introducing them with a solemn and authoritative Thus saith Jehovah. But this novel and supreme truth of vicarious and redemptive suffering, this passion and virtue which crowns the Servant's office, is introduced to us, not by the mouth of God, but by the lips of penitent men; not as an oracle, but as a confession; not as the commission of Divine authority laid beforehand upon the Servant like his other duties, but as the conviction of the human conscience after the Servant has been lifted up before it. In short, by this unusual turn of his art, the prophet seeks to teach us, that vicarious suffering is not a dogmatic, but an experimental truth. The substitution of the Servant for the guilty people, and the redemptive force of that substitution, are no arbitrary doctrine, for which God requires from man a mere intellectual assent; they are no such formal institution of religion as mental indolence and superstition delight to have prepared for their mechanical adherence: but substitutive suffering is a great living fact of human experience, whose outward features are not more evident to men's eyes than its inner meaning is appreciable by their conscience, and of irresistible effect upon their whole moral nature.

Is this lesson of our prophet's art not needed? Men have always been apt to think of vicarious suffering, and of its function in their salvation, as something above and apart from their moral nature, with a value known only to God and not calculable in the terms of conscience or of man's moral experience; nay, rather as something that conflicts with man's ideas of morality and justice. Whereas both the fact and the virtue of vicarious suffering come upon us all, as these speakers describe the vicarious sufferings of the Servant to have come upon them, as a part of inevitable experience. If it be natural, as we saw, for men to be bewildered by the first sight of suffering, to scorn it as futile and to count it the fault of the sufferer himself, it is equally natural and inevitable that these first and hasty theories should be dispelled by the longer experience of life and the more thorough working of conscience. The stricken are not always bearing their own sin. "Suffering is the minister of justice. This is true in part, yet it also is inadequate to explain the facts. Of all the sorrow which befalls humanity, how small a part falls upon the specially guilty; how much seems rather to seek out the good! We might almost ask whether it is not weakness rather than wrong that is punished in this world." [227] In every nation, in every family, the innocent suffer for the guilty. Vicarious suffering is not arbitrary or accidental; it comes with our growth; it is of the very nature of things. It is that part of the Service of Man, to which we are all born, and of the reality of which we daily grow more aware.

But even more than its necessity life teaches us its virtue. Vicarious suffering is not a curse. It is Service--Service for God. It proves a power where every other moral force has failed. By it men are redeemed, on whom justice and their proper punishment have been able to effect nothing. Why this should be is very intelligible. We are not so capable of measuring the physical or moral results of our actions upon our own characters or in our own fortunes as we are upon the lives of others; nor do we so awaken to the guilt and heinousness of our sin as when it reaches and implicates lives, which were not partners with us in it. Moreover, while a man's punishment is apt to give him an excuse for saying, I have expiated my sin myself, and so to leave him self-satisfied and with nothing for which to be grateful or obliged to a higher will; or while it may make him reckless or plunge him into despair; so, on the contrary, when he recognises that others feel the pain of his sin and have come under its weight, then shame is quickly born within him, and pity and every other passion that can melt a hard heart. If, moreover, the others who bear his sin do so voluntarily and for love's sake, then how quickly on the back of shame and pity does gratitude rise, and the sense of debt and of constraint to their will! For all these very intelligible reasons, vicarious suffering has been a powerful redemptive force in the experience of the race. Both the fact of its beneficence and the moral reasons for this are clear enough to lift us above a question, which sometimes gives trouble regarding it,--the question of its justice. Such a question is futile about any service for man, which succeeds as this does where all others have failed, and which proves itself so much in harmony with man's moral nature. But the last shred of objection to the justice of vicarious suffering is surely removed when the sufferer is voluntary as well as vicarious. And, in truth, human experience feels that it has found its highest and its holiest fact in the love that, being innocent itself, stoops to bear its fellows' sins,--not only the anxiety and reproach of them, but even the cost and the curse of them. Greater love hath no man than this, that a man lay down his life for his friends; and greater Service can no man do to man, than to serve them in this way.

Now in this universal human experience of the inevitableness and the virtue of vicarious suffering, Israel had been deeply baptized. The nation had been served by suffering in all the ways we have just described. Beginning with the belief that all righteousness prospered, Israel had come to see the righteous afflicted in her midst; the best Israelites had set their minds to the problem, and learned to believe, at least, that such affliction was of God's will,--part of His Providence, and not an interruption to it. Israel, too, knew the moral solidarity of a people: that citizens share each other's sorrows, and that one generation rolls over its guilt upon the next. Frequently had the whole nation been spared for a pious remnant's sake; and in the Exile, while all the people were formally afflicted by God, it was but a portion of them whose conscience was quick to the meaning of the chastisement, and of them alone, in their submissive and intelligent sufferance of the Lord's wrath, could the opening gospel of the prophecy be spoken, that they had accomplished their warfare, and had received of the Lord's hand double for all their sins. But still more vivid than these collective substitutes for the people were the individuals, who, at different points in Israel's history, had stood forth and taken up as their own the nation's conscience and stooped to bear the nation's curse. Far away back, a Moses had offered himself for destruction, if for his sake God would spare his sinful and thoughtless countrymen. In a psalm of the Exile it is remembered that,

He said, that He would destroy them, Had not Moses His chosen stood before Him in the breach, To turn away His wrath, lest He should destroy. [228]

And Jeremiah, not by a single heroic resolve, but by the slow agony and martyrdom of a long life, had taken Jerusalem's sin upon his own heart, had felt himself forsaken of God, and had voluntarily shared his city's doom, while his generation, unconscious of their guilt and blind to their fate, despised him and esteemed him not. And Ezekiel, who is Jeremiah's far-off reflection, who could only do in symbol what Jeremiah did in reality, was commanded to lie on his side for days, and so bear the guilt of his people. [229]

But in Israel's experience it was not only the human Servant who served the nation by suffering, for God Himself had come down to carry His distressed and accursed people, and to load Himself with them. Our prophet uses the same two verbs of Jehovah as are used of the Servant. [230] Like the Servant, too, God was afflicted in all their affliction; and His love towards them was expended in passion and agony for their sins. Vicarious suffering was not only human, it was Divine.

Was it very wonderful that a people with such an experience, and with such examples, both human and Divine, should at last be led to the thought of One Sufferer, who would exhibit in Himself all the meaning, and procure for His people all the virtue, of that vicarious reproach and sorrow, which a long line of their martyrs had illustrated, and which God had revealed as the passion of His own love? If they had had every example that could fit them to understand the power of such a sufferer, they had also every reason to feel their need of Him. For the Exile had not healed the nation; it had been for the most of them an illustration of that evil effect of punishment to which we alluded above. Penal servitude in Babylon had but hardened Israel. God poured on him the fury of anger, and the strength of battle: it set him on fire round about, yet he knew not; and it burned him, yet he laid it not to heart. [231] What the Exile, then, had failed to do, when it brought upon the people their own sins, the Servant, taking these sins upon himself, would surely effect. The people, whom the Exile had only hardened, his vicarious suffering should strike into penitence and lift to peace.

IV. Ch. liii. 7-9.

It is probable that with ver. 6 the penitent people have ceased speaking, and that the parable is now taken up by the prophet himself. The voice of God, which uttered the first strophe, does not seem to resume till ver. 11.

If strophe iii. confessed that it was for the people's sins the Servant suffered, strophe iv. declares that he himself was sinless, and yet silently submitted to all which injustice laid upon him.

Now Silence under Suffering is a strange thing in the Old Testament--a thing absolutely new. No other Old Testament personage could stay dumb under pain, but immediately broke into one of two voices,--voice of guilt or voice of doubt. In the Old Testament the sufferer is always either confessing his guilt to God, or, when he feels no guilt, challenging God in argument. David, Hezekiah, Jeremiah, Job, and the nameless martyred and moribund of the Psalms, all strive and are loud under pain. Why was this Servant the unique and solitary instance of silence under suffering? Because he had a secret which they had not. It had been said of him: My Servant shall deal wisely or intelligently, shall know what he is about. He had no guilt of his own, no doubts of his God. But he was conscious of the end God had in his pain, an end not to be served in any other way, and with all his heart he had given himself to it. It was not punishment he was enduring; it was not the throes of the birth into higher experience, which he was feeling: it was a Service he was performing,--a service laid on him by God, a service for man's redemption, a service sure of results and of glory. Therefore as a lamb to the slaughter is led, and as a sheep before her shearers is dumb, he opened not his mouth.

The next two verses (8, 9) describe how the Servant's Passion was fulfilled. The figure of a sick man was changed in ver. 5 to that of a punished one, and the punishment we now see carried on to death. The two verses are difficult, the readings and renderings of most of the words being very various. But the sense is clear. The Servant's death was accomplished, not on some far hill top by a stroke out of heaven, but in the forms of human law and by men's hands. It was a judicial murder. By tyranny and by judgement,--that is, by a forced and tyrannous judgement,--he was taken. To this abuse of law the next verse adds the indifference of public opinion: and as for his contemporaries, who of them reflected that he was cut off from, or cut down in, the land of the living,--that in spite of the form of law that condemned him he was a murdered man,--that for the transgression of my people the stroke was his? So, having conceived him to have been lawfully put to death, they consistently gave him a convict's grave: they made his grave with the wicked, and he was with the felon in his death, though--and on this the strophe emphatically ends--he was an innocent man, he had done no harm, neither was guile in his mouth.

Premature sickness and the miscarriage of justice,--these to Orientals are the two outstanding misfortunes of the individual's life. Take the Psalter, set aside its complaints of the horrors of war and of invasion, and you will find almost all the rest of its sighs rising either from sickness or from the sense of injustice. These were the classic forms of individual suffering in the age and civilisation to which our prophet belonged, and it was natural, therefore, that when he was describing an Ideal or Representative Sufferer, he should fill in his picture with both of them. If we remember this, [232] we shall feel no incongruity in the sudden change of the hero from a sick man to a convict, and back again in ver. 10 from a convict to a sick man. Nor, if we remember this, shall we feel disposed to listen to those interpreters, who hold that the basis of this prophecy was the account of an actual historical martyrdom. Had such been the case the prophet would surely have held throughout to one or the other of the two forms of suffering. His sufferer would have been either a leper or a convict, but hardly both. No doubt the details in vv. 8 and 9 are so realistic that they might well be the features of an actual miscarriage of justice; but the like happened too frequently in the Ancient East for such verses to be necessarily any one man's portrait. Perverted justice was the curse of the individual's life,--perverted justice and that stolid, fatalistic apathy of Oriental public opinion, which would probably regard such a sufferer as suffering for his sins the just vengeance of heaven, though the minister of this vengeance was a tyrant and its means were perjury and murder. Who of his generation reflected that for the transgression of my people the stroke was on him!

V. Ch. liii. 10-12.

We have heard the awful tragedy. The innocent Servant was put to a violent and premature death. Public apathy closed over him and the unmarked earth of a felon's grave. It is so utter a perversion of justice, so signal a triumph of wrong over right, so final a disappearance into oblivion of the fairest life that ever lived, that men might be tempted to say, God has forsaken His own. On the contrary--so strophe v. begins--God's own will and pleasure have been in this tragedy: Yet it pleased the LORD to bruise him. The line as it thus stands in our English version has a grim, repulsive sound. But the Hebrew word has no necessary meaning of pleasure or enjoyment. All it says is, God so willed it. His purpose was in this tragedy. Deus vult! It is the one message which can render any pain tolerable or light up with meaning a mystery so cruel as this: The LORD Himself had purposed to bruise His Servant, the LORD Himself had laid on him sickness (the figure of disease is resumed).

God's purpose in putting the Servant to death is explained in the rest of the verse. It was in order that through his soul making a guilt-offering, he might see a seed, prolong his days, and that the pleasure of the Lord might prosper by his hand.

What is a guilt-offering? The term originally meant guilt, and is so used by a prophet contemporary to our own. [233] In the legislation, however, both in the Pentateuch and in Ezekiel, it is applied to legal and sacrificial forms of restitution or reparation for guilt. It is only named in Ezekiel along with other sacrifices. [234] Both Numbers and Leviticus define it, but define it differently. In

Numbers (v. 7, 8) it is the payment, which a transgressor has to make to the human person offended, of the amount to which he has harmed that person's property: it is what we call damages. But in Leviticus it is the ram, exacted over and above damages to the injured party (v. 14-16; vi. 1-7), or in cases where no damages were asked for (v. 17-19), by the priest, the representative of God, for satisfaction to His law; and it was required even where the offender had been an unwitting one. By this guilt-offering the priest made atonement for the sinner and he was forgiven. It was for this purpose of reparation to the Deity that the plagued Philistines sent a guilt-offering back with the ark of Jehovah, which they had stolen. [235] But there is another historical passage, which though the term guilt-offering is not used in it, admirably illustrates the idea. [236] A famine in David's time was revealed to be due to the murder of certain Gibeonites by the house of Saul. David asked the Gibeonites what reparation he could make. They said it was not a matter of damages. But both parties felt that before the law of God could be satisfied and the land relieved of its curse, some atonement, some guilt-offering, must be made to the Divine Law. It was a wild kind of satisfaction that was paid. Seven men of Saul's house were hung up before the Lord in Gibeon. But the instinct, though satisfied in so murderous a fashion, was a true and a grand instinct,--the conscience of a law above all human laws and rights, to which homage must be paid before the sinner could come into true relations with God, or the Divine curse be lifted off.

It is in this sense that the word is used of the Servant of Jehovah, the Ideal, Representative Sufferer. Innocent as he is, he gives his life as satisfaction to the Divine law for the guilt of his people. His death was no mere martyrdom or miscarriage of human justice: in God's intent and purpose, but also by its own voluntary offering, it was an expiatory sacrifice. [237] By his death the Servant did homage to the law of God. By dying for it He made men feel that the supreme end of man was to own that law and be in a right relation to it, and that the supreme service was to help others to a right relation. As it is said a little farther down, My Servant, righteous himself, wins righteousness for many, and makes their iniquities his load.

It surely cannot be difficult for any one, who knows what sin is, and what a part vicarious suffering plays both in the bearing of the sin and in the redemption of the sinner, to perceive that at this point the Servant's service for God and man reaches its crown. Compare his death and its sad meaning, with the brilliant energies of his earlier career. It is a heavy and an honourable thing to come from God to men, laden with God's truth for your charge and responsibility; but it is a far heavier to stoop and take upon your heart as your business and burden men's suffering and sin. It is a needful and a lovely thing to assist the feeble aspirations of men, to put yourself on the side of whatever in them is upward and living,--to be the shelter, as the Servant was, of the bruised reed and the fading wick; but it is more indispensable, and it is infinitely heavier, to seek to lift the deadness of men, to take their guilt upon your heart, to attempt to rouse them to it, to attempt to deliver them from it. It is a useful and a glorious thing to establish order and justice among men, to create a social conscience, to inspire the exercise of love and the habits of service, and this the Servant did when he set Law on the Earth, and the Isles waited for his teaching; but after all man's supreme and controlling relation is his relation to God, and to this their righteousness the Servant restored guilty men by his death.

And so it was at this point, according to our prophecy, that the Servant, though brought so low, was nearest his exaltation; though in death, yet nearest life, nearest the highest kind of life, the seeing of a seed, the finding of himself in others; though despised, rejected and forgotten of men, most certain of finding a place among the great and notable forces of life,--therefore do I divide him a share with the great, and the spoil he shall share with the strong. Not because as a prophet he was a sharp sword in the hand of the Lord, or a light flashing to the ends of the earth, but in that--as the prophecy concludes, and it is the prophet's last and highest word concerning him--in that he bare the sin of the many, and interposed for the transgressors.

**

We have seen that the most striking thing about this prophecy is the spectral appearance of the Servant. He haunts, rather than is present in, the chapter. We hear of him, but he himself does not speak. We see faces that he startles, lips that the sight of him shuts, lips that the memory of him, after he has passed in silence, opens to bitter confession of neglect and misunderstanding; but himself we see not. His aspect and his bearing, his work for God and his influence on men, are shown to us, through the recollection and conscience of the speakers, with a vividness and a truth that draw the consciences of us who hear into the current of the confession, and take our hearts captive. But when we ask, Who was he then? What was his name among men? Where shall we find himself? Has he come, or do you still look for him?--neither the speakers, whose conscience he so smote, nor God, whose chief purpose he was, give us here any answer. In some verses he and his work seem already to have happened upon earth, but again we are made to feel that he is still future to the prophet, and that the voices, which the prophet quotes as speaking of having seen him and found him to be the Saviour, are voices of a day not yet born, while the prophet writes.

But about five hundred and fifty years after this prophecy was written, a Man came forward among the sons of men,--among this very nation from whom the prophecy had arisen; and in every essential of consciousness and of experience He was the counterpart, embodiment and fulfilment of this Suffering Servant and his Service. Jesus Christ answers the questions, which the prophecy raises and leaves unanswered. In the prophecy we see one, who is only a spectre, a dream, a conscience without a voice, without a name, without a place in history. But in Jesus Christ of Nazareth the dream becomes a reality; He, whom we have seen in this chapter only as the purpose of God, only through the eyes and consciences of a generation yet unborn,--He comes forward in flesh and blood; He speaks, He explains Himself, He accomplishes almost to the last detail the work, the patience and the death that are here described as Ideal and Representative.

The correspondence of details between Christ's life and this prophecy, published five hundred and fifty years before He came, is striking; if we encountered it for the first time, it would be more than striking, it would be staggering. But do not let us do what so many have done--so fondly exaggerate it as to lose in the details of external resemblance the moral and spiritual identity.

For the external correspondence between this prophecy and the life of Jesus Christ is by no means perfect. Every wound that is set down in the fifty-third of Isaiah was not reproduced or fulfilled in the sufferings of Jesus. For instance, Christ was not the sick, plague-stricken man, whom the Servant is at first represented to be. The English translators have masked the leprous figure, that stands out so clearly in the original Hebrew,--for acquainted with grief, bearing our griefs, put him to grief, we should in each case read sickness. Now Christ was no Job. As Matthew points out, the only way He could be said to bear our sicknesses and to carry our pains was by healing them, not by sharing them.

And again, exactly as the judicial murder of the Servant, and the entire absence from his contemporaries of any idea that he suffered a vicarious death, suit the case of Christ, the next stage in the Servant's fate was not true of the Victim of Pilate and the Pharisees. Christ's grave was not with the wicked. He suffered as a felon without the walls on the common place of execution, but friends received the body and gave it an honourable burial in a friend's grave. Or take the clause, with the rich in his death. It is doubtful whether the word is really rich, and ought not to be a closer synonym of wicked in the previous clause; but if it be rich, it is simply another name for the wicked, who in the East, in cases of miscarried justice, are so often coupled with the evildoers. It cannot possibly denote such a man as Joseph of Arimathea; nor, is it to be observed, do the Evangelists in describing Christ's burial in that rich and pious man's tomb take any notice of this line about the Suffering Servant.

But the absence of a complete incidental correspondence only renders more striking the moral and spiritual correspondence, the essential likeness between the Service set forth in ch. liii. and the work of our Lord.

The speakers of ch. liii. set the Servant over against themselves, and in solitariness of character and office. They count him alone sinless where all they have sinned, and him alone the agent of salvation and healing where their whole duty is to look on and believe. But this is precisely the relation which Christ assumed between Himself and the nation. He was on one side, all they on the other. Against their strong effort to make Him the First among them, it was, as we have said before, the constant aim of our Lord to assert and to explain Himself as The Only.

And this Onlyness was to be realised in suffering. He said, I must suffer; or again, It behoves the Christ to suffer. Suffering is the experience in which men feel their oneness with their kind. Christ, too, by suffering felt His oneness with men; but largely in order to assert a singularity beyond. Through suffering He became like unto men, but only that He might effect through suffering a lonely and a singular service for them. For though He suffered in all points as men did, yet He shared none of their universal feelings about suffering. Pain never drew from Him either of those two voices of guilt or of doubt. Pain never reminded Christ of His own past, nor made Him question God.

Nor did He seek pain for any end in itself. There have been men who have done so; fanatics who have gloried in pain; superstitious minds that have fancied it to be meritorious; men whose wounds have been as mouths to feed their pride, or to publish their fidelity to their cause. But our Lord shrank from pain; if it had been possible He would have willed not to bear it: Father, save Me from this hour; Father, if it be Thy will, let this cup pass from Me. And when He submitted and was under the agony, it was not in the feeling of it, nor in the impression it made on others, nor in the manner in which it drew men's hearts to Him, nor in the seal it set on the truth, but in something beyond it, that He found His end and satisfaction. Jesus looked out of the travail of His soul and was satisfied.

For, firstly, He knew His pain to be God's will for an end outside Himself,--I have a baptism to be baptized with, and how am I straitened till it be accomplished: Father, save Me from this hour, yet for this cause came I to this hour: Father, Thy will be done,--and all opportunities to escape as temptations.

And, secondly, like the Servant, Jesus dealt prudently, had insight. The will of God in His suffering was no mystery to Him. He understood from the first why He was to suffer.[238]

The reasons He gave were the same two and in the same order as are given by our prophet for the sufferings of the Servant,--first, that fidelity to God's truth could bring with it no other fate in Israel;[239]

then that His death was necessary for the sins of men, and as men's ransom from sin. In giving the first of these reasons for His death, Christ likened Himself to the prophets who had gone before Him in Jerusalem; but in the second He matched Himself with no other, and no other has ever been known in this to match himself with Jesus.

When men, then, stand up and tell us that Christ suffered only for the sake of sympathy with His kind, or only for loyalty to the truth, we have to tell them that this was not the whole of Christ's own consciousness, this was not the whole of Christ's own explanation. Suffering, which leads men into the sense of oneness with their kind, only made Him, as it grew the nearer and weighed the heavier, more emphatic upon His difference from other men. If He Himself, by His pity, by His labours of healing (as Matthew points out), and by all His intercourse with His people, penetrated more deeply into the participation of human suffering, the very days which marked with increasing force His sympathy with men, only laid more bare their want of sympathy with Him, their incapacity to follow into that unique conscience and understanding of a Passion, which He bore not only with, but, as He said, for His brethren. Who believed that which we heard, and to whom was the arm of the Lord revealed? As to His generation, who reflected ... that for the transgression of my people He was stricken? Again, while Christ indeed brought truth to earth from heaven, and was for truth's sake condemned by men to die, the burden which He found waiting Him on earth, man's sin, was ever felt by Him to be a heavier burden and responsibility than the delivery of the truth; and was in fact the thing, which, apart from the things for which men might put Him to death, remained the reason of His death in His own sight and in that of His Father. And He told men why He felt their sin to be so heavy, because it kept them so far from God, and this was His purpose, He said, in bearing it--that He might bring us back to God; not primarily that He might relieve us of the suffering which followed sin, though He did so relieve some when He pardoned them, but that He might restore us to right relations with God,--might, like the Servant, make many righteous. Now it was Christ's confidence to be able to do this, which distinguished Him from all others, upon whom has most heavily fallen the conscience of their people's sins, and who have most keenly felt the duty and commission from God of vicarious suffering. If, like Moses, one sometimes dared for love's sake to offer his life for the life of his people, none, under the conscience and pain of their people's sins, ever expressed any consciousness of thereby making their brethren righteous. On the contrary, even a Jeremiah, whose experience, as we have seen, comes so wonderfully near the picture of the Representative Sufferer in ch. liii.,--even a Jeremiah feels, with the increase of his vicarious pain and conscience of guilt, only the more perplexed, only the deeper in despair, only the less able to understand God and the less hopeful to prevail with Him. But Christ was sure of His power to remove men's sins, and was never more emphatic about that power than when He most felt those sins' weight.

And He has seen His seed; He has made many righteous. We found it to be uncertain whether the penitent speakers in ch. liii. understood that the Servant by coming under the physical sufferings, which were the consequences of their sins, relieved them of these consequences; other passages in the prophecy would seem to imply, that, while the Servant's sufferings were alone valid for righteousness, they did not relieve the rest of the nation from suffering too. And so it would be going beyond what God has given us to know, if we said that God counts the sufferings on the Cross, which were endured for our sins, as an equivalent for, or as sufficient to do away with, the sufferings which these sins bring upon our minds, our bodies and our social relations. Substitution of this kind is neither affirmed by the penitents who speak in the fifty-third of Isaiah, nor is it an invariable or essential part of the experience of those who have found forgiveness through Christ. Every day penitents turn to God through Christ, and are assured of forgiveness, who feel no abatement in the rigour of the retribution of those laws of God, which they have offended; like David after his forgiveness, they have to continue to bear the consequences of their sins. But dark as this side of experience undoubtedly is, only the more conspicuously against the darkness does the other side of experience shine. By believing what they have heard, reaching this belief through a quicker conscience and a closer study of Christ's words about His death, men, upon whom conscience by itself and sore punishment have worked in vain, have been struck into penitence, have been assured of pardon, have been brought into right relations with God, have felt all the melting and the bracing effects of the knowledge that another has suffered in their stead. Nay, let us consider this--the physical consequences of their sins may have been left to be endured by such men, for no other reason than in order to make their new relation to God more sensible to them, while they feel those consequences no longer with the feeling of penalty, but with that of chastisement and discipline. Surely nothing could serve more strongly than this to reveal the new conscience towards God that has been worked within them. This inward righteousness is made more plain by the continuance of the physical and social consequences of their sins than it would have been had these consequences been removed.

Thus Christ, like the Servant, became a force in the world, inheriting in the course of Providence a portion with the great and dividing the spoils of history with the strong. As has often been said, His Cross is His Throne, and it is by His death that He has ruled the ages. Yet we must not understand this as if His Power was only or mostly shown in binding men, by gratitude for the salvation He won them, to own Him for their King. His power has been even more conspicuously proved in making His fashion of service the most fruitful and the most honoured among men. If men have ceased to turn from sickness with aversion or from weakness with contempt; if they have learned to see in all pain some law of God, and in vicarious suffering God's most holy service; if patience and self-sacrifice have come in any way to be a habit of human life,--the power in this change has been Christ. But because these two--to say, Thy will be done, and to sacrifice self--are for us men the hardest and the most unnatural of things to do, Jesus Christ, in making these a conscience and a habit upon earth, has indeed shown Himself able to divide the spoil with the strong, has indeed performed the very highest Service for Man of which man can conceive.

Footnotes:

203. Thus Ewald supposed ch. lii. 13-liii. to be an elegy upon some martyr in the persecutions under Manasseh. Professor Briggs, as we have noticed before, claims to have discovered that all the passages in the Servant are parts of a trimeter poem, older than the rest of the prophecy, which he finds to be in hexameters. See p. [39]315.

204. I may quote Dillmann's opinion on this last point: "Andererseits sind nicht blos die Grundgedanken und auch einzelne Wendungen wie 52, 13-15. 53, 7. 11. 12 durch 42, 1 ff. 49, 1 ff. 50, 3 ff. so wohl vorbereitet und so sehr in Übereinstimmung damit, dass an eine fast unveränderte Herübernahme des Abschnitts aus einer verlornen Schrift (Ew.) nicht gedacht werden kann, sondern derselbe doch wesentlich als Werk des Vrf. angesehen werden muss" (Commentary 4th ed., 1890, p. 453).

205. This verb best gives the force of the Hebrew, which means both to deal prudently and to prosper or succeed. See p. [40]346.

206. Vulgate finely: "extolletur, sublimis erit et valde elatus."

207. "The term rendered 'startle' has created unnecessary difficulty to some writers. The word means to 'cause to spring or leap;' when applied to fluids, to spirt or sprinkle them. The fluid spirted is put in the accusative, and it is spirted upon the person. In the present passage the person, 'many nations,' is in the accusative, and it is simply treason against the Hebrew language to render 'sprinkle.' The interpreter who will so translate will 'do anything.'"--A. B. Davidson, Expositor, 2nd series, viii., 443. The LXX. has thaumasontai ethne polla. The Peschitto and Vulgate render sprinkle.

208. And not our report, or something we caused to be heard, as in the English Version,--smvh is the passive participle of sm, to hear, and not of hsmy, to cause to hear. The speakers are now the penitent people of God who had been preached to, and not the prophets who had preached.

209. Tender shoot. Masculine participle, meaning sucker, or suckling. Dr. John Hunter (Christian Treasury) suggests succulent plant, such as grow in the desert. But in Job viii. 16; xiv. 7; xv. 30, the feminine form is used of any tender shoot of a tree, and the feminine plural in Ezek. xvii. 22 of the same. The LXX. read paidion, infant. Before Him, i.e. Jehovah. Cheyne, following Ewald, reads before us. So Giesebrecht.

210. Took for his burden. Loaded himself with them. The same grievous word which God uses of Himself in ch. xlvi. See p. [41]180.

211. There is more than afflicted (Authorised Version) in this word. There is the sense of being humbled, punished for his own sake.

212. The possessive pronoun has been put to the end of the lines, where it stands in the original, producing a greater emphasis and even a sense of rhyme.

213. The possessive pronoun has been put to the end of the lines, where it stands in the original, producing a greater emphasis and even a sense of rhyme.

214. The possessive pronoun has been put to the end of the lines, where it stands in the original, producing a greater emphasis and even a sense of rhyme.

215. klnv Kullanu so rendered instead of "all of us," in order to be assonant with the close of the verse, as the original is, which closes with kullam.

216. That is, by a form of law that was tyranny, a judicial crime.

217. Cut off violently, prematurely, unnaturally.

218. See p. [42]368.

219. The verbs, hitherto in the perfect in this verse, now change to the imperfect; a sign that they express the purpose of God. Cf. Dillmann, in loco.

220. From the travail of his soul shall he see, and by his knowledge be satisfied. Taking vdtv with ysv instead of with ytsdyq. This reading suggested itself to me some years ago. Since then I have found it only in Prof. Briggs's translation, Messianic Prophecy, p. 359. It is supported by the frequent parallel in which we find seeing and knowing in Hebrew.

221. Some translate many, i.e., the many to whom he brings righteousness, as if he were a victor with a great host behind him.

222. Jer. xxiii. 5.

223. Hitzig (among others) held that it is the prophets who are the speakers of ver. 1, and that the voices of the penitent people come in only with ver. 2 or ver. 3. In that case smvtynv would mean what we heard from God (smvh is elsewhere used for the prophetic message) and delivered to the people. This interpretation multiplies the dramatis personæ, but does not materially alter the meaning, of the prophecy. It merely changes part of the penitent people's self-reproach into a reproach cast on them by their prophets. But there is no real reason for introducing the prophets as the speakers of ver. 1.

224. For the argument that it is Israel who speaks here, see Hoffmann (Schriftbeweis), who was converted from the other view, and Dillmann, 4th ed., in loco. A very ingenious attempt has been made by Giesebrecht (Beiträge zur Jesaia Kritik, 1890, p. 146 ff.), in favour of the interpretation that the heathen are the speakers. His reasons are these: 1. It is the heathen who are spoken of in lii. 13-15, and a change to Israel would be too sudden. Answer: The heathen are not exclusively spoken of in lii. 13-15; but if they were a change in the next verse to Israel would not be more rapid than some already made by the prophet. 2. The words in liii. 1 suit the heathen. They have already received the news of the exaltation of the Servant, which in lii. 15 was promised them. This is the smvtnv, that is news we have just heard. h'myn is a pluperfect of the subjunctive mood: Who could or who would have believed this news of the exaltation we have just heard, and the arm of Jehovah to whom was it revealed! i.e., it was revealed to nobody. Answer: besides the precariousness of taking h'myn as a pluperfect subjunctive, this interpretation is opposed to the general effort of the prophecy, which is to expose unbelief before the exaltation, not after it. 3. To get rid of the argument--that, while the speakers own that the Servant bears their sins, it is said the Servant was stricken for the sins of my people, and that therefore the speakers must be the same as "my people":--Giesebrecht would utterly alter the reading of ver. 8 from mphs mv nn lmv, for the transgression of my people was the stroke to him to mpsm ynn, for their stroke was he smitten.

225. ns' and svl. In speaking of his country's woes, Jeremiah (x. 19) says: This is sickness, or my sickness, and I must bear it, v's'ny zh chly. Ezekiel (iv. 4) is commanded to lie on his side, and in that symbolic position to bear the iniquity of His people, ts' vnm. One of the Lamentations (v. 7) complains: Our fathers have sinned and are not, and we bear (svl) their iniquities. In these cases the meaning of both ns' and svl is simply to feel the weight of, be involved in. The verbs do not convey the sense of carrying off or expiating. But still it had been said of the Servant that in his suffering he would be practical and prosper; so that when we now hear that he bears his people's sins, we are ready to understand that he does not do this for the mere sake of sharing them, but for a practical purpose, which, of course, can only be their removal. There is, therefore, no need to quarrel with the interpretation of ver. 4, that the Servant carries away the suffering with which he is laden. Matthew makes this interpretation (viii. 17) in speaking of Christ's healing. But it is a very interesting fact, and not without light upon the free and plastic way in which the New Testament quotes from the Old, that Matthew has ignored the original and literal meaning of the quotation, which is that the Servant shared the sicknesses of the people: a sense impossible in the case for which the Evangelist uses the words.

226. But they do not tell us, whether they were totally exempted from suffering by the Servant's pains, or whether they also suffered with him the consequence of their misdeeds. For that question is not now present to their minds. Whether they also suffer or not (and other chapters in the prophecy emphasize the people's bearing of the consequences of their misdeeds), they know that it was not their own, but the Servant's suffering, which was alone the factor in their redemption.

227. Mystery of Pain, by James Hinton, p. 27.

228. Psalm cvi. 23; cf. also ver. 32, where the other side of the solidarity between Moses and the people comes out. They angered Him also at the waters of Strife, so that it went ill with Moses for their sakes ... he spake unadvisedly with his lips.

229. See p. [43]352.

230. Isa. xlvi. 3, 4. See pp. [44]179, [45]180 of this volume.

231. Ch. xlii. 25.

232. If we remember this we shall also feel more reason than ever against perceiving the Nation, or any aspect of the Nation, in the Sufferer of ch. liii. For he suffers, as the individual suffers, sickness and legal wrong. Tyrants do not put whole nations through a form of law and judgement. Of course, it is open to those, who hold that the Servant is still an aspect of the Nation, to reply, that all this is simply evidence of how far the prophet has pushed his personification. A whole nation has been called "The Sick Man" even in our prosaic days. But see pp. [46]268-[47]76.

233. Jer. li. 4.

234. xl. 39; xlii. 13; xliv. 29; xlvi. 20.

235. 1 Sam. vi. 13.

236. Cf. Wellhausen's Prolegomena, ch. ii., 2.

237. There is no exegete but agrees to this. There may be differences of opinion about the syntax,--whether the verse should run, though Thou makest his soul guilt, or a guilt-offering; or, though his soul

make a guilt-offering; or (reading ysym for tsym), while he makes his soul a guilt-offering,--but all agree to the fact that by himself or by God the Servant's life is offered an expiation for sin, a satisfaction to the law of God.

238. Cf. Baldensperger (Das Selbstbewusstsein Jesu, p. 119 ff.) on the genuineness of Christ's predictions and explanations of His sufferings.

239. Cf. p. [48]330.

BOOK IV

THE RESTORATION.

We have now reached the summit of our prophecy. It has been a long, steep ascent, and we have had very much to seek out on the way, and to extricate and solve and load ourselves with. But although a long extent of the prophecy, if we measure it by chapters, still lies before us, the end is in sight; every difficulty has been surmounted which kept us from seeing how we were to get to it, and the rest of the way may be said to be down-hill.

To drop the figure--the Servant, his vicarious suffering and atonement for the sins of the people, form for our prophet the solution of the spiritual problem of the nation's restoration, and what he has now to do is but to fill in the details of this.

We saw that the problem of Israel's deliverance from Exile, their Return, and their Restoration to their position in their own land as the Chief Servant of God to humanity, was really a double problem-- political and spiritual. The solution of the political side of it was Cyrus. As soon as the prophet had been able to make it certain that Cyrus was moving down upon Babylon, with a commission from God to take the city, and irresistible in the power with which Jehovah had invested him, the political difficulties in the way of Israel's Return were as good as removed; and so the prophet gave, in the end of ch. xlviii., his great call to his countrymen to depart. But all through chs. xl.-xlviii., while addressing himself to the solution of the political problems of Israel's deliverance, the prophet had given hints that there were moral and spiritual difficulties as well. In spite of their punishment for more than half a century, the mass of the people were not worthy of a return. Many were idolaters; many were worldly; the orthodox had their own wrong views of how salvation should come (xlv. 9 ff.); the pious were without either light or faith (l. 10). The nation, in short, had not that inward righteousness, which could alone justify God in vindicating them before the world, in establishing their outward righteousness, their salvation and reinstatement in their lofty place and calling as His people. These moral difficulties come upon the prophet with greater force after he has, with the close of ch. xlviii., finished his solution of the political ones. To these moral difficulties he addresses himself in xlix.-liii., and the Servant and his Service are his solution of them:--the Servant as a Prophet and a Covenant of the People in ch. xlix. and in ch. l. 4 ff.; the Servant as an example to the people, ch. l. ff.; and finally the Servant as a full expiation for the people's sins in ch. lii. 13-liii. It is the Servant who is to raise up the land, and to bring back the heirs to the desolate heritages, and rouse the Israel who are not willing to leave Babylon, saying to the bound, Go forth; and to them that sit in darkness, Show yourselves (xlix. 8, 9). It is he who is to sustain the weary and to comfort the pious in Israel, who, though pious, have no light as they walk on their way back (l. 4, 10). It is the Servant finally who is to achieve the main problem of all and make many righteous (liii. 11). The hope of restoration, the certainty of the people's redemption, the certainty of the rebuilding of Jerusalem, the certainty of the growth of the people to a great multitude, are, therefore, all woven by the prophet through and through with his studies of the Servant's work in xlix., l., and lii. 13- liii.,--woven so closely and so naturally that, as we have already seen (pp. [49]313 f., [50]336 ff.), we cannot take any part of chs. xlix.-liii. and say that it is of different authorship from the rest. Thus in ch. xlix. we have the road to Jerusalem pictured in vv. 9b-13, immediately upon the back of the Servant's call to go forth in ver. 9a. We have then the assurance of Zion being rebuilt and thronged by her children in vv. 14-23, and another affirmation of the certainty of redemption in vv. 24-26; In l. 1-3 this is repeated. In li.-lii. 12 the petty people is assured that it shall grow innumerable again; new affirmations are made of its ransom and return, ending with the beautiful prospect of the feet of the heralds of deliverance on the mountains of Judah (lii. 7b) and a renewed call to leave Babylon (vv. 11, 12). We shall treat all these passages in our Twenty-First Chapter.

And as they started naturally from the Servant's work in xlix. 1-9a and his example in l. 4-11, so upon his final and crowning work in ch. liii. there follow as naturally ch. liv. (the prospect of the seed that liii. 10 promised he should see), and ch. lv. (a new call to come forth). These two, with the little pre-exilic prophecy, ch. lvi. 1-8, we shall treat in our Twenty-Second Chapter.

Then come the series of difficult small prophecies with pre-exilic traces in them, from lvi. 9-lix. They will occupy our Twenty-Third Chapter. In ch. lx. Zion is at last not only in sight, but radiant in the rising of her new day of glory. In chs. lxi. and lxii. the prophet, having reached Zion, "looks back," as

Rev. George Adam Smith, M.A.

Dillmann well remarks, "upon what has become his task, and in connection with that makes clear once more the high goal of all his working and striving." In lxiii. 1-6 the Divine Deliverer is hailed. We shall take lx.-lxiii. 6 together in our Twenty-Fourth Chapter.

Ch. lxiii. 7-lxiv. is an Intercessory Prayer for the restoration of all Israel. It is answered in ch. lxv., and the lesson of this answer, that Israel must be judged, and that all cannot be saved, is enforced in ch. lxvi. Chs. lxiii. 7-lxvi. will therefore form our Twenty-Fifth and closing Chapter.

Thus our course is clear, and we can overtake it rapidly. It is, to a large extent, a series of spectacles, interrupted by exhortations upon duty; things, in fact, to see and to hear, not to argue about. There are few great doctrinal questions, except what we have already sufficiently discussed; our study, for instance, of the term righteousness, we shall find has covered for us a large part of the ground in advance. And the only difficult literary question is that of the pre-exilic and post-exilic pieces, which are alleged to form so large a part of chs. lvi.-lix. and lxiii.-lxvi.

CHAPTER XXI

DOUBTS IN THE WAY.

Isaiah xlix.-lii. 12.

Chapters xlix.-liii. are, as we have seen, a series of more or less closely joined passages, in which the prophet, having already made the political redemption of Israel certain through Cyrus, and having dismissed Cyrus from his thoughts, addresses himself to various difficulties in the way of restoration, chiefly moral and spiritual, and rising from Israel's own feelings and character; exhorts the people in face of them by Jehovah's faithfulness and power; but finds the chief solution of them in the Servant and his prophetic and expiatory work. We have already studied such of these passages as present the Servant to us, and we now take up those others, which meet the doubts and difficulties in the way of restoration by means of general considerations drawn from God's character and power. Let it be noticed that, with one exception (ch. l. 11), [240] these passages are meant for earnest and pious minds in Israel,--for those Israelites, whose desires are towards Zion, but chill and heavy with doubts.

The form and the terms of these passages are in harmony with their purpose. They are a series of short, high-pitched exhortations, apostrophes and lyrics. One, ch. liii. 9-12, calls upon the arm of Jehovah, but all the rest address Zion,--that is, the ideal people in the person of their mother, with whom they ever so fondly identified themselves; or Zion's children; or them that follow righteousness, or ye that know righteousness; or my people, my nation; or again Zion herself. This personification of the people under the name of their city, and under the aspect of a woman, whose children are the individual members of the people, will be before us till the end of our prophecy. It is, of course, a personification of Israel, which is complementary to Israel's other personification under the name of the Servant. The Servant is Israel active, comforting, serving his own members and the nations; Zion, the Mother-City, is Israel passive, to be comforted, to be served by her own sons and by the kings of the peoples.

We may divide the passages into two groups. First, the songs of return, which rise out of the picture of the Servant and his redemption of the people in ch. xlix. 9b, with the long promise and exhortation to Zion and her children, that lasts till the second picture of the Servant in ch. lii. 4; and second, the short pieces which lie between the second picture of the Servant and the third, or from the beginning of ch. li. to ch. lii. 12.

I.

In ch. xlix. 9b God's promise of the return of the redeemed proceeds naturally from that of their ransom by the Servant. It is hailed by a song in ver. 13, and the rest of the section is the answer to three doubts, which, like sobs, interrupt the music. But the prophecy, stooping, as it were, to kiss the trembling lips through which these doubts break, immediately resumes its high flight of comfort and promise. Two of these doubts are: ver. 14, But Zion hath said, Jehovah hath forsaken me, and my Lord hath forgotten me; and ver. 24, Shall the prey be taken from the mighty or the captives of the terrible be delivered? The third is implied in ch. l. 1.

The promise of return is as follows: On roads shall they feed, and on all bare heights shall be their pasture. They shall not hunger nor thirst, nor shall the mirage nor the sun smite them: for He that yearneth over them shall lead them, even by springs of water shall He guide them. And I will set all My mountains for a way, and My high ways shall be exalted. Lo, these shall come from far: and, lo, these from the North and from the West, and these from the land of Sinim. [241] Sing forth, O heavens; and be glad, O earth; let the mountains break forth into singing: for Jehovah hath comforted His people, and over His afflicted He yearneth.

Now, do not let us imagine that this is the promise of a merely material miracle. It is the greater glory of a purely spiritual one, as the prophet indicates in describing its cause in the words, because He that yearneth over them shall lead them. The desert is not to abate its immemorial rigours; in itself the way shall still be as hard as when the discredited and heart-broken exiles were driven down it from home to servitude. But their hearts are now changed, and that shall change the road. The new faith, which has made the difference, is a very simple one, that God is Power and that God is Love. Notice the possessive pronouns used by God, and mark what they put into His possession: two kinds of things,-- powerful things, I will make all My mountains a way; and sorrowful things, Jehovah hath comforted His people, and will have compassion on His afflicted. [242] If we will steadfastly believe that everything in the world which is in pain, and everything which has power, is God's, and shall be used by Him, the one for the sake of the other, this shall surely change the way to our feet, and all the world around to our eyes.

1. Only it is so impossible to believe it when one looks at real fact; and however far and swiftly faith and hope may carry us for a time, we always come to ground again and face to face with fact. The prophet's imagination speeding along that green and lifted highway of the Lord lights suddenly upon the end of it,--the still dismantled and desolate city. Fifty years Zion's altar fires have been cold and her walls in ruin. Fifty years she has been bereaved of her children and left alone. The prophet hears the winds blow mournfully through her fact's chill answer to faith. But Zion said, Forsaken me hath Jehovah, and my Lord hath forgotten me! Now let us remember, that our prophet has Zion before him in the figure of a mother, and we shall feel the force of God's reply. It is to a mother's heart God appeals. Doth a woman forget her sucking child so as not to yearn over the son of her womb? yea, such may forget, but I will not forget thee, desolate mother that thou art! [243] Thy life is not what thou art in outward show and feeling, but what thou art in My love and in My sight. Lo, upon both palms have I graven thee; thy walls are before Me continually. The custom, which to some extent prevails in all nations, of puncturing or tattooing upon the skin a dear name one wishes to keep in mind, is followed in the East chiefly for religious purposes, and men engrave the name of God or some holy text upon the hand or arm for a memorial or as a mark of consecration. It is this fashion which God attributes to Himself. Having measured His love by the love of a mother, He gives this second human pledge for His memory and devotion. But again He exceeds the human habit; for it is not only the name of Zion which is engraved on His hands, but her picture. And it is not her picture, as she lies in her present ruin and solitariness, but her restored and perfect state: thy walls are continually before Me. For this is faith's answer to all the ruin and haggard contradiction of outward fact. Reality is not what we see: reality is what God sees. What a thing is in His sight and to His purpose, that it really is, and that it shall ultimately appear to men's eyes. To make us believe this is the greatest service the Divine can do for the human. It was the service Christ was always doing, and nothing showed His divinity more. He took us men and He called us, unworthy as we were, His brethren, the sons of God. He took such an one as Simon, shifting and unstable, a quicksand of a man, and He said, On this rock I will build My Church. A man's reality is not what he is in his own feelings, or what he is to the world's eyes; but what he is to God's love, to God's yearning, and in God's plan. If he believe that, so in the end shall he feel it, so in the end shall he show it to the eyes of the world.

Upon those great thoughts, that God's are all strong things and all weak things, and that the real and the certain in life is His will, the prophecy breaks into a vision of multitudes in motion. There is a great stirring and hastening, crowds gather up through the verses, the land is lifted and thronged. Lift up thine eyes round about, and behold: all of them gather together, they come unto thee. As I live, saith Jehovah, thou shalt surely clothe thyself with them all as with an ornament, and gird thyself with them, like a bride. For as for thy waste places and thy desolate ones and thy devastated land--yea, thou wilt now be too strait for the inhabitants, and far off shall be they that devoured thee. Again shall they speak in thine ears,--the children of thy bereavement (that is, those children who have been born away from Zion during her solitude), Too strait for me is the place, make me room that I may dwell. And thou shalt say in thine heart, Who hath borne me these,--not begotten, as our English version renders, because the question with Zion was not who was the father of the children, but who, in her own barrenness, could possibly be the mother,--Who hath borne me these, seeing I was first bereft of my children, and since then have been barren, an exile and a castaway! And these, who hath brought them up! Lo, I was left by myself. These,--whence are they! Our English version, which has blundered in the preceding verses, requires no correction in the following; and the first great Doubt in the Way being now answered, for they that wait on the Lord shall not be ashamed, we pass to the second, in ver. 24.

2. Can the prey be taken from the mighty, or the captives of the tyrant [244] be delivered? Even though God be full of love and thought for Zion, will these tyrants give up her children? Yea, thus saith Jehovah, Even the captives of the mighty shall be taken, and the prey of the tyrant be delivered; and with him that quarreleth with thee will I quarrel, and thy children will I save. And I will make thine oppressors to eat their own flesh, and as with new wine with their blood shall they be drunken, that all flesh may know that I am Jehovah thy Saviour, and thy Redeemer the Mighty One of Jacob.

3. But now a third Doubt in the Way seems to have risen. Unlike the two others, it is not directly stated, but we may gather its substance from the reply which Jehovah makes to it (l. 1). Thus saith Jehovah, What is this bill of divorce of your mother whom I have sent away, or which of My creditors is it to whom I have sold you? The form, in which this challenge is put, assumes that the Israelites themselves had been thinking of Jehovah's dismissal of Israel as an irrevocable divorce and a bankrupt sale into slavery. [245]

"What now is this letter of divorce,--this that you are saying I have given your mother? You say that I have sold you as a bankrupt father sells his children,--to which then of my creditors is it that I have sold you?"

The most characteristic effect of sin is that it is always reminding men of law. Whether the moral habit of it be upon them or they are entangled in its material consequences, sin breeds in men the conscience of inexorable, irrevocable law. Its effect is not only practical, but intellectual. Sin not only robs a man of the freedom of his own will, but it takes from him the power to think of freedom in others, and it does not stop till it paralyses his belief in the freedom of God. He, who knows himself as the creature of unchangeable habits or as the victim of pitiless laws, cannot help imputing his own experience to what is beyond him, till all life seems strictly lawbound, the idea of a free agent anywhere an impossibility, and God but a part of the necessity which rules the universe.

Two kinds of generations of men have most tended to be necessitarian in their philosophy,--the generations which have given themselves over to do evil, and the generations whose political experience or whose science has impressed them with the inevitable physical results of sin. If belief in a Divine Redeemer, able to deliver man's nature from the guilt and the curse of sin, is growing weak among us to-day, this is largely due to the fact that our moral and our physical sciences have been proving to us what creatures of law we are, and disclosing, especially in the study of disease and insanity, how inevitably suffering follows sin. God Himself has been so much revealed to us as law, that as a generation we find it hard to believe that He ever acts in any fashion that resembles the reversal of a law, or ever works any swift, sudden deed of salvation.

Now the generation of the Exile was a generation, to whom God had revealed Himself as law. They were a generation of convicts. They had owned the justice of the sentence which had banished and enslaved them; they had experienced how inexorably God's processes of judgement sweep down the ages; for fifty years they had been feeling the inevitable consequences of sin. The conscience of Law, which this experience was bound to create in them, grew ever more strong, till at last it absorbed even the hope of redemption, and the God, who enforced the Law, Himself seemed to be forced by it. To express this sense of law these earnest Israelites--for though in error they were in earnest--went to the only kind of law, with which they were familiar, and borrowed from it two of its forms, which were not only suggested to them by the relations in which the nation and the nation's sons respectively stood to Jehovah, as wife and as children, but admirably illustrated the ideas they wished to express. There was, first, the form of divorce, so expressive of the ideas of absoluteness, deliberateness and finality;--of absoluteness, for throughout the East power of divorce rests entirely with the husband; of deliberateness, for in order to prevent hasty divorce the Hebrew law insisted that the husband must make a bill or writing of divorce instead of only speaking dismissal; and of finality, for such a writing, in contrast to the spoken dismissal, set the divorce beyond recall. The other form, which the doubters borrowed from their law, was one, which, while it also illustrated the irrevocableness of the act, emphasized the helplessness of the agent,--the act of the father, who put his children away, not as the husband put his wife in his anger, but in his necessity, selling them to pay his debts and because he was bankrupt.

On such doubts God turns with their own language. "I have indeed put your mother away, but where is the bill that makes her divorce final, beyond recall? You indeed were sold, but was it because I was bankrupt? To which, then, of My creditors (note the scorn of the plural) was it that I sold you? Nay, by means of your iniquities did you sell yourselves, and by means of your transgressions were you put away. But I stand here ready as ever to save, I alone. If there is any difficulty about your restoration it lies in this, that I am alone, with no response or assistance from men. Why when I came was there no man? when I called was there none to answer? Is My hand shortened at all that it cannot redeem? or is there in it no power to deliver?" And so we come back to the truth, which this prophecy so often presents to us, that behind all things there is a personal initiative and urgency of infinite power, which moves freely of its own compassion and force, which is hindered by no laws from its own ends, and needs no man's co-operation to effect its purposes. The rest of the Lord's answer to His people's fear, that He is bound by an inexorable law, is simply an appeal to His wealth of force. This omnipotence of God is our prophet's constant solution for the problems which arise, and he expresses it here in his favourite figures of physical changes and convulsions of nature. Lo, with My rebuke I dry up the sea, I make rivers a wilderness: their fish stinketh, because there is no water, and dieth for thirst. I clothe the heavens with blackness, and sackcloth I set for their covering. The argument seems to be: if God can work those sudden revolutions in the physical world, those apparent interruptions of law in that sphere, surely you can believe Him capable of creating sudden revolutions also in the sphere of history, and reversing those laws and processes, which you feel to be unalterable. It is an argument from the physical to the moral world, in our prophet's own analogical style, and like those we found in ch. xl.

II. li.-lii. 12.

Passing over the passage on the Servant, ch. l. 4-11, we reach a second series of exhortations in face of Doubts in the Way of the Return. The first of this new series is li. 1-3.

Their doubts having been answered with regard to God's mindfulness of them and His power to save them, the loyal Israelites fall back to doubt themselves. They see with dismay how few are ready to achieve the freedom that God has assured, and upon how small and insignificant a group of individuals the future of the nation depends. But their disappointment is not made by them an excuse to desert the purpose of Jehovah: their fewness makes them the more faithful, and the defection of their countrymen drives them the closer to their God. Therefore, God speaks to them kindly, and answers their last sad doubt. Hearken unto Me, ye that follow righteousness, that seek Jehovah. Righteousness here might be taken in its inward sense of conformity to law, personal rightness of character; and so taken it would well fall in with the rest of the passage. Those addressed would then be such in Israel, as in face of hopeless prospects applied themselves to virtue and religion. But righteousness here is more probably used in the outward sense, which we have found prevalent in "Second Isaiah," of vindication and victory; the "coming right" of God's people and God's cause in the world, their justification and triumph in history. [246] They who are addressed will then be they who, in spite of their fewness, believe in this triumph, follow it, make it their goal and their aim, and seek Jehovah, knowing that He can bring it to pass. And because, in spite of their doubts, they are still earnest, and though faint are yet pursuing, God speaks to comfort them about their fewness. Their present state may be very small and unpromising, but let them look back upon the much more unpromising character of their origin: look unto the rock whence ye were hewn, and the hole of the pit whence ye were digged. To-day you may be a mere handful, ridiculous in the light of the destiny you are called to achieve, but remember you were once but one man: look unto Abraham your father, and to Sarah who bare you: for as one I called him and blessed him, that I might make of him many.

When we are weary and hopeless it is best to sit down and remember. Is the future dark: let us look back and see the gathering and impetus of the past! We can follow the luminous track, the unmistakable increase and progress, but the most inspiring sight of all is what God makes of the individual heart; how a man's heart is always His beginning, the fountain of the future, the origin of nations. Lift up your hearts, ye few and feeble; your father was but one when I called him, and I made him many!

Having thus assured His loyal remnant of the restoration of Zion, in spite of their fewness, Jehovah in the next few verses (4-8) extends the prospect of His glory to the world: Revelation shall go forth from Me, and I will make My Law to light on the nations. Revelation and Law between them summarise His will. As He identified them both with the Servant's work (ch. xl. 11), so here He tells the loyal in Israel, who were in one aspect His Servant, that they shall surely come to pass; and in the next little oracle, vv. 7, 8, He exhorts them to do that in which the Servant has been set forth as an example: fear ye not the reproach of men, neither be dismayed at their revilings. For like a garment the moth shall eat them up, and like wool shall the worm devour them. It is a response in almost the same words to the Servant's profession of confidence in God in ch. l. 7-9. By some it is used as an argument to show that the Servant and the godly remnant are to our prophet still virtually one and the same; but we have already seen (ch. l. 10) the godfearing addressed as distinct from the Servant, and can only understand here that they are once more exhorted to take him as their example. But if the likeness of the passage on the Servant to this passage on the suffering Remnant does not prove that Remnant and Servant are the same, it is certainly an indication that both passages, so far from being pieced together out of different poems, are most probably due to the same author and were produced originally in the same current of thought.

When all Doubts in the Way have now been removed, what can remain but a great impatience to achieve at once the near salvation? To this impatience the loosened hearts give voice in vv. 9-11: Awake, awake, put on strength, Arm of Jehovah; awake as in the days of old, ages far past! Not in vain have Israel been called to look back to the rock whence they were hewn and the hole of the pit whence they were digged. Looking back, they see the ancient deliverance manifest: Art thou not it that hewed Rahab in pieces, that pierced the Dragon! Art thou not it that dried up the sea, waters of the great flood; that did set the hollows of the sea a way for the passage of the redeemed. Then there breaks forth the March of the Return, which we heard already in the end of ch. xxxv., [247] and to His people's impatience Jehovah responds in vv. 9-16 in strains similar to those of ch. xl. The last verse of this reply is notable for the enormous extension which it gives to the purpose of Jehovah in endowing Israel as His prophet,--an extension to no less than the renewal of the universe,--in order to plant the heavens and found the earth; though the reply emphatically concludes with the restoration of Israel, as if this were the cardinal moment in the universal regeneration,--and to say to Zion, My people art thou. The close conjunction, into which this verse brings words already applied to Israel as the Servant and words which describe Israel as Zion, is another of the many proofs we are discovering of the impossibility of breaking up "Second Isaiah" into poems, the respective subjects of which are one or other of these two personifications of the nation. [248]

But the desire of the prophet speeds on before the returning exiles to the still prostrate and desolate city. He sees her as she fell, the day the Lord made her drunken with the cup of His wrath. With urgent passion he bids her awake, seeking to rouse her now by the horrid tale of her ruin, and now by his exultation in the vengeance the Lord is preparing for His enemies (li. 17-23). In a second strophe he addresses her in conscious contrast to his taunt-song against Babel. Babel was to sit throneless and stripped of her splendour in the dust; but Zion is to shake off the dust, rise, sit on her throne and assume her majesty. For God hath redeemed His people. He could not tolerate longer the exulting of their tyrants, the blasphemy of His name (lii. 1-6). All through these two strophes the strength of the passion, the intolerance of further captivity, the fierceness of the exultation of vengeance, are very remarkable.

But from the ruin of his city, which has so stirred and made turbulent his passion, the prophet lifts his hot eyes to the dear hills that encircle her; and peace takes the music from vengeance. Often has Jerusalem seen rising across that high margin the spears and banners of her destroyers. But now the lofty skyline is the lighting place of hope. Fit threshold for so Divine an arrival, it lifts against heaven, dilated and beautiful, the herald of the Lord's peace, the publisher of salvation.

How beautiful upon the mountains are the feet of him that bringeth good tidings, that publisheth peace, that bringeth good tidings of good, that publisheth salvation! Hark thy watchmen! they lift up the voice, together they break into singing; yea, eye to eye do they see when Jehovah returneth to Zion.

The last verse is a picture of the thronging of the city of the prophets by the prophets again--so close, that they shall look each other in the face. For this is the sense of the Hebrew to see eye in eye, and not that meaning of reconciliation and agreement which the phrase has come to have in colloquial English. The Exile had scattered the prophets and driven them into hiding. They had been only voices to one another, like Jeremiah and Ezekiel with the desert between the two of them, or like our own prophet, anonymous and unseen. But upon the old gathering-ground, the narrow but the free and open platform of Jerusalem's public life, they should see each other face to face, they should again be named and known. Break out, sing together, ye wastes of Jerusalem: for Jehovah has comforted His people, has redeemed Jerusalem. Bared has Jehovah His holy arm to the eyes of all the nations, and see shall all ends of the earth the salvation of our God.

Thus the prophet, after finishing his long argument and dispelling the doubts that still lingered at its close, returns to the first high notes and the first dear subject with which he opened in ch. xl. In face of so open a way, so unclouded a prospect, nothing remains but to repeat, and this time with greater strength than before, the call to leave Babylon:

Draw off, draw off, come forth from there, touch not the unclean; Come forth from her midst; be ye clean that do bear the vessels of Jehovah. Nay, neither with haste shall ye forth, nor in flight shall ye go, For Jehovah goeth before thee, and Israel's God is thy rearward.

Footnotes:

240. See p. [51]334.

241. The question whether this is the land of China is still an open one. The possibility of intercourse between China and Babylon is more than proved. But that there were Jews in China by this time (though they seem to have found their way there by the beginning of the Christian era) is extremely unlikely. Moreover, the possibility of such a name as Sinim for the inhabitants of China at that date has not been proved. No other claimants for the name, however, have made good their case. But we need not enter further into the question. The whole matter is fully discussed in Canon Cheyne's excursus, and by him and Terrien de Lacouperie in the Babylonian and Oriental Record for 1886-87. See especially the number for September 1887.

242. His humbled, His poor in the exilic sense of the word. See Isaiah i.-xxxix., pp. [52]432 ff.

243. On the "Motherhood of God" cf. Isaiah i.-xxxix., p. 245 ff.

244. For tsdyq, the righteous or just, which is in the text, the Syr., Vulg., Ewald, and others read ryts, as in the following verse, terrible or terribly strong. Dillmann, however (5th ed., 1890, p. 438), retains tsdyq takes the terms mighty and just as used of God, and reads the question, not as a question of despair uttered by the people, but as a triumphant challenge of the prophet or of God Himself. He would then make the next verse run thus: Nay, for the captives of the mighty may be taken, and the prey of the delivered, but with him who strives with thee I will strive.

245. The English version, Where is the bill, is incorrect. The phrase is the same as in lxvi. ver. 1, What is this house that ye build for Me? what is this place for My rest? It implies a house already built; and so in the text above What is this bill of divorce implies one already thought of by the minds of the persons addressed by the question.

246. Cf. p. [53]221. Dillmann's view that righteousness means here personal character is contradicted by the whole context, which makes it plain that it is something external, the realisation of which those addressed are doubting. What troubles them is not that they are personally unrighteous, but that they are so few and insignificant. And what God promises them in answer is something external, the establishment of Zion. Cf. also the external meaning of righteousness in vv. 5, 6.

247. Isaiah. i.-xxxix., p. [54]441.

248. Cf. p. [55]315.

Rev. George Adam Smith, M.A.

CHAPTER XXII

ON THE EVE OF RETURN.

Isaiah liv.-lvi. 8.

One of the difficult problems of our prophecy is the relation and grouping of chs. liv.-lix. It is among them that the unity of "Second Isaiah," which up to this point we have seen no reason to doubt, gives way. Ch. lvi. 9-lvii. is evidently pre-exilic, and so is ch. lix. But in chs. liv., lv., and lvi. 1-8 we have three addresses, evidently dating from the Eve of the Return. We shall, therefore, treat them together.

I. The Bride the City (ch. liv.).

We have already seen why there is no reason for the theory that ch. liv. may have followed immediately on ch. lii. 12. [249] And from Calvin to Ewald and Dillmann, critics have all felt a close connection between ch. lii. 13-liii. and ch. liv. "After having spoken of the death of Christ," says Calvin, "the prophet passes on with good reason to the Church: that we may feel more deeply in ourselves what is the value and efficacy of His death." Similar in substance, if not in language, is the opinion of the latest critics, who understand that in ch. liv. the prophet intends to picture that full redemption which the Servant's work, culminating in ch. liii., could alone effect. Two keywords of ch. liii. had been a seed and many. It is the seed and the many whom ch. liv. reveals. Again, there may be, in ver. 17 of ch. liv., a reference to the earlier picture of the Servant in ch. l., especially ver. 8. But this last is uncertain; and, as a point on the other side, there are the two different meanings, as well as the two different agents, of righteousness in ch. liii. 11, My Servant shall make many righteous, and in ch. liv. 17, their righteousness which is of Me, saith Jehovah. In the former, righteousness is the inward justification; in the latter, it is the external historical vindication.

In ch. liv. the people of God are represented under the double figure, with which the Book of Revelation has made us familiar, of Bride and City. To imagine a Nation or a Land as the spouse of her God is a habit natural to the religious instinct at all times; the land deriving her fruitfulness, the nation her standing and prestige, from her connection with the Deity. But in ancient times this figure of wedlock was more natural than it is among us, in so far as the human man and wife did not then occupy that relation of equality, to which it has been the progress of civilisation to approximate; but the husband was the lord of his wife,--as much her Baal as the god was the Baal of the people,--her lawgiver, in part her owner, and with full authority over the origin and subsistence of the bond between them. Marriage thus conceived was a figure for religion almost universal among the Semites. But as in the case of so many other religious ideas common to the Hebrews and their heathen kin, this one, when adopted by the prophets of Jehovah, underwent a thorough moral reformation. Indeed, if one were asked to point out a supreme instance of the operation of that unique conscience of the religion of Jehovah, which was spoken of before, [250] one would have little difficulty in selecting its treatment of the idea of religious marriage. By the neighbours of Israel, the marriage of a god to his people was conceived with a grossness of feeling and illustrated by a foulness of ritual, which thoroughly demoralised the people, affording, as they did, to licentiousness the example and sanction of religion. So debased had the idea become, and so full of temptation to the Hebrews were the forms in which it was illustrated among their neighbours, that the religion of Israel might justly have been praised for achieving a great moral victory in excluding the figure altogether from its system. But the prophets of Jehovah dared the heavier task of retaining the idea of religious marriage, and won the diviner triumph of purifying and elevating it. It was, indeed, a new creation. Every physical suggestion was banished, and the relation was conceived as purely moral. Yet it was never refined to a mere form or abstraction. The prophets fearlessly expressed it in the warmest and most familiar terms of the love of man and woman. With a stern and absolute interpretation before them in the Divine law, of the relations of a husband to his wife, they borrowed from that only so far as to do justice to the Almighty's initiative and authority in His relation with mortals; and they laid far more emphasis on the instinctive and spontaneous affections, by which Jehovah and Israel had been drawn together. Thus, among a people naturally averse to think or to speak of God as loving [251] men, this close relation to Him of marriage was expressed with a warmth, a tenderness and a delicacy, that exceeded even the two other fond forms in which the Divine grace was conveyed,--of a father's and of a mother's love.

In this new creation of the marriage bond between God and His church, three prophets had a large share,--Hosea, Ezekiel and the author of "Second Isaiah." To Hosea and Ezekiel it fell to speak chiefly of unpleasant aspects of the question,--the unfaithfulness of the wife and her divorce; but even then, the moral strength and purity of the Hebrew religion, its Divine vehemence and glow, were only the more evident for the unpromising character of the materials with which it dealt. To our prophet, on the contrary, it fell to speak of the winning back of the wife, and he has done so with wonderful delicacy and tenderness. Our prophet, it is true, has not one, but two, deep feelings about the love of God: it passes through him as the love of a mother, as well as the love of a husband. But while he lets us see the former only twice or thrice, the latter may be felt as the almost continual undercurrent of his prophecy, and often breaks to hearing, now in a sudden, single ripple of a phrase, and now in a long tide of marriage music. His lips open for Jehovah on the language of wooing,--speak ye to the heart of Jerusalem; and though his masculine figure for Israel as the Servant keeps his affection hidden for a time, this emerges again when the subject of Service is exhausted, till Israel, where she is not Jehovah's Servant, is Jehovah's Bride. In the series of passages on Zion, from ch. xlix. to ch. lii., the City is the Mother of His children, the Wife who though put away has never been divorced. In ch. lxii. she is called Hephzi-Bah, My-delight-is-in-her, and Beulah, or Married,--for Jehovah delighteth in thee, and thy land shall be married. For as a youth marrieth a maiden, thy sons shall marry thee; and with the joy of a bridegroom over a bride, thy God shall joy over thee. [252] But it is in the chapter now before us that the relation is expressed with greatest tenderness and wealth of affection. Be not afraid, for thou shalt not be shamed; and be not confounded, for thou shalt not be put to the blush: for the shame of thy youth thou shalt forget, and the reproach of thy widowhood thou shalt not remember again. For thy Maker is thy Husband, Jehovah of Hosts is His name; and thy Redeemer the Holy of Israel, God of the whole earth is He called. For as a wife forsaken and grieved in spirit thou art called of Jehovah, even a wife of youth, when she is cast off, saith thy God. For a small moment have I forsaken thee, but with great mercies will I gather thee. In an egre of anger [253] I hid My face a moment from thee, but with grace everlasting will I have mercy upon thee, saith thy Redeemer Jehovah.

In this eighth verse we pass from the figure of the Bride to that of the City, which emerges clear through flood and storm in ver. 11. Afflicted, Storm-beaten, Uncomforted, Lo, I am setting in dark metal (antimony, used by women for painting round the eyes, so as to set forth their brilliance more) thy stones,--that they may shine from this setting like women's eyes,--and I will found thee in sapphires: as heaven's own foundation vault is blue, so shall the ground-stones be of the New Jerusalem. And I will set rubies for thy pinnacles, and thy gates shall be sparkling stones, [254] and all thy borders stones of delight,--stones of joy, jewels. The rest of the chapter paints the righteousness of Zion as her external security and splendour.

II. A Last Call to the Busy (ch. lv.).

The second address upon the Eve of Return is ch. lv. Its pure gospel and clear music render detailed exposition, except on a single point, superfluous. One can but stand and listen to those great calls to repentance and obedience, which issue from it. What can be added to them or said about them? Let one take heed rather to let them speak to one's own heart! A little exploration, however, will be of advantage among the circumstances from which they shoot.

The commercial character of the opening figures of ch. lv. arrests the attention. We saw that Babylon was the centre of the world's trade, and that it was in Babylon that the Jews first formed those mercantile habits, which have become, next to religion, or in place of religion, their national character. Born to be priests, the Jews drew down their splendid powers of attention, pertinacity and imagination from God upon the world, till they equally appear to have been born traders. They laboured and prospered exceedingly, gathering property and settling in comfort. They drank of the streams of Babylon, no longer made bitter by their tears, and ceased to think upon Zion.

But, of all men, exiles can least forget that there is that which money can never buy. Money and his work can do much for the banished man,--feed him, clothe him, even make for him a kind of second home, and in time, by the payment of taxes, a kind of second citizenship; but they can never bring him to the true climate of his heart, nor win for him his real life. And of all exiles the Jew, however free and prosperous in his banishment he might be, was least able to find his life among the good things--the water, the wine and the milk--of a strange country. For home to Israel meant not only home, but duty, righteousness and God. [255] God had created the heart of this people to hunger for His word, and in His word they could alone find the fatness of their soul. Success and comfort shall never satisfy the soul which God has created for obedience. The simplicity of the obedience that is here asked from Israel, the emphasis that is laid upon mere obedience as ringing in full satisfaction, is impressive: hearken diligently, and eat that which is good; incline your ear and come unto Me, hear and your soul shall live. It suggests the number of plausible reasons, which may be offered for every worldly and material life, and to which there is no answer save the call of God's own voice to obedience and surrender. To obedience God then promises influence. In place of being a mere trafficker with the nations, or, at best, their purveyor and money-lender, the Jew, if he obeys God, shall be the priest and prophet of the peoples. This is illustrated in vv. 4b-6, the only hard passage in the chapter. God will make His people like David; whether the historical David or the ideal David described by Jeremiah and Ezekiel is uncertain. [256] God will conclude an everlasting covenant with them, equivalent to the sure favours showered on him. As God set him for a witness (that is, a prophet) to the peoples, a prince and a leader to the peoples, so (in phrases that recall some used by David of himself in the eighteenth Psalm) shall they as prophets and kings influence strange nations--calling a nation thou knowest not, and nations that have not known thee shall run unto thee. The effect of the unconscious influence, which obedience to God, and surrender to Him as His instrument, are sure to work, could not be more grandly stated. But we ought not to let another point escape our attention, for it has its contribution to make to the main question of the Servant. As explained in the note to a sentence above, it is uncertain whether David is the historical king of that name, or the Messiah still to come. In either case, he is an individual, whose functions and qualities are transferred to the people, and that is the point demanding attention. If our prophecy can thus so easily speak of God's purpose of service to the Gentiles passing from the individual to the nation, why should it not also be able to speak of the opposite process, the transference of the service from the nation to the single Servant? When the nation were unworthy and unredeemed, could not the prophet as easily think of the relegation of their office to an individual, as he now promises to their obedience that that office shall be restored to them?

The next verses urgently repeat calls to repentance. And then comes a passage which is grandly meant to make us feel the contrast of its scenery with the toil, the money-getting and the money-spending from which the chapter started. From all that sordid, barren, human strife in the markets of Babylon, we are led out to look at the boundless heavens, and are told that as they are higher than the earth, so are God's ways higher than our ways, and God's reckonings than our reckonings; we are led out to see the gentle fall of rain and snow that so easily maketh the earth to bring forth and bud, and give seed to the sower and bread to the eater, and are told that it is a symbol of God's word, which we were called from our vain labours to obey; we are led out to the mountains and to the hills breaking before you into singing, and to the free, wild natural trees [257] tossing their unlopped branches; we are led to see even the desert change, for instead of the thorn shall come up the fir-tree, and instead of the nettle shall come up the myrtle; and it shall be to Jehovah for a name, for an everlasting sign that shall not be cut off. Thus does the prophet, in his own fashion, lead the starved worldly heart, that has sought in vain its fulness from its toil, through scenes of Nature, to that free omnipotent Grace, of which Nature's processes are the splendid sacraments.

III. Proselytes and Eunuchs (ch. lvi. 1-8).

The opening verse of this small prophecy, My salvation is near to come, and My righteousness to be revealed, attaches it very closely to the preceding prophecy. If ch. lv. expounds the grace and faithfulness of God in the Return of His people, and asks from them only faith as the price of such benefits, ch. lvi. 1-8 adds the demand that those who are to return shall keep the law, and extends their blessings to foreigners and others, who though technically disqualified from the privileges of the born and legitimate Israelite, had attached themselves to Jehovah and His Law.

Such a prophecy was very necessary. The dispersion of Israel had already begun to accomplish its missionary purpose; pious souls in many lands had felt the spiritual power of this disfigured people, and had chosen for Jehovah's sake to follow its uncertain fortunes. It was indispensable that these Gentile converts should be comforted against the withdrawal of Israel from Babylon, for they said, Jehovah will surely separate me from His people, as well as against the time when it might become necessary to purge the restored community from heathen constituents. [258] Again, all the male Jews could hardly have escaped the disqualification, which the cruel custom of the East inflicted on some, at least, of every body of captives. It is almost certain that Daniel and his companions were eunuchs, and if they, then perhaps many more. But the Book of Deuteronomy had declared mutilation of this kind to be a bar against entrance to the assembly of the Lord. It is not one of the least interesting of the spiritual results of the Exile, that its necessities compelled the abrogation of the letter of such a law. With a freedom that foreshadows Christ's own expansion of the ancient strictness, and in words that would not be out of place in the Sermon on the Mount, this prophecy ensures to pious men, whom cruelty had deprived of the two things dearest to the heart of an Israelite,--a present place, and a perpetuation through his posterity, in the community of God,--that in the new temple a monument [259] and a name should be given, better and more enduring than sons or daughters. This prophecy is further noteworthy as the first instance of the strong emphasis which "Second Isaiah" lays upon the keeping of the Sabbath, and as first calling the temple the House of Prayer. Both of these characteristics are due, of course, to the Exile, the necessities of which prevented almost every religious act save that of keeping fasts and Sabbaths and serving God in prayer. On our prophet's teaching about the Sabbath there will be more to say in the next chapter.

Footnotes:

249. Cf. pp. [56]336 ff.

250. See pp. [57]247 ff.

251. "Das eigentliche Wort 'Liebe' kommt im A. T. von Gott fast gar nicht vor,--und wo es, bei einem späten Schriftsteller, vorkommt, ist es Bezeichnung seiner besondren Bundes-liebe zu Israel, deren natürliche Kehrseite der Hass gegen die feindlichen Völker ist."--Schultz, A. T. Theologie, 4th ed., p. 548.

252. The reserve of this--the limitation of the relation to one of feeling--is remarkable in contrast to the more physical use of the same figure in other religions.

253. Egre, or sudden rush of the tide, or spate, or freshet. The original is assonant: B^eshesseph qesseph.

254. So literally; LXX. crystals, carbuncles or diamonds.

255. Cf. Isaiah i.-xxxix., pp. [58]440 ff.

256. The structure of this difficult passage is this. Ver. 3 states the equation: the everlasting covenant with the people Israel=the sure, unfailing favours bestowed upon the individual David. Vv. 4 and 5 unfold the contents of the equation. Each side of it is introduced by a Lo. Lo, on the one side, what I have done to David; Lo, on the other, what I will do to you. As David was a witness of peoples, a prince and commander of peoples, so shalt thou call to them and make them obey thee. This is clear enough. But who is David? The phrase the favours of David suggests 2 Chron. vi. 42, remember the mercies of David thy servant; and those in ver. 5 recall Psalm xviii. 43 f.: Thou hast made me the head of nations; A people I know not shall serve me; As soon as they hear of me they shall obey me; Strangers shall submit themselves to me. Yet both Jeremiah and Ezekiel call the coming Messiah David. Jer. xxx. 9: They shall serve Jehovah their God and David their King. Ezek. xxxiv. 23: And I will set up a shepherd over them, and he shall feed them, and he shall be their shepherd. And I Jehovah will be their God, and My servant David prince among them. After these writers, our prophet could hardly help using the name David in its Messianic sense, even though he also quoted (in ver. 5) a few phrases recalling the historical David. But the question does not matter much. The real point is the transference of the favours bestowed upon an individual to the whole people.

257. English version, trees of the field, but the field is the country beyond the bounds of cultivation; and as beasts of the field means wild beasts, so this means wild trees,--unforced, unaided by man's labour.

258. Neh. xiii.

259. The original is a hand; a term applied (perhaps because it consisted of tapering stones) to an index, or monument of victory, 1 Sam. xv. 12; or to a sepulchral monument, 2 Sam. xviii. 18.

Rev. George Adam Smith, M.A.

CHAPTER XXIII

THE REKINDLING OF THE CIVIC CONSCIENCE.

Isaiah lvi. 9-lix.

It was inevitable, as soon as their city was again fairly in sight, that there should re-awaken in the exiles the civic conscience; that recollections of those besetting sins of their public life, for which their city and their independence were destroyed, should throng back upon them; that in prospect of their again becoming responsible for the discharge of justice and other political duties, they should be reminded by the prophet of their national faults in these respects, and of God's eternal laws concerning them. If we keep this in mind, we shall understand the presence in "Second Isaiah" of the group of prophecies at which we have now arrived, ch. lvi. 9-lix. Hitherto our prophet, in marked contrast to Isaiah himself, has said almost nothing of the social righteousness of his people. Israel's righteousness, as we saw in our fourteenth chapter, has had the very different meaning for our prophet of her pardon and restoration to her rights. But in ch. lvi. 9-lix. we shall find the blame of civic wrong, and of other kinds of sin of which Israel could only have been guilty in her own land; we shall listen to exhortations to social justice and mercy like those we heard from Isaiah to his generation. Yet these are mingled with voices, and concluded with promises, which speak of the Return as imminent. Undoubtedly exilic elements reveal themselves. And the total impression is that some prophet of the late Exile, and probably the one, whom we have been following, collected these reminiscences of his people's sin in the days of their freedom, in order to remind them, before they went back again to political responsibility, why it was they were punished and how apt they were to go astray. Believing this to be the true solution of a somewhat difficult problem, we have ventured to gather this mixed group of prophecies under the title of the Rekindling of the Civic Conscience. They fall into three groups: first, ch. lvi. 9-lvii.; second, ch. lviii.; third, ch. lix. We shall see that, while there is no reason to doubt the exilic origin of the whole of the second, the first and third of these are mainly occupied with the description of a state of things that prevailed only before the Exile, but they contain also exilic observations and conclusions.

I. A Conscience but no God (ch. lvi. 9-lvii.).

This is one of the sections which almost decisively place the literary unity of "Second Isaiah" past possibility of belief. If ch. lvi. 1-8 flushes with the dawn of restoration, ch. lvi. 9-lvii. is very dark with the coming of the night, which preceded that dawn. Almost none dispute, that the greater part of this prophecy must have been composed before the people left Palestine for exile. The state of Israel, which it pictures, recalls the descriptions of Hosea, and of the eleventh chapter of Zechariah. God's flock are still in charge of their own shepherds (lvi. 9-12),--a description inapplicable to Israel in exile. The shepherds are sleepy, greedy, sensual, drunkards,--victims to the curse, against which Amos and Isaiah hurled their strongest woes. That sots like them should be spared while the righteous die unnoticed deaths (lvii. 1) can only be explained by the approaching judgement. No man considereth that the righteous is taken away from the Evil. The Evil cannot mean, as some have thought, persecution,--for while the righteous are to escape it and enter into peace, the wicked are spared for it. It must be a Divine judgement,--the Exile. But he entereth peace, they rest in their beds, each one that hath walked straight before him,--for the righteous there is the peace of death and the undisturbed tomb of his fathers. What an enviable fate when emigration, and dispersion through foreign lands, are the prospect of the nation! Israel shall find her pious dead when she returns! The verse recalls that summons in Isa. xxvi., in which we heard the Mother Nation calling upon the dead she had left in Palestine to rise and increase her returned numbers.

Then the prophet indicts the nation for a religious and political unfaithfulness, which we know was their besetting sin in the days before they left the Holy Land. The scenery, in whose natural objects he describes them seeking their worship, is the scenery of Palestine, not of Mesopotamia,--terebinths and wâdies, and clefts of the rocks, and smooth stones of the wâdies. The unchaste and bloody sacrifices with which he charges them bear the appearance more of Canaanite than of Babylonian idolatry. The humiliating political suits which they paid--thou wentest to the king with ointment, and didst increase thy perfumes, and didst send thine ambassadors afar off, and didst debase thyself even unto Sheol (ver. 9)--could not be attributed to a captive people, but were the sort of degrading diplomacy that Israel learned from Ahaz. While the painful pursuit of strength (ver. 10), the shabby political cowardice (ver.

11), the fanatic sacrifice of manhood's purity and childhood's life (ver. 5), and especially the evil conscience which drove their blind hearts through such pain and passion in a sincere quest for righteousness (ver. 12), betray the age of idolatrous reaction from the great Puritan victory of 701,--a generation exaggerating all the old falsehood and fear, against which Isaiah had inveighed, with the new conscience of sin which his preaching had created. [260] The dark streak of blood and lust that runs through the condemned idolatry, and the stern conscience which only deepens its darkness, are sufficient reasons for dating the prophecy after 700. The very phrases of Isaiah, which it contains, have tempted some to attribute it to himself. But it certainly does not date from such troubles as brought his old age to the grave. The evil, which it portends, is, as we have seen, no persecution of the righteous, but a Divine judgement upon the whole nation,--presumably the Exile. We may date it, therefore, some time after Isaiah's death, but certainly--and this is the important point--before the Exile. This, then, is an unmistakably pre-exilic constituent of "Second Isaiah."

Another feature corroborates this prophecy's original independence of its context. Its style is immediately and extremely rugged. The reader of the original feels the difference at once. It is the difference between travel on the level roads of Mesopotamia, with their unchanging horizons, and the jolting carriage of the stony paths of Higher Palestine, with their glimpses rapidly shifting from gorge to peak. But the remarkable thing is that the usual style of "Second Isaiah" is resumed before the end of the prophecy. One cannot always be sure of the exact verse at which such a literary change takes place. In this case some feel it as soon as the middle of ver. 11, with the words, Have not I held My peace even of long time, and thou fearest Me not? [261] It is surely more sensible, however, after ver. 14, in which we are arrested in any case by an alteration of standpoint. In ver. 14 we are on in the Exile again--before ver. 14 I cannot recognise any exilic symptom--and the way of return is before us. And one said,--it is the repetition to the letter of the strange anonymous voice of ch. xl. 6,--and one said, Cast ye up, Cast ye up, open up, or sweep open, a way, lift the stumbling block from the way of My people. And now the rhythm has certainly returned to the prevailing style of "Second Isaiah," and the temper is again that of promise and comfort.

These sudden shiftings of circumstance and of prospect are enough to show the thoughtful reader of Scripture how hard is the problem of the unity of "Second Isaiah." On which we make here no further remark, but pass at once to the more congenial task of studying the great prophecy, vv. 14-21, which rises one and simple from these fragments as does some homogeneous rock from the confusing débris of several geological epochs.

For let the date and original purpose of the fragments we have considered be what they may, this prophecy has been placed as their conclusion with at least some rational, not to say spiritual, intention. As it suddenly issues here, it gathers up, in the usual habit of Scripture, God's moral indictment of an evil generation, by a great manifesto of the Divine nature, and a sharp distinction of the characters and fate of men. Now, of what kind is the generation, to whose indictment this prophecy comes as a conclusion? It is a generation which has lost its God, but kept its conscience. This sums up the national character which is sketched in vv. 3-13. These Israelites had lost Jehovah and His pure law. But the religion into which they fell back was not, therefore, easy or cold. On the contrary, it was very intense and very stern. The people put energy in it, and passion, and sacrifice that went to cruel lengths. Belief, too, in its practical results kept the people from fainting under the weariness in which its fanaticism reacted. In the length of thy way thou wast wearied, yet thou didst not say, It is hopeless; life for thy hand--that is, real, practical strength--didst thou find: wherefore thou didst not break down. And they practised their painful and passionate idolatry with a real conscience. They were seeking to work out righteousness for themselves (ver. 12 should be rendered: I will expose your righteousness, the caricature of righteousness which you attempt). The most worldly statesman among them had his sincere ideal for Israel, and intended to enable her, in the possession of her land and holy mountain, to fulfil her destiny (ver. 13). The most gross idolater had a hunger and thirst after righteousness, and burnt his children or sacrificed his purity to satisfy the vague promptings of his unenlightened conscience.

It was indeed a generation which had kept its conscience, but lost its God; and what we have in vv. 15 to 21 is just the lost and forgotten God speaking of His Nature and His Will. They have been worshipping idols, creatures of their own fears and cruel passions. But He is the high and lofty one--two of the simplest adjectives in the language, yet sufficient to lift Him they describe above the distorting mists of human imagination. They thought of the Deity as sheer wrath and force, scarcely to be appeased by men even through the most bloody rites and passionate self-sacrifice. But He says, The high and the holy I dwell in, yet with him also that is contrite and humble of spirit, to revive the spirit of the humble, and to revive the heart of the contrite ones. The rest of the chapter is to the darkened consciences a plain statement of the moral character of God's working. God always punishes sin, and yet the sinner is not abandoned. Though he go in his own way, God watches his ways in order to heal him. I create the fruit of the lips, that is, thanksgivings: Peace, peace, to him that is far off and him that is near, saith Jehovah, and I will heal him. But, as in ch. xlviii. and ch. l., a warning comes last, and behind the clear, forward picture of the comforted and restored of Jehovah we see the weird background of gloomy, restless wickedness.

II. Social Service and the Sabbath (ch. lviii.).

Several critics (including Professor Cheyne) regard ch. lviii. as post-exilic, because of its declarations against formal fasting and the neglect of social charity, which are akin to those of post-exilic prophets like Zechariah and Joel, and seem to imply that the people addressed are again independent and responsible for the conduct of their social duties. The question largely turns on the amount of social responsibility we conceive the Jews to have had during the Exile. Now we have seen that many of them enjoyed considerable freedom: they had their houses and households; they had their slaves; they traded and were possessed of wealth. They were, therefore, in a position to be chargeable with the duties to which ch. lviii. calls them. The addresses of Ezekiel to his fellow-exiles have many features in common with ch. lviii., although they do not mention fasting; and fasting itself was a characteristic habit of the exiles, in regard to which it is quite likely they should err just as is described in ch. lviii. Moreover, there is a resemblance between this chapter's comments upon the people's enquiries of God (ver. 2) and Ezekiel's reply when certain of the elders of Israel came to enquire of Jehovah. [262] And again vv. 11 and 12 of ch. lviii. are evidently addressed to people in prospect of return to their own land and restoration of their city. We accordingly date ch. lviii. from the Exile. But we see no reason to put it as early as Ewald does, who assigns it to a younger contemporary of Ezekiel. There is no linguistic evidence that it is an insertion, or from another hand than that of our prophet. Surely there were room and occasion for it in those years which followed the actual deliverance of the Jews by Cyrus, but preceded the restoration of Jerusalem,--those years in which there were no longer political problems in the way of the people's return for our prophet to discuss, and therefore their moral defects were all the more thrust upon his attention; and especially, when in the near prospect of their political independence, their social sins roused his apprehensions.

Those, who have never heard an angry Oriental speak, have no idea of what power of denunciation lies in the human throat. In the East, where a dry climate and large leisure bestow upon the voice a depth and suppleness prevented by our vulgar haste of life and teasing weather, men have elaborated their throat-letters to a number unknown in any Western alphabet; and upon the lowest notes they have put an edge, that comes up shrill and keen through the roar of the upper gutturals, till you feel their wrath cut as well as sweep you before it. In the Oriental throat, speech goes down deep enough to echo all the breadth of the inner man; while the possibility of expressing within so supple an organ nearly every tone of scorn or surprise preserves anger from that suspicion of spite or of exhaustion, which is conveyed by too liberal a use of the nasal or palatal letters. Hence in the Hebrew language to call with the throat means to call with vehemence, but with self-command; with passion, yet as a man; using every figure of satire, but earnestly; neither forgetting wrath for mere art's sake, nor allowing wrath to escape the grip of the stronger muscles of the voice. It is to lift the voice like a trumpet,--an instrument, which, with whatever variety of music its upper notes may indulge our ears, never suffers its main tone of authority to drop, never slacks its imperative appeal to the wills of the hearers.

This is the style of the chapter before us, which opens with the words, Call with the throat, spare not, lift up thy voice like a trumpet. Perhaps no subject more readily provokes to satire and sneers than the subject of the chapter,--the union of formal religion and unlovely life. And yet in the chapter there is not a sneer from first to last. The speaker suppresses the temptation to use his nasal tones, and utters, not as the satirist, but as the prophet. For his purpose is not to sport with his people's hypocrisy, but to sweep them out of it. Before he has done, his urgent speech, that has not lingered to sneer nor exhausted itself in screaming, passes forth to spend its unchecked impetus upon final promise and gospel. It is a wise lesson from a master preacher, and half of the fruitlessness of modern preaching is due to the neglect of it. The pulpit tempts men to be either too bold or too timid about sin; either to whisper or to scold; to euphemise or to exaggerate; to be conventional or hysterical. But two things are necessary,--the facts must be stated, and the whole manhood of the preacher, and not only his scorn or only his anger or only an official temper, brought to bear upon them. Call with the throat, spare not, like a trumpet lift up thy voice, and publish to My people their transgression, and to the house of Jacob their sin.

The subject of the chapter is the habits of a religious people,--the earnestness and regularity of their religious performance contrasted with the neglect of their social relations. The second verse, "the descriptions in which are evidently drawn from life," [263] tells us that the people sought God daily, and had a zeal to know His ways, as a nation that had done righteousness,--fulfilled the legal worship,--and had not forsaken the law [264] of their God: they ask of Me laws [265] of righteousness,--that is, a legal worship, the performance of which might make them righteous,--and in drawing near to God they take delight. They had, in fact, a great greed for ordinances and functions, [266] --for the revival of such forms as they had been accustomed to of old. Like some poor prostrate rose, whose tendrils miss the props by which they were wont to rise to the sun, the religious conscience and affections of Israel, violently torn from their immemorial supports, lay limp and windswept on a bare land, and longed for God to raise some substitute for those altars of Zion by which, in the dear days of old, they had lifted themselves to the light of His face. In the absence of anything better, they turned to the chill and shadowed forms of the fasts they had instituted. [267] But they did not thereby reach the face of God. Wherefore have we fasted, say they, and Thou hast not seen? we have humbled our souls, and Thou takest no notice? The answer comes swiftly: Because your fasting is a mere form! Lo, in the very day of your fast ye find a business to do, and all your workmen you overtask. So formal is your fasting that your ordinary eager, selfish, cruel life goes on beside it just the same. Nay, it is worse than usual, for your worthless, wearisome fast but puts a sharper edge upon your temper: Lo, for strife and contention ye fast, to smile with the fist of tyranny. And it has no religious value: Ye fast not like as you are fasting to-day so as to make your voice heard on high. Is such the fast that I choose,--a day for a man to afflict himself? Is it to droop his head like a rush, and grovel on sackcloth and ashes? Is it this thou wilt call a fast and a day acceptable to Jehovah? One of the great surprises of the human heart is, that self-denial does not win merit or peace. But assuredly it does not, if love be not with it. Though I give my body to be burned and have not love, it profiteth me nothing. Self-denial without love is self-indulgence. Is not this the fast that I choose? to loosen the bonds of tyranny, to shatter the joints of the yoke, to let the crushed go free, and that ye burst every yoke. Is it not to break to the hungry thy bread, and that thou bring home wandering poor? [268] when thou seest one naked that thou cover him, and that from thine own flesh thou hide not thyself? Then shall break forth like the morning thy light, and thy health [269] shall immediately spring. Yea, go before thee shall thy righteousness, the glory of Jehovah shall sweep thee on, literally, gather thee up. Then thou shalt call, and Jehovah shall answer; thou shalt cry, and He shall say, Here am I. If thou shalt put from thy midst the yoke, and the putting forth of the finger, and the speaking of naughtiness--three degrees of the subtlety of selfishness, which when forced back from violent oppression will retreat to scorn and from open scorn to backbiting,--and if thou draw out to the hungry thy soul,--tear out what is dear to thee in order to fill his need, the strongest expression for self-denial which the Old Testament contains,--and satisfy the soul that is afflicted, then shall uprise in the darkness thy light, and thy gloom shall be as the noonday. And guide thee shall Jehovah continually, and satisfy thy soul in droughts, and thy limbs make lissom; and thou shalt be like a garden well-watered, [270] and like a spring of water whose waters fail not. And they that are of thee shall build the ancient ruins; the foundations of generation upon generation thou shalt raise up, and they shall be calling thee Repairer-of-the-Breach, Restorer-of-Paths-for-habitation. [271] Thus their righteousness in the sense of external vindication and stability, which so prevails with our prophet, shall be due to their righteousness in that inward moral sense in which Amos and Isaiah use the word. And so concludes a passage, which fills the earliest, if not the highest, place in the glorious succession of Scriptures of Practical Love, to which belong the Sixty-first chapter of Isaiah, the Twenty-fifth of Matthew and the Thirteenth of First Corinthians. Its lesson is,--to go back to the figure of the draggled rose,--that no mere forms of religion, however divinely prescribed or conscientiously observed, can of themselves lift the distraught and trailing affections of man to the light and peace of Heaven; but that our fellow-men, if we cling to them with love and with arms of help, are ever the strongest props by which we may rise to God; that character grows rich and life joyful, not by the performance of ordinances with the cold conscience of duty, but by acts of service with the warm heart of love.

And yet such a prophecy concludes with an exhortation to the observance of one religious form, and places the keeping of the Sabbath on a level with the practice of love. If thou turn from the Sabbath thy foot, from doing thine own business on My holy day; [272] and callest the Sabbath Pleasure,--the word is a strong one, Delight, Delicacy, Luxury,--Holy of Jehovah, Honourable; and dost honour it so as not to do thine own ways, or find thine own business, or keep making talk: then thou shalt find thy pleasure, or thy delight, in Jehovah,--note the parallel of pleasure in the Sabbath and pleasure in Jehovah,--and He shall cause thee to ride on the high places of the land, and make thee to feed upon the portion of Jacob thy father: yea, the mouth of Jehovah hath spoken.

Our prophet, then, while exalting the practical Service of Man at the expense of certain religious forms, equally exalts the observance of Sabbath; his scorn for their formalism changes when he comes to it into a strenuous enthusiasm of defence. This remarkable fact, which is strictly analogous to the appearance of the Fourth Commandment in a code otherwise consisting of purely moral and religious laws, is easily explained. Observe that our prophet bases his plea for Sabbath-keeping, and his assurance that it must lead to prosperity, not on its physical, moral or social benefits, but simply upon its acknowledgment of God. Not only is the Sabbath to be honoured because it is the Holy of Jehovah and Honourable, but making it one's pleasure is equivalent to finding one's pleasure in Him. The parallel between these two phrases in ver. 13 and ver. 14 is evident, and means really this: Inasmuch as ye do it unto the Sabbath, ye do it unto Me. The prophet, then, enforces the Sabbath simply on account of its religious and Godward aspect. Now, let us remember the truth, which he so often enforces, that the Service of Man, however ardently and widely pursued, can never lead or sum up our duty; that the Service of God has, logically and practically, a prior claim, for without it the Service of Man must suffer both in obligation and in resource. God must be our first resort--must have our first homage, affection

Rev. George Adam Smith, M.A.

and obedience. But this cannot well take place without some amount of definite and regular and frequent devotion to Him. In the most spiritual religion there is an irreducible minimum of formal observance. Now, in that wholesale destruction of religious forms, which took place at the overthrow of Jerusalem, [273] there was only one institution, which was not necessarily involved. The Sabbath did not fall with the Temple and the Altar: the Sabbath was independent of all locality; the Sabbath was possible even in exile. It was the one solemn, public and frequently regular form in which the nation could turn to God, glorify Him and enjoy Him. Perhaps, too, through the Babylonian fashion of solemnising the seventh day, our prophet realised again the primitive institution of the Sabbath, and was reminded that, since seven days is a regular part of the natural year, the Sabbath is, so to speak, sanctioned by the statutes of Creation.

An institution, which is so primitive, which is so independent of locality, which forms so natural a part of the course of time, but which, above all, has twice--in the Jewish Exile and in the passage of Judaism to Christianity--survived the abrogation and disappearance of all other forms of the religion with which it was connected, and has twice been affirmed by prophecy or practice to be an essential part of spiritual religion and the equal of social morality,--has amply proved its Divine origin and its indispensableness to man.

III. Social Crimes (ch. lix.).

Ch. lix. is, at first sight, the most difficult of all of "Second Isaiah" to assign to a date. [274] For it evidently contains both pre-exilic and exilic elements. On the one hand, its charges of guilt imply that the people addressed by it are responsible for civic justice to a degree, which could hardly be imputed to the Jews in Babylon. We saw that the Jews in the Exile had an amount of social freedom and domestic responsibility which amply accounts for the kind of sins they are charged with in ch. lviii. But ver. 14 of ch. lix. reproaches them with the collapse of justice in the very seat and public office of justice, of which it was not possible they could have been guilty except in their own land and in the days of their independence. On the other hand, the promises of deliverance in ch. lix. read very much as if they were exilic. Judgement and righteousness are employed in ver. 9 in their exilic sense, [275] and God is pictured exactly as we have seen Him in other chapters of our prophet.

Are we then left with a mystery? On the contrary, the solution is clear. Israel is followed into exile by her old conscience. The charges of Isaiah and Ezekiel against Jerusalem, while Jerusalem was still a "civitas," ring in her memory. She repeats the very words. With truth she says that her present state, so vividly described in vv. 9-11, is due to sins of old, of which, though perhaps she can no longer commit them, she still feels the guilt. Conscience always crowds the years together; there is no difference of time in the eyes of God the Judge. And it was natural, as we have said already, that the nation should remember her besetting sins at this time; that her civic conscience should awake again, just as she was again about to become a civitas. [276] [277]

The whole of this chapter is simply the expansion and enforcement of the first two verses, that keep clanging like the clangour of a great, high bell: Behold, Jehovah's hand is not shortened that it cannot save, neither is His ear heavy that it cannot hear; but your iniquities have been separators between you and your God, and your sins have hidden His face from you, that He will not hear. There is but one thing that comes between the human heart and the Real Presence and Infinite Power of God; and that one thing is Sin. The chapter labours to show how real God is. Its opening verses talk of His Hand, His Ear, His Face. And the closing verses paint Him with the passions and the armour of a man,-- a Hero in such solitude and with such forward force, that no imagination can fail to see the Vivid, Lonely Figure. And He saw that there was no man, and He wondered that there was none to interpose; therefore His own right arm brought salvation unto Him, and His righteousness it upheld Him. And He put on righteousness like a breastplate and salvation for an helmet upon His head; and He put on garments of vengeance for clothing, and wrapped Himself in zeal like a robe. Do not let us suppose this is mere poetry. Conceive what inspires it,--the great truth that in the Infinite there is a heart to throb for men and a will to strike for them. This is what the writer desires to proclaim, and what we believe the Spirit of God moved his poor human lips to give their own shape to,--the simple truth that there is One, however hidden He may be to men's eyes, who feels for men, who feels hotly for men, and whose will is quick and urgent to save them. Such an One tells His people, that the only thing which prevents them from knowing how real His heart and will are--the only thing which prevents them from seeing His work in their midst--is their sin.

The roll of sins to which the prophet attributes the delay of the people's deliverance is an awful one; and the man who reads it with conscience asleep might conclude that it was meant only for a period of extraordinary violence and bloodshed. Yet the chapter implies that society exists, and that at least the forms of civilisation are in force. Men sue one another before the usual courts. But none sueth in righteousness or goeth to the law in truth. They trust in vanity and speak lies. All these charges might be true of a society as outwardly respectable as our own. Nor is the charge of bloodshed to be taken literally. The Old Testament has so great a regard for the spiritual nature of man, that to deny the individual his rights or to take away the peace of God from his heart, it calls the shedding of innocent blood. Isaiah reminds us of many kinds of this moral murder when he says, your hands are full of blood: seek justice, relieve the oppressed, judge the fatherless, plead for the widow. Ezekiel reminds us of others when he tells how God spake to him, that if he warn not the wicked, and the same wicked shall die in his iniquity, his blood will I require at thy hand. And again a Psalm reminds us of the time when the Lord maketh inquisition for blood, He forgetteth not the cry of the poor. [278] This is what the Bible calls murder and lays its burning words upon,--not such acts of bloody violence as now and then make all humanity thrill to discover that in the heart of civilisation there exist men with the passions of the ape and the tiger, but such oppression of the poor, such cowardice to rebuke evil, such negligence to restore the falling, such abuse of the characters of the young and innocent, such fraud and oppression of the weak, as often exist under the most respectable life, and employ the weapons of a Christian civilisation in order to fulfil themselves. We have need to take the bold, violent standards of the prophets and lay them to our own lives,--the prophets that call the man who sells his honesty for gain, a harlot, and hold him blood-guilty who has wronged, tempted or neglected his brother. Do not let us suppose that these crimson verses of the Bible may be passed over by us as not applicable to ourselves. They do not refer to murderers or maniacs: they refer to social crimes, to which we all are in perpetual temptation, and of which we all are more or less guilty,--the neglect of the weak, the exploitation of the poor for our own profit, the soiling of children's minds, the multiplying of temptation in the way of God's little ones, the malice that leads us to blast another's character, or to impute to his action evil motives for which we have absolutely no grounds save the envy and sordidness of our own hearts. Do not let us fail to read all such verses in the clear light which John the Apostle throws on them when he says: He that loveth not abideth in death. Whosoever hateth his brother is a murderer.

Footnotes:

260. See vol. i., pp. 363, 364.

261. So Ewald, Cheyne and Briggs. Ewald takes lvi. 9-lvii. 11a as an interruption, borrowed from an earlier prophet in a time of persecution, of the exilic prophecy, which goes on smoothly from lvi. 8 to lvii. 11b. We have seen that it is an error to suppose that lvi. 9-lvii. rose from a time of persecution.

262. Ezek. xxi.; cf. xxxiii. 30 f.

263. Delitzsch.

264. Mishpat and mishpatim, cf. p. [59]299.

265. Mishpat and mishpatim, cf. p. [60]299.

266. Such as is also expressed by exiles in Psalms xlii., xliii. and lxiii., but there with what spiritual temper, here with what a hard legal conception of righteousness.

267. For these see p. [61]61.

268. Literally, the poor, the wandering. It was a frequent phrase in the Exile: Lam. iii. 19, Remember mine affliction and my homelessness; i. 7, Jerusalem in the day of her affliction and her homelessness. LXX. astegoi, roofless.

269. Probably the fresh flesh which appears through a healing wound. Made classical by Jeremiah, who uses it thrice of Israel,--in the famous text, Is there no balm, etc., x. 22; and in xxx. 17; xxxiii. 6.

270. Jer. xxxi. 12.

271. Cf. Job xxiv. 13.

272. Cf. Amos viii. 5.

273. See pp. [62]43 f.

274. Ewald conceives chs. lviii., lix. to be the work of a younger contemporary of Ezekiel, to which the chief author of "Second Isaiah" has added words of his own: lviii. 12, lix. 21. The latter is evidently an insertion; cf. change of person and of number, etc. Delitzsch puts the passage down to the last decade of the Captivity, when for a little time Cyrus had turned away from Babylon, and the Jews despaired of his coming to save them.

275. See pp. [63]219 ff.

276. Another slight trace reveals the conglomerate nature of the chapter. If, as the earlier verses indicate, it was Israel that sinned, then it is the rebellious in Israel who should be punished. In ver. 18a, therefore, the adversaries or enemies ought to be Israelites. But in 18b the foreign islands are included. The LXX. has not this addition. Bredenkamp takes the words for an insertion. Yet the consequences of Israel's sin, according to the chapter, are not so much the punishment of the rebellious among the people as the delay of the deliverance for the whole nation,--a deliverance which Jehovah is represented as rising to accomplish, the moment the people express the sense of their rebellion and are penitent. The adversaries and enemies of ver. 18, therefore, are the oppressors of Israel, the foreigners and heathen; and 18b with its islands comes in quite naturally.

277. Note on mishpat and Ssedhaqah in ch. lix. This chapter is a good one for studying the various meanings of mishpat. In ver. 4 the verb shaphat is used in its simplest sense of going to law. In vv. 8 and

14 mishpat is a quality or duty of man. But in ver. 9 it is rather what man expects from God, and what is far from man because of his sins; it is judgement on God's side, or God's saving ordinance. In this sense it is probably to be taken in ver. 15,--Ssedhaqah follows the same parallel. This goes to prove that we have two distinct prophecies amalgamated, unless we believe that a play upon the words is intended.

278. Isa. i. 17; Ezek. ii. 18; Psalm ix. 12.

CHAPTER XXIV

SALVATION IN SIGHT.

Isaiah lx.-lxiii. 7.

The deliverance from Babylon has long been certain, since ch. xlviii.; all doubts in the way of Return have been removed, ch. xlix.-lii. 12; the means for the spiritual Restoration of the people have been sufficiently found, ch. liii. and preceding chapters on the Servant; Zion has been hailed from afar, ch. liv.; last calls to leave Babylon have been uttered, ch. lv.; last councils and comforts, lvi. 1-8; and the civic conscience has been rekindled, ch. lvi. 9-lix. There remains now only to take possession of the City herself; to rehearse the vocation of the restored people; and to realise all the hopes, fears, hindrances and practical problems of the future. These duties occupy the rest of our prophecy, chs. lx.-lxvi.

Ch. lx. is a prophecy as complete in itself as ch. liv. The City, which in liv. was hailed and comforted from afar, is in ch. lx. bidden rise and enjoy the glory that has at last reached her. Her splendours, hinted at in ch. liv., are seen in full and evident display. In chs. lxi.-lxii. her prophet, her genius and representative, rehearses to her his duties, and sets forth her place among the peoples. And in ch. lxiii. 1-7 we have another of those theophanies or appearances of the--Sole Divine Author of His people's salvation, which, abrupt and separate as if to heighten the sense of the solitariness of their subject--occur at intervals throughout our prophecy,--for instance, in ch. xlii., vv. 10-17, and in ch. lix. 16-19. These three sections, ch. lx., chs. lxi.-lxii. and ch. lxiii. 1-7, we will take together in this chapter of our volume.

I. Arise, Shine (ch. lx.)

The Sixtieth chapter of Isaiah is the spiritual counterpart of a typical Eastern day, with the dust laid and the darts taken out of the sunbeams,--a typical Eastern day in the sudden splendour of its dawn, the completeness and apparent permanence of its noon, the spaciousness it reveals on sea and land, and the barbaric profusion of life, which its strong light is sufficient to flood with glory.

Under such a day we see Jerusalem. In the first five verses of the chapter, she is addressed, as in ch. liv., as a crushed and desolate woman. But her lonely night is over, and from some prophet at the head of her returning children the cry peals, Arise, shine, for come hath thy light, and the glory of Jehovah hath risen upon thee. In the East the sun does not rise; the word is weak for an arrival almost too sudden for twilight. In the East the sun leaps above the horizon. You do not feel that he is coming, but that he is come. This first verse is suggested by the swiftness with which he bursts upon an Eastern city, and the shrouded form does not, as in our twilight, slowly unwrap itself, but shines at once, all plates and points of glory. Then the figure yields: for Jerusalem is not merely one radiant point in a world equally lighted by the sun, but is herself Jehovah's unique luminary. For behold the darkness shall cover the earth, and gross darkness the peoples, but upon thee shall Jehovah arise, and His glory upon thee shall be seen. And nations shall come to thy light, and kings to the brightness of thy rising. In the next two verses it is again a woman who is addressed. Lift up thine eyes round about and see, all of them have gathered, have come to thee: thy sons from afar are coming, and thy daughters are carried in the arms. [279] Then follows the fairest verse in the chapter. Then thou shalt see and be radiant, and thy heart shall throb and grow large; for there shall be turned upon thee the sea's flood-tide, and the wealth of the nations shall come to thee. The word which the Authorised English version translated shall flow together, and our Revised Version lightened, means both of these. It is liquid light,--light that ripples and sparkles and runs across the face; as it best appears in that beautiful passage of the thirty-fourth Psalm, they looked to Him and their faces were lightened. Here it suggests the light which a face catches from sparkling water. The prophet's figure has changed. The stately mother of her people stands not among the ruins of her city, but upon some great beach, with the sea in front,--the sea that casts up all heaven's light upon her face and drifts all earth's wealth to her feet, and her eyes are upon the horizon with the hope of her who watches for the return of children.

The next verses are simply the expansion of these two clauses,--about the sea's flood and the wealth of the Nations. Vv. 6-9 look first landward and then seaward, as from Jerusalem's own wonderful position on the high ridge between Asia and the sea: between the gates of the East and the gates of the West. On the one side, the city's horizon is the range of Moab and Edom, that barrier, in

Rev. George Adam Smith, M.A.

Jewish imagination, of the hidden and golden East across which pour the caravans here pictured. Profusion of camels shall cover thee, young camels of Midian and Ephah; all of them from Sheba shall come: gold and frankincense shall they bring, and the praises of Jehovah shall they publish. All the flocks of Kedar shall be gathered to thee, the rams of Nebaioth shall minister to thee: they shall come up with acceptance on Mine altar, and the house of My glory will I glorify. These were just what surged over Jordan from the far countries beyond, of which the Jews knew little more than the names here given,--tawny droves of camels upon the greenness of Palestine like a spate of the desert from which they poured; rivers of sheep brimming up the narrow drove-roads to Jerusalem:--conceive it all under that blazing Eastern sun. But then turning to Judah's other horizon, marked by the yellow fringe of sand and the blue haze of the sea beyond, the prophet cries for Jehovah: Who are these like a cloud that fly, and like doves to their windows? Surely towards Me the Isles [280] are stretching, and ships of Tarshish in the van, to bring thy sons from afar, their silver and their gold with them, to the Name of Jehovah of Hosts and to the Holy of Israel, for He hath glorified thee. The poetry of the Old Testament has been said to be deficient in its treatment of the sea; and certainly it dwells more frequently, as was natural for the imagination of an inland and a highland people to do, upon the hills. But in what literature will you find passages of equal length more suggestive of the sea than those short pieces in which the Hebrew prophet sought to render the futile rage of the world, as it dashed on the steadfast will of God, by the roar and crash of the ocean on the beach; [281] or painted a nation's prosperity as the waves of a summer sea; [282] or described the long coastlands as stretching out to God, and the white-sailed ships coming up the horizon like doves to their windows!

The rest of the chapter, from ver. 10 onwards, is occupied with the rebuilding and adornment of Jerusalem, and with the establishment of the people in righteousness and peace. There is a very obvious mingling of the material and the moral. The Gentiles are to become subject to the Jew, but it is to be a voluntary submission before the evidence of Jerusalem's spiritual superiority. Nothing is said of a Messiah or a King. Jerusalem is to be a commonwealth; and, while her magistracy shall be Peace and her overseers Righteousness, God Himself, in evident presence, is to be her light and glory. Thus the chapter ends with God and the People, and nothing else. God for an everlasting light around, and the people in their land, righteous, secure and growing very large. The least shall become a thousand, and the smallest a strong nation: I Jehovah will hasten it in its time.

This chapter has been put through many interpretations to many practical uses:--to describe the ingathering of the Gentiles to the Church (in the Christian year it is the Lesson for Epiphany), to prove the doctrine that the Church should live by the endowment of the kingdoms of this world, and to enforce the duty of costliness and magnificence in the public worship of God. The glory of the Lebanon shall come unto thee, fir-tree, plane-tree and sherbin together, to beautify the place of My sanctuary, and I will make the place of My feet glorious.

The last of these duties we may extend and qualify. If the coming in of the Gentiles is here represented as bringing wealth to the Church, we cannot help remembering that the going out to the Gentiles, in order to bring them in, means for us the spending of our wealth on things other than the adornment of temples; and that, besides the heathen, there are poor and suffering ones for whom God asks men's gold, as He asked it in olden days for the temple, that He may be glorified. Take that last phrase:--And--with all that material wealth which has flowed in from Lebanon, from Midian, from Sheba--I will make the place of My feet glorious. When this singular name was first uttered it was limited to the dwelling-place of the Ark and Presence of God, visible only on Mount Zion. But when God became man, and did indeed tread with human feet this world of ours, what were then the places of His feet? Sometimes, it is true, the Temple, but only sometimes; far more often where the sick lay, and the bereaved were weeping,--the pool of Bethesda, the death-room of Jairus' daughter, the way to the centurion's sick servant, the city gateways where the beggars stood, the lanes where the village folk had gathered, against His coming, their deaf and dumb, their palsied and lunatic. These were the places of His feet, who Himself bare our sicknesses and carried our infirmities; and these are what He would seek our wealth to make glorious. They say that the reverence of men builds now no cathedrals as of old; nay, but the love of man, that Christ taught, builds far more of those refuges and houses of healing, scatters far more widely those medicines for the body, those instruments of teaching, those means of grace, in which God is as much glorified as in Jewish Temple or Christian Cathedral.

Nevertheless He, who set the place of His feet, which He would have us to glorify, among the poor and the sick, was He, who also did not for Himself refuse that alabaster box and that precious ointment, which might have been sold for much and given to the poor. The worship of God, if we read Scripture aright, ought to be more than merely grave and comely. There should be heartiness and lavishness about it,--profusion and brilliance. Not of material gifts alone or chiefly, gold incense or rare wood, but of human faculties, graces and feeling; of joy and music and the sense of beauty. Take this chapter. It is wonderful, not so much for the material wealth which it devotes to the service of God's house, and which is all that many eyes ever see in it, as for the glorious imagination and heart for the beautiful, the joy in light and space and splendour, the poetry and the music, which use those material things simply as the light uses the wick, or as music uses the lyre, to express and reveal itself. What a call this chapter is to let out the natural wonder and poetry of the heart, its feeling and music and exultation,--all that is within us, as the Psalmist says,--in the Service of God. Why do we not do so? The answer is very simple. Because, unlike this prophet, we do not realise how present and full our salvation is; because, unlike him, we do not realise that our light has come, and so we will not arise and shine.

II. The Gospel (chs. lxi.-lxii.)

The speaker in ch. lxi. is not introduced by name. Therefore he may be the Prophet himself, or he may be the Servant. The present expositor, while feeling that the evidence is not conclusive against either of these, and that the uncertainty is as great as in ch. xlviii. 16, [283] inclines to think that there is, on the whole, less objection to its being the prophet who speaks than to its being the Servant. See the appended note. But it is not a very important question, which is intended, for the Servant was representative of prophecy; and if it be the prophet who speaks here, he also speaks with the conscience of the whole function and aim of the prophetic order. That Jesus Christ fulfilled this programme does not decide the question one way or the other; for a prophet so representative was as much the antetype and foreshadowing of Christ as the Servant himself was. On the whole, then, we must be content to feel about this passage, what we must have already felt about many others in our prophecy, that the writer is more anxious to place before us the whole range and ideal of the prophetic gift than to make clear in whom this ideal is realised; and for the rest Jesus of Nazareth so plainly fulfilled it, that it becomes, indeed, a very minor question to ask whom the writer may have intended as its first application.

If ch. lx. showed us the external glory of God's people, ch. lxi. opens with the programme of their inner mission. There we had the building and adornment of the Temple, that Jehovah might glorify His people: here we have the binding of broken hearts and the beautifying of soiled lives, that Jehovah may be glorified. But this inner mission also issues in external splendour, in a righteousness, which is like the adornment of a bride and like the beauty of spring.

The commission of the prophet is mainly to duties we have already studied in preceding passages, both on himself and on the Servant. It will be enough to point out its special characteristics. The Spirit of my Lord Jehovah is upon me, for that Jehovah hath anointed me to bring good tidings to the afflicted; He hath sent me to bind up the broken-hearted, to proclaim to the captive liberty, and to the prisoners open ways; [284] to proclaim an acceptable year for Jehovah, and a day of vengeance for our God; to comfort all that mourn; to offer to the mourners of Zion, to give unto them a crest [285] for ashes, the oil of joy for mourning, the mantle of praise for the spirit of dimness; [286] so that men may call them Oaks-of-Righteousness, the planting of Jehovah, that He may break into glory.

There are heard here all the keynotes of our prophet, and clear, too, is that usual and favourite direction of his thoughts from the inner and spiritual influences to the outward splendour and evidence, the passage from the comfort and healing of the heart to the rich garment, the renown, and his own dearest vision of great forest trees,--in short, Jehovah Himself breaking into glory. But one point needs special attention.

The prophet begins his commission by these words, to bring good tidings to the afflicted, and again says, to proclaim to the captive. The afflicted, or the poor, as it is mostly rendered, is the classical name for God's people in Exile. We have sufficiently moved among this people to know for what reason the bringing of good tidings should here be reckoned as the first and most indispensable service that prophecy could render them. Why, in the life of every nation, there are hours, when the factors of destiny, that loom largest at other times, are dwarfed and dwindle before the momentousness of a piece of news,--hours, when the nation's attitude in a great moral issue, or her whole freedom and destiny, are determined by telegrams from the seat of war. The simultaneous news of Grant's capture of Vicksburg and Meade's defeat of Lee, news that finally turned English opinion, so long shamefully debating and wavering, to the side of God and the slave; the telegrams from the army, for which silent crowds waited in the Berlin squares through the autumn nights of 1870, conscious that the unity and birthright of Germany hung upon the tidings,--are instances of the vital and paramount influence in a nation's history of a piece of news. The force of a great debate in Parliament, the expression of public opinion through all its organs, the voice of a people in a general election, things in their time as ominous as the Fates, all yield at certain supreme moments to the meaning of a simple message from Providence. Now it was for news from God that Israel waited in Exile; for good tidings and the proclamation of fact. They had with them a Divine Law, but no mere exposition of it could satisfy men who were captives and waited for the command of their freedom. They had with them Psalms, but no beauty of music could console them: How should we sing the Lord's song in a strange land? They had Prophecy, with its assurance of the love and the power of their God; and much as there was in it to help them to patience and to hope, general statements were not enough for them. They needed the testimony of a fact. Freedom and Restoration had been promised them: they waited for the proclamation that it was coming, for the good news that it had arrived. Now our prophecy is mainly this proclamation and good news of fact. The prophet uses before all other words two,--to call or proclaim, kara, and to tell good tidings, bisser. We found them in his opening chapter: we find them again here when he sums up his mission. A third goes along with them, to comfort, naham, but it is the accompaniment, and they are the burden, of his prophecy.

But good tidings and the proclamation meant so much more than the mere political deliverance of Israel--meant the fact of their pardon, the tale of their God's love, of His provision for them, and of His wonderful passion and triumph of salvation on their behalf--that it is no wonder that these two words came to be ever afterwards the classical terms for all speech and prophecy from God to man. We actually owe the Greek words of the New Testament for gospel and preaching to this time of Israel's history. The Greek term, from which we have evangel, evangelist and evangelise, originally meant good news, but was first employed in a religious sense in the Greek translation of our prophecy. And our word "preach" is the heir, though not the lineal descendant, through the Latin prædicare and the Greek kerussein, of the word, which is translated in ch. lx. of our prophet to proclaim, but in ch. xl. to call or cry. It is to the Exile that we trace the establishment among God's people of regular preaching side by side with sacramental and liturgical worship; for it was in the Exile that the Synagogue arose, whose pulpit was to become as much the centre of Israel's life as was the altar of the Temple. And it was from the pulpit of a synagogue centuries after, when the preaching had become dry exposition or hard lawgiving, that Jesus re-read our prophecy and affirmed again the good news of God.

What is true of nations is true of individuals. We indeed support our life by principles; we develop it by argument;--we cannot lay too heavy stress upon philosophy and law. But there is something of far greater concern than either argument or the abstract principles from which it is developed; something that our reason cannot find of itself, that our conscience but increases our longing for. It is, whether certain things are facts or not; whether, for instance, the Supreme Power of the Universe is on the side of the individual combatant for righteousness; whether God is love; whether Sin has been forgiven; whether Sin and Death have ever been conquered; whether the summer has come in which humanity may put forth their shoots conscious that all the influence of heaven is on their side, or whether, there being no heavenly favours, man must train his virtue and coax his happiness to ripen behind shelters and in conservatories of his own construction. Now Christ comes to us with the good news of God that it is so. The supreme force in the Universe is on man's side, and for man has won victory and achieved freedom. God has proclaimed pardon. A Saviour has overcome sin and death. We are free to break from evil. The struggle after holiness is not the struggle of a weakly plant in an alien soil and beneath a wintry sky, counting only upon the precarious aids of human cultivation; but summer has come, the acceptable year of the Lord has begun, and all the favour of the Almighty is on His people's side. These are the good tidings and proclamation of God, and to every man who believes them they must make an incalculable difference in life.

As we have said, the prophet passes in the rest of this prophecy from the spiritual influences of his mission to its outward effects. The people's righteousness is described in the external fashion, which we have already studied in Chapter Fourteen; Zion's espousals to Jehovah are celebrated, but into that we have also gone thoroughly (pp. ^{64}398 ff.); the restoration of prophecy in Jerusalem is described (lxii. 6-9), as in ch. lii. 8; and another call is given to depart from Babylon and every foreign city and come to Zion. This call coming now, so long after the last, and when we might think that the prophet had wholly left Babylon behind, need not surprise us. For even though some Jews had actually arrived at Zion, which is not certain, others were hanging back in Babylon; and, indeed, such a call as this might fitly be renewed for the next century or two: so many of God's people continued to forget that their citizenship was in Zion.

III. The Divine Saviour (ch. lxiii. 1-7).

Once again the prophet turns to hail, in his periodic transport, the Solitary Divine Hero and Saviour of His people.

That the writer of this piece is the main author of "Second Isaiah" is probable, both because it is the custom of the latter to describe at intervals the passion and effort of Israel's Mighty One, and because several of his well-known phrases meet us in this piece. The speaker in righteousness mighty to save recalls ch. xlv. 19-24; and the day of vengeance and year of my redeemed recalls ch. lxi. 2; and I looked, and there was no helper, and I gazed, and there was none to uphold, recalls lix. 16. The prophet is looking out from Jerusalem towards Edom,--a direction in which the watchmen upon Zion had often in her history looked for the return of her armies from the punishment of Israel's congenital and perpetual foe. The prophet, however, sees the prospect filled up, not by the flashing van of a great army, but by a solitary figure, without ally, without chariot, without weapons, swaying on in the wealth of his strength. The keynote of the piece is the loneliness of this Hero. A figure is used, which, where battle would only have suggested complexity, enthrals us with the spectacle of solitary effort,--the figure of trampling through some vast winefat alone. The Avenging Saviour of Israel has a fierce joy in being alone: it is his new nerve to effort and victory,--therefore mine own right arm, it brought salvation to me. We see One great form in the strength of one great emotion. My fury, it upheld me.

The interpretation of this chapter by Christians has been very varied, and often very perverse. To use the words of Calvin, "Violenter torserunt hoc caput Christiani." But, as he sees very rightly, it is not the Messiah nor the Servant of Jehovah, who is here pictured, but Jehovah Himself. This Solitary is the Divine Saviour of Israel, as in ch. xlii. 7 f. and in ch. lix. 16 f. In Chapter Eight of this volume we spoke so fully of the Passion of God, that we may now refer to that chapter for the essential truth which underlies our prophet's anthropomorphism, and claims our worship where a short sight might only turn the heart away in scorn at the savage and blood-stained surface. One or two other points, however, demand our attention before we give the translation.

Why does the prophet look in the direction of Edom for the return of his God? Partly, it is to be presumed, because Edom was as good a representative as he could choose of the enemies of Israel other than Babylon. [287] But also partly, perhaps, because of the names which match the red colours of his piece,--the wine and the blood. Edom means red, and Bossrah is assonant to Bôsser, a vinedresser. [288] Fitter background and scenery the prophet, therefore, could not have for his drama of Divine Vengeance. But we must take care, as Dillmann properly remarks, not to imagine that any definite, historical invasion of Edom by Israel, or other chastening instrument of Jehovah, is here intended. It is a vision which the prophet sees of Jehovah Himself: it illustrates the passion, the agony, the unshared and unaided effort which the Divine Saviour passes through for His people.

Further, it is only necessary to point out, that the term in ver. 1 given as splendid by the Authorised Version, which I have rendered sweeping, is literally swelling, and is, perhaps, best rendered by sailing on or swinging on. The other verb which the Revised Version renders marching means swaying, or moving the head or body from one side to another, in the pride and fulness of strength. In ver. 2 like a wine-treader is literally like him that treadeth in the pressing-house--Geth (the first syllable of Gethsemane, the oil-press). But vr h in ver. 3 is the pressing-trough.

Who is this coming from Edom,
Raw-red his garments from Bossrah!
This sweeping on in his raiment,
Swaying in the wealth of his strength?
I that do speak in righteousness,
Mighty to save!
Wherefore is red on thy raiment,
And thy garments like to a wine-treader's?
A trough I have trodden alone,
Of the peoples no man was with me.
So I trod them down in my wrath,
And trampled them down in my fury;
Their life-blood sprinkled my garments,
And all my raiment I stained.
For the day of revenge in my heart,
And the year of my redeemed has come.
And I looked, and no helper;
I gazed, and none to uphold!
So my righteousness won me salvation;
And my fury, it hath upheld me.
So I stamp on the peoples in my wrath,
And make them drunk with my fury,
And bring down to earth their life-blood.

Footnotes:

279. Literally, on the side or hip, the Eastern method of carrying children.
280. Or coasts. See pp. [65]109 ff.
281. Isa. xiv.; Isaiah i.-xxxix., pp. [66]281 ff.
282. Isa. xlviii. 18.
283. See p. [67]210, note. Some points of the speaker's description of himself--for example, the gift of the Spirit and the anointing--suit equally well any prophet, or the unique Servant. The lofty mission and its great results are not too lofty or great for our prophet, for Jeremiah received his office in terms as large. That the prophet has not yet spoken at such length in his own person is no reason why he should not do so now, especially as this is an occasion on which he sums up and enforces the whole range of prophecy. It can, therefore, very well be the prophet who speaks. On the other hand, to say with Diestel that it cannot be the Servant because the personification of the Servant ceases with ch. liii. is to beg the question. A stronger argument against the case for the Servant is that the speaker does not call himself

by that name, as he does in other passages when he is introduced; but this is not conclusive, for in l. 4-9 the Servant, though he speaks, does not name himself. To these may be added this (from Krüger), that the Servant's discourse never passes without transition into that of God, as this speaker's in ver. 8, but the prophet's discourse often so passes; and this, that vsr, qr' and nchm are often used of the prophet, and not at all of the Servant. These are all the points in the question, and it will be seen how inconclusive they are. If any further proof of this were required, it would be found in the fact that authorities are equally divided. There hold for the Servant Calvin, Delitzsch, Cheyne (who previously took the other view), Driver, Briggs, Nägelsbach and Orelli. But the Targums, Ewald, Hitzig, Diestel, Dillmann, Bredenkamp and Krüger hold by the prophet. Krüger's reasons, Essai sur la Théologie d'Isaïe xl.-lxvi., p. 76, are specially worthy of attention.

284. Literally, opening; but the word is always used of opening of the eyes. Ewald renders open air, Dillmann hellen Blick.

285. Any insignia or ornament for the head.

286. The same word as in xlii. 3, fading wick.

287. See Isaiah i.-xxxix., pp. [68]438-[69]40.

288. Cf. Krüger, Essai sur la Théologie d'Isaïe xl.-lxvi., pp. 154-55. Lagarde has proposed to read m'dm, past participle, for m'dm and mbtsr for mbtsrh. Who is this that cometh dyed red, redder in his garments than a vinedresser?

CHAPTER XXV

A LAST INTERCESSION AND THE JUDGEMENT.

Isaiah lxiii. 7-lxvi.

We might well have thought, that with the section we have been considering the prophecy of Israel's Redemption had reached its summit and its end. The glory of Zion in sight, the full programme of prophecy owned, the arrival of the Divine Saviour hailed in the urgency of His feeling for His people, in the sufficiency of His might to save them,--what more, we ask, can the prophecy have to give us? Why does it not end upon these high notes? The answer is, the salvation is indeed consummate, but the people are not ready for it. On an earlier occasion, let us remember, when our prophet called the nation to their Service of God, he called at first the whole nation, but had then immediately to make a distinction. Seen in the light of their destiny, the mass of Israel proved to be unworthy; tried by its strain, part immediately fell away. But what happened upon that call to Service happens again upon this disclosure of Salvation. The prophet realises that it is only a part of Israel who are worthy of it. He feels again the weight, which has been the hindrance of his hope all through,--the weight of the mass of the nation, sunk in idolatry and wickedness, incapable of appreciating the promises. He will make one more effort to save them--to save them all. He does this in an intercessory prayer, ch. lxiii. 7-lxiv., in which he states the most hopeless aspects of his people's case, identifies himself with their sin, and yet pleads by the ancient power of God that we all may be saved. He gets his answer in ch. lxv., in which God sharply divides Israel into two classes, the faithful and the idolaters, and affirms that, while the nation shall be saved for the sake of the faithful remnant, Jehovah's faithful servants and the unfaithful can never share the same experience or the same fate. And then the book closes with a discourse in ch. lxvi., in which this division between the two classes in Israel is pursued to a last terrible emphasis and contrast upon the narrow stage of Jerusalem itself. We are left, not with the realisation of the prophet's prayer for the salvation of all the nations, but with a last judgement separating its godly and ungodly portions.

Thus there are three connected divisions in lxiii. 7-lxvi. First, the prophet's Intercessory Prayer, ch. lxiii. 7-lxiv.; second, the Answer of Jehovah, ch. lxv.; and third, the Final Discourse and Judgement, ch. lxvi.

I. *The Prayer for the Whole People (ch. lxiii. 7-lxiv.).*

There is a good deal of discussion as to both the date and the authorship of this piece,--as to whether it comes from the early or the late Exile, and as to whether it comes from our prophet or from another. It must have been written after the destruction and before the rebuilding of the Temple; this is put past all doubt by these verses: Thy holy people possessed it but a little while: our adversaries have trodden down Thy sanctuary. Thy holy cities are become a wilderness, Zion has become a wilderness, Jerusalem a desolation. The house of our holiness and of our ornament, wherein our fathers praised Thee, is become for a burning of fire, and all our delights are for ruin. [289]

This language has been held to imply that the disaster to Jerusalem was recent, as if the city's conflagration still flared on the national imagination, which in later years of the Exile was impressed rather by the long, cold ruins of the Holy Place, the haunt of wild beasts. But not only is this point inconclusive, but the impression that it leaves is entirely dispelled by other verses, which speak of the Divine anger as having been of long continuance, and as if it had only hardened the people in sin; compare ch. lxiii. 17 and lxiv. 6, 7. There is nothing in the prayer to show that the author lived in exile, and accordingly the proposal has been made to date the piece from among the first attempts at rebuilding after the Return. To the present expositor this seems to be certainly wrong. The man who wrote vv. 11-15 of ch. lxiii. had surely the Return still before him; he would not have written in the way he has done of the Exodus from Egypt unless he had been feeling the need of another exhibition of Divine Power of the same kind. The prayer, therefore, must come from pretty much the same date as the rest of our prophecy,--after the Exile had long continued, but while the Return had not yet taken place. Nor is there any reason against attributing it to the same writer. It is true the style differs from the rest of his work, but this may be accounted for, as in the case of ch. liii., by the change of subject. Most critics, who hold that we still follow the same author, take for granted that some time has elapsed since the prophet's triumphant strains in chs. lx.-lxii. This is probable; but there is nothing to make it certain.

What is certain is the change of mood and conscience. The prophet, who in ch. lx. had been caught away into the glorious future of the people, is here as utterly absorbed in their barren and doubtful present. Although the salvation is certain, as he has seen it, the people are not ready. The fact he has already felt so keenly about them,--see ch. xlii., vv. 24, 25,--that their long discipline in exile has done the mass of them no good, but evil, comes forcibly back upon him (ch. lxiv. 5b ff.). Thou wast angry, and we sinned only the more: in such a state we have been long, and shall we be saved! The banished people are thoroughly unclean and rotten, fading as a leaf, the sport of the wind. But the prophet identifies himself with them. He speaks of their sin as ours, of their misery as ours. He takes of them the very saddest view possible, he feels them all as sheer dead weight: there is none that calleth on Thy name, that stirreth himself up to take hold on Thee: for Thou hast hid Thy face from us, and delivered us into the power of our iniquities. But the prophet thus loads himself with the people in order to secure, if he can, their redemption as a whole. Twice he says in the name of them all, Doubtless Thou art our Father. His great heart will not have one of them left out; we all, he says, are the work of Thy hand, we all are Thy people.

But this intention of the prayer will amply account for any change of style we may perceive in the language. No one will deny that it is quite possible for the same man now to fling himself forward into the glorious vision of his people's future salvation, and again to identify himself with the most hopeless aspects of their present distress and sin; and no one will deny that the same man will certainly write in two different styles with regard to each of these different feelings. Besides which, we have seen in the passage the recurrence of some of our prophecy's most characteristic thoughts. We feel, therefore, no reason for counting the passage to be by another hand than that which has mainly written "Second Isaiah." It may be at once admitted that he has incorporated in it earlier phrases, reminiscences and echoes of language about the fall of Jerusalem in use when the Lamentations were written. But this was a natural thing for him to do in a prayer, in which he represented the whole people and took upon himself the full burden of their woes.

If such be the intention of chs. lxiii. 7-lxiv., then in them we have one of the noblest passages of our prophet's great work. How like he is to the Servant he pictured for us! How his great heart fulfils the loftiest ideal of Service: not only to be the prophet and the judge of his people, but to make himself one with them in all their sin and sorrow, to carry them all in his heart. Truly, as his last words said of the Servant, he himself bears the sin of many, and interposes for the transgressors. Before we see the answer he gets, let us make clear some obscure things and appreciate some beautiful ones in his prayer.

It opens with a recital of Jehovah's ancient lovingkindness and mercies to Israel. This is what perhaps gives it connection with the previous section. In ch. lxii. the prophet, though sure of the coming glory, wrote before it had come, and urged upon the Lord's remembrancers to keep no silence, and give Him no silence till He establish and till He make Jerusalem a praise in the earth. This work of remembrancing, the prophet himself takes up in lxiii. 7: The lovingkindnesses of Jehovah I will record, literally, cause to be remembered, the praises of Jehovah, according to all that Jehovah hath bestowed upon us. And then he beautifully puts all the beginnings of God's dealings with His people in His trusting of them: For He said, Surely they are My people, children that will not deal falsely; so He became their Saviour. In all their affliction He was afflicted, the Angel of His Face saved them. This must be understood, not as an angel of the Presence, who went out from the Presence to save the people, but, as it is in other Scriptures, God's own Presence, God Himself; and so interpreted, the phrase falls into line with the rest of the verse, which is one of the most vivid expressions that the Bible contains of the personality of God. [290] In His love and in His pity He redeemed them, and bare them, and carried them all the days of old. Then he tells us how they disappointed and betrayed this trust, ever since the Exodus, the days of old. But they rebelled and grieved the Spirit of His holiness: therefore He was turned to be their enemy, He Himself fought against them. This refers to their history down to, and especially during, the Exile: compare ch. xlii., vv. 24, 25. Then in their affliction they remembered the days of old--the English version obscures the sequence here by translating he remembered--and then follows the glorious account of the Exodus. In ver. 13 the wilderness is, of course, prairie, flat pasture-land; they were led as smoothly as a horse in a meadow, that they stumbled not. As cattle that come down into the valley--cattle coming down from the hill sides to pasture and rest on the green, watered plains--the Spirit of Jehovah caused them to rest: so didst Thou lead Thy people to make Thyself a glorious name. And then having offered such precedents, the prophet's prayer breaks forth to a God, whom His people feel no longer at their head, but far withdrawn into heaven: Look down from heaven, and behold from the habitation of Thy holiness and Thy glory: where is Thy zeal and Thy mighty deeds? the surge of Thy bowels and thy compassions are restrained towards me. Then he pleads God's fatherhood to the nation, and the rest of the prayer alternates between the hopeless misery and undeserving sin of the people, and, notwithstanding, the power of God to save as He did in times of old; the willingness of God to meet with those who wait for Him and remember Him; and, once more, His fatherhood, and His power over them, as the power of the potter over the clay.

Two points stand out from the rest. The Divine Trust, from which all God's dealing with His people is said to have started, and the Divine Fatherhood, which the prophet pleads.

He said, Surely they are My people, children that will not deal falsely: so He was their Saviour. The "surely" is not the fiat of sovereignty or foreknowledge: it is the hope and confidence of love. It did not prevail; it was disappointed.

This is, of course, a profound acknowledgment of man's free will. It is implied that men's conduct must remain an uncertain thing, and that in calling men God cannot adventure upon greater certainty than is implied in the trust of affection. If one asks, What, then, about God's foreknowledge, who alone knoweth the end of a thing from the beginning, and His sovereign grace, who chooseth whom He will? are you not logically bound to these?--then it can only be asked in return, Is it not better to be without logic for a little, if at the expense of it we obtain so true, so deep a glimpse into God's heart as this simple verse affords us? Which is better for us to know--that God is Wisdom which knows all, or Love that dares and ventures all? Surely, that God is Love which dares and ventures all with the worst, with the most hopeless of us. This is what makes this single verse of Scripture more powerful to move the heart than all creeds and catechisms. For where these speak of sovereign will, and often mock our affections with the bare and heavy (if legitimate) sceptre they sway, this calls forth our love, honour and obedience by the heart it betrays in God. Of what unsuspicious trust, of what chivalrous adventure of love, of what fatherly confidence, does it speak! What a religion is this of ours in the power of which a man may every morning rise and feel himself thrilled by the thought that God trusts him enough to work with His will for the day; in the power of which a man may look round and see the sordid, hopeless human life about him glorified by the truth, that for the salvation of such God did adventure Himself in a love that laid itself down in death. The attraction and power of such a religion can never die. Requiring no painful thought to argue it into reality, it leaps to light before the natural affection of man's heart; it takes his instincts immediately captive; it gives him a conscience, an honour and an obligation. No wonder that our prophet, having such a belief, should once more identify himself with the people, and adventure himself with the weight of their sin before God.

The other point of the prayer is the Fatherhood of God, concerning which all that is needful to say here is that the prophet, true to the rest of Old Testament teaching on the subject, applies it only to God's relation to the nation as a whole. In the Old Testament no one is called the son of God except Israel as a people, or some individual representative and head of Israel. And even of such the term was seldom employed. This was not because the Hebrew was without temptation to imagine his physical descent from the gods, for neighbouring nations indulged in such dreams for themselves and their heroes; nor because he was without appreciation of the intellectual kinship between the human and the Divine, for he knew that in the beginning God had said, Let us make man in our own image. But the same feeling prevailed with him in regard to this idea, as we have seen prevailed in regard to the kindred idea of God as the husband of His people. [291] The prophets were anxious to emphasize that it was a moral relation,--a moral relation, and one initiated from God's side by certain historical acts of His free, selecting, redeeming and adopting love. Israel was not God's son till God had evidently called and redeemed him. Look at how our prophet uses the word Father, and to what he makes it equivalent. The first time it is equivalent to Redeemer: Thou, O Lord, art our Father; our Redeemer from old is Thy name (lxiii. 16b). The second time it is illustrated by the work of the potter: But now, O Lord, Thou art our Father; we are the clay, and Thou our potter; and we are all the work of Thy hand (lxiv. 8). Could it be made plainer in what sense the Bible defines this relation between God and man? It is not a physical, nor is it an intellectual relation. The assurance and the virtue of it do not come to men with their blood or with the birth of their intellect, but in the course of moral experience, with the sense that God claims them from sin and from the world for Himself; with the gift of a calling and a destiny; with the formation of character, the perfecting of obedience, the growth in His knowledge and His grace. And because it is a moral relation time is needed to realise it, and only after long patience and effort may it be unhesitatingly claimed. And that is why Israel was so long in claiming it, and why the clearest, most undoubting cries to God the Father, which rise from the Greek in the earliest period of his history, reach our ears from Jewish lips only near the end of their long progress, only (as we see from our prayer) in a time of trial and affliction.

We have a New Testament echo of this Old Testament belief in the Fatherhood of God, as a moral and not a national relation, in Paul's writings, who in the Second Epistle to the Corinthians (vi. 17, 18) urges thus: Wherefore come out from among them, and be ye separate, saith the Lord, and touch not the unclean thing; and I will receive you, and will be a Father unto you, and ye shall be My sons and daughters, saith the Lord Almighty.

On these grounds, then,--that God in His great love had already adventured Himself with this whole people, and already by historical acts of election and redemption proved Himself the Father of the nation as a whole,--does our prophet plead with Him to save them all again. The answer to this pleading he gets in ch. lxv.

II. God's Answer to the Prophet's Intercession (ch. lxv.).

God's answer to his prophet's intercession is twofold. First, He says that He has already all this time been trying them with love, meeting them with salvation; but they have not turned to Him. The prophet has asked, Where is Thy zeal? the yearning of Thy bowels and Thy compassions are restrained towards me. Thou hast hid Thy face far from us. Wilt Thou refrain Thyself for these things, O Jehovah? wilt Thou hold Thy peace and afflict us very sore. And now, in the beginning of ch. lxv., Jehovah answers, not with that confusion of tenses and irrelevancy of words with which the English version makes Him speak; but suitably, relevantly and convincingly. I have been to be inquired of those who asked not for Me. I have been to be found of them that sought Me not. I have been saying, I am here, I am here, to a nation that did not call on My name. I have stretched out My hands all the day to a people turning away, who walk in a way that is not good, after their own thoughts; a people that have been provoking Me to My face continually,--and then He details their idolatry. This, then, is the answer of the Lord to the prophet's appeal. "In this I have not all power. It is wrong to talk of Me as the potter and of man as the clay, as if all the active share in salvation lay with Me. Man is free,--free to withhold himself from My urgent affection; free to turn from My outstretched hands; free to choose before Me the abomination of idolatry. And this the mass of Israel have done, clinging, fanatical and self-satisfied, to their unclean and morbid imaginations of the Divine, all the time that My great prophecy by you has been appealing to them." This is a sufficient answer to the prophet's prayer. Love is not omnipotent; if men disregard so open an appeal of the Love of God, they are hopeless; nothing else can save them. The sin against such love is like the sin against the Holy Ghost, of which our Lord speaks so hopelessly. Even God cannot help the despisers and abusers of Grace.

The rest of God's answer to His prophet's intercession emphasizes that the nation shall be saved for the sake of a faithful remnant in it (vv. 8-10). But the idolaters shall perish (vv. 11, 12). They cannot possibly expect the same fare, the same experience, the same fate, as God's faithful servants (vv. 13-15). But those who are true and faithful Israelites, surviving and experiencing the promised salvation, shall find that God is true, and shall acknowledge Him as the God of Amen, because the former troubles are forgotten--those felt so keenly in the prophet's prayer in ch. lxiv.--and because they are hid from Mine eyes. The rest of the answer describes a state of serenity and happiness wherein there shall be no premature death, nor loss of property, nor vain labour, nor miscarriage, nor disappointment of prayer nor delay in its answer, nor strife between man and the beasts, nor any hurt or harm in Jehovah's Holy Mountain. Truly a prospect worthy of being named as the prophet names it, a new heaven and a new earth!

Ch. lxv. is thus closely connected, both by circumstance and logic, with the long prayer which precedes it. The tendency of recent criticism has been to deny this connection, especially on the line of circumstance. Ch. lxv. does not, it is argued, reflect the Babylonish captivity as ch. lxiii. 7-lxiv. so clearly does; but, on the contrary, "while some passages presuppose the Exile as past, others refer to circumstances characteristic of Jewish life in Canaan." [292] But this view is only possible through straining some features of the chapter adaptable either to Palestine or Babylon, and overlooking others which are obviously Babylonian. Sacrificing in gardens and burning incense on tiles were practices pursued in Jerusalem before the Exile, but the latter was introduced there from Babylon, and the former was universal in heathendom. The practices in ver. 5 are never attributed to the people before the Exile, were all possible in Babylonia, and some we know to have been actual there. [293] The other charge of idolatry in ver. 11 "suits Babylonia," Cheyne admits, "as well as (probably) Palestine." [294] But what seems decisive for the exilic origin of ch. lxv. is that the possession of Judah and Zion by the seed of Jacob is still implied as future (ver. 9). Moreover the holy land is alluded to by the name common among the exiles in flat Mesopotamia, My mountains, and in contrast with the idolatry of which the present generation is guilty the idolatry of their fathers is characterised as having been upon the mountains and upon the hills, and again the people is charged with forgetting My holy mountain, a phrase reminiscent of Psalm cxxxvii., ver. 4, and more appropriate to a time of exile, than when the people were gathered about Zion. All these resemblances in circumstance corroborate the strong logical connection which we have found between ch. lxiv. and ch. lxv., and leave us no reason for taking the latter away from the main author of "Second Isaiah," though he may have worked up into it recollections and remains of an older time.

III. The Last Judgement (ch. lxvi.).

Whether with the final chapter of our prophecy we at last get footing in the Holy Land is doubtful. [295] It was said on p. [70]20 that, "in vv. 1 to 4 of this chapter the Temple is still unbuilt, but the building would seem to be already begun." This latter clause should be modified to, "the building would seem to be in immediate prospect." The rest of the chapter, vv. 6-24, has features that speak more definitely for the period after the Return; but even they are not conclusive, and their effect is counterbalanced by some other verses. Ver. 6 may imply that the Temple is rebuilt, and ver. 20 that the sacrifices are resumed; but, on the other hand, these verses may be, like parts of ch. lx., statements of the prophet's vivid vision of the future. [296] Vv. 7 and 8 seem to describe a repeopling of Jerusalem that has already taken place; but ver. 9 says, that while the bringing to the birth has already happened, which is, as we must suppose, the deliverance from Babylon,--or is it the actual arrival at Jerusalem?--the bringing forth from the womb, that is, the complete restoration of the people, has still to take place. Ver. 13 is certainly addressed to those who are not yet in Jerusalem.

These few points reveal how difficult, nay, how impossible, it is to decide the question of date, as between the days immediately before the Return and the days immediately after. To the present expositor the balance of evidence seems to be with the later date. But the difference is very small. We are at least sure--and it is really all that we require to know--that the rebuilding of Jerusalem is very near, nearer than it has been felt in any previous chapter. The Temple is, so to speak, within sight, and the prophet is able to talk of the regular round of sacrifices and sacred festivals almost as if they had been resumed.

To the people, then, either in the near prospect of Return, or immediately after some of them had arrived in Jerusalem, the prophet addresses a number of oracles, in which he pursues the division, that ch. lxv. had emphasized, between the two parties in Israel. These oracles are so intricate, that we are compelled to take up the chapter verse by verse. The first of them begins by correcting certain false feelings in Israel, excited by former promises of the rebuilding and the glory of the Temple. Thus saith Jehovah, The heavens are My throne, and earth is My footstool: what is this for a house that ye will build--or, are building--Me, and what is this for a place for My rest? Yea, all these things--that is, all the visible works of God in heaven and earth--My hand hath made, and so came to pass all these things, saith Jehovah. But unto this will I look, unto the humble and contrite in spirit, and that trembleth at My word. These verses do not run counter to, or even go beyond, anything that our prophet has already said. They do not condemn the building of the Temple: this was not possible for a prophecy which contains ch. lx. They condemn only the kind of temple which those whom they address had in view,--a shrine to which the presence of Jehovah was limited, and on the raising and maintenance of which the religion and righteousness of the people should depend. While the former Temple was standing, the mass of the people had thus misconceived it, imagining that it was enough for national religion to have such a structure standing and honoured in their midst. And now, before it is built again, the exiles are cherishing about it the same formal and materialistic thoughts. Therefore the prophet rebukes them, as his predecessors had rebuked their fathers, and reminds them of a truth he has already uttered, that though the Temple is raised, according to God's own promise and direction, it will not be to its structure, as they conceive of it, that He will have respect, but to the existence among them of humble and sincere personal piety. The Temple is to be raised: the place of His feet God will make glorious, and men shall gather round it from the whole earth, for instruction, for comfort and for rejoicing. But let them not think it to be indispensable either to God or to man,--not to God, who has heaven for His throne and earth for His footstool; nor to man, for God looks direct to man, if only man be humble, penitent and sensitive to His word. These verses, then, do not go beyond the Old Testament limit; they leave the Temple standing, but they say so much about God's other sanctuary man, that when His use for the Temple shall be past, His servant Stephen [297] shall be able to employ these words to prove why it should disappear.

The next verse is extremely difficult. Here it is literally: A slaughterer of the ox, a slayer of a man; a sacrificer of the lamb, a breaker of a dog's neck; an offerer of meat-offering, swine's blood; the maker of a memorial offering of incense, one that blesseth an idol, or vanity. Four legal sacrificial acts are here coupled with four unlawful sacrifices to idols. Does this mean that in the eye of God, impatient even of the ritual He has consecrated, when performed by men who do not tremble at His word, each of these lawful sacrifices is as worthless and odious as the idolatrous practice associated with it,--the slaughter of the ox as the offering of a human sacrifice, and so forth? Or does the verse mean that there are persons in Israel who combine, like the Corinthians blamed by Paul, [298] both the true and the idolatrous ritual, both the table of the Lord and the table of devils? Our answer will depend on whether we take the four parallels with ver. 2, which precedes them, or with the rest of ver. 3, to which they belong, and ver. 4. If we take them with ver. 2, then we must adopt the first, the alternative meaning; if with ver. 4, then the second of these meanings is the right one. Now there is no grammatical connection, nor any transparent logical one, between vv. 2 and 3, but there is a grammatical connection with the rest of ver. 3. Immediately after the pairs of lawful and unlawful sacrificial acts, ver. 3 continues, yea, they have chosen their own ways, and their soul delighteth in their abominations. That surely signifies that the unlawful sacrifices in ver. 3 are things already committed and delighted in, and the meaning of putting them in parallel to the lawful sacrifices of Jehovah's religion is either that Israelites have committed them instead of the lawful sacrifices, or along with these. In this case, vv. 3, 4 form a separate discourse by themselves, with no relation to the equally distinct oracle in vv. 1 and 2. The subject of vv. 3 to 4 is, therefore, the idolatrous Israelites. They are delivered unto Satan, their choice; they shall have no part in the coming Salvation. In ver. 5 the faithful in Israel, who have obeyed God's word by the prophet, are comforted under the mocking of their brethren, who shall certainly be put to shame. Already the prophet

Rev. George Adam Smith, M.A.

hears the preparation of the judgement against them (ver. 6). It comes forth from the city where they had mockingly cried for God's glory to appear. The mocked city avenges itself on them. Hark, a roar from the City! Hark, from the Temple! Hark, Jehovah accomplishing vengeance on His enemies!

A new section begins with ver. 7, and celebrates to ver. 9 the sudden re-population of the City by her children, either as already a fact, or, more probably, as a near certainty. Then comes a call to the children, restored, or about to be restored, to congratulate their mother and to enjoy her. The prophet rewakens the figure, that is ever nearest his heart, of motherhood,--children suckled, borne and cradled in the lap of their mother fill all his view; nay, finer still, the grown man coming back with wounds and weariness upon him to be comforted of his mother. As a man whom his mother comforteth, so will I comfort you, and ye shall be comforted in Jerusalem. And ye shall see, and rejoice shall your heart, and your bones shall flourish like the tender grass. But this great light shines not to flood all Israel in one, but to cleave the nation in two, like a sword of judgement. The hand of Jehovah shall be known towards His servants, but He will have indignation against His enemies,--enemies, that is, within Israel. Then comes the fiery judgement, For by fire will Jehovah plead, and by His sword with all flesh; and the slain of Jehovah shall be many. Why there should be slain of Jehovah within Israel is then explained. Within Israel there are idolaters: they that consecrate themselves and practise purification for the gardens, after one in the middle;[299] eaters of swine's flesh, and the Abomination, and the Mouse. They shall come to an end together, saith Jehovah, for I know, or will punish,[300] their works and their thoughts. In this eighteenth verse the punctuation is uncertain, and probably the text is corrupt. The first part of the verse should evidently go, as above, with ver. 17. Then begins a new subject.

It is coming to gather all the nations and the tongues, and they shall come and shall see My glory; and I will set among them a sign,--a marvellous and mighty act, probably of judgement, for he immediately speaks of their survivors,--and I will send the escaped of them to the nations Tarshish, Put[301] and Lud, drawers of the bow, to Tubal and Javan,--that is, to far Spain, and the distances of Africa, towards the Black Sea and to Greece, a full round of the compass,--the isles far off that have not heard report of Me, nor have seen My glory; and they shall recount My glory among the nations. And they shall bring all your brethren from among all the nations an offering to Jehovah, on horses and in chariots and in litters, and on mules and on dromedaries, up on the Mount of My Holiness, Jerusalem, saith Jehovah, just as when the children of Israel bring the offering in a clean vessel to the house of Jehovah. And also from them will I take to be priests, to be Levites, saith Jehovah. For like as the new heavens and the new earth which I am making shall be standing before Me, saith Jehovah, so shall stand your seed and your name. But again the prophecy swerves from the universal hope into which we expect it to break, and gives us instead a division and a judgement: the servants of Jehovah on one side occupied in what the prophet regards as the ideal life, regular worship--so little did he mean ver. 1 to be a condemnation of the Temple and its ritual!--and on the other the rebels' unburied carcases gnawed by the worm and by fire, an abomination to all. And it shall come to pass from new moon to new moon, and from sabbath to sabbath, all flesh shall come to worship before Me, saith Jehovah: and they shall go out and look on the carcases of the men who have rebelled against Me; for their worm dieth not, and their fire is not quenched, and they shall be an abhorrence to all flesh.

We have thus gone step by step through the chapter, because its intricacies and sudden changes were not otherwise to be mastered. What exactly it is composed of must, we fear, still remain a problem. Who can tell whether its short, broken pieces are all originally from our prophet's hand, or were gathered by him from others, or were the fragments of his teaching which the reverent hands of disciples picked carefully up that nothing might be lost? Sometimes we think it must be this last alternative that happened; for it seems impossible that pieces so strange to each other, so loosely connected, could have flowed from one mind at one time. But then again we think otherwise, when we see how the chapter as a whole continues the separation made evident in ch. lxv., and runs it on to a last emphatic contrast.

***

So we are left by the prophecy,--not with the new heavens and the new earth which it promised: not with the holy mountain on which none shall hurt nor destroy, saith the Lord; not with a Jerusalem full of glory and a people all holy, the centre of a gathered humanity,--but with the city like to a judgement floor, and upon its narrow surface a people divided between worship and a horrible woe.

O Jerusalem, City of the Lord, Mother eagerly desired of her children, radiant light to them that sit in darkness and are far off, home after exile, haven after storm,--expected as the Lord's garner, thou art still to be only His threshing-floor, and heaven and hell as of old shall, from new moon to new moon, through the revolving years, lie side by side within thy narrow walls! For from the day that Araunah the Jebusite threshed out his sheaves upon thy high windswept rock, to the day when the Son of Man standing over against thee divided in His last discourse the sheep from the goats, the wise from the foolish, and the loving from the selfish, thou hast been appointed of God for trial and separation and

The Expositor's Bible: The Book of Isaiah Volumes I & II
judgement.

It is a terrible ending to such a prophecy as ours. But is any other possible? We ask how can this contiguity of heaven and hell be within the Lord's own city, after all His yearning and jealousy for her, after His fierce agony and strife with her enemies, after so clear a revelation of Himself, so long a providence, so glorious a deliverance? Yet, it is plain that nothing else can result, if the men on whose ears the great prophecy had fallen, with all its music and all its gospel, and who had been partakers of the Lord's Deliverance, did yet continue to prefer their idols, their swine's flesh, their mouse, their broth of abominable things, their sitting in graves, to so evident a God and to so great a grace.

It is a terrible ending, but it is the same as upon the same floor Christ set to His teaching,--the gospel net cast wide, but only to draw in both good and bad upon a beach of judgement; the wedding feast thrown open and men compelled to come in, but among them a heart whom grace so great could not awe even to decency; Christ's Gospel preached, His Example evident, and Himself owned as Lord, and nevertheless some whom neither the hearing nor the seeing nor the owning with their lips did lift to unselfishness or stir to pity. Therefore He who had cried, Come all unto Me, was compelled to close by saying to many, Depart.

It is a terrible ending, but one only too conceivable. For though God is love, man is free,--free to turn from that love; free to be as though he had never felt it; free to put away from himself the highest, clearest, most urgent grace that God can show. But to do this is the judgement.

Lord, are there few that be saved? The Lord did not answer the question but by bidding the questioner take heed to himself: Strive to enter in at the strait gate.

***

Almighty and most merciful God, who hast sent this book to be the revelation of Thy great love to man, and of Thy power and will to save him, grant that our study of it may not have been in vain by the callousness or carelessness of our hearts, but that by it we may be confirmed in penitence, lifted to hope, made strong for service, and above all filled with the true knowledge of Thee and of Thy Son Jesus Christ. Amen.

Footnotes:

289. Ch. lxiii. 18 and lxiv. 10, 11. In the Hebrew ch. lxiv. begins a verse later than it does in the English version.

290. Semites had a horror of painting the Deity in any form. But when God had to be imagined or described, they chose the form of a man and attributed to Him human features. Chiefly they thought of His face. To see His face, to come into the light of His countenance, was the way their hearts expressed longing for the living God. Exod. xxiii. 14; Psalm xxxi. 16, xxxiv. 16, lxxx. 7. But among the heathen Semites God's face was separated from God Himself, and worshipped as a separate god. In heathen Semitic religions there are a number of deities who are the faces of others. But the Hebrew writers, with every temptation to do the same, maintained their monotheism, and went no farther than to speak of the angel of God's Face. And in all the beautiful narratives of Genesis, Exodus and Judges about the glorious Presence that led Israel against their enemies, the angel of God's face is an equivalent of God Himself. Jacob said, the God which hath fed me, and the angel which hath redeemed me, bless the lads. In Judges this angel's word is God's Word.

291. See pp. [71]398 ff.

292. Cheyne. Similarly Bredenkamp, who contends that the prophecy is Isaianic, and to be dated from the time of Manasseh.

293. Cf. Dillmann, in loco.

294. Among Orientals the planets Jupiter and Venus were worshipped as the Larger and the Lesser Luck. They were worshipped as Merodach and Istar among the Babylonians. Merodach was worshipped for prosperity (cf. Sayce, Hibbert Lectures, pp. 460, 476, 488). It may be Merodach and Istar, to whom are here given the name Gad, or Luck (cf. Genesis xxii. 11, and the name Baal Gad in the Lebanon valley) and Meni, or Fate, Fortune (cf. Arabic al-manijjat, fate; Wellhausen, Skizzen, iii., 22 ff., 189). There was in the Babylonian Pantheon a "Manu the Great who presided over fate" (Lenormant, Chaldean Magic, etc., p. 120). Instances of idolatrous feasts will be found in Sayce, op. cit., p. 539; cf. 1 Cor. x. 21, Ye cannot partake of the table of the Lord and of the table of devils. See what is said in p. [72]62 of this volume about the connection of idolatry and commerce.

295. Bleek (5th ed., pp. 287, 288) holds ch. lxvi. to be by a prophet who lived in Palestine after the resumption of sacrificial worship (vv. 3, 6, 30), that is, upon the altar of burnt-offering which the Returned had erected there, and at a time when the temple-building had begun. Vatke also holds to a post-exilic date, Einleitung in das A.T., pp. 625, 630. Kuenen, too, makes the chapter post-exilic. Bredenkamp takes vv. 1-6 for Palestinian, but pre-exilic, and ascribes them to Isaiah. With ver. 1 he

compares 1 Kings viii. 27; and as to ver. 6 he asks, How could the unbelieving exiles be in the neighbourhood of the Temple and hear Jehovah's voice in thunder from it? Vv. 7-14 he takes as exilic, based on an Isaianic model.

296. So Dillmann and Driver; Cheyne is doubtful.

297. Acts vii. 49.

298. 1 Cor. x.

299. So, in literal translation of the text, the One being a master of ceremonies, who, standing in the middle, was imitated by the worshippers (cf. Baudissin, Studien zur Semitischen Religionsgeschichte, i., p. 315, who combats Lagarde's and Selden's view, that 'hd, one, stands for the God Hadad). The Massoretes read the feminine form of one, which might mean some goddess.

300. Know, Pesh. and some editions of the LXX.; punish, Delitzsch and Cheyne.

301. The Hebrew text has Pul, the LXX. Put. Put and Lud occur together, Ezek. xxvii. 10-xxx. 5. Put is Punt, the Egyptian name for East Africa. Lud is not Lydia, but a North African nation. Jeremiah, xlvi. 9, mentions, along with Cush, Put and the Ludim in the service of Egypt, and the Ludim as famous with the bow.

www.ingramcontent.com/pod-product-compliance
Lightning Source LLC
Chambersburg PA
CBHW032018230426
43671CB00005B/125